CONVEYANCING
LAW AND PRACTICE IN SCOTLAND

CONVEYANCING
LAW AND PRACTICE
IN SCOTLAND

by

JOHN M. HALLIDAY

C.B.E., M.A., LL.B. (Glasgow), LL.D. (Edin.).

*Emeritus Professor of Conveyancing in the
University of Glasgow*

Volume III

Leases and Heritable Securities

Published under the auspices of

THE SCOTTISH UNIVERSITIES LAW INSTITUTE

EDINBURGH

W. GREEN & SON LTD.

1987

First published in 1987

© 1987 THE SCOTTISH UNIVERSITIES LAW INSTITUTE

ISBN 0 414 00815 4
Typeset by Columns of Reading

Printed in Great Britain
at the University Printing House, Oxford

PREFACE

THIS volume deals with transactions relating to leases and heritable securities, and also floating charges.

I have again to express my gratitude for the continuing assistance of Professor J.A.M. Inglis and Emeritus Professor A.J. McDonald who have suggested many valuable additions and improvements to the draft text. I must also thank the Deputy Keeper, Mr. John Robertson, who has found time among his many other commitments to guide me on matters relating to registration of title. Again, too, I am indebted to Mr. I.J.S. Talman who has read and constructively criticised the whole text.

I have had generous help from many of my colleagues in the legal profession who had particular expertise on various specialised topics; I record my thanks in particular to Professor R.B. Jack, Mr. James H. Campbell, Mr. John H. Greene, Mr. D.B. Malloy and Mr. David Semple. I am grateful also to Mr. J. Muir Watt who made most helpful comments on the chapter relating to agricultural leases.

For permission to utilise styles of deeds I have to thank the Law Society of Scotland, the City of Glasgow District Council, Clydesdale Bank plc and Alliance & Leicester Building Society.

Miss Shelagh Barclay and Mrs. Fiona Halliday have again produced the entire typescript, and my wife has compiled the tables of cases and statutes and undertaken much detailed work of checking. I owe much to their patient industry.

Last but not least I again thank the publishers, W. Green & Son Ltd., who have maintained their high standards of excellence in preparing the volume for printing and supervising its production.

The law is stated as at December 31, 1986.

J.M. HALLIDAY

CONTENTS

LIST OF ABBREVIATIONS

Bell, *Comm.*	Professor G.J. Bell, *Commentaries on the Law of Scotland and the Principles of Mercantile Jurisprudence*, 7th ed., 1870.
Bell, *Prin.*	Professor G.J. Bell, *Principles of the Law of Scotland*, 10th ed., 1899.
Bell, (Montgomerie)	Professor A.M. Bell, *Lectures on Conveyancing*, 3rd ed., 1882.
Burns	John Burns, *Conveyancing Practice according to the Law of Scotland*, 4th ed., 1957.
Craigie, *Heritable Rights*	John Craigie, *Scottish Law of Conveyancing, Heritable Rights*, 3rd ed., 1899.
Duncan and Hope	A.G.M. Duncan and J.A.D. Hope, *The Rent (Scotland) Act 1984*, 1986.
Encyclopaedia	*Encyclopaedia of the Laws of Scotland*, 1926–1933.
Ersk.	Professor John Erskine of Carnock, *An Institute of the Law of Scotland*, 8th ed., 1871.
Gill	B. Gill, *The Law of Agricultural Holdings in Scotland*, 1982.
Gloag, *Contract*	Professor W.M. Gloag, *Law of Contract*, 2nd ed., 1929.
Gloag and Henderson	Professor W.M. Gloag and Professor R.C. Henderson, *Introduction to the Law of Scotland*, 8th ed. by A.B. Wilkinson and W.A. Wilson, 1980.
Gloag and Irvine	Professor W.M. Gloag and J.M. Irvine, *Law of Rights in Security*, 1897.
Greene and Fletcher	J.H. Greene and I.M. Fletcher, *The Law and Practice of Receivership in Scotland*, 1987.
Halliday	Professor J.M. Halliday, *Conveyancing and Feudal Reform (Scotland) Act 1970*, 2nd ed., 1977.
McKerrell	Douglas G. McKerrell, *The Rent Acts – A Practitioner's Guide*, 1985.
Menzies, *Lectures*	Professor Allan Menzies, *Lectures on Conveyancing according to the Law of Scotland*, revised ed., 1900.
Paton and Cameron	G.C.H. Paton and J.G.S. Cameron, *The Law of Landlord and Tenant in Scotland*, 1967.
Rankine, *Leases*	Sir John Rankine, *Law of Leases in Scotland*, 3rd ed., 1916.
R.T.P.B.	Registration of Title Practice Book, 1981.
Ross and McKichan	Murray J. Ross and D.J. McKichan, *Drafting and Negotiating Commercial Leases in Scotland*, 1985.

Stair	Sir James Dalrymple, Viscount Stair, *Institutions of the Law of Scotland*, Tercentenary ed., 1981.
Walker, Prin.	Professor D.M. Walker, *Principles of Scottish Private Law*, 3rd ed., 1982.
Walker and Walker	A.G. Walker and N.M.L. Walker, *The Law of Evidence in Scotland*, 1964.
Wood, *Lectures*	Professor J.P. Wood, *Lectures on Conveyancing*, 1903.

TABLE OF CASES

TABLE OF STATUTES

PART I

LEASES

CHAPTER 25

NATURE AND CONSTITUTION OF LEASES

Introduction

25–01   This work is concerned only with the conveyancing aspects of leases: for the substantive law of leases reference may be made to the undernoted texts.[1] Likewise it is beyond the scope of this work to consider in detail the various statutory provisions regulating leases of particular kinds of subjects such as the Agricultural Holdings Acts, the Rent (Scotland) Acts and the Tenancy of Shops (Scotland) Act, but important matters to be kept in view in relation to leases of such subjects are noticed briefly.

Nature and characteristics of leases

25–02   In principle a lease is a personal contract between a landlord and a tenant for the use of heritable property, but in certain circumstances the tenant may have a real right which enables him to maintain his possession of the subjects against persons other than the landlord who granted the lease.[2] For the features which distinguish a lease from other rights to the use of land such as feus, sales, licences or security rights reference may be made to standard textbooks.[3] The essential elements of a lease are a contract (1) with *consensus in idem* constituted in the manner required by law (2) for the use and enjoyment of heritable property (3) in return for a rent (4) for a period specified or ascertainable.

---

[1] Rankine, *Leases*; Paton and Cameron, *Landlord and Tenant*; Walker, *Prin.*, III, Chap. 5.15.
[2] See paras. 25–38 to 25–41.
[3] Paton and Cameron, *Landlord and Tenant*, 8–15; Walker, *Prin.*, III, 214, 215.

CONSTITUTION OF LEASES

Contracts of lease

25-03   A valid contract of lease may be created between parties who have the capacity to grant and take lands on lease if it contains the essential elements of a lease and is executed with the formalities required by law for the particular lease. These requirements are considered in more detail in the following paragraphs.

(A) Capacity of Parties

Granter's infeftment

25-04   The proper title of the granter of a lease who is the proprietor of the subjects is his infeftment,[4] but the lack of infeftment may be cured by his subsequent completion or acquisition of title on the principle of accretion so long as no impediment has intervened.[5] So a lease granted by an uninfeft proprietor, such as a person who has right to the land within the meaning of section 4 of the Conveyancing (Scotland) Act 1924 and who subsequently completes his title by expeding and recording a notice of title, or a beneficiary in whose favour executors of the deceased proprietor subsequently grant a docket of transfer of the subjects in terms of section 15(2) of the Succession (Scotland) Act 1964 upon which a recorded notice of title has followed, or a purchaser under missives in whose favour a disposition of the subjects is subsequently granted and recorded or used to obtain a registered interest in the subjects in the Land Register, is thereby validated. If the granter is not infeft and accretion has not operated, the lease is binding on the parties and their respective executors or representatives as a personal contract but not upon singular successors such as purchasers or heritable creditors who have not consented to the lease. Where a lease has been granted by a person who had an invalid title, or one which although *ex facie* regular has subsequently been reduced, it may be impugned by the true owner or by the tenant, and a subsequent assignation of the original granter's right to the true owner does not validate the lease since the granter had nothing to assign.[6]

Granters having a right to the subjects for a limited period

25-05   Such persons may grant leases but only for a period within the duration of their right to the subjects. So a liferenter having a beneficial right may grant a lease but only for a period not exceeding the currency of the liferent, and a lessee may, unless prohibited in

---

[4]Bell, *Prin.*, s. 1181.
[5]As to the conditions for operation of accretion, see Vol. II, paras. 24–59 to 24–62.
[6]*Reid's Tr.* v. *Watson's Trs.* (1896) 23 R. 636.

terms of the lease, grant a sub-lease but only for a period which expires at or before the endurance of the head lease.

Pupils

25–06   As to the rights of tutors of pupils to grant leases, subject to the possible risk of reduction within the *quadriennium utile*, reference may be made to Volume I, paragraphs 2–10 to 2–12 and 2–26 and 2–27.

Minors

25–07   As to the rights of minors having no curator, or minors with consent of curators, to grant leases, again subject to possible reduction within the *quadriennium utile*, see Volume I, paragraphs 2–24, 2–26 and 2–27.

Trustees

25–08   **(a) Lessors**. The rights of trustees to grant leases are outlined in Volume I, paragraphs 2–57 to 2–60. As to non-Scottish trustees see the undernoted case.[7]

(b) Lessees. See Volume I, paragraph 2–62.

Judicial factors

25–09   As to the general powers of a judicial factor reference may be made to Volume I, paragraphs 2–80 to 2–83.

Lessors. A judicial factor, being a trustee within the definition in section 2 of the Trusts (Scotland) Act 1921, may exercise the powers conferred by section 4 of that Act so far as not at variance with the terms or purposes of his office. These include power to grant leases of any duration (including mineral leases).[8]

Lessees. There is no general power given to trustees (including judicial factors) to take heritable property on lease but they may do so if required for the provision of a suitable residence for occupation by any of the beneficiaries.[9]

Companies

25–10   Normally the memorandum of association contains express power to grant or take leases, but even in the absence of a specific power the right to do so will in appropriate circumstances be authorised by the general power in the memorandum to do any acts incidental or conducive to the company's objects. Further, the provisions of section

[7]*Pender's Trs*. (1903) 5 F. 504.
[8]Trusts (Scotland) Act 1921, s. 4(1)(*c*).
[9]Trusts (Scotland) Act 1921, s. 4(1)(*ee*) added by Trusts (Scotland) Act 1961, s. 4.

35 of the Companies Act 1985 to the effect that, in favour of a person dealing with a company in good faith, any transaction entered into by the directors (which would include a lease) is deemed to be one which is within the capacity of the company to enter into and the power of the directors to bind the company is deemed to be free of any limitation under the memorandum or articles, nor is a party to such a transaction bound to inquire as to any such capacity or limitation.

Receivers

25–11   A receiver has, in relation to any heritable property of the company which is attached by the floating charge by virtue of which he was appointed, the powers given by the instrument which created the charge and also, in so far as not inconsistent with any provision in that instrument, the power to grant any lease of that property and to take on lease any property required or convenient for the business of the company.[10] These powers are subject to the rights of any person who has effectually executed diligence against the property or of any heritable creditor having a fixed security over it or the holder of a floating charge having priority over, or ranking *pari passu* with, the floating charge by virtue of which the receiver was appointed.[11]

Partnerships

25–12   Heritable property is normally held by trustees for the partnership and leases of it should be granted by the infeft trustees with the consent of all the partners. In strict theory a lease granted by the trustees confers an unchallengeable title on the lessee by virtue of section 2 of the Trusts (Scotland) Act 1961, but the usual and best practice is to have the lease signed by all the partners.[12] Leases in favour of a partnership may be taken in favour of the partnership *socio nomine*, but it is preferable in practice to take leases in favour of the partners and the survivors and survivor as trustees for the firm.[13]

Heritable creditors in possession

25–13   A creditor under a standard security who is in lawful possession of the security subjects, *e.g.* by agreement or after due legal process, may let the security subjects or any part of them for a period not exceeding seven years. If he desires to let for any longer period he may apply to the sheriff for a warrant to do so. The application will state the proposed tenant and duration and conditions of the proposed lease, and will be served on the proprietor of the security subjects and on any

---

[10]Companies Act 1985, s. 471(1)(*p*).
[11]*Ibid.*, s. 471(2).
[12]See Vol. I, para. 2–127.
[13]Paton and Cameron, *Landlord and Tenant*, 63.

other heritable creditor having interest as such in the subjects.[14] The court has discretion to grant, vary or refuse the application.[15]

25–14 A bondholder in possession under a bond and disposition in security has powers of leasing the security subjects broadly similar to those of a creditor in possession under a standard security.[16]

25–15 The grantee of an *ex facie* absolute disposition where the relative agreement has not been recorded has on the face of the record a title of ownership which enables him to grant an effective lease of the subjects or any part of them. If the granting of a lease by the creditor infringes the terms of the agreement, however, the creditor may incur liability for breach of the agreement. On the other hand, if the relative agreement had been recorded or otherwise brought to the notice of the prospective lessee and it contained a prohibition of or restriction upon the granting of leases by the creditor, the lease would be vulnerable to challenge by the debtor, at least if prejudice to his interest could be established.

Debtors under heritable securities

25–16 The owner of property who has granted a standard security on the standard conditions is under obligation not to let or agree to let the security subjects or any part thereof without the prior consent of the creditor.[17] The rights of heritable creditors to reduce a lease granted in breach of that obligation are not affected although the debtor has previously undertaken to grant a lease in terms of an unrecorded document,[18] unless the heritable creditors had knowledge when the standard security was granted that the lessee already had some sort of right which was capable of becoming a real right in the security subjects, with the result that the creditors were not in good faith.[19]

25–17 There is no such statutory restriction on the right of an owner of property who has granted a bond and disposition in security and remains in possession of the property. Unless some restraint upon his power to let has been included in the recorded bond and disposition in security the owner remains entitled to grant leases of the subjects or any part of them, provided that they are not in terms unduly favourable to the tenant with the effect of prejudicing the security.[19a]

25–18 The right of a proprietor to grant leases of property which has been conveyed to a creditor by an *ex facie* absolute disposition but remains in possession of the subjects depends upon (1) a mandate, express or implied, by the creditor or (2) the circumstance that the owner, before

[14]Conveyancing and Feudal Reform (Scotland) Act 1970, s. 20(3).
[15]*Ibid.*, s. 20(4).
[16]Heritable Securities (Scotland) Act 1894, ss. 6,7.
[17]Conveyancing and Feudal Reform (Scotland) Act 1970, Sched. 3, condition 6.
[18]*Trade Development Bank* v. *Warriner & Mason (Scotland) Ltd.*, 1980 S.C. 74; *Trade Development Bank* v. *David W. Haig (Bellshill) Ltd.*, 1983 S.L.T. 510.
[19]*Trade Development Bank* v. *Crittall Windows Ltd.*, 1983 S.L.T. 510.
[19a]*Reid* v. *McGill*, 1912 2 S.L.T. 246.

granting the *ex facie* absolute disposition, has been infeft in the subjects. As to mandate, the fact that the creditor has permitted the debtor to remain in possession and manage the property implies, in the absence of any provision to the contrary in the agreement qualifying the absolute disposition which is known to the lessee, a power to grant leases which confer a real right on the tenant.[20] The implied mandate authorises lets which are within the scope of normal administration of the property, is personal to the debtor and is not transmissible[21] and may be recalled by the creditor. Apart from implied mandate, however, the debtor's power to let may be based on his having been infeft in the subjects when the absolute disposition was granted. The *locus classicus* in which this basis was explained is the statement of Lord Kinnear:[22]

> "The doctrine is that a security in the form of an absolute disposition but qualified by a back-bond declaring the title to be limited to a definite security is neither more nor less than a heritable security, and therefore that the granter's title of property remains entire subject to the security. It follows that the granter of the disposition remaining in possession has a perfectly valid and sufficient title to dispose of the property in any way provided he does not trench on the security. Nothing hinders him to sell, subject of course to the security, or to make an entail, or to grant other postponed securities, either in the same form or any other. But the principle is that a security in this form, being merely a security after all, although in form a disposition absolute, does not divest the granter even feudally, and he is therefore in a position to deal with his estate by virtue of his own original title, and requires no other right or authority, so long as he leaves his creditor's security unimpaired."

It was held in *Ritchie* that the debtor was entitled to grant a lease and the principle has been subsequently affirmed.[23] Lord Kinnear distinguished the case where the debtor had never been infeft, as where he had simply consented to a disposition by a former owner in favour of the creditor, in which circumstance the debtor, unless he can establish mandate, is not entitled to grant leases.

Joint proprietors

25–19   All the *pro indiviso* proprietors of heritable property must concur in granting a lease of the property or any part of it.[24]

Agents

25–20   The powers of factors, attorneys or other agents to grant leases

---

[20]*Abbott* v. *Mitchell* (1870) 8 M. 791; *Edinburgh Entertainments Ltd.* v. *Stevenson*, 1926 S.C. 363.
[21]*Ritchie* v. *Scott* (1899) 1 F. 728 at 735.
[22]*Ritchie* v. *Scott, supra,* at 736.
[23]*Edinburgh Entertainments Ltd.* v. *Stevenson, supra.*
[24]*Campbell and Stewart* v. *Campbell*, Jan. 24, 1809, F.C. See also *Higgins* v. *Assessor for Lanarkshire*, 1911 S.C. 931 and *Barr* v. *Turner* (1904) 12 S.L.T. 369.

depend upon the scope of their mandates, which may be determined by express writing or by parole evidence on the ordinary rules relating to proof of agency. It was stated by Rankine[25] that in the old law a factor could not, without express powers, grant a lease, and it has been held that a solicitor, even though he was employed to collect the rents and attend to the repairs of a property, had no general authority to grant leases.[26] On the other hand it seems reasonably clear that a solicitor, employed to adjust the terms of a lease on behalf of a client, has implied authority to sign a contract of lease which is binding on his client.

Local authorities

25–21   A local authority may let property subject only to the general restriction that the period of lease of a dwelling-house may not exceed 20 years,[27] and a secure tenancy cannot be created for more than that period.[28] The former restrictions upon the powers of a local authority to let more than seven years imposed by section 165 of the Local Government (Scotland) Act 1947 no longer apply.[29]

Heirs of entail in possession

25–22   As to the powers of heirs of entail in possession to grant leases and undertake obligations under leases, see the undernoted texts.[30,31]

Fiduciary fiars

25–23   In terms of section 8(2) of the Trusts (Scotland) Act 1921 a fiduciary fiar may apply to the Court of Session to exercise any of the powers of a trustee including power to grant leases. Alternatively he may apply to the court to appoint a trustee or trustees who may exercise such powers.

Fiars

25–24   A fiar of property which is subject to a liferent cannot grant a lease which takes effect during the subsistence of the liferent without the consent of the liferenter, but may grant a lease which will take effect after the death of the liferenter.[32]

Effect of diligence and insolvency

25–25   (a) **Granter of lease.** An inhibition used against the owner of

---

[25] Leases, 46.
[26] Danish Dairy Co. Ltd. v. Gillespie, 1922 S.C. 656.
[27] Land Tenure Reform (Scotland) Act 1974, s. 8.
[28] Tenant's Rights, Etc. (Scotland) Act 1980, Sched. 1, para. 1. But see Housing (Scotland) Act 1986, s. 10.
[29] section 165 repealed—Local Government (Scotland) Act 1973, Sched. 29.
[30] Paton and Cameron, Landlord and Tenant, 55, 56.
[31] Burns, 605, 606.
[32] Rankine, Leases, 78.

property does not strike at a lease granted subsequently, provided that it is in ordinary course of administration of the property and is for a fair rent and of normal duration: that does not prejudice the inhibitor. If, however, a grassum is payable or the lease is on terms unduly favourable to the tenant, the inhibitor may be prejudiced and the lease may be reduced at his instance. The position is similar if the property has been rendered litigious by a notice of litigiosity.[33] A lease may be challengeable as an illegal preference under the Bankruptcy Act 1696 or as a gratuitous alienation under the Bankruptcy Act 1621, or as an unfair preference or gratuitous alienation under section 36 or 34 of the Bankruptcy (Scotland) Act 1985, as the case may be, but only if it was granted for an inadequate consideration or is not otherwise exempt from challenge on any of the grounds of defence available under the relevant statute.[34] A bankrupt, however, may not grant a lease after the first deliverance or the award of sequestration. Nor may an owner of property who has granted a trust deed for creditors which has become a protected trust deed[34a] grant a lease of the property while the trust deed is in operation.

(b) **Grantee of lease**. An inhibition or notice of litigiosity against a tenant who has power to assign or sub-let may affect his right to exercise these powers. On the other hand an inhibition against a tenant who holds under a lease under which assignees or sub-tenants are excluded, or excluded except with the consent of the landlord, is ineffective since there is no right in the tenant which can be adjudged, and in such a case the tenant may renounce the lease in favour of the landlord.[35] An assignation, renunciation or sub-lease may be challengeable under the Bankruptcy Acts 1621 or 1696, or under the Bankruptcy (Scotland) Act 1985 in the same way as a lease by the proprietor.[36]

(B) Leases and Agreements to Let—Form and Execution

Leases for not more than one year

25–26   A lease for not more than one year may be constituted orally or by informal writing and may be proved *prout de jure*.[37]

Leases for more than one year

25–27   A lease for a period of more than one year should be constituted in

---

[33]Rankine, *Leases*, 51, 52.
[34]See *Gorrie's Tr.* v. *Gorrie* (1890) 17 R. 1051; Bankruptcy (Scotland) Act 1985, ss. 34(4) and 36(2).
[34a]As to protected trust deed see Bankruptcy (Scotland) Act 1985, Sched. 5.
[35]*Fraser* v. *Marquis of Abercorn* (1835) 14 S. 77.
[36]See *Paterson's Tr.* v. *Paterson's Trs.* (1891) 19 R. 91.
[37]Paton and Cameron, *Landlord and Tenant*, 19, 20; Walker, *Prin.*, III, 215.

writing, attested or holograph or adopted as holograph, of both parties[38] or their authorised agents, but may be constituted by informal writing or oral agreement if followed by actings which amount to homologation or *rei interventus* which bar *locus poenitentiae*.[39] An agreement to let advertising space, being a document *in re mercatoria*, does not require to satisfy those requirements.[39a] The parties must have reached agreement on all the essential elements of a lease,[40,41] but some conditions, if not expressed, may be implied, *e.g.* the date of entry, if not specified, will be deemed to be immediate.[42]

Practice

25–28   Leases of unfurnished or furnished dwelling-houses in the private sector of relatively short duration are normally entered into by missives, the tenant's signature being attested and the signature of the landlord or his factor being either attested or adopted as holograph.[43] Tenancies of unfurnished dwelling-houses in the public sector usually take the form of a tenancy agreement in a standard form, the signatures of the tenant and the factor for the landlords being formally attested.[44] Leases of agricultural property are usually formally authenticated and may be preceded by missives adopted as holograph by agents for both parties, but frequently the formal lease gives effect to arrangements made verbally or by informal writings. The practice in relation to leases of commercial or industrial property varies, lets of relatively short duration being sometimes left to rest upon missives or agreements, attested or holograph or adopted as holograph by the parties or their agents, but leases of longer duration usually are, and if they are registrable must be, formally attested.[45]

Duration

25–29   Subject to the qualification aftermentioned as regards leases of dwelling-houses, a lease may be for any period.[46] In *Campbell* v. *McLean*[47] a building lease for 99 years, renewable for ever on payment of a grassum, was held valid for 99 years, the question of its being

---

[38]*Walker* v. *Flint* (1863) 1 M. 417; *Gibson* v. *Adams* (1875) 3 R. 144.

[39]*Walker* v. *Flint*, *supra*; *Sellar* v. *Aiton* (1875) 2 R. 381; *Station Hotel, Nairn Ltd.* v. *Macpherson* (1905) 13 S.L.T. 456; *Wight* v. *Newton*, 1911 S.C. 762; *Morrison-Low* v. *Paterson*, 1985 S.L.T. 255. See also *Campbeltown Coal Co. Ltd.* v. *Duke of Argyll*, 1926 S.C. 126 and *Pickard* v. *Ritchie*, 1986 S.L.T. 466.

[39a]*United Kingdom Advertising Co. Ltd.* v. *Glasgow Bag-Wash Laundry*, 1926 S.C. 303.

[40]See para. 25–02.

[41]*Erskine* v. *Glendinning* (1871) 9 M.656; *Buchanan* v. *Duke of Hamilton* (1878) 5 R.(H.L.) 69; *Wight* v. *Newton*, *supra*; *Gray* v. *Edinburgh University*, 1962 S.C. 157.

[42]*Christie* v. *Fife Coal Co. Ltd.* (1899) 2 F. 192.

[43]See para. 25–27.

[44]See para. 27–46.

[45]See para. 26–02.

[46]*Frazer* v. *Lord Advocate* (1762) 2 Pat. App. 66 (1140 years); *Carron Co.* v. *Henderson's Trs.* (1896) 23 R. 1042 (171 years); *Crawford* v. *Livingstone's Trs.*, 1938 S.C. 609 (354 years).

[47](1870) 8 M.(H.L.) 40.

renewable thereafter being left for later decision. There is, however, an important statutory restriction upon the duration of the lease of a dwelling-house. In terms of section 8 of the Land Tenure Reform (Scotland) Act 1974 no part of property which is subject to a lease for more than 20 years executed after September 1, 1974 may be used as or as part of a dwelling-house.[48] There are excepted from this statutory prohibition (1) use of part of the subjects as ancillary to the use of the remainder,[48a] (2) caravan sites,[49] and (3) agricultural holdings, small landholdings and crofts.[50] It is not permissible to contract out of the statutory prohibition.[51] A breach of the prohibition does not render the lease void or unenforceable but entitles the landlord to give notice to the tenant to terminate the use within 28 days from the date of notice, failing which the landlord may raise an action of removing.[52] A lease may provide for breaks in the option of either or both parties, usually at stated periods on prescribed notice. Options to break in favour of the tenant are frequently included in mineral leases to allow for termination when the minerals have been extracted to an extent that the remaining minerals are no longer workable commercially. Options to break in favour of the landlord are commonly included in agricultural leases to permit of development of the land for other purposes: often the landlord in such leases reserves a right to resume the land or part of it at any time upon giving stipulated notice.[53] For a fuller discussion of breaks see the undernoted text.[54] The duration of a lease may be prolonged by tacit relocation if the stipulated period of the lease expires without either party having given notice of his intention to terminate it and there has been nothing in the conduct of parties to rebut the presumption that renewal of the lease was intended.[54a] When tacit relocation operates, the lease is continued for a further period of one year or in cases where the lease was for a period of less than a year, for a further duration of that period, and so on successively for further periods until one party gives due notice of termination; all the terms and conditions of the original lease remain in force so far as they are not inconsistent with any implied term of the new contract.[55]

---

[48]But see Law Reform (Miscellaneous Provisions) (Scotland) Act 1985, s. 1 which permits renewal of pre-1974 leases under an obligation therein.
[48a]1974 Act, s. 8(3).
[49]Ibid., s. 8(2).
[50]Ibid., s. 8(5).
[51]Ibid., s. 21.
[52]Ibid., s. 9. As to the consequences of failure by the tenant to obtemper the notice see Halliday, Land Tenure Reform (Scotland) Act 1974, 31, 32; McKerrell, The Rent Acts, 126–128.
[53]See para. 28–14.
[54]Paton and Cameron, Landlord and Tenant, 242–244.
[54a]Buchanan v. Harris & Sheldon (1900) 2 F. 935; McFarlane v. Mitchell (1900) 2 F. 901; Kirkpatrick's Exrx. v. G. & A. Kirkpatrick, 1983 S.L.T. 191.
[55]See further Paton and Cameron, op. cit., Chap. XIV; Walker, Prin., III, 229, 230, 249; A.G.M. Duncan, "Tacit Relocation in Leases," 1978 S.L.T. (News) 157.

Subjects

25–30   The subjects of a lease must be heritable property including incorporeal rights annexed to it, whether capable of feudalisation or not. Salmon fishings, being a distinct feudal hereditament, may be the subject of a lease. Trout fishings can be let, but until recently a lease of fishings separately from a lease of the riparian land was not binding upon successors of the landlord[56]: the Freshwater and Salmon Fisheries (Scotland) Act 1976[57] now provides that a written contract for consideration and for a period of not less than one year which confers a right of fishing for freshwater fish is deemed to be a lease to which the Leases Act 1449 applies and so is valid against the landlord's successors. Shootings may be let separately from the land for any period within the duration of the landlord's ownership of the land, but, as a personal privilege which cannot be made a real burden, a lease for beyond that period is not binding upon successors of the landlord.[58] If, however, the lease is of the land or heritable property together with a right of shootings, it may qualify for the purposes of the Leases Act 1449 and be valid against the landlord's singular successors.[59] Ordinarily a lease confers on the tenant a right of enjoyment of the subjects and their fruits, but a mineral lease is really a sale of the minerals with a licence for a period to enter on the lands and extract and take away the minerals on payment of a rent in the form of a royalty on the amount of minerals taken, perhaps with an alternative fixed rent which merges in the royalty. Leases of certain types of subjects, such as unfurnished and furnished dwelling-houses, shops, agricultural holdings, small landholdings and crofts are subject to important statutory regulations and controls which are noticed briefly later in relation to the particular subjects.

Rent

25–31   The necessary element of rent is usually a sum specified or to be ascertained in terms of the lease payable at stated terms during the currency of the tenancy. In leases of relatively short duration, *e.g.* not exceeding five years, the rent may be a fixed amount which remains unchanged throughout the period of the lease, but in longer leases, and sometimes even in shorter leases, provision is made for increases or reviews of rent in order to reflect decreases in the value of money or increases in the recoverable rent of property of the kind involved. In leases of dwelling-houses in the private sector the initial period of let is usually short so that on due notice of termination the rent can be renegotiated, and in the case of regulated tenancies under the Rent

---

[56]*Earl of Galloway* v. *Duke of Bedford* (1902) 4 F. 851.
[57]s. 4.
[58]*Beckett* v. *Bisset*, 1921 2 S.L.T. 33.
[59]*Farquharson* (1870) 9 M. 66.

Acts there are detailed statutory conditions for the assessment of a fair rent.[60] In leases of dwelling-houses in the public sector the landlord is free to fix and adjust levels of rent subject only to certain limitations or fiscal constraints, and normally reserves the right to alter the rent at any monthly period upon specified notice.[61] In the field of commercial and industrial leases, where the duration of leases is normally longer, an initial rent is stipulated reviewable upwards at stated review dates, the amount of the increase being determined either in relation to an appropriate published index or by agreement, which failing, by reference to an expert or arbiter.[62] In leases executed after September 1, 1974, it is unlawful to stipulate for payment of any casualty, but it is permissible to stipulate for review of rent or for a permanent or periodical variation of rent on terms prescribed in the lease.[62a]

Obligations of parties

25–32   The common law obligations of landlord and tenant in leases of dwelling-houses and agricultural subjects have been significantly altered by legislation and are more conveniently discussed in the relevant Chapters 27 and 28 *infra*. The obligations of parties in leases of commercial and industrial subjects, although comparatively unaffected by legislation, have in modern practice been substantially changed by the introduction of the concept of the full repairing and insuring lease and are considered in Chapter 29 *infra*.

Remedies of landlord

25–33   (1) **Personal action**. A landlord may enforce payment of rent by a personal action for recovery of the amount due and use any appropriate diligence thereon. If the lease contains a consent to registration for execution summary diligence on a six days' charge is competent.[63] A landlord may enforce other obligations of the tenant by personal action requiring implement and may restrain any continuing breach of the tenant's obligations by interdict.

25–34   (2) **Hypothec**. In leases of urban subjects including dwelling-houses and commercial and industrial property a landlord has at common law a right of hypothec which confers a right in security over the *invecta et illata* in the premises let and to recover any such articles and effects from those in possession of them if they have been removed in breach of the right. The right is effectively excluded in leases of land let for agriculture or pasture exceeding two acres in extent by the Hypothec Abolition (Scotland) Act 1880 and is restricted as regards the items

---

[60]See para. 27–13.
[61]See para. 27–47.
[62]See paras. 29–22 to 29–24.
[62a]Land Tenure Reform (Scotland) Act 1974, s. 16.
[63]See Vol. I, paras. 4–60 to 4–76.

which may be the subject of the hypothec in leases of certain small dwelling-houses to which the House Letting and Rating (Scotland) Act 1911 applies. The items covered are furniture, plenishing, stock-in-trade, goods and equipment and moveables generally, including articles on hire-purchase, but not money, the tenant's clothing and tools of trade, nor does it cover articles belonging to a third party.[63a] The landlord may interdict the tenant from removing articles which are subject to hypothec and, if they have been removed, may obtain judicial warrant to have them brought back. The right of hypothec secures one year's rent due or current, but not arrears, and must be enforced within three months of the last term of payment. The right is enforced by a petition for sequestration in the sheriff court, followed by a warrant for sale of the sequestrated effects. The landlord's right of hypothec is preferable to the rights of unprivileged diligence creditors, the tenant's trustee in bankruptcy[64] or a liquidator in the winding-up of a company tenant,[65] but is not preferred to preferential claims in bankruptcy or liquidation.[66]

25–35   **(3) Irritancy and extraordinary removing**. At common law and by statute[67] a landlord had a right to irritate a lease for non-payment of rent, but in the case of leases of dwelling-houses and agricultural subjects these have in practice been effectively superseded by modern statutes and in leases of commercial or industrial property by conventional provisions in leases. The current law in relation to irritancies in leases of residential property and agricultural subjects is considered in Chapters 27[68] and 28[69] respectively: conventional irritancies in leases of commercial or industrial subjects, as affected by the Law Reform (Miscellaneous Provisions) (Scotland) Act 1985, are dealt with in Chapter 29.[70]

Remedies of tenant

25–36   Failure by the landlord to implement any of his obligations under the lease may entitle the tenant to claim damages or, where the failure is substantial, to retain the rent or to obtain an abatement of rent, or, if the subjects have been destroyed or rendered uninhabitable, to abandon the lease without further liability for payment of rent.[71]

[63a] As to hired articles see *Ditchburn Organisation (Sales) Ltd.* v. *Dundee Corporation*, 1971 S.L.T. 218, and as to brewers' kegs see *Scottish & Newcastle Breweries Ltd.* v. *Edinburgh District Council*, 1979 S.L.T. (Notes) 11.

[64] Bankruptcy (Scotland) Act 1913, s. 115; Bankruptcy (Scotland) Act 1985, s. 33(2).

[65] Companies Act 1985, s. 623; *Anderson's Trs.* v. *Donaldson & Co. Ltd. (in liquidation)*, 1908 S.C. 38.

[66] For a fuller account of the landlord's right of hypothec, see Paton and Cameron, *op. cit.*, Chap. XIII.

[67] Act of Sederunt, Dec. 14, 1756.

[68] para. 27–02.

[69] para. 28–32.

[70] para. 29–33.

[71] Walker, *Prin.*, III, 243, 244.

Warrandice

25–37   Subject to any qualification stated in the lease the landlord warrants that the tenant shall have a valid title to possession at the date of entry and that there will be no encroachment on the tenant's possession during the currency of the let.[72] Eviction, total or partial, founds a claim based on warrandice.[73] The landlord's warrandice does not cover loss resulting from *damnum fatale* or supervenient legislation,[74] but if the eviction is total or substantial the tenant may abandon the lease on the principle of *rei interitus*. The liability of the landlord under warrandice may be excluded also in circumstances where the tenant had knowledge of possible defects in the landlord's title or the loss was due to the fault of the tenant, *e.g.* by his failure to take protective measures to avoid the loss.[75] As to warrandice generally, reference may be made to Volume I, paragraphs 4–36 and 4–38. At common law warrandice implies that the subjects are reasonably fit for the purposes of the lease including, where applicable, the landlord's obligation to keep the premises wind and watertight.[76]

LEASE AS A REAL RIGHT

Common law

25–38   At common law a lease was simply a personal contract of location, binding upon the parties and their executors or representatives but not conferring rights on the tenant which were effective in a question with singular successors of the landlord such as purchasers of the subjects from him.

Leases Act 1449

25–39   This Act, as interpreted by judicial decisions, confers upon tenants a real right in heritable property capable of being let as separate subjects provided that the lease satisfies certain conditions. The conditions are: (1) The lease, if for more than one year, must be in writing, either attested, holograph or adopted as holograph, although informal writing if supported by *rei interventus* is sufficient.[77] Verbal alterations of a written lease are not enforceable in a question with a singular successor of the landlord.[78] (2) The subjects of the lease must be land or heritable property capable of separate possession such as houses, minerals, quarries, ferries, harbours, salmon fishings, land with

---

[72] Gloag, *Contract*, 297; *Shawsrigg Fireclay Co.* v. *Larkhall Collieries* (1903) 5 F. 1131 at 1138; *Huber* v. *Ross*, 1912 S.C. 898 at 912, 913.
[73] *Dougall* v. *Magistrates of Dunfermline*, 1908 S.C. 151.
[74] *Tay Salmon Fisheries* v. *Speedie*, 1929 S.C. 593; *Mackeson* v. *Boyd*, 1942 S.C. 56.
[75] See Paton and Cameron, *op. cit.*, 129.
[76] *Ibid.*, 130–134.
[77] *Buchanan* v. *Harris & Sheldon* (1900) 2 F. 935.
[78] Paton and Cameron, *op. cit.*, 107.

shootings or sporting rights and rights of trout fishings for not less than a year granted for a consideration.[79] (3) The tenant must have taken possession under the lease,[80] but limited acts of possession before the date of entry are not enough.[81] (4) There must be a definite ish although not necessarily a fixed or certain one, e.g. the lease may be for the duration of a liferent. The grant must not be in perpetuity but a lease for 19 years or other period, renewable thereafter for further periods, will be valid against singular successors of the landlord for the defined period then current.[82] (5) It is necessary that there be a definite rent, not necessarily a full rent,[83] but an illusory rent is insufficient.[84] It does not affect the protection given to the tenant by the Act that a grassum has been paid as well as a rent, but if a grassum only has been paid without a continuing rent that is insufficient.[85] Where a garage was let for 10 years in return for a single payment of £200 but the tenant was entitled to terminate the contract and to receive payment of a sum equal to £20 per annum for the unexpired period, it was held that in the absence of a stipulation for rent the tenant had only a personal right of occupation not enforceable against a singular successor of the landlord.[86]

Registration of Leases (Scotland) Act 1857

25–40   A real right may also be created in favour of the tenant by registration of a long lease under this Act on certain conditions provided in the statute as amended.[87]

Personal conditions in leases

25–41   Even although a lease has created a real right in the tenant, not every condition stipulated in it will be binding upon singular successors of the landlord. In general, conditions which are *inter naturalia* of a lease run with the lands, but conditions which are purely personal do not bind successors of the landlord. For particulars of conditions which do, or do not, bind singular successors of the landlord see the undernoted texts and authorities there cited.[88]

SPECIAL TENURES

Kindly tenancy

25–42   The kindly tenants of Lochmaben hold on a tenure which in effect is

---

[79]Freshwater and Salmon Fisheries (Scotland) Act 1976, s. 4.
[80]Bell, *Prin.*, ss. 1209 to 1211; *Johnston* v. *Cullen* (1676) Mor. 15231.
[81]*Millar* v. *McRobbie*, 1949 S.C. 1.
[82]*Wight* v. *Earl of Hopeton* (1763) Mor. 10461; *Campbell* v. *McLean* (1870) 8 M.(H.L.) 40.
[83]Bell, *Prin.*, s. 1201.
[84]Ersk., II,vi,24.
[85]Bell, *Prin.*, s. 1201; Rankine, *Leases*, 144.
[86]*Mann* v. *Houston*, 1957 S.L.T. 89. See also *Wallace* v. *Simmers*, 1960 S.C. 255.
[87]See Chap. 26.
[88]Paton and Cameron, *op. cit.*, 95–97; Walker, *Prin.*, III, 219.

more akin to full ownership than leasehold. See Volume II, paragraph 16–17.

Tenancy-at-will

25–43 A tenancy-at-will is an anomalous type of tenancy which is found occasionally in certain rural and mining areas. It involves the renting of land for building a house without formal title but subject to payment of a rent, transferable by receipt for the price and intimation of the change to the landlord or his factor. The holding is perpetual, without any specified ish. There were disadvantages in this type of holding in respect that the tenant, having no formal title, could not readily borrow on the security of his house and could not require the landlord to grant a formal title. In terms of section 20 of the Land Registration (Scotland) Act 1979 a tenant-at-will who wishes to acquire his landlord's interest may serve a notice in, or as nearly as may be in, the form in Schedule 1 to the Act. The price payable by the tenant-at-will to his landlord as compensation is such amount as, failing agreement, is equal to either (a) the value of the land excluding any buildings thereon but on the assumption that planning permission for residential purposes has been granted in respect of it, or (b) one twenty-fifth of the value of the land including any buildings on it, whichever is the lesser, together with (i) the amount required to discharge any heritable security over the tenancy land or, where the security is over land including the tenancy land, a proportion of the amount lent reasonably attributable to the tenancy land which would be required to restrict the security so as to disburden the tenancy land, subject to a maximum of 90 per cent of the amount of the price payable by the tenant to the landlord for acquisition of the tenancy land, and (ii) the amount required to redeem any feuduty, ground annual or other periodic payment falling to be redeemed under section 5 of the Land Tenure Reform (Scotland) Act 1974. On tender of compensation ascertained as above and the expenses reasonably incurred by the landlord in conveying his interest in the tenancy land and the expenses of discharge or restriction of any heritable security and any redemption of feuduty, etc., the landlord is required to convey such interest on terms or conditions to be agreed between the parties or, failing agreement to be determined by the Lands Tribunal for Scotland as appropriate to the circumstances of the case.[89] Detailed provisions as to the jurisdiction of the tribunal and the procedure in determining references to it on the matter and execution of any necessary conveyance by the sheriff clerk in pursuance of an order by the sheriff in circumstances where the landlord fails to grant a conveyance or cannot be found are contained in section 21 of the Act, and provisions as to the rights and obligations of heritable creditors involved are

---

[89]Land Registration (Scotland) Act 1979, s. 20.

contained in section 22 of the Act. The Act requires the landlord to "convey" his interest in the tenancy land: the deed takes the form of a feu grant or, if the landlord is himself a tenant, an assignation of his lease but only *quoad* the land which is the subject of the tenancy-at-will (1979 Act, s. 21(10)). In terms of section 21(7) of the 1979 Act a landlord has power to execute a valid conveyance notwithstanding that he may be under any such disability as is mentioned in section 7 of the Lands Clauses Consolidation (Scotland) Act 1845, so that persons having a partial or qualified interest, including guardians, may execute an effective conveyance.

STAMP DUTY ON LEASES

Leases—no premium

25–44   Stamp duty on leases of unfurnished subjects is payable in accordance with the following table:

Annual rent		Term not exceeding 7 years or indefinite	Term exceeding 7 years but not exceeding 35 years	Term exceeding 35 years but not exceeding 100 years	Term exceeding 100 years
exceeds	does not exceed				
£	£		£ p	£ p	£ p
	5	Nil	10	60	1·20
5	10	Nil	20	1·20	2·40
10	15	Nil	30	1·80	3·60
15	20	Nil	40	2·40	4·80
20	25	Nil	50	3·00	6·00
25	50	Nil	1·00	6·00	12·00
50	75	Nil	1·50	9·00	18·00
75	100	Nil	2·00	12·00	24·00
100	150	Nil	3·00	18·00	36·00
150	200	Nil	4·00	24·00	48·00
200	250	Nil	5·00	30·00	60·00
250	300	Nil	6·00	36·00	72·00
300	350	Nil	7·00	42·00	84·00
350	400	Nil	8·00	48·00	96·00
400	450	Nil	9·00	54·00	108·00
450	500	Nil	10·00	60·00	120·00
500		50p per £50 or part of £50	£1 per £50 or part of £50	£6 per £50 or part of £50	£12 per £50 or part of £50

Furnished lettings—no premium

A letting agreement for any definite term less than a year of any furnished dwelling-house or apartment where the rent for the term exceeds £500 attracts a fixed duty of £1. No stamp duty is payable where the rent for the term does not exceed £500.

Lease with premium

Stamp duty on premium as for a conveyance on sale.

Duplicates

Where the stamp duty on a lease is less than 50p a duplicate must bear the same stamp: in any other case it must bear a stamp of 50p. A duplicate must also bear a stamp denoting that the original has been duly stamped.

CHAPTER 26

RECORDED LEASES AND REGISTERED INTERESTS IN LEASES

RECORDED LEASES

REGISTERED INTERESTS IN LEASES

PROCEDURE

(1) Recorded Leases

(2) Registered Interests in Leases

RECORDED LEASES

Introduction

26–01   The requirement of possession to confer a real right on the tenant under the Leases Act 1449 made it virtually impracticable for the tenant to use his lease as a fund of credit since there was no method of giving a creditor a real right in security without ceding possession.[1] The principal object of the Registration of Leases (Scotland) Act 1857 was to enable leases which satisfied certain criteria and assignations, including assignations in security, of such leases to be recorded in the Register of Sasines with the effect of making the right of the lessee or assignee real without the necessity of possession.

Requirements for a registrable lease

26–02   The requirements of the 1857 Act, as subsequently amended,[2] for a lease to be recorded are: (1) The lease must be probative and the absence of probative writing cannot be supplied by *rei interventus*.[3] (2) It must be of a duration exceeding 20 years[4] or contain an obligation on the lessor to renew at fixed periods or upon the termination of a life or lives so as to endure for more than that period,[5] thus excluding leases of subjects which, or any part of which, may be used as a dwelling-house.[6] Burns[7] questions whether breaks would disqualify, but it is thought, on analogy with the definition of a long lease in section 8(4) of the Land Tenure Reform (Scotland) Act 1974, that they would not have that effect.[8] Other requirements originally specified in the 1857 Act, such as that the extent of the land should not exceed 50 acres, and that registration be effected at or after the term of entry, have been removed with retrospective effect, principally by the Land Tenure Reform (Scotland) Act 1974, Sched. 6.

---

[1] *Brock* v. *Cabbell* (1831) 5 W. & S. 476.
[2] Registration of Leases (Scotland) Amendment Act 1877. s. 1; Conveyancing (Scotland) Act 1924, ss. 24, 47; Long Leases (Scotland) Act 1954, ss. 26, 27; Succession (Scotland) Act 1964. Sched. 3; Land Tenure Reform (Scotland) Act 1974, s. 18 and Sched. 6.
[3] 1857 Act, s. 1.
[4] Land Tenure Reform (Scotland) Act 1974, Sched. 6, para. 1.
[5] 1857 Act, s. 17, as amended.
[6] Land Tenure Reform (Scotland) Act 1974, s. 8.
[7] at p. 388.
[8] The analogy is admittedly imperfect, since s. 8(4) refers to an agreement between the parties whereas a break is normally exercisable in the sole option of one party.

Description of subjects

26–03   The description of the subjects in a lease which is to be recorded should be more precise than in a lease which is not. In the latter a general description or one which is defined simply by reference to the possession of the landlord or tenant may suffice, but for a recorded lease the description of the subjects must be sufficiently detailed to enable them to be identified by the Keeper for the purposes of the search sheet.[9]

Effect of recording

26–04   A lease duly recorded is, by virtue of such registration, effectual against any singular successor of the lessor whose infeftment is posterior to the date of such registration,[10] a recorded assignation of a registered lease effectually vests the assignee in the right of the granter of the assignation without prejudice to the hypothec or other rights of the landlord,[11] and a recorded assignation of a registered lease gives a real security to the assignee.[12] Registration of a lease is not, however, equivalent to infeftment, and so a purchaser of property held on registered lease was found entitled to resile when it was disclosed that the seller had not a feudal title.[13]

Real right—requirements for recorded and unrecorded leases

26–05   The requirements for creation of a real right in the case of a recorded lease are different in important respects from those in the case of an unrecorded lease, notably that (1) possession is unnecessary to confer a real right—recording has an equivalent effect and so enables a security right to be created over the lessee's interest by recording the security deed without dispossessing the debtor; (2) a recorded lease must be probative whereas informal writing followed by *rei interventus* may be effective in constituting an unrecorded lease; (3) in a recorded lease the rent may be illusory; and (4) there is no requirement that a recorded lease should have a definite ish provided that its duration exceeds the period of 20 years.

Recording equivalent to possession

26–06   Registration affords an alternative method of completing a real right in the lessee; it does not exclude the other mode of creating a real right by possession.[14] From dicta in *Rodger* v. *Crawfords*[15] it was clear that in a competition between an assignee of a recorded lease who had

---

[9]See Vol. II, para. 18–06.
[10]1857 Act, s. 2.
[11]*Ibid*., s. 3.
[12]*Ibid*., s. 4, but see para. 26–11.
[13]*McConnell* v. *Chassels* (1903) 10 S.L.T. 790.
[14]1857 Act, s. 16.
[15](1867) 6 M. 24.

recorded his assignation and an assignee whose assignation had not been recorded the criterion of preference was the date on which the rights of the respective parties were completed by registration or possession, the right of the party who first completed it by either method being preferable. It followed that a purchaser of a registered lease was exposed to the risk that the lease had already been assigned to a third party who, without recording the assignation, had entered into possession, a fact that a search did not disclose. The risk was particularly great if the property had been sub-let since the civil possession of the third party by drawing the rents from the subtenants would not always be evident on inspection of the subjects. That risk has now been substantially removed by the provisions of paragraph 3 of Schedule 6 to the Land Tenure Reform (Scotland) Act 1974 which provides that the registration of any long lease or assignation thereof on or after September 1, 1974 completes the right under it so as to establish a preference over the right of any party to any other registrable lease or writ granted after that date and not registered at the time of the registration of the first-mentioned lease or writ. The provisions in paragraph 3 are without prejudice to section 2 of the Prescription and Limitation (Scotland) Act 1973 so that, if the grantee of a lease or assignation thereof whose title has not been completed by registration possesses the subjects for 20 years or more so that his right has been validated by positive prescription, his title will prevail over that of a grantee of a lease of the subjects or an assignation thereof who has recorded his title but has not had possession, but that is a somewhat unlikely event. In a competition between two parties, both of whom have recorded titles to a lease or assignations thereof, the party whose title is first recorded will prevail.[16]

Method of recording

26–07   Recording of registrable leases or assignations, assignations in security, discharges or renunciations of registered leases in the Register of Sasines is effected by placing a warrant of registration on the deed in the same way as is done in the case of feu grants or dispositions.[17] Where the person effecting registration is not the original grantee of a lease which has not been recorded he may present the lease with a notice of title in Form No. 2 of Schedule B to the Conveyancing (Scotland) Act 1924, adapted to incorporate a description of the lease as prescribed in Schedule J to that Act; the warrant of registration on the notice of title will run:

Register on behalf of the within named A in the Register of the

[16] 1857 Act, s. 12.
[17] See Vol. II, para. 24–13.

County of   along with the (lease) docqueted
with reference hereto,

and the lease will be docqueted:

Docqueted with reference to the notice of title in favour of A
recorded of even date herewith.[18]

Conversion of long leases into feus

26–08   The Long Leases (Scotland) Act 1954 enabled the tenants of
dwelling-houses under leases for a period of not less than 50 years
granted before August 10, 1914 to give notice to the landlord to grant
a feu right on making a payment to the landlord calculated in the way
prescribed in the Act. Since notice required to be given within five
years of the commencement of the Act (September 1, 1954), however,
the rights conferred by it are no longer exercisable.

REGISTERED INTERESTS IN LEASES

Long leases and shorter leases

26–09   Section 28(1) of the Land Registration (Scotland) Act 1979 defines a
long lease as a probative lease (a) exceeding 20 years or (b) which is
subject to any provision whereby any person holding the interest of the
grantor is under a future obligation, if so requested by the grantee, to
renew the lease so that the total duration could (in terms of the lease,
as renewed, and without any subsequent agreement, express or
implied, between the persons holding the interests of the grantor and
the grantee) extend for more than 20 years. This definition is similar in
effect to, but not identical with, the definition of long lease in section
8(4) of the Land Tenure Reform (Scotland) Act 1974. In this chapter
the term "shorter lease" is used to describe a lease which is not a long
lease as defined in the 1979 Act.

Shorter leases

26–10   Shorter leases are excluded from the definition of an interest in
land[19] and so are not registrable under the 1979 Act. They are
overriding interests but, unlike other overriding interests, they cannot
be noted on the Register.[20] The reasons for their exclusion are that
they are numerous and of a short-term and transitory nature,[21] and
may have been terminated or expired or continued by tacit relocation
without the Keeper's knowledge.

---

[18]Conveyancing (Scotland) Act 1924, s. 24 and Sched. J.
[19]Land Registration (Scotland) Act 1979, s. 28(1).
[20]Ibid., s. 6(4).
[21]Report by Committee on Registration of Title (Henry Report), Cmnd. 4137 (1969), para. 45.

Registration of long leases

26–11   Once an area has become operational for the purposes of registration of title, a lessee under a long lease can obtain a real right *only* by registration of his interest in the Land Register.[22] The practical consequences of this provision after the date when an area has become operational (the operational date) may be analysed as follows:

(1) Interest created by lease. If the lessee's interest has been or is created by execution and delivery of a lease in his favour but has not been made real before the operational date by recording in the Register of Sasines or by possession, the lessee can obtain a real right only by registration of his interest in the Land Register.

(2) Interest acquired by assignation or succession. If the lessee's interest has been acquired by assignation, whether for value or by way of gift, or by succession, and his interest has not been made real before the operational date then, even if the interest of the lessee's author has been made real by recording in the Register of Sasines or by possession, the interest of the assignee or successor can be made real only by registration of it in the Land Register.

(3) Interest acquired by partial assignation or sub-lease. If an interest in or under a lease has been acquired by the grantee of a partial assignation or a sub-lease and that interest has not been made real before the operational date, then, even if the interest of his author has been made real by recording in the Register of Sasines or by possession, the interest of the grantee of the partial assignation or sub-lease can be made real only by registration of it in the Land Register.

(4) Securities. The position in relation to the creation of securities over a lessee's interest differs from that where the lessee's interest itself is being acquired. A lessee whose interest has already been made real by recording in the Register of Sasines may grant a standard security over his interest after the operational date, and the creditor's title can be completed by recording the standard security in the Register of Sasines. Likewise, if the lessee has a right which has already been made real by possession before the operational date he may record the lease in the Register of Sasines and grant a standard security over his interest, which can be made a real right in security by recording in the Register of Sasines.[23]

(5) Dealings with interests of lessees already registered in Land Register. When the interest of a lessee under a long lease has been registered in the Land Register all subsequent dealings with it, whether assignations, registrable sub-leases or the granting of standard securities, will be registered in the Land Register.

---

[22]Land Registration (Scotland) Act 1979, s. 3(3).
[23]See R.T.P.B., paras. D.4.17 to D.4.19.

Description of subjects

26–12 **(1) First registration**. When first registration is induced by the grant of a long lease or by transfer of the interest of the tenant in such a lease, it is necessary to describe the subjects as in sasine practice.[24] Further, the description must be sufficient to enable the Keeper to identify the subjects on the Ordnance Map.

(2) Long lease of whole registered interest. Where a long lease is granted over the whole of a proprietor's interest that has already been registered, the subjects should be described by reference to the title number of the registered interest, thus:

> All and Whole the subjects (*insert postal address if appropriate*) registered under Title Number(s)

(3) Long lease of part of registered interest. Where a long lease is of a part of a proprietor's registered interest the part let should be described in sufficient detail to enable it to be identified on the Ordnance Map and a plan is desirable. The description might be as follows:

> All and Whole (*describe so as to enable identification on Ordnance Map*) being part of the subjects registered under Title Number(s)

Alternatively the part let may be described as the whole of the subjects under exception of a specified part, thus:

> All and Whole the subjects registered under Title Number(s) with the exception of (*describe so as to enable identification on Ordnance Map*).

If the part let is one or more parcels separately described in the title sheet of the registered interest, it may be sufficiently described by reference to the particular parcel or parcels in the title sheet of the registered interest, thus:

> All and Whole the subjects (*insert postal address if appropriate*) (First) *or* (First) and (Second) registered under Title Number

> or

> All and Whole the subjects (*insert postal address if appropriate*) marked plot(s) number(s)   on the plan of Title Number

(4) Dealing with lease which is a registered interest. Where the tenant's interest under a long lease has already been registered the subjects may be described in any subsequent dealing with it, *e.g.* an assignation or renunciation of or standard security over it, by reference to the title number of the tenant's registered interest in the lease, thus:

---

[24] See para. 26–03.

All and Whole the subjects (*insert postal address if appropriate*) registered under Title Number

(5) Dealing with part of lease which is a registered interest. Where the dealing is with part only of the tenant's registered interest in the lease, the part should be described on the same lines as already indicated in sub-paragraph (3) above in relation to a part of a registered interest.[25]

PROCEDURE

(1) Recorded Leases

Examination of title

26–13   In a transaction where a lease is being granted which is to be recorded in the Register of Sasines the granter's title should be examined in the same way as in a transaction of purchase of the subjects.[26] In particular, attention should be directed to the following matters:

(1) Granter's infeftment. It is essential that the granter be infeft in the subjects. It is not sufficient that he has a right to the subjects within the meaning of section 3 of the Conveyancing (Scotland) Act 1924 since deduction of title is not competent in a lease; in such a case he should complete title by a notice of title, duly recorded.

(2) Searches. These should be provided with an interim report to, as nearly as practicable, the date of entry or settlement. It has been held that failure by a prospective lessee to search the record before entering into a lease was an element in putting him *in mala fide*.[27] A letter of obligation regarding searches should be obtained at entry in the form, appropriately adapted, of that recommended in a purchase and sale transaction.

(3) Heritable securities. If a search discloses the existence of a heritable security burdening the lessor's title, the consent of the heritable creditor to the lease should be obtained. If the security is a standard security a long lease granted by the debtor is reducible unless standard condition 6 of Schedule 3 to the Conveyancing and Feudal Reform (Scotland) Act 1970 has been varied to permit such a lease, which would seldom be the case. If the security was in the form of a bond and disposition in security the granting of a long lease would seldom be an act of ordinary administration, and if the security had been created by *ex facie* absolute disposition it would be difficult to justify the granting of a long lease under an implied mandate or as an act which did not trench on the security. In any event, whatever the form of the

---

[25] See R.T.P.B., paras. D.4.22 and E.42.
[26] See Vol. II, Chap. 21.
[27] *Trade Development Bank* v. *Warriner & Mason (Scotland) Ltd.*, 1980 S.C. 74 at 94.

security, a long lease granted without the consent of the heritable creditor would be reducible if the creditor subsequently enforced his security by sale.[28]

(4) **Conditions of title**. It should be checked that any buildings, existing or to be erected by the lessee on the leasehold subjects, or the proposed use of them by the lessee, are not or would not be in contravention of conditions of the lessor's title.

Possession

26–14   Normally it is contemplated that the lessee under a long lease will receive vacant possession. In such circumstances it should be confirmed that the proprietor of the subjects has or will have physical possession of the subjects on the date of entry under the proposed lease. If there are any existing tenancies of the subjects or any part of them it should have been stipulated in the missives for the new lease that the lessor will have given valid notice to terminate such tenancies with effect before or at the date of entry under the proposed new lease. The possibility of the right to terminate such tenancies being precluded or restricted by statute, *e.g.* the Agricultural Holdings Acts or the Tenancy of Shops (Scotland) Act 1949 as renewed or the Rent (Scotland) Acts should be kept in view by the lessor. If the subjects let include a matrimonial home, a lease is a dealing in terms of the Matrimonial Homes (Family Protection) (Scotland) Act 1981 and so a consent or renunciation by the non-entitled spouse or an affidavit by the entitled spouse will be required in whichever of the forms contained in paragraph 21–29, 21–30 or 21–31 of Volume II may be appropriate.

Terms and conditions of lease

26–15   The adjustment of the terms and conditions of the lease to be granted is a matter for negotiation between the parties and is considered more fully later in relation to particular kinds of subjects.[29] Suffice to say that in long leases matters of particular importance are restrictions on assignation or sub-letting, rent and rent reviews, restrictions on use, the lessee's obligations as to permitted buildings in the case of a building lease, the lessee's obligations as to repair and maintenance and possibly rebuilding and conventional irritancy on contravention of conditions of the lease.

Conveyancing procedures

26–16   The conveyancing procedures in the transaction will be on the same

---

[28]See *Cumming* v. *Stewart*, 1928 S.C. 296.
[29]See Chaps. 27, 28 and 29.

lines as those already outlined in relation to the sale and purchase of heritable property[30] *mutatis mutandis.*

(2) Registered Interests in Leases

First registration

26–17   When a long lease is granted over subjects situated in whole or in part within an operational area, whether or not the interest of the proprietor of the subjects has yet been registered, the interest of the lessee can become a real right only by registration in the Land Register.[31] Registration is effected by an application on Form 1 accompanied by a sufficient progress of titles establishing the lessor's ownership and all prior writs containing burdens or rights affecting the subjects, any existing heritable securities affecting the subjects with any necessary consent to the lease (if not incorporated therein), any P16 report and any other relevant documents.[32] If any heritable security is being created contemporaneously over the lessee's interest application for registration of the security should be made on Form 2.

26–18   **Examination of title.** In a transaction inducing first registration of the lessee's interest the title of the lessor should be examined in the same way as already indicated in the case of a lease which is to be recorded in the Register of Sasines.[33]

(1) *Granter's infeftment.* This is necessary. If the granter is not infeft the Keeper will normally register the lessee's interest but with exclusion of indemnity.

(2) *Reports.* Form 10 and Form 11 reports should be obtained as in the case of a transaction of purchase and sale which induces first registration.[34] If doubt exists as to the boundaries of the subjects, a P16 report may be obtained which should accompany the application for registration.

(3) *Heritable securities and conditions of lessor's title.* Investigations on these matters should be made as in a transaction for the granting of a lease to be recorded in the Register of Sasines.[35]

The Keeper will also examine the lessor's title before registering the lessee's interest in the lease but it is preferable that any defects should be discovered and, unless they are such as may be accepted by the Keeper without exclusion of indemnity in the exercise of his discretion,

---

[30]Vol. II, para. 23–02.
[31]See para. 26–11 and R.T.P.B., paras. D.1.07 and D.1.08.
[32]R.T.P.B., para. B.3.01.
[33]See para. 26–13.
[34]See Vol. II, paras. 23–18 to 23–20.
[35]See para. 26–13.

remedied where practicable before submission of the application for registration.

26–19 **Possession**. Where it is intended that the lessee under the long lease is to have vacant possession of the subjects it is necessary to ensure that there are no existing leases or tenancies of the subjects or any part of them which have been made real by possession, or that any such leases or tenancies have been or will be terminated before or at the date of entry under the proposed long lease,[36] since any existing unrecorded leases will be overriding interests which are excluded from the Keeper's indemnity.[37] If the subjects are or include a matrimonial home the procedure in paragraph 26–14 *supra* should be adopted. Any existing long lease recorded in the Register of Sasines or the tenant's interest in which has been registered in the Land Register will, of course, be disclosed in the Form 10 or Form 11 report. It is peculiarly important that the possession of the lessee under the long lease being now registered should commence immediately on the date of entry if the Keeper's indemnity is excluded because the lessor is not infeft, so that the period of 10 years may commence to run on the expiry of which the exclusion may be removed.[38]

26–20 **Terms and conditions of lease**. See paragraph 26–15, *supra*.

26–21 **Conveyancing procedures**. The conveyancing procedures in the transaction will be on the same lines as those already outlined in relation to a sale and purchase which induces first registration in the Land Register[39] *mutatis mutandis*.

Leases out of registered interests

26–22 Where a long lease is being granted of the whole or part of the interest of a proprietor which has been registered in the Land Register, or where a long sub-lease is being granted out of the interest of an existing lessee which has been so registered, the interest of the new lessee or sub-lessee can be made real only by registration in the Land Register. In any such transaction, whether the new lease or sub-lease is of the whole or part of the subjects comprised in the registered interest of the proprietor or head lessee, as the case may be, application for the registration of the interest of the lessee or sub-lessee under the new lease or sub-lease should be made on Form 3.[40] If the registered proprietor of the interest has died and his executor has not yet completed title the application by the lessee for registration of his interest under the lease does not have the effect of completing the title

---

[36]See para. 26–14.
[37]Land Registration (Scotland) Act 1979, s. 12(3)(*h*).
[38]R.T.P.B., para. C.63.
[39]See Vol. II, para. 23–17.
[40]R.T.P.B., para. D.2.17.

of the executor of the proprietor or lessor so as to satisfy the common law rule which requires infeftment of the landlord. To obtain that result it is necessary for the executor to apply on Form 2 together with the land certificate in name of the deceased proprietor and the confirmation establishing the executor's right, when the executor's title will be completed without the need of a notice of title being expede.[41]

26–23 **Examination of title**. It is unnecessary to examine the title of the proprietor or head lessee, as the case may be, whose interest has been registered but, if there have been any subsequent dealings with or transmissions of the registered interest which have not entered the Land Register, the sufficiency of the relevant links or midcouples should be checked. Form 12 and Form 13 reports should be obtained. If there are any existing heritable securities over the registered interest of the proprietor or head lessee the consent of the heritable creditor to the new lease or sub-lease should be obtained.

26–24 **Possession**. If vacant possession of the subjects of the new long lease is to be given it should be confirmed that there are no existing shorter leases affecting the subjects or, if there are any, that valid notice terminating them has been given to take effect before or at the date of entry under the new lease. If the subjects include a matrimonial home the procedure suggested in paragraph 26–14 *supra* should be adopted. Any existing long leases will be disclosed in the Form 12 or Form 13 report, unless the lessee has prior to the commencement of the Land Registration (Scotland) Act 1979 acquired a real right to the subjects of the lease by virtue of possession.

26–25 **Terms and conditions of lease**. See paragraph 26–15, *supra*.

26–26 **Conveyancing procedures**. The conveyancing procedures in the transaction will be similar to those already outlined in relation to a transaction of sale and purchase of a registered interest[42] *mutatis mutandis*.

INTERPOSED LEASES

Introduction

26–27   Where a long lease is being granted it may be that the subjects are already let under shorter leases or long leases and it is intended that the new lessee will have only civil possession, *i.e.* he will step into the shoes of the lessor and receive the rents payable by the existing tenants. Before the Land Tenure Reform (Scotland) Act 1974 was passed, it was thought that there was no power in a proprietor who had

---

[41]Land Registration (Scotland) Act 1979. s. 3(6) and rule 9(1) of the Land Registration (Scotland) Rules 1980. (S.I. 1980 No. 1413) (S.114).

[42]See Vol. II. para. 23–26.

already granted a lease or leases to interpose another party as tenant so as to degrade an existing tenant into the position of sub-tenant,[43] and a lease of lands already let was regarded as not being a lease at all.[44] Section 17 of the 1974 Act has removed this difficulty by permitting the proprietor to interpose a lease, whether longer or shorter or of the same duration as the existing tenancy or tenancies, with the effect that the new lessee becomes the lessor under the existing lease or leases as if the existing lease or leases had been assigned to the grantee of the interposed lease. On the termination, for any reason, of the interposed lease any remaining rights and obligations of the grantee of it vest or will be deemed to have vested in the person in right of the granter of the interposed lease on the same terms and conditions as if that lease had not been granted. The interposed lease may be granted by "the person in right of the lessor of a lease," *i.e.* by the original lessor or his successor. That could be (1) the proprietor of the subjects leased or (2) a lessee who had granted a sub-lease, since there is nothing in the word "lessor" that restricts its meaning to a proprietor. The section is retroactive and validates interposed leases granted prior to the passing of the 1974 Act.

Use

26–28   A typical situation in which the facility of the interposed lease is useful is where a company has constructed, or acquired and modernised, an office block and granted leases, shorter or long, of several office premises therein. The developing company's organisation is not geared to continuing management of property but it nevertheless wishes to obtain a return upon its investment in the form of income from the rents, increasing with periodical rent reviews. In these circumstances it may grant an interposed lease in favour of a property management company at an initial rent which is slightly less than the total of the rents receivable under the existing leases, with provisions for rent review, perhaps determined in relation to increasing rents from the existing leases. The benefits to the developing company are that it is relieved of the task of continuing administration and management of the block and also has the personal obligation of a responsible management company for payment of the rent imposed in the interposed lease. The management company effectively receives remuneration for its services in the difference between the total of the rents payable under the existing leases (now effectively sub-leases) and the lower rent payable under the interposed lease.

Conveyancing aspects

26–29   Where an interposed lease is to be recorded in the Register of

---

[43] *Wilson* v. *Wilson* (1859) 21 D. 309 at 312.
[44] *Bruce* v. *Assessor for Zetland* (1882) 10 R. 34.

Sasines (in non-operational areas) or induces first registration in the Land Register (operational areas) the granter's title should be examined as in the case of any new long lease.[45] Where it is to be granted out of a registered interest examination of title is restricted as explained in paragraph 26–23 *supra*.

It is also necessary to examine the existing leases as to the validity of their constitution and to ensure that none of their terms or conditions are inconsistent with those to be inserted in the interposed lease. In particular the amount of the rents and the provisions for rent review must be noted in order to negotiate the initial rent and provisions for review to be contained in the interposed lease. Irritancy clauses should also be examined; the provisions in respect of irritancy in the interposed lease must not be more severe than those in the existing leases.

The interposed lease, where the subjects are situated in an area which is not yet operational, will be recorded with a warrant of registration in the Register of Sasines. Where the subjects are situated in an operational area, application for registration of the lessee's interest in the Land Register will be made on Form 1 or Form 3, as appropriate.[46]

---

[45]See para. 26–13.
[46]See paras. 26–17 and 26–22.

CHAPTER 27

LEASES OF RESIDENTIAL PROPERTY

(B) Furnished Lettings

(C) Prior Notice

(D) Heritable Securities

THE PUBLIC SECTOR

Introduction

27–01   The letting of urban dwelling-houses is subject to important statutory controls and it is essential that practitioners in framing leases of dwelling-houses should have the relevant legislation in mind. The principal statutory provisions are now consolidated in the Rent (Scotland) Act 1984 and, particularly as regards leases in the public sector, the Tenants' Rights, Etc. (Scotland) Act 1980.[1] A full

---

[1]Minor amendments to the 1984 Act have been made by the Rent (Amendment) Act 1985, s. 1, the Housing (Consequential Provisions) Act 1985, Sched. 2 and the Law Reform (Miscellaneous Provisions) (Scotland) Act 1985, Sched. 2; and important amendments to the 1980 Act have been made by the Tenants' Rights, Etc. (Scotland) Amendment Act 1980, the Local Government (Miscellaneous Provisions) (Scotland) Act 1981, the Social Security and Housing Benefits Act 1982, the Tenants' Rights, Etc. (Scotland) Amendment Act 1984, the Rent (Scotland) Act 1984 and the Housing (Scotland) Act 1986.

treatment of the statutory provisions is outwith the scope of this work, but some of the more important matters from a conveyancing aspect are noticed briefly *infra* in respect of leases of dwelling-houses in the private sector[2] and in the public sector.[3] For an up-to-date account of the relevant statutory provisions reference may be made to the undernoted texts.[4] As regards leases of dwelling-houses associated with agricultural holdings the provisions of the Agricultural Holdings Acts may also be relevant.

THE PRIVATE SECTOR

Protected tenancies

27–02   A protected tenancy or sub-tenancy of a dwelling-house or part of a dwelling-house as defined in Part I of the Rent (Scotland) Act 1984 has certain important aspects, principally (1) the rent stipulated in the document of lease may be altered at the instance of the landlord or the tenant in accordance with the procedure prescribed in the Act and determined by the rent officer or the Rent Assessment Committee on the basis of the concept of "fair rent,"[5] (2) the landlord's right to recover possession of the subjects on breach of conditions by the tenant or on expiry of the term of the lease is restricted, notably by a discretion exercisable by the sheriff,[6] and (3) the right to the tenancy continues after the death of the tenant to a successor as a statutory tenant and on the death of a statutory tenant to his or her successor.[7]

27–03   **Definition—the valuation roll limit**. A tenancy or sub-tenancy is unprotected if (1) in the case of a dwelling-house which was shown on the valuation roll on March 23, 1965 its rateable value exceeded £200 per annum, or (2) in the case of a dwelling-house which first entered on the valuation roll on or after April 1, 1978 the rateable value exceeded £600 per annum, or (3) in the case of a dwelling-house which first entered the valuation roll on or after April 1, 1985 the rateable value was or is more than £1,600 per annum.[8] It follows that a tenancy of which the rateable value on the appropriate day did not exceed the relevant limit stated is a protected tenancy unless it falls within any of the exceptions aftermentioned.[9]

27–04   **Exceptions**. A tenancy which would otherwise be a protected tenancy is nevertheless not protected in certain circumstances, namely (1) if it

---

[2]paras. 27–02 to 27–37.
[3]paras. 27–38 to 27–49.
[4]D.G. McKerrell, *The Rent Acts* (1985); A.G.M. Duncan and J.A.D. Hope, *The Rent (Scotland) Act 1984*.
[5]Rent (Scotland) Act 1984, ss. 28–54.
[6]*Ibid.*, ss. 11–21.
[7]*Ibid.*, s. 3 and Sched. 1. See D.G. McKerrell, *op. cit.*, 13 to 19.
[8]*Ibid.*, s. 1; Protected Tenancies and Part VII Contracts (Rateable Value Limits) (Scotland) Order 1985 (S.I. 1985 No. 314).
[9]See paras. 27–04 to 27–06.

is a tenancy at a low rent,[10] (2) if it is a tenancy of a dwelling-house *bona fide* let at a rent which includes payments in respect of board or attendance,[11] (3) if it is a tenancy granted to a person who is pursuing or intends to pursue a course of study provided by an institution specified by the Secretary of State and is so granted by that institution or by another specified institution or body of persons,[12] (4) if it is a tenancy for the purpose of conferring on the tenant the right to occupy the dwelling-house for a holiday,[13] (5) if it is a tenancy of a dwelling-house let with agricultural land exceeding two acres in extent,[14] (6) if the tenancy is of a dwelling-house where the landlord's interest belongs to the Crown,[15] (7) if the tenancy is one when at any time the interest of the landlord belongs to a local authority or other housing body specified,[16] (8) if the tenancy is of a dwelling-house forming part of a building where the landlord's interest belongs to a resident landlord,[17] (9) if the tenancy is of a dwelling-house which consists of or comprises premises licensed for the sale of exciseable liquor for consumption on the premises,[18] or (10) if the tenancy is one to which the Tenancy of Shops (Scotland) Act 1949 applies.[19]

Of those exceptions the only ones commonly encountered which are of particular relevance to the framing of leases are:

No. (2) above (tenancies let at a rent which includes payments in respect of board or attendance) which are considered in paragraphs 27–05 and 27–30 *infra*.

No. (5) above (tenancies of dwelling-houses let with agricultural land) which are treated in Chapter 28 *infra*.[19a]

No. (7) above (tenancies where landlord is a local authority) which are leases in the public sector considered in paragraphs 27–38 to 27–49 *infra*.

No. (8) above (tenancy with resident landlord) which is treated in paragraph 27–06 *infra*.

Nos. (9) and (10) above (tenancies of licensed premises and shops) which are commercial leases considered in Chapter 29 *infra*.

27–05 **Tenancies let at rent which includes payment for board or attendance.** A tenancy is unprotected under this heading only if (a) the tenancy is a "bona fide" let[20]; (b) "board" is something more than an early-

---

[10]Rent (Scotland) Act 1984, s. 2(1)(a). For illustrations of the application of the exception, see D.G. McKerrell, *op. cit.*, 4.

[11]Rent (Scotland) Act 1984, s. 2(1)(b) and (4).

[12]*Ibid.*, s. 2(1)(c).

[13]*Ibid.*, s. 2(1)(d).

[14]*Ibid.*, ss. 1(3) and 2(1)(e).

[15]*Ibid.*, s. 4.

[16]*Ibid.*, s. 5. As to tenancies in the public sector, see paras. 27–38 to 27–49.

[17]*Ibid.*, s. 6.

[18]*Ibid.*, s. 10(1).

[19]*Ibid.*, s. 10(2).

[19a]The relevant point of time at which the character of the subjects as falling within this exception is determined is the date when recovery of possession is sought, not the date of the granting of the lease: *Campbell* v. *McQuillan*, 1983 S.L.T. 210.

[20]1984 Act, s. 2(1)(b).

morning cup of tea[21] but a continental breakfast may be sufficient.[22] The payment in respect of attendance must, having regard to the value of the attendance to the tenant, form a substantial part of the whole rent.[23] "Attendance" means service personal to the tenant[24] provided under the contract of tenancy.[25] Services which are not for the tenant's exclusive benefit, *e.g.* the heating of a communal water supply or the cleaning of common passages, vestibules or stairways do not amount to attendance,[26] but if the services, although supplied also to other tenants in a block of flats, have some personal element such as carrying fuel to an individual flat, they may amount to attendance.[27] Where personal services are given by an employee of the landlord to several tenants, the wages of the employee must be apportioned among the tenants for the purpose of determining whether the payment for provision of the services forms a substantial part of the rent,[28] but the court may take into account what the tenant would have had to pay if the landlord did not provide the service.[29] For provisions that may be inserted in a style of lease with board and/or attendance which would not create a protected tenancy, see paragraph 27–30 *infra*.

27–06 **Tenancies where landlord resident**. A tenancy is not protected in terms of section 6 of the Rent (Scotland) Act 1984 if it satisfies certain specified conditions. Broadly these are: (1) the subjects let are a dwelling-house (not being a whole flat in a purpose-built block of flats[29a]) which forms part only of a building; (2) when the tenancy was granted by the landlord he must have occupied as his residence another dwelling-house which also forms part of the same building with the qualification, if the landlords are trustees, that occupation of the other dwelling-house may be by a liferenter or fiar under the trust; and (3) at all times since the tenancy was granted the landlord's interest has belonged to a person who, at the time he owned that interest, occupied as his residence another dwelling-house which also formed part of the building. The provisions of section 6 can be of use where the owner-occupier of a large house subdivides it into several flats, continuing to occupy one flat himself. If the dwelling-house is purchased with a view to subdivision into flats to be let with retention of one flat for occupation by the purchaser himself, the landlord must

[21]*Wilkes* v. *Goodwin* [1923] 2 K.B. 86.
[22]*Holiday Flat Co.* v. *Kuczera*, 1978 S.L.T. (Sh.Ct.) 47. See also *Gavin* v. *Lindsay*, 1987 S.L.T. (Sh.Ct.) 12.
[23]Rent (Scotland) Act 1984, s. 2(4). "Substantial" should be at least 23 per cent—A.G.M. Duncan and J.A.D. Hope, *op. cit.*, 58/2.
[24]*Palser* v. *Grinling, Property Holding Co. Ltd.* v. *Mischeff* [1948] A.C. 291, 310.
[25]*Michael* v. *Phillips* [1924] 1 K.B. 16, 25, C.A.
[26]*Palser* v. *Grinling, Property Holding Co. Ltd.* v. *Mischeff, supra; Engvall* v. *Ideal Flats Ltd.* [1945] 1 All E.R. 230, 233, C.A.
[27]*Nye* v. *Davis* [1922] 2 K.B. 56; *Palser* v. *Grinling, Property Holding Co. Ltd.* v. *Mischeff, supra* at 311.
[28]*Palser* v. *Grinling, Property Holding Co. Ltd.* v. *Mischeff, supra* at 318, 319.
[29]*Maltby* v. *Butler* (1950) 155 E.G. 247.
[29a]For definition see 1984 Act, s. 8(*a*).

(a) enter into occupation of his own flat *before* he grants tenancies of the other flats, *or* (b) actually occupy the retained flat within 28 days of the date of the conveyance of the building to him,[30] *or* (c) notify the tenant of the let flat in writing within that period of 28 days that he intends to occupy the retained flat as his residence and actually occupy it (i) within six months of the date of the conveyance (settlement) or (ii) before the date when he ceases to be the landlord, *e.g.* on sale of the building, whichever is the earlier.

There is a saving provision that the tenancy of a let flat does not cease to be unprotected by reason of the failure of the landlord to occupy his part of the building for a period of not more than 24 months after the landlord's death during which his interest is vested in his executor.[31] As to an appropriate provision to be inserted in a lease of another flat by a resident landlord, see paragraph 27–26 *infra*.

7–07 **Statutory tenants and tenancies.** The rights of a statutory tenant and his successors on the death of a tenant of a dwelling-house let under a protected tenancy should be kept in view by a solicitor acting for a prospective granter of a tenancy which is or may become protected and explained to his client as one of the elements of a protected tenancy.[32]

7–08 **Security of tenure.** The most important feature of a protected tenancy is the security of tenure given to the tenant and any statutory tenant or successor by reason of the restrictions imposed by the Rent Acts upon the right of the landlord to recover possession of the let dwelling-house. The circumstances in which the court *may* grant an order for recovery of possession (the discretionary cases) are listed in Part I of Schedule 2 to the Rent (Scotland) Act 1984: the circumstances in which the court *must* grant an order for recovery of possession (the mandatory cases) are listed in Part II of that Schedule. Practising solicitors should be familiar with the various discretionary and mandatory cases and a helpful modern commentary upon them is contained in the undernoted text.[33] Reference to them, so far as relevant to the framing of leases, is made in the styles contained in this chapter.

In addition, the Matrimonial Homes (Family Protection) (Scotland) Act 1981 confers occupancy rights upon the spouse of the tenant of a dwelling-house which is a matrimonial home.[34] If the dwelling-house is a matrimonial home the landlord cannot recover possession if the tenant renounces the let unless the non-entitled spouse has consented

---

[30]Although in subs. (8)(c) of s. 6 "conveyance" is defined as including the grant of the tenancy, in Scottish practice this date would probably be construed as the date of settlement since until delivery of the disposition there has not been effective transfer of ownership.

[31]For details see the Rent (Scotland) Act 1984, s. 6(3)(c) and D.G. McKerrell, *op. cit.*, 7–9.

[32]1984 Act, s. 3. As to the need for possession see A.G.M. Duncan and J.A.D. Hope, *op. cit.*, 58/3: for a convenient summary of the rights of statutory tenants see D.G. McKerrell, *op cit.*, 7–9.

[33]D.G. McKerrell, *op. cit.*, 25–34.

[34]s. 1.

to the renunciation nor can he do so even where the tenant has abandoned the subjects, a ground which might otherwise have entitled him to repossess. A person co-habiting with the tenant may obtain similar rights under an order of the court.[35] For the purposes of the Act "tenant" includes a sub-tenant and a statutory tenant under the Rent Acts.[36] Accordingly the 1981 Act imposes restraints upon the landlord's right to recover possession in addition to those under the Rent (Scotland) Act 1984.

27–09   **Service tenancies and service occupancies.** There is a well-recognised distinction in law between a service tenancy and a service occupancy. A service tenancy is one where a person, although employed by the proprietor of the house, occupies it *qua* tenant, and the character of the right as being a true tenancy may be indicated by an agreement providing for payment of rent and termination on notice and by the fact that the tenant is not bound to occupy the house as a condition of his employment.[37] On the other hand a service occupancy is one where the house is occupied by an employee as such and the right to occupy is a condition of employment,[38] is in the nature of a licence rather than a tenancy and is not a protected tenancy under the Rent (Scotland) Act 1984 although the occupier has a measure of protection against eviction without due process of law under Part III of the Act. From the point of view of the employer/landlord, where he wishes to create a service occupancy so that he may recover possession of the house on termination of the occupier's employment, the safest method is to charge no rent or a low rent within the meaning of section 2(1)(a) of the 1984 Act and to make occupancy a condition of employment under the service contract. If the occupancy is truly a service occupancy of a matrimonial home and the lease is subject to a requirement that the entitled spouse must reside therein, the non-entitled spouse cannot apply for an order transferring the tenancy to her.[39]

27–10   **Short tenancies.** A new type of tenancy, a short tenancy, was introduced by the Tenants' Rights, Etc. (Scotland) Act 1980.[40] The relevant provisions of the 1980 Act contained in sections 34, 35 and 36 are now reproduced in sections 9, 13 and 14 of the Rent (Scotland) Act 1984 read along with Schedule 2, Part II, Case 15 which replaces the former Case 11D introduced in 1980. Although a short tenancy is a protected tenancy it has the important advantage that possession can

---

[35] 1981 Act, s. 18.

[36] *Ibid.*, s. 22.

[37] *MacGregor* v. *Dunnett*, 1949 S.C. 510; *British Transport Commission* v. *Assessor for Inverness*, 1952 S.C. 511, 519.

[38] *Marquis of Bute* v. *Prenderleith*, 1921 S.C. 281.

[39] Matrimonial Homes (Family Protection) (Scotland) Act 1981, s. 13(7).

[40] Amended by the Tenants' Rights, Etc. (Scotland) Amendment Acts 1980 and 1984, the Local Government (Miscellaneous Provisions) (Scotland) Act 1981, s. 35 and the Local Government and Planning (Scotland) Act 1982, ss. 53–55.

be recovered by the landlord at the end of the stipulated period of the lease subject to observance of the provisions as to service of notice of intention to apply for an order to recover possession prescribed in section 14 of the 1984 Act.

27–11   As regards creation of a short tenancy, the following matters in framing the lease and the procedures to be followed are important:

(1) Before the creation of the short tenancy the landlord must give an appropriate written notice to the prospective tenant informing him that the tenancy will be a short tenancy for the purposes of the 1984 Act.[41]

(2) Either the rent, at the commencement of the tenancy, has been registered or the landlord has applied for and been granted a certificate of fair rent and within 14 days after the commencement of the tenancy makes application for that fair rent to be registered, and the application cannot be withdrawn.[42]

(3) It is necessary that, immediately before the creation of the short tenancy, the tenant was not a protected or statutory tenant unless as the result of a previous short tenancy.[43] (This requirement is designed to prevent the conversion of an existing protected tenancy into a short tenancy.)

(4) The period of the short tenancy specified in the agreement must be not less than one nor more than five years.[44] (That normally involves that the agreement must be in probative or holograph writing.)

(5) The tenancy agreement must not contain any provision whereby the landlord may terminate the tenancy before the expiry of the specified period other than for non-payment of rent or breach of any other obligation of the tenancy.[45] (So there cannot be an earlier break in the option of the landlord.)

(6) The tenancy agreement must be stamped appropriately if the rent exceeds £500 per annum.[46]

27–12   As to termination of the tenancy and recovery of possession:

(a) The landlord may recover possession on or after the termination of the tenancy by serving on the tenant a notice in writing of his intention to apply to the court for termination of the tenancy and thereafter applying to the court for such an order. The notice should be served before or not less than three months after the expiry of the period of the lease stated in the agreement to let and the application to the court must be made not less than three nor more than six months

---

[41]1984 Act, s. 9(1)(d). For the form of notice see Short Tenancies (Prescribed Information) (Scotland) Order 1980 (S.I. 1980 No. 1666).
[42]Ibid., s. 9(1)(e) and (2). As to registration of rents see para. 27–13.
[43]Ibid., s. 9(1)(a).
[44]Ibid., s. 9(1)(b).
[45]Ibid., s. 9(1)(c).
[46]Stamp Act 1891. See para. 25–44.

after service of the notice. If the landlord fails to serve the notice timeously the tenancy continues for a period of 12 months from the stipulated period of its expiry. In addition the landlord must serve on the tenant a formal notice to quit not less than 40 days before the ish.[47] In effect, therefore, if the date of the ish under the tenancy agreement is June 30, 1995 and the landlord wishes to recover possession on that date he must (1) serve the notice of intention to apply to the court before March 31, 1995 (since he cannot apply to the court earlier than three months after service of the notice), (2) serve a formal notice to quit not later than 40 days before June 30, 1995, and (3) apply to the court not earlier than three months after service of the notice of intention.

(b) The tenant may terminate the tenancy by giving notice to the landlord (i) where the period of the tenancy is two years or less, one month's notice or (ii) where the period of the tenancy is more than two years, three months' notice.[48]

If the tenant dies before the ish, any statutory tenant by succession under Schedule 1 to the 1984 Act is entitled to retain possession only until the expiry of the remaining period of duration in the tenancy agreement. If the tenancy is terminated for any reason before the expiry of the period specified in the tenancy agreement, any sub-tenant is entitled to retain possession only until the expiry of that period.[49]

For provisions to be inserted in an agreement for a short tenancy, see paragraph 27–25 *infra*.

27–13 **Determination of fair rent.** A basic principle of the Rent Acts is the right of either party to a regulated tenancy[50] to apply for registration of the rent to the rent officer who will then determine a fair rent, and no greater amount of rent is recoverable by the landlord. In the case of a short tenancy the rent must be registered.[51] Parts IV and V of the 1984 Act contain detailed provisions as to the principles and procedure for determination of fair rents, appeals from the decision of the rent officer to the rent assessment committee, increases in rent and the determination by the sheriff of additional payments for the use of furniture and services, increases of rent or increases in rates (where paid by the landlord), etc. Details of these matters are outwith the scope of this book but reference may be made to A.G.M. Duncan and J.A.D. Hope, *op. cit.*, pages 58/28 to 58/55–56, D.G. McKerrell, *op. cit.*, pages 71 to 96 and the helpful booklets issued by the Scottish Development Department who are responsible for the rent registration service.

---

[47] 1984 Act, ss. 13, 14, 112 and Sheriff Courts (Scotland) Act 1907, ss. 37, 38. S. 112 of the 1984 Act requires a minimum period of four weeks, but s. 37 of the 1907 Act requires notice of 40 days. The form of notice is prescribed by the Notices to Quit (Prescribed Information) (Protected Tenancies and Part VII Contracts) (Scotland) Regulations 1980 (S.I. 1980 No. 1667).
[48] 1984 Act, s. 13(2).
[49] *Ibid.*, s. 13(5).
[50] Defined as a protected or statutory tenancy: 1984 Act, s. 8.
[51] See para. 27–11.

27–14   **Part VII contracts—furnished lettings**. Part VII contracts are defined in section 63 of the 1984 Act but broadly they are contracts for lets of dwelling-houses or parts of dwelling-houses in consideration of a rent which includes payment for the use of furniture or for services (not board if the value of the board to the tenant forms a substantial portion of the whole rent) and the rateable value of the dwelling-house does not exceed the limits mentioned in paragraph 27–03 *supra*. Normally it is a private sector tenancy. Such a contract may be referred to a rent assessment committee, which may approve, reduce or increase the contractual rent, and the rent so determined remains, in the absence of any significant change in the condition of the premises or of the furniture or services, determined for three years unless on a joint reference to the committee by both parties. The committee maintains a register of rents of Part VII contracts which contains particulars of any approved and increased or reduced rents and is available for public inspection. There can be some overlap in the protection given to a furnished letting as being a protected or regulated tenancy or a Part VII contract. If the tenancy is regulated the full protection given to a protected tenancy is available. If, however, the tenancy is excluded from protection, *e.g.* by reason of the landlord being resident (paragraph 27–06 *supra*), it may still be a Part VII contract and subject to determination and registration of the rent by the rent officer or the rent assessment committee on a reference by either party with the consequential restrictions upon the landlord's right to recover possession after notice to quit provided in sections 71 to 75 of the 1984 Act.

27–15   **Premiums and deposits**. Part VIII of the 1984 Act prohibits the taking of a premium or deposit as a condition of the grant, renewal or continuance of a protected tenancy and also restricts the taking of a premium or deposit upon assignation of a protected tenancy. There is an important exception, however, where a deposit is taken as security for the tenant's obligations for accounts for supplies of gas, electricity, telephone or other domestic supplies and for damage to the dwelling-house or contents, provided that the amount of the deposit does not exceed two months' rent.[52]

Notices to quit

27–16   It is a prerequisite of any court action by a landlord for termination of a tenancy that a notice to quit in appropriate form has been served on the tenant. If a valid notice to quit has not been served timeously the tenancy continues by tacit relocation[53] for a further 12 months if the period of the lease was one year or more. If the period of the lease was less than one year, it is continued successively for that period until

---

[52]1984 Act, s. 90(3).
[53]See para. 25–29.

due notice is given. The requirements for a valid notice to quit and the period of notice are governed by the provisions of the Sheriff Courts (Scotland) Act 1907[54] and the Rent (Scotland) Act 1984.[55] The minimum periods of notice to be received by the tenant prior to the date of termination of the tenancy are:

(1) In *all* cases, not less than four weeks.[56]

(2) In the case of houses let for one year or more with or without land not exceeding two acres in extent, 40 days.[57] Short tenancies are within this category.

(3) In the case of dwelling-houses let for any period exceeding four months but less than one year, in the absence of any express stipulation, 40 days.[58]

(4) In the case of dwelling-houses let for a period not exceeding four months, in the absence of any express stipulation, one-third of the full period of the let,[59] but subject to the above minimum of 28 days.

If the tenancy is a protected tenancy or under a Part VII contract the notice must be in a prescribed form.[60] Further, in the case of Part VII contracts, there are special rules applicable in particular situations.[61]

In all cases notices should be given by messenger-at-arms or sheriff officer or by registered letter or recorded delivery.[62]

Policy and practice

27–17   The effect of 70 years of almost continuous regulation of letting of dwelling-houses in the private sector has been largely to inhibit the former practice of creating new tenancies of unfurnished houses which would be protected under the Rent Acts, save in exceptional circumstances for special reasons. A substantial number of dwelling-houses are still being let but normally where the tenancy will be unprotected, *e.g.* if the valuation of the house on the appropriate day exceeds the valuation limit or the tenant is a company or the landlord is resident in the building or board and attendance is provided or the arrangement is a student or holiday letting, or, if the tenancy will be protected, the circumstances are such as to enable the landlord to recover possession since it is within one of the mandatory cases under Part II of Schedule 2 to the Rent (Scotland) Act 1984 or the contract is a short tenancy within the meaning of section 9 of the Act. For a commentary on the circumstances in which these various exemptions from protection or rights to recover possession will be available and

---

[54]ss. 37, 38 and 38A and Sched. 1, rr. 103–107.
[55]s. 112.
[56]1907 Act, s. 38; 1984 Act, s. 112.
[57]1907 Act, s. 37.
[58]*Ibid.*, s. 38.
[59]*Ibid.*, s. 38.
[60]The form is prescribed in the Notices to Quit (Prescribed Information) (Protected Tenancies and Part VII Contracts) (Scotland) Regulations 1980 (S.I. 1980 No. 1667).
[61]1984 Act, ss. 71–76.
[62]1907 Act, r. 106; 1984 Act, s. 114.

the provisions of leases and the procedures necessary for their application reference may be made to the following paragraphs:

Paragraph

27–05, 27–30	s. 2(1)(*b*) (let with board and attendance).
27–30	s. 2(1)(*c*) (student lettings).
27–31	s. 2(1)(*d*) (holiday lettings).
27–06, 27–26	s. 6 (resident landlord).
27–21	Case 11 (let by owner-occupier).
27–22	Case 12 (let pending retirement).
27–31	Cases 13 and 14 (letting for brief periods).
27–10, 27–25	s. 9 and Case 15 (short tenancy).
27–23	Cases 16, 17, 18, 19 and 21 (various special cases).
27–24	Case 20 (house designed or adapted for special needs).

In appropriate cases it is also necessary to keep in view the possible rights of a non-entitled spouse of the tenant under the matrimonial homes legislation.

Preliminary inquiries and procedures

27–18   Before a lease of a dwelling-house is framed and adjusted certain matters require attention of which the more important are outlined in this paragraph.

(1) Type of lease. The lease will normally be of a kind which will create either a tenancy which is not a protected tenancy or, if protected, will enable the landlord to recover possession on its expiry since the tenancy will satisfy the conditions specified in one of the mandatory cases or will be a short tenancy. It is essential that the landlord's solicitor should have a clear view of the category into which the tenancy will fall and examine the relevant statutory provisions to ensure that any necessary preliminary notices are given and that the lease as framed will satisfy the requirements for exemption from protection or for recovery of possession, as the case may be.

(2) Landlord's identity and title. It is still a requirement for the granting of a lease that the landlord is infeft. Where the lease is of relatively brief duration it is not the practice to examine the landlord's title with the same particularity as is usual in a transaction of purchase or lending on security, but at least the tenant's solicitor should see up-to-date searches or reports in the Register of Sasines or the Land Register, including personal searches. It is important, particularly when the preparation of the lease is instructed by an agent for the landlord, that the full name and place of abode or business of the landlord is made available to his solicitor and in the case of a company the names and addresses of the directors and secretary, since that information must be supplied at any time in response to written request by the tenant.[63]

(3) Heritable securities. If any subsisting heritable security is disclosed by the searches, the consent of the creditor to the lease should be taken.

(4) Subjects. The subjects should be described so as to identify them. If the subjects let are part of a larger unit, appropriate provisions should be included as to sharing of common services, definition of areas of exclusive or common garden ground, parking area, etc. In the case of furnished lets an inventory of the contents should be prepared for annexation to the lease or tenancy agreement.

(5) Prior notices. In short tenancies the landlord must before the creation of the tenancy give an appropriate notice and the statutory provisions as to registration of the rent must have been complied with.[64] Further, where a regulated tenancy falls within any of the categories in Part II of Schedule 2 to the 1984 Act (other than case 20), it is a condition of the right to recover possession in terms of the relevant case that prior notice of the nature of the tenancy is given by the landlord to the tenant not later than the commencement of the tenancy.[65]

(6) Rent allowance scheme. The landlord has a duty to give notice to a tenant under a regulated tenancy of the rent allowance scheme operated by the relevant local authority[66] and transmit to the tenant the information furnished by the local authority with regard to the scheme within one month of its receipt.

Styles

27–19   Paragraph 27–20 *infra* is a skeleton style containing clauses which are common to all or many leases of dwelling-houses. Paragraphs 27–21 to 27–31 *infra* contain variations appropriate to different categories of lettings. A general style of prior notice is given in paragraph 27–34 *infra* which requires adaptation appropriate to the circumstances of different kinds of leases.

(A) Unfurnished Lets

Skeleton style of lease of dwelling-house[67]

---

[63]Rent (Scotland) Act 1984, s. 108(3).
[64]See para. 27–11.
[65]1984 Act, Sched. 2, Part III, para. 2.
[66]Housing (Financial Provisions) (Scotland) Act 1972, s. 20; Rent Allowance Scheme (Duty of Landlords) (Scotland) Regulations 1972 (S.I. 1972 No. 1377) (S.107); Rent Allowance Scheme (Duty of Landlords) (Scotland) Amendment Regulations 1973 (S.I. 1973 No. 1411) (S.105).
[67]As to prior notice see paras. 27–32 to 27–35.

27–20

LEASE
between
A, (*designed*), (hereinafter referred to as "the Landlord")
and
B, (*designed*), (hereinafter referred to as "the Tenant")

FIRST
Subjects of Let
and Period

The Landlord hereby lets to the Tenant but expressly excluding assignees legal or conventional and sub-tenants [without the written consent of the Landlord] ALL and WHOLE that detached dwelling-house containing two public rooms, study, kitchen, laundry apartment, hall, cloak-room, four bedrooms and bathroom known as Dunottar, 12 Grange Road, Aviemore, with the garden ground pertaining thereto and the garage, greenhouse and implement shed erected on the said garden ground (*or otherwise as the case may be*) and the whole fixtures and fittings herein (all hereinafter referred to as "the premises") and that for the period from   (hereinafter referred to as "the date of entry") to   .

SECOND
Rent

The Tenant shall pay to the Landlord for the premises rent at the rate of £   per calendar month payable monthly in arrears[68] the first payment being due on   and subsequent payments on the   day of each month thereafter. The rent will be paid by standing order to the (*specify name and address of Landlord's bank*) into Account No.   .

THIRD
Deposit

A deposit of £   [69] shall be paid by the Tenant at the date of entry as security for the Tenant's obligations for accounts for supplies of [gas], electricity, telephone and other domestic supplies and for damage to the premises. Such deposit or any balance thereof not required for those purposes shall be refunded to the Tenant on termination of the lease, without interest.

FOURTH
Supplies and
Services

The Tenant shall pay promptly and relieve the Landlord of liability for all charges incurred for [gas], electricity, telephone, [coal] [oil for the central heating system] and other supplies or services in respect of the premises during the currency

---

[68] Any requirement that rent for a protected tenancy which is a regulated tenancy shall be payable before the beginning of the relevant rental period or more than six months before the end of the relevant rental period (if that period is more than six months) is void: 1984 Act, s. 89.

[69] The amount of the deposit must not exceed two months' rent: 1984 Act, s. 90(3).

of his tenancy. In the event of any of these services being cut off the Tenant will pay the reconnection charges. [The Tenant shall pay the local rates in respect of the period of his tenancy]. [The Landlord will be responsible for payment of local rates.]

FIFTH
Maintenance and
Repair

The Tenant accepts the premises as being in good tenantable condition and repair and shall be bound to maintain the interior of the premises throughout the period of the Lease and to leave them at the termination thereof for any reason in the like good tenantable condition and repair and in good decorative order. The Tenant shall require the written consent of the Landlord before commencing any internal redecoration. The Landlord undertakes to maintain the structure and the exterior of the premises in water tight condition and will keep in repair and good working order the installations in the premises for the supply of water, [gas], electricity, sanitation [and central heating,] provided always that any defects in such installations are not due to improper use of them or neglect by the Tenant.[70]

SIXTH
Cleaning

The Tenant undertakes throughout the period of his tenancy to keep regularly cleaned all windows and to have chimney vents swept by a reputable firm and to leave all windows and vents so cleaned and swept at his outgoing. The Tenant also undertakes to maintain the garden ground in a neat and tidy condition and to regularly cut and trim all grass and hedges and to keep all boundary fences in good order and condition.

SEVENTH
Use

The premises shall be used as a private dwelling-house for occupation by a single family only and the Tenant is prohibited from using the premises or permitting them to be used for any other purpose whatever. No caravans or high-sided vehicles shall be brought on to the premises save furniture vans at the commencement or termination of the tenancy. No dogs, cats or other animals or pets shall be kept in the premises without the written consent of the Landlord. The Tenant will not do or permit to be done on the premises anything which in the opinion of the Landlord may be a nuisance or a cause of annoyance to the

---

[70] In leases for less than seven years granted after July 3, 1962 an obligation on the landlord in those terms is implied by statute and conventional provisions to the contrary are ineffective—Housing (Scotland) Act 1966, ss. 8, 10.

EIGHTH
Alterations

NINTH
Access

TENTH
Indemnity

ELEVENTH
Insurance

TWELFTH
Temporary Failure

THIRTEENTH
Prohibition of
Assignation or
Sub-letting

FOURTEENTH
Removal

Landlord or to the occupiers of adjoining property nor leave the premises unoccupied without prior notice to the Landlord.

The Tenant shall not carry out or permit to be carried out any structural or other alterations or additions to the premises nor erect any additional buildings or structures without the prior written consent of the Landlord.

The Landlord or his agent or any other person authorised by him shall have a right of access to the premises at all reasonable times on giving prior notice to the Tenant for the purpose of inspection of the premises and effecting repairs or maintenance thereof or other necessary purpose.

The Tenant shall indemnify the Landlord against all liability for which the Landlord may become responsible as a result of anything done or omitted to be done on the premises by the Tenant, his servants or agents or any other party for whom the Tenant may be responsible and against all relative or consequential expenses. The Landlord undertakes on receipt of a written warning from the Tenant to take reasonable precautions to prevent any loss or damage occurring to the premises.

The Landlord agrees to insure the said dwelling-house against fire and other risks against which dwelling-houses are normally insured and to pay the premiums in respect thereof. The insurance of all contents of the premises shall be the sole responsibility of the Tenant.

The Landlord shall not be liable for the temporary deprivation of the occupancy or the full use and enjoyment of the premises through the bursting, leaking or failure of water supply, waste or soil pipes or the choking, stoppage or overflow thereof or of the drains, gutters, rhones or conductors or from the failure, fusing or breakdown of [the central heating system], electric cables, wires or appliances.[71]

The Tenant shall not assign this Lease in whole or in part nor sub-let nor part with the possession of the premises or any part thereof.

The Tenant binds himself to flit and remove with all his goods and gear on the expiry or earlier or agreed date of termina-

---

[71]See *Golden Casket (Greenock) Ltd.* v. *B.R.S. (Pickfords) Ltd.*, 1972 S.L.T. 146.

tion of his tenancy hereunder without any warning away or process of removal and to make good any damage caused by the removal of any fittings which he may be entitled to remove.

FIFTEENTH
Irritancy

If the rent or any instalment or part thereof is in arrears and the Tenant has failed to make payment of such arrears for a period of 14 days after he has been required by notice from the Landlord to do so the Landlord may terminate this Lease and resume possession of the premises. If the Tenant shall be in breach of or fail to implement any of his other obligations under this Lease and shall have failed to remedy such breach or implement such obligation within a period of one month after being requested by the Landlord to do so the Landlord may terminate this Lease and resume possession of the premises and may also recover from the Tenant all loss or damage which the Landlord may sustain from such breach or non-implement.[72]

SIXTEENTH

[*Here insert a brief description of any circumstances in which the Landlord may be entitled to terminate the tenancy under statute. For an example see paragraph 27–21 infra.*].

SEVENTEENTH
Expenses

The Tenant will be responsible for the whole costs of preparation of this Lease and for any stamp duty payable thereon[73] [*or otherwise as may be agreed*].

EIGHTEENTH
Registration

Both parties consent to the registration hereof for preservation and execution.

(*To be attested*)
(*Stamp duty—see para. 25–44*)

Lease of unfurnished dwelling-house by owner-occupier—Case 11

27–21   The style in paragraph 27–20 *supra* may be used, inserting as Clause SIXTEENTH the following:

SIXTEENTH

The Tenant acknowledges that the Landlord may make application to the court for possession of the premises under any of the Cases contained in Schedule 2 to the Rent (Scotland) Act 1984 and any other Act or Order amending the same and without prejudice to the foregoing generality the Tenant acknowledges to have received

---

[72]The provisions of ss. 4 and 5 of the Law Reform (Miscellaneous Provisions) (Scotland) Act 1985 do not apply to residential property—see s. 7(1)(*a*).
[73]See para. 25–44.

a notice served in accordance with the requirements of Case 11 of Schedule 2 to the said Act.[74]

Lease of unfurnished dwelling-house pending retirement of owner—Case 12

27–22 The style in paragraph 27–20 *supra* may be used, inserting as Clause SIXTEENTH a clause in the form in paragraph 27–21 *supra* with the substitution of a reference to Case 12.[74]

Lease of unfurnished dwelling-house—Case 16, 17, 18, 19 or 21

27–23 A lease granted in the circumstances envisaged in any of those cases may be framed generally in accordance with the style in paragraph 27–20 *supra* with appropriate adaptation of Clause SIXTEENTH on the lines indicated in paragraph 27–21 *supra* substituting a reference to the relevant case. If desired a brief description of the circumstances may be inserted.[74]

Lease of unfurnished dwelling-house adapted for special needs of tenant—Case 20

27–24 In this case prior notice is not required by the 1984 Act, but it is suggested that such notice should nevertheless be given. The style of lease in paragraph 27–20 *supra* may be used with a clause on the lines of Clause SIXTEENTH suitably adapted or alternatively, if notice has not been given, with an introductory narrative of the circumstances of special design or adaptation of the premises.

Lease of unfurnished dwelling-house—short tenancy—section 9 and Case 15[75]

27–25 The style in paragraph 27–20 *supra* may be used with the following modifications of clauses:

FIRST	The period specified should be not less than one nor more than five years.
SECOND	The rent must be the fair rent registered and may be payable in advance.
FOURTEENTH	The obligation to remove should be expressed in relation to the expiry of the period of the tenancy.
SIXTEENTH	This clause should run: The Tenant acknowledges that the tenancy hereby created is a short tenancy within the meaning of Section 9 of the Rent

---

[74] As to prior notice, see paras. 27–32 to 27–36.
[75] As to matters to be observed in relation to a short tenancy, see para. 27–11.

> (Scotland) Act 1984 and that the requirements of that section have been complied with and further that the Landlord may make application to the court to recover possession of the premises under Case 15 of Schedule 2 to the said Act.

Lease of unfurnished dwelling-house or apartments—resident landlord

27–26   Leases of this kind may be either for a relatively short or a longer term. It is essential to ensure that the terms and conditions of the let and the whole circumstances satisfy the conditions for exemption from protection contained in section 6 of the 1984 Act.[76]

Where the lease is for a relatively long period the lease may be formal and attested on the lines of that in paragraph 27–20 *supra*, subject to appropriate variations in some of the clauses, viz.:

FIRST
: The flat let will be described so as to identify it, with any garage included in the tenancy and rights of access by any common entrance or vestibule and stairway. If desired, there may be added to the period a provision that the lease will continue after the contractual duration until terminated by two calendar months' notice[77] in writing by either party.

SECOND
: The rent inserted will be that initially agreed but the amount may be referred by either party to the rent assessment committee.[78] If the lease is for a very long period, periodic increases in rent should be considered.

SIXTH
: Provision for contribution to the expense of cleaning and redecoration of the common parts of the building should be included.

SIXTEENTH
: "In respect that the premises consist of a flat in the said building known as (*describe by postal address*) which is not a purpose-built block of flats and that the Landlord resides in (*identify Landlord's flat*) forming part of the said building the Tenant accepts that the tenancy hereby created is a tenancy within the meaning of section 6 of the Rent (Scotland) Act 1984."

Where the let is for a relatively short period the lease may take the form of missive letters attested, holograph or adopted as holograph in the style suggested in paragraph 27–27 *infra* but with the inclusion of a provision on the lines of clause SIXTEENTH above.

---

[76]See para. 27–06.
[77]Minimum period 40 days.
[78]1984 Act, ss. 98(1) and 65.

Skeleton style of tenancy agreement—unfurnished dwelling-house

27–27   This style will normally, unless the rateable value of the subjects on the appropriate day exceeded or exceeds the valuation limit, create a protected tenancy. For that reason it will seldom be used in practice unless in circumstances where exemption from protection is available under section 2 or section 6 of the Rent (Scotland) Act 1984 or it is a short tenancy within the meaning of section 9 thereof or is granted in circumstances falling within one of the cases specified in Part II of Schedule 2 to the Act so that the landlord would be entitled to recover possession. For suggestions in the case of particular kinds of leases or missives of let as to matters which may be included in styles to achieve one of these results, see the undernoted paragraphs.[79]

Tenancy agreement—unfurnished flat—short period

To Messrs (*name and address of proprietor's agents*)
   I hereby agree to take on let from you as Agents for (*name and address of proprietor*) as Proprietor that flat (*identify flat and address*) on the following terms and conditions:
1.   The tenancy shall initially be from   for three months from 1st April 1988 to 30th June 1988 and thereafter on a month to month agreement until terminated by either party giving one month's notice in writing to the other.[80]
2.   The rent shall be at the rate of £120 per month payable monthly in advance on 2nd April 1988 for that month of April and on the second day of each month thereafter during the currency of the tenancy.[81]
3.   I shall also pay an initial deposit of £100 as security for my obligations in respect of supplies of gas, electricity, telephone or other domestic supplies and any damage to the flat. The deposit or any unused balance thereof shall be repaid on termination of the tenancy, without interest.[82]
4.   I shall pay the cost of all heating and lighting used and telephone rental and calls made during my tenancy. The proprietor will pay the local rates.
5.   I shall plenish the flat so as to afford adequate security for the rent and shall keep the flat properly aired and fired during the subsistence of my tenancy and shall concur with the tenants or owners of other flats in the building in maintaining the entrance and stairs of the building clean and tidy.

---

[79]para. 27–30—s. 2(1)(*b*) (let with board or attendance); para. 27–30—s. 2(1)(*c*) (student letting); para. 27–31—s. 2(1)(*d*) (holiday letting); para. 27–26—s. 6 (resident landlord); para. 27–21—Case 11 (let by owner-occupier); para. 27–22—Case 12 (let pending retirement); para. 27–31—Cases 13 and 14 (letting for brief periods); para. 27–25—s. 9 and Case 15 (short tenancy); para. 27–24—Case 20 (house designed or adapted for special needs).
[80]As to minimum notice and form of notice in the case of a protected tenancy, see para. 27–16.
[81]Payments in advance *before the beginning* of a rental period are prohibited—Rent (Scotland) Act 1984, s. 89.
[82]The amount of the deposit must not exceed two months' rent.

6. I accept the flat as being in good and tenantable condition and repair and will keep the same in the like condition during the subsistence of the tenancy and leave it so on the termination thereof.

7. No dogs or other animals shall be kept in the flat unless with the written consent of the Proprietor or his agents.

8. The Proprietor shall keep the main structure of the said building wind and water tight, but (a) he shall not be liable for any loss or damage arising from the bursting or leakage or overflow of any service pipes or tanks or flooding from within or without from any cause and (b) I shall be responsible for the repair of any windows that may be broken.[83] Notice in writing must be given to you as Agents of any essential structural repairs required.

9. I shall be responsible for the interior decoration of the flat and also for the cost of repair of broken plaster on the walls of the flat due to the stripping of wall paper or any other cause whatsoever.

10. The Proprietor or any authorised agent or tradesmen employed by him shall be entitled at any time to enter and inspect the flat on giving 24 hours' notice and I shall afford all reasonable facilities for the execution of any repairs authorised by him.

11. No alterations to the flat other than interior decoration shall be made without the prior written consent of the Proprietor or his Agents.

12. If the rent is in arrear or if I desert the flat or am in breach of any other obligation of this agreement the Proprietor shall be entitled to irritate the tenancy or take any other procedures competent at law to enforce implement hereof.

13. [If the tenancy agreement is one in which the landlord is entitled to recover possession (mandatory case) here insert an acknowledgment of the relevant circumstances and of receipt of the necessary prior notice, *e.g.* as in paragraph 27–21 *supra*.]

14. I agree to pay any stamp duty payable in respect of this agreement.[84]

Dated the   day of   1988.

(To be attested or holograph)

(name and address of Agents)
On behalf of (*name and address of proprietor*) we hereby confirm the foregoing agreement.

Dated the   day of   1988

(To be attested, holograph or adopted as holograph by Agents)

In practice the agreement and confirmation may be printed or reproduced in standard form with appropriate minor adjustments.

---

[83]Normally a landlord's responsibility: *Hastie* v. *City of Edinburgh District Council*, 1981 S.L.T. (Sh.Ct.) 61.

[84]See para. 25–44.

(B) *Furnished Lettings*

General

27–28 Furnished lettings may also be protected tenancies under the Rent (Scotland) Act 1984. Additional provisions to be inserted in the style in paragraph 27–20 *supra* (formal lease), or in paragraph 27–27 *supra* (tenancy agreement) when the lease or let includes furniture, are suggested in paragraph 27–29 *infra*. Special clauses which may be included in leases or lets which are usually with furniture in order to obtain exemption from protection or to facilitate recovery of possession are considered in paragraphs 27–30 and 27–31 *infra*.

Provisions regarding furniture

27–29 Where the lease is of a furnished dwelling-house the following additions may be made to the style in paragraph 27–20 *supra*:

FIRST — *Insert after the description of the premises* together with the furniture, furnishings and other effects specified in the Inventory thereof annexed and signed as relative hereto

FIFTH — *Add* The Tenant shall keep the furniture, furnishings and other effects in the premises in good order and clean condition and shall replace or repair any of them which may be broken, missing or damaged.

A detailed inventory of the individual items of furniture, etc., should be annexed to the lease, noting any existing defects or damage in any particular items. The inventory will be signed at the end by the parties.

Where the document is a tenancy agreement in the style in paragraph 27–27 *supra*, provisions similar to those suggested in this paragraph should be inserted in any appropriate clause or clauses of the agreement and an inventory attached and signed.

Furnished letting with board or attendance

27–30 The style suggested in this paragraph is a form of tenancy agreement suitable for short-term furnished letting with board. If the let is to students the tenancy will not be exempt from protection as a student letting under section 2(1)(c) of the Rent (Scotland) Act 1984 unless the landlord is a specified educational institution or body: exemption from protection will normally depend upon the board provision in section 2(1)(b) of the Act. As to the statutory requirements, see paragraph 27–05 *supra*.

TENANCY AGREEMENT
between
A B Limited (*designed*) (the Landlord)
and
C (*designed*) (the Tenant)

The Landlord hereby lets to the Tenant the two apartments consisting of a sitting room and bedroom known as Apartment No. 6 in the building situated at 73 Hillhead Street, Glasgow, with the furniture and fittings specified in Schedule I annexed hereto (which apartments and furniture are hereinafter comprehended in the expression "the premises") on the following terms and conditions:—

1. The let will be for the period of nine months from 1st October 1988 until 30th June 1989 and thereafter from month to month until terminated by either party on 40 days' prior notice in writing.

2. The Landlord will provide to the Tenant during the period of the tenancy a continental breakfast each morning (except Sundays and public holidays) between the hours of 8.30 a.m. and 9.30 a.m. on the conditions specified in the Regulations in Schedule II hereto.

3. The rent payable by the Tenant, which includes the provision of breakfast, shall be £   per month, payable monthly on the 2nd day of each calendar month for the month then current.

4. On or before the commencement of the tenancy the Tenant will (i) provide an acceptable Banker's reference and (ii) deposit the sum of £   as security for payment of heating and lighting charges and telephone incurred by him in respect of the premises and any damage to the premises or their contents.[85]

5. In addition to the rent the Tenant shall pay punctually when due the cost of all heating and lighting supplied to the premises [and the telephone rental and calls made from the telephone installed in the premises].

6. The items specified in Schedule I hereto will be checked immediately before the Tenant's entry to the premises and again on termination of the tenancy and the Tenant will replace all items which are missing or irreparably damaged and will repair all repairable items which have been damaged during the tenancy.

7. Any person authorised by the Landlord will be entitled at any time on 24 hours' notice to enter and inspect the premises and the Tenant shall be bound to afford all reasonable facilities for the execution of any repairs or maintenance for which the Landlord is responsible.

8. In the event of the rent for any month not being paid when due or the Tenant being guilty of any conduct which in the opinion of the Landlord is a nuisance or annoyance to the occupiers of other flats in the said building or causing or permitting the condition of the said apartments or the furniture therein to deteriorate through neglect or ill-treatment or committing any breach of the conditions hereof or of the said regulations which the Landlord may deem to be material, the

---

[85]The amount of the deposit must not exceed two months' rent.

Landlord shall be entitled to serve on the Tenant a notice to quit the premises.[86]

9. The Tenant is prohibited from assigning the tenancy or sub-letting the premises or any part thereof without the prior written consent of the Landlord.

10. The Regulations in Schedule II hereto shall form part of this Agreement.

11. The Tenant shall bear the cost of any stamp duty payable in respect of this agreement.   (*To be signed by parties*)

SCHEDULE I
INVENTORY OF FURNITURE AND EFFECTS

Item	*Quantity*	*General Condition*

(*To be signed by parties*)

SCHEDULE II
REGULATIONS

Occupants

1. The premises shall be used for the accommodation of the Tenant and not more than two other persons of his immediate family. No other persons will occupy the premises.

Breakfast

2. Breakfast for the Tenant is included in the rent. Breakfast for any additional persons will be provided at a tariff of £ per person, provided notice at least 24 hours previously is given. The breakfast will be a continental breakfast. Breakfast will be provided each morning between the hours of 8.30 a.m. and 9.30 a.m. except on Sundays and public holidays. Breakfast may be provided in the discretion of the Landlord on Sundays at an additional tariff of £ per person if advance notice 48 hours before is given. The Landlord reserves the right to increase the tariff on giving 14 days notice in writing. Breakfast will be available as above but the Landlord will not be responsible for any failure to provide it due to reasons outwith his control.

Inventories

3. The Tenant will co-operate with the Landlord or any person acting on his behalf in checking and agreeing the items in the inventory in Schedule I on ingoing and outgoing of the Tenant.[87]

[86]Unless it can be established that the tenancy is not protected by virtue of s. 2(1)(*b*) the provisions of this clause will be enforceable only if the court is satisfied that the provisions of Case 1, 2, 3 or 4 of Pt. I of Sched. 2 to the Rent (Scotland) Act 1984 apply.

[87]For cases where failure to complete an inventory was held not to be a suspensive condition which rendered a lease incomplete, see *Steuart* v. *Neilsons* (1864) 2 M. 817; *Elliot* v. *Erickson*, 1960 S.L.T. (Sh.Ct.) 28.

Insurance

4. The Landlord will be responsible for insurance of the structure of the premises let. The Tenant will keep the items of furniture provided by the Landlord and all items brought by the Tenant into the premises properly insured to their full replacement value at the expense of the Tenant.

Use

5. No parties of more than six persons shall be held in the premises at any time. No noise or disturbance which may cause annoyance to other occupants of the building is permitted and, in particular, no music or other sound which may be audible outwith the premises shall be permitted in the premises between the hours of 11.00 p.m. and 8.00 a.m. No trade, business or profession shall be carried on in the premises. No portable heating appliance of any kind shall be used in the premises other than electric fires.

Alterations and Decoration

6. No alterations shall be made on any part of the structure of the premises and any redecoration of the premises shall be made in such a way as to avoid any insertions in walls or the application of adhesives thereto other than paste. Any internal redecoration shall require the prior written approval of the Landlord and no external painting or the showing or affixing of any external signs or notices is permitted.

Cleaning

7. The Tenant will keep the premises in a clean and tidy condition throughout the period of the tenancy and will leave them so at its termination.

Vestibule and Common Parts

8. The Landlord shall be responsible for cleaning and decorating the vestibule, stairs, bathrooms and toilets in the building used in common by more than one tenant. The Tenant shall not leave in any such common parts any articles or obstructions.

Television and Radio

9. Not more than one television set and one radio set shall be used in the premises. The Tenant will be solely responsible for payment of the licence fees therefor.

Notices

10. All notices and communications should be addressed or given to   , the managing agent for the Landlord.

(To be signed by parties)

Furnished lettings for holidays or brief periods

27–31   A holiday let will normally be with furniture and does not constitute a protected tenancy.[87a] A tenancy agreement based on the style suggested in paragraph 27–27 *supra* adapted and simplified as appropriate, may be used with provisions as to furniture as indicated in paragraph 27–29 *supra*.

Furnished lettings for periods not exceeding eight months or 12 months[87b] may be in the form of tenancy agreements as suggested above in this paragraph, but (a) these may create protected tenancies and (b) prior notice must be given if the landlord is to have the right to recover possession.

(C) *Prior Notice*

The statutory requirement

27–32   A feature of the legislation in the Rent Acts is the requirement of prior notice being given by the landlord to the tenant of the nature of the tenancy as being within one of the categories of regulated tenancy in which the landlord may recover possession. The Rent (Scotland) Act 1984 requires such notice as a condition of the landlord's right to recover possession in the mandatory Cases 11, 12, 13, 14, 15, 16, 17, 18, 19 and 21: although not required in Case 20 it may be prudent to give notice also in circumstances where the house has been adapted for the special needs of the tenant before the tenancy is created. It is essential that the requisite notice is given not later than the commencement of the regulated tenancy.

Practice

27–33   Sometimes the notice is incorporated only as a specific clause in the tenancy agreement, but that practice is not recommended. It involves the risk, particularly in circumstances where the period of tenancy is not more than one year, that the tenant may be permitted to take entry in reliance on a verbal agreement or informal correspondence and the lease or tenancy agreement is adjusted and signed shortly thereafter; the tenant's possession following upon the informal arrangement may result in the tenancy having effectively commenced before the formal document containing the notice has been signed so that the notice will have been given later than the commencement of the tenancy. In addition it may be prudent to incorporate in the lease or tenancy agreement an acknowledgment that the necessary prior notice has been given.[88]

Form of notice

27–34   The 1984 Act does not prescribe a form of notice. A letter on the following lines is suggested:

[87a]Rent (Scotland) Act 1984, s. 2(1)(*d*).
[87b]Case 13 or Case 14 tenancies: 1984 Act, Sched. 2.
[88]See for example para. 27–21.

To (*name and address of tenant*)
We (*name and address of landlord's agents*) as agents for AB, (*designed*), the proprietor, hereby give you notice that the dwelling-house known as   which is about to be let to you [furnished] for a period of   commencing on   in terms of [Lease] [Tenancy Agreement] between the said AB and you [dated   ] [about to be executed] was previously occupied by the said AB as his residence and accordingly the said AB is an owner-occupier within the meaning of Case 11 contained in Schedule 2 to the Rent (Scotland) Act 1984 and possession may be recovered under the said Case 11.

(*Signed*)

Where the right to recover possession is based on the circumstances in cases other than Case 11 the wording of the notice will be adapted appropriately.

Service of notice

27–35   In terms of section 114 of the 1984 Act any notice requiring to be served on the tenant may be given (a) by delivering it to him, (b) by leaving it at his proper address or (c) by sending it to him by recorded delivery at that address. In practice method (c) should be adopted, and, although not required by the Act, the notice should be served in duplicate with a form of acknowledgment of receipt endorsed on the duplicate copy to be signed by the tenant and returned.

Additional notices and procedures

27–36   It may be useful to remind readers of the further obligations of the landlord to notify the tenant of the rent allowance scheme[89] and, in the case of short tenancies under section 9 of the 1984 Act and Case 15 of Schedule 2, to procure registration of the rent[90] and, if he desires to recover possession on the expiry of the term of the tenancy, to serve not later than three months before the date of its expiry, a notice of intention to apply to the court for termination of the tenancy.[91] Moreover in all cases timeous notice to quit will require to be given if a tenancy is to be terminated.[92]

(D) Heritable Securities

Regulated heritable securities

27–37   The statutory restrictions upon the increase of rates of interest or the calling-up of principal and enforcement by sale or foreclosure in the

---

[89]para. 27–18(6).
[90]para. 27–11.
[91]para. 27–12.
[92]para. 27–16.

case of heritable securities over property which is subject to regulated tenancies remain as a legacy from the old Increase of Rent and Mortgage Restrictions Acts. The current provisions regarding them are contained in Part IX of the Rent (Scotland) Act 1984. Such regulated heritable securities are now only those created before December 8, 1965 or, if over dwelling-houses subject to a regulated furnished tenancy, before August 14, 1974. As to the current law in relation to such securities, see the undernoted text.[93]

THE PUBLIC SECTOR

Secure tenancies[93a]

27–38   The concept of secure tenancies in the public sector (broadly equivalent to protected tenancies in the private sector) is defined in Part II of the Tenants' Rights, Etc. (Scotland) Act 1980 as amended.[94] In order to be a tenancy which is secure the following conditions must be satisfied:

(1) the dwelling-house must be let as a separate dwelling;

(2) the tenant must be an individual and the dwelling-house must be his only or principal home, and

(3) the landlord must be one of the bodies listed in section 10(2) of the 1980 Act, viz.—

(a) an islands or district council, or a joint board or joint committee of an islands or district council or the common good of such a council, or any trust under the control of such a council;

(b) a development corporation established by an order made, or having effect as if made, under the New Towns (Scotland) Act 1968;

(c) the Scottish Special Housing Association;

(d) the Housing Corporation;

(e) a registered housing association within the meaning of the Housing Act 1974;

(f) a housing co-operative within the meaning of section 5 of the Housing Rents and Subsidies (Scotland) Act 1975; and

(g) any housing trust which was in existence on November 13, 1953 or any authorised society within the meaning of the Housing Act 1914.

If the tenancy is held jointly by two or more individuals it is sufficient to constitute the tenancy as a secure tenancy if at least one of the joint tenants occupies the dwelling-house as his only or principal resi-

[93]D.G. McKerrell, *The Rent Acts*, 109–111.
[93a]The law is stated as at December 31, 1986 but it should be noted that as from January 7, 1987 substantial changes have been made by the Housing (Scotland) Act 1986. Broadly the effect is to extend the categories of landlords in para. 27–38(3) to include regional councils and police and fire authorities so that in general virtually all categories of public sector tenancies are secure.
[94]Tenants' Rights, Etc. (Scotland) Amendment Act 1980; Local Government (Miscellaneous Provisions) (Scotland) Act 1981, s. 35 and Sched. 3; Matrimonial Homes (Family Protection) (Scotland) Act 1981, s. 13; Tenants' Rights, Etc. (Scotland) Amendment Act 1984; Rent (Scotland) Act 1984, Scheds. 8 and 10; Housing (Scotland) Act 1986.

dence.[95] Security of tenure is not lost if the tenant acquires another dwelling-house, even although the house of which he has security of tenure no longer remains his only or principal home.[96]

Non-secure tenancies

27–39   A tenancy is not a secure tenancy if it falls within any of the categories listed in Schedule 1 to the 1980 Act, *viz.*—

(1) If the tenancy is for a period exceeding 20 years.[97]

(2) If the tenant is an employee of the landlord or of any local authority or development corporation and his contract of employment requires him to occupy the dwelling-house for the better performance of his duties.

(3) If the dwelling-house was let by the landlord expressly on a temporary basis to a person moving into an area in order to take up employment there, and for the purpose of enabling him to seek accommodation in the area.

(4) If the dwelling-house was let by the landlord to the tenant expressly on a temporary basis pending development affecting it.

(5) If the dwelling-house is occupied by the tenant while works are being carried out on the dwelling-house which he normally occupies as his home, and if he is entitled to return there after the works are completed by agreement or by virtue of an order of the sheriff under section 15(5) of the 1980 Act.

(6) If the dwelling-house is being let to the tenant expressly on a temporary basis in fulfilment of a duty imposed on a housing authority by the Housing (Homeless Persons) Act 1977.

(7) If the dwelling-house (a) is let together with agricultural land exeeding two acres in extent, or (b) consists of or includes premises which are used as a shop or office for business, trade or professional purposes, or (c) consists of or includes premises licensed for the sale of exciseable liquor, or (d) is let in conjunction with any purpose mentioned in (b) or (c) above.

Succession to secure tenancies—qualified persons

27–40   In the public sector there are rights of succession to a secure tenancy in favour of "qualified persons" (a phrase broadly equivalent to the expression "statutory tenant" in the private sector). On the death of a secure tenant the right to continue the tenancy passes to any qualified person being (1) the spouse of the secure tenant, (2) the survivor of individuals who were joint tenants, or (3) where there is no person falling within (1) or (2) above a member of the tenant's family over 16 years of age, with the further condition that the dwelling-house was the only or principal home of the qualified person at the time of the

---

[95]1980 Act, s. 10(3).
[96]*Ibid.*, s. 10(5).
[97]Repealed as from January, 7, 1987 by Housing (Scotland) Act 1986, s. 10.

tenant's death or in case (3) above had been his/her principal home throughout the 12 months immediately preceding the tenant's death. There is no further entitlement to a secure tenancy on a second occasion when the qualified person dies, but a qualified person would be entitled to continue as tenant for six months.[98]

Termination of secure tenancies

27–41   A secure tenancy may be terminated:

(1) on the death of the secure tenant where there is no qualified person entitled to succeed to the tenancy;

(2) on the death of the secure tenant and the qualified person declines the tenancy by notice in writing within four weeks of the tenant's death[99] or on the death of a qualified person who has succeeded to the secure tenancy[1];

(3) by written agreement between the landlord and the tenant;

(4) if the dwelling-house is unoccupied and the procedure of notice by the landlord in accordance with section 19 of the 1980 Act has been followed;

(5) if an order for recovery of possession has been made by the court[2]; or

(6) by four weeks' notice given by the tenant.

Recovery of possession

27–42   (a) **Grounds.** Part I of Schedule 2 to the 1980 Act as amended specifies 14 grounds on which possession may be recovered of a dwelling-house which is subject to a secure tenancy, and a further ground (15) was added by section 6 of the Tenants' Rights, Etc. (Scotland) Amendment Act 1984. Briefly, the 15 grounds are:

(1) The rent is in arrear or any other obligation of the tenancy has been broken.

(2) The tenant (or any one of joint tenants) or any person lodging with him or any sub-tenant has been convicted of using the dwelling-house or allowing it to be used for immoral or illegal purposes.

(3) The condition of the dwelling-house has deteriorated by acts of waste by, or neglect or default of, the tenant or any person residing or lodging with him or any sub-tenant.

(4) The condition of any furniture provided for use under the tenancy has deteriorated owing to ill-treatment.

(5) The tenant and his or her spouse have been absent from the dwelling-house without reasonable cause for a continuous period

---

[98] 1980 Act, s. 13, *q.v.* for further details.
[99] *Ibid.*, s. 13(4).
[1] *Ibid.*, s. 13(5).
[2] For the circumstances in which such an order may be made, see para. 27–42.

exceeding six months or have ceased to occupy it as their principal home.

(6) The landlord wishes to transfer the secure tenancy to (a) the tenant's spouse or former spouse or (b) a person with whom the tenant has been living as husband and wife, who has applied to the landlord for such transfer, and either of the parties no longer wishes to live together with the other in the house.[2a]

(7) The tenant or joint tenant or any person residing or lodging with him or any sub-tenant has been guilty of conduct in or in the vicinity of the dwelling-house which is a nuisance or annoyance and it is not reasonable in all the circumstances that the landlord should be required to make other accommodation available to him.[3]

(8) Conduct as in ground 7 above where in the opinion of the landlord it is appropriate in the circumstances to require the tenant to move to other accommodation.

(9) The dwelling-house is overcrowded within the meaning of section 89 of the Housing (Scotland) Act 1966, in such circumstances as to render the occupier guilty of an offence.

(10) The landlord intends within a reasonable period of time to demolish, or carry out substantial work on, the building or a part of the building which comprises or includes the dwelling-house and it cannot reasonably do so without obtaining possession of the dwelling-house.

(11) The dwelling-house has been designed or adapted for occupation by a person whose special needs require accommodation of the kind provided by it and (a) there is no longer a person with such special needs occupying it and (b) the landlord requires it for occupation by a person who has such special needs.

(12) Similar circumstances as in (11) above in a case where the dwelling-house forms part of a group of houses which has been designed, or provided with or located near facilities for persons in need of special social support.

(13) The landlord is a housing association whose objects include the housing of persons who are in a special category by reason of age, infirmity, disability or social circumstances and the tenant, having been granted a tenancy as a person falling within such a special category, has ceased to be in the special category, or for other reasons the accommodation in the dwelling-house is no longer suitable to his needs and is required for someone who is in a special category.

(14) The interest of the landlord in the dwelling-house is that of a lessee under a lease and that lease has terminated or will do so within six months.

(15) The landlord is an islands council, the dwelling-house is held by

---

[2a]Housing (Scotland) Act, 1986, s. 11.
[3]See *Scottish Special Housing Association* v. *Lumsden*, 1984 S.L.T. (Sh.Ct.) 71.

the council for the purposes of its functions as education authority and is required for a person who is or will be employed by the council for those purposes, the council cannot reasonably provide suitable alternative accommodation for such person and the tenant or his predecessor in the secure tenancy was employed by the council for the purposes of its functions as education authority and that employment has terminated or notice of its termination has been given.

In all cases possession can be recovered on one of the foregoing grounds only by an order of the sheriff.[4] If the ground upon which an order is sought falls within any of Cases 1 to 5 and 7 above the court has a discretion to make the order if the sheriff considers it reasonable to do so,[5] but if the ground upon which an order is sought falls within any of the Cases 6 and 8 to 15 above the sheriff will make the order if it appears to him that other suitable accommodation will be available to the tenant when the order takes effect.[6] In the former situation the court has a wide discretion on consideration of all the circumstances, but in the latter the court must make the order if it is satisfied that there is other suitable accommodation, a much more limited discretion. Further, if the ground of application for an order falls within any of the Cases 1 to 6 above the court may adjourn the proceedings for a period or periods with or without conditions as to payment of rent or other conditions.[7]

7-43 **(b) Procedure**. The procedure for recovering possession on any of the above grounds is:

(1) The landlord must serve a notice on the tenant in prescribed form.[8]

(2) Not earlier than (a) four weeks from the date of service of the notice or (b) the date on which the tenancy could have been brought to an end by service of a notice to quit if the tenancy had not been a secure tenancy, whichever is later, the landlord may raise proceedings for recovery of possession by way of summary cause in the sheriff court of the district where the dwelling-house is situated.[8a]

(3) The notice must still be in force when the proceedings are raised (the notice ceases to be in force after six months from the date specified in it).[9]

Abandonment

7-44 Sections 18 to 20 of the 1980 Act contain provisions which enable

---

[4]See para. 27–43.
[5]1980 Act, s. 15(2)(*a*).
[6]*Ibid.*, s. 15(2)(*b*); as to the criteria for determining whether other accommodation is suitable see Sched. 2, Pt. II of the Act.
[7]*Ibid.*, s. 15(1).

[8]The form of notice is prescribed in the Secure Tenancies (Proceedings for Possession) (Scotland) Order 1980 (S.I. 1980 No. 1389) (S.110).
[8a]1980 Act, s. 14.
[9]1980 Act, s. 14(4).

the landlord to recover possession of a dwelling-house let under a secure tenancy where the landlord has reason to believe that the tenant has ceased to occupy it and does not intend to occupy it as his home, and prescribe the notice and proceedings required.

Lease or tenancy agreement—preparation and execution

27–45   A lease or tenancy agreement creating a secure tenancy must be in writing probative or holograph of the parties.[10] The deed should be executed before the commencement of the tenancy, and it is the duty of the landlord to draw up the document or documents, to ensure that they are duly executed and to supply a copy to the tenant.[11] The landlord may make a summary application to the sheriff where the tenant refuses or fails duly to execute the document or documents and the tenant may make such an application where he considers that a lease or tenancy agreement does not fairly reflect the existing terms of the tenancy.[12] The tenant is not to be required to pay any fees for preparation of the document or documents[13]: any fees for doing so are in practice paid or provided for by the landlord.

Style—tenancy agreement—secure tenancy

27–46   The following style of tenancy agreement has been provided by courtesy of the City of Glasgow District Council.

TENANCY AGREEMENT
between
THE CITY OF GLASGOW DISTRICT COUNCIL
("the Council")
and

("the Tenant" whether the tenancy is to one person or jointly to more than one person)

This Tenancy Agreement sets out the terms on which the Tenant occupies the house situated at   ("the house") and the duties and obligations of the Council and the Tenant under the Agreement.

1. APPLICA-
   TION FORM

The Agreement is granted on the strength of the statements made in (a) the Tenant's application form for the tenancy of a Council house and/or (b) any transfer application form and (c) revisals of these. If the Tenant either intentionally or negli-

---

[10]1980 Act, s. 16(1).
[11]Ibid., s. 16(3).
[12]Ibid., s. 16(4) and (5).
[13]Ibid., s. 16(6).

gently misrepresents any circumstances in these forms and, in consequence, is granted the tenancy, this Agreement will be null and void.

2. COMMENCEMENT The tenancy shall commence on (regardless of the date of signing of the Agreement) and shall be for a period of one month from that date and shall continue on a monthly basis thereafter until terminated in terms of Clause 10 of this Agreement and Part 1 of the attached Schedule ("the Schedule").

3. RENT AND RATES The initial rent is per annum[14] payable at per monthly period and the initial rates are per annum payable monthly at amounts to be notified. The rent must be paid in advance to the Council along with the local rates payable for the house. The Council must give the Tenant twenty-eight days written notice of alterations of rent.

4. SERVICE CHARGE Where the Council provides chargeable services such as District Heating a service charge shall be payable by the Tenant. The income raised by such service charges on a city-wide basis will, taking one year with another, not exceed the cost of providing the services. Any service charge shall be paid along with rent and rates.

5. SECURITY OF TENANCY The tenancy is a secure tenancy in terms of the Tenants' Rights, Etc. (Scotland) Act 1980, as amended, under which the Tenant has the right to occupy the house without disturbance.

6. ABANDONMENT OF SECURE TENANCY If the Council has reasonable ground for believing that the house is unoccupied and that the Tenant does not intend to occupy it as his or her home, the Council shall be entitled to enter the house at any time, by force if necessary, for the purpose of securing the house and its contents against vandalism and may take possession of the house in accordance with Section 19 of the Tenants' Rights, Etc. (Scotland) Act 1980.

7. SUCCESSION TO TENANCY This Agreement confers on qualified persons a right of succession to tenancy. This right and the rules governing succession are set out in Part 2 of the Schedule.

8. OBLIGATIONS OF COUNCIL AND OF TENANT The Council and the Tenant must carry out the responsibilities under this Agreement listed in Part 3 of the Schedule. If the Council fails to fulfil its obligations the Tenant may recover from the Council any

---

[14] See para. 27–47.

resultant loss or damages suffered by him or her. In addition to any rights provided for by legislation or by other Clauses in this Agreement, the Tenant shall be entitled to withhold all or part of the rent due in the event of the Council failing to:—

(i) Give the Tenant full possession of the house;

(ii) Make the house tenantable and habitable, and thus structurally sound, wind- and water-tight and in a reasonable state of repair and maintenance;

(iii) Execute repairs which are the Council's responsibility and which have resulted in injury, loss or damage sustained by the Tenant or persons residing with him or her without payment of compensation by the Council after a reasonable time.

The Tenant is strongly advised to seek legal advice before deciding whether or not to withhold rent.

The Tenant must:—

(a) Give the Council reasonable time in which to take remedial action before withholding rent;

(b) Notify the Council of his or her intention to withhold the rent;

(c) Continue to pay rates and other charges collectable by the Council.

If the Tenant fails to fulfil his or her obligations the Council may recover from the Tenant any resultant loss or damages suffered by the Council and may terminate the Agreement.

9. LODGERS, SUB-LETTING, ASSIGNATION, ETC.   The Tenant is entitled to take in lodgers or to assign, sub-let or otherwise give up to another person possession of the house or any part of it, provided that the Tenant complies with the provisions of Part 4 of the Schedule.

10. TERMINATION   This Agreement may be terminated if any of the events listed in paragraph 2 of Part 1 of the Schedule occurs. The Tenant shall be responsible for all sums due in respect of the occupation of the house up to the date of termination of the Agreement or removal from the house, whichever is the later, including without prejudice to this generality arrears of rent, rates and service charges and re-chargeable repair costs.

11. DISPUTES   If the Tenant and the Council are in dispute about any matter of fact or interpretation or law arising out of this Agreement or about whether the Council's consent to any proposed action by the Tenant has been unreasonably withheld, the matter may be referred by agreement between the Tenant and the Council to an Arbitration Tribunal. Recourse to this Tribunal will not affect any rights which the Council or the Tenant may have to raise legal proceedings.

The Arbitration Tribunal will consist of one Councillor who shall be appointed by and selected from a panel of 10 such Councillors, one Tenants' Representative who shall be appointed by and selected from a panel of 10 Tenants' Representatives and one independent person who shall be appointed by and selected from a panel of 10 such persons.

The panel of 10 Councillors shall be appointed by the City of Glasgow District Council Housing Committee. The panel of 10 Tenants' Representatives shall be appointed by a meeting of all Tenants' Associations arranged by the Glasgow Council of Tenants' Associations. The panel of 10 independent persons shall be appointed by the Councillor's panel and the Tenants' Representatives' panel meeting together.

Regulations governing the Tribunal's proceedings shall be drawn up by the panels aforementioned, in consultation with the Glasgow Council of Tenants' Associations and individual Tenants' Associations and shall be subject to the approval of the Council prior to adoption. The regulations shall be in accordance with the principles of natural justice. The panel shall have no powers to award expenses against a Tenant except in the case of frivolous and vexatious applications, where the Tenant has been warned of this prior to the hearing of his or her application.

The administrative costs of the Arbitration Tribunal proceedings shall be borne by the Council.

IN WITNESS WHEREOF this Agreement typewritten and printed on this and the preceding page(s) and the attached Schedule are executed as follows.

1. By the Tenant at   on
   the   day of
   before the witnesses hereto
   subscribing
   First Witness.....................
   Address...........................
   Occupation.......................
   Second Witness.................
   Address ....
   Occupation.. .

2. By a duly authorised official of the City of Glasgow District
Council at   on the   day of
                    before the witnesses hereto subscribing
First Witness......................
Address...........................
Occupation.......................

....
for the Council

Second Witness ....
Address...........................
Occupation.......................

SCHEDULE
Part 1
Security of Tenancy—Termination of Agreement[15]

1.   This tenancy is a secure tenancy in terms of the Tenants'
Rights, Etc. (Scotland) Act 1980, as amended ("the Act")
(a) if the Tenant is an individual and the house is his or her
only or principal home, or (b) if the tenancy of the house is
held jointly by two or more individuals and at least one of
the joint Tenants occupies the house as his or her only or
principal home.

2.   This secure tenancy may be brought to an end:—
(a)   where the Tenant has given to the Council four weeks
written notice of termination (if the Tenant is married
or lives with another person as man and wife, the
Tenant's partner must complete a form issued by the
Housing Department to the effect that he or she also
wishes to end the tenancy); or
(b)   by written agreement between the Council and the
Tenant; or
(c)   where the death occurs of the Tenant (or if the
tenancy is held jointly by more than one individual of
any one of the joint tenants) and no one is qualified to
succeed to the tenancy in terms of Part 2 of the
Schedule; or
(d)   where all persons qualified to succeed to the tenancy
under Part 2 of the Schedule have declined the
tenancy by giving the Council notice in writing to that
effect within four weeks of the Tenant's death and
have vacated the house within three months thereafter
(any such person must pay the rent and other charges
which become due in respect of any period during any
part of which he or she has occupied the house after
the death); or
(e)   where the tenancy appears to have been abandoned
and the Council has served notice under Section 19(2)
of the Act bringing the tenancy to an end in the belief
that the house is unoccupied and that the Tenant does

---

[15]See paras. 27–41, 27–42, 27–43.

not intend to occupy it as his or her house, subject to the right of a Tenant aggrieved by such action of recourse to the Sheriff Court in terms of Section 20 of the Act; or

(f) where an order has been made by the Sheriff for recovery of possession under Section 15 of the Act following a request by the Council for recovery of possession on any of the following grounds:—

(i) Rent lawfully due from the Tenant has not been paid or any other obligation of the tenancy has been broken. (The Council will not use warrant sales or poinding to recover rent arrears. Arrestment of wages will be used only as a last resort.)

(ii) The Tenant (or any one of joint Tenants) or any person living or lodging in the house or any sub-tenant has been convicted of using the house or allowing it to be used for immoral or illegal purposes.

(iii) The condition of the house or any of the common parts has deteriorated owing to acts of waste by or the neglect or default of the Tenant, or any person living or lodging with the Tenant, or any sub-tenant, subject, in the case of acts by a person living in the house or a sub-tenant, to the Tenant not having taken reasonable steps to remove the lodger or sub-tenant. "The common parts" means any part of a building containing the house and any other premises which the Tenant is entitled in terms of the Tenancy Agreement to use in common with occupiers of other houses.

(iv) The condition of any furniture provided for use under the tenancy or for use in any of the common parts (as defined in (iii) above) has deteriorated owing to ill-treatment by the Tenant or any person living or lodging in the house or any sub-tenant, subject, in the case of ill-treatment by a person living in the house or a sub-tenant, to the Tenant not having taken reasonable steps to remove the lodger or sub-tenant.

(v) The Tenant and the Tenant's spouse have been absent from the house without reasonable cause for a continuous period of over six months or have ceased to occupy the house as their principal home.

(vi) The Tenant or any person living or lodging in the house or any sub-tenant has been guilty of conduct in or in the vicinity of the house which is a nuisance or annoyance to neighbours and it is not reasonable in all the circumstances that the Council should require to make other housing available to him or her.

(vii) The Tenant or any person living or lodging in the house or any sub-tenant has been guilty of conduct in or in the vicinity of the house which is a nuisance or annoyance to neighbours and in the opinion of the Council it is appropriate in the circumstances to require the Tenant to move to other housing.

(viii) The house is overcrowded within the meaning of Section 89 of the Housing (Scotland) Act 1966, in such circumstances as to render the occupier guilty of an offence.

(ix) The Council intends within a reasonable period of time to demolish or carry out substantial work on the building or a part of the building which comprises or includes the house and it cannot reasonably do so without obtaining possession of the house.

(x) The house has been designed or adapted for occupation by a person whose special needs require housing of the kind provided by the house and (a) there is no longer a person with such special needs occupying the house and (b) the Council requires it for occupation (whether alone or with other members of his family) by a person who has such special needs.

(xi) The house forms part of a group of houses which has been designed or which has been provided with or located near facilities for persons in need of special social support and (a) there is no longer a person with such a need occupying the house and (b) the Council requires it for occupation (whether alone or with other members of his family) by a person who has such a need.

(xii) The interest of the Council in the house is that of a lessee under a lease and that lease either (a) has terminated or (b) will terminate within six months from the date of raising proceedings for recovery of possession.

(In relation to grounds (i) to (vi) above, the Sheriff can grant an order for recovery of possession only if he or she is satisfied that it is reasonable to do so.

In relation to grounds (vii) to (xii) above, the Council must prove to the Sheriff that alternative housing suitable for the needs of the Tenant and his or her family is available. In determining the suitability of the alternative housing offered, the Sheriff will have regard to (a) its proximity to the place of work (including attendance at an educational institution) of the Tenant and of other members of his or her family compared to his or her existing house, (b) the size of house required by the Tenant and his or her family, (c) the character of the house compared to the Tenant's existing house, (d) the terms on which the alternative housing is offered to the Tenant compared to the terms of the existing Tenancy Agreement, (e) if any furniture is provided by

> the Council for use under the existing tenancy, whether furniture is to be provided for use under the new tenancy which is of a comparable nature in relation to the needs of the Tenant and his or her family and (f) any special needs of the Tenant or his or her family.)

3. If a matrimonial dispute arises between two persons who are living together as man and wife, whether they are married or not, either spouse or co-habitee who is not the "sole" Tenant may apply to the Court for an order in terms of the Matrimonial Homes (Family Protection) (Scotland) Act 1981, regulating the occupancy of the marital home or transferring the tenancy. The Council must comply with such an order.

   If the Tenant leaves the house and is willing voluntarily to transfer the tenancy to the other spouse, the Council will agree to transfer the tenancy.

   Any rent arrears owed by the former Tenant shall not be passed on to the new Tenant, and the new tenancy shall be offered on the same terms and conditions as the previous tenancy. The Council will provide an equivalent standard of housing to the spouse made homeless by a matrimonial dispute.

Part 2
Succession to Secure Tenancy[16]

1. On the death of a Tenant under a secure tenancy, the tenancy shall pass to:—

   (a) The Tenant's spouse or co-habitee where the house was his or her only or principal home at the time of the Tenant's death;

   (b) A surviving Tenant where the tenancy was held jointly by two or more individuals and the house was that person's only or principal home at the time of the Tenant's death;

   (c) A member of the Tenant's family over the age of 16 years where there is no person falling within paragraphs (a) or (b) above and the house or any other Council house or accommodation let by the Tenant was that member's only or principal home throughout the period of 12 months immediately preceding the Tenant's death;

   (d) A member of the Tenant's household where there is no person falling within paragraphs (a), (b) or (c) and the house or any other Council house or accommodation let by the Tenant was the member's only or principal home throughout the period of 12 months immediately preceding the Tenant's death.

2. If no person qualifies for succession to the secure tenancy as outlined above the tenancy shall be ended.

3. If a person qualifies to succeed to the secure tenancy but declines the tenancy he or she must give the Council written notice declining the tenancy within four weeks of the death

---

[16]See para. 27–40.

of the Tenant. Such a person must vacate the house within three months from the date of notice declining the tenancy and will be liable for rent and other charges for any period during which he or she has occupied the house after the death of the Tenant.

4. If more than one person qualifies to succeed to the secure tenancy they shall all decide by agreement which one or more of them shall succeed to the tenancy.

5. If there is no agreement by qualified persons in terms of paragraph 4 above the Council shall decide which person or persons shall succeed to the tenancy.

6. There shall be no limit to the number of times on which the right of succession may operate.

7. Where the Tenant gives up the tenancy, leaving any of his or her household in the house, the secure tenancy may pass to any remaining member of the household in terms of the above paragraphs.

8. The Council may at its discretion reduce the 12-month period referred to in paragraph 1(c) and (d).

Part 3
Obligations of the Council and of the Tenant

1. RENT — The tenant must pay the rent regularly and promptly.

2. INSPECTION PRIOR TO START OF TENANCY: REPAIR OF DEFECTS BY COUNCIL — At the start of the tenancy the Council is solely responsible for ensuring that the house is tenantable and habitable, thus to make the house structurally sound, in a wind- and water-tight condition and in a reasonable state of repair and maintenance. Prior to the start of the tenancy a representative from the Housing Department will accompany the prospective tenant in inspecting the house and drawing up a mutually agreed list of outstanding repairs, both external and internal, required to make the house tenantable and habitable, and thus structurally sound, wind- and water-tight and in a reasonable state of repair and maintenance. A copy of this list will be given to the Tenant. If the Tenant finds defects in the house after the joint inspection, any such repairs may be added to the list of outstanding repairs by mutual agreement.

The Council will then carry out all the repairs required within a reasonable time. If there are any fixtures and fittings in the house which have been installed by a previous tenant, such items will be detailed in the inspection list as being present in the house.

The Council will repair and thereafter maintain any standard items which the Council itself might have installed as part of a modernisation scheme and for the maintenance of which it has become liable in terms of its statutory responsibilities or has currently assumed responsibility.

**3. SUBSE-
QUENT
REPAIRS**

Following the completion of the repairs referred to in Clause 2 above, the Council is solely responsible throughout the tenancy for maintaining the house in a tenantable and habitable condition, thus to make the house structurally sound, wind- and water-tight and in a reasonable state of repair and maintenance, and generally otherwise adhering to the requirements of the Housing (Scotland) Act 1966, Section 8, and the Housing (Scotland) Act 1974, Sections 13 and 14.

Without prejudice to this generality, the Council is therefore specifically responsible for:—

(a) keeping in repair the structure and exterior of the house (including drains, gutters and external pipes) and

(b) keeping in repair and proper working order the installations in the house (i) for the supply of water, gas and electricity and for sanitation (including basins, sinks, baths and sanitary conveniences but not unless otherwise agreed fixtures, fittings and appliances for making use of the supply of water, gas or electricity) and (ii) for space heating or heating water.

The Council will be responsible also for ensuring that the house is substantially free from rising or penetrating damp, has satisfactory provision for natural lighting, ventilation and heating and adequate electrical wiring and basic fitments to provide satisfactory artificial lighting, has an adequate piped supply of wholesome water available within the house, has a sink provided with a satisfactory supply of both hot and cold water within the house, has a water closet available for the exclusive use of the occupants of the house and suitably located within the house, has an effective system for the drainage and disposal of foul or surface water, has an electricity or gas supply to the cooking of food within the house and has satisfactory access to all external doors and outbuildings.

The Tenant is solely responsible for the repair and maintenance of non-standard fixtures or fittings voluntarily accepted at the commencement of the tenancy. The repair and maintenance of standard fittings and fixtures by the Council is subject to the qualifications referred to in the last sentence of Paragraph 2 of this part of the Schedule.

Otherwise the Tenant is responsible for keeping and leaving the house clean and in a reasonable state of repair, ordinary fair wear and tear excepted. The Tenant is specifically responsible for internal painting and decoration of the house except where the Council agree to undertake such work at the start of the tenancy or otherwise.

The Tenant must notify the Council of the need for any repair or replacement which is the Council's responsibility. The Council will in addition be responsible for regular inspections of the condition of the house at a reasonable frequency. When the need for a repair or replacement is reported or ascertained in the course of inspection, the Council will carry out the repair or make the required replacement within a reasonable time of becoming aware of the defect. If the Tenant feels that any time limit set by the Council for the carrying out of any particular repair is excessively long or has not been adhered to, he or she has a right to withhold rent in terms of Clause 8 of this Agreement or to take the matter up with the courts. The Tenant may also, in terms of Clause 11 of this Agreement, refer any dispute as regards time limits to the Arbitration Tribunal.

Where the need for any repair or replacement arises as a result of damage caused by misuse or neglect on the part of the Tenant or any persons living or lodging in the house or any sub-tenant, or any person visiting the house at the invitation or with the consent of the Tenant or any other person living in the house, the Tenant or sub-tenant shall be liable for the cost of such repairs even although the Council may carry out the work. Where the need for any such repair or replacement arises as a result of damage, misuse or neglect by a third party not connected with the Tenant, the Tenant shall not be liable for the cost of such work.

Where the Council undertakes works of repair or improvement, the Council shall ensure that such works are carried out in a good and workmanlike manner and with good and proper materials. A sample of all completed work shall be inspected by officials of the Council.

Where the need for any repair or replacement of items which are the responsibility of the Tenant arises from negligence on the Council's part in carrying out work in the house or where the Tenant suffers any material loss directly caused by such negligent work, the Council is responsible for reinstatement of the damaged items and for reimbursement of any material loss.

4. EMERGENCY REPAIRS
The Council will take any action, including entry to the house, which is necessary to remove or prevent danger to life, personal injury or health, to prevent substantial damage or further damage to property, to make the premises secure and to restore essential services where reasonably possible within 24 hours of such repairs being notified.

5. INSPECTION
The Council will give the Tenant reasonable notice of the week during which any proposed visit by its staff to carry out an inspection and/or repairs will be made, where possible in accordance with previous access information given by the Tenant, except in the case of an emergency where no notice is required and immediate entry must be given. The Council and the Tenant will make every endeavour to ensure that previously notified access arrangements are adhered to.

6. COMMON PARTS OF BUILDING
(a) The Council will regularly inspect the common parts of the building and must keep in good repair the entrance steps, common doorways, doors, entrance hall, passages, staircases, banisters, landings, windows, ceilings, roofs, external walls, walls surrounding the close and all other parts of the block or property of which the house forms part, including open areas and bin shelters. The Council will so far as reasonably practicable keep the common parts of the building in a satisfactory state of decoration.

(b) In turn with other tenants, the Tenant must wash and clean the common stairs, landings, windows, banisters and bin-chute accesses and must ensure that all these common areas and the drying green are cleaned and tidied not less than once per week. It is particularly agreed that:—

(i) Tenants of houses on the ground floor will be responsible for washing and cleaning of all ground floor passages, entrances, doors and windows;

(ii) Tenants of houses on all floors above the ground floor will be responsible for washing and cleaning of landings, passages, banisters, windows, etc., on their floor and for the section of staircase leading to their floor from the floor below;

(iii) All Tenants will take in rotation their turn for cleaning the bin-chute accesses and tidying the drying green;

(iv) All Tenants shall have chimney vents or gas flues regularly cleared and shall employ a qualified tradesman for that purpose.

7. INSTALLA-TIONS

The Council must maintain close communication with the appropriate authorities responsible for the supply of all services such as water, gas, electricity, heating and television aerials.

8. OPEN SPACES

(a) The Council must maintain in a safe, clean and tidy condition all pathways and parking spaces, and cultivated areas not under the direct responsibility of the Tenant and which are owned by the Council. The Council will advise Strathclyde Regional Council of any defects reported in relation to roadways, pavements or other areas which are the responsibility of the Regional Council.

(b) Applications from a group of tenants representing the whole of or at least one block of houses for permission to cultivate or otherwise change open space areas will be considered. Otherwise the Tenant must not interfere with open space areas in housing developments.

9. USE OF PROPERTY

(a) The Tenant shall use the house only as a private dwellinghouse and must not carry out any business activity without the prior written consent of the Council. The Tenant shall not without the written permission of the Council affix to the house or exhibit any business sign or deface the exterior. Consent to operate a business will not be unreasonably withheld by the Council but permission shall be withdrawn should evidence be found of persistent noise, nuisance or inconvenience being caused to the Tenant's neighbours. Where permission is granted to operate a business activity the Council may review the rent for the house and impose a supplementary charge for its use for trade, professional or business purposes.

(b) The Tenant shall not cause or allow members of his or her family to cause serious or deliberate nuisance or annoyance to neighbours.

(c) The keeping of dogs, other domestic pets and fowls, pigeons or other livestock in multi-storey flats is not allowed. Otherwise the Tenant shall keep dogs and other domestic pets under proper control and not give cause for complaint to neighbours.

(d) The use or storage of bottled gas in any form within the house and the common parts of the building of which the house forms part is prohibited. The use of paraffin is not prohibited but the limit of paraffin to be stored inside the house shall be two gallons and outside shall be five gallons. The Tenant is warned that the use of paraffin in the house constitutes a fire and explosion risk unless due precautions are taken and may cause condensation unless the house is sufficiently well ventilated to remove the water vapour which the burning of paraffin generates.

(e) The Tenant shall not leave the house unfurnished or unoccupied for more than 21 days without previously informing the Council.

10. ALTERA-
TIONS

The Tenant may carry out structural alterations to the house, alter fittings and fixtures or decorate the exterior of the building with the prior written consent of the Council. Such consent shall not be unreasonably withheld but if the Tenant is dissatisfied with the Council's decision he or she may refer the matter to arbitration in terms of Clause 11 of this Agreement or raise the matter in the Sheriff Court in terms of the Act.

If the Council fails to reply within one month to a written request for consent to make alterations, permission is considered to have been given.

The Tenant may erect any buildings, fences or structures of any kind, fixed or portable, within the house or ground or make any alterations to or remove any of the fittings in the house or make alterations to garden ground, paths and railings, gates or chespale fencing with the written consent of the Council. No outhouse other than a garage shall be of greater dimension than 2.5 metres by 2 metres by 2 metres to eaves and no garage shall be of greater dimension than 5 metres by 2.5 metres by 2.3 metres to eaves. Outhouses or garages will be permitted on ground attached to tenements but only in accordance with a scheme approved by all the tenants in the tenement and by the Council.

Where alterations and additions are made by the Tenant with the permission of the Council the Council will maintain any items which the Council itself might have installed as part of a modernisation scheme and for the maintenance of which it has become liable in terms of its statutory responsibilities or has currently assumed responsibility.

11. IMPROVEMENTS BY TENANT

Where the Tenant carries out improvements to the fabric of the house or heritable fixtures in the house with the prior written consent of the Council in the course of a secure tenancy, e.g. by providing a new bathroom suite, installing new power points, central heating, sink units, etc., the Council will pay to the Tenant on termination of the tenancy a sum not exceeding the original cost of such improvements.

If the secure tenancy is terminated by the death of the Tenant, payment will be made to the succeeding Tenant or the Tenant's personal representatives if none succeeds to the tenancy.

The amount of the payment shall not exceed the original cost of the works less any funds from any public source. Improvements made by the Tenant will not by themselves affect the rent payable for the house, but may affect the rateable value of the house.

12. GARDEN GROUND

The Tenant must keep free of litter and in good and proper condition the garden ground attached to the house, paths and hedges, such hedges not to exceed 1 metre in height where the vision of motorists would be impeded, and 2 metres else-where.

The Tenant must not top, lop, pollard or fell trees without the prior written consent of the Council. The Council will make regular inspections of the garden ground.

13. GARAGE Where a garage integral to the house is provided by the Council the Tenant is responsible for keeping and leaving the garage clean and carrying out any internal painting which is required. The Council will regularly inspect such a garage and keep it in repair and proper working order. Where the need for any repair or replacement arises as a result of damage caused by misuse or neglect on the part of the Tenant or any persons living or lodging in the house or any sub-tenant or any person visiting the house at the invitation or with the consent of the Tenant or any other person living in the house, the Tenant or sub-tenant shall be liable for the cost of such repairs even although the Council may carry out the work.

14. VEHICLES, ETC. The Tenant may park motor vehicles, caravans or boats on vehicle runways approved by the Council, but not otherwise on garden ground or on areas of ground or approaches in the immediate vicinity of multi-storey developments.

15. AERIALS The Tenant may attach aerial installations to the exterior of the house or building or install an aerial on garden ground or in loft space but only with the prior written consent of the Council. Such consent shall not be unreasonably withheld and if the Tenant is dissatisfied with a Council decision on this matter he or she may refer the matter to arbitration in terms of Clause 11 of this Agreement or alternatively raise the matter in the Sheriff Court in terms of the Act. If the Council fails to reply within one month to a written request to attach an aerial, permission will be deemed to have been given.

The cost of repairing any damage to the roof, chimneyhead or any other part of the house or building due to the erection of an aerial shall be met by the Tenant.

16. INSPECTION AT END OF TENANCY At the end of the tenancy the Tenant must (a) permit a representative of the Housing Department to inspect the house in the presence of the Tenant or his or her representative for any damage due to the Tenant's fault or negligence, (b) replace any fixtures or fittings which have been removed without consent during the period of the tenancy or pay the Council the cost of their replacement, (c) pay for the repair of any damage due to his or her negligence or fault, it being agreed that the Tenant is not responsible however for fair wear and tear to the house, and (d) clear out any rubbish or personal possessions from the house, loft, garage, garden or any other part of the house or its surrounds.

Part 4
Regulations Governing Sub-letting, etc.[17]

1. A Tenant wishing to take in a lodger or lodgers or to assign or sub-let the whole or part of the house to another person must seek the written consent of the Council. Consent shall not be unreasonably withheld. If the Council fails to reply within one month to a written request to take in a lodger or assign or sub-let all or part of the house, consent is considered to have been given.

2. The Council may refuse consent if it considers that:—
    (a) The proposed rent is unreasonable;
    (b) Any returnable deposit to be charged as security for the payment of bills for gas, electricity, telephone or other domestic supplies and for any damage to the house and its contents is unreasonable;
    (c) Overcrowding, as defined in Part 5 of the Schedule, will result;
    (d) The rooms likely to be used by a lodger or sub-tenant will be affected by works to be carried out in the house or building by the Council; or
    (e) The request does not conform to a Code of Practice covering the taking in of lodgers or sub-letting or assignation agreed between the Council and the Glasgow Council of Tenants' Associations.

3. If consent is refused and the Tenant is not satisfied, he or she may refer the matter to arbitration in terms of Clause 11 of this Agreement or appeal to the Sheriff Court on grounds (c), (d) or (e) of paragraph 2 above.

4. A Tenant must warn a sub-tenant that where the need for any repair or replacement of Council property arises as a result of damage, misuse or neglect on the part of the sub-tenant, the sub-tenant shall be liable for the cost of such repair or replacement even though the Council may carry out the work.

Part 5
Overcrowding

The Council will not without the Tenant's written consent let any house to a Tenant where overcrowding as defined by the Housing (Scotland) Act 1966, will result.

Where a Tenant notifies the Council that he or she wishes to be transferred because his or her house is overcrowded, the Council will provide suitable alternative housing as soon as possible.

---

[17]See para. 27–48.

Part 6
Variation of Agreement[18]

1. The Tenant shall be given a copy of the Tenancy Agreement on demand.
2. The Council shall not change the Agreement except for the level of rent and service charges after it has been signed by the Tenant without the consent of the Tenant.
3. If the Tenant does not consent to any proposed change by the Council, other than rent or service charges, the Council may request the Sheriff to authorise the change.
4. If the Tenant considers any existing provision of the Agreement to be unreasonable or unfair he or she can ask the Council to alter it. If the Council refuses, the Tenant can request the Sheriff to order the provision to be changed.
5. The Council undertakes that before it makes any policy changes or alterations affecting all Tenancy Agreements which affect secure tenancies it will inform the Glasgow Council of Tenants' Associations and all Tenants' Organisations and Community Councils of the proposed changes.
6. The Council will consider any representations made by the Glasgow Council of Tenants' Associations, Tenants' Organisations and Community Councils before reaching any decision on proposed changes and will give the organisations a reasonable time in which to consider the proposals.

(*To be signed by or on behalf of the parties*)

Rent

7–47   Landlords in the public sector have a large measure of freedom in imposing and reviewing the rents of dwelling-houses forming part of their housing stock. Local authorities may charge such reasonable rents as they may determine and review rents from time to time and make changes in rents either generally or in particular cases as circumstances may require, but no account is to be taken of the personal circumstances of tenants.[19] There are, however, limitations of a fiscal character on this freedom where a local authority in disregard of Government guidelines is charging inadequate rents.

Assignation and sub-letting

7–48   It is a term of every secure tenancy that the tenant shall not assign, sub-let or otherwise give up to another person possession of the dwelling-house except with the consent in writing of the landlord, which shall not be unreasonably withheld. The landlord may refuse consent if it appears that a payment is to be received by the tenant other than (a) a rent which in the landlord's opinion is reasonable or

---

[18]See para. 27–49.
[19]Housing Rents and Subsidies (Scotland) Act 1975, s. 1 as amended.

(b) a deposit returnable at the termination of the assignation, sub-let or other transaction given for security for the sub-tenant's obligations for accounts for supplies of gas, electricity, telephone or other domestic supplies and for damage to the dwelling-house or contents, which in the landlord's opinion is reasonable.[20] Ground rules for assigning, sub-letting, etc., are set out in Schedule 3 to the 1980 Act, and include a right to the tenant who is aggrieved by a refusal of consent by the landlord to raise proceedings by way of summary application to the sheriff against such refusal.

Variations

27–49   The terms of a secure tenancy may be varied only by agreement between the landlord and the tenant, or under subsection (2) or (4) of section 17 of the Tenants' Rights, Etc. (Scotland) Act 1980, and it is not permissible to contract out.[21] An agreement to vary the terms of the tenancy must be in probative or holograph writing and it is the duty of the landlord to prepare the document and ensure that it is duly executed.[22] Subsection (2) of section 17 permits increase of the rent or any other charge after written notice of not less than four weeks before the beginning of the rental period or any earlier date on which the payment of rent in respect of that period falls to be made. Subsections (3) and (4) of section 17 provide for an order by the sheriff varying any term of the tenancy (other than rent) on summary application by the landlord or the tenant. Such an application may be made by the landlord where the tenant refuses to agree to a variation proposed by the landlord. An application may be made by the tenant on one of three grounds, namely: (1) by reason of changes in the character of the dwelling-house or of the neighbourhood or other circumstances which the sheriff may deem material, the term has become unreasonable or inappropriate; (2) the term is unduly burdensome compared with any benefit which would result from its performance; or (3) the existence of the term impedes some reasonable use of the dwelling-house, and the landlord refuses to agree to the variation.[23] The expression of those three grounds echoes the language of section 1(3)(*a*), (*b*) and (*c*) of the Conveyancing and Feudal Reform (Scotland) Act 1970 in respect of the variation or discharge of land obligations, and presumably the sheriff would adopt similar criteria for decision to those used by the Lands Tribunal for Scotland in deciding upon applications under that subsection of the 1970 Act.[24] Neither an increase of rent in pursuance of section 17(2) of the 1980 Act nor an order of the sheriff varying the terms of the tenancy under section

[20]Tenants' Rights, Etc. (Scotland) Act 1980, s. 21.
[21]1980 Act, s. 17(1).
[22]*Ibid.*, s. 17(6).
[23]*Ibid.*, s. 17(3).
[24]See Vol. II, paras. 19–64 to 19–94.

17(4) of the Act has the effect of terminating the tenancy. In any lease of a dwelling-house granted after July 3, 1962 for a period of less than seven years it is an implied obligation of the landlord to repair the structure and installations for the supply of water, gas, electricity and for sanitation and it is not permissible to contract out of that obligation.[25] The tenant under a secure tenancy may carry out repairs which the landlord is under obligation to carry out and recover the cost from the landlord, all in terms and subject to the conditions of regulations by the Secretary of State for Scotland.[26]

---

[25] Housing (Scotland) Act 1966, ss. 8, 10.
[26] 1980 Act, s. 17A added by the Tenants' Rights, Etc. (Scotland) Amendment Act 1984, s. 7. The regulations have not yet been promulgated.

CHAPTER 28

LEASES OF LAND AND AGRICULTURAL SUBJECTS

AGRICULTURAL HOLDINGS

AGRICULTURAL HOLDINGS

Introduction

28–01   A lease of an agricultural holding within the meaning of the Agricultural Holdings (Scotland) Act 1949[1] is defined in section 93(1) of the Act as "a letting of land for a term of years, or for lives, or for lives and years, or from year to year"; if the period is less than from year to year it takes effect as a lease from year to year.[2] From the conveyancing aspect the principles of common law regulate the capacity of parties and the methods of constitution and proof of leases of agricultural holdings, and the Leases Act 1449 and, in the relatively few cases where it is applicable, the Registration of Leases (Scotland) Act 1857 as amended apply to such leases. They are, however, governed by important statutory restrictions under the Agricultural Holdings (Scotland) Act 1949 and related legislation.[3] For a fuller treatment of the relevant substantive law, reference may be made to the undernoted specialist texts.[4] A basic style of a lease of an

---

[1] ss. 1, 93. For further definition and relevant authorities see Gill, *Law of Agricultural Holdings in Scotland*, Chap. 2.

[2] 1949 Act, s. 2.

[3] The principal statutes are the Agriculture (Scotland) Act 1948, the Agricultural Holdings (Scotland) Act 1949, the Agriculture Act 1958, the Succession (Scotland) Act 1964, the Agriculture (Miscellaneous Provisions) Acts 1968 and 1976, the Agricultural Holdings (Amendment) (Scotland) Act 1983 and the Agriculture Act 1986.

[4] Gill, *Law of Agricultural Holdings in Scotland* (1982); Connell, *The Agricultural Holdings (Scotland) Acts* (6th ed., 1970); Muir Watt, *Agricultural Holdings* (12th ed., 1967), and supplements; *Aspects of Agricultural Law* (Law Society of Scotland, 1981).

agricultural holding, designed primarily for an arable and stock-rearing farm, adjusted by the Law Society of Scotland in 1980, is reproduced with the permission of the Society in paragraph 28–02 *infra*, and a commentary on its provisions is offered in paragraphs 28–03 to 28–34 *infra*. Variations on the style for a pastoral farm are suggested in paragraph 28–45 *infra*. In practice it is now comparatively unusual for a landowner to enter into a lease of an arable farm in precisely the form suggested. In open-market lettings the limited partnership device is now frequently used whereby the tenant is a limited partnership constituted under the Limited Partnership Act 1907, the landlord or his nominee being the limited partner and the real tenant being the general partner. The deed of partnership is framed in terms which enable the limited partner to dissolve the partnership, thus terminating the lease and circumventing the statutory protections as to security of tenure which an agricultural tenant would otherwise have.[4a] Sometimes a lease of the kind in the style may be used in a sale and lease-back transaction, or where a tenant has been in possession without a written lease and exercises his right under section 4 of the 1949 Act to require one, although in the last-mentioned circumstances the tenant will usually seek to have a lease in terms which contain only the provisions required by common law or statute.

Style of agricultural lease—arable farm

28–02

LEASE
between

(who and whose successors as Landlord under this Lease are hereinafter referred to as "the Landlord")
and

(hereinafter referred to as "the Tenant")
IT IS AGREED between the parties hereto as follows:

The Landlord in consideration of the rent and other benefits and with and under the reservations, conditions and others hereinafter specified, hereby lets to the Tenant, excluding successors, assignees and subtenants whether legal or conventional without the written consent of the Landlord ALL and WHOLE the Farm of

Subjects let

extending to   all as delineated on the plan thereof annexed and signed as relative hereto together with the farmhouse and all other buildings thereon

---

[4a] A device analogous to this has recently encountered difficulties in England—see *Featherstone* v. *Staples* [1986] E.G.L.R. 6 (C.A.).

(which subjects are hereinafter referred to as "the Farm").

Duration The Farm is let from   for a period of   .

Rent The yearly rent payable by the Tenant will initially be   payable in equal instalments at Fifteenth May and Eleventh November in each year, beginning the first payment at   for the term preceding and the next payment at and so forth half-yearly thereafter with interest on any sum outstanding (whether in respect of rent or otherwise) at a rate three percentage points above the Base Rate of the   Bank of   in force from time to time. The Landlord will not at any time be barred from claiming damages from the Tenant for failure to implement any obligation under this Lease by reason of the fact that the rent may have been accepted by the Landlord.

Rent Review The rent will be subject to review every **(delete if Lease for** three years, the first review date being **five years or less)**   and the subsequent review dates occurring at intervals of three years thereafter. The new rent (which will take effect from the relevant review date) will be fixed by agreement between the Landlord and the Tenant, failing which by arbitration.

RESERVATIONS

There are reserved to the Landlord:

Minerals (A) the whole ores, minerals and mineral substances, whether metalliferous or not, including precious and other metals, and sand, gravel and building stone on or under the Farm with full power to do everything necessary to prospect for, work, win and carry away, let or dispose of the same, including power to erect buildings and plant in connection therewith, but subject to payment for surface damage (which in the case of crops shall include temporary grass) or for damage to fixed equipment or other property of the Tenant and to an adjustment of rent which, failing agreement, will be fixed by arbitration;

Alter marches, (B) power to alter marches and excamb **etc.** land with any neighbouring proprietor, an adjustment of rent being made on the basis of the annual values of any additions to or deductions from the Farm, which adjustment will, failing agreement, be fixed by arbitration;

Resumption (C) power at any time to resume any part

or parts of the Farm for any purpose other than agricultural purposes on giving at least   months' written notice;

Water

(D) all water in rivers, streams, burns, springs, lochs, ponds, wells, reservoirs, dams, drains, conduits, canals, or underground channels with all necessary rights of access thereto subject to the use thereof by the Tenant for the proper purposes of the Farm only;

Game

(E) the whole shootings and fishings on the Farm with the exclusive right of sporting, shooting, fishing, trapping and snaring, subject to the Tenant's common law and statutory rights; declaring that the Tenant is hereby granted permission to kill deer if found on arable land or enclosed pasture; and the period of twelve months ending Thirty-First October in each year will be substituted for the calendar year for the purposes of Section 15(1) of the Agricultural Holdings (Scotland) Act 1949; and the Tenant, so far as in his power and subject as aforesaid, will protect the game on the Farm and will prevent all poachers and others from trespassing thereon and will immediately give notice to the Landlord of poaching, suspected poaching or trespassing;

Woods and plantations

(F) all woods, trees, brushwood and plantations (with grass therein) and the ground occupied thereby on the Farm; with power on payment for surface damage (i) to cut, prune and remove the same and to plant others in their place; (ii) to fence the same and also the stools of trees and shrubs when cut; (iii) to enclose any unenclosed woods and plantations, all without compensation to the Tenant, it being understood that all such plantations or woodlands occupied by the Tenant will be so occupied by mere tolerance and such permission may be withdrawn by the Landlord at any time; and (iv) to cart wood through the Farm from the woods and plantations thereon or from neighbouring woods or plantations; declaring that if any trees, woods or plantations and the fences round the same are destroyed or injured by the Tenant or his employees or by the Tenant's machinery or by the Tenant's livestock, the Tenant will be liable to the Landlord for the damage so done;

Wayleaves

(G) all existing rights of way, wayleaves and servitudes, with power to grant further wayleaves and servitudes, subject to payment for surface damage (which in the case of crops shall include temporary grass);

Roads

(H) a right to use all roads and means of access over the Farm to other lands and subjects;

Access by the Landlord

(I) the right to enter and to authorise others to enter all parts of the Farm for the purpose of satisfying the Landlord that the conditions of this Lease are being properly carried out, or fulfilling the Landlord's obligations or exercising his rights hereunder; declaring that if any ground damaged or resumed under any of the foregoing powers is restored to an arable state and if possession thereof is given to the Tenant at any time during the currency of this Lease, the abatement of rent in respect of such ground will cease and the Tenant will thereafter be bound to cultivate such land along with the rest of the Farm in accordance with the terms of this Lease.

FURTHER CONDITIONS

Rates, etc.

1 The Tenant will pay all rates, taxes and other charges, including water rates, usually payable by tenants or occupiers.

Landlord's obligation to reinstate and insure

2 The Landlord will reinstate or replace any building on the Farm which is damaged or destroyed by fire if its reinstatement or replacement is required to enable him to fulfil his obligation to manage the Farm in accordance with the rules of good estate management; and the Landlord will also effect in his own name a policy or policies of insurance against damage by fire for all buildings on the Farm to their full reinstatement value.[4b]

Tenant's obligation to insure crops, etc.

3 The Tenant will in the event of the destruction by fire of harvested crops grown on the Farm for consumption thereon return to the Farm the full equivalent manurial value of the crops so destroyed insofar as the return thereof is required for the fulfilment of his obligation to farm in accordance with the rules of good husbandry; and the Tenant will insure to their full value against damage by fire, all live and dead stock on the Farm and all such harvested crops as aforesaid with an insurance office to be reasonably approved

---

[4b] It may be desired to add a provision that in the event of any of the farm buildings being destroyed or damaged by fire so as not to be reasonably capable of being used for its purpose the rent will be abated appropriately by an amount to be agreed or failing agreement determined by arbitration until the building is replaced or repaired but the lease shall not terminate.

of by the Landlord and will exhibit the receipts for the premiums paid therefor to the Landlord and, if required, will assign the policy or policies of assurance to the Landlord who will be entitled to recover any sum due under the same and to apply such sum in payment of all or part of the rent due or current at the time and any other sums due by the Tenant to the Landlord, and if the Tenant fails to pay the premiums on the said policy or policies as they become due, the Landlord will be entitled to do so and recover payment thereof from the Tenant; [the Tenant will also insure the stock against anthrax and foot and mouth disease and brucellosis].

Landlord's obligation for fixed equipment

4 The Landlord undertakes to put the fixed equipment on the Farm into a thorough state of repair, and to provide such buildings and other fixed equipment as will enable the Tenant, provided he is reasonably skilled in husbandry, to maintain efficient production as respects both the kind of produce specified in the Lease and the quality and quantity thereof; and will, during the tenancy, effect such replacement or renewal of the fixed equipment as may be rendered necessary by natural decay or by fair wear and tear.

Tenant's obligation for fixed equipment

5 The Tenant agrees that the undertaking of the Landlord to put the fixed equipment on the Farm in a thorough state of repair has been duly implemented; and the Tenant binds himself during this Lease to maintain the fixed equipment on the Farm in as good a state of repair (natural decay and fair wear and tear excepted) as it was in immediately after it was put in repair as aforesaid, or, in the case of equipment provided, improved, replaced or renewed during the tenancy, as it was immediately after it was so provided, improved, replaced or renewed, the dykes and fences having the cope and wire on (as the case may be); and all being left "slap free," natural decay and ordinary fair wear and tear alone being excepted.

Notwithstanding the foregoing, the cost of maintaining or replacing those fences which form the boundaries of the Farm will, where the Farm adjoins other subjects belonging to the Landlord, be shared equally between the Tenant and the Landlord.

Tenant's other obligations

6 Without prejudice to the generality of the foregoing obligation to uphold the fixed

equipment, the Tenant undertakes:

(a) to employ skilled tradesmen as necessary to replace loose or broken slates and glass, overhaul roofs, chimneys, rhones, gutters, pipes, roads and bridges, walls, dykes and fences, gates and gate pillars and to scour the ditches, drains and water courses;

(b) to keep all tile and surface drains and sewage disposal systems clear and efficient, and to repair all burst and choked drains;

(c) to dig and clean the roots of and switch all the hedges, and not to remove or destroy any hedges on the Farm;

(d) to cut down and spray all thistles, dockens and weeds on the Farm once before they come into flower and again in August in each year, and to take all practicable steps to prevent the growth of wild oats;

(e) to keep down all rabbits, moles, rats and other vermin and pests on the Farm;

(f) to paint, once in every   years, the whole outside woodwork and ironwork of the buildings on the Farm in such manner as shall be approved by the Landlord;

(g) to paint, once in every   years, the internal walls and woodwork of the farmhouse which have previously been painted in such manner as shall be approved by the Landlord;

(h) to whitewash or limewash, once in every   years, all those parts of the farmhouse and other buildings which have previously been whitewashed or limewashed.

If any of the foresaid operations is neglected or not duly performed, the Landlord shall have power to employ workmen to execute the necessary operation and the Tenant will be bound to meet the expenditure thereby incurred; and the Tenant will perform free of charge all cartage of materials required for any improvements or repairs which may be executed or made on the Farm during the currency of this Lease. No capital improvements will be carried out by the Tenant except with the prior written consent of the Landlord.

Record   7 The Landlord and the Tenant agree that a record of the condition of the fixed equipment on, and the cultivation of, the

Farm will be made at the commencement of this Lease. At the termination of this Lease the Tenant will have a right to compensation for improvements and the Landlord to compensation for dilapidations.

Alteration to fixed equipment

8 The Tenant will not alter or add to any or erect new fixed equipment unless with the prior written consent of the Landlord.

Tenant's fixtures

9 The Tenant's fixtures are specified in Schedule I annexed hereto. At the termination of this Lease the Landlord or the incoming tenant will take over at valuation all the Tenant's fixtures. These fixtures will be kept in proper repair by the Tenant at all times.

Stock

10 The Tenant will always keep the Farm fully stocked and equipped with his own stock and crop and the Tenant accepts the Farm at entry in the then state of cultivation without claim or objection; and the Tenant will manage, manure, labour and crop the Farm as an arable and/or livestock rearing farm only, according to the rules of good husbandry in all respects and shall not use the Farm or any part or parts of it for any other business whatsoever; declaring that, subject to the provisions of section 9 of the Agricultural Holdings (Scotland) Act 1949 as amended, no permanent pasture land (or any part of the hill) will be broken up without the prior written permission of the Landlord, and in the last year of this Lease the Tenant will be bound to have the Farm under a rotation according to the rules of good husbandry as recognised and practised in the district; and the Tenant binds himself not to sell or remove from the Farm, but to consume thereon, the whole straw, turnips, and fodder (except potatoes and grain) growing yearly thereon and to apply to the Farm yearly the whole dung thereon and to manure the same and to leave the whole dung made thereon and not used at the expiry of this Lease to the Landlord or incoming tenant who will take over the dung at a valuation to be fixed, failing agreement, by arbitration.

Quotas

10A (1) The Tenant shall not permit or suffer any milk quota or any basic quota under any marketing scheme to lapse or be reduced through any failure to produce a sufficient quantity of milk or any produce now or hereafter the subject of any marketing scheme which is or has been produced on the Farm.

(2) The Tenant shall not sell or otherwise dispose of the whole or any part of any milk quota or any basic quota under any marketing scheme allotted to the Farm or to the Tenant in respect of the Farm.

(3) On termination of the tenancy hereunder the Tenant shall nominate the Landlord or the incoming tenant as his successor in respect of any milk quota and any basic quota under any marketing scheme in respect of which the Tenant has the right of nomination.

Muirburn
11 The Tenant may burn one-tenth of the heather, muir, whins or bracken on the Farm in each year, but only on written intimation to the Landlord before the Twentieth day of March in each year. The Tenant will, when appropriate, give notice to neighbouring occupiers of his intention to burn and will take every precaution to avoid injuring any wood or trees and generally to control the burning.

No camping or caravanning
12 The Tenant will ensure that no part of the Farm is used for camping or caravanning.

Market gardening and dairy farming
13 If the Tenant uses any part of the Farm as a market garden or for commercial flower or vegetable cultivation, or as a dairy farm, or for pig or poultry production, he will have no claim against the Landlord for alterations or improvements or for compensation at the termination of this Lease.

Last year
14 The Tenant will at the proper season in the last year of this Lease, sow, if required so to do by the Landlord or incoming tenant, with such kinds and quantities of clover and grass seed as either of them may specify, such part of the Farm in grain crop in that year as may be fixed by the Landlord or incoming tenant; the Tenant will be bound to harrow and roll in said seed and protect the grass therefrom against injury by cattle or sheep or otherwise, all free of charge, the Landlord or incoming tenant paying for the grass seed; and further, in the last year of this Lease, the Tenant will allow the Landlord or incoming tenant to enter into such part of the Farm as may be intended for fallow at the separation of the penultimate crop from the ground and to labour, manure and dress the same accordingly; and generally in the last year the Tenant will allow the Landlord or incoming tenant access to the whole land under crop as soon as the crops

are carried off the ground; and the Landlord or incoming tenant will take the whole of the waygoing fodder and grain crop and outgoing turnip crop of the last year of this Lease at a valuation to be fixed, failing agreement, by arbitration; and the Tenant further binds himself at the termination of this Lease to leave the Landlord or incoming tenant the one year old grass and all straw on the Farm, and to plough and harrow the fallow ground.

Residence on farm

15 The Tenant will reside in the farmhouse, and the habitable buildings will be occupied only by employees of the Tenant unless the Landlord agrees otherwise in writing.

Waste ground

16 The Tenant will be bound at his own expense to reclaim any areas of waste ground on the Farm which are capable of being reclaimed as soon as it is practical to do so.

Irritancy

17 If, during this Lease, the Tenant becomes notour bankrupt or grants a Trust Deed for behoof of his creditors or, without the prior written consent of the Landlord, assigns this Lease or sub-lets the Farm or any part or parts of it, or allows one half-year's rent to remain unpaid for one month after it has become due or for fourteen days after receipt of a written demand from the Landlord, whichever is the later, or fails to cultivate the Farm according to the rules of good husbandry, or if the farmhouse or buildings is or are not occupied in accordance with Condition 15 hereof, or if the Tenant fails within a reasonable time to remedy any breach, capable of being remedied, of any condition of this Lease, not inconsistent with his responsibilities as Tenant, or commits a breach of a condition of this Lease which materially prejudices the Landlord and is not capable of being remedied, then and in any of these events, it will be in the power of the Landlord by written intimation addressed to the Tenant at the Farm and sent by Recorded Delivery post or Registered Letter to put an end to this Lease on a specified date being not less than three months after the date of such intimation and to resume possession of the Farm in whatever state it may then be without any declarator or process of law and without prejudice to the Landlord's claim for past due and current rents and all other claims competent to him, and neither

the Tenant nor any of his creditors will in such an event have any right or claim for improvements or otherwise against the Landlord.

Removing

18 The Tenant binds and obliges himself to flit and leave the Farm vacant for the Landlord or incoming tenant at the termination of this Lease without the necessity of any warning or process of removing.

Registration

19 The parties consent to registration hereof for preservation and execution.

(To be attested)
(Stamp duty—see para. 25–44)
SCHEDULE I
Tenant's Fixtures
(To be signed by parties)

3–03 Parties. The parties must be named.[5] As indicated in paragraph 28–01 *supra*, the tenant in leases negotiated on a commercial basis will frequently be a limited partnership. As to the parties to a lease of an agricultural holding and changes in the personnel of landlords or tenants, reference may be made to Gill, *Law of Agricultural Holdings in Scotland*, Chapter 3.

3–04 *Successors*. As to the rights of successors of the tenant of an agricultural holding, whether by bequest or on intestacy, at common law as altered by the Agricultural Holdings (Scotland) Act 1949[6] and the Succession (Scotland) Act 1964,[7] reference may be made to the undernoted text[8] and the Agricultural Holdings (Amendment) (Scotland) Act 1983.[9]

As regards a testamentary bequest it appears that, despite the wide terms of section 20(1) of the 1949 Act, it is competent to contract out of the section.[10] Nor is the right to contract out negatived by the 1964 Act, since section 29(1) provides that such a bequest shall not be treated as invalid by reason only that there is among the conditions of the tenancy or lease an *implied* condition prohibiting assignation whereas the normal practice, as in the style in paragraph 28–02 *supra*, is to insert an *express* exclusion of successors or assignees.

As regards succession on intestacy, it is unclear in the absence of a directly relevant judicial decision whether it is competent to contract out of the provisions of section 16 of the 1964 Act. In the first place, if the deceased tenant "immediately before his death held the interest of

[5] 1949 Act. Sched. 5, para. 1.
[6] ss. 20, 21.
[7] ss. 14, 16 and 29.
[8] Gill, *op. cit.*, Chaps. 32 and 33. See also Vol. IV.
[9] s. 4.
[10] *Kennedy* v. *Johnstone*, 1956 S.C. 39, referred to and not disapproved in the House of Lords decision in *Johnson* v. *Moreton* [1980] A.C. 37.

a tenant under a tenancy or lease which was not expressed to expire on his death"[11] the tenant's right under the lease forms part of his estate and vests for the purposes of administration in his executor,[12] and notwithstanding a prohibition of assignation in the lease may be transferred by the executors to any one of the persons entitled to succeed to the deceased's intestate estate.[13] If the provisions of section 16 are to be excluded it would appear that the safe course is to ensure that the tenant's right to the lease expires on his death.[14] It seems doubtful whether the exclusion of successors and assignees in the style in paragraph 28–02 *supra* would achieve this result and, in the comparatively few cases where a lease is granted to an individual and not to a limited partnership, it is for consideration whether there should be added "under declaration that this lease shall expire on the death of the tenant." A prospective tenant, however, may be unwilling to accept such a qualification.

Where the lease contains a special destination applicable on the death of the tenant which could not be, or has not in fact been evacuated, his interest does not form part of his estate and the operation of section 16 of the 1964 Act is excluded.[15]

From the point of view of the tenant, consideration should be given as to the potential liability to inheritance tax on the value of the tenant's interest passing on his death in the various circumstances of a bequest of the tenancy, succession to the tenancy under a special destination or acquisition of the tenancy by transfer by the executor.[16]

28–05   *Assignees.* The exclusion of assignees (a term which includes legatees by what is effectively an assignation *mortis causa*)[17] of a lease of an agricultural holding is implied at common law in leases of ordinary duration[17a] but is usually expressed.

28–06   *Sub-tenants.* The exclusion of sub-tenants is also implied at common law but is likewise usually made express in the lease. In the unusual case where sub-tenancies are permitted by the lease or expressly agreed to by the landlord the 1949 Act makes specific provision, particularly in relation to notices to quit.[18]

---

[11] 1964 Act, s. 36(2).
[12] *Ibid.*, s. 14.
[13] *Ibid.*, s. 16.
[14] It is competent to have a lease for the lifetime of the tenant—*Macalister* v. *Macalister* (1859) 21 D. 560; *Inland Revenue* v. *Graham's Trs.*, 1971 S.C. (H.L.) 1; *Cormack* v. *McIldowie's Exrs.*, 1974 S.L.T. 178 at 183, 1975 S.L.T. 214 at 221, although a lease for lifetime of the tenant may not be within the definition of a lease of an agricultural holding—1949 Act, s. 93(1).
[15] 1964 Act, s. 36(2), proviso (a). As to what constitutes a special destination, see *Reid's Trs.* v. *Macpherson*, 1975 S.L.T. 101 and *Cormack* v. *McIldowie's Exrs.*, *supra*.
[16] See *Aspects of Agricultural Law* (Law Society of Scotland, 1981), 11, 87, 88; Inheritance Tax Act 1984, s. 171.
[17] See *Kennedy* v. *Johnstone*, 1956 S.C. 39 at 47.
[17a] See para. 31–02.
[18] 1949 Act, s. 27: see Gill, *op. cit.*, para 32 and *Aspects of Agricultural Law* (Law Society of Scotland, 1981), 9, 10.

3–07 Subjects let. In proper practice the description of the subjects let should be by reference to a plan, as in the style in paragraph 28–02 *supra*. In terms of section 4(1)(*b*) of the Agricultural Holdings (Scotland) Act 1949 where a lease of an agricultural holding contains no provision for any of the matters specified in the Fifth Schedule to the Act, the landlord or the tenant may require a lease which contains such a provision and one of the requirements specified in paragraph 2 of the Schedule is a description by reference to a map or plan. Landlord's and tenant's fixtures are dealt with later in the style.

3–08 Duration. A period of several years is contemplated in the style in paragraph 28–02 *supra* with reviews of rent at three-yearly intervals. In practice it is suggested that a lease be from year to year or, if longer, with breaks exercisable by the landlord at three-yearly intervals, so that on notice to quit being given the rent can be renegotiated more frequently. Even where notice to quit is served under section 25(2)(*e*) of the 1949 Act because of failure by the tenant to remedy a breach of his obligations under the lease, it appears that such a notice can be given only at a break in or expiry of the lease.[19] Moreover, if a near relative of a deceased tenant has acquired right to the lease and the landlord wishes to serve notice to quit on the ground of the lack of sufficient training or experience,[20] it would appear that he can only do so with effect on the expiry of the lease which may be a considerable time afterwards in the case of a lease for several years. If the date of entry is stated in a lease of an agricultural holding as the term of Whitsunday or Martinmas, that is defined as May 28 or November 28.[21]

3–09 Rent. Section 19 of the Agricultural Holdings (Scotland) Act 1949 entitles the landlord to raise an action of removing if the rent is six months in arrear, but this statutory irritancy is purgeable by the tenant by making payment of the arrears or by finding caution to the satisfaction of the sheriff for the arrears and for one further year's rent. Since purgation can be made the remedy is not particularly effective, and the imposition of an obligation to pay interest on arrears included in the style in paragraph 28–02 *supra* is a useful compulsitor. The old legal irritancy in agricultural leases under the Act of Sederunt of December 14, 1756,[22] incurred when two years' rent is unpaid, has in practice been superseded by section 19 of the 1949 Act.

Any provision in a lease which makes provision for payment of a higher rent or liquidated damages in the event of a breach or non-fulfilment of any of the terms or conditions of the lease is not

---

[19]*Macnabb* v. *A. & J. Anderson*, 1955 S.C. 38.
[20]1949 Act, s. 26A and Ninth Sched. added by Agricultural Holdings (Amendment) (Scotland) Act 1983, s. 4.
[21]1949 Act, s. 93(1); *Austin* v. *Gibson*, 1979 S.L.T. (Land Ct.) 12.
[22]C.A.S., L., xv.

enforceable: the landlord in such an event is not entitled to recover any sum in excess of the damage actually suffered by him in consequence of the breach or non-fulfilment.[22a]

28–10 *Acceptance of rent as bar to enforcement of tenant's obligations.* The clause in the above-mentioned style to the effect that acceptance of rent does not bar the landlord from claiming damages for failure of the tenant to implement any obligation under the lease is substantially declaratory of the existing law. The relevant decisions to that effect are based mainly on the principle that the terms of a formal lease are not easily altered by actings of parties,[23] and that the action of the landlord in not enforcing timeously an obligation of the tenant does not normally involve prejudice to the tenant.[24] The express provision in the style may be of value, however, in the unusual case where the tenant can establish prejudice.

28–11 *Rent review.* A provision for rent review is now usual in leases for a period of years, but it may be preferable to let for a much shorter period without the need to provide for reviews of rent.[25] The rent review clause in the style in paragraph 28–02 is less sophisticated than those which are now inserted in commercial or industrial leases,[26] but in agricultural leases a simple provision for determination of the increase in rent by an arbiter experienced in agricultural practice is all that is required. Section 7 of the Agricultural Holdings (Scotland) Act 1949, as amended by section 2 of the Agriculture Act 1958 and section 2 of the Agricultural Holdings (Amendment) (Scotland) Act 1983, and also, as to disregard of increases in rental value due to transferred milk quota paid for by the tenant, section 16 of the Agriculture Act 1986 relate to the basis of determination by the arbiter of the variation in rent on the occasion of a review and the periods when a reference to arbitration on the matter may be demanded, now in general at intervals of not less than three years from the commencement of the lease or the last variation in rent. The arbitration proceedings must be set in motion by the landlord or the tenant serving notice in writing demanding a reference to arbitration of the question what rent should be payable as from the next ensuing day on which the tenancy could have been terminated by a notice to quit given at the date of demanding the reference.

28–12 **Reservation of minerals.** Clause (A) of the section of the style in paragraph 28–02 *supra* contemplates the working of minerals by underground operations; in general if the extraction of minerals involves opencast or surface workings the landlord will resume

---

[22a]1949 Act, s. 16.
[23]*Carron Co.* v. *Henderson's Trs.* (1896) 23 R. 1042.
[24]*Morrison-Low* v. *Howison*, 1961 S.L.T. (Sh.Ct.) 53 at 58.
[25]See para. 28–08.
[26]See Chap. 29.

possession of the necessary portions of the surface under clause (C).[27] The reservation may be important, since the working of sand or gravel which lie near the surface may effectively destroy the land for agricultural purposes, at least for a period until reinstatement (which is now usually required as a condition of planning consent for mineral workings) is carried out. The compensation for surface damage will be determined by arbitration.[28]

8–13 Alteration of marches and excambion. Clause (B) of the reservations in the above-mentioned style, at least as regards excambions, appears to apply to exchanges of ground between proprietors. It may be advisable to extend the wording of the clause to permit expressly alteration of marches and exchanges of ground between tenants of the same landlord.

8–14 Resumption. At common law the landlord has no right of resumption: an express clause in a lease conferring the power is necessary and almost invariably is inserted. On the basis of the decision in *Kininmonth* v. *British Aluminium Co.*[29] no period of notice is required in Scotland where the lease has permitted resumption at any time, but the English courts have decided that, since notice of at least two months is required to enable the tenant to serve timeous notice of claims for removal of fixtures, disturbance compensation or high farming compensation, any stipulation in a lease for a lesser period of notice is invalid.[30] It is unclear whether the Scottish courts would follow the English decisions but in practice it is advisable to stipulate for at least two months' notice. The exception from the right to resume of a resumption for agricultural purposes (clause (C) of Reservations in the style) is based on the view that a resumption for that purpose would be contrary to the good faith of the lease.[31] It is unnecessary and inadvisable to specify the purposes for which land may be resumed; the various possible circumstances in which the landlord may wish to exercise the power cannot be predicted. It is not in the landlord's interest to specify any limit of the extent of the land which may be resumed, but it should be kept in view that if the location or extent of land which the landlord proposes to resume is such that the tenant is prevented from making profitable use of the remainder for agricultural purposes it may be contrary to the faith of the lease.[32]

8–15 Water. Reservation (D) of the style is merely declaratory of the

---

[27]See para. 28–14.
[28]1949 Act, ss. 68, 74.
[29]1915 S.C. 271.
[30]*Re Disraeli's Agreement* [1939] Ch. 382; *Coates* v. *Diment* [1951] 1 All E.R. 890.
[31]See *The Admiralty* v. *Burns*, 1910 S.C. 531; *Turner* v. *Wilson*, 1954 S.C. 296; *Pigott* v. *Robson*, 1958 S.L.T. 49.
[32]*Turner* v. *Wilson, supra* at 302. See also *Trotter* v. *Torrance* (1891) 18 R. 848 and *Glencruitten Trs.* v. *Love*, 1966 S.L.T. (Land Ct.) 5.

common law which entitles the tenant to use water for ordinary agricultural purposes.

28–16   Game. Subject to the statutory rights of a tenant to kill ground game for protection of his crops the landlord's sporting rights do not pass to an agricultural tenant unless conferred in the lease,[33] but it is desirable to define the rights of the parties clearly in the lease as in reservation (E) of the style. As to the statutory rights of the tenant in respect of ground game and deer, reference may be made to the undernoted text.[34]

28–17   Woods and plantations. It is advisable to regulate the rights of parties in relation to timber on the land on the lines of reservation (F) in the style.

28–18   Access. At common law the landlord has a right to enter on the holding for inspection and he has also a statutory right to do so.[35] It is for consideration whether in appropriate cases the landlord might stipulate for a more extensive right of access than that provided for in reservation (I) of the style, *e.g.* access for other purposes or by vehicles on making good any damage caused. The declaration as to the return of ground restored after resumption with cessation of the abatement of rent is broadly reasonable; if the ground as restored is less valuable for farming purposes that should be reflected in the rent at the next review.

28–19   Insurance. The obligations imposed on the landlord and the tenant respectively in conditions 2 and 3 of the style as to insurance and reinstatement of buildings damaged by fire and insurance of dead stock and harvested crops are required by the Fifth Schedule to the 1949 Act.[36] The obligation of the tenant to have the insurance office approved by the landlord is a normal provision in leases and the extension of the insurance to cover the risk of diseases affecting livestock is a sensible provision in appropriate cases. A requirement that the tenant is obliged to pay any premium in respect of insurance of fixed equipment on the holding is invalid.[37]

28–20   Fixed equipment

(a) *Landlord's obligations*. Condition 4 of the style substantially reproduces the obligations of the landlord required by the 1949 Act and must be carried out at the commencement of the tenancy or as soon as reasonably possible thereafter.[38]

---

[33]*Wemyss* v. *Gulland* (1847) 10 D. 204; *Copland* v. *Maxwell* (1871) 9 M. (H.L.) 1.
[34]Gill, *op. cit.*, Chap. 11.
[35]Agricultural Holdings (Scotland) Act 1949, s. 18.
[36]*Ibid.*, Fifth Sched., paras. 5 and 6.
[37]*Ibid.*, s. 5(4).
[38]*Ibid.*, s. 5(2)(*a*).

(b) *Tenant's obligations*. Condition 5 of the style likewise substantially reproduces the obligations of the tenant stipulated in the 1949 Act,[39] with the addition only of the provision as to repair and replacement of fences.[40] The obligations of the tenant for repair and maintenance of fixed equipment are subject to the exception of fair wear and tear, and do not extend to renewal or replacement of fixed equipment which has succumbed to natural decay not caused by misuse or neglect on the part of the tenant.[41]

It should be noted that the obligations of the landlord and the tenant cannot effectively be varied in the lease from those prescribed by section 5 of the 1949 Act; any material alteration which the parties may adjust should be incorporated in a separate agreement entered into *after* the commencement of the tenancy as permitted by section 5(3) of the Act. An illustration of such an agreement follows.

AGREEMENT[42]

between

A B, (*designed*), (hereinafter called "the Landlord")

and

C D, (*designed*), (hereinafter called "the Tenant")

The parties agree that their obligations under the Lease of the Farm of   dated   shall be varied as follows:—

1. Notwithstanding the terms of the said Lease the Tenant accepts the fixed equipment on the Farm as being in a thorough state of repair and sufficient in all respects to enable him to maintain efficient production, and further the Tenant undertakes that he will during the tenancy effect at his own expense on behalf of the Landlord such replacement or renewal of the buildings or other fixed equipment on the Farm as may be rendered necessary by natural decay or by fair wear and tear.

2. Except in so far as varied hereby, the parties confirm the terms of the said Lease.

(*To be attested*)   (*Stamp duty nil*)

It should be kept in view that this statutory licence to alter the terms of a lease by subsequent agreement is restricted to a variation in the terms of the lease as regards fixed equipment.

28–21   **Other obligations of tenant**. The provisions as to other obligations of the tenant contained in clause 6 of the style are usual in most agricultural leases, but any which are inappropriate to the particular subjects may be omitted. The right of the landlord to implement any of

---

[39] *Ibid.*, s. 5(2)(*b*).

[40] As to replacement, as distinct from repair, of fences being a landlord's obligation see *Mackay* v. *Duke of Sutherland's Trs.*, 1970 S.L.C.R. App. 140.

[41] *Turner's Trs.* v. *Steel* (1900) 2 F. 363 at 368; *Johnstone* v. *Hughan* (1894) 21 R. 777. See "Fair Wear and Tear in Agricultural Leases" (1962) 3 Conv. Rev. 80.

[42] Based on style suggested by Styles Committee of the Law Society of Scotland.

the obligations which are neglected by the tenant does not prevent the
landlord from founding on the tenant's failure and serving a notice to
quit based upon such breach of the tenant's obligations; the remedy of
permitting the landlord to carry out the operations is supplementary to
any other remedies competent to him.[43]

28–22   **Capital improvements**. In terms of clauses 6 and 8 of the style the prior
written consent of the landlord is required for any capital improvements or alterations or additions to fixed equipment by the tenant. If
the landlord's consent is not given, however, the tenant may seek to
have such operations authorised by the Land Court, using the
procedure in section 52 of the 1949 Act.

28–23   **Record of the holding**. Clause 7 of the style provides for a record of the
condition of the fixed equipment on, and the cultivation of, the farm to
be made at the commencement of the lease. In terms of the 1949 Act
either the landlord or the tenant may at any time, whether at the
commencement of the lease or during its currency, require such a
record to be made[44] and indeed in post-1949 leases a record of the
condition of the fixed equipment is required on the lease being entered
into,[45] although in practice that is not always done. The tenant may
also require that a record be made of existing improvements either
carried out by him or for which he, with the landlord's consent, has
paid compensation to an outgoing tenant and of any fixtures or
buildings which he is entitled to remove under section 14 of the 1949
Act.[46] The importance of a proper record is that it is a prerequisite to
certain statutory claims, *e.g.* a claim by the tenant for high farming[47] or
claims by the landlord for compensation for dilapidation or deterioration[48] or for general deterioration.[49] Such a record will, when
required, be made by a person appointed by the Secretary of State, the
expense of making the record being borne, unless otherwise agreed,
equally by the parties.[50]

28–24   **Tenant's fixtures**. Section 14 of the 1949 Act entitles the tenant to
remove fixed equipment installed by him or buildings erected by him,
subject to the right of the landlord to acquire them at valuation.
Clause 9 of the style contracts out of the statutory provision (which is
permissible in relation to section 14) by providing that the landlord will
take over all the tenant's fixtures at valuation.

28–25   **Stock and permanent pasture**. Clause 10 is appropriate to a cropping

---

[43] *Halliday* v. *Fergusson*, 1961 S.C. 24.
[44] 1949 Act, s. 17.
[45] *Ibid.*, s. 5(1).
[46] *Ibid.*, s. 17.
[47] *Ibid.*, s. 56.
[48] *Ibid.*, s. 57(1).
[49] *Ibid.*, s. 58.
[50] *Ibid.*, s. 17(8).

and stock-rearing farm.[51] The responsibility of the tenant to farm in accordance with the rules of good husbandry is defined in the Sixth Schedule to the Agriculture (Scotland) Act 1948 and if he fails to do so the landlord may apply to the Land Court under section 28 of the 1949 Act and if he obtains a certificate that the tenant has so failed may serve an incontestable notice to quit.[52] As regards permanent pasture it is suggested that the style would be improved by specifying in the lease the particular areas of permanent pasture to which clause 10 refers.[53]

8–26 **Muirburn**. Regular muirburning is a recognised element in good husbandry, particularly in the case of sheep farms.[54] A statutory right of muirburn is conferred on a tenant by the Hill Farming Act 1946 which contains detailed provisions as to the periods and times of day within which it may be carried out, notice to the landlord and proprietors of adjoining lands or woodlands and the obligation of due care in its performance.[55] All that is necessary in a lease is to insert any further provisions, not being inconsistent with the 1946 Act, which the landlord may consider desirable. In clause 11 of the style the further provisions are (1) specification of the limit of extent of muirburn in each year, (2) a statement of the date before which notice must be given to the landlord and (3) an extension of the statutory obligation to the effect of giving notice to neighbouring occupiers and not merely to proprietors of adjoining lands or woodlands.

8–27 **Prohibition of camping or caravanning**. The prohibition in clause 12 of the style is not unreasonable; the subjects are let for agricultural purposes and improperly supervised camping and caravanning may adversely affect amenity.

8–28 **Market gardening and dairy farming**. The object of clause 13 of the style is to avoid liability on the landlord to pay compensation for the provision of specialist equipment such as greenhouses, etc., of market gardens or pig houses or poultry houses for battery production of chickens.

8–29 **Cropping—last year**. The tenant is free to practise any system of cropping arable lands which does not result in deterioration of the holding, but that freedom does not apply during the last year of a lease[56] and so detailed provisions imposing specific obligations on the tenant in the last year such as those included in clause 14 of the style may competently be inserted.

---

[51]For variations in a lease of a pastoral farm, see para. 28–45.
[52]1949 Act, s. 25(2)(d).
[53]See 1949 Act, s. 9.
[54]See Agriculture (Scotland) Act 1948, s. 26(2) and Fifth and Sixth Scheds.
[55]Hill Farming Act 1946, ss. 23–27.
[56]1949 Act, s. 12.

28–30   Residence. The requirement of residence by the tenant on the farm is usual (clause 15 of the style). As to what is sufficient residence see the undernoted decisions.[57]

28–31   Waste ground. Whether or not a provision on the lines of that in clause 16 of the style should be included is a matter for consideration. The 1949 Act provides[58] that in leases entered into before January 1, 1921 the tenant is not entitled to compensation for any improvements which he was required to carry out by the terms of his tenancy, but in modern leases the reclamation of waste land is an improvement under Part II of the First Schedule to the 1949 Act in respect of which, where due notice has been given to the landlord, compensation is payable,[59] although in the ascertainment of compensation an element to be taken into account is any benefit which under an agreement in writing the landlord has given to the tenant in consideration of his carrying out the improvement.[60] The clause in the style may provide a basis for a contention by the landlord that the obligation imposed on the tenant to reclaim waste land so far as practical was an element in the adjustment of the rent, but it is thought that this contention would succeed only if it could be established that reclamation of a particular area or areas was in contemplation of the parties when the lease was negotiated and was taken into account in the negotiations.

28–32   Irritancy. A conventional irritancy is now almost invariably inserted in an agricultural lease for the reasons that (1) the statutory irritancy for non-payment of rent in section 19 of the 1949 Act is purgeable on payment of arrears or finding caution and is not a particularly effective remedy,[61] (2) it enables the notice-to-quit provisions of sections 24 and 25 of the Act to be by-passed since the landlord's right to enforce an irritancy is preserved by section 24(5) and is enforceable at any time when an irritancy has been incurred,[61a] and (3) the tenant is not entitled to compensation for disturbance under section 35 of the Act when the tenancy is terminated by reason of irritancy. The statutory restrictions upon the exercise of irritancy clauses in leases contained in sections 4 to 6 of the Law Reform (Miscellaneous Provisions) (Scotland) Act 1985 do not apply to leases of agricultural holdings.[62] The principle that an irritancy in a lease, once incurred, cannot be purged remains applicable.[63]

---

[57]*Stuart* v. *Warnocks* (1883) 20 S.L.R. 863; *Blair Trust Co.* v. *Gilbert*, 1940 S.L.T. 322; *Lloyds Bank Ltd.* v. *Jones* [1955] 2 Q.B. 298; *Morrison-Low* v. *Howison*, 1961 S.L.T. (Sh.Ct.) 53.

[58]s. 48.

[59]s. 51.

[60]s. 49(2).

[61]See para. 28–09.

[61a]It has been decided in England that notice of forfeiture must be of sufficient length to enable the tenant to claim timeously compensation in respect of high farming—hence the provision for three months' notice in cl. 17 of style in para. 28–02.

[62]Law Reform (Miscellaneous Provisions) (Scotland) Act 1985. s. 7.

[63]*McDouall's Trs.* v. *MacLeod*, 1949 S.C. 593. The principle was subsequently affirmed in *Dorchester Studios (Glasgow) Ltd.* v. *Stone*, 1975 S.C. (H.L.) 56.

28–33   As regards the terms of clause 17 of the style the following comments are offered:

(a) If the tenant is a company there should be included a further event upon which irritancy will be incurred, namely, the tenant going into liquidation whether compulsory or voluntary save for the purpose of amalgamation or reconstruction of a solvent company.

(b) The condition as to the tenant failing to remedy a breach "within a reasonable time" may lead to argument. From the landlord's point of view it may be preferable to omit the phrase so that the irritancy is incurred upon breach. In practice it would be sensible for the landlord to notify the tenant that he requires the breach to be remedied within a stated reasonable period and to raise irritancy proceedings only after expiry of that period, but he is in the strong position that strictly the irritancy has been incurred in terms of the lease whenever the breach occurred.

(c) It is doubtful whether or to what extent the final provision of the clause in the style as to the tenant having no claim for improvements or otherwise against the landlord is legally enforceable. Section 48 of the 1949 Act provides that the tenant "at the termination of the tenancy, on quitting the holding" shall be entitled to compensation for a new improvement, and in terms of section 64 of the Act the tenant's entitlement to such compensation exists notwithstanding any agreement to the contrary. The question therefore is whether, when an irritant clause is enforced, that event comes within the ambit of the phrase above quoted. There can be an argument based on the decision in *Marquis of Breadalbane* v. *Stewart*[64] that the enforcement of an irritancy is not the same as termination of the lease and that a clause of irritancy should be enforced in accordance with its terms. On the other hand it may be contended that the definition of termination of the tenancy in section 93(1) of the 1949 Act, namely, "the termination of the lease by reason of effluxion of time or from any other cause" is wide enough to comprehend termination by reason of an irritancy having been incurred. Moreover, the principle explained in the recent decision of the House of Lords in *Johnson* v. *Moreton*,[65] that provisions of the legislation may be in the public interest as well as the private interest, could found an argument that the encouragement of improvements in agricultural holdings by provision for compensation on waygoing is in the public interest as evidenced by the prohibition of contracting-out in section 64 of the Act and that a clause of irritancy, in so far as it purports to defeat that objective, is not enforceable. It is thought that the latter view is correct. Nevertheless, it is suggested that a provision on the lines of that contained in the style may be inserted *quantum valeat*.

28–34   Upon the occurrence of the breach the landlord may serve notice on

---

[64](1904) 6 F.(H.L.) 23.
[65][1980] A.C. 37.

the tenant specifying the breach and requiring the tenant to remove. If that is resisted the landlord may raise an action of declarator of irritancy and removing.[66] If the tenant defends the action on the ground that an irritancy has not been incurred, it will be sisted for arbitration to determine the issue.[67] Possible defences to the action are (1) denial of the breach,[68] (2) oppression by the landlord,[69] (3) breach by the landlord of an obligation incumbent on him under the lease,[70] or (4) acquiescence implying waiver by the landlord.[71]

28–35   **Notices to quit.** The complex provisions of the 1949 Act as to termination of the tenancy of an agricultural holding by notice given by either party are outwith the scope of a work on conveyancing but are analysed in Chapter 16 of Gill, *Law of Agricultural Holdings in Scotland* as recently amended in relation to the termination of tenancies acquired by succession by sections 3 and 4 of the Agricultural Holdings (Amendment) (Scotland) Act 1983. It should be noted, however, that it is incompetent to contract out of the statutory provisions in a lease,[72] and conveyancers should also keep in view the effect of the sale of an agricultural holding upon a notice to quit and the procedures to be observed in such circumstances.[73]

Compensation

28–36   A fundamental feature of the statutory code for agricultural holdings is the right of compensation available to the tenant or the landlord in certain circumstances and, from the point of view of the landlord, the extent to which the obligation to pay compensation to the tenant may be modified by agreement.

Tenant's rights
28–37   (1) *Improvements.* A tenant is entitled on quitting the holding to compensation for certain improvements.[74] Sections 36 to 55 of the 1949 Act and the First, Second and Third Schedules set out the rules which govern the tenant's rights to compensation for improvements. The rules, which are somewhat complex, are analysed and explained in Gill, *The Law of Agricultural Holdings in Scotland*, Chapter 26. Broadly the improvements for which the tenant may claim compensation may be classified as (i) "old" or "new" improvements in accordance with the dates when they were begun, (ii) those which require or do not require the consent of or notice to the landlord, and

---

[66]*Edmond* v. *Reid* (1871) 9 M. 782; *Duke of Argyll* v. *Campbeltown Coal Co.*, 1924 S.C. 844.
[67]1949 Act, s. 74; *British Transport Commission* v. *Forsyth*, 1963 S.L.T. (Sh.Ct.) 32.
[68]*Stuart* v. *Warnocks* (1883) 20 S.L.R. 863; *Blair Trust Co.* v. *Gilbert*, 1940 S.L.T. 322; *British Transport Commission* v. *Forsyth, supra.*
[69]See *McDouall's Trs.* v. *MacLeod*, 1949 S.C. 593.
[70]*Macnab* v. *Willison*, 1960 S.L.T. (Notes) 25; *British Transport Commission* v. *Forsyth, supra.*
[71]*Lamb* v. *Mitchell's Trs.* (1883) 10 R. 640.
[72]1949 Act, s. 24(1), proviso.
[73]1949 Act, s. 31; Gill, *op. cit.*, Chap. 19.
[74]1949 Act, s. 36(1).

(iii) permanent or temporary improvements. Under each of the First, Second and Third Schedules to the 1949 Act the claims are categorised as Part I, Part II and Part III improvements. Part I improvements are permanent improvements to which the consent of the landlord is required, Part II improvements are those for which notice to the landlord is required and include improvement of land drainage and the erection or alteration of buildings, while Part III improvements are temporary improvements which may be carried out by the tenant as part of the ongoing practice of good husbandry and require neither the consent of, nor notice to, the landlord.

From the conveyancing aspect it is important to know whether the statutory provisions as to the tenant's right to compensation can be modified by agreement. The general rule is that contracting out of the statutory provisions is not permitted.[75] There are, however, particular provisions of the 1949 Act which provide for some modification of that rule, *viz*.

(a) A tenant is not entitled to claim compensation, where the lease was entered into before January 1, 1921, for an improvement which he was required to carry out in terms of the lease.[76]

(b) For old improvements the tenant may claim compensation under custom, agreement or otherwise in lieu of any compensation provided by section 37[77] and for new improvements the tenant may claim compensation under an agreement in writing in lieu of any compensation provided by section 48.[78]

(c) In all cases of Part I improvements, whether old or new, where the landlord's consent was given on agreed terms of compensation, the compensation payable under the agreement is substituted for compensation under the 1949 Act.[79]

(d) In the case of Part II improvements the parties may enter into an agreement in writing as to the terms of compensation or otherwise at the stage when the tenant gives notice in writing of the improvements which he intends to carry out, and if the parties agree in writing, whether in the lease or subsequently, to dispense with such notice, the agreement may also regulate the terms in respect of compensation. The compensation payable in terms of any such agreement will rule in lieu of the statutory provisions as to compensation.[80]

(e) A compensation agreement entered into in writing before January 1, 1921 in respect of an old improvement specified in Part III of the Second or Third Schedule to the 1949 Act will regulate the compensation payable so long as it is fair and reasonable having regard

---

[75] 1949 Act, s. 64(1).
[76] *Ibid.*, s. 37(1), proviso; s. 48(1), proviso.
[77] *Ibid.*, s. 37(2).
[78] *Ibid.*, s. 48(2).
[79] *Ibid.*, s. 39(2); s. 50(2); Sixth Sched., para. 12.
[80] *Ibid.*, s. 51(2) and (3).

to the circumstances existing at the time of making the agreement.[81]

(f) In the situation where a tenancy is terminating and the farm is being re-let to an incoming tenant, any agreement between the landlord and the incoming tenant whereby the latter undertakes to pay to the outgoing tenant any compensation payable by the landlord under the 1949 Act or the Agricultural Holdings (Scotland) Acts 1923 to 1948 in respect of improvements or to refund to the landlord any such compensation which has been paid by the landlord to the outgoing tenant is null and void,[82] subject only to the exception that such an agreement in writing which is in respect of new improvements under Part III of the First Schedule may be made, up to a maximum amount specified in the agreement.[83]

Notice of intention to claim compensation for improvements must be given within two months after termination of the tenancy.[84]

28–38 (2) *High farming.* Section 56(1) of the 1949 Act entitles the tenant to claim compensation for the continuous adoption of a standard of farming or a system of farming (usually known as high farming) which has been more beneficial to the holding than the standard or system required by the lease. It is a precondition of any such claim that a record of the condition of the holding has been made under section 17 of the Act and notice of intention to claim compensation under this head must be given in writing by the tenant to the landlord not later than one month before the termination of the tenancy and should state that the claim is being made under and in terms of section 56.

28–39 (3) *Disturbance and reorganisation.* Section 35 of the 1949 Act provides for payment to the tenant for disturbance in five sets of circumstances.[85] The compensation is one year's rent at the rate payable immediately before termination of the tenancy, but the tenant may claim a greater amount up to a maximum of two years' rent if he gives not less than one month's notice of the sale of goods, implements, fixtures, produce or stock and affords the landlord a reasonable opportunity of making a valuation thereof. Section 9 of the Agricultural Holdings (Miscellaneous Provisions) Act 1968 entitles the tenant to a sum in addition to compensation for disturbance to assist in the reorganisation of his affairs. The amount payable is four times the annual rent of the holding. The landlord may be exempt from liability to make the reorganisation payment in any of the circumstances specified in section 11 of the 1968 Act.[86,87] It is not permissible to contract out of the liability for a reorganisation payment.[88]

---

[81] *Ibid.*, s. 42.
[82] *Ibid.*, s. 11(1).
[83] *Ibid.*, s. 11(2).
[84] *Ibid.*, s. 68(2).
[85] For a convenient summary of these see Gill, *op. cit.*, Chap. 28.
[86] *Barns-Graham* v. *Lamont*, 1971 S.C. 170; *Copeland* v. *McQuaker*, 1973 S.L.T. 186.
[87] For further details see Gill, *op. cit.*, Chap. 28.
[88] 1968 Act, s. 11(4).

28–39A (4) *Milk quotas.* A tenant who has a registered milk quota in relation to the holding is entitled on termination of the lease and quitting the holding to compensation in respect of the value of the quota calculated in accordance with Schedule 2 to the Agriculture Act 1986.[88a] The tenant may be entitled to compensation for milk quota under an agreement in writing in lieu of the payment provided by the Act.[88b]

28–40 (5) *Early resumption.* In the event of the landlord exercising his right to resume part of the holding before the expiry of the lease the tenant may make certain claims under the 1949 and 1968 Acts. These cannot be defeated by any provisions of the lease: the tenant may enforce his statutory rights if they are more advantageous than any rights of compensation stated in the lease.

(a) The tenant may claim a reduction in rent, including elements for severance and injurious affection loss, under section 34 of the 1949 Act.

(b) He may also claim in respect of disturbance under sections 35 and 60 of the 1949 Act based upon the rental value of the land resumed.

(c) He may also claim under sections 47 to 49 and 60 of the 1949 Act for improvements carried out on the land resumed.

(d) He may also claim under section 15(3) of the 1968 Act for any loss of benefit which would have accrued to him if the resumption had taken place approximately 12 months later.

(e) In addition he will be entitled under sections 9 and 11(6) of the 1968 Act to a reorganisation payment of four times the rental value of the resumed land.

28–41 (6) *Common law claims.* In addition to the statutory claims above mentioned in paragraphs 28–37 to 28–40 *supra* the tenant may claim at common law for ploughing and cultivation for any crop which he will not reap, grass seed sown with the waygoing white crop, surplus dung, fodder and grain crop and turnip crop.[88c]

Landlord's rights

28–42 *Dilapidation and deterioration.* On the tenant quitting the holding upon termination of the tenancy the landlord has a statutory right under section 57 of the 1949 Act to claim compensation for any dilapidation or deterioration of, or damage to, any part of the holding, or anything in or on the holding, caused by failure by the tenant to farm in accordance with the rules of good husbandry. The amount of the compensation payable is the cost of making good the dilapidation, deterioration or damage. Alternatively the landlord may claim for such

[88a]1986 Act, s. 14.
[88b]*Ibid.,* Sched. 2, para. 2(4).
[88c]See D.L. Laird, *Aspects of Agricultural Law,* 50. See also style in para. 28–02, cond. 14.

matters under a written lease, but he cannot claim both under the Act and under a lease, except as regards a statutory claim under section 6(1) of the 1949 Act.[89]

Under section 58 of the 1949 Act the landlord may also claim compensation for general deterioration of the holding, the onus being upon the landlord to show that the value of the holding has been reduced, whether by reason of any such dilapidation, deterioration or damage as is mentioned in section 57 or otherwise by non-fulfilment by the tenant of his responsibilities to farm in accordance with the rules of good husbandry. It is a necessary condition of a claim by the landlord under section 57 or 58 that a record of the holding has been made under section 17 of the 1949 Act.[90] Claims, if made under section 57 or 58, require to be preceded by a written notice of intention to claim not later than three months before the termination of the tenancy,[91] but if made under a lease must be made within two months after the termination.[92] The landlord may also claim on the termination of the tenancy for injury to or deterioration of the holding due to the exercise by the tenant of his rights of freedom of cropping and disposal of the produce,[93] the amount of compensation being the cost of putting the holding into the condition in which it should have been but for the actings of the tenant.[94]

Arbitration

28-43 (a) **Statutory arbitrations**. The 1949 Act contains numerous specific provisions for arbitration and a general provision in section 74 of the Act requiring arbitration on any question of any kind between the landlord and the tenant in accordance with rules prescribed in section 75 of and the Sixth Schedule to the Act as now amended by section 5 of the Agricultural Holdings (Amendment) (Scotland) Act 1983. It is not permissible to contract out of those statutory provisions in the lease or otherwise.[95]

(b) **Common law arbitrations**. Waygoing valuations of sheep stocks, dung, fallow, straw, crops, fences and other specific things the property of an outgoing tenant, agreed under a lease to be taken over at the termination of the tenancy by the landlord or an incoming tenant, are excluded from the arbitration provisions of sections 74 and 75 of the 1949 Act.[96] The lease usually provides for valuations of those

---

[89] 1949 Act. s. 57(3).
[90] *Ibid.*, s. 59(2).
[91] *Ibid.*, s. 59(1).
[92] *Ibid.*, s. 68(1)(*a*) and (2).
[93] *Ibid.*, s. 12(2)(*b*).
[94] *Fraser* v. *McDonald* (1834) 12 S. 684.
[95] 1949 Act, s. 75(1).
[96] *Ibid.*, s. 75(4).

excluded matters being made by arbitration.[97] As regards sheep stock valuations see paragraph 28–45 *infra*.

28–44   As to procedure in common law and statutory arbitrations reference should be made to the chapter on "Arbitration" by K.M. Campbell, *Aspects of Agricultural Law* (1981), pages 20 to 33. In relation to statutory arbitrations, however, the amendments made to section 75 of and the Sixth Schedule to the 1949 Act by section 5 of the Agricultural Holdings (Amendment) (Scotland) Act 1983 should be borne in mind. In relation to waygoing claims and valuations, reference should be made to the chapter in the same text by D.L. Laird at pages 47 to 54. These chapters, contributed by authors with wide experience in the field of agricultural arbitrations, contain much detailed practical advice on the relevant procedures.

Style of lease—sheep farm

28–45   The style of lease of an arable farm in paragraph 28–02 *supra* may be used for a lease of a sheep farm subject to the following variations:

Rent. The rent of a pastoral farm is legally due one-half at Whitsunday on entry and the other half at Martinmas following, but the terms of payment may be varied contractually.

Stock. Where the farm is wholly pastoral, clause 10 of the style will be altered to read:

> The Tenant will always maintain on the Farm a sheep stock of a suitable breed and type in regular ages (so far as reasonably practicable) in accordance with the recognised practices of hill sheep farming [and in particular without prejudice to that generality he shall (i) use lug, horn or other stock marks for the purpose of determining ownership of the sheep stock, (ii) ensure the regular selection and retention of the best family stock for breeding and (iii) ensure the regular selection and use of tups, choosing the qualities most suitable for the flock]. The stock shall be bound to the ground, and on the expiry of the lease whether at the natural ish or any other period the Tenant shall be bound to leave and sell the same to the Landlord or incoming tenant and the Landlord or incoming tenant shall be bound to take and pay for the same. Failing agreement the price shall be fixed by arbitration in accordance with a valuation to be made in terms of the Sheep Stocks Valuation (Scotland) Act 1937 and the Hill Farming Act 1946 as amended. No permanent pasture land (or any part of the hill(s)) will be broken up without the prior written permission of the Landlord.

Last year. Clause 14 of the style is appropriate to a cropping farm, but may be included in the lease of a predominantly pastoral farm as regards any part of the farm where cropping may be practised.

---

[97]See style in para. 28–02, cond. 14.

SMALL LANDHOLDINGS AND CROFTS

Small landholdings

28–46   Small agricultural holdings as defined in the Small Landholders (Scotland) Act 1911 constitute a special type of holding regulated by the provisions of the Small Landholders (Scotland) Acts 1886 to 1931 as amended by the Crofters (Scotland) Acts 1955 and 1961 and the Crofting Reform (Scotland) Act 1976. For a summary of the principal features of these holdings reference may be made to Walker, *Principles of Scottish Private Law*, Volume III, pages 278 to 280. From a conveyancing aspect it should be noted that such holdings, although they may be renounced, are not assignable, save in special circumstances to a member of the landholder's family with the leave of the Land Court.[98]

Crofts

28–47   Crofting tenure is now regulated by the Crofters Holdings (Scotland) Act 1886, parts of the Small Landholders (Scotland) Acts 1911, 1919 and 1931, the Crofters (Scotland) Acts 1955 and 1961, the Crofting Reform (Scotland) Act 1976 and the Law Reform (Miscellaneous Provisions) (Scotland) Act 1985.[99] The Acts regulate crofting holdings in the crofting counties and contain *inter alia* provisions as to security of tenure, determination of fair rents by the Land Court, bequests of the tenancy by the crofter and succession rights of his heir and compensation to the tenant for improvements or to the landlord for deterioration. The crofter may renounce his tenancy at any term of Whitsunday or Martinmas on one year's written notice to the landlord[1] but he can assign it only with the written consent of the Crofters' Commission or, with the consent of the landlord, to a member of his family.[2] The 1976 Act conferred power on a crofter to acquire ownership of his croft, failing agreement with the landlord, by an order made by the Land Court on terms and conditions specified in the Act.[3] For a summary of the principal statutory provisions see the undernoted text.[4]

SPORTING LEASES

Parties

28–48   Normally the granter of a game or sporting lease must be the

---

[98]Crofters Holdings (Scotland) Act 1886, s. 1 as amended by Small Landholders (Scotland) Act 1911, s. 21.
[99]ss. 30, 31 and 32.
[1]1955 Act, s. 7 as amended by 1961 Act, Sched. 1.
[2]1955 Act, s. 8 as amended by 1976 Act, s. 15.
[3]ss. 1–6.
[4]Walker, *Prin.*, III, 281–286.

proprietor of the lands over which the right is granted. It is competent for a person who has a real right to the shootings or fishings which is not merely a personal privilege to grant a lease of the sporting rights, but in practice the lease from the proprietor of the land will prohibit assignees or sub-tenants. An agricultural lease will not be presumed to carry a right of fishing or shooting,[5] other than the right of the agricultural tenant to shoot rabbits and hares to protect his crops under the Ground Game Act 1880.

Sporting leases as real rights

8–49   A lease of salmon fishings is binding upon singular successors of the landlord.[6] So also is a lease of a deer forest for stalking.[7] If the lease is simply of a right of shooting, even where a lodge is let with the right, the older authorities are to the effect that it is not binding upon singular successors of the landlord.[8] A lease of trout fishings for consideration and for a period of not less than one year is now deemed to be one to which the Leases Act 1449 applies and so is valid in a question with successors of the landlord.[9] Something depends upon the actual terms of the document which confers the right, particularly whether it is properly construed as a lease or a mere licence.[10]

Style—lease of fishings

8–50   **MINUTE OF LEASE**
between
AB, (*designed*), (hereinafter
called "the landlord")
and
CD, (*designed*), (hereinafter
called "the tenant")
1. The landlord hereby lets to the tenant [and his executors] excluding assignees or sub-tenants except with the prior written consent of the landlord [which consent shall not be unreasonably withheld] [the exclusive[11] right of fishing for salmon on the river within the boundaries of the landlord's estate of X in the County of   ] [a right in common with other persons entitled to exercise such right of fishing for salmon, trout and other freshwater fish in Loch   ].
2. The duration of the let is from (*date*) to (*date*) both dates inclusive in each of the   years 19   to 19   [12]

---

[5]*Copland* v. *Maxwell* (1871) 9 M.(H.L.) 1.
[6]*Gemmill* v. *Riddell* (1847) 9 D. 727.
[7]*Farquharson* (1870) 9 M. 66.
[8]*Pollock, Gilmour & Co.* v. *Harvey* (1828) 6 S. 913; *Birkbeck* v. *Ross* (1865) 4 M. 272. See also *Beckett* v. *Bisset*, 1921 2 S.L.T. 33.
[9]Freshwater and Salmon Fisheries (Scotland) Act 1976, s. 4.
[10]*Inland Revenue* v. *Anderson*, 1922 S.C. 284.
[11]If the right is not exclusive there should be a stipulated limit on the number of other persons to whom the right may be given.
[12]The duration must be not less than one year if a lease of trout fishing is to be binding on singular successors of the landlord.

3. The rent for each season is £   payable on   in each year.[13] The landlord shall pay all rates and taxes on occupation of the estate and fishings.

4. The landlord will provide at his expense the [exclusive] services of a competent keeper or water bailiff to supervise the river [loch] and protect fish therein and expel unauthorised persons poaching or trespassing for the purpose of fishing. The tenant will obey the reasonable demands of such keeper or water bailiff.[14]

[5. The landlord shall provide one boat on the said river [loch] for the exclusive use of the tenant which shall be returned to the landlord in good order and condition on the termination of this lease.]

6. The tenant shall fish by rod and line only and shall exercise the right of fishing in a sportsmanlike manner. In particular, without prejudice to that generality, the tenant shall not capture or permit the capture of fish by netting and shall not take or kill any salmon of less than   pounds in weight but in the event of any such salmon being caught shall forthwith return it to the river [loch].

7. The tenant shall exercise the right of fishing so as to do as little injury to the banks of the said river and land adjoining them as possible and shall make adequate compensation for any such injury.[15]

[8. The tenant shall not invite more than   persons to exercise in company with the tenant at any one time the right of fishing hereby granted, and shall not invite or authorise or permit any person to exercise such right in the absence of the tenant.]

9. The tenant shall co-operate with the keeper or water bailiff in preserving the fishings and shall use his best endeavours to prevent injury or damage thereto by unauthorised persons.

10. The landlord reserves the right to terminate this lease in the event of the rent being unpaid for 21 days after the due date or in the event of the tenant being in breach of or failing to fulfil any of the conditions of this lease, but without prejudice to the right of the landlord to claim damages caused by any such breach or failure.

11. The expenses of this lease shall be borne [by the parties equally] [wholly by the tenant].

(*To be attested*)   (*Stamp duty—see para. 25–44*)

Style—lease of shootings

28–51   MINUTE OF LEASE
                                                    between
                                      AB, (*designed*), (hereinafter
                                        called "the landlord")
                                                    and
                                      CD, (*designed*), (hereinafter
                                        called "the tenant")
1. The landlord hereby lets to the tenant [and his executors]

---

[13]Normally rent is payable at the beginning of the season.

[14]Usually keepers are employed by the landlord. If not, the provisions of this clause may impose on the tenant an obligation to employ keepers.

[15]Applicable to river fishing only.

excluding assignees or sub-tenants except with the prior written
consent of the landlord [which consent shall not be unreasonably
withheld] the shooting of the estate of X in the County of
              [but excluding (*specify any areas of the estate to
be excluded*)].
2. The duration of the let is from (*date*) to (*date*) both dates
inclusive in each of the years 19   to 19   .
3. The rent for each season is £   payable on   in
each year.[16] The landlord shall pay all rates and taxes on
occupation of the estate and the shootings.
4. The landlord shall provide, at his expense competent keepers
and the exclusive use of   trained and efficient ponies and
        trained and efficient dogs and shall provide housing near the
shoot and feeding for the ponies and dogs.[17]
5. The right of shooting hereby granted is restricted to shooting
of the following birds only, namely, (*list of kinds of birds which
may be shot*). [No more than   grouse,   partridges and
        pheasants may be shot in any one season.] A fair stock of
birds shall be left on the land at the close of each season unless
prevented by circumstances outwith the tenant's control. The
tenant shall exercise the right hereby granted in a sportsmanlike
manner. There shall be no driving of grouse before   August
in each season.
[6. The tenant shall not do or suffer to be done any unnecessary
damage to lands, fences or crops, whether by permitting the
stock of game unreasonably to increase or by the way in which
the right of shooting is exercised or otherwise so far as
attributable to the tenant, and shall compensate the agricultural
tenant or occupier for any such damage and keep the landlord
indemnified against any claims for compensation by the agricultural tenant or occupier in respect of any such damage and the
expenses involved in relation to any such claims.][18]
7. [*As in clause* 9 of style in para. 28–50 *supra* adapted to
shootings].
8. [*As in clause* 10 of style in para. 28–50 *supra*].
9. [*As in clause* 11 of style in para. 28–50 *supra*].

(*To be attested*)   (*Stamp duty—see para. 25–44*)

---

[16]Normally payable at the beginning of the season.
[17]If the arrangement is otherwise in any respect, the clause will be amended appropriately.
[18]Applicable where any part of the shootings is over agricultural land. As to the rights of an
agricultural tenant to claim such damage and the notice of any such claim to be given by the landlord
to the shooting tenant see Walker, *Prin.*, 287.

CHAPTER 29

COMMERCIAL AND INDUSTRIAL LEASES

INTRODUCTION

PRELIMINARY CONSIDERATIONS

THE LEASE

A. Drafting Problems

INTRODUCTION

Evolution

29–01   Leases of commercial or industrial property in their modern form are of comparatively recent growth in Scotland. Originally a lease was a personal contract which, if it satisfied certain conditions, could create a real right in the tenant by virtue of the Leases Act 1449 or the Registration of Leases (Scotland) Act 1857,[1] the rent throughout the period of the lease was normally a fixed sum and, apart from building leases, the obligation of keeping the subjects wind and water tight rested on the landlord. In the post-war period the commercial philosophy of landlords has significantly changed. Much of the most valuable heritable property, industrial estates or building developments in urban areas, is owned by bodies which derive their finance from governmental or local authority sources or by companies whose business is the acquisition, development and management of property. In different degree landlords regard property as an investment and their objective is to secure a revenue return, increasing from time to time to reflect the decrease in the value of money or the commercial success or attractiveness of a development, which will accrue to them as far as possible clear of any continuing expenditure on their part. Hence the full repairing and insuring lease, which places the whole responsibility of repairing, maintaining and renewing the subjects of

---

[1] See Chap. 25.

the lease upon the tenant, has become the norm. The abolition of owner's rates by the Valuation and Rating (Scotland) Act 1956 facilitated the achievement of that objective and the Land Tenure Reform (Scotland) Act 1974 removed the alternative method of obtaining a revenue yield from heritable property in the form of feuduties or ground annuals.

The English influence

29–02   Investment leases have a longer history in England than in Scotland and there are many more decisions of the English courts which interpret the legal result of particular clauses than are as yet available in Scotland. Moreover, much Scottish heritable property is owned by English companies who seek to insert in Scottish leases provisions with an effect equivalent to those in their leases of English property with which they are familiar. The achievement of this objective poses difficulties for the draftsman of a Scottish lease because of the differences between the laws of the two countries. In England a lease confers on the tenant an estate in land and in some important respects the relationship of landlord and tenant is governed by statute, principally the Landlord and Tenant Acts of 1927, 1954 and 1962. Some of the more important differences between the relevant Scottish and English law are: (1) A tenant of business premises in England may obtain a renewal of his tenancy on application to the court[2]: in Scotland, apart from the relatively short extension of a tenancy of a shop which may be obtained by a tenant from the court in terms of the Tenancy of Shops (Scotland) Acts 1949 and 1964, the tenant of business premises has no such protection. (2) In England the circumstances in which the principle of frustration of the contract terminates a lease are rare[3]: in Scotland leases are terminated *rei interitu* on destruction of the premises.[4] Accordingly, if it is desired that a Scottish lease will continue notwithstanding the destruction of the let premises, a specific provision to that effect or words clearly indicating that intention must be inserted in the lease. (3) In England a tenant may make improvements to the premises after notice to the landlord and, if the landlord does not object or the court certifies the improvement as a proper one despite objection by the landlord, the tenant is entitled to claim compensation for the improvement on the termination of the lease.[5] In Scotland there is no comparable provision in relation to leases of commercial or industrial premises. (4) In most English leases it is implied, notwithstanding any express provision to

---

[2]Landlord and Tenant Act 1954, Pt. II.
[3]*National Carriers Ltd.* v. *Panalpina (Northern) Ltd.* [1981] 2 W.L.R. 45, H.L.; *Cricklewood Property and Investment Trust Ltd.* v. *Leighton's Investment Trust Ltd.* [1945] A.C. 221.
[4]*Duff* v. *Fleming* (1870) 8 M. 769; *Tay Salmon Fisheries Co.* v. *Speedie*, 1929 S.C. 593; *Mackeson* v. *Boyd*, 1942 S.C. 56; *Cantors Properties (Scotland) Ltd.* v. *Swears & Wells Ltd.*, 1980 S.L.T. 165.
[5]Landlord and Tenant Act 1927, Pt. I.

the contrary, that the consent of the landlord to assignation of the lease or sub-letting or the making of improvements will not be unreasonably withheld.[5a] There is no such implication in Scottish law. (5) Upon assignment of a lease in English law both the original tenant who assigns and the assignee are liable to the landlord to perform the covenants in the lease but the law implies,[6] and there is frequently expressed in the assignment, an obligation upon the assignee to indemnify the original tenant. In Scotland an assignation of a lease permitted or not prohibited by the landlord terminates the liability of the original tenant for performance of obligations arising after the assignation. (6) The relief against forfeiture of an English lease upon non-payment of rent or breach of other covenants of the lease, originally given by the Court of Chancery and now by statute,[7] and the restrictions upon exercise of a right of irritancy in a Scottish lease in terms of sections 4 to 7 of the Law Reform (Miscellaneous Provisions) (Scotland) Act 1985, are broadly similar in effect but with differences of detail and procedure.

Bibliography

29–03 The legal profession in Scotland now has available an excellent up-to-date textbook: *Drafting and Negotiating Commercial Leases in Scotland*, by Murray J. Ross and D.J. McKichan. Reference may also be made to Volume 27 of *Halsbury's Laws of England* (4th edition) and English textbooks on the subject, but these should be used with care in view of the differences between English and Scots law referred to in paragraph 29–02 *supra*.

PRELIMINARY CONSIDERATIONS

Parties

29–04 Since a lease will involve a continuing relationship, it is prudent for each party to make preliminary inquiries as to the financial status and reputation of the other.

The landlord is concerned to inquire that the tenant is a substantial and established company or firm or a responsible individual since liquidation, receivership or bankruptcy of the tenant during the currency of the lease may result in disclaimer of the contract and the necessity of re-letting, possibly in circumstances where the market for the premises is temporarily depressed. If the tenant is a company a search of the Register of Charges and examination of the company's file may provide relevant information[8]: if the tenant is a firm or individual a banker's reference should be requested. If there is

---

[5a]*Ibid.*, s. 19.
[6]Law of Property Act 1925, s. 77(1)(D) and Sched. 2, Pt. X.
[7]Law of Property Act 1925, s. 146.
[8]See para. 29–18.

reasonable doubt as to the financial status of the tenant, the landlord should require a responsible guarantor to join in the lease.[9]

The tenant also has an interest to assess the status and reputation of the landlord. Preferably the landlord should be a local authority or public agency or a substantial public limited company having a continuing policy of commercial or industrial letting of property. The response of a liquidator or receiver to requests for consent to change of use, assignation, sub-letting or renewal of the lease may be less accommodating than that of the original landlord since the primary objective of a liquidator or receiver may be the realisation of capital rather than continuance of income.

The premises

29-05   The prospective tenant must be satisfied that the subjects of let are suitable for his business purposes. Relevant matters are: (1) the usable floor area; (2) the load-bearing strength of floors, particularly where heavy machinery or equipment of significant weight is to be installed or where storage accommodation for raw materials or finished products in substantial quantities will be required; (3) the general condition and decoration of the structure; (4) the adequacy of toilet and other facilities in relation to the requirements under the Factories Acts, the Offices, Shops and Railway Premises Act, the Health and Safety at Work Act and/or the Fire Precautions Act, as the case may be; and (5) the condition of electric wiring and gas, oil or other installations. A professional survey of the premises should be instructed by the prospective tenant before entering into a lease.

Services

29-06   It should be confirmed that public services of electricity, gas, water and drainage are available and, where industrial processes are in contemplation, that any special demands for any such services can be met. If special plumbing or electrical connections are to be installed, it should be verified that there will be no objection to such installations either from the landlord or the supplying authority and that the structure of the building and the nature of the existing services will enable installation of such special services at acceptable cost.

Access

29-07   If the lease is of a commercial building or offices within it, either suitable access and parking accommodation should be included in the premises let or rights to an adequate number of spaces in a shared parking area should be given. Such a facility is now almost essential for

[9] See para. 29–37.

office accommodation of good quality in an urban area. In the case of industrial buildings or units therein it is necessary to verify that there will be available suitable access for vehicles and loading and unloading during business hours and parking accommodation for vehicles overnight or when waiting for loads during business hours.

Light and air

29–08 Where the landlord does not own the adjoining property there will not be any restraint, except in the unlikely event of the existence of a negative servitude in favour of the let premises, upon building development which may adversely affect the light of the premises which are the subject of the proposed let. All that can be done is to assess from the nature and age of the adjoining buildings whether any such building development is probable. If the landlord owns adjoining buildings or land the tenant may seek to ensure that rights of light and air enjoyed by the premises to be let are protected, but the landlord may consider it inadvisable to restrict possible development of his adjoining property by agreeing to concede any such protection and indeed may often reserve the right to make such development.

Servitudes and burdens upon the premises

29–09 It is essential to ensure that there are no existing servitudes, rights of way or burdens or conditions in the landlord's title which will preclude or restrict the use of the premises to be let or any development which is contemplated by the tenant.[10]

Local circumstances

29–10 It is important for the prospective tenant to ensure that there will be no significant change of circumstances affecting properties in the neighbourhood or developments which may adversely affect the premises or their proposed use. Inquiries of the local planning authority as to the zoning of the area, possible road or other developments, etc., should be made, and any survey of the premises should be obtained from a surveyor with knowledge of the area who should be able to supply or obtain such information. Where the premises involve a retail business appropriate market research will include an assessment of pending changes which will be relevant to the prospective market.

Proposed use

29–11 The tenant must be satisfied that the proposed use of the premises will be permitted under the Town and Country Planning Acts. He must be satisfied that such use is authorised by an express planning

---

[10]See *Armia Ltd.* v. *Daejan Developments Ltd.*, 1979 S.C. (H.L.) 56.

permission or an existing use certificate or evidence that the premises have been used since before January 1, 1965 in the way proposed.[11] He must also be satisfied that there are no restrictions in the title of the landlord or, in the case of a sub-lease, the titles of the proprietor or the head landlord which would prevent or limit such use.

Title and searches

29–12   Where the landlord is the proprietor of the subjects of let his proper title is infeftment and the tenant should confirm that he has a real right perfected by recording in the Register of Sasines or by registration of his interest as proprietor in the Land Register, so that the tenant will be protected against singular successors of the landlord under the Leases Act 1449. As already mentioned, the tenant should also be satisfied from examination of the landlord's title that there are no burdens or conditions which would preclude or restrict the tenant's proposed use of the premises. Searches should be instructed in the property and personal registers to ensure that there are no heritable securities burdening the premises or larger subjects of which the premises form part, since the consent of the heritable creditor will be required to the letting of the premises.[12]

Duration of lease

29–13   One important preliminary matter which requires decision by both parties is the duration of the proposed lease. Primarily the period will be determined by policy and commercial considerations. The tenant's wishes will be influenced by his confidence in the prospects of success of the business for which he requires the premises. If he has reason to doubt that the business will be successful he should seek a let for a reasonably short period since, if he should wish to be rid of the liability for payment of rent and the other obligations of the lease before its expiry, there may be valid reasons for the landlord withholding consent to assignation or sub-letting. If, however, the tenant has an established business for which he is seeking more suitable premises it is in his interest to negotiate a lease for a longer period since the good-will of his business in a particular location, a matter which should be disregarded by express provision in reviews of rent, may well be an element which the landlord will take into account in open negotiations for a renewal of the lease on its expiry. The policy of the landlord will normally be to secure letting to responsible tenants with periodical reviews of rent for as long a period as can be negotiated within the anticipated life of the building in its existing condition, but not for any greater period since, if major alteration or reconstruction is contem-

---

[11] Town and Country Planning (Scotland) Act 1972, ss. 90, 91.
[12] Conveyancing and Feudal Reform (Scotland) Act 1970, Sched. 3, cond. 6; *Trade Development Bank* v. *Warriner & Mason (Scotland) Ltd.*, 1980 S.C. 74.

plated in order to maximise the commercial potential of the site, the existence of unexpired leases may be an impediment to the achievement of that objective.

It is desirable that the detailed terms of the lease should be agreed before the parties are committed to the transaction. If by reason of pressure of time some quicker procedure is adopted (although that is not recommended) the principal matters should be agreed with a further provision that the terms of the lease will be "in accordance with the landlord's normal conditions of letting for the property" or "fair and reasonable as between the landlord and the tenant" or "of a kind appropriate to commercial lettings of property of this kind in accordance with current practice," plus an agreement to refer to a local solicitor or property agent, acting as an expert and not as an arbiter, to determine the terms of the lease if the parties fail to agree.

Expenses

29–14   It is now usual for the landlord to stipulate that the whole expenses of negotiating and adjusting a commercial lease, including the legal costs incurred by the landlord and stamp duty, should be borne by the tenant. The acceptance of such a stipulation depends upon the negotiating strength of the respective parties, but it is often accepted by the tenant. It is suggested that in such circumstances the tenant's solicitor should seek to impose a limit upon the legal costs of the landlord which bears some reasonable relationship to the importance of the transaction since the length of the lease, and consequently the legal costs of its preparation, are substantially within the control of the landlord whose solicitor prepares the initial draft. A further development in a situation where the tenant is prepared to meet the landlord's legal costs may be that the landlord's solicitor seeks an undertaking that the tenant will pay the landlord's legal charges and disbursements whether or not the transaction proceeds.[13] In principle such an undertaking should not be given, although again much depends upon the negotiating strength of the parties. A tenant may be prepared to accept liability for the landlord's costs as part of the price of obtaining the benefit of suitable premises, but may reasonably regard that as unacceptable in the circumstances of abortive negotiations from which no benefit accrues to either party. At the very least the tenant's solicitor should stipulate that his client will not be responsible for the landlord's legal charges if the transaction does not proceed for reasons unrelated to the negotiations between the parties.

Stamp duty and registration charges

29–15   (1) *Stamp duty*. The rate of stamp duty upon a lease depends in part

---

[13]See Ross and McKichan, *op. cit.*, para. 2.2.

upon its duration, increasing in stages of 7, 35 and 100 years.[13a] Economy in stamp duty is effected if the period of the lease is just within any of these stages.

(2) *Registration.* If the subjects of the lease are situated within an operational area for the purposes of registration of title and the lease is for a period exceeding 20 years or is subject to any provision whereby the granter is under a future obligation, if so requested by the grantee, to renew the lease so that its total duration could extend for more than 20 years, then a real right can be obtained by the tenant only by registration of his interest in the Land Register.[14] Even where the subjects are situated in an area which is not yet operational the tenant will usually find it practicable to obtain a secured loan over his interest only if he records the lease in the Register of Sasines. It should be kept in view that leases for a period exceeding 20 years will involve the tenant in the costs of registration or recording.

Taxation

29–16   The landlord, if not aware from experience of the taxation implications of leasing property, should obtain professional advice on the matter. For a convenient summary of the more important liabilities to income or corporation tax, capital gains tax and value added tax reference may be made to the undernoted text.[15]

Negotiation of terms

29–17   The negotiations for concluding a contract of lease of commercial or industrial premises are often protracted. Ideally the missives, in addition to specific matters such as identification of the premises, initial rent and review periods and provisions peculiar to the particular lease, should include the adjustment of a *pro forma* or draft lease, and considerable correspondence and/or meetings between solicitors of the parties may be required. Sometimes the need of the tenant to secure speedy occupation of the premises requires a more expeditious conclusion of missives. The solicitors for the parties should, if practicable, avoid short-circuiting the negotiating procedures since the result may be that issues which could have more readily been resolved when both parties were anxious to complete the bargain are postponed to be settled in a contested arbitration or in court proceedings after both parties are committed to it under a missive of lease which has failed adequately to provide for the rights of the parties in the relevant circumstances.[15a]

[13a]See table in para. 25–44.
[14]Land Registration (Scotland) Act 1979, ss. 3(3), 28(1).
[15]Ross and McKichan, *op. cit.*, para. 2.18. See also Vol. IV.
[15a]See para. 29–13.

For a useful check list of matters to be considered in the negotiation of a lease see Ross and McKichan, *op. cit.*, Appendix 2.

THE LEASE

A. Drafting Problems

Parties

29–18 It is essential to check that the landlord is infeft in the property.[16] In the case of a sub-lease it is necessary to check also that the granter is tenant of the premises and that the duration of his tenancy under the head lease is equivalent to or greater than the proposed duration of the sub-lease. If either party to the proposed lease is a limited company the name of the company must be precisely in accordance with its registered name, since otherwise the lease may be granted by or to a non-entity. Specification of the registration number of a company which is a party to the lease or a guarantor will facilitate reference for any particulars that may be required, *e.g.* the registered office of the company may be required for the purpose of serving formal notices.

Nature of premises—scheme of drafting

29–19 The provisions of a lease vary considerably in relation to (1) the location of the premises either in a private industrial estate owned by the landlord or in an existing developed urban area and (2) the physical characteristics of the premises themselves as being either the whole of a building or only part of a multiple-tenancy building.

(1) **Whole building in industrial estate**. The landlord will wish to retain control of the unlet parts of the estate and to use or develop these from time to time as he may decide, and as an aid to drafting these may be defined as retained parts although strictly a definition is unnecessary since the definition of the let premises automatically excludes the unlet parts of the estate. Within the retained parts are access roadways, landscaped areas and service connections used or enjoyed by the tenants of premises on the estate and the most convenient drafting method is to define these as retained or common parts to which rights of use and enjoyment are given to the tenants, subject to payment to the landlord of an appropriate service charge for their maintenance or renewal.

(2) **Whole building in developed urban area**. In a lease of such premises the landlord will not usually own other property in the vicinity, and streets and service connections will be provided by the relevant public

---

[16]See para. 25–04.

authority. A definition of common parts and rights to use them is normally unnecessary except in the case where parking areas or accesses are used in common with adjacent or nearby properties.

(3) **Units in multiple-tenancy buildings**. Leases of premises of this kind present much more complex problems of drafting. The description of the premises must identify the let unit clearly with definition of its precise boundaries and specification of the parts of the building which are common for the benefit of all the tenants. In view of the possible variations in the construction of particular buildings[17] it is recommended that the description of the unit and common parts be adjusted with the advice of a surveyor. Further, if the unit is in a building situated in an industrial estate there may also be provision as to liability for a share of the maintenance of roadways, amenity ground and service connections provided by the landlord of the estate. Again if the unit is a retail shop there will be further variations, the maintenance of the shop window(s) being the exclusive liability of the tenant, and provision may also be required in respect of the maintenance of accesses to the rear or side of the shop, either exclusive or shared. It is evident that the mode of definition of the premises let and the common parts and the liability for maintenance thereof should be consistent as between all units in the same building and before the lease of the first unit is granted careful consideration must be given to ensure that the leases of all units in the building will be framed in one consistent scheme determined before the first lease of a unit is adjusted and adhered to in leases of all other units. For an illustration see paragraph 29–20 *infra*.

Description of premises

29–20   In all cases the let premises should be described so as to identify them clearly. The description should preferably be by reference to a plan, declared to be demonstrative and not taxative, with a conveyancing description by reference to the title description of the premises or of larger subjects of which they form part. Where the landlord's interest in the premises or larger subjects is registered in the Land Register the description should be by reference to the title number. Since usable floor area may be a relevant element, particularly in relation to the allocation of liability for the maintenance and management of the common parts and the selection of comparable premises for the purpose of rent reviews, it is helpful to specify it if that can conveniently be done.

The problems of definition of boundaries of the let premises and of the retained or common parts in a multiple-tenancy building have already been mentioned in paragraph 29–19 *supra*. By way of

---

[17] As to the structure of modern buildings and the problems of defining boundaries and common and mutual parts, see Ross and McKichan, *op. cit.*, paras. 3.9–3.14.

illustration a description of a suite of office premises and the retained or common parts in a building of steel and concrete construction may, subject to the advice of a surveyor in respect of the particular building, be as follows:

The Premises

The northmost office premises situated on the first floor above the ground floor of the building known as   Street, Glasgow comprising approximately   square [feet] [metres] (which area is demonstrative only and not taxative), which building is erected on the subjects described and disponed in (*short conveyancing description as in Landlord's title*) as the said premises (herein called "the Premises") are delineated within the boundaries coloured   on the plan annexed and executed as relative hereto, and without prejudice to that generality the Premises include the following parts of or within them:— (a) the plaster covering or other finish of the interior of all walls enclosing the Premises (b) the interior surfaces and parts of all windows and window frames (c) the coverings and screeds of the floors (d) the plaster or other finish of the ceilings and any suspended non-structural ceilings (e) all non-structural walls and partitions wholly within the Premises (f) all additions, alterations or improvements to or erections on the Premises (except the Tenant's trade fixtures or fittings) (g) all Landlord's plant, fittings and fixtures used exclusively by the Tenant and (h) all [gas,] electricity, water, telephone and other supply or drainage pipes, cables and conductors situated within and serving exclusively the Premises and relative apparatus and appurtenances (except so far as belonging to the relevant supply authorities), but exclude any load bearing pillars within the Premises.

The Common Parts

The whole parts of the said building known as   Street, Glasgow excepting the Premises and other parts of the said building let or intended to be let as or as part of separate premises (the Premises and such other premises being herein called "lettable premises") including without prejudice to that generality the foundations and roof, the external and internal structural walls (excluding the interior surfaces and parts of all windows and window frames in, and the covering or other finish of the interior of walls enclosing, lettable premises), all load bearing pillars, the floors and ceilings (excluding the coverings and screeds of floors and the plaster or other finish of ceilings and any suspended non-structural ceilings so far as enclosing or within lettable premises), the entrance vestibule, stairs and landings (including the windows, walls and ceilings thereof), elevator(s) and shaft(s), and all [gas], electricity, water, telephone and other supply or drainage pipes, cables and conductors serving more than one of the lettable premises and relative apparatus and appurtenances (except so far as belonging to the relevant supply authorities) and including also any additions, alterations or improvements thereto made during the currency of the Lease.

Fixtures

29–21   In many cases there will be on the premises fixtures and fittings belonging to the landlord and he may instal additional or replacement fixtures or fittings during the currency of the lease. There may also be fixtures or fittings installed by the tenant for his business purposes which as trade fixtures may be removed by him on termination of the lease subject to any special provisions on the matter specified in the lease.[18]

An inventory or schedule of the landlord's fixtures and fittings should be prepared at the commencement of the lease and any defects therein noted or rectified at the landlord's expense.

As regards tenant's fixtures or fittings the landlord may wish to have the option of acquiring these or any of them at valuation on the termination of the lease, and a stipulation to that effect may be inserted in the lease.

Rent review or escalation

29–22   In modern leases of considerable duration a provision for the review of the rent at stated intervals is now almost invariably included in order to maintain the value of the rent in economic terms and to reflect improvement in the market for the premises. In Scottish practice the revised rent at each review term is normally determined, failing agreement of parties, by an independent expert or arbiter based on agreed criteria as to matters to be assumed and disregarded, a review properly so-called. Sometimes, although much less commonly, the increased rent may be arrived at by reference to a published index selected as appropriate to the type of premises, which is strictly an escalating rent stipulated in advance.

29–23 **Rent review.** The principal elements to be considered in framing a rent review clause are:

(1) *Period.* The tendency in stipulating review periods is towards reviews at shorter intervals. Seven years was until recently not uncommon, but now five years or even three years may be stipulated.

(2) *Activation—time of the essence.* In earlier practice stipulations were often inserted whereby the landlord required to give advance notice before each review date activating the procedure for review, often with "fail-safe" provisions if he overlooked the time limit, but now it is usual simply to provide that the rent will be reviewed at stated intervals leaving either party to initiate the procedure.[19] There has

---

[18]See *Dowall* v. *Miln* (1874; 1 R. 1180) *Brand's Trs.* v. *Brand's Trs.* (1876) 3 R. (H.L.) 16; *Miller* v. *Muirhead* (1894) 21 R. 658; *Cliffplant Ltd.* v. *Kinnaird, Mabey Bridge Co. Ltd.* v. *Kinnaird,* 1982 S.L.T. 2.

[19]Primarily the interest to have the rent reviewed is that of the landlord, but the tenant may also wish it in certain circumstances—see Ross and McKichan, *op. cit..,* para. 6.7.

been considerable litigation upon the question whether a landlord who has failed to have the rent reviewed until after the relevant review date is past, has thereby lost the right to require a review of rent with retroactive effect from the stipulated date. The legal principle is whether, on a proper construction of the lease, time has been made of the essence of the bargain. In general the trend of the relevant decisions has been that a rent review clause confers an option on the landlord and that procedural time limits are not of the essence of the contract,[20] but there may be provisions of the lease which rebut that presumption.[21] and a long delay in activating the review may be regarded as a waiver by the landlord of his right to require it.[22] The safe course is to state expressly in the lease that time is not of the essence.[23] For a more detailed discussion of the relevant authorities in relation to particular provisions of leases, including the legal implications of trigger notices, see the undernoted text.[24]

(3) *The criteria*. A properly-framed rent review clause sets out the criteria upon which the revised rent is to be determined. Normally it will be an annual amount, payable until the next review date, which represents the rental value of the premises, without any premium, as between a willing landlord and a willing tenant if offered on the open market with vacant possession on certain assumptions and disregarding certain matters. Among the assumptions usually stated are that the premises are in good repair and that the tenant has complied with the provisions of the lease and that there shall be disregarded the effect on rent of any goodwill attached to the premises as a result of the trading of the tenant, the fact that the tenant or any permitted sub-tenants have been in occupation of the premises, any voluntary improvements to the premises made by the tenant and any damage to or destruction of the premises. Other matters to be considered in relation to rent review clauses are:

(i) The revised rent is determined in respect of the open-market rental value of a lease of the premises which contains the same conditions as the current lease. So, if there are special rights or privileges given to the tenant, these should be incorporated in the lease; any subsequent informal concessions should be made conditional upon their being taken into account in reviews of rent.

(ii) It is assumed that the notional open-market rent will be fixed on the basis that the premises are let as a whole for the same use,

---

[20]*United Scientific Holdings Ltd.* v. *Burnley Borough Council, Cheapside Land Development Co. Ltd.* v. *Messels Service Co.* [1978] A.C. 904; *Touche Ross & Co.* v. *Secretary of State for the Environment* (1982) 265 E.G. 982.

[21]*Al Saloom* v. *Shirley James Travel Service Ltd.* (1981) 259 E.G. 420; *Lewis* v. *Barnett* (1982) 264 E.G. 1079; *Henry Smith's Charity Trs.* v. *AWADA Trading and Promotion Services Ltd.* (1983) 269 E.G. 729.

[22]*Banks* v. *Mecca Bookmakers (Scotland) Ltd.*, 1982 S.L.T. 150.

[23]See para. 29–43, Schedule, para. 9.

[24]Ross and McKichan, *op. cit.*, paras. 6.12–6.19.

although that would normally be implied if the lease contained the usual prohibition against sub-letting of parts.[25]

(iii) The duration of the lease to be taken into account in determining the hypothetical rent recoverable in the open market should be specified in the rent review clause. Possible choices are:— (a) a period of 10 years, (b) the unexpired period of the lease or (c) the whole period of the lease as originally entered into, in each case with reviews of rent at the review dates specified in the lease. A preference for the last alternative was expressed by the joint committee set up by the Law Society of England and Wales and the Royal Institution of Chartered Surveyors,[26] and is probably the most appropriate provision in most cases.[27]

(4) *Expert or arbiter.* If the parties fail to reach agreement on the revised rent the usual provision is that the amount will be determined by an independent surveyor, and it is important to state whether he is to act as an expert or as an arbiter. If he acts as an expert the parties are relying entirely on his experience, skill and judgment, he is under no obligation to allow the parties to make representations or to consider them if made,[28] his decision is not subject to appeal,[29] and the only possible ground of objection would be that he acted negligently.[30] On the other hand, if he acts as an arbiter he must observe the ordinary rules of conduct of an arbitration and hear the parties and any relevant evidence and representations, and, unless the application of section 3 of the Administration of Justice (Scotland) Act 1972 is excluded, an appeal from his decision on questions of law may be made to the Court of Session.[31] It is suggested that in important leases involving a substantial rent the safe course is to appoint the independent surveyor as arbiter. In less important leases at smaller rentals, of premises of a common type with many comparable premises in the neighbourhood, where the rent review clause is in normal terms, the alternative of appointing the independent surveyor as an expert may be adopted, since the time and expense of arbitration may be largely avoided. Provision should be made for the appointment of another person as arbiter or expert, in the event of the death of the surveyor originally appointed or his failure to make a decision within a reasonable stated period.

(5) *Late determination of revised rent.* The procedure for determination of the revised rent may extend beyond the stipulated review date,[32]

---

[25]*Plinth Property Investment Ltd.* v. *Mott, Hay and Anderson* (1978) 249 E.G. 1167, C.A.
[26]Report (1980) 77 L.S. Gaz. 1982.
[27]For a full discussion of the criteria to be adopted in rent reviews, see Ross and McKichan, *op. cit.*, paras. 6.20–6.51.
[28]*Regis Property Co. Ltd.* v. *Lewis & Peat Ltd.* [1970] Ch. 695.
[29]*Campbell* v. *Edwards* [1976] 1 W.L.R. 403.
[30]Supply of Goods and Services Act 1982, s. 13. See *Belvedere Motors Ltd.* v. *King* (1981) 260 E.G. 813.
[31]See Vol. I, Chap. 14.
[32]See, *e.g. Scottish Development Agency* v. *Morrisons Holdings Ltd.*, 1986 S.L.T. 59.

and provision should be made for continued payment of the existing rent at the due term or terms, and payment of the difference between it and the revised rent when ascertained with interest thereon at a stipulated rate in respect of the period from the review date until payment.[32a]

9–24 **Escalating rent—indexing.** An alternative to a rent review clause is a provision for an index-linked rent increasing at stated periods in proportion to the increase in a selected published index over the same period. This method has the advantage of avoiding the expense and possible delay of the rent review procedure, but it is not normally acceptable in commercial lettings. The first difficulty is the selection of an appropriate index; the General Index of Retail Prices gives a measure of the changes in prices of a large variety of goods and services and, although there are other published indices for different sectors of trade and industry, there is none which accurately reflects changes in the recoverable rental of property and even less that of a particular kind of property. Nevertheless index-linking of rent may be acceptable in leases of property in developments which are financed wholly or partly from public funds where the primary objective is the attraction of trade to the area and the provision of employment, and the maximisation of recoverable rent, although not unimportant, is not the only consideration. In very large developments of that kind the recurring administrative expense involved in rent review procedures may be substantial. In such cases the adoption of index-linking of rents will require the approval of the funding authority. In addition there are two problems, namely: (i) the selected index reflects changes which have occurred in the year preceding each date of its publication and the last available issue of the index may have been published up to a year prior to the date of revision of the rent, so that there can be a significant time-lag; and (ii) comparison by a valuer of the record of increases shown by the index over a period with increases (based on his experience) in open-market rentals of premises of the kind being let over a comparable period may demonstrate that the latter have outstripped the former to a calculable extent. Both of these problems are superable, however, by stipulating in the lease for the addition of an appropriate plus factor, determined by a valuer, to the increase as shown by the selected index. It is possible that publication of the selected index may cease or that its constituents may be substantially altered: for such eventualities the lease should provide for review of rent in normal terms.

Insurance

9–25 For a full account of the matters to be considered in adjusting the

---

[32a] See para. 29–43, Schedule, para. 6.

provisions of a lease relating to the insurance of the premises, reference may be made to the undernoted text.[32b] The following suggestions are offered on the principal matters:

(1) **Who effects the policy**. Insurance of a multiple-tenancy building should always be effected by the landlord, with provision for reimbursement of the premiums by the tenants in appropriate proportions. In the event of damage to or destruction of the premises by any of the insured risks the landlord will be obliged to apply the insurance moneys in the repair or reinstatement of the premises, not necessarily in exactly the same form as the original building (since the use of modern building methods and materials may be preferable and planning or building regulations may dictate a different style of construction) but so as to provide equivalent or comparable accommodation for the tenant. Where the premises let comprise a whole building it is still preferable that the insurance be effected by the landlord, but insurance by a responsible tenant may be permitted provided that the landlord controls the choice of the insurer, the risks covered and the amount of the cover, that the landlord's interest is endorsed on the policy and that the tenant is under obligation to make up any deficiency between the proceeds of the insurance and the cost of repair or reinstatement in the event of damage or destruction by any of the insured risks. Even in such a case it is recommended that the insurance should be effected in joint names of landlord and tenant. If the insurance is effected by the tenant he must be obliged in terms of the lease to insure for its full replacement value.[32c] The landlord has a paramount interest in securing that his property is adequately insured and that premiums are duly paid: hence the general rule that the insurance is effected by him in his name, and that course also facilitates the interest of a heritable creditor being noted on the policy.

(2) **The insured risks**. The risks to be covered should be specified in the lease. They should include all risks to the property which are normally insurable plus loss of rent for the period reasonably estimated to be required for the work of repair or reinstatement, since the rent will be abated or payment of it suspended during that period. The tenant should be made liable for any loss or restriction in the amount payable by the insurers which has been caused by improper acts of or use of the premises by the tenant or persons for whom he is responsible.

(3) **The amount of cover**. The landlord should ensure that the amount of cover is fully adequate for reinstatement of the premises in the event of their total destruction, making due allowance for site clearance, escalating costs of building and architect's and other professional fees.

[32b]Ross and McKichan, *op. cit.*, Chap. 10.
[32c]See *Fehilly* v. *General Accident Fire and Life Assurance Corporation Ltd.*, 1983 S.L.T. 141.

(4) Continuance of the lease. In commercial lettings the objective of the landlord is to ensure that, despite damage or destruction by any of the insured risks, the rental yield from his investment should resume after repair or reinstatement, the loss from abated or suspended rent in the intervening period being recouped from the insurance for loss of rent. The attainment of that objective may be frustrated, however, if any necessary planning or other permission for the work of repair or reinstatement is refused or granted only upon conditions which are unacceptable, in which event the lease should terminate and the proceeds of the insurance should be retained by the landlord. Even where repair or reinstatement is practicable, however, in certain cases it may be sensible to provide an option, exercisable by either the landlord or the tenant, to terminate the lease upon giving notice within a brief stated period, say three to six months, after the occurrence of the damage or destruction. The situation in which the provision of such an option may be considered is where the premises comprise the whole of an old building and the rent is modest. The landlord in such circumstances may wish to maximise the site value by demolishing and erecting a different type of building for which at the time there is a good market. The dislocation of the tenant's business and loss of trade (unless the tenant has effected insurance against the risk) together with the expense of finding and removing to temporary premises may impair the ability of the tenant to resume payments of rent after repair and reinstatement, and he may prefer to be free to resume his business elsewhere.

Repairing obligations

29–26   There are certain principles of common law which must be borne in mind by a landlord when a full repairing and insuring lease is being adjusted, *viz.* (i) The landlord impliedly warrants that the premises are reasonably fit for the purposes of the lease.[33] (ii) The landlord has a duty to keep the premises wind and water tight and in tenantable condition by carrying out any repairs required for that purpose.[34] (iii) If the premises are seriously damaged or destroyed by *damnum fatale* or otherwise cease to be available to the tenant, the tenant may abandon the lease.[35]

The liability of the landlord under the warranty of the condition of the premises is elided by a provision of the lease whereby the tenant accepts the premises as in good and substantial repair and condition and fit for the purposes for which they are let.[36]

---

[33]Paton and Cameron, *Landlord and Tenant*, 130.
[34]*Dickie* v. *Amicable Property Investment Building Society*, 1911 S.C. 1079; *Gunn* v. *National Coal Board*, 1982 S.L.T. 526.
[35]*Duff* v. *Fleming* (1870) 8 M. 769; *Tay Salmon Fisheries* v. *Speedie*, 1929 S.C. 593; *Mackeson* v. *Boyd*, 1942 S.C. 56; *Cantors Properties (Scotland) Ltd.* v. *Swears & Wells Ltd.*, 1980 S.L.T. 165.
[36]See style in para. 29–43, clause 6.2.

The landlord is relieved of responsibility for keeping the premises wind and water tight and in tenantable condition by a term of the lease which imposes on the tenant an obligation to repair and if necessary renew, rebuild or reinstate the premises throughout the period of the lease and to leave them in good tenantable repair and condition at its termination. The acceptance of such an obligation and the adjustment of its precise terms, however, must always be carefully considered by the tenant and his advisers since in the event of major damage or destruction by a non-insured risk the potential liability could be substantial. If the damage is relatively minor, *e.g.* want of restoration or reinstatement of alterations made by the tenant, the liability of the tenant may be restricted to the loss thereby suffered to the landlord.[36a] It should be noted that this decision was pronounced in a situation where the lease had ended: where the lease is still current there seems no reason why the landlord should not be entitled to insist upon performance of the tenant's obligation. The undertaking of such a responsibility has particular danger where the premises consist of a unit in a multiple-occupancy building, since other tenants may not be bound in similar terms and, even if they are, may not be in a financial position to meet their proportion of the expense. For these reasons the adjustment of the repairing and reinstatement obligations is in practice a battleground of tough negotiations. A compromise solution in the lease of a single building may be to leave responsibility upon the landlord for the repair of structural defects, the tenant undertaking liability for repair or renewal of items such as elevators, electrical installations or other supply systems and interior decoration which would normally require such works during the period of the lease, but there can be difficulties in defining the respective areas of responsibility with the necessary precision.[37]

The common law rule which entitles the tenant to abandon the lease *rei interitu* is almost invariably expressly negatived in the lease, since the landlord's interest is to ensure a continuing revenue from his investment in all foreseeable circumstances. In the majority of cases the cost of repair or reinstatement will be covered by insurance, but there can be damage or destruction through uninsured risks. As to the situation where the damage or destruction is covered by insurance, see paragraph 29–25 *supra*. Since the possibility of major damage or destruction resulting from an uninsured risk is in most cases relatively remote, a provision as to continuance of the lease is frequently accepted by the tenant, but if there is reason to suspect that it may occur as affecting the particular premises the tenant's advisers should be wary of accepting the provision without qualification.

[36a] *Prudential Assurance Co. Ltd.* v. *James Grant & Co. (West) Ltd.*, 1982 S.L.T. 423.
[37] See Ross and McKichan, paras. 8.4–8.36 and authorities there cited. As to windows being part of the main walls, see also *Hastie* v. *City of Edinburgh District Council*, 1981 S.L.T. (Sh.Ct.) 61.

Use

9–27   The landlord should confirm that the proposed use of the premises does not contravene the conditions of his title to the property and, in the case of a sub-lease, the conditions of the head lease. If the premises include any dwelling-house accommodation (i) it is necessary to prohibit the creation of any sub-tenancy which would be a protected tenancy under the Rent (Scotland) Act 1984 since the statutory rights of the sub-tenant might preclude the obtaining of vacant possession of the whole premises on termination of the lease, and (ii) the Land Tenure Reform (Scotland) Act 1974 imposes restrictions upon the creation of the tenancy of a dwelling-house which will endure for more than 20 years. The landlord should also bear in mind that for the purposes of rent review a too-restrictive category of permitted use will militate against the amount of the revised rent since the hypothetical letting will be calculated on the assumption that the other terms of the lease, including the restriction on use, will apply.[38] Use should be limited to premises within the relevant use class under the Town and Country Planning (Use Classes) (Scotland) Order 1973,[39] unless in a shopping precinct it is desired to restrict competition in particular retail trades or in an industrial estate a local authority or government agency wishes to ensure the continuance of a use which involves the employment of significant manpower. Again, to modify the effect of restriction of use on recoverable rent for the purpose of rent reviews it is suggested that in all cases the prohibition of other uses should be qualified by "except with the consent of the landlord which shall not be unreasonably withheld." There should also be inserted a prohibition against any use which may constitute a nuisance or cause disturbance, inconvenience or damage to the landlord or his other tenants or the occupiers of adjacent or neighbouring premises.

From the point of view of the tenant it is essential that the terms of the use clause are wide enough to embrace his existing business and any potential variations of or additions to it and, if assignation or a sub-let of the whole or part of the premises is a possibility, wording which will comprehend any business within a particular use class may be desirable.

Other stipulations as to use may be inserted in leases of particular premises. If the premises are a suite of offices in a multiple-tenancy building specification of the hours of the day on which the premises will be available for use may be reasonable in order to restrict the times during which the landlord will require to provide the services of a caretaker or other personnel. In general it is in the interest of the landlord to stipulate that the premises will be occupied and open for

---

[38] As to the effect of a restricted use clause on recoverable rent, see *Plinth Property Investment Ltd.* v. *Mott, Hay and Anderson* (1978) 249 E.G. 1167.
[39] S.I. 1973 No. 1165 (S.90).

trade during normal business hours and, particularly in the case of a shopping precinct, that an adequate window display will be maintained.

Statutory and title obligations

29–28   It is usual to impose on the tenant the obligation of complying with statutory obligations relating to the premises.[40] There are several statutes which may require operations on premises,[41] sometimes at considerable expense. The tenant should be satisfied before entering into the lease that all relevant statutory requirements have been complied with to ensure so far as possible that he will not be liable to meet the cost of works required to comply with any statute or regulations, particularly as any enhancement of the rental value of the premises will not be disregarded in rent reviews since the work will have been required in pursuance of an obligation to the landlord. It is possible, however, that the tenant may obtain a decision from the sheriff that a reasonable part of the cost of such works should be borne by the landlord by reason of provisions to that effect in the relevant statute.[42]

When the tenant's solicitor is examining the title of the landlord to confirm that he is infeft, he should also note whether the obligations and conditions in the title *prima facie* have been implemented. If that is not the case, then in effect the tenant may require to relieve the landlord of the cost of any works required by the superior in enforcing conformity with the title conditions, and again any resulting improvement in the rental value of the premises will not be disregarded in subsequent reviews of rent. In practice there is much to be said for the landlord incorporating in the lease any relevant obligations and conditions of the title: the need for the tenant's solicitor to examine the landlord's title and the delay in doing so will thereby be avoided.

Alienation

29–29   **(1) Part of premises.** An assignation of part only of the premises is usually prohibited completely: the landlord does not wish to incur the administrative expense and inconvenience of dealing with several tenants. In the exceptional case where the premises are large and the tenant insists upon the right of partial assignation (i) the number of partial assignations should be limited and the parts in respect of which the lease may be assigned should be specified, and (ii) the right to assign should be qualified by the requirement of the landlord's consent, which should not be unreasonably withheld where the

---

[40]See para. 29–43, cl. 6.10.
[41]*e.g.* Factories Act 1961, s. 170; Offices, Shops and Railway Premises Act 1963, s. 7(2); Fire Precautions Act 1971, s. 28; Health and Safety at Work, etc. Act 1974, Pt. III.
[42]See Ross and McKichan, *op. cit.*, para. 7.21.

proposed assignee is of good financial standing and the business to be conducted is within the ambit of the use clause.

Sub-letting of part of the premises is also usually prohibited but again, in the case of larger premises, it may be permitted subject to conditions similar to those suggested above in the case of partial assignations with conditions as to the terms of a sub-lease on the lines of those suggested below in relation to sub-leases of the whole premises. In retail shops it is now common to have "shop-within-a-shop" arrangements whereby a specialist retailer other than the tenant occupies an area within the premises for the sale of particular goods: such arrangements should be in the form of licences, not sub-lets, and the consent of the landlord should be required.

(2) Whole of premises. Where the period of the lease is long the tenant will normally seek the right to assign the whole of the premises: he does not wish to be committed to a liability for a lengthy period from which he cannot escape. The landlord will be well advised to permit such an assignation, subject to the usual qualification requiring his consent not to be unreasonably refused, because an absolute prohibition of assignation could adversely affect the hypothetical rental value of the premises for the purposes of rent reviews. It may be advisable in relation to refusal of consent to stipulate that the assignee should be a reputable person or company of good financial standing, demonstrably capable of performing the obligations of the tenant under the lease. Where the assignee is a subsidiary company of the tenant company the landlord may stipulate that as a condition of his consent to the assignation the parent company should remain liable for or guarantee performance by the assignee of the tenant's obligations in terms of the lease.

If an assignation of the whole of the premises is permitted subject to consent not to be unreasonably withheld, there can be an argument that the right to sub-let the whole of the premises need not also be given.[43] A right to sub-let the whole of the premises, subject to consent as above mentioned, should be made conditional upon there being no premium payable to the tenant, the rent being not less than the rent payable under the lease or the current open market rental value of the premises and payable on the same dates as in the head lease with corresponding reviews of rent and the form of the sub-lease being approved by the landlord and an extract of it furnished to the landlord for his records.[44] An alternative course of action is that the landlord should not concern himself with the terms of the sub-lease and rely on the head lease.

Consent not unreasonably withheld

29–30   The question whether a landlord is unreasonably withholding

---

[43]See Ross and McKichan, *op. cit.*, para. 7.5
[44]See para. 29–43, cl. 6.14.4.

consent arises principally in relation to (i) change of use of the premises or (ii) assignation or sub-letting. Whether consent is being unreasonably refused has been a fertile field of litigation, and although most of the decisions have been made by English courts in relation to the statutorily implied provision that the landlord's consent to assigning or underletting shall not be unreasonably withheld,[45] the reasoning of the English courts will have persuasive effect in Scotland in so far as the decisions are not based on specialties of English law. It is outwith the scope of this work to analyse all the decisions of the courts on the subject, but some broad conclusions can be derived from them.

It may be stated as a general proposition that the onus of establishing unreasonableness rests on the tenant: it is not for the landlord to prove that the withholding of consent was justified.[46] Further, it will normally be held unreasonable refusal if the object of the landlord is to obtain a money payment in exchange for his consent.[47]

As regards consent to change of use it would probably be a proper ground for withholding consent if the change would diminish the value of the premises or any neighbouring premises belonging to the landlord.[48] For example, where the landlord owns other properties containing retail shops in the vicinity, a change of use of premises from a shop of a kind which catered for day-to-day shopping to a business which did not, could diminish the attractiveness of the precinct as a regular shopping area offering a wide variety of goods in frequent demand. It would also be a proper ground for refusal of consent if the proposed use might constitute a nuisance or cause inconvenience to other premises in the neighbourhood. On the other hand, refusal of consent for reasons unconnected with the use of the premises would generally be held to be unjustified.

As regards refusal of consent to assignation or sub-letting, it will generally be unreasonable if the grounds of refusal are unconnected with the personality or financial status of the assignee or sub-tenant or the use to which he proposes to put the premises.[49] The personality or financial standing of the assignee or sub-tenant may be a proper ground of refusal,[50] but not for reasons of the sex[51] or race[52] of the

---

[45]Landlord and Tenant Act 1927, s. 19(1)(a).

[46]*Mills* v. *Cannon Brewery Co. Ltd.* [1920] 2 Ch. 38 at 46.

[47]This is a statutory provision in England—Landlord and Tenant Act 1927, s. 19(3)—but the rationale would probably apply in Scotland.

[48]Also statutory in England—1927 Act, s. 19(2).

[49]*Re Gibbs and Houlder Bros. & Co. Ltd.'s Lease, Houlder Bros. & Co. Ltd.* v. *Gibbs* [1925] Ch. 575, C.A.; *Viscount Tredegar* v. *Harwood* [1929] A.C.72, H.L.; *Bickel* v. *Duke of Westminster* [1977] Q.B. 517.

[50]*Shanly* v. *Ward* (1913) 29 T.L.R. 714, C.A.; *Cohen* v. *Popular Restaurants Ltd.* [1917] 1 K.B. 480; *Whiteminster Estates Ltd.* v. *Hodges Menswear Ltd.* (1974) 232 E.G. 715.

[51]Sex Discrimination Act 1975, s. 1(1)(a).

[52]Race Relations Act 1976, s. 1(1).

person. It is unreasonable for a landlord to refuse consent if his object is to engineer a surrender of the lease.[53]

On the subject of the reasonableness or otherwise of a landlord in refusing consent see the article[54] and two recent decisions under-noted.[55]

Services

29-31   **(1) Whole building in industrial estate.** In a lease of such premises the obligation of maintaining, cleaning, repairing and rebuilding the premises will normally have been undertaken by the tenant, save in the exceptional case where the landlord has agreed to be responsible for major structural defects.[56] In addition, however, there may be access roads and pathways, amenity ground, private supply or sewerage services, etc., provided by the landlord for the whole estate which will require maintenance and gardening or other services for which an annual service charge will be imposed apportioned amongst all the tenants on the estate.

(2) Whole building in developed urban area. In a lease of premises of this kind the roads and supply and sewerage connections outwith the building will usually be maintained by the relevant public authority and the obligation of maintenance, repair and rebuilding the premises let will have been imposed on the tenant. There may, however, be rights to private parking accommodation or accesses which are shared with other properties, in which case it is necessary to provide that the tenant will pay to the landlord the proportion applicable to the premises of his contribution to the maintenance and repair of such facilities.

(3) Unit in multiple-tenancy building. In a lease of such premises the services to be provided by the landlord, the cost of which will be reimbursed by the tenant, are much more extensive and include items such as maintenance, repair and if necessary renewal of common parts of the structure which are not in the ordinary use of language comprehended in the term "services." The usual drafting scheme of the lease is to exclude the common parts of the building from the definition of the let unit which forms the premises, but the tenant is given the right to use the common parts for the purposes of his tenancy.[57] There will also be included in the description of the services items which are services in ordinary parlance, such as the costs of administering and managing the building, the remuneration of a

---

[53] *Bates* v. *Donaldson* [1896] 2 Q.B. 241, C.A.; *Re Winfrey & Chatterton's Agreement* [1921] 2 Ch. 7.
[54] A.I. Phillips, "Consent not to be unreasonably withheld" (1960) *Conveyancing Review* II, 41.
[55] *Ponderosa International Development Inc.* v. *Pengap Securities (Bristol) Ltd.* (1986) 277 E.G. 1252; *British Bakeries (Midlands) Ltd.* v. *Michael Testler & Co. Ltd.* (1986) 277 E.G. 1245.
[56] See para. 29-26.
[57] See para. 29-43, cl. 1 and Schedule, Pt. IV.

caretaker and cleaners and workmen for the cleaning, redecoration and when necessary repair or replacement of vestibule, stairs, elevators and pipes, cables, drains, etc., which are used in common by the tenants of the building. In addition, if the building is situated in an industrial estate, the services may require to include those mentioned in sub-paragraph (1) of this paragraph or, in the case of a building in an urban area where there are common parking accommodation and accesses, those mentioned in sub-paragraph (2) above.

All the items to be specified as services should be clearly identified in the lease or relative schedule with a general phrase which will comprehend other possible services that may be required in future, e.g.

> "all other services provided by the landlord from time to time during the period of the lease which are capable of being enjoyed by the tenant [along with other tenants or occupiers of the building] or reasonably necessary for the maintenance or cleaning of the building or are consonant with its good management."

For examples of possible services which may be specified according to the nature of the particular premises see paragraph 29–43, Schedule, Part III.

Service charges

29–32   Liability to reimburse the expenses of providing the services should be imposed on all the tenants whose premises benefit from the services, payment to be made by tenants annually or at other convenient period on demand, possibly with an initial provisional payment in the first year of the lease which will be adjusted subsequently when the actual amount of the expense of providing the services is ascertained. The total costs of providing the services will be apportioned amongst the tenants whose premises are benefited on some equitable basis, e.g. rateable values or floor areas. In the first instance the expense of providing the services will be calculated by the landlord's surveyor or factor and apportioned amongst the tenants on the agreed basis, but there should be a right of appeal to an independent expert or arbiter if the amount or the allocation can reasonably be disputed.[58] The service charge may include, in addition to the sum necessary to meet the costs actually incurred, a contribution to a sinking fund in order to provide for a major expenditure that may be required in the future and to ensure that any such extraordinary charge will be equitably spread amongst past and existing tenants.

Irritancy

29–33   At common law there is an old legal irritancy where the tenant has

---

[58]The amount of the service charge will not usually be so great as to justify appeal, but it is proper that tenants should have some safeguard against extravagant or unnecessary costs.

failed to pay rent for two years which is applicable to commercial or industrial leases,[59] but in practice such leases almost always contain provisions for a conventional right of irritancy exercisable in the event of failure in punctual payment of rent, bankruptcy or insolvency of the tenant or breach of any of the tenant's obligations under the lease. Unlike irritancies in feus, a conventional irritancy in a lease, once incurred, was not purgeable; the landlord was entitled to enforce it by an action of declarator that the tenant had incurred an irritancy and for an order ordaining him to remove.[60] Delay in payment of rent for even a comparatively short period after the payment term entitled the landlord to enforce the irritancy.[61] The court might refuse a declarator of irritancy if oppression by the landlord could be established, but a plea of oppression could only succeed where there had been no oversight or negligence on the part of the tenant.[62]

The rigour of the law has recently been modified in sections 4 to 6 of the Law Reform (Miscellaneous Provisions) (Scotland) Act 1985. If the breach consists in failure to pay rent timeously the landlord, before he is entitled to rely upon a conventional irritancy, must after payment of the rent has become due serve a notice on the tenant to make payment of the rent and any interest thereon payable in terms of the lease within a specified period being not less than 14 days from the service of the notice or any greater period between the service of the notice and the expiry of any time provided for in the lease or otherwise for the late payment of the rent.[63] If the breach is of a condition of the lease other than payment of rent, the landlord may rely upon a conventional irritancy only if in all the circumstances of the case a fair and reasonable landlord would seek to do so: if the breach is capable of being remedied within a reasonable time, the court will have regard to whether a reasonable opportunity has been afforded to the tenant to enable the breach to be remedied.[64] It is not permissible for the parties to contract out of these statutory provisions.[65]

As regards policy in drafting an irritancy clause in a lease: (1) Since it is incompetent to contract out of the provisions of the 1985 Act, the clause should be expressed as subject to them. (2) In order to avoid confusion in the mind of persons studying the lease, any detailed expression of the right of irritancy should be in terms at least as liberal as those laid down by the 1985 Act. (3) In circumstances where the tenant has become insolvent it may be sensible, and in the interest of both parties, to allow the trustee in bankruptcy or under a protected trust deed, the liquidator or receiver or a heritable creditor of the

---

[59]Rankine, *Leases*, 533; Paton and Cameron, *Landlord and Tenant*, 229.

[60]*Stewart* v. *Watson* (1864) 2 M. 1414; *McDouall's Trs.* v. *MacLeod*, 1949 S.C. 593; *Lucas's Exrs.* v. *Demarco*, 1968 S.L.T. 89; *Dorchester Studios (Glasgow) Ltd.* v. *Stone*, 1975 S.C. (H.L.) 56.

[61]*H.M.V. Fields Properties Ltd.* v. *Tandem Shoes Ltd.*, 1983 S.L.T. 114.

[62]*H.M.V. Fields Properties Ltd.* v. *Skirt 'n' Slack Centre of London Ltd.*, 1982 S.L.T. 477.

[63]s. 4.

[64]s. 5.

[65]s. 6(1).

tenant a reasonable period to dispose of the tenant's interest under the lease on condition that personal responsibility is undertaken by such person for implement of the whole obligations of the tenant in terms of the lease both those outstanding at the time and during the period until disposal of the lease to an acceptable assignee.[66] The landlord could normally offer such a concession at the relevant time without committing himself to do so in the lease, but the advisers of the tenant or a heritable creditor should seek to have it included in the lease as a contractual right.

Waiver

29–34   It is important that the landlord does not in the administration of a lease depart or permit departure from the conditions of a lease to such an extent that he will be held to have waived the condition. In the context of leases, waiver is most frequently pled against a landlord where (1) he suffers without objection use of the premises by the tenant for purposes other than the use permitted by the lease, (2) he continues for a period after a rent review date to accept the amount of rent payable prior to that date, or (3) he continues to accept payment of rent after serving a notice exercising his option to irritate the lease on account of a breach of its conditions. The nature of waiver as a legal concept in Scots law was examined by Lord Fraser of Tullybelton and Lord Keith of Kinkel in *Armia Ltd.* v. *Daejan Developments Ltd.*,[67] and their views were adopted by Lord Grieve in relation to a lease in *Banks* v. *Mecca Bookmakers (Scotland) Ltd.*[68] The conclusion was that: "whether or not there has been waiver of a right is a question of fact to be determined objectively upon a consideration of all the relevant evidence."[69] It was also made clear in *Banks* that, since the abandonment inferred from waiver is a question of fact, the question cannot be affected one way or the other by prejudice suffered by the person who alleges that the right has been abandoned.[70]

In *Banks* it was decided that acceptance of the pre-review rent for approximately two years after the review date was past inferred abandonment of the right of review. In the suggested style regarding the procedure in rent reviews[71] express provision is made for continued payment of the old rent when the revised rent has not been ascertained timeously and the lease contains a specific clause[72] negativing the inference of abandonment.

As regards departure from the permitted use the landlord should decide whether, if he is willing to allow an extended use, it is to be a

---

[66]See para. 29–43, cl. 10.
[67]1979 S.C.(H.L.) 56.
[68]1982 S.L.T. 150.
[69]*Banks* v. *Mecca Bookmakers (Scotland) Ltd., supra* at 152.
[70]*Supra* at 153.
[71]para. 29–43, Schedule, para. 6.
[72]para. 29–43, cl. 12.

concession personal to the tenant in occupation of the premises at the time or a more permanent concession which amounts to an alteration of the use clause. In the former case the landlord should give permission by letter expressed as a personal licence not binding upon successors of either party; in the latter case a formal memorandum altering the terms of the use clause should be executed by the parties and endorsed on or attached to the lease.

The most potentially serious application of the principle of waiver is where the landlord has given notice exercising his right of irritancy with immediate effect but subsequently by inadvertence accepts payment of the rent. In theory the effect of a notice of irritancy, although a declarator of irritancy by the court may subsequently be required, is that as from the effective date of the notice the tenancy ceases to exist and acceptance of rent thereafter is inconsistent with that situation. In England the rule that acceptance of rent after service of a notice of forfeiture amounts to a waiver of the notice has been strictly applied,[73] although it is subject to the qualification that if the landlord has shown a final determination to enforce the forfeiture, as by commencing an action to recover possession, no subsequent act, even receipt of rent, will operate as a waiver.[74] English law involves the principle of estoppel, which is not necessarily identical in effect with personal bar in Scotland,[75] and in one Scottish case[76] where one payment of rent was accepted by the landlords and not refused until much later the landlords were held entitled to irritate, although a plea of personal bar was departed from by the tenant and so waiver was not put in issue. In practice a landlord should ensure that any agency collecting the rent, such as the landlord's bank to which payment of the rent is made by banker's order, should be instructed immediately when a notice of irritancy is served that any payment of rent tendered must be rejected. A clause negativing the inference of waiver[77] may be inserted in the lease, but its efficacy when acts which would otherwise found a plea of waiver have occurred has not yet been judicially assessed.

Waiver of the requirement of punctual payment of rent on the due dates is not easily inferred from past indulgences by the landlord's predecessors in accepting rent paid late.[78]

Interest

29–35   It is usual to provide in a lease for payment of interest on arrears of

---

[73]*Windmill Investments (London) Ltd.* v. *Milano Restaurant Ltd.* [1962] 2 Q.B. 373; *Central Estates (Belgravia) Ltd.* v. *Woolgar (No. 2)* [1972] 1 W.L.R. 1048.
[74]*Evans* v. *Enever* [1920] 2 K.B. 315; *Civil Service Co-operative Society* v. *McGrigor's Tr.* [1923] 2 Ch. 347.
[75]*Armia Ltd.* v. *Daejan Developments Ltd.*, *supra per* Lord Keith at 72.
[76]*H.M.V. Fields Properties Ltd.* v. *Skirt 'n' Slack Centre of London Ltd.*, 1982 S.L.T. 477.
[77]*e.g.* para 29–43, cl. 12.
[78]*What Every Woman Wants (1971) Ltd.* v. *Wholesale Paint and Wallpaper Co. Ltd.*, 1984 S.L.T. 133.

rent or late payment of other sums due under the lease.[79] The rate of interest should not be so great as to be challengeable as a penalty; 3 or 4 per cent above the base rate of a specified joint-stock bank is usual. Where liability for payment of interest is so imposed the landlord should in practice issue notices for payment of rent before each rental period.

Value added tax

29–36   The grant, assignation or surrender of a lease is exempt from liability to value added tax,[80] but there may be other payments, not being payments of rent, for special facilities, *e.g.* parking spaces, in respect of which the tax is payable. Where, as is customary, the lease provides for payment by the tenant of the landlord's legal expenses in connection with the preparation of the lease it is improper for the landlord's solicitors to address the invoice to the tenant: it should be addressed to the landlord with a note that it is payable by the tenant.[81]

Guarantees

29–37   Guarantees of the obligations of the tenant must be framed with care, keeping in mind that they will be strictly construed and that the guarantor may be released from his obligation by acts which may prejudice him, such as giving time to the tenant to pay rent or granting other indulgences to the tenant or variation of the lease so that it differs from that under which the obligations were guaranteed.[82] It is usual to provide in the lease that a guarantor shall not be discharged or released by acts which otherwise would in law have that effect,[83] and also to provide that, on bankruptcy or liquidation of the tenant and disclaimer of the lease by the trustee in bankruptcy or liquidator, the guarantor may be required to take a lease on the same terms,[84] and that if the guarantor dies or becomes insolvent the tenant may be required to procure a new guarantor.[85] The obligation of the guarantor should be expressed as enforceable only on being required to implement it by the landlord, so that the *terminus a quo* of negative prescription of it will commence only when he is so required.[86] For the protection of the guarantor a stipulation should be included that he will be released from his guarantee upon assignation of the lease, when his guarantee will *ipso facto* terminate.

---

[79] *e.g.* para. 29–43, cl. 6.1.8.
[80] Value Added Tax Act 1983, Sched. 6.
[81] See L.S. Gaz., July 1983.
[82] See Vol. I, Chap. 6.
[83] See para. 29–43, cl. 9.2.
[84] *Ibid.*, cl. 9.3. Alternatively or additionally the guarantor may stipulate for a right to take up the lease in such circumstances.
[85] *Ibid.*, cl. 9.4.
[86] Prescription and Limitation (Scotland) Act 1973, s. 6(3).

B. Style and Format of Lease

Selection of style

9-38   In current practice, leases of commercial or industrial property frequently extend to a size and complexity which appear to the parties, particularly to the tenant who is usually asked to meet the whole costs of their preparation, to be inordinate. To some extent this is inevitable in a document which will regulate a continuing relationship lasting for a period of years, where the duty of a solicitor is to provide adequately for every contingency which is reasonably foreseeable. On the other hand, a tenant under a short lease of premises of relatively small value understandably considers that a massive document involving costs disproportionate to the importance of the transaction is unacceptable. To this problem there is no ideal solution. This chapter contains specimen clauses appropriate to a long-term lease in full form and also an example of a shorter style of lease which may be used in less-important transactions, but leaves many matters of detail to be determined by existing law or established practice.

Format of lease

9-39   The most convenient arrangement of a lease in full form is:

(1) a frontispiece or cover which contains sufficient information to enable the particular lease to be identified from the landlord's store of leasehold titles, possibly printed on distinctively-coloured paper or cardboard for each different property or estate;

(2) an index of clauses in the lease and relative schedule, which will facilitate reference to particular provisions;

(3) the lease itself which contains the principal rights and obligations of the parties; and

(4) a schedule dealing with more detailed matters.

Side-headings for individual clauses may be included for ease of reference, if desired.

Variations appropriate to different kinds of premises

9-40   It is impracticable to offer standard clauses which could to any significant extent be incorporated in all or a large number of leases, since the variations required on account of the different characteristics of particular properties and the requirements of individual landlords and tenants render the automatic adoption of any style of clause a dangerous proceeding. The specimen clauses offered must be regarded only as possible versions, and are accompanied by a warning that the draftsman must consider their appropriateness to the particular lease and make such variations as may be necessary to comply with the instructions of the parties and the characteristics of the premises.

Cover or frontispiece

29–41
19

LEASE
between

and

_____

Premises

Period (*e.g. 7 years from*   *19* .)

Initial Rent

Rent Review Dates

Guarantor (if any)

(*Landlord or Solicitors*)
Reference No.

29–42
INDEX
Lease

Specimen clauses

9–43

CONTRACT OF LEASE
between

the Landlord specified in the following Particulars (hereinafter called "the Landlord")

and

the Tenant specified in the following Particulars (hereinafter called "the Tenant")

[and

the Guarantor specified in the following Particulars (hereinafter called "the Guarantor")]

1.   PARTICULARS
The following Particulars form part of this Deed:—

Landlord[87]	(*Name and address*) [Company Registration No.]
Tenant[87]	(*Name and address*) [Company Registration No.]
[Guarantor[87]	(*Name and address*) [Company Registration No.]]
Premises	The subjects described in the Particulars and more particularly in Part I of the Schedule with all alterations thereon and additions thereto made during the Period of the Lease and the pertinents thereof and all landlord's fixtures and fittings which are or at any time during the Period of the Lease may be in or on the Premises, and references to the Premises in the absence of any provision to the contrary include references to any part thereof.[88]
Date of Entry	19 .
Date of Termination	19 .
Initial Rent	£ per annum.
Rental Dates	[Quarterly] on in each year during the Period of the Lease commencing on 19 .[89]
Review Dates	19 and each [third] subsequent anniversary of that date during the Period of the Lease

[87]See para. 29–18.
[88]See *Esdaile* v. *Lewis* [1956] 2 All E.R. 357, C.A.
[89]If a rent-free period is allowed, this date will differ from the date of entry.

Permitted Use[90] (*Specify*) and not for any other purpose.

Decorating Periods Every year (exterior) and every year (interior) and in both cases in the last six months before the Date of Termination.

2. **DEFINITIONS**

In this Deed the following expressions shall have the following meanings:

"Particulars" The Particulars in Clause 1 hereof.

"this Deed" The Lease, any Plan and the Schedule.

"Lease" This Lease and any Plan.

"Clause" A clause in the Lease.

"Plan" Any plan or plans and drawing or drawings annexed hereto which shall be demonstrative only and not taxative.

"Schedule" The Schedule annexed hereto.

"Paragraph" A paragraph in the Schedule.

"Period of the Lease" The duration of the Lease whether terminated before the Date of Termination or continued thereafter by tacit relocation or otherwise.

"Revised Rent" The increased rent determined at each of the Review Dates in accordance with Part II of the Schedule.

"Interest" Interest from the date when any payment under this Deed is due to the date when it is made at the Interest Rate.

"Interest Rate" per cent per annum above the Base Rate of (*Bank*) at the relevant time or any other comparable rate agreed by the parties or, failing agreement, as shall be deter-

---

[90] As to the effect of a severe restriction on use upon the revised rent on rent review, see para. 29–27.

	mined conclusively by the Surveyor.
"Insured Risks"	The risks insured against specified in Clause 5.3.
"Insurers"	The insurance company or underwriters selected by the Landlord to cover the Insured Risks.
"Conductors"	Any pipes, cables, wires, sewers, drains, gutters, watercourses, channels, conduits, shafts, ducts, flues, and other conducting media by or through which any electricity, gas, power, air, water or waste or other facility may pass including all relative fittings and appurtenances.
"Surveyor"	Any qualified surveyor (who may be an individual, firm or company) appointed by the Landlord to provide professional services in relation to this Deed and matters arising therefrom.
"Planning Acts"	The Town and Country Planning (Scotland) Acts 1972 and 1977 and the Local Government and Planning (Scotland) Act 1982 and the Town and Country Planning Act 1984.
["Estate"	The Industrial Estate being the subjects in the County of more particularly described in (insert identifying conveyancing description, by short reference if practicable)][91]
["Services"	The services specified in Part III of the Schedule.][92]
["Service Charge"	The service charge specified in Part III of the Schedule.][92]
["Common Parts"	The parts of and service connections to and from the Estate which are used in common by the Tenant and other proprietors or tenants on the Estate.][93]

---

[91] Appropriate where the premises are situated in an industrial estate. See paras. 29–19 and 29–20.
[92] Appropriate where services and service charges are involved. See para. 29–19.
[93] Appropriate where the premises are situated in an industrial estate but may require more detailed specification—see para. 29–19.

["Building"]   The building known as (*describe
                    shortly by postal address or
                    otherwise sufficient to identify*) in
                    which the Premises are
                    situated.][94]

["Common Parts"]   The parts of and service connec-
                    tions to and from the Building
                    which are used in common by
                    the Tenant with the Landlord
                    and/or other occupiers of the
                    Building.][95]

3.   INTERPRETATION

The words and phrases specified or defined in the
Particulars and Definitions in Clauses 1 and 2 shall in
this Deed have the meanings therein attributed to
them.

In this Deed:

(i) The word "Landlord" means the Landlord and
includes all persons who may succeed to the interest of
the Landlord under this Deed and where the context
so admits includes their respective successors in title.

(ii) The word "Tenant" means the Tenant and
includes the permitted assignees of the Tenant and all
persons who may succeed to the interest of the Tenant
and in the case where the Tenant is an individual
includes his personal representatives.

[(iii) The word "Guarantor" means the Guarantor
specified in the Particulars and includes any other
person who may at any time undertake to guarantee
any of the obligations of the Tenant under this Deed
and where the Guarantor is an individual includes his
personal representatives.]

(iv) Where the Tenant [or the Guarantor] for the
time being are two or more persons obligations
imposed on or undertaken by them shall be binding on
such persons jointly and severally.

(v) Where the Tenant is a firm or partnership the
obligations of the Tenant under this Deed shall be
binding jointly and severally on all persons who are or
become members of the firm at any time during the
Period of the Lease and their respective executors and
representatives whomsoever and also on the firm and
its whole assets without the necessity of discussing
them in their order[95a] and such obligations shall
remain in full force and effect notwithstanding any
change or changes which may occur in the firm
whether by the assumption of a new partner or
partners or by the retiral, bankruptcy or death of any
individual partner.

---

[94] Appropriate where the premises are part of a building—see para. 29–19.
[95] Appropriate where the premises are part of a building and will usually require more detailed
specification—see paras. 29–19 and 29–20.
[95a] This may be unduly comprehensive: the tenant may seek exclusion of liability of deceased or
outgoing partners or their representatives.

(vi) Where any act by the Tenant is not permitted or prohibited the Tenant shall be under obligation not to permit or suffer such act to be done.

(vii) Where any consent or approval of the Landlord is required such consent or approval shall be construed as one given in writing and not otherwise.

(viii) Where any right is conferred on the Landlord to have access to the Premises it shall be construed as extending to all persons authorised by the Landlord including agents, professional advisers, contractors and workmen and the person exercising such right shall be responsible for making good any damage caused by his operations but shall not otherwise be liable for any compensation.

(ix) Words importing the singular include the plural and vice versa.

(x) Words importing one gender include all other genders.

(xi) References to any Act or statute include references to any Acts or statutes amending the same and to any orders or regulations made thereunder.

4.   GRANT

In consideration of the rents and other prestations specified in this Deed the Landlord LETS to the Tenant, excluding assignees and sub-tenants legal or voluntary and creditors or managers for creditors in any form except where permitted under this Deed, the Premises together with (so far as the Landlord has power to grant the same) the rights specified in Part IV of the Schedule but under reservation and exception of the rights, burdens, servitudes, conditions and others specified or referred to in Parts V and VI of the Schedule AND THAT for the period from the Date of Entry until the Date of Termination: FOR which CAUSES the Tenant UNDERTAKES (First) throughout the Period of the Lease (1) to pay to the Landlord the Initial Rent specified in Clause 1 or, when appropriate, the Revised Rent defined in Clause 2, payable by banker's order without any deduction by equal quarterly payments in advance on the Rental Dates in each year, the first of such payments to be made on the Date of Entry,[96] and proportionately for any period less than a quarter, (2) to refund to the Landlord and to pay the insurance premiums in terms of Clause 5 of the Lease, [(3) to pay to the Landlord on demand the Service Charge payable in terms of Part III of the Schedule][97] (4) to pay to the Landlord all other sums whatsoever that may be or become payable to the Landlord in terms of this Deed and (5) to pay to the Landlord Interest on all rents and other sums payable or refundable to the Landlord in terms

[96]May require alteration if an initial rent-free period is given.
[97]Appropriate when a service charge is imposed.

of Clause 6.1.8 of this Deed and (Second) to implement the whole other obligations of the Tenant under or arising from the provisions of this Deed.

5. **INSURANCE AND REINSTATEMENT**[98]

5.1. The Tenant warrants that prior to the execution of this Deed there have been disclosed to the Landlord any or all circumstances which are likely to affect the decision of any insurance company or underwriters to grant or continue insurance against any of the Insured Risks.

5.2. Subject to reimbursement of the premiums by the Tenant in terms of Clause 5.4 the Landlord will insure and keep insured the Premises throughout the Period of the Lease [in joint names of the Landlord and the Tenant], subject to such excesses, exclusions or limitations as the Landlord or the Insurers may impose, with such insurance company or underwriters as may be selected by the Landlord for such amount as the Landlord shall from time to time determine as being the full cost of rebuilding or reinstatement of the Premises including relative demolition and site clearance costs and the fees of architects and other appropriate professional advisers.

5.3. Such insurance shall be against the following Insured Risks:
(a) loss or damage by fire, lightning, explosion, [subsidence,] flood, storm or tempest, earthquake, bursting or overflowing of water pipes or tanks, aircraft and (in peace time) articles dropped therefrom, riot and civil commotion, malicious damage, impact by road vehicles and such other risks as may reasonably be requested by the Tenant and agreed to by the Landlord,
(b) loss of rent payable under the Deed (including potential increases of rent upon rent reviews) in the event of partial or total destruction of the Premises for the period which the Landlord may reasonably consider to be required for rebuilding or reinstatement, and
(c) public liability of the Landlord arising from or in connection with any matter relating to the Premises.

5.4. The Tenant will reimburse the Landlord on demand all sums which the Landlord may from time to time pay for insuring and keeping insured the Premises against the Insured Risks.[98a]

5.5. Neither the Tenant nor any person acting with the

---

[98]See para. 29–25.
[98a]Appropriate to lease of whole building. Where premises are a unit in a multiple-tenancy building, consider specifying proportion of premium which the tenant is liable to reimburse.

authority or under the control of the Tenant will do or omit to do anything which will result in the policy or policies of insurance effected by the Landlord in terms of Clause 5.2 being vitiated or the insurance thereunder prejudiced or which result in the Insurers refusing payment thereunder in whole or in part; if payment is so refused by reason of the actings or omissions of the Tenant or other person aforesaid the Tenant will pay to the Landlord on demand the amount so refused.

5.6. The Tenant (a) will not store at the Premises any explosive or inflammable goods or substances or do anything which will increase the rate of the insurance premium (b) will not obstruct the access to any means of escape from the Premises and (c) will keep at the Premises any fire fighting equipment required by the relevant Fire Authority or the Insurers and will maintain the same in good order and will not obstruct the access thereto.

5.7. If the Premises or any part thereof are destroyed or damaged by any of the Insured Risks so as to be unfit for occupation and use and there have been no acts or default by the Tenant or any person acting with its authority or under its control which will have caused the policy or policies of insurance to be vitiated or payment thereunder to be refused in whole or in part:—
    (a) Subject to Clause 5.7(c), the Landlord will apply the net proceeds of the insurance (save in respect of loss of rent) in repairing the damage and reinstating or reconstructing the Premises in accordance with any current planning permission and building regulations so as to provide for the Tenant a substantially comparable area to that contained in the Premises before such damage and the Tenant will pay and make available to the Landlord any excess applicable to such insurance[98b];
    (b) Until such repair, reinstatement or reconstruction has been completed payment by the Tenant of a fair proportion of the rent shall be suspended, the said proportion, failing agreement, to be determined by a surveyor appointed by the parties or, in default of agreement by the parties, by a surveyor acting as an expert appointed by the Chairman for the time being of the Scottish Branch of the Royal Institution of Chartered Surveyors on the application of either party, but the Lease will continue notwithstanding such destruction or damage or any rule of law to the contrary; and

---

[98b]This clause obliges the Landlord to apply the insurance moneys. If they are insufficient, who provides the deficiency? Theoretically it should be the Landlord who controls the amount of the sum insured, and it is a reasonable counterpart to the continuance of the lease that the Tenant should have comparable premises fully completed.

(c) In the event of any necessary permission or approval for such repair, reinstatement or reconstruction being refused by the competent authority or granted only with unacceptable conditions (after all appeals procedure has been exhausted) all sums received in respect of such insurance will be retained by the Landlord and all sums payable by the Tenant under Clause 5.7(a) will forthwith be paid to the Landlord and thereupon the Lease will terminate.

5.8.   The Tenant throughout the Period of the Lease will insure and keep insured in joint names of the Landlord and the Tenant the plate glass in the Premises against breakage with an insurance company approved by the Landlord and will pay punctually the premiums in respect thereof and produce to the Landlord, if requested, receipts for the premiums. All sums received from such insurance will be applied in reinstating the plate glass and any additional cost involved will be met by the Tenant.

5.9.   The cost of any valuations of the Premises instructed by the Landlord for insurance purposes from time to time, but not more frequently than once in every three years, shall be reimbursed to the Landlord by the Tenant on demand.

6.   OBLIGATIONS OF THE TENANT
6.1.   *Monetary Obligations*
6.1.1.   The Tenant shall pay punctually when due the Initial Rent and, when appropriate, the Revised Rent in terms of Clause 4.
6.1.2.   The Tenant shall on demand pay to the Landlord the whole sums reimbursable or payable to the Landlord in respect of insurance of the Premises and shall pay the premiums for insurance of plate glass in the Premises, all in accordance with Clause 5.[98c]
6.1.3.   The Tenant shall pay when due and indemnify the Landlord against all rates, taxes, assessments, duties, charges, impositions and outgoings (whether or not of a capital or non-recurring nature) which are or during the Period of the Lease become payable by the owner or occupier in respect of the Premises other than taxes on the rent payable under the Lease or taxes arising on the disposal or deemed disposal of, or other dealing by the Landlord with, its interest in the Premises.
6.1.4.   The Tenant shall pay and indemnify the Landlord against any amount of Value Added Tax or any tax of a similar nature which may be substituted for it or levied in addition to it which shall be legally payable in respect of any payment made by the Tenant under the

---

[98c]See n. 98a as to amendment in the case of a unit in a multiple-tenancy building.

Lease and which is not recoverable by the Landlord from Her Majesty's Customs and Excise.[99]

6.1.5. [The Tenant shall pay to the Landlord [annually] on demand the Service Charge provided for in Part III of the Schedule.]

6.1.6. The Tenant shall pay to the suppliers of and indemnify the Landlord against all charges for, electricity, gas and other services consumed or used at or in relation to the Premises (including rents of meters or apparatus) where a separate supply is provided to the Premises.

6.1.7. The Tenant shall pay to the Landlord on demand the whole costs, expenses and outlays (including all legal and professional costs and fees) reasonably incurred by the Landlord:

(a) in relation to the negotiation and preparation of this Deed;

(b) in respect of any application for consent or approval required by this Deed whether granted or not;

(c) incidental to the preparation and service of all notices and schedules relating to deficiencies of repair or requiring the Tenant to remedy breach of any of its obligations under this Deed whether the same be served before or after the expiry of the Period of the Lease;

(d) in the preparation and service of a schedule of dilapidations before or after the expiry of the Period of the Lease;

(e) in procuring the remedy of any breach of an obligation of the Tenant including without prejudice to that generality the payment of arrears of rent or other sums due by the Tenant under this Deed.

6.1.8. The Tenant shall pay to the Landlord Interest (a) on any instalment of the Initial Rent or the Revised Rent from the date when the same was due for payment[1] until payment is actually made by the Tenant and (b) on any other sum payable or reimbursable by the Tenant to the Landlord under this Deed from a date being 14 days after payment is demanded by or on behalf of the Landlord until payment is actually made by the Tenant, but nothing contained in this sub-clause shall entitle the Tenant to withhold or delay payment of any instalment of rent or other sum foresaid nor prejudice the other rights or remedies of the Landlord arising from failure by the Tenant to make punctual payment of any instalment of rent or other such sum.[2]

6.2 *Maintenance, Repair and Renewal*[3]

The Tenant accepts the Premises [the Common Parts

---

[99]See para. 29–36.
[1]Days of grace may be allowed—if so, appropriate amendment will be required.
[2]See para. 29–35.
[3]See para. 29–26.

and the Services] at the Date of Entry as in all respects in good substantial and tenantable condition and repair and fit for the purposes for which the Premises are let and undertakes at all times throughout the Period of the Lease to keep the Premises in the like good substantial and tenantable condition and if and when necessary to renew, reinstate and rebuild the same [irrespective of the cause of damage necessitating any repair, renewal, reinstatement or rebuilding][4] [except where the damage necessitating such repair, renewal, reinstatement or rebuilding arises from a latent or inherent defect in the main structure of the Premises][5] and to replace from time to time the Landlord's fixtures and fittings in the Premises which may become beyond repair at any time during the Period of the Lease or on its expiry, but excepting always damage by any of the Insured Risks where the payment received from the Insurers is sufficient to cover the cost of repair, renewal, reinstatement or rebuilding. Subject to Clause 5.7.(c), the Lease shall not be terminated by reason of any damage to or destruction of the Premises but shall remain in full force and effect notwithstanding any rule of law to the contrary.

6.3. *Cleaning*

The Tenant undertakes throughout the Period of the Lease to keep the Premises and all Conductors serving the Premises in a clean and tidy condition and to clean all windows and glass in the Premises at least once per week.

6.4. *Decoration*

6.4.1. The Tenant undertakes at each of the appropriate Decorating Periods

(a) to paint all such parts of the exterior of the Premises as are usually painted with a priming coat and three coats of good quality paint of such colours as may be approved by the Landlord, and

(b) to paint or paper all such parts of the interior of the Premises as are usually painted or papered, such painting to consist of three coats of good quality paint and such papering to be of good quality paper all to the reasonable satisfaction of the Landlord. Painting and papering of the interior to be done at the final Decorating Period shall be of such colours or patterns as the Landlord may require.

6.4.2. The Tenant also undertakes to clean and point all stonework and/or brickwork on the exterior of the Premises at any time when reasonably required by the Landlord to the reasonable satisfaction of the Landlord.

---

[4]This is the usual provision in a clear lease.
[5]Alternative provision in the interest of the tenant, if negotiable.

6.5.   *Servicing of Plant and Machinery*
The Tenant undertakes throughout the Period of the
Lease at the Tenant's expense to enter into such
contracts as the Landlord or the Insurers may
reasonably require for the inspection and servicing of
all plant and machinery in or about the Premises.

6.6.   *Access*
The Tenant shall permit the Landlord and all persons
authorised by it to enter upon the Premises at all times
during the Period of the Lease on giving reasonable
notice (except in emergency),

(a)   to inspect the condition of the Premises and
prepare schedules of dilapidations, inventories of
the Landlord's fixtures and fittings and plant and
machinery and exercise any of the rights conferred on or reserved to the Landlord under this
Deed,

(b)   to carry out any works of decoration, repair or
construction upon any neighbouring premises on
condition of making good any damage thereby
caused to the Premises and

(c)   in the last six months of the Period of the Lease,
howsoever determined, to exhibit in or on the
Premises signs indicating that the Premises or
any part thereof are for sale or to let.

6.7.   *Compliance with Obligations*
If at any time during the Period of the Lease the
Landlord becomes aware from inspection or otherwise
of any breaches of the Tenant's obligations under this
Deed the Landlord may give notice in writing to the
Tenant specifying the breaches and requiring the same
to be remedied, and if the Tenant shall fail within 21
days of the date of such notice, or immediately in case
of emergency, to commence to take effective steps to
comply with such notice the Landlord may enter upon
the Premises with any persons authorised by it and
cause to be carried out all or any of the works referred
to in such notice or remedy the breach and the whole
costs incurred by the Landlord for that purpose shall
be repaid by the Tenant to the Landlord on demand.

6.8.   *Alterations or Additions*
The Tenant shall not erect or construct any new or
additional structure on the Premises nor make any
alterations or additions to any part of the Premises nor
cut, injure or remove any structural parts of the
Premises nor alter the appearance or design of the
Premises, provided always that the Tenant may with
the prior written consent of the Landlord erect
partitions in or carry out non-structural alterations
upon the Premises but any such partitions or non-
structural alterations shall be removed not later than
the Date of Termination but only if the Landlord so
requests, any damage to the Premises or any part

thereof occasioned by such removal to be made good by or at the expense of the Tenant.

6.9. *Use*[6]

6.9.1. At all times during the Period of the Lease the Tenant shall use the Premises only for the Permitted Use specified in the Particulars in Clause 1 and not for any other purpose without the prior consent of the Landlord [which consent shall not be unreasonably withheld] and shall not leave the Premises or any substantial part thereof vacant.

6.9.2. The Premises shall be kept open for business or trading during normal business hours for the area in which the Premises are situated and the Tenant shall use his best endeavours to promote business or trade in the Premises.

6.9.3. The Tenant shall not
(a) use the Premises for any noisy, offensive or noxious trade or business nor for any illegal or immoral purpose nor hold on the Premises any sale by auction,
(b) allow empty containers or rubbish of any kind to accumulate upon or about the Premises,
(c) discharge into any Conductor any deleterious or dangerous effluent or substance,
(d) overload any floors or other part of the Premises or machinery or apparatus therein and in general not subject the Premises or any part thereof to strains which they are not designed to bear,
(e) overload any electrical cables, wires or circuits,
(f) discharge from the Premises into the atmosphere any noxious, corrosive or harmful vapours, fumes or gases,
(g) stop up or darken or obstruct any windows or light in or affecting the Premises,
(h) erect or display on or in any part of the Premises any pole or flag or any bill, placard, poster or sign or affix to or display the same on the windows of the Premises without the prior consent of the Landlord, provided always that the Tenant may with the approval of the Landlord affix to the exterior of the Premises or display in a window a sign or notice showing the Tenant's name and business which the Tenant shall remove on the expiry of the Period of the Lease and restore any damage to the Premises caused by its affixing or its removal, nor
(i) obstruct any access, footpath, pavement or forecourt in the vicinity of the Premises.

6.9.4. The Tenant shall comply. with all regulations reasonably made by the Landlord from time to time for the management and use of the Premises and any other land or premises that may be used in common with any other person.

[6]See para. 29–27.

6.9.5.   [The Tenant shall at all times during the Period of the Lease display in the window(s) of the Premises a reasonable quantity of goods for sale and shall keep such window(s) clean and well illuminated.][6a]

6.10.   *Statutory and Title Obligations*[7]
6.10.1.   The Tenant shall at all times during the Period of the Lease observe and comply with and at its own expense implement all requirements or orders of any government, local or other competent authority applicable to the Premises or to the trade or business carried on by the Tenant therein.
6.10.2.   The Tenant shall observe and perform all obligations, conditions, burdens and others contained or referred to in the title deeds specified in Part VI of the Schedule.[7a]

6.11.   *Servitudes*
6.11.1.   The Tenant shall not interrupt or obstruct any right of the nature of a servitude, wayleave, privilege or encroachment enjoyed by any existing premises nor permit any new such right to be acquired over, under or in the Premises, and if any claim or attempt to exercise any such right shall be made the Tenant shall give immediate notice thereof to the Landlord and permit the Landlord and its agents to enter upon the Premises for the purpose of ascertaining the nature of any such right and at the request of the Landlord, but at the expense of the Tenant, adopt such means as may be reasonably required or deemed proper for preventing the acquisition of such right.
6.11.2.   The Tenant shall not give to any third party any acknowledgment that the Tenant enjoys any right relating to the Premises by the consent of such third party nor pay to such third party any sum of money or enter into any agreement with such third party for the purpose of inducing or obliging such third party to abstain from interrupting or obstructing such right, and if any of the owners or occupiers of neighbouring buildings or land does or threatens to do anything which interrupts or obstructs such right, the Tenant shall forthwith give notice thereof to the Landlord.

6.12.   *Planning Acts*
6.12.1.   The Tenant shall comply with the provisions of the Planning Acts in relation to the Premises.
6.12.2.   The Tenant shall obtain at its expense from the appropriate authorities all permissions, licences or consents which may be required for the carrying out of any operations or use of the Premises.
6.12.3.   The Tenant shall not apply for any planning permission without first obtaining the prior consent of the Landlord and shall furnish to the Landlord copies of any

---

[6a]Appropriate to shop premises.
[7]See para. 29–28.
[7a]Appropriate to lease of whole building: modify *quoad* unit in multiple-tenancy building.

planning permission granted and shall not proceed to carry out any operations or make any change of use authorised by such permission until the Landlord has confirmed that the terms of the permission are acceptable to it.

6.12.4. Unless the Landlord shall otherwise in writing direct the Tenant shall carry out and complete before the Date of Termination any works stipulated to be carried out to the Premises as a condition of any planning permission granted during the Period of the Lease and to be implemented by or on behalf of the Tenant, whether or not the date by which the planning permission requires such works to be carried out falls within the Period of the Lease.

6.12.5. If the Landlord reasonably so requires the Tenant shall provide adequate security for the compliance with any conditions stipulated in any planning permission granted in respect of the Premises and in that event the Tenant shall not proceed with any operations authorised by such permission until such security has been provided.

6.12.6. The Tenant shall at its expense appeal against any refusal of any planning permission in respect of the Premises or conditions imposed thereby, if reasonably required by the Landlord to do so.

6.12.7. The Tenant shall satisfy itself that there are no provisions of the Planning Acts or the title deeds of the Premises which prohibit or restrict the use of the Premises for the Permitted Use and nothing in this Deed or otherwise shall constitute or imply any warranty by the Landlord that the Premises may be used for the Permitted Use. If the performance or observance of any of the obligations, conditions or provisions of this Deed shall hereafter become impossible or illegal or restricted by reason of provisions of the Planning Acts the Lease and the rents payable thereunder shall not terminate but shall continue in full force and effect.

6.13. *Communication of Notices*
The Tenant shall furnish to the Landlord particulars of any notice, permission, order or proposal relevant to the Premises or the use thereof received by the Tenant or the occupier of the Premises from any planning, local or other competent authority within seven days of the receipt thereof and shall, if the Landlord so requires but at the Tenant's expense, either take all necessary steps to comply therewith or make or join with the Landlord in making objections or representations against or in respect of such notice, permission, order or proposal.

6.14. *Alienation*[8]
6.14.1. The Tenant shall not

---

[8]See para. 29–29.

    (a)   assign, sub-let, or grant security over or part with or share the possession or occupation of any part (as distinct from the whole) of the Premises nor enter into any agreement to do so, or

    (b)   assign, sub-let, or grant security over or part with the possession or occupation of the whole of the premises otherwise than by a formal assignation, sub-lease, or security and with the prior consent of the Landlord, which consent shall not be unreasonably withheld.[9]

6.14.2.   In the case of any permitted assignation or sub-lease

    (a)   the assignee or sub-tenant shall be a responsible person or body who is in the opinion of the Landlord of good financial standing, and

    (b)   the Tenant shall procure, if required by the Landlord, that a guarantor or guarantors acceptable to the Landlord undertake direct responsibility to the Landlord for implement of the obligations of the assignee or sub-tenant.

6.14.3.   In the case of any permitted sub-lease the Tenant shall procure that

    (a)   the sub-lease shall be granted without any fine, premium or grassum,

    (b)   the rent shall not be less than the higher of the rent payable under this Deed or the open market rental value of the Premises (as determined by the Surveyor) at the time when the sub-lease is granted and shall be payable in advance on the dates on which rent is payable under this Deed with provisions for review of the rent corresponding as to dates and terms with those stipulated in this Deed, with right to the Landlord to make representations to any arbiter who may determine the amount of the increased rent, and

    (c)   the sub-lease shall contain the same terms, *mutatis mutandis*, as those contained in this Deed and in particular without prejudice to that generality shall contain a prohibition against assigning, sub-letting, or granting securities over or otherwise dealing with the Premises or any part thereof without the prior consent of the Landlord and a condition that any sub-under-lease granted out of the sub-lease shall contain the like provisions.

6.14.4.   Any permitted assignation or sub-lease shall be in a form approved by the Landlord prior to its execution, and an extract thereof shall be furnished to the Landlord or its solicitors or the Surveyor within one month after such execution.[9a]

6.14.5.   In the event of any breach or non-performance of any of the conditions or provisions of this Deed by any

---

[9] See para. 29–30.
[9a] As to an alternative course of action, see para. 29–29.

permitted sub-tenant or occupier of the Premises the Tenant shall forthwith at its own expense institute all appropriate proceedings and take all necessary steps to procure the remedy of such breach or non-performance, but without prejudice to the rights and claims of the Landlord arising directly or indirectly therefrom.

6.15. *Indemnity*
The Tenant shall indemnify the Landlord against all liabilities and claims which may be prestable against the Landlord arising directly or indirectly from
(a) any breach or non-performance of any of the obligations, conditions or provisions of this Deed,
(b) any act, omission or negligence of the Tenant or any person acting expressly or impliedly with the authority of the Tenant in relation to the Premises and
(c) the whole expenses of any actions or proceedings arising therefrom.

6.16. *Notice of Defects*
The Tenant shall notify the Landlord of any defect in the Premises which might involve the Landlord in responsibility for taking any action which may be required of the Landlord in order to comply with any of the provisions of this Deed or any duty imposed on the Landlord by law in relation to the Premises and shall display on, in or about the Premises all notices which the Landlord may reasonably require to be so displayed.

6.17. *Outgoing*
6.17.1. On the expiry of the Period of the Lease (however it may be terminated) the Tenant shall
(a) remove from the Premises and yield possession thereof to the Landlord in good and substantial condition and repair, return the keys and remove all tenant's fixtures, signs and lettering installed in or erected or placed on the Premises and make good any damage to the Premises occasioned by such removal,
(b) if so requested by the Landlord remove all additions and alterations made to the Premises with the approval of the Landlord during the Period of the Lease and restore any damage caused to the Premises by such removal, and
(c) if the Premises are not in a state of repair and decoration in accordance with the obligations of the Tenant under this Deed the Tenant shall if the Landlord so requires pay to the Landlord (i) such sum as shall in the opinion of the Surveyor be required to make good the deficiencies in such repair and decoration and (ii) the rent at the rate last payable immediately before the expiry of the Period of the Lease for the period

estimated by the Surveyor as reasonably necessary for remedying such deficiencies.

6.17.2. If after the expiry of the Period of the Lease there remains in or about the Premises any property of the Tenant and the Tenant shall fail to remove the same within seven days after being requested by the Landlord to do so, the Landlord shall be entitled to sell or dispose of the same but shall account to the Tenant for any proceeds of such sale or disposal at any time within six months after the expiry of the Period of the Lease on being requested by the Tenant so to account.

7. OBLIGATIONS OF THE LANDLORD

Subject to the implement by the Tenant of its whole obligations under and compliance by the Tenant with the whole provisions incumbent on it in terms of this Deed and under reservation of the rights excepted or reserved to the Landlord in terms of Part V of the Schedule, the Landlord grants absolute warrandice.

[8. SERVICES[10]

Subject to the Tenant paying to the Landlord the Service Charge and complying with the whole obligations of the Tenant under this Deed the Landlord will throughout the Period of the Lease provide the Services as specified in Part III of the Schedule, but the Landlord will not be liable to the Tenant in respect of any interruption or failure of any of the Services by reason of necessary work of repair, maintenance or replacement or damage from any cause outwith the control of the Landlord [or due to omission or negligence on the part of any person undertaking or maintaining or supervising the Services on behalf of the Landlord].]

9. [GUARANTEES[11]

9.1. The Guarantor undertakes to the Landlord at any time but only when and if required in writing by the Landlord to pay the foregoing rents and other monetary obligations due by the Tenant and to implement and perform the whole other obligations undertaken or binding upon the Tenant under this Deed and to pay or make good all loss, damage and expenses sustained by the Landlord arising directly or indirectly from the failure of the Tenant to implement or perform such obligations or any of them in whole or in part.

9.2. Notwithstanding any rule of law or practice to the contrary the Guarantor shall not be released or

---

[10]See para. 29–31.
[11]See para. 29–37.

discharged from the undertaking foresaid by (a) the Landlord releasing or discharging any of the persons if more than one comprised in the Tenant or the Guarantor (b) the Landlord giving time or any other indulgence to the Tenant or (c) the variation of any of the terms of the Deed.

9.3. If the Tenant (being a company) shall go into liquidation or (not being a company) shall become bankrupt or enter into a composition or arrangement or trust deed for behoof of creditors and the liquidator, trustee in bankruptcy or trustee under the trust deed shall disclaim the Lease or if the Tenant shall be wound up or cease to exist or if the Landlord shall become entitled to irritate the Lease, then the Guarantor shall, if required by the Landlord by written notice given to the Guarantor within three months after such disclaimer or entitlement procure the renunciation of the Lease by the Tenant and accept a lease of the Premises for a period commensurate with the remainder of the Period of the Lease if such disclaimer or entitlement to irritate or renunciation had not been made at the same rent and on the same conditions in all respects (other than this Clause 9) as are contained in this Deed and the Guarantor shall be responsible for the whole costs and expenses of the Landlord and his professional advisers in relation to such new lease.[11a]

9.4. Within one month after the death of any Guarantor (being an individual) or of any Guarantor becoming bankrupt or, being a company, passing a resolution to wind up or being liquidated or having a receiver appointed on any of its assets or entering into an arrangement or composition for the benefit of creditors, the Tenant shall notify the Landlord in writing of the occurrence of any such event and shall, if so required by the Landlord, procure some other person acceptable to the Landlord to execute a guarantee in respect of the Tenant's obligations under this Deed in similar terms to those undertaken by the Guarantor in terms of this Clause 9.]

10. IRRITANCY[12]

Subject to the provisions of sections 4, 5, and 6 of the Law Reform (Miscellaneous Provisions) (Scotland) Act 1985, if at any time during the Period of the Lease (a) any rents or other monetary obligations of the Tenant under this Deed shall be in arrear and unpaid for 14 days after becoming payable, or (b) there shall be any breach, non-performance or non-observance by the Tenant of any of the obliga-

---

[11a] For a possible corresponding right to guarantor, see para. 29–37.
[12] See para. 29–33.

tions or conditions of this Deed, or

(c) the Tenant (being an individual or firm) (i) becomes apparently insolvent or is sequestrated or (ii) (being a company) enters into liquidation whether voluntary or compulsory (save for the purpose of amalgamation or reconstruction of a solvent company) or has a receiver appointed of its undertaking or has an administration order made in relation to it or (in either case) enters into an arrangement or composition for the benefit of its creditors or suffers any diligence to be done or execution to be levied on its goods, then and in any of those events the Landlord shall be entitled forthwith to terminate this Lease and treat this Lease and all transmissions thereof with all that has followed or can competently follow thereon as void and null and that without the necessity of any declarator, process of removal or other legal procedure and the Premises shall thereupon revert to the Landlord and it shall be lawful for the Landlord or any person or persons authorised by the Landlord to enter upon the possession of the Premises or any part thereof and to uplift rents, eject tenants and occupiers and thereafter use, possess and enjoy the same free of all claims by the Tenant as if this Deed had never been granted without prejudice to any right of action or remedy of the Landlord in respect of the premature termination of this Lease or of any antecedent breach by the Tenant of any of the conditions contained in this Deed, which irritancy is hereby declared to be pactional and not penal and shall not be purgeable at the Bar; [Provided always that, for the protection of [every creditor in any existing heritable security over the Tenant's interest in the Lease which has been notified to the Landlord and] any permanent trustee in bankruptcy of, or trustee under a protected trust deed granted by, the Tenant or any administrator or liquidator of or receiver appointed on the undertaking of the Tenant (any of such persons being hereinafter called "the affected person") the Landlord shall not be entitled to terminate this Lease on the occurrence of any of the events specified in sub-paragraphs (a) to (c) of this Clause without first allowing the affected person a period of one year thereafter in which to dispose of the Tenant's interest in this Lease and shall be entitled to terminate this Lease only if the Tenant's interest has not been disposed of within that period, but always subject to the conditions that

(i) the affected person shall within two months of the occurrence of any such event personally accept in probative writing liability for the whole obligations of the Tenant under this Deed (whether occurring before such acceptance or during the period until such disposal) and shall if reasonably requested by the Landlord find caution for performance of such obligations in an amount acceptable to the Landlord

(ii) make payment upon the date of such acceptance of

all sums of money due under the Lease which are then in arrear and

(iii) the Landlord shall deal with any request for consent to an assignation of the Lease by the affected person in the same manner as if the request had been made by the Tenant.]

11. CONTINUANCE OF THE LEASE

Except as otherwise provided in this Deed the Deed shall not terminate as the result of damage to or destruction of the Premises or any part thereof.

12. WAIVER[13]

Each obligation of the Tenant under this Deed shall continue in full force and effect notwithstanding that the Landlord shall have failed to enforce the same for a temporary period or granted a licence personal to the Tenant for the time being to depart from such obligation. In particular acceptance by the Landlord after any Review Date of the rent payable immediately before such Review Date or acceptance by the Landlord of rent after notice has been given by the Landlord of termination of the Lease under Clause 10 shall not imply waiver of the right to require payment of the appropriate Revised Rent from the Review Date or waiver of the notice of termination, as the case may be, unless such acceptance of rent has continued for a period of more than two years after the Review Date or service of the notice of termination, as the case may be.

13. THE SCHEDULE

The whole provisions of the Schedule form part of this Deed and are binding upon the Landlord and the Tenant [and the Guarantor].

14. NOTICES

Any notice, request, demand, consent or approval under this Lease shall be in writing and shall be sufficiently served if sent by registered post or recorded delivery service to or left addressed to the party concerned (if the party concerned is a body incorporated in the United Kingdom) at its registered office or (if the party concerned is an individual or firm) if so sent to or left at his or its last known address in the United Kingdom or in either case so sent to or left at the Premises. Any notice sent by registered post or recorded delivery service shall be deemed to have been duly served at the expiration of 48 hours after the time of posting. In proving service it shall be sufficient to prove that the envelope contain-

---

[13]See para. 29–34.

ing the notice was duly addressed to the party concerned in accordance with this Clause and posted to or left at the place to which it was so addressed. If at the request of the Landlord, a notice has instead to be served on an agent of the Landlord, it shall be deemed to be duly served if service on the agent complies with the relevant provisions of this Clause. If the Landlord at the relevant time is a limited company or other corporate body any notice, request, demand, consent or approval shall be sufficiently given if signed by a Director, the Secretary or other duly authorised officer of the Landlord or by the Surveyor on behalf of the Landlord.

15.   APPLICABLE LAW

The Deed shall be construed in accordance with the law of Scotland and the parties hereto prorogate the jurisdiction of the Court of Session in Scotland in all actions arising out of or in connection with this Deed and also to all lawful execution which may follow as a result of the registration of this Deed for execution.

16.   CONSENT TO REGISTRATION

The parties hereto consent to registration of this Deed and of any certificate issued thereunder for preservation and execution.

(*To be attested*)   (*Stamp duty—see para. 25–44*)

SCHEDULE
PART I
The Premises

1.   (*See paragraphs 29–05, 29–20 and 29–21 supra*)

PART II
Rent Review[14]

2.   On each of the Review Dates during the Period of the Lease the rent shall be increased to an amount (being the Revised Rent) which is equal to the open market rental value of the Premises current at the relevant Review Date.

3.   The open market rental value of the Premises shall be an amount to be agreed between the Landlord and the Tenant or, failing such agreement, to be determined in accordance with Paragraph 4 which shall represent the rental value of the Premises as between a willing landlord and a willing tenant without a premium if offered for rent on the open market with vacant possession subject to the provisions of the Deed for a duration equal to the Period of the Lease. In

---

[14]See paras. 29–22 and 29–23.

determining such value (1) it shall be assumed that the Premises are in good and substantial repair and that all the obligations of the Landlord and the Tenant under the Deed have been complied with and (2) there shall be disregarded any effect on rent of (i) the fact that the Tenant or its sub-tenants or their respective predecessors in title have been in occupation of the Premises (ii) any goodwill attaching to the Premises by reason of any trade or business carried on therein by the Tenant or its sub-tenants (iii) any improvements carried out by the Tenant or its sub-tenants during the Period of the Lease otherwise than in pursuance of an obligation to the Landlord and (iv) any damage to or destruction of the Premises.

4. If three months before any Review Date the Landlord and the Tenant shall have failed to agree upon the open market value of the Premises at such Review Date it shall be determined by an independent surveyor [as arbiter] [who shall act and be deemed to act as an expert and not as an arbiter] to be agreed upon by the parties to the Lease or, failing such agreement, by a surveyor experienced in the valuation of properties comparable to the Premises in the area where the Premises are situated to be nominated by the parties or, failing agreement, by the Chairman for the time being of the Scottish Branch of the Royal Institution of Chartered Surveyors at the request of either the Landlord or the Tenant, and the determination by such surveyor shall be binding upon both the Landlord and the Tenant. If the surveyor shall fail to determine the Revised Rent within three months after his appointment or dies or relinquishes his appointment another surveyor may be appointed in his place by agreement of the Landlord and Tenant or, failing such agreement, by the said Chairman at the request of either the Landlord or the Tenant. [As regards any decision of an arbiter in pursuance of this Paragraph the application of section 3 of the Administration of Justice (Scotland) Act 1972 is expressly excluded.]

5. Notwithstanding anything contained in this Part of the Schedule the Revised Rent payable after each Review Date shall not be less than the rent payable by the Tenant immediately before such Review Date.

6. If by any Review Date the relevant Revised Rent has not been ascertained by agreement or determination as aforesaid then in respect of the period between the relevant Review Date and the date when the Revised Rent is so ascertained the Tenant shall pay (i) on the Rental Date or Rental Dates the rent at the rate payable immediately before the relevant Review Date and (ii) immediately upon the Revised Rent having been ascertained an amount equal to the difference between the Revised Rent so ascertained and the rent actually paid in respect of the period since the relevant

Review Date apportioned on a daily basis together with Interest on the amount of such difference.[14a]

7. If at any Review Date there shall be in force any statute or other provision of law which shall restrain, restrict or modify the Landlord's right to review the rent and/or to recover any increase thereof, then within [6] months (time being of the essence of the contract) after any such restraint, restriction, or modification is removed, relaxed or modified the Landlord shall be entitled to require the rent to be reviewed so far as permissible by law in accordance with the procedure for review of rent on a Review Date contained in this Schedule and the Revised Rent shall be deemed to be payable as from the earliest date permitted by law. The provisions of this Part of the Schedule shall apply with the substitution of references to the said earliest date for references to the relevant Review Date.

8. As soon as the Revised Rent has been ascertained in accordance with this Schedule the parties shall execute a Memorandum recording the Revised Rent. The parties shall bear their own legal costs in respect thereof but the Tenant shall pay any stamp duty thereon and, if required by either party, the dues of registering the same in the Books of Council and Session and in an appropriate case in the Register of Sasines or the Land Register of Scotland.

9. As regards all periods of time specified or referred to in this Part of the Schedule (except that mentioned in Paragraph 7) time shall be deemed not to be of the essence.

PART III
Services[15]

10. Subject to the provisions of Clause 8 the Landlord will provide the following Services:

[Maintaining, repairing, altering or reinstating and where appropriate cleaning, painting and redecorating the Common Parts at such times and to such extent as the Landlord may consider adequate.]

[Inspecting, servicing, cleaning and where necessary repairing or renewing all Conductors serving the Premises and also other parts of the [Building] [Estate] but not those which serve only the Premises.]

[Inspecting, maintaining and when necessary renewing all elevators, fire alarms and fire apparatus and fire fighting equipment, boilers and central heating system which serve the whole Building but not any of these which serve only the Premises.]

[14a]A rate lower than the interest rate may be appropriate if the interest is paid promptly after the revised rent has been ascertained.

[15]See paras. 29–31 and 29–32.

[Keeping the Common Parts adequately lighted during all times during which the use of the Premises is permitted.]

[Supplying, providing, maintaining and renewing and keeping in good working order all apparatus, equipment, waste receptacles, appliances and other things which the Landlord shall consider necessary for the use and appearance of the [Building] [Estate].]

[Providing and maintaining plants, shrubs or grassed areas of the Estate and keeping the same free from weeds and the grass mown.]

[Collecting and disposing of refuse from the [Building] [Estate].]

Any other services to the [Building] [Estate] which the Landlord may provide from time to time and which the Landlord considers are consistent with its good management.

11. The Tenant will pay annually on demand to the Landlord the Service Charge being a fair and reasonable contribution towards the annual cost of providing the Services, the amount of such contribution to be assessed by the Surveyor, and such contribution shall in default of payment be recoverable as rent in arrear.[15a] The decision of the Surveyor shall be final and conclusive as regards the need for or desirability of any works to be performed for the repair, maintenance or replacement of any of the Services, but any dispute or difference as to the cost of providing the Services or the amount of the Tenant's contribution thereto shall be determined by an arbiter to be agreed by the parties or failing agreement to be nominated by the Chairman of the Scottish Branch of the Royal Institution of Chartered Surveyors whose decision shall be final and binding [the application of section 3 of the Administration of Justice (Scotland) Act 1972 being expressly excluded.]

PART IV
Rights Granted

12. The right to the Tenant and all persons expressly or impliedly authorised by the Tenant, in common with the Landlord and all other persons having the like right, of access to and egress from the Premises with or without vehicles for all purposes connected with the use of the Premises (but not for any other purpose) over and by any access roads and footways on ground belonging to or under the exclusive control of the Landlord.

13. The right to the Tenant in common with the Landlord

[15a]The procedure may if desired be elaborated in detail fixing an annual or shorter period for computation of the cost of the services, arranging for an initial payment to account and subsequent adjustment to the actual cost, etc. See Ross and McKichan, *op. cit.*, Chap. 11.

and all other persons having the like right to use the Common Parts for all proper purposes in connection with the use of the Premises.

14.   The right to the Tenant in common with the Landlord and all other persons having the like right to the free passage of water, soil, gas, electricity and other services and facilities through the Conductors now serving the Premises subject to all reasonable regulations made by the Landlord from time to time and subject also to temporary interruption for repair, alteration or replacement.

PART V
Rights Excepted or Reserved

15.   The following rights are excepted and reserved to the Landlord and any persons having the authority of the Landlord:

(a)   The free and uninterrupted passage of all services and facilities now or at any time during the Period of the Lease in, upon, under or through the Premises for the benefit of any property adjacent to or in the vicinity of the Premises with right to repair, alter or renew all Conductors of such services or facilities and to have access to and through the Premises for those purposes upon giving reasonable notice to the Tenant (except in case of emergency).

(b)   The right to build, alter, repair or rebuild or execute other works upon any building now or at any time during the Period of the Lease erected upon land adjacent to or in the vicinity of the Premises, to build into any external wall of the Premises in the execution of such works, to erect scaffolding for the construction, repair, or renewal or the cleaning or maintenance of any such building and to have temporary access through the Premises for any of those purposes upon giving reasonable notice to the Tenant.

(c)   The right to support from the Premises for any buildings erected or to be erected adjacent to or in the vicinity of the Premises.

16.   The Landlord shall not incur any liability to the Tenant in respect of any temporary inconvenience, loss or damage resulting from the exercise of any of the foregoing rights nor shall the Landlord incur any such liability resulting from any permanent loss or impairment of light or air to the Premises or interference with the access to or amenity of the Premises which may result from the exercise of any of the foregoing rights.

PART VI
Title Deeds referred to for Burdens and Conditions[16]

---

[16] See para. 29–28.

C. Shorter Forms of Lease

Use of shorter forms

29–44 Reference has already been made to the problem of lengthy draft leases of commercial or industrial premises being submitted by landlords (with correspondingly substantial legal charges usually paid by tenants) where the period of the let is relatively short and the rental is modest.[17] In such cases the adoption of a briefer style of lease (although in this context "briefer" is necessarily a relative term) may be economically justifiable, albeit that it lacks detailed specification on several matters which may require to be determined, if any of them later becomes an issue, by law and practice. As an illustration there is reproduced with the permission of the Law Society of Scotland in paragraph 29–45 *infra* the model style of commercial lease prepared by the Styles Committee of the Society[18] with certain minor amendments. It should be noted that this style is appropriate to a lease of a single building: suitable amendments will be required if the premises are a unit in a multiple-tenancy building.

29–45

LEASE

between ,

(designation)

(hereinafter called "the Landlord")[19]

and

[whose Registered Office is at

(hereinafter called "the Tenant")][20]

[whose principal place of business

is at   (hereinafter called "the Tenant")][21]

[residing at

(hereinafter called "the Tenant")][22]

and

[*(designation)*

(hereinafter called "the Guarantor")][23]

Interpreta- 1.   In this Lease unless there is something in
tion   the context inconsistent therewith

     1.1.   (a) words importing the masculine include the feminine and words importing the neuter include the masculine and the feminine;

---

[17]para. 29–38.
[18](1980) 25 J.L.S. W117.
[19]If a company, company registration number may be mentioned.
[20]Where tenant is an incorporated body—see also n. 19.
[21]Where tenant is a firm—see also cl. 1.1(g).
[22]Where tenant is an individual—see also cl. 1.1(f).
[23]Where there is a guarantor—see also cl. 1.1(f).

(b) words importing the singular include the plural and vice versa;

(c) words importing persons include corporations and vice versa;

(d) any reference to an Act of Parliament includes any modification, extension or re-enactment thereof for the time being in force and all instruments, orders, regulations, permissions and directions for the time being made or given thereunder or deriving validity therefrom;

[(e) where any matter is expressed to require the consent or approval of the Landlord it shall be implied that the same is in writing and, unless otherwise stated, that such consent or approval shall not be unreasonably withheld;]

[(f) where the Tenant [or the Guarantor] are two or more persons obligations imposed on or undertaken by them shall be binding on such persons jointly and severally;]

[(g) where the Tenant is a firm (*insert provision as in Clause 3(v) in para. 29–43 supra*)]

Definitions   1.2.   the following expressions shall have the meanings hereinafter mentioned:

(a) "Clause" means a clause of the Lease;

(b) "Insured Risks" means such of the following risks namely, loss or damage by fire, lightning, explosion, aircraft and other aerial devices (other than such aircraft and other aerial devices as are hostile) or articles dropped therefrom, earthquake, [subsidence], riot and civil commotion and malicious damage, storm or tempest, bursting or overflowing of water apparatus or pipes, flood, impact by road vehicles and such other risks as are from time to time included in any policy of insurance effected under the Lease; the Insured Risks to be such risks as are reasonably determined in the first instance by the Landlord and to include such additional risks as the Tenant may reasonably require;

(c) "the Insurers" means such insurance office or underwriter of repute as is nominated by the Landlord;

(d) "the Landlord" means the Landlord and all persons succeeding to the interest of the Landlord in the Premises;

(e) "Lease" means this lease and the Schedule hereto;

(f) "Loss of Rent" means such a sum of money as the Landlord may reasonably estimate represents the loss of rent payable hereunder in the event of partial or total destruction of the Premises having regard to the period required for reinstatement and potential increases in rent under the rent review provisions hereinafter contained or such greater sum as the Tenant may reasonably require;

(g) "Paragraph" means a paragraph of the Schedule;

(h) "the Planning Acts" means the Town and Country Planning (Scotland) Acts 1972 and 1977 and the Local Government and Planning (Scotland) Act 1982;

(i) "Premises" means the subjects (or any part thereof) described in Part I of the Schedule, all alterations or additions thereto which may be made during the Period of the Lease and every part and pertinent thereof and all landlord's fixtures and fittings in or about the same;

(j) "Prescribed Rate" means the rate of interest which is 3 percentage points above the Base Rate for the time being of [Bank];

(k) "Reinstatement Value" means the cost which would be incurred (including fees and the cost of shoring up, demolition and site clearance) in reinstating the Premises in accordance with the requirements of the Lease as reasonably determined in the first instance by the Landlord or such greater amount as the Tenant may reasonably require;

(l) "Schedule" means the Schedule annexed and executed as relative hereto;

(m) "Tenant" means the Tenant and its permitted assignees or sub-tenants and in the case of an individual shall include his executors and representatives whomsoever;

(n) "Term Date" means any of the dates on which rent is payable under Clause 2;

(o) "Date of Expiry" means the date of expiry or sooner termination of the Lease (however the same shall be determined);

[(p) "Guarantor" means the Guarantor and in the case of an individual shall include his executors and representatives whomsoever;]

(q) "Title Deeds" means the title deeds which are specified in Part IV of the Schedule.

Premises
Period of
the Lease
and Rent

2 IN CONSIDERATION OF the rents and other prestations hereinafter specified the Landlord hereby Lets to the Tenant but excluding always assignees and sub-tenants legal or voluntary and creditors and

managers for creditors in any form except where permitted under the Lease the Premises subject to the reservations in Part V of the Schedule and that for the period from the   day of   One thousand nine hundred and (hereinafter called "the Date of Entry") until   thousand and   (hereinafter called "the Period of the Lease"), FOR WHICH CAUSES the Tenant accepts the Premises in their present condition and HEREBY UNDERTAKES (FIRST) to pay to the Landlord the yearly rent of   or when appropriate the revised rent as provided in Part II of the Schedule by equal [quarterly] payments in advance at the terms of [   ] clear of all deductions whatsoever, the first of such payments to be made on the Date of Entry[24] such rent or revised rent to be paid without any written demand and, if the Landlord so requires, by Banker's Order and (SECOND) to make all other payments and fulfil the other obligations undertaken by the Tenant under the Lease.

Tenant's
Monetary
Obligations
Rent
Insurance

3 The Tenant HEREBY UNDER-TAKES throughout the Period of the Lease:
(1) To pay the rent and the revised rent herein stipulated on the dates and in the manner foresaid;
(2) To reimburse the Landlord on demand all sums which the Landlord may from time to time pay for insuring and keeping insured the Premises against the Insured Risks and for the Loss of Rent and for insuring and keeping insured the plate glass if the Tenant fail to keep the plate glass insured in accordance with the obligation of the Tenant contained in Paragraph 6 of Part III of the Schedule;

Rates and
other
charges

(3) To pay when due all rates, taxes, duties, charges, assessments, impositions and outgoings whatsoever (whether or not of a capital or non-recurring nature) which are, at any time during the Period of the Lease, payable by the owner or occupier in respect of the Premises other than taxes on the rent payable under the Lease or taxes

---

[24]If the date of entry does not coincide with a term date add: "the appropriate proportion of such payment for the period from the Date of Entry until the term of   to be made on the Date of Entry."

arising on the disposal or deemed disposal by the Landlord of or other dealing by the Landlord with its interest in the Premises;

Contribution to Costs of Common Subjects

(4) To reimburse the Landlord on demand all payments due under and in terms of the Title Deeds including contributions towards expenditure on the maintenance of subjects common to the Premises and other premises, but only so far as applicable to the Premises.

VAT

(5) To pay to the Landlord such amount of Value Added Tax at the rate for the time being in force as shall be legally payable to and irrecoverable by the Landlord from Her Majesty's Customs and Excise in respect of all moneys undertaken to be paid by the Tenant under this Lease[25];

Interest on Payments in Arrear

(6) To pay on demand to the Landlord, without prejudice to any other right, remedy or power herein contained or otherwise available to the Landlord, interest at the Prescribed Rate on any rent or any other sum of money payable or reimbursable to the Landlord under the Lease which shall have become due but remain unpaid for fourteen days, such interest to run as well after as before any judgment from the date when the same shall become due until payment thereof.[26]

Tenant's Further Obligations

4 The Tenant FURTHER UNDER-TAKES throughout the Period of the Lease to fulfil the obligations contained in Part III of the Schedule.

Landlord's Obligations

5 (1) The Landlord HEREBY UNDER-TAKES to insure and keep insured the Premises in joint names of the Landlord and the Tenant and such additional names as the Landlord or the Tenant may reasonably request at all times during the Period of the Lease (unless such insurance shall be vitiated by any act, neglect, default or omission of the Tenant) against the Insured Risks with the Insurers in the Reinstatement Value thereof and for the Loss of Rent and if required to produce to the Tenant a certificate from the Insurer stating for what sums and against what risks the Premises are insured and to what date the premiums have been paid and in case of damage by any of the Insured Risks (unless this Lease has been terminated by *rei*

---

[25]See para. 29–36.
[26]See para. 29–35.

interitus in consequence of such damage) with all reasonable speed to cause all moneys received in respect of such insurance (other than in respect of Loss of Rent) to be forthwith laid out in reinstating the Premises.[27]

(2) The Landlord undertakes to repair, renew and rebuild the Premises to the extent of any damage caused by a latent or inherent defect in the main structure of the Premises unless this Lease has been terminated by *rei interitus* in consequence of such damage.

(3) If the Premises shall at any time during the Period of the Lease be so damaged or destroyed as to render the Premises unfit for occupation and use in whole or in part in accordance with the terms and provisions of the Lease, then (unless this Lease has been terminated by *rei interitus* in consequence of such damage) the rents herein provided for or a fair proportion thereof according to the nature and extent of the damage sustained shall be suspended (but if such destruction or damage is attributable to an Insured Risk to the extent only that the Insurers meet the Landlord's claim under the policy for the Loss of Rent) until the Premises shall again be rendered fit for occupation and use, or if such destruction or damage is attributable to an Insured Risk until the Loss of Rent insurance effected by the Landlord shall be exhausted, if earlier.

Irritancy

6 Subject to the provisions of sections 4 to 6 of the Law Reform (Miscellaneous Provisions) (Scotland) Act 1985, if the rent herein stipulated or any part thereof shall at any time be in arrear for twenty-one days after the same shall have become due whether legally demanded or not and shall remain unpaid for a further period of fourteen days after demand by the Landlord under threat of irritancy, or if there shall be a breach of any of the obligations undertaken by the Tenant under the Lease which shall not be remedied by the Tenant within such reasonable period as shall be allowed by the Landlord in a notice requesting the remedy of such breach under threat of irritancy, or if the Tenant shall become apparently insolvent or shall make any arrangement with creditors or

---

[27]See para. 29–35.

being a company shall go into liquidation whether voluntary or compulsory, otherwise than a voluntary liquidation of a solvent company for the purpose of amalgamation or reconstruction, or has an administration order made in relation to it, or being a firm shall be sequestrated, then and in any such case it shall be lawful for the Landlord by notice to the Tenant to bring the Lease to an end forthwith and to repossess the Premises as if the Lease had not been granted but without prejudice to any right of action or remedy of the Landlord in respect of any previous breach of any of the obligations undertaken by the Tenant under the Lease.[28]

Provisos and Reservations

7 The provisos, conditions, disclaimers and reservations contained in Part V of the Schedule shall form part of the Lease.

Guarantee

[8 The Guarantor HEREBY UNDERTAKES to the Landlord that the Tenant will at all times during the Period of the Lease pay the stipulated rent on the date and in the manner foresaid, make all other payments under the Lease as aforesaid and fulfil the other obligations undertaken by the Tenant under the Lease and that, if the Tenant shall default in making of any of the said payments or in fulfilling any of the said obligations, then and in every such case the Guarantor on demand by the Landlord will make such payments to the Landlord and fulfil such obligations including all loss, damage and expense sustained by the Landlord through such default PROVIDED ALWAYS that the Guarantor shall have no liability in respect of any such default by an assignee with the Landlord's consent of the Tenant's interest in the Premises.][29]

Notices

9 Any notice, request, demand, consent or approval under the Lease shall be in writing and shall be deemed to be sufficiently served at the expiry of forty-eight hours after posting if sent by Recorded Delivery Post. Any notice to the Tenant [or the Guarantor] shall be sent (if an incorporated body) to its Registered Office and (if a person) to his last known address in Great Britain or Northern Ireland or to the Premises and (in any other case) to the

[28]See para. 29–33.
[29]See para. 29–37.

Tenant at the Premises. Any notice to the Landlord (if an incorporated body) shall be sent to its Registered Office and (if a person) sent to him at his last known address in Great Britain or Northern Ireland. If, at the request of the Landlord, a notice has instead to be served on its agent it shall be deemed duly served if service complies with the relevant foregoing provisions. In proving service it shall be sufficient to prove that the envelope containing the notice was duly addressed and posted in accordance with the provisions of this Clause.

Consent to Registration

10 The parties consent to registration hereof for preservation and execution. IN WITNESS WHEREOF

SCHEDULE REFERRED TO IN THE FOREGOING LEASE

PART I

The Premises[30]

1 The Premises
(Including pertinents, servitudes and exceptions and reservations as described in the Landlord's Title.)

PART II

Rent Review[31]

Date of Review

2 (1) At the expiry of the   year and each period of   years thereafter during the Period of the Lease (the date of expiry of each such period being hereinafter called the "Date of Review") the rent shall be increased to an amount (hereinafter called the "Revised Rent") equal to the market rental value of the Premises at the Date of Review.

Valuation

(2) The market rental value of the Premises shall be such an amount as shall be agreed between the Landlord and the Tenant or shall be determined in accordance with subparagraph (3) of this Paragraph as representing the rental value of the Premises as between a willing lessor and a willing lessee if offered for let on the open market under a lease for a period of [   ] years with

---

[30] See para. 29–20.
[31] See para. 29–23.

vacant possession and upon the supposition (if not a fact) that the Tenant has complied with all the obligations undertaken by him under the Lease and taking no account of:

(i) any goodwill attributable to the Premises by reason of any trade or business carried on therein by the Tenant;

(ii) any improvements to the Premises carried out by the Tenant otherwise than in pursuance of an obligation to the Landlord;

(iii) the destruction of or damage to the Premises; and

(iv) the fact that the Tenant has been in occupation of the Premises.

Decision on Rent Value

(3) If the Landlord and the Tenant shall be unable to agree on the market rental value it shall be determined by a surveyor (who shall act and be deemed to act as an expert and not as an arbiter) to be agreed upon by the parties to the Lease or, if they fail so to agree, by a surveyor experienced in the valuation of properties comparable to the Premises in the area where the Premises are situated to be nominated at the request of the Landlord or Tenant by the Chairman for the time being of the Scottish Branch of the Royal Institution of Chartered Surveyors, and the determination by such surveyor shall be binding on both the Landlord and the Tenant.

Upwards only

(4) Notwithstanding any determination by such surveyor the rent payable by the Tenant after each Date of Review shall not be less than the rent payable by the Tenant immediately before such Date of Review.

Payment after Date of Review

(5) If by any Date of Review the amount of the relevant revised rent has not been agreed between the parties hereto or determined as aforesaid, then in respect of the period of time beginning with the relevant Date of Review and ending on the Term Date immediately following the date upon which the amount of the Revised Rent is agreed or determined as aforesaid the Tenant shall pay to the Landlord rent at the yearly rate payable immediately before the relevant Date of Review, and at the expiry of the said period of time there shall be due as a debt payable by the Tenant to the Landlord on demand an amount equal to the difference between the Revised Rent and the rent actually paid in respect of the said period of time apportioned on a daily basis.

Memorandum

(6) As soon as the Revised Rent has been agreed or determined as aforesaid the parties hereto will forthwith endorse a memorandum thereof on the Lease or (at the option of the Landlord) execute a separate memorandum specifying the Revised Rent, and any stamp duty payable in respect thereof shall be borne by the Tenant.

PART III

Obligations of the Tenant

To repair, maintain or renew

3 At all times throughout the Period of the Lease at the Tenant's expense well and substantially to repair and maintain or renew the Premises except where the damage necessitating such repair, maintenance or renewal arises from a latent or inherent defect in the main structure of the Premises or is caused by any of the Insured Risks and the insurance moneys have not nor shall become irrecoverable through any act or default of the Tenant.[32]

To permit entry by Landlord and others

4 To permit the Landlord and its agents with or without workmen, at all reasonable times on giving reasonable notice (except in emergency) to the Tenant to enter the Premises to inspect the same, view the state of repair and condition thereof, prepare a schedule of the Landlord's fixtures and of any dilapidations and exercise the rights reserved to or conferred upon the Landlord by the Lease.

To comply with notices to repair

5 Well and substantially to make good all deficiencies in maintenance, repair and renewal of which notice shall be given to, or left on the Premises for the Tenant by the Landlord and for which the Tenant is liable under the Lease within [   ] calendar months after the giving or leaving of such notice (or sooner if requisite), and if the Tenant shall fail to comply with any such notice to permit the Landlord to enter the Premises to make good the same at the cost of the Tenant, which cost shall be repaid by the Tenant to the Landlord on demand with interest thereon at the Prescribed Rate from the date of payment by the Landlord together with all solicitors' and surveyors' fees and other expenses

---

[32]See para. 29–26.

which may be properly incurred by the Landlord in connection therewith.

Plate Glass Insurance

6 To insure and keep insured in the joint names of the Landlord and the Tenant all the plate glass forming part of the Premises against breakage for a sum not less than the full reinstatement cost thereof for the time being with the Insurers and, whenever reasonably required by the Landlord, to produce the relevant policy of insurance or a copy thereof and the receipt for the current year's premium, and forthwith to lay out all moneys received under such insurance and such other money as may be necessary in reinstating the glass with glass of the same quality and thickness.

To decorate interior and exterior

7 (1) In every third year during the Period of the Lease and during the last year thereof (however the same may be determined) to paint all such outside parts of the Premises as are usually painted in such manner and in such colour as shall be approved by the Landlord and to restore, point and make good the brickwork, [stairs if any] and stonework where necessary to the reasonable satisfaction of the Landlord. (2) In every seventh year during the Period of the Lease and during the last year thereof (however the same may be determined) to paint all such interior parts of the Premises as are usually painted in such manner and in such colour as shall be approved by the Landlord and otherwise to redecorate the interior parts of the Premises to the reasonable satisfaction of the Landlord. (3) At regular intervals throughout the Period of the Lease to clean and treat all other materials, surfaces and finishes of the interior and exterior of the Premises to the reasonable satisfaction of the Landlord.

To service fixed equipment

8 At the request of the Landlord but at the cost of the Tenant to enter into such contracts as the Landlord may reasonably consider advisable with persons of repute previously approved by the Landlord for the regular maintenance, inspection and servicing of the [lifts (if any), boilers (if any), central heating (if any) and air-conditioning apparatus (if any)] from time to time in and about the Premises.

To keep clean and tidy

9 At all times during the Period of the Lease to keep the Premises in a clean and

tidy condition and clear of all rubbish, and to clean at least once every month the inside and outside of the windows and window-frames of the Premises and all the glass (if any) in the entrance door thereto.

Not to use otherwise than for specified purpose

10 Not to use the Premises or permit them to be used for any noisy, offensive or dangerous trade or business, nor for any illegal or immoral purpose, nor to do or permit to be done on the Premises anything which, in the reasonable opinion of the Landlord, may be or may tend to become a nuisance or cause disturbance or inconvenience to the owners or occupiers of any adjoining or neighbouring premises or to the prejudice of the Landlord, nor to hold or permit or suffer to be held upon the Premises any sale by auction or public exhibition or public show or spectacle or political meeting or gambling, nor to use or permit the Premises to be used otherwise than as [   ] without the consent of the Landlord.[33]

Not to introduce dangerous things

11 Not to bring or permit to be brought into the Premises any article or thing which is or may become dangerous, offensive, radioactive or explosive, nor to carry on or do or permit to be carried on or done therein any hazardous trade or act in consequence of which the Landlord would be prevented from insuring the Premises or any other property for the time being owned by the Landlord or in which the Landlord has an insurable interest at the ordinary rate of premium or whereby any insurance effected in respect of the Premises or any such other property would be vitiated or prejudiced, nor without the consent of the Landlord to do or allow to be done anything whereby any additional premium may become payable for the insurance of the Premises or any such other property; and if the Premises or such other property or any part thereof are destroyed or damaged by any of the Insured Risks and the insurance money under any insurance against the same is wholly or partly irrecoverable by reason solely or in part of any act or default of the Tenant or the Tenant's servants or agents, forthwith to pay to the Landlord the whole or (as the case may be) the irrecoverable portion of

the cost (including professional and other fees) of completely rebuilding and reinstating the same.

Not to overload

12 Not to place or keep or permit to be placed or kept in the Premises any heavy articles in such position or in such quantity or otherwise in such manner as to overload or cause damage to or be in the reasonable opinion of the Landlord likely to overload or cause damage to the Premises, and not to permit the electrical circuits or the lifts in the Premises to be overloaded.

Not to harm drains

13 Not to allow to pass into the sewers, drains or watercourses serving the Premises any effluent or other substance which might cause any obstruction in or damage to the said sewers, drains or watercourses and in the event of any such obstruction or damage forthwith to make good the same to the reasonable satisfaction of the Landlord.

Not to make alterations

14 Not to divide, alter or damage the Premises nor merge the Premises with any adjoining premises, nor make any alterations or additions to the Premises except with the previous consent of the Landlord and in accordance with drawings and specifications previously submitted to and approved by the Landlord; provided always that the Landlord may as a condition of giving such consent require the Tenant to enter into such undertakings with the Landlord as the Landlord may reasonably require in regard to the execution of any such works and the reinstatement of the Premises at the Date of Expiry or otherwise.

Not to prejudice servitudes

15 (1) Not by building or otherwise to interrupt or obstruct any right of the nature of a servitude, wayleave, privilege or encroachment enjoyed by any existing premises, nor to permit any new such right to be acquired over, under or into the Premises; and if any claim or attempt to exercise any such right shall be made, to give immediate notice thereof to the Landlord and to permit the Landlord and its agents to enter upon the Premises for the purpose of ascertaining the nature of any such right and at the request of the Landlord, but at the cost of the Tenant, to adopt such means as may be reasonably required or deemed proper for preventing

Not to acknowledge servitude

the acquisition of any such right.

(2) Not to give to any third party any acknowledgment that the Tenant enjoys any such right over, under or into the Premises by the consent of such third party, nor to pay to such third party any sum of money or to enter into any agreement with such third party for the purpose of inducing or obliging such third party to abstain from interrupting or obstructing such right, and if any of the owners or occupiers of adjacent land or buildings does or threatens to do anything which interrupts or obstructs such right, forthwith to give notice thereof to the Landlord.

To obtain permission for signs

16 Not at any time during the Period of the Lease to affix or exhibit or permit to be affixed or exhibited in or on the Premises or on the forecourt in front thereof any bill, placard, advertisement or other sign visible from the outside of the Premises without the prior approval in writing of the Landlord.

Alienation

17 (1) Not at any time to assign, sub-let or otherwise dispose of or for any purpose or in any way deal with the Tenant's interest in or part with or share possession or occupation of part only of the Premises.

(2) Not at any time to assign, sub-let or otherwise dispose of or for any purpose or in any way deal with the Tenant's interest in or part with or share possession or occupation of the whole of the Premises without the consent of the Landlord.

(3) Not at any time to sub-let or agree to sub-let the Premises except at a rent which at the date of entry under such sub-lease is not less than the market rental value as defined in Part II of this Schedule, nor to permit a reduction in the rent payable by any sub-tenant, and to ensure that in any permitted sub-lease there shall be provisions that:

(i) the rent payable under such sub-lease shall be payable no more than one [quarter] in advance and shall be subject to review in an upward direction only no less frequently than and in such manner as to coincide with the rent reviews provided for under the Lease; and

(ii) the sub-tenant shall be prohibited from granting any assignation or any further sub-lease without the consent of the Landlord.[34]

Intimation of devolution of Tenant's interest

18 Within twenty-one days after the date of any assignation of the Lease or the grant of any sub-lease or any assignation of such a sub-lease or any devolution of the Lease or of any such sub-lease by will, intestacy or operation of law to provide or cause to be provided to the Landlord for registration a certified copy of the deed, document or instrument effecting such assignation, sub-lease, assignation of sub-lease or devolution.

To observe statutory requirements

19 At the Tenant's own expense to execute all such works as are under or in pursuance of any Act of Parliament directed or required to be executed on or in respect of the Premises or the Tenant's use thereof whether by the owner thereof and/or the Landlord and/or the Tenant and to comply with all the requirements of any relevant Act of Parliament and all relevant notices which may be served by any Public, Local or Statutory Authority and not to do or permit to be done on the Premises anything whereby the Landlord may become liable to pay any penalty imposed by, or to bear the whole or any part of any expenses incurred under, any such Act, direction, requirement or notice as aforesaid.[35]

Planning

20 (1) During the period of the Lease to comply in all respects with the Planning Acts and to keep the Landlord indemnified in respect thereof.
(2) Not to make any application for planning permission or give any notice to any relevant authority of an intention to commence or to carry out any development without the previous consent of the Landlord and forthwith after the grant or refusal of such application to supply to the Landlord (free of cost) a copy thereof for retention.
(3) Not to implement any such planning permission until any conditions attached thereto have been submitted to and approved by the Landlord.
(4) Unless the Landlord shall otherwise direct to carry out before the Date of

---

[34]See para. 29–29.
[35]See para. 29–28.

Expiry any works stipulated to be carried out to the Premises by a date subsequent to such Date of Expiry as a condition of any such planning permission.

(5) Forthwith after receiving notice of the same to give full particulars to the Landlord of any notice or proposal for a notice or order or proposal for an order given, made or issued to the Tenant by any competent authority under or by virtue of the Planning Acts and, if so required by the Landlord, to produce such notice, order or proposal to the Landlord.

(6) To make or join with the Landlord in making such objection or representation against or in respect of any proposal for such a notice or order as the Landlord shall deem expedient.[35]

To inform Landlord of notices

21 Upon the occurrence of any event or upon the receipt of any notice, order, requisition or direction which may be capable of adversely affecting the Landlord's interest in the Premises forthwith at its own expense to deliver full particulars or a copy thereof to the Landlord.

Re-letting Notices

22 To permit the Landlord to fix and retain for a period not exceeding six months prior to the Date of Expiry in a conspicuous position on the Premises, but not so as to obscure the fascia or restrict or interfere unreasonably with the access of light and air to the Premises, a notice-board for the re-letting of the Premises and not to obscure the said notice-board and to permit all persons authorised in writing by the Landlord or by its agents to view the Premises at all reasonable hours upon prior appointment having been made.

To inform Landlord of defects

23 To inform the Landlord immediately of any defect in the Premises which might give rise to a duty imposed by the title deeds, common law or statute on the Landlord in favour of any person.

To observe title conditions

24 To perform and comply with the burdens, conditions and others contained or referred to in the Title Deeds so far as applicable to the Premises and still subsisting and to keep the Landlord indemnified against all actions, proceedings, expenses, claims and demands in any way relating thereto.[35]

To remove

25(1) Immediately prior to the Date of Expiry at the cost of the Tenant:

(a) to replace any of the Landlord's fixtures and fittings which shall be missing, broken, damaged or destroyed with others of a similar character and quality;

(b) to remove every sign or painting of the name or business of the Tenant or other occupier from the Premises and to remove all tenant's fixtures and fittings, furniture and effects from the Premises, making good to the reasonable satisfaction of the Landlord all damage caused by such removal;

(c) if so requested by the Landlord, to remove and make good all alterations or additions made to the Premises at any time during the Period of the Lease and well and substantially to reinstate the Premises in such manner as the Landlord shall reasonably direct and to its reasonable satisfaction.

(2) At the Date of Expiry to remove from and leave vacant and clear the Premises leaving unless and except so far as otherwise requested as aforesaid by the Landlord all fixtures and fittings therein and improvements and additions thereto (other than tenant's fixtures and fittings) in such good and substantial repair and condition as shall be in accordance with the obligations undertaken by the Tenant under the Lease, provided that if at the Date of Expiry the Premises shall not be in such good and substantial repair and condition the Tenant shall carry out at its expense the works necessary to put the Premises into such repair and condition and if the Tenant fails to do so, the Landlord shall be entitled to carry out such works at the expense of the Tenant; whether such works are carried out by the Tenant or, on the failure of the Tenant as aforesaid, by the Landlord, there shall be paid to the Landlord by the Tenant a sum equivalent to the loss of rent suffered by the Landlord in respect of the period from the Date of Expiry to the date when such works have been completed to the reasonable satisfaction of the Landlord.

To pay
Landlord's costs

26 To reimburse the Landlord all expenses reasonably incurred by the Landlord:

(1) incidental to the preparation and service of all notices and schedules relating to deficiencies of repair or

requiring the Tenant to remedy breach of any of its obligations under the Lease whether the same be served before or after the Date of Expiry;

(2) in the preparation and service of a schedule of dilapidations before or after the Date of Expiry;

(3) in procuring the remedy of any breach of an obligation or the payment of arrears due by the Tenant under the Lease.

To pay
Landlord's costs
of applications
for consent

27 Upon making an application for any consent or approval which is required under the Lease to disclose to the Landlord such information as the Landlord may reasonably require and pay the Landlord's proper expenses in connection therewith (including applications where consent is refused or an application is withdrawn).

PART IV

Title Deeds referred to for Burdens

28 Writs referred to for burdens, conditions etc.

PART V

Provisos, Conditions and Disclaimers

No restrictions
on adjoining
property

29 Nothing herein contained or implied shall impose or be deemed to impose any restriction on the use of any land or building or premises not comprised in the Lease or prevent or restrict in any way the development of any such land or building or premises, provided that such use or development does not substantially interfere with or affect the quiet enjoyment and use of the Premises by the Tenant.

Reservations

30 There is reserved to the Landlord, its servants and agents with or without workmen, at all reasonable times so far as may be necessary or desirable, the right on giving reasonable notice (except in emergency) to the Tenant to enter and remain upon the Premises with all necessary tools, appliances and materials for the purpose of repairing, altering or rebuilding any adjoining or neighbouring premises belonging to the Landlord and in order to cleanse, empty and repair any of the sewers, drains and gutters belonging to the same, making

good all damage occasioned thereby to the Premises.

Disclaimer of
Liability

31 The Landlord shall at no time become liable to the Tenant for any loss, damage or expense sustained by the Tenant through any defect or deficiency in the Premises arising from the choking, bursting, stoppage or failure of any water supply, waste or other pipes, drains, sewers, rhones, conductors, gutters, ducts, water courses, cisterns or others.

CHAPTER 30

LEASES OF SPECIAL SUBJECTS

(1) GROUND OR BUILDING LEASES

(1) GROUND OR BUILDING LEASES

History

30–01   It was formerly the practice to lease vacant ground for the erection of houses or other buildings, usually for a period of 99 years or 999 years, registered under the Registration of Leases (Scotland) Act 1857, containing provisions for the type of buildings to be erected and their maintenance on the lines of the conditions in a feu grant in less or similar detail, often with imposition of casualties such as a duplicand on the succession of heirs or an extra year's rent upon an assignation to singular successors.[1] Many of these leases, where the property or a part thereof was occupied as a private dwelling-house forming the usual residence of the lessee and the lease had been granted before August 10, 1914 for a period of not less than 50 years, were converted into feus by the occupying lessee exercising the right conferred by the Long Leases (Scotland) Act 1954.[2]

Modern practice

30–02   Building leases for more than 20 years of ground for the erection of

---

[1] There could be variants, *e.g.* payment of a full year's rent of what the subjects should be worth at the time in full of that year's rent—*Crawford* v. *Campbell*, 1937 S.C. 596.

[2] The right of conversion to a feu was available only if notice was given by the lessee before September 1, 1959—1954 Act, s. 1(2).

property which may be used as or as part of a dwelling-house are now obsolete on account of the limitations imposed by section 8 of the Land Tenure Reform (Scotland) Act 1974. Ground leases for long periods are still in use for developments relating to commercial or industrial property in circumstances where the owner of the ground wishes to have it developed and then leased back to him at an initial rent often expressed as a percentage of the total costs of the development with periodic rent reviews both of the rent payable under the ground lease and the occupational rent payable in respect of the developed property. Alternatively, the developer will market the developed property by granting either short or long leases. In accordance with the philosophy of securing to the owner the continuing economic worth of the site and the benefit of any enhancement of its value it is now customary to insert in the ground lease a provision for review of rent, but there is an awkward drafting problem as to the determination of the proportion of the increase in value of the developed property which is properly attributable to the site. The style of ground lease in paragraph 30–03 *infra* incorporates one solution to that problem.

Style—ground or building lease

0–03

LEASE
between

AB Limited (*designed*)[3] (who and whose successors in the ownership of the ground aftermentioned are referred to whenever the expression "the Landlords" is hereinafter used)

and

XY Limited (*designed*)[3] (who and their successors in the right of occupancy under this Lease are referred to whenever the expression "the Tenants" is hereinafter used).

FIRST
Grant
and Rents

The Landlords in consideration of the rents and other prestations hereinafter specified hereby LET to the Tenants but excluding assignees legal or conventional and sub-tenants except as permitted in terms of Clause FIFTH hereof ALL and WHOLE that area of ground containing square [yards] [metres] or thereby (which area is demonstrative only and not taxative) delineated and tinted red on the plan annexed and executed as relative hereto[4] (which area of ground is hereinafter called

---

[3] Quote companies registration number in designation.
[4] Describe also by boundaries and measurements, if desirable.

"the red area") being part of the subjects in the County of   described and disponed in Disposition by CD in favour of the Landlords dated   and recorded in the Division of the Register of Sasines for the County of   on 1982,[5] together with a right of access to and egress from the red area by   Road,   AND THAT for the period from (hereinafter called "the Date of Entry") until   [6] FOR WHICH CAUSES the Tenants UNDERTAKE to pay to the Landlords (1) from   [7] (hereinafter called "the Rent Commencement Date") until   [8] rent at the rate of £   per annum (hereinafter called "the Initial Rent") and (2) from and after   [8] such increased rent per annum as may become payable in terms of Part I of the Schedule annexed and executed as relative hereto. The said rents shall be paid (by banker's order if the Landlords so require) without the necessity of any demand by equal quarterly payments in advance without any deduction on   ,   ,   and   in each year commencing on the Rent Commencement Date in respect of the quarter succeeding and so forth quarterly thereafter during the currency of this Lease, with interest at   per cent per annum on any of such quarterly payments from the date when such payment falls due until paid.

SECOND
Construction
of Property

The Tenants UNDERTAKE to commence forthwith and to complete not later than   [9] on the red area the construction of an office block with a surface car park and accesses and pathways to yield an initial annual rental or rentals totalling at least £   per annum (hereinafter called "the Estimated Initial Rental")[10] all in accordance with the plans and specifications which have been approved by the

---

[5]If a registered title, describe by reference to title number.

[6]The period will be at least as long as the anticipated life of the buildings to be erected, possibly with an option to renew for a further specified period.

[7]The date to be inserted is normally that by which the proposed buildings will be completed, the preceding period being a rent-free period.

[8]The first date at which the rent will be reviewed.

[9]Insert date by which works are to be completed, e.g. two or three years after date of entry.

[10]The total anticipated recoverable rentals when the property is completed will be agreed between the surveyors of the parties when the lease is entered into.

Landlords[11] and in accordance with the provisions of any relevant statutes, bye-laws and regulations made by any competent authority (which office block, surface car park, accesses and pathways and any other permitted erections on the red area are hereinafter called "the Property"). The Tenants shall also comply with the whole provisions contained in Part II of the said Schedule.

THIRD
Consents and
Practicability

The Tenants shall be deemed to have satisfied themselves that all necessary permissions, consents and approvals by the relevant local authorities or other competent bodies have been or will be obtained so far as required for the implementation of the whole obligations under this Lease and generally as to the practicability of such implementation and the Landlords have given and give no warranty in respect of any such matters.

FOURTH
Maintenance,
Use and
Insurance of
Property

The Tenants further UNDERTAKE following the construction and completion of the Property and throughout the currency of this Lease, to implement and fulfil the whole provisions and conditions specified in Part III of the said Schedule.

FIFTH
Alienation
and
Securities

The Tenants shall not be entitled to assign their right and interest under this Lease in respect of a part only of the subjects let but may assign such right and interest over the whole of the said subjects with the prior written consent of the Landlords which shall not be unreasonably withheld. The Tenants shall also be entitled to grant a security or charge over their said right and interest in the whole, but not part, of the said subjects for *bona fide* advances with the prior written consent of the Landlords which shall not be unreasonably withheld. The Tenants shall also be entitled to sub-let parts or the whole of the said subjects at rents which represent the open market rental value thereof at the time with provision for review of such rents at the same periods and on the same conditions *mutatis mutandis* as are provided in Part I of the said Schedule but shall inform the Landlords within thirty days after the execution of each of such sub-leases of the

---

[11]Normally detailed plans and specifications of the building will have been submitted to and approved by the landlords as part of the preliminary negotiations before the lease is executed.

name and designation of the sub-tenant, the period of the sub-lease and the initial rent payable thereunder and shall, if so required by the Landlords, furnish an extract of the sub-lease to the Landlords.[12]

SIXTH
Breaches by
Sub-tenants

In the event of any breach, non-performance or non-observance of any of the provisions or obligations hereof by any sub-tenant or occupier of the Property or any part thereof the Tenants shall forthwith at their own expense take all necessary steps and carry out any procedures required to procure the remedy of such breach, non-performance or non-observance but without prejudice to the rights of the Landlords arising from such breach, non-observance or non-performance.

SEVENTH
Reserved
Rights of
Landlord in
respect of
adjacent land

The Landlords reserve the right by themselves or other persons authorised by them to deal as they may think fit with any land or buildings adjacent to or in the vicinity of the red area and the Property and in particular without prejudice to that generality to erect on such land or to alter or reconstruct, demolish or rebuild any such buildings notwithstanding that any of the foresaid operations may affect or diminish the light or air enjoyed or that may during the currency of this Lease be enjoyed by the Property.

EIGHTH
Servitudes

The Tenants shall not during the currency of this Lease become entitled to or acquire any servitude, right or privilege over or affecting any other land or property which now belongs or may hereafter belong to the Landlords other than the red area.

NINTH
Effect of
Waiver

Each of the Tenants' obligations hereunder shall remain in full force and effect notwithstanding that the Landlords may have released or failed to enforce it for a period not exceeding two years, nor shall acceptance of rent for the like period after the breach of any such obligation or, where for any reason the Revised Rent has not been agreed or determined on any Date of Review in accordance with Part I of the

---

[12]The provision as to sub-letting is appropriate where it is intended that the property will be sub-let in suites of offices. It would be administratively inconvenient if the consent of the landlords as owners of the ground were required to each sub-let but the minimal information stipulated will enable the landlords to monitor the policy of the tenants and ensure that the property is being efficiently administered. If it is intended that the property be occupied as a single unit, a prohibition of sub-lets of parts or the whole of the property except with the consent of the landlords, not to be unreasonably withheld, may be appropriate.

said Schedule, shall acceptance by the Landlords for a period not exceeding two years after the relevant Date of Review of the rent payable immediately before such Date of Review imply any departure from the Landlords' rights to enforce the whole obligations of the Tenants hereunder.[13]

TENTH
Continuance
of Lease

This Lease shall continue in full force and effect notwithstanding any damage to or destruction of the Property or any part thereof.

ELEVENTH
Irritancy

[Irritancy clause as in clause 10 in paragraph 29–43 supra][14]

TWELFTH
Notices

[As in clause 14 in para. 29–43 supra]

THIRTEENTH
Expenses

The Tenants shall pay and indemnify the Landlords against all costs, charges and expenses and outlays (including legal and surveyors' and other professional fees and charges) reasonably incurred by the Landlords in respect of the negotiation and preparation of and stamp duty on this Lease, the preparation and service of all notices to the Tenants, any application for consent or approval made by the Tenants and procuring the remedying of any breaches by the Tenants of any of their obligations hereunder including without prejudice to that generality proceedings for recovery of arrears of rent or other payments due by the Tenants to the Landlords under or arising from this Lease.

FOURTEENTH
Arbitration

Any dispute or difference between the Landlords and the Tenants which in accordance with the provisions hereof falls to be determined by arbitration or any dispute or difference with respect to the construction or effect of this Lease, or as to the respective rights, duties or obligations of the parties, or as to any other matter or thing arising out of or connected with this Lease shall (except where otherwise expressly provided) be referred to an arbiter to be appointed by the parties or, failing agreement on such appointment, to be nominated by the Chairman for the time being of the Scottish Branch of the Royal Institution of Chartered Surveyors whose

[13]See para. 29–34.
[14]See para. 29–33.

decision shall be final and binding on the parties. [The application of section 3 of the Administration of Justice (Scotland) Act 1972 is hereby expressly excluded.]

FIFTEENTH   The Landlords and the Tenants consent to registration hereof for preservation and execution.   (*To be attested*)
(*Stamp duty—see para. 25–44*)

PLAN

SCHEDULE

In this Schedule expressions defined in the foregoing Lease (hereinafter called "the Lease") shall have the meanings thereby respectively attributed to them.

PART I
Rents and Rent Reviews

1. On   [15] and each period of five years thereafter during the currency of the Lease (the date of expiry of each such period being hereinafter called the "Date of Review") the rent payable under the Lease shall be increased to an amount (hereinafter called the "Revised Rent") calculated in accordance with paragraph 2 hereof.

2. (a) There shall be ascertained the open market rental value of the Property as at the Date of Review, being the annual rent or aggregate of annual rents at which the Property might reasonably be expected to be let without premium in the open market as between a willing landlord and a willing tenant or tenants under a lease for a period of   [16] years with vacant possession on the basis that the tenant or tenants undertook to pay all usual tenant's rates and taxes and to bear the cost of repairs, insurances and other expenses necessary to maintain the Property in a state to command such rent or rents and upon the assumption that the Tenants have observed and performed all the obligations undertaken by them under the Lease but disregarding any effect on rent of (i) the fact that the Tenants or any person or persons deriving title from the Tenants have been in occupation of the Property, (ii) any goodwill attaching to the Property by reason of the carrying on thereat of the business of the Tenants or of any person or persons deriving title from the Tenants, (iii) any improvements carried out by the Tenants or any person or persons deriving title from the Tenants otherwise than in pursuance of an obligation to the Landlords, and (iv) the destruction of or damage to the Property or any part thereof.

(b) There shall be calculated the amount which bears to the open market rental value ascertained under sub-paragraph (a) above the same ratio that the Initial Rent payable under Clause FIRST of the Lease bears to the Estimated Initial Rental

---

[15] Assuming five-yearly reviews this date will be five years after the rent commencement date.
[16] The whole period of the lease.

specified in Clause SECOND of the Lease and if the amount so calculated exceeds the Initial Rent the difference plus the Initial Rent shall be the Revised Rent.[17]

3. If the Landlords and the Tenants shall be unable to agree on the open market rental value of the Property at the Date of Review the same shall be determined by a surveyor (who shall be deemed to act as an expert and not as an arbiter)[18] to be agreed upon by the Landlords and the Tenants or, if they fail so to agree, to be determined by a surveyor to be nominated by the Chairman for the time being of the Scottish Branch of the Royal Institution of Chartered Surveyors, and the determination of such surveyor shall be binding upon both the Landlords and the Tenants.

4. Notwithstanding any determination by such surveyor the rent payable by the Tenants after each Date of Review shall not be less than the rent payable by the Tenants immediately before such Date of Review.

5. If by any Date of Review the amount of the relevant Revised Rent has not been agreed or determined as aforesaid, then in respect of the period of time beginning with the relevant Date of Review and ending with the date when the amount of the Revised Rent is agreed or determined as aforesaid, the Tenants shall pay to the Landlords rent at the annual rate payable immediately before the relevant Date of Review, and at the expiry of the said period of time there shall be due as a debt payable by the Tenants to the Landlords the difference between the Revised Rent and the rent actually paid in respect of the said period of time apportioned on a daily basis.[19]

6. As soon as the Revised Rent has been agreed or determined as aforesaid the Landlords and the Tenants shall forthwith endorse on the Lease and execute a memorandum specifying the Revised Rent, any stamp duty thereon being borne by the Tenants.

7. The Revised Rent agreed or determined at any Date of Review as aforesaid shall be payable thereafter at the dates and in the manner provided in Clause FIRST of the Lease and shall remain payable until further increased at any subsequent Date of Review or until expiry of the period of the Lease (whichever shall first occur).

PART II
Construction of Property

8. The Tenants shall not depart from the approved plans and specifications referred to in Clause SECOND of the Lease in any

---

[17]Assuming initial rent £1,000, estimated initial rental £10,000 and open market rental value at date of review £25,000:

Ratio of initial rent/estimated initial rental = 1/10.
1/10 of £25,000 = £2,500.
Difference over initial rent (£2,500 − £1,000) = £1,500.
New rent (£1,500 + £1,000) = £2,500.

[18]In this case it may be preferred to avoid the expense of arbitration proceedings.

[19]Provision may be made for payment of interest on the difference at a stated rate.

respect without the consent in writing of the Landlords which consent shall not be unreasonably withheld and in constructing the Property the Tenants bind and oblige themselves as follows:—

(a) They shall not use any materials other than those specified in the said approved plans or the detailed plans, sections, elevations and specifications approved by the Landlords without the prior consent in writing of the Landlords, which consent shall not be unreasonably withheld or delayed.

(b) They shall take down and remove all work and materials which shall be unsound or unfit for the purpose intended and which shall not be in accordance with any relevant statute or regulations or with the layout in the said approved plans or with the said detailed plans, sections, elevations and specifications within such reasonable period as may be prescribed in any notice given on behalf of the Landlords and shall also repair and make good any defects or omissions in the Property in such manner and within such reasonable time as may be specified in such notice and if the Tenants shall neglect so to do within the period specified in such notice it shall be lawful for the Landlords or their servants, contractors, agents, or workmen to remove all non-complying materials and to substitute others therefor and to remove or make good all non-complying works and all expenses of so doing shall be paid to the Landlords by the Tenants within twenty eight days of a written demand in that behalf, provided that if the Tenants shall reply to any notice requiring such taking down, removal or repair within 14 days of the service thereof, with a counter-notice disputing the reasonableness of either the requirement or the length of notice given, then failing agreement as to such reasonableness the Landlords' notice shall not have effect until confirmed by the Arbiter under Clause FOURTEENTH of the Lease.

(c) They shall not erect or build or permit to be erected or built any building, structure or erection (except such temporary structures or buildings required in connection with the building operations as shall have been previously approved in writing by the Landlords) or any sign or advertisement of any kind otherwise than in conformity with the said detailed plans, sections, elevations and specifications; declaring however that nothing contained in this sub-clause shall prevent the display of notice boards customarily displayed by building contractors or developers or notice boards relating to the letting of the buildings to be erected by the Tenants; but no such notice boards shall be affixed to the hoardings or fences enclosing the subjects let.

(d) They shall not deposit, make up or manufacture or permit to be deposited, made up or manufactured upon the red area any building or other materials except such as may be actually required for the Property and shall so soon as the Property shall be completed forthwith remove from the red area all building and other materials and rubbish whatever.

(e) They shall carry out their operations in such a manner as to avoid as far as reasonably possible any disturbance or annoyance to the owners or occupiers of buildings in the neighbourhood and shall indemnify the Landlords from and against all actions, proceedings, costs, damages, claims and demands arising from such operations; declaring, however, that the Landlords shall be obliged to give to the Tenants immediate written notice of any claim received by the Landlords in respect of such matters and shall not settle or compromise any such claim without the previous concurrence of the Tenants.

(f) They shall do all acts and things required by and perform the works in conformity in all respects with the provisions of the statutes applicable thereto and with the bye-laws, regulations, orders, town planning provisions or other regulations for the time being in force relating to buildings and the Tenants shall give all necessary and usual notices under any building or other Acts or bye-laws; declaring that the building works shall be carried out as herein provided under the inspection and to the reasonable satisfaction of the duly authorised officers or agents of the Landlords.

(g) They shall maintain the Property in good order and condition and if any defect shall appear in any part thereof or any accident shall occur thereto such defect or the damage caused by any such accident shall as soon as reasonably practicable be made good and repaired by the Tenants to the reasonable satisfaction of the Landlords and if the Tenants shall for forty days after notice from the Landlords refuse or neglect to make good and repair any such defect or damage (but subject to a like right of appeal by the Tenants to the Arbiter as under sub-paragraph (b) of this paragraph) the Landlords by their servants, contractors, agents and workmen may execute any necessary works and the cost thereof shall be paid to the Landlords by the Tenants within twenty eight days of a written demand in that behalf; and the Tenants shall take all reasonable care to avoid damage to adjoining roads including footpaths and on demand shall repay to the Landlords the reasonable costs as certified by the engineer of the Landlords for the time being of making good any damages thereto or to the sewers, drains, pipes or cables or other works thereon or thereunder caused or arising from any act or omission of the Tenants or their agents in relation to the construction of the Property or any part thereof.

(h) They shall not, without the consent in writing of the Landlords (which consent shall not be unreasonably withheld) remove or permit or suffer to be removed until after the completion of the building works in connection with which they are to be employed any building materials (other than inferior or unfit materials removed for the purpose of being replaced by proper materials) or plant which shall be brought upon the red area for the purpose of such building works.

(i) They shall erect on the red area such temporary fences, not exceeding six feet in height, as the Landlords shall reasonably require and on the completion of the Property they shall erect on the red area (where not occupied by buildings) such permanent fences as may be envisaged by the said detailed plans, sections, elevations and specifications.

(j) They shall permit the Landlords by their officers, servants, workmen and others duly authorised by them to enter upon the red area or any part thereof at any reasonable time the Landlords so desire for the purpose of viewing and examining the progress of construction of the Property or any part thereof and of inspecting and testing the materials being used in connection therewith and the workmanship thereof and of ascertaining generally that the agreements, conditions and stipulations contained in this paragraph have been and are being duly observed and performed and (subject to giving at least forty eight hours previous written notice) for the purposes of laying, constructing, repairing or cleansing any sewer, drain or water main or other public utility services from any adjoining land or public highway; declaring however that in the exercise of the aforesaid rights the Landlords shall cause the least possible interference and inconvenience and shall make good all damage occasioned thereby with all due dispatch.

(k) They shall insure the structures as existing from time to time in accordance with either the current Schedule of Conditions of Building Contract issued under the sanction of the Royal Institute of British Architects or paragraph 11 hereof.

(l) They shall indemnify and keep indemnified the Landlords against all liability, actions, claims, demands, losses, charges, damages and expenses in respect of any loss or injury or damage whatsoever arising out of or in the course of or by reason of the erection and execution of the Property provided however that the Landlords shall be obliged to give to the Tenants immediate written notice of any claim received by the Landlords in respect of such matters and shall not settle or compromise any such claim without the previous consent of the Tenants.

(m) As soon as practicable after the completion of the construction of the Property, the Tenants shall remove from the subjects let all temporary structures erected during construction and all surplus materials and shall lay out and landscape all unbuilt on ground not utilised as a surface car park or as roads or paths, all to the satisfaction of the Landlords.

PART III
Maintenance, Use and Insurance of Property

9. The Tenants undertake, following the construction and completion of the Property and throughout the currency of the Lease either to procure that sub-tenants or occupiers of the Property and every part thereof shall implement and fulfil the obligations and conditions in this paragraph, or the Tenants shall themselves implement and fulfil the said obligations and conditions, namely:

(a) All existing and future outgoings payable by law in respect of the Property or any part thereof either by the owners or occupiers thereof shall be paid punctually when due and without prejudice to the foregoing generality all rates, taxes, duties, charges, assessments, impositions and outgoings whatsoever of a recurring nature (whether parliamentary, county, municipal, parochial, local or of any other description) which are now or may at any time hereafter be assessed, charged or imposed upon or payable in respect of the Property and others on the red area shall be so paid, excepting always feuduties and ground annuals and taxes assessed on the Landlords in respect of the rent payable under the Lease; and all obligations (whether relating to the Property or any business permitted to be carried on therein) imposed by any Act or Acts of Parliament, statutory instruments, or the rules, bye-laws, regulations and notices or orders of any local or other authority for the time being in force shall be duly complied with and all such works as under or by virtue of any such Act or Acts, statutory instruments, rules, bye-laws, regulations, notices or orders as are or shall be properly directed or necessary to be done or executed on or in respect of the Property or the red area or any part thereof, whether by the owner, landlord, tenant or occupier, shall be so done or executed timeously, and the Landlords shall be indemnified against all claims, demands and liability in respect thereof.

(b) The Property and every part thereof and the red area shall be kept and repaired, maintained, renewed and rebuilt in good and substantial condition and decorated, paved and cleaned, all to the reasonable satisfaction of the Landlords. In the event of any damage to the Property or the red area by any of the insured risks referred to in paragraph 11 of this Schedule the whole moneys payable under the insurance policy or policies shall be applied at the sight of and to the satisfaction of the Landlords in repair or rebuilding of the Property, and if payment of any amount for which the said policy or policies was or were effected shall be refused in whole or in part by reason of any act, neglect or default by the Tenants or their servants or agents or any sub-tenants, occupiers or any other person for whom the Tenants are responsible, or if such moneys are insufficient to repair or rebuild the Property, the Tenants shall be responsible for supplying the deficiency.

(c) In the   year after   [20] and in every   year thereafter and also in the last year of the Lease howsoever determined all exterior parts of the Property which ought to be painted shall be painted in a proper and workmanlike manner to the reasonable satisfaction of the Landlords and to a colour scheme approved by the Landlords with two coats of good quality undercoat paint and one coat of good quality gloss or other suitable top coat paint and all exterior parts of the Property which ought to be so treated shall be waxed, polished or otherwise treated with good quality materials and all the outside hardwood and metal and other work not required to be painted or polished shall be cleaned and treated in a suitable manner for its maintenance in good condition.

(d) In the   year after   [21] and in every   year thereafter and also in the last year of the Lease howsoever determined all the inside wood, metal and other parts of the Property usually, or requiring to be, painted, shall be painted in a proper and workmanlike manner with one coat at least of good quality undercoat paint and one coat of good quality top coat paint, and also, with every such internal painting, all such interior parts of the Property as have been or ought properly to be so treated shall be whitewashed, colour-washed, distempered, grained, varnished or polished or papered or otherwise decorated or treated with good quality materials, all such work to be carried out to the reasonable satisfaction of the Landlords, and so that in the last year of the Lease the tints, colours and patterns of such works of internal painting and decoration shall be such as shall previously be approved by the Landlords in writing.

---

[20] The date when the property is to be completed in terms of clause second of the lease.
[21] Insert date as in n. 20.

(e) At all times throughout the period of the Lease the walls or fences, if any, erected on the boundaries of the red area shall be kept and maintained in good repair, order and condition to the reasonable satisfaction of the Landlords.

(f) The Property or any part thereof shall not be altered either externally or internally (except as regards internal partitioning of a temporary nature and internal decoration and finishes) nor shall there be erected any further or replacement buildings upon the red area without the prior written approval of the Landlords (which approval shall not be unreasonably withheld) to the plans, sections, elevations and specifications of the proposed alterations or of the further or replacement buildings and the materials to be used in the construction thereof, nor without such approval as aforesaid shall any external projection from any of the buildings on the red area be made or any alteration be made upon the existing external design or external appearance or the external decoration scheme of the Property.

(g) No buildings other than permanent buildings shall be erected on the red area.

(h) The red area or the Property shall not be used for any noisy, noxious or offensive trade or for industrial purposes or for the holding of auction sales or for roundabouts, shooting galleries, pin tables, amusement arcades, swings, games, lotteries or competitions, or any similar purpose or for any illegal or immoral purposes or for any other purpose which the Landlords may reasonably consider to be detrimental to the amenity of the neighbourhood.

(i) The Landlords or their representatives, with or without workmen, shall be entitled by prior appointment during reasonable hours to enter upon the subjects let and the Property or any part thereof from time to time as the Landlords may consider necessary for the purpose of inspecting the state and condition thereof and if, following any such inspection, written notice shall be given by the Landlords to the Tenants of any defect or want of repair which has been found, within thirty five days after such notice such defect or want of repair shall be well and sufficiently repaired or made good or restored. The Landlords reserve the right themselves to carry out such repairs and charge the cost thereof to the Tenants if the said repairs are not carried out within the said period, provided that such extension of time will be granted as may be reasonably necessary for the execution of major repairs which cannot be completed within the said period.

(j) The Landlords or their representatives or workmen and any other person or persons authorised by the Landlords (including any statutory undertakers, their representatives or workmen in respect of any apparatus retained in, under or over the unbuilt part of the subjects let) shall be entitled at all reasonable times during the currency of the Lease (after at least forty eight hours written notice, except in the case of emergency) to enter into and upon the red area and the Property for the purpose of constructing, laying down, altering, repairing, cleansing, emptying or inspecting any sewers, water courses, gutters, drains, water pipes, telephone cables and wires, electric mains and wires or gas mains and pipes in connection with or for the accommodation of any neighbouring or adjoining land and buildings or of developing such adjoining land, provided that the Landlords and others as aforesaid shall inconvenience the Tenants as little as possible and shall make good all damage and loss thereby occasioned.

(k) No oil, grease or other deleterious matter or substance shall be allowed to enter from the Property the drains and sewers of the local authority and any plant necessary for treating any deleterious effluent before permitting the same to enter such drains and sewers shall be provided and installed by the Tenants as may be reasonably required by the Landlords from time to time in accordance with the best modern practice.

(l) No refuse dump or rubbish or scrap heap shall be formed on the unbuilt parts of the red area and all refuse, rubbish and scrap (other than any refuse which the local authority are under statutory obligation to remove) which may have accumulated on the red area and all used tins, cans, boxes and other containers shall be regularly removed and generally the red area shall be kept clear and in good order at all times.

10. (a) For the prevention of pollution of the air the Tenants shall not cause or permit any smoke, effluvia, vapour or grit to be emitted from the red area or the Property, declaring however, that, in the use of any fuel burning apparatus or appliance approved as aftermentioned, this requirement will be held to be satisfied if the fuel utilised therein is one of the fuels authorised by any regulations made under the Clean Air Act 1956 or any Acts replacing or amending the same or is a liquid fuel and if the apparatus or appliance is so maintained and operated as to minimise the emission of smoke.

(b) Any fuel burning apparatus or appliance to be installed, other than oil, gas or electric heaters complying with a specification approved by the British Standards Institution, shall be of such a type as shall be previously approved in writing by the Landlords, which approval shall not be unreasonably withheld, and such approved fuel burning apparatus or appliance shall not be altered or replaced without the previous consent in writing of the Landlords.

(c) Such approved fuel burning apparatus or appliance shall, at all times throughout the currency of the Lease, be kept in repair and maintained to the reasonable satisfaction in all respects of the Landlords.

(d) All chimneys in connection with such approved fuel burning apparatus or appliances shall be erected and thereafter maintained throughout the period of the Lease to the reasonable satisfaction in all respects of the Landlords.

11. (a) The Property shall be insured and at all times kept insured by the Tenants with a reputable insurance office for an amount to be approved in writing by the Landlords sufficient to cover the cost of repairing all damage or of completely reinstating it in the event of destruction, together with site clearance costs and the fees of architects and surveyors and other professional fees and expenses incidental thereto against loss or damage by fire, lightning, storm and tempest, subsidence, flood, explosion, riot or civil commotion and (in peace time) aircraft and articles dropped therefrom and also three years' rent of the Property as sub-let at the time, and all premiums payable for such insurance shall be paid when due and receipts for such premiums shall whenever required be produced to the Landlords. If the Property

at any time is not so kept insured or receipts for premiums are not so produced when required the Landlords may effect and maintain such insurance and any sums expended by the Landlords for that purpose shall be repaid by the Tenants to the Landlords on demand. The Landlords shall be entitled to have their interest endorsed on any policy or policies of insurance effected by the Tenants or their sub-tenants in fulfilment of obligations under this paragraph.

(b) The Tenants shall not do or permit to be done in or about the Property anything which might render the said policy or policies of insurance void or voidable or restrict or modify the amounts for which the same were effected or would be likely to increase the risk of fire or explosion or increase the amount of premiums payable for such insurance.

(c) In the event of the Property or any part thereof being destroyed or damaged by fire or any other risks foresaid the Tenants shall apply the whole moneys payable under the said policy or policies in repairing and rebuilding the Property in fulfilment of their obligations under sub-paragraph (b) of paragraph 9 of this Schedule.

(To be executed by parties)

(2) MINERAL LEASES

Introduction

30–04   Since the nationalisation of coal and associated minerals by the Coal Industry Nationalisation Act 1946 conveyancing practice in relation to the working of minerals has significantly changed. Leases of minerals to be extracted by underground working are relatively uncommon: the minerals which can be exploited commercially in the private sector comprise principally those which occur near or on the surface such as sand and gravel or bings or debris heaps from disused coal, shale, ironstone or fireclay mines or rock extracted by quarrying operations. Where the extraction of the minerals involves permanent, or at least long-term, destruction of the surface the usual practice is that the mineral operator purchases the land including the minerals, when the seller may be content to leave the regulation of access and working practice to statutory control[22] and of restoration of the surface to the conditions imposed in that regard by the relevant planning authority upon the permission to work the minerals,[23] but may in particular cases enter into an agreement with the purchaser having continuing effect or insert conditions in the disposition of the land for the protection of the amenity of other land in the vicinity. In the case of bings or debris heaps the conveyancing method may be a lease or an absolute disposition of the bing itself with provisions as to access and restoration of the ground.

---

[22]*e.g.* Mines and Quarries Act 1954 as amended.
[23]Town and Country Planning (Scotland) Act 1972, ss. 19, 27.

Lease or sale

30–05   The choice between granting a lease of minerals or selling the land including the minerals or selling as a separate subject minerals on the surface such as debris heaps may have important consequences as regards valuation for rating[24] and liability to capital gains tax as a disposal or part-disposal.[25] Discussion of the rating and taxation aspects is outwith the scope of this work, but professional advisers should be consulted when any such transaction is contemplated.

Capacity of parties

30–06   A lease of minerals is in effect a sale of part of heritable subjects with a licence to extract and remove the minerals. Trustees of trusts as defined in the Trusts (Scotland) Act 1921 have power to grant mineral leases provided that to do so is not at variance with the terms or purposes of their trust,[26] but a tutor, curator or judicial factor for an individual, whose primary duty is to preserve the estate rather than to alter its character, may consider that the granting of a new mineral lease which is in reality a disposal of part of the estate with damaging effect on the amenity of the remainder is at variance with the purposes of his office.[27] In the case of family trusts the granting of a lease of minerals would seldom be consonant with the terms or purposes of the trust and an express power would require to have been conferred in the trust deed.[28]

Underground minerals

30–07   Leases of minerals to be extracted by underground working from mines or pits vary in form according to the nature of the mineral strata and the surface, but the principal matters for which provision is usually made are:

(1) Description of mineral area. This is almost invariably described by reference to an annexed plan possibly showing also in vertical section the upper and lower limits of the seam where these can be defined.

(2) Consideration. Usually an annual fixed rent is stipulated which merges in lordships or royalties based on the quantity of minerals won, the greater of the fixed rent or lordships in any year being payable. It is in the interest of the landlord to negotiate a fixed rent which will ensure that the minerals will be worked promptly so that he will obtain as quickly as practicable the greater rental yield from lordships, and to

---

[24]*McCosh* v. *Assessor for Ayrshire*, 1945 S.C. 260; *Secretary of State for Scotland* v. *Assessor for Invernessshire*, 1948 S.C. 334; *Moray Estates Development Co.* v. *Inland Revenue*, 1951 S.C. 754.
[25]Capital Gains Tax Act 1979, ss. 19, 37.
[26]s. 4(1)(c).
[27]*Campbell* v. *Wardlaw* (1883) 10 R. (H.L.) 65.
[28]As to powers of various parties to grant leases of minerals, see Vol. I, paras. 2–11, 2–57, 2–82 and 2–102.

discourage the tenant from using the lease for securing a bank or stock of minerals which will be extracted later when either market conditions or his business policy dictate. Frequently a "shorts" clause is included which entitles the tenant to recoup the excess of fixed rent over lordships paid in any year from the excess of lordships over fixed rent payable in a subsequent year. The lordship may be determined on a sliding scale in relation to the market price of the minerals at each term of payment of the lordship—a provision which was relatively unusual in older leases but may now merit consideration as a form of inflation-proofing.[29] Whatever its form, whether fixed rent or lordship or royalty, the annual payment is in law a rent, and the landlord may exercise his right of hypothec in the event of non-payment.[30]

(3) **Duration**. The period of the lease should be long enough to permit complete extraction of the minerals so far as commercially workable. That may be difficult to estimate accurately, and the tenant will normally seek to negotiate a duration which is ample, with breaks in his option at stated periods to enable him to abandon the lease if the minerals are earlier exhausted or for any reason are found to be unworkable at a profit.[31] Where provision is made for breaks, the tenant cannot terminate or reduce the lease at any other time on the ground that the minerals cannot be worked at a profit.[32] Where no breaks are provided for in the lease the tenant is not entitled to abandon it on the ground that the difficulties of working were such that the minerals could not be won at a profit,[33] but may only do so if the minerals are exhausted.[34]

(4) **Tenant's rights**. The lease will confer on the tenant all rights necessary for the working of the minerals, such as power to search for and extract and dispose of the minerals, to sink pits or drive mines, to use specified parts of the surface for the erection of machinery, ventilation shafts, access roads and deposit of debris, and to divert watercourses and/or use water therefrom, etc. If necessary, access rights may be granted over other land belonging to the landlord. Payment for use of the surface or wayleaves over other land may be imposed in addition to the rent or royalties on the minerals.

(5) **Tenant's obligations**. These will include payment of the fixed rent or royalties, to keep, and permit the landlord from time to time to inspect, proper records of the quantities of minerals extracted and to

---

[29] Alternatively there may be provision for review of fixed rent and lordships at stated periods, although the intervals between review periods would normally be greater than in an ordinary commercial lease, *e.g.* 10 or 15 years.

[30] *Liquidators of Linlithgow Oil Co. Ltd.* v. *Earl of Rosebery* (1903) 6 F. 90.

[31] *Waddell's Trs.* v. *Monkland Iron Co.* (1885) 13 R. 237; *Ebbw Vale Steel Co.* v. *Wood's Tr.* (1898) 25 R. 439.

[32] *Fleeming* v. *Baird & Co.* (1871) 9 M. 730; *Gowans* v. *Christie* (1873) 11 M.(H.L.) 1.

[33] *Dixon* v. *Campbell* (1824) 2 Sh.App. 175.

[34] *Murdoch* v. *Fullerton* (1829) 7 S. 404.

render accounts of the total weight thereof within three months after each rental term for the purpose of calculating royalties, to extract the minerals in a skilful and workmanlike manner and to observe all relevant statutory regulations, to keep and have available up-to-date plans of the workings for inspection by the landlord or his surveyor and to deliver plans of the completed workings on termination of the lease, to leave underground barriers within the let area, to fence off the surface of the let area, to obtain all necessary planning and other consents, to purify any outflow from the workings, not to assign the lease nor sub-let, to insure the whole plant, machinery and works and to indemnify the landlord against all claims arising from the tenant's operations and to pay the expenses of the lease and the expenses incurred by the landlord in relation to the exercise of his rights arising from it.

(6) Damage from subsidence. The tenant will be obliged to work the minerals in such a manner as to prevent so far as practicable or to minimise damage to the surface of the area let or to any adjacent land. In the event of any such damage being caused by the tenant's operations to land or buildings belonging to the landlord provision will be made for payment by the tenant of compensation to be determined, failing agreement, by arbitration; the mineral tenant will also be bound to pay and indemnify the landlord against liability for damage to property of feuars or tenants of the landlord and to adjoining or neighbouring property which may be damaged by the mineral workings.

(7) Irritancy. A conventional irritancy, subject to sections 4 to 6 of the Law Reform (Miscellaneous Provisions) (Scotland) Act 1985, will be included in the event of arrears of rents or royalties, breach of the tenant's obligations or bankruptcy, liquidation or insolvency of the tenant, but without any right to a trustee in bankruptcy, heritable creditors or a liquidator to take up the lease.

(8) Termination. On termination of the lease the tenant will be obliged to restore the surface, fill up mines or pits and remove all buildings and erections. The landlord will usually have an option to purchase the tenant's machinery and plant at a price agreed or determined by an independent valuer[35]; if the option is not exercised the tenant will be obliged to remove them.

(9) Arbitration.

(10) Consent to registration for preservation and execution.

The stamp duty is on the lease scale (see paragraph 25–44) plus £2 in respect of the varying lordship rent.[36]

---

[35]See *Wilson* v. *Douglas* (1868) 7 M. 112.
[36]Stamp Act 1891, s. 4(*b*), Sched. Lease or Tack, para. (4); Finance Act 1974, s. 49(1), Sched. 11, para. 10(2).

Bings or debris heaps

30–08   The material in bings is purchased or leased for making bricks or
other products and the principal elements in determining market value
are the suitability of the material for the manufacture of the products
and the distance between the site of the bing and the manufacturing
works since carriage is an important factor in the total cost of the raw
material. From the point of view of the seller or lessor his interests are
to obtain the proceeds of the sale or lease and to have the site cleared
and restored for agricultural purposes and improvement of amenity.
The terms of the agreement for sale or the lease are negotiated, the
seller or lessor seeking to have the contents of the bing removed and
the ground restored as quickly as practicable while the purchaser's or
lessee's objective depends mainly upon the urgency of his commercial
need to use the materials and the stocks of similar material obtainable
from bings which are more conveniently situated to his brickworks or
other manufactory, the particular bing being secured to be worked
when more economically viable stocks have been exhausted. If the
transaction takes the form of a sale, the agreement will normally
contain a stipulation for removal of the bing within a stated period,
and may include an option to re-purchase the restored site at an agreed
price. If the transaction takes the form of a lease, the lessor will seek a
duration that is as nearly as possible the estimated time required for
complete removal of the material. The consideration on sale may be a
lump sum or a royalty based on the weight of the material removed;
the consideration in a lease will be either a fixed rent merging in
royalties or simply a rent calculated only upon royalties. The
responsibility for constructing and maintaining any necessary access
roadway is that of the lessee or purchaser, possibly, where access is
obtained over land belonging to the seller or lessor, with provision for
a wayleave charge. In the case of a lease the lessor may reserve an
option to require an access roadway to remain or be removed by the
lessee as part of the restoration process; provision for a similar option
may be made part of an agreement for sale so far as the roadway
extends over retained land belonging to the seller or land which he has
an option to re-purchase. Special consideration is required as to
insertion in a lease of an irritancy clause: on balance it is usually
desirable that the lease should include one although, depending on
circumstances, damages for breach may be a preferable remedy. It
may be advisable for more detailed provision to be made with regard
to restoration of the site than is required by the conditions of planning
permission.

Opencast or surface workings

30–09   Apart from coal now vested in the National Coal Board, the
minerals most frequently worked commercially by excavation from the
surface are sand and gravel for the manufacture of cement. These

minerals are usually obtained by purchase of the land for a lump sum, or possibly for a price calculated as a royalty on tonnage, and leases of them are relatively uncommon.

Quarries

30–10   Rock or stone quarried is usually worked from land purchased, since restoration of the surface to its former state is impracticable.

CHAPTER 31

ASSIGNATIONS, SUB-LEASES AND VARIATION AND TERMINATION OF LEASES

ASSIGNATIONS

SUB-LEASES

ASSIGNATIONS

Legal effect

31–01 When a lease has been assigned and, where the consent of the
landlord is required, the landlord has accepted the assignee as tenant,
the assignee is liable for all obligations under the lease which become
prestable thereafter. On the principle of delegation the assignor ceases
to be liable for all future obligations under the lease[1] unless in terms of
the lease the obligations were imposed on the tenant and his assignees
jointly and severally,[2] but the assignor remains liable for implement of
obligations which became prestable before the effective date of the
assignation.[3]

---

[1] *Skene* v. *Greenhill* (1825) 4 S. 25.
[2] *Burns* v. *Martin* (1887) 14 R.(H.L.) 20.
[3] Gloag, *Contract*, 264.

In the case of long leases which may be recorded under the
Registration of Leases (Scotland) Act 1857 as amended by Schedule 6
to the Land Tenure Reform (Scotland) Act 1974, the effect of an
assignation is to vest in the assignee the right of the assignor in and to
the lease to the extent assigned.[3a]

Assignability

31–02   The general principle is that leases involve the element of *delectus
personae* and the interest of the tenant is not assignable unless
expressly declared to be so or with the consent of the landlord.[4] Leases
of exceptional duration or of particular subjects, however, may be
assigned.[5] In leases of unfurnished urban property, whether residential
or commercial subjects, the presumption is that no element of *delectus
personae* is involved and the tenant may assign his interest, but his
right to do so is usually excluded in terms of the lease except with the
consent of the landlord, often with the qualification that such consent
will not be unreasonably withheld.[6] However, leases of furnished
houses incorporate hire of the furniture and are not assignable,[7] and
the terms of the lease may be such as to infer *delectus personae*.[8] It has
been stated that an exclusion of assignees might be ineffectual in a
lease of such duration that it amounts to an alienation,[9] but with the
modern practice of very long leases of commercial property this
statement must be regarded as doubtful.[10] Leases of rural subjects of
ordinary duration are not assignable.[11] In leases of agricultural subjects
it has been decided that leases for 19 or 21 years are of ordinary
duration and do not imply a power to assign,[12] whereas leases for the
life of the lessee[13] or for a period unusually long in the case of
particular subjects[14] imply the right of the tenant to assign. Sporting
leases plainly involve *delectus personae* and cannot effectually be
assigned without the permission of the landlord.[15] The opinion has
been expressed that a mineral lease for 31 years is not of extraordinary
duration and so is not assignable without the landlord's consent.[16]

The right of a tenant to bequeath a lease, or the statutory right of his
executor to assign a lease on intestacy, with special provisions in

---

[3a]1857 Act, s. 3.
[4]Rankine, *Leases*, 171.
[5]*Elliot* v. *Duke of Buccleuch* (1747) Mor. 10329. As to exceptional duration and particular subjects,
see this paragraph *infra*.
[6]See, *e.g.* styles in paras. 27–20 and 27–46 (residential property) and 29–43 and 29–45 (commercial
property).
[7]Rankine, *op. cit.*, 175.
[8]*Earl of Elgin* v. *Walls* (1833) 11 S.585.
[9]*Bain* v. *Mackenzie* (1896) 23 R. 528 *per* Lord McLaren at 532 and Lord Kinnear at 533.
[10]Paton and Cameron, *Landlord and Tenant*, 152.
[11]Bell, *Prin.*, s. 1216.
[12]*Alison* v. *Proudfoot* (1788) Mor. 15290; *Earl of Cassillis* v. *Macadam* (1806) Mor. App. v. Tack,
No. 14.
[13]Rankine, *op. cit.*, 173.
[14]Hume, *Lectures*, IV 95.
[15]*Mackintosh* v. *May* (1895) 22 R. 345.
[16]*Duke of Portland* v. *Baird & Co.* (1865) 4 M. 10 at 16, 19, 22; Rankine, *op. cit.*, 175–176.

relation to crofting or agricultural leases, are treated in Volume IV.

31–03 **Exclusion of assignees and sub-tenants**. In leases which otherwise might be assignable it is the usual practice to exclude assignees or sub-tenants expressly. An exclusion of "assignees and sub-tenants", without more, excludes both voluntary and judicial assignees, such as a trustee in sequestration, liquidator or judicial factor, and quasi-judicial assignees such as a trustee under a trust deed for creditors,[17] but it is usual expressly to exclude assignees whether legal or conventional.[18] If the exclusion is not express but is implied from *delectus personae*, however, only conventional but not judicial or quasi-judicial assignees are excluded.[19] Where a mineral lease was granted in favour of trustees for a firm with a provision excluding assignees legal and conventional, it was held that sequestration of the firm terminated the lease.[20]

Frequently the exclusion is qualified by wording such as: "without the consent in writing of the landlord which shall not be unreasonably withheld." The effect of this phrase in the field of commercial and industrial leases where it has been most widely canvassed has already been considered in paragraph 29–30 *supra*.

Preliminary considerations

31–04 In the negotiation of assignations of leases there are many preliminary matters which require consideration by the parties and their advisers. This paragraph and paragraphs 31–05 to 31–09 deal with matters for examination and inquiry which are necessary in all such transactions, irrespective of the nature of the premises: further items for consideration in assignations of commercial or industrial premises are treated *infra*.[21]

31–05 **(1) Title**. The assignee is concerned to ensure that the title to the lease itself and the title of the assignor, where there have been previous assignations or transmissions of the tenant's interest, are valid. As regards the original lease he should be satisfied that the landlord was duly infeft, that the consent of any heritable creditor to the lease was obtained, that the lease and the permitted use do not infringe any conditions of the landlord's title and that the lease was sufficient in point of form and properly executed. In the case of a long lease[22] the assignees should be satisfied that

(i) where the lease was granted before the area in which the premises are situated became operational for the purposes of

---

[17]Rankine, *op. cit.*, 177.
[18]See styles in paras. 27–20, 29–43 and 29–45.
[19]Rankine, *op. cit.*, 177.
[20]*Walker* v. *McKnights* (1886) 13 R. 599.
[21]See para. 31–12.
[22]*i.e.* of more than 20 years' duration (Land Tenure Reform (Scotland) Act 1974, Sched. 6; Land Registration (Scotland) Act 1979, s. 28(1)).

registration of title it was duly recorded in the Register of Sasines or the tenant's right had become real by possession and that any subsequent assignations or transmissions of the tenant's interest were valid and effectual,

(ii) where either the lease itself or any subsequent assignation or transmission of it occurred after the area in which the premises are situated became so operational, the interest of the tenant for the time being was made real by registration of it in the Land Register,[23] and

(iii) searches in the property and personal registers, or a Form 10 or Form 12 report, as may be appropriate, show clear records in the same way as is required in a purchase of land.[24]

In the case of assignations of all leases where a company has been involved as the granter of the lease or of any assignations of it during the appropriate period of positive prescription,[25] a search should also be made in the Companies Register of Charges and the company files—see Volume II, paragraph 21–87 *supra*. Also, in the case of assignations of all leases, it should be verified that, when the lease was granted, the landlord's title was not subject to any heritable security or that, if it was so subject, any necessary consent of the heritable creditor to the lease was obtained—see paragraph 25–16 *supra*. It should also be confirmed that the title of the assignor was not burdened by any heritable security or affected by diligence, so that the assignee will receive an unburdened and valid title. In the case of assignations of long leases the searches or reports already mentioned should disclose any such burdens or diligences. In the case of assignations of shorter leases the creation of effective heritable securities is impracticable, but the right of the assignor may be affected by an inhibition so that a search of the Register of Inhibitions and Adjudications should be instructed and, if the assignor is a company, its right may be the subject of a floating charge but that should be disclosed by the search above suggested in the Register of Charges.

31–06   (2) **Right to assign.** If the right of assignation of the lease is excluded expressly or by implication of law, the consent of the landlord to the proposed assignation will be required. The terms of the lease and the relevant circumstances may entitle the landlord to refuse consent to the assignation, or to permit it subject to the imposition of additional or altered conditions. The assignor should verify that the landlord's consent will be given before missives for sale or transfer of the lease

---

[23]The interest of the original tenant can be made real only by such registration. The right of any person acquiring the tenant's interest by assignation or transmission, even if the original tenant's right had previously been made real by possession or recording in the Register of Sasines, can only be made real by registration of the interest acquired by assignation or transmission after the area became operational in the Land Register (Land Registration (Scotland) Act 1979, s. 3(3); R.T.P.B., para. D.4.18).

[24]See Vol. II, paras. 21–73 to 21–87, 23–18 and 23–27.

[25]Ten years (recorded or registered leases), 20 years (unrecorded leases)—Prescription and Limitation (Scotland) Act 1973, ss. 1, 2.

have been concluded.[25a] It is preferable that the landlord's consent should be incorporated in the assignation; if it is in a separate writing, that should be carefully preserved with the assignation.[26]

31–07 (3) **Terms of lease**. The assignee should examine carefully the whole terms and conditions of the lease which will continue to regulate his right of tenancy. The right further to assign or to sub-let, the rent and any provisions as to its review, the unexpired period of the lease, the permitted use of the premises, repair and maintenance obligations and the terms of the irritancy clause are of particular importance. As regards these matters in assignations of commercial or industrial premises, see the undernoted paragraph.[27]

31–08 (4) **Condition of premises—survey**. Where the value of the premises is substantial, a report from a professional surveyor on the condition of the premises should be obtained either by the assignee or by the assignor and the assignee jointly. A copy of the lease should be furnished to the surveyor so that he may confirm that the obligations of repair, maintenance, renewal or reinstatement have been satisfactorily implemented.

31–09 (5) **Apportionments**. The parties to the assignation will require to agree upon the apportionment of rent, rates, any service charge and other monetary obligations of the tenant.

Domestic property

31–10 Assignations of leases of domestic property are comparatively uncommon, the preferred method being renunciation of the existing lease and the granting of a new lease by the landlord to the proposed assignee. The right to assign will be impliedly excluded by law in the case of furnished lettings and may be so excluded in unfurnished lets of short duration but in any event is almost always conventionally excluded in terms of the lease, so that the landlord in most cases will require to be consulted. Leases of houses in the private sector often do not contain provisions for review of the rent, and it is in the interests of the landlord to obtain the current rental value of the subjects by way of a new lease to the incoming tenant. Moreover it is usually more satisfactory that the existing lease is renounced, a record of the condition of the house and any furniture is made and any wants of repair or loss or breakages of furniture adjusted between the landlord and the outgoing tenant, and a new lease granted to the incoming

[25a] Alternatively missives should be concluded conditional upon the consent of the landlord being obtained.

[26] The usual practice of solicitors is to register such writings in the Books of Council and Session, but registration of large numbers of ancillary documents of temporary importance increases unnecessarily the burden of administration of the Register. Once the landlord has accepted rent from the assignee for (say) two years, any right to object to the assignation will effectively have been waived.

[27] para. 31–12.

tenant. In the public sector the right to increase the rent is invariably reserved to the landlord and assignation of the lease with the landlord's consent, subject to the ground rules in Schedule 3 to the Tenants' Rights, Etc. (Scotland) Act 1980, is practicable, although even in such cases a renunciation and new lease may be preferred. It should be kept in view that any assignation of a lease of a house which is or is capable of being a matrimonial home or any renunciation of the tenancy of such a subject requires the consent or renunciation of the non-entitled spouse or an affidavit by the entitled spouse: as to forms of consent, renunciation or affidavit, see paragraphs 21–29, 21–30 or 21–31 in Volume II *supra*.

Agricultural subjects, building leases and mineral leases

31–11   Assignations of leases of agricultural holdings between tenants in arm's-length transactions are comparatively rare: when assignations are made they are usually by the tenant to another member of his family or to a family partnership in a form appropriate to an unrecorded or a recorded or registered lease as the case may be.

Assignations of building leases and mineral leases are also seldom encountered in practice. If desired, assignations should be in a form appropriate to a shorter lease or a recorded or registered long lease as may be appropriate.

Commercial or industrial premises

31–12   The principal matters to be considered are:

(1) A premium may be asked by the assignor as a consideration for the assignation. The amount depends upon the level of the existing rent and the period which will elapse before the rent next falls due for review. Theoretically the premium is being paid for the benefit of enjoyment of the existing rent for that period since the assumption is that as from the next review the assignee will be required to pay a full open-market rental, but the actual amount payable will be influenced by other considerations such as the anxiety of the assignor to free himself of liability under the lease and of the assignee to secure the premises. The value of tenant's improvements which may be suitable for the purpose of the assignee may also in certain cases be an element in determining the premium payable.

(2) The length of the unexpired period of the lease is also important, because on expiry of the lease there will be an open negotiation for its renewal between the landlord and the assignee which will not be regulated by the terms of a rent review clause.

(3) The assignee must be satisfied that the purposes for which he proposes to use the premises are within the ambit of the use clause; if not, an extension of the use clause will require to be negotiated with the landlord. Even if the permitted use is sufficient to permit of the use proposed by the assignee, it may be so restrictive that the assignee will

have a relatively narrow market should he seek to dispose of the lease before its expiry.

(4) The terms of the repair and maintenance clauses should be considered and a professional survey of the premises should be commissioned to ensure that there are no outstanding or contingent liabilities which may be prestable.

(5) The irritancy clause should be examined and it should be confirmed from the landlord that the assignor has complied with all his obligations under the lease and that no event has occurred which would entitle the landlord to commence irritancy proceedings. A landlord may safely give such confirmation as regards past monetary obligations of the assignor but he should be wary of giving an unqualified assurance as regards repair and maintenance obligations lest in future some remedial work is required which can be shown to stem from some act or omission of the assignor with the result that the landlord may be barred from enforcing his rights against the assignee by reason of the assurance given. Further, if the assignee is granting a heritable security over his interest and the lease does not contain provision for the benefit of a heritable creditor such as that suggested in the style in Clause 10 of paragraph 29–43 *supra*, a variation of the irritancy clause may require to be negotiated with the landlord. Since the landlord may be unwilling to give any such confirmation or assurance or to agree to such variation the assignee's offer should be made conditional upon them being obtained or procured.[28]

(6) Where the consent of the landlord to assignation is required, as it almost invariably is, it will be a condition of the assignee's offer that the consent will be procured.[29]

(7) If fittings of the assignor are being purchased, it should be checked that they are not subject to hire purchase or conditional sale agreements and are not in fact landlord's fixtures. Where a price is being paid it should be apportioned between the premium for the lease and the amount paid in respect of the acquisition of tenant's fittings since that may affect stamp duty and the tenant's accountants should advise on liability for value-added tax.

Form of assignation

31–13   (1) **Recorded or registered leases.** A form of assignation of leases which have been recorded in the Register of Sasines under the Registration of Leases (Scotland) Act 1857 is provided in Schedule A to the Act. The statutory form as amended by subsequent legislation runs[29a]:

---

[28]See cl. 12(4), para. 31–15 as regards confirmation that there have been no previous breaches of obligations.

[29]See cl. 7(d), para. 31–15. As to circumstances in which the landlord's consent is unreasonably withheld, see para. 29–30.

[29a]This is the basic statutory form; for a fuller modern style, see para. 31–17.

> I, AB, (*designation*), in consideration of the sum of
> now paid to me (*or otherwise as the case may be*) assign to CD,
> (*designation*), a lease granted by EF, (*designation*), in my favour
> (*or if not in assignor's favour name and design grantee*) of the
> subjects therein described lying in the County of
> dated   and recorded in the Register of Sasines for
> the County of   on   [but (*where the*
> *lease is assigned in part only*) in so far only as regards the
> following portion of the subjects leased; viz. (*specify particularly*
> *the portion*)]; with entry as at (*term of entry*); And (*where sub-*
> *lease*) I assign the rents from (*term*); And I grant warrandice;
> And I bind myself to free and relieve the said CD of all rents and
> burdens due to the landlord or others at and prior to the term of
> entry in respect of said lease; And I consent to registration for
> preservation and execution.   (*Stamp clause, if required*).
> (*To be attested*)

The form can be adapted for use in an assignation of the interest of a lessee which has been registered in the Land Register, describing the lease by reference to its title number. Section 16(3) of the Land Registration (Scotland) Act 1979 (which specifies the effect when the obligation of relief is omitted) is wide enough to include an assignation of a recorded lease or a registered leasehold interest, but the definition of the effect of a deed where there is such an omission is not in terms precisely appropriate to such an assignation and it is better to include the clause.

An assignation of a recorded lease may competently be granted by a person who has right to the lease by deducing his title in the assignation from the person having the last recorded title to it.[29b] If the assignor is not the original lessee but has a recorded title, specification of his title is unnecessary.[29c]

Before December 30, 1985, it was doubtful whether additional real conditions which would be binding on successors of the assignee could be effectively included in a partial assignation of a lease, although in practice that course was often adopted. Section 3 of the Law Reform (Miscellaneous Provisions) (Scotland) Act 1985 now permits that to be done with retrospective effect, and allows deeds of conditions authorised by section 32 of the Conveyancing (Scotland) Act 1874 and section 17 of the Land Registration (Scotland) Act 1979 to be used in relation to assignations of recorded leases or registered leasehold interests with the effect of creating the conditions real when the deed is recorded in the Register of Sasines or the obligation is registered in the Land Register. In consonance with the provisions of the Land Tenure Reform (Scotland) Act 1974, however, the only obligations of periodical payment which can thus be made real are payments (1) of rent or of an apportionment of rent, (2) in defrayal of a contribution towards some continuing cost related to the subjects of

---

[29b]Conveyancing (Scotland) Act 1924, s. 24.
[29c]Conveyancing and Feudal Reform (Scotland) Act 1970, s. 47 and Sched. 11.

the lease assigned or (3) under a heritable security. If an assignation purports to impose an obligation of periodical payment other than those mentioned, the assignation is not rendered void or unenforceable but has effect as if the improperly-included obligation had not been imposed.

(2) Other leases. There is no statutorily-prescribed form of assignation of leases which have not been recorded or where the lessee's interest has not been registered in the Land Register, and such assignations should be framed in accordance with traditional conveyancing practice.[30]

Conveyancing procedures

31–14   After appropriate investigation on preliminary matters has been made,[31] formal missives should be adjusted and completed.[32] Thereafter, in the case of recorded or registered leasehold interests the procedures outlined in Chapter 23 *supra* in the sale and purchase of heritable property should be followed *mutatis mutandis*, and the assignation should be recorded in the Register of Sasines or the assignee's interest registered in the Land Register as may be appropriate.[33]

Offer to purchase—commercial premises

31–15   The style of offer to purchase a lease of commercial premises will vary according to the characteristics of the premises and any special arrangements between the parties, but the following basic style covers matters which will normally be contained in it. The offer is framed on behalf of the assignee and not all of the conditions will in many cases be acceptable to the assignor.

> On behalf of our clients (*name and designation of purchasers*) (hereinafter called "the Assignee") we hereby offer to take from your clients (*name and designation of sellers*) (hereinafter called "the Assignor"), the tenants under a Lease dated
> between (*name and designation of landlord*) and [the Assignor] [(*name and designation of original tenant*) under which the Assignor is now tenant] of the subjects known as
> [and for the purpose of identification edged red on the plan annexed and signed as relative hereto, which plan is demonstrative only and not taxative], together with the landlord's and tenant's fittings and fixtures therein and thereon and the whole rights, common, mutual and exclusive, relative thereto as at present enjoyed in connection therewith (hereinafter called "the Premises") on the following terms and conditions:—

---

[30] For an illustration see para. 31–16.
[31] See paras. 31–04 to 31–09 and 31–12.
[32] For an example see para. 31–15.
[33] See para. 31–19.

1. The Assignee shall pay to the Assignor a premium of £ payable on the date of entry aftermentioned. The said premium shall be apportioned between the price payable for assignation of the said Lease and for the tenant's fittings and fixtures[33a] as such apportionment shall be agreed between the Assignor and the Assignee or failing agreement shall be determined by an expert to be appointed, failing agreement by the parties, by the Chairman for the time being of the Scottish Branch of the Royal Institution of Chartered Surveyors on the application of either party.

2. Entry and vacant possession of the Premises shall be given on or such later date as may be agreed by the Assignee.

3. Prior to the date of entry the Assignor shall produce letters, dated within 30 days before the date of entry, from the appropriate local or other relevant authority to the effect that (a) the roads, lanes, footpaths and sewers bounding or serving the Premises are public and maintained by the relevant local authority, (b) the Premises comply with the Offices, Shops and Railway Premises Act 1963 and the Health and Safety at Work, etc. Act 1974 and relative regulations, (c) the existing use of the Premises is the permitted use, free from conditions, under the Town and Country Planning (Scotland) Acts, (d) the Premises or the building of which they form part are not situated within a Redevelopment Area or Conservation Area and are not listed as being of architectural or historic interest and (e) there are no outstanding notices, orders or proposals under the Town and Country Planning (Scotland) Acts or other statutes or regulations or orders made thereunder which in the opinion of the Assignee would be likely to affect the Premises adversely. The Assignor will also produce a current unconditional Fire Certificate in respect of the Premises.

4. If any structural alterations have been made to the Premises within 10 years before the date of this offer the Assignor will exhibit in respect thereof all necessary planning consents and building warrants and certificates of completion under the Building (Scotland) Acts and the written consent thereto of the landlord under the said Lease and (if necessary) of the superior of the property which includes the Premises.

5. It is a suspensive condition of this offer that the Assignee obtains a report, in terms satisfactory to the Assignee, by a surveyor as to the structural condition of the Premises and the Assignor will permit access by the surveyor for such survey.

6. The Assignor warrants that the Premises contain no blue asbestos or other type of asbestos that may involve danger to occupiers and that no high alumina cement, calcium chloride or wood-wool slabs are incorporated in the structure of the Premises.

7. As regards the said Lease the Assignor will forthwith after conclusion of the missives following hereon (a) exhibit the Lease duly executed and a valid title to the tenant's interest thereunder (b) produce to the Assignee any amendments to or variations of the Lease, formal or informal, (c) satisfy the Assignee that there

---

[33a] An inventory specifying the tenant's fixtures and fittings included in the sale may be annexed for identification.

has been no breach of the obligations of the landlord or tenant under the said Lease, and (d) exhibit written evidence of the landlord's consent to the assignation of the said Lease to the Assignee or its nominees, to the proposed use of the Premises as [and to any alterations to the Premises proposed by the Assignee]. It is a condition of this offer that the whole terms and conditions of the said Lease and any amendments to or variations thereof are to the reasonable satisfaction of the Assignee.

8. As regards the property of which the Premises form part and the title of the landlord thereto the Assignor will after conclusion of the missives following hereon and before the date of entry satisfy the Assignee that (a) at the time when the said Lease was granted the landlord was heritable proprietor duly infeft in the said property with a valid marketable title thereto and clear searches in the Property and Personal Registers and that nothing has subsequently occurred which affects the validity of the said Lease, (b) any ground burdens affecting the said property have been redeemed in terms of the Land Tenure Reform (Scotland) Act 1974, (c) the said property and the use thereof are in conformity with the provisions and conditions of the title deeds thereof and there are no unduly onerous or unusual conditions contained therein and (d) there are no servitudes, wayleaves or other burdens in favour of third parties affecting the Premises.

9. The Assignor shall be responsible for the maintenance of the Premises in their present condition from the date of this offer until the date of entry and the Assignee shall have no liability for such maintenance, and the Assignor shall implement at its expense any statutory notices in respect of the Premises served prior to the date of entry.

10. In the event of failure by the Assignor to implement any of the conditions 7, 8 or 9 of this offer before the date of entry or in the event of the report of the surveyor in terms of condition 5 hereof not being satisfactory to the Assignee, the Assignee shall be entitled in its option either to waive such condition or to resile from the contract embodied in the missives to follow hereon without liability for damages.

11. The rent and all other monetary obligations of the tenant in terms of the said Lease shall be apportioned between the Assignor and the Assignee as at the date of entry.

12. In exchange for the premium the Assignor will at settlement:
(1) deliver a duly executed assignation of the said Lease in favour of the Assignee or its nominee;
(2) deliver or exhibit a good marketable title and [34][clear searches in the Property Register for 40 years prior to the date of registration of the said assignation or for such lesser period as the Assignee may agree and in the Personal Register against all relevant parties for the period of five years prior to the said date] [35][(i) a Form 10 Report brought down to the date of settlement and showing no entries prejudicial to the Assignor's interest, the cost (if any) of the said Report being the responsibility of the Assignor, and (ii) such documents and evidence including a plan as the Keeper may require to enable the Keeper to issue a Land

---

[34]Where assignation to be recorded in Register of Sasines—see para. 31–19.
[35]Where assignation induces first registration in Land Register—see para. 31–19.

Certificate in the name of the Assignee or its nominee as the registered tenant under the said Lease of the whole Premises and containing no exclusion of indemnity in terms of section 12(2) of the Land Registration (Scotland) Act 1979. The Land Certificate to be issued to the Assignee or its nominee will disclose no entry, deed or diligence prejudicial to the interest of the Assignee or its nominee other than such as are created by or against the Assignee or its nominee, or have been disclosed to and accepted by the Assignee prior to the date of settlement] *or* [36][(i) a Land Certificate (containing no exclusion of indemnity under section 12(2) of the Land Registration (Scotland) Act 1979) and all necessary links in title evidencing the Assignor's exclusive right as tenant of the Premises under the said Lease, (ii) a Form 12 Report brought down to the date of settlement and showing no entries prejudicial to the interest of the Assignor, the cost (if any) of such Report being the responsibility of the Assignor, and (iii) such documents and evidence as the Keeper may require to enable registration of the interest of the Assignee or its nominee as the registered tenant under the said Lease of the whole Premises without exclusion of indemnity under the said section 12(2). The Land Certificate to be issued to the Assignee or its nominee will disclose no entry, deed or diligence prejudicial to the Assignee or its nominee other than such as are created by or against the Assignee or its nominee, or have been disclosed to and accepted by the Assignee prior to the date of settlement]; [37][and also (a) deliver or exhibit searches in the Companies Register of Charges and the Company Files against the Assignor and all companies interested in the said Lease within the appropriate period of positive prescription brought down to the said date of entry and which disclose no notice or entry affecting the right of the Assignor to grant and deliver the said Assignation, (b) deliver an undertaking to continue the said searches to a date 30 days after the said date of entry which will also disclose no such notice or entry, (c) grant a certificate that no deeds have been granted by or with the consent of the Assignor other than those disclosed in the searches in the relevant Property Register, Companies Register of Charges or Company Files affecting the said property or the said Lease and that there are no circumstances known to the Assignor whereby proceedings for its liquidation have been or might be initiated before the expiry of 30 days after the said date of entry and (d) if any Floating Charge over the assets of the Assignor exists at the said date of entry procure and deliver a certificate from the holder thereof that the said Floating Charge has not crystallised and that there are no circumstances known to such holder which would indicate the possibility of the said Floating Charge crystallising within the said period of 30 days;][38]

(3) deliver a certificate from the landlord under the said Lease that (a) the terms and conditions thereof have not been subject to any amendment or variation, formal or informal, other than those already exhibited by the Assignor in accordance with clause 7 hereof and (b) neither the landlord nor the tenant is in breach

---

[36]Where tenant's interest already registered in Land Register—see para. 31–19.
[37]Applicable where the assignor is an incorporated company—see Vol. II, para. 21–87.
[38]See Vol. II, para. 21–87.

of any of their respective obligations under the said Lease and there are no outstanding disputes or claims thereunder; and
(4) deliver the said Lease or an official extract thereof and all documents ancillary thereto.
13. The missives of which this offer forms part shall remain in full force and effect until fully implemented, notwithstanding payment of the premium and delivery of the said Assignation.
14. This offer, unless previously withdrawn, will be deemed to be withdrawn unless an acceptance is received by us not later than

(To be attested or adopted as holograph)

Assignation of unrecorded or unregistered lease

31–16 We, AB Limited, *(designation)*, (hereinafter called "the Assignors") the Tenants under the Lease hereinafter assigned IN CONSIDERATION of £   paid to us by CD Limited, *(designation)*, hereby with the consent and concurrence of XY Limited, *(designation)*, being in right of the landlord's part of the said Lease (who and their successors in such right are hereinafter called "the Landlords") ASSIGN to the said CD Limited and their successors and permitted assignees (hereinafter called "the Assignees") the Lease between the said XY Limited and us the said AB Limited *(or otherwise as the case may be)* dated   and registered in the Books of Council and Session on   both in the year
(hereinafter called "the Lease") of ALL and WHOLE *(identifying description of let premises)* together with the fittings and fixtures therein and the parts, privileges and pertinents thereof (all which are hereinafter called "the Premises") and our whole right, title and interest in and to the Lease during the whole terms and years thereof still to run and with and under the whole clauses, rights and obligations therein contained AND THAT as from   19   (hereinafter called "the Date of Entry"); with power to the Assignees during the remaining period of the Lease to occupy the Premises, surrogating and substituting the Assignees in our full right and place in the Premises with full power to them to do everything requisite or necessary concerning the same which we could have done ourselves before the granting hereof, providing always as it is hereby expressly provided and declared that the Assignees shall be bound and obliged as by their execution hereof they bind and oblige themselves to make payment to the Landlords of the whole rents and others stipulated in the Lease to be paid by the tenants and to perform, implement and observe the whole other terms, conditions and obligations contained in the Lease so far as incumbent on the tenants thereunder but that in respect only of the period from the Date of Entry until termination of the Lease; And we the Assignors bind and oblige ourselves to free and relieve the Assignee of all rents and obligations and liabilities due to and prestable by the Landlords and others under the Lease in respect of the period prior to the Date of Entry; And the Landlords by their execution hereof accept the Assignees in full

right and place of the Assignors under the Lease:[39] [And the
Landlords agree and confirm that the whole obligations and
liabilities of the Assignors as tenants in terms of the Lease have
been fully met, implemented and fulfilled as at the Date of Entry
and that there are no circumstances existing in respect of the
Premises as at the Date of Entry which would entitle the
Landlords to irritate or terminate the Lease, or alternatively, in
so far as any of the said obligations or liabilities have not been so
met, implemented or fulfilled or the conditions of the Lease have
been infringed, breached or otherwise departed from by the
Assignors, then such acts, omissions or neglect (if any) of the
Assignors shall be held to have been acquiesced in and condoned
by the Landlords for the remaining period of the Lease but
without prejudice to any legal rights or remedies not affecting the
rights of the Assignees hereunder which the Landlords may have
against the Assignors arising from such acts, omissions or
neglect:] (*If Assignors not the original tenants, insert brief
deduction of their title to the Lease*)[40]: [And we the Assignors
undertake to pay all reasonable costs, charges, fees and expenses
of the Landlords and their solicitors in respect of the consideration, execution and completion of this Assignation:][41] And we
the Assignors grant warrandice. (*Stamp clause, if required*)

(To be attested)
(Stamp)[42]

Assignation of recorded lease[43]

31–17   We, AB Limited, (*designation*), IN CONSIDERATION of the
sum of £   now paid to us hereby [with the consent of XY
Limited, (*designation*), (who and their successors as landlords
under the Lease hereby assigned are hereinafter called "the
Landlords")] ASSIGN to CD Limited, (*designation*), a Lease
dated   and recorded in the Division of the Register
of Sasines for the County of   on   both in
the year 19   granted by the said XY Limited in our favour (*or
otherwise as the case may be*) of ALL and WHOLE (*identifying
description of subjects leased*) in the Parish of   and
County of   [but (*where the lease is assigned in part
only*) in so far only as regards the following portion of the
subjects leased, viz: (*specify particularly the portion*)], together
with the fittings and fixtures therein and the parts, privileges
and pertinents thereof; with entry as at   :[44] [And
(*where sub-lease*) I assign the rents from (*term*);] (*If the assignees
are to be expressly bound to implement the obligations of the
tenant for the remaining period of the lease insert a provision to*

---

[39]Landlords may be unwilling to have the following bracketed provisions or all of them
included—see para. 31–12.

[40]Deduction of title is normal practice in unrecorded or unregistered assignations where the granter
is not the grantee of the lease whereby the right assigned was created.

[41]The provision as to payment of the landlord's costs will vary according to the bargain.

[42]See para. 31–21.

[43]Based on statutory form—Registration of Leases (Scotland) Act 1857, s. 3 and Sched. A.

[44]If granter, although not the original lessee, has a recorded title no deduction of title is
required—Conveyancing and Feudal Reform (Scotland) Act 1970, s. 47 and Sched. 11. If the granter
has right to the lease by a title which has not been recorded in the Register of Sasines insert a
deduction of title as in note 4 to Sched. J to the Conveyancing (Scotland) Act 1924.

that effect as in paragraph 31–16): (*Insert any confirmation by the Landlords as to implement of obligations before the date of entry as in paragraph 31–16*): And we the said AB Limited grant warrandice; and we bind ourselves to free and relieve the said CD Limited of all rents and burdens due to the Landlords and others at and prior to the said date of entry in respect of the said Lease. (*Stamp clause, if required*).
(*To be attested*)

(*Stamp*)[45]

Assignation of tenant's interest registered in the Land Register

31–18   We, AB Limited, (*designation*), IN CONSIDERATION of the sum of £   paid to us by CD Limited, (*designation*), ASSIGN to the said CD Limited ALL and WHOLE the subjects (*postal address if appropriate or other short description*) registered under Title Number   [46] and the fittings and fixtures therein and the parts, privileges and pertinents thereof: With entry as at   : And we XY Limited, (*designation*), the Landlords in the Lease between us and the said AB Limited dated   , the interest of the tenant under which Lease constitutes the title registered under the said Title Number, hereby CONSENT to this Assignation: (*Insert any confirmation by the Landlords as to implement of obligations before date of entry as in paragraph 31–16*): (*If the assignees are to be expressly bound to implement the obligations of the tenant for the remaining period of the lease insert a provision to that effect as in paragraph 31–16*): And we the said AB Limited grant warrandice; and we the said AB Limited bind ourselves to free and relieve the said CD Limited of all rents and burdens due to the said XY Limited and others at and prior to the said date of entry in respect of the said Lease.   (*Stamp clause, if required*).
(*To be attested*)
(*Stamp*)[47]

Completion of assignee's title

31–19   **(1) Shorter leases.** Where the duration of the lease does not exceed 20 years the assignation should be intimated to the landlord by sending to the landlord by registered post or recorded delivery service a copy of the assignation, unless the landlord's consent was incorporated in the assignation. Registration of the assignation in the Books of Council and Session is not sufficient intimation.

(2) Long leases (duration more than 20 years). Where the premises are situated in an area which has not, at the time when the assignee's title is being completed, become operational for the purposes of registration of title, the assignation should be recorded in the Register of

---

[45]See para. 31–21.
[46]If part only of leasehold subjects is assigned the description should be of "ALL and WHOLE (describe the part so as to identify it clearly preferably with reference to a plan) being part of " and continue with reference to the whole subjects as registered under their title number.
[47]See para. 31–21.

Sasines. Where the premises are situated in an area which has, at the time when the assignee's title is being completed, become operational the right of the assignee can be made real only by registration of his interest in the Land Register even if (i) the lease itself was recorded in the Register of Sasines or the tenant's right was completed simply by possession, or (ii) the assignation was executed or delivered before the area became operational.[48] Also if the original tenant's right under the lease or the right of a previous assignee was registered in the Land Register the right of the current assignee must also be registered in the Land Register since all subsequent dealings with a registered interest require to be so registered.

Where recording of the assignation in the Register of Sasines is appropriate and the assignor has a recorded title or has deduced title in the assignation,[49] then the assignation may be recorded with a warrant of registration on behalf of the assignee. Where the lease has not been recorded but the assignee wishes to have a recorded title, *e.g.* in order to grant a standard security, a notice of title in favour of the assignee should be expede and recorded along with the lease docqueted with reference to the notice of title and the warrant of registration should refer to the lease.[50]

Where registration of the assignee's interest in the Land Register is appropriate then (a) if the assignor's title is recorded in the Register of Sasines, or is deduced from the title of his author so recorded, application for registration should be made by the assignee on Form 1, or (b) if the assignor's interest has already been registered in the Land Register application for registration should be made by the assignee on Form 2 (assignation of whole registered interest) or Form 3 (partial assignation of registered interest), as the case may be. In the circumstances where the lease has not been recorded in the Register of Sasines but the assignee wishes to have his interest registered the Keeper should be consulted as to the appropriate procedure, but in principle the assignee, as the person now entitled to the tenant's interest under the lease, may apply on Form 1 for registration of that interest, the application being accompanied by the lease and any deeds whereby the right to the tenant's interest has been acquired by the assignor.

Incorporation of additional real conditions in assignations

31–20   Where it is desired to take advantage of the facility, created by section 3 of the Law Reform (Miscellaneous Provisions) (Scotland) Act 1985, of introducing in an assignation of a long lease additional conditions which will be binding on singular successors of the

---

[48]R.T.P.B., para. D.4.18.
[49]See para. 31–17, n. 44.
[50]Conveyancing (Scotland) Act 1924. s. 24(3). Sched. J, note 5, Sched. B, note 7, and Sched. F. note 5.

assignee,[51] the following points should be noted:

(1) If the additional conditions affect the interests of the landlord and the tenant *inter se* the consent of the landlord will be required.

(2) The statutory limitations upon obligations of periodical payment must be observed.[52]

The facility will be most useful when a number of partial assignations of the tenant's interest in the let premises are being granted. It is permissible to insert the additional conditions in each partial assignation, but in most cases the use of a deed of conditions which can be incorporated by reference in each of the partial assignations will be the more convenient method. Note that a deed of conditions will automatically create the conditions real when it is recorded in the Register of Sasines or the obligations are registered in the Land Register, as the case may be, unless the application of section 17 of the Land Registration (Scotland) Act 1979 is expressly excluded in the deed.

Stamp duty

1–21 An assignation of a lease for a premium or other valuable consideration is liable to stamp duty as a conveyance on sale.[53] If any sum is paid in respect of moveable fittings or fixtures it should be excluded from the premium for the assignation of the tenant's right to the lease shown in the assignation. As to the assessment of stamp duty on assignations of building leases, see Volume II, paragraph 22–34 *supra*.

SUB-LEASES

Power to sub-let

1–22 In general the right of a tenant to sub-let at common law is regulated by the same rules as apply to his right to assign.[54] The duration of the sub-let cannot be greater than that of the main lease. Sub-letting is usually prohibited contractually in leases of residential property in the private sector and prohibited except with the consent of the landlord in leases of such property in the public sector. Leases of agricultural holdings also usually prohibit sub-letting except with the consent of the landlord. In leases of commercial or industrial premises sub-letting of part of the premises is normally prohibited absolutely, but sub-letting of the whole premises may be permitted with the consent of the landlord.

---

[51]See para. 31–13.
[52]1985 Act, s. 3(3)—see para. 31–13.
[53]See Vol. II, para. 22–32.
[54]See para. 31–02.

Legal effect of sub-letting

31–23   An effective sub-lease gives a real right to the sub-tenant under the Leases Act 1449 or the Registration of Leases (Scotland) Act 1857 in a question with both the head landlord and the tenant who has granted it, subject to the qualification that if the sub-lease is a long lease of more than 20 years' duration and the premises are situated in an area which has become operational for the purposes of registration of title a real right can be obtained only by registration of the sub-tenant's interest in the Land Register.[55] As between the landlord and the principal tenant the latter remains liable for all his obligations under the principal lease. There is no privity of contract between the principal landlord and the sub-tenant and there is no right of action *ex contractu* between them, but the sub-tenant is exposed to risk of irritancy of the head lease, which will effectively also terminate the sub-lease, in the event of breach by the sub-tenant of a condition of the head lease. As between the principal tenant and the sub-tenant their respective rights and obligations are regulated by the sub-lease.[56] From a conveyancing aspect the result is that the sub-tenant is concerned to ensure the validity of the main lease and the continued observance of the obligations of the principal tenant thereunder and also the validity of the sub-lease and the consonance of its provisions with those of the head lease.

Preliminary considerations

31–24   The matters to be considered in a transaction of sub-letting to some extent are similar to those already discussed in relation to the grant of an assignation of a lease[57] with the addition of others peculiar to the granting of a sub-lease.

31–25   **(1) Title**. The title of the landlord to grant the principal lease should be checked as in the case of an assignation.[58] Further it is necessary to verify that the principal tenant's title is valid, which involves the validity of the principal lease and, if a long lease, its recording or the registration of the principal tenant's interest. If the principal lease has been assigned the sufficiency of the title of the assignee who is now granting the sub-lease should likewise be verified.

31–26   **(2) Right to sub-let**. The right of the principal tenant to grant the sub-lease should be confirmed and any necessary consent of the landlord obtained and incorporated in the sub-lease.

31–27   **(3) The principal lease**. The principal lease should be examined in detail to ensure that its terms, with which the sub-lease must be

---

[55]Land Registration (Scotland) Act 1979, s. 3(3).
[56]For a fuller account of the relationships of parties, see Paton and Cameron, *op. cit.*, 167–169.
[57]See paras. 31–04 to 31–08.
[58]See para. 31–05.

consonant, are acceptable. It should also be confirmed, preferably in the form of a certificate from the principal landlord if obtainable, that the whole obligations as to payment of rent, and otherwise, have been duly implemented by the principal tenant.

31–28 **(4) Condition of premises—survey.** A report by a professional surveyor should be obtained as to the condition of the premises. If the sub-lease is of a part only of the premises let under the principal lease the report should not be restricted to the part to be sub-let; it is important to know that the whole of the premises let under the principal lease have been properly maintained in accordance with the principal tenant's obligations thereunder.

31–29 **(5) Heritable securities.** If there is an existing standard security over the subjects owned by the proprietor or over the recorded principal lease or the registered interest of the principal tenant therein, the consent of the heritable creditor to the sub-lease must be obtained.[59]

Drafting problems

31–30 **Choice of method.** Where the whole subjects of the principal lease are being sub-let the object of the principal tenant is to pass on to the sub-tenant all the obligations of the principal tenant under the head lease, except with regard to the duration and rent and any for which the principal tenant proposes to retain liability. The duration of the sub-lease cannot exceed the unexpired period of the head lease; the rent is negotiable but the head lease may have imposed conditions on that matter, *e.g.* the charge of a premium may have been prohibited and it may have been stipulated that the sub-rent should not be less than that payable under the head lease. Moreover the obligations of the sub-tenant must be consistent with those imposed on the principal tenant in terms of the head lease. That result may be achieved either (1) by specifying only the essential elements of the sub-lease and any particular provisions which differ from those in the head lease (which must nevertheless be compatible with them) and on other matters incorporating the relevant provisions of the head lease by reference or (2) by framing the sub-lease at length incorporating such provisions as differ from those of the head lease and repeating *ad longum* the other obligations thereof. Either method requires careful drafting but the first method results in a shorter document and diminishes the risk of inaccurate reproduction of many of the terms of the head lease: that is the method adopted in the style of sub-lease in paragraph 31–35 *infra*. Whichever method is employed the draftsman must beware of slavishly adopting or repeating all the provisions of the principal lease. For example, if certain acts are prohibited in the principal lease except with the consent of the landlord which shall not be unreasonably

---

[59]Conveyancing and Feudal Reform (Scotland) Act 1970, Sched. 3, s.c. 6; *Trade Development Bank* v. *Warriner & Mason (Scotland) Ltd.*, 1980 S.C. 74.

withheld, there is a case for prohibiting such actions in the sub-lease except with the consent of the granter without any qualification as to consent not being unreasonably withheld. That will obviate a separate argument with the sub-tenant as to the reasonableness of refusal of consent. Again, if certain clauses of the principal lease are badly or ambiguously framed, the opportunity may be taken of restating them in clear terms in the sub-lease; if that is done, however, the draftsman must ensure that the reframed clauses are not more favourable to the sub-tenant than the corresponding clauses of the principal lease.

Where only a part of the premises in the principal lease is being sub-let (which is seldom permitted) the drafting problems may be more complex. The part sub-let must be described and, in a long sub-lease where the interest of the sub-tenant is to be registered in the Land Register, the description should be made by reference to the title number of the head lease and to a plan which will enable the Keeper to identify the sub-let subjects on the Ordnance Map. The same choice of method as already outlined in a sub-lease of the whole premises is available but in a sub-lease of part the second *ad longum* method may be easier to handle.

31–31   Rent review. In a sub-lease of the whole premises let by the principal lease either (1) the sub-lease may specify a separate procedure for review of rent with independent provisions for arbitration, although theoretically that may result in the rents payable under the principal lease and the sub-lease being different, or (2) the sub-lease may provide for the sub-rent being increased automatically in accordance with variations under the rent review clause of the principal lease. The latter alternative may not be acceptable to the sub-tenant since he will have no locus to make representations in the proceedings for review and, if adopted, provision should be made for a right of representation being given to the sub-tenant in the rent review negotiations and in any arbitration proceedings.

In a sub-lease of part of the premises in the principal lease the like choice of method is available, but if the first method is adopted the sub-lease should provide that in the event of arbitration being required the same arbiter should determine the increase of rent under both the principal lease and the sub-lease. If the second method is adopted, the increase in the sub-rent being a stated proportion of the increase in the principal rent, a right of representation should be given to the sub-tenant in the rent review negotiations and in any arbitration proceedings.

31–32   Insurance. In the usual situation where under the principal lease the landlord insures the premises but the premiums are reimbursed by the tenant, a sub-lease of the whole premises should provide for repayment of the premiums by the sub-tenant to the principal tenant, who should be obliged to enforce the principal landlord's obligations in the event of damage or destruction resulting from an insured risk. If the rent payable under the sub-lease is greater than that payable under the principal lease the insurance against loss of rent will require to be increased appropriately, the sub-tenant being obliged to pay the difference in the premium in respect of the excess cover.

In a sub-lease of part only of the premises let in the principal lease, an agreed proportion of the insurance premium will be repayable by the sub-tenant to the principal tenant.

31–33 **Repair and maintenance**. The terms of the sub-lease as regards the obligations of repair, maintenance and reinstatement depend to some extent upon the duration of the sub-lease. If the sub-lease is for a lengthy period, the principal tenant will wish to be relieved of these obligations by the sub-tenant (in the case of a sub-lease of part *quoad* that part) and the sub-tenant may reasonably be asked to do so. On the other hand if the sub-lease is for a relatively short period the sub-tenant should be wary of undertaking an obligation which is potentially onerous, and the matter will require to be resolved by negotiation between the parties and the careful adjustment of the agreed obligations of the sub-tenant to be inserted in the sub-lease.

31–34 **Irritancy**. A sub-tenant may lose his right of tenancy by irritancy either of the sub-lease or of the principal lease. In the latter circumstance the sub-tenant, if the irritancy was not incurred by reason of any act or omission of the sub-tenant or any person for whose actions he was responsible, will have a claim of damages against the principal tenant, but that may be of little value in the events which have occurred. The sub-tenant may seek protection by stipulating for an undertaking by the proprietor that, if the principal lease is irritated by reason of breaches or in circumstances for which the sub-tenant was not responsible, the proprietor will grant a direct lease of the sub-let premises to the sub-tenant for the unexpired period of the sub-lease and otherwise on the terms and conditions thereof.[59a] The proprietor, however, will not always be willing to give such an undertaking, especially if sub-letting has been adopted in preference to assignation because the proprietor was not satisfied with the financial status of the sub-tenant. A compromise solution may be to make the undertaking conditional upon the provision, if the proprietor so requires, of an acceptable guarantee.

[59a] It will be appreciated that this undertaking will be enforceable only against the proprietor who grants it and will not bind singular successors.

Style of sub-lease[60]

31–35

SUB-LEASE
between
XY Limited, (*designation*)
Companies Regn. No.
(hereinafter called "the Mid-landlord")
and
GH Limited, (*designation*)
Companies Regn. No.
(hereinafter called "the Sub-tenant")

1. *Definitions and Interpretation*
In this sub-lease unless there is something in the subject or context inconsistent therewith:

(1) "Lease" means the lease of the Premises between (*name and designation of proprietor*) ("the Landlord") and the Mid-landlord dated   and registered in the Books of Council and Session on   [61];

(2) "Sub-lease" means this sub-lease;

(3) "Mid-landlord" comprises the Mid-landlord above specified and all persons succeeding to the interest of the Mid-landlord in the Premises;

(4) "Sub-tenant" comprises the Sub-tenant above specified and its permitted assignees or sub-under-tenants and in the case of an individual shall include his executors or representatives;

(5) the interpretation provisions contained in clause 1 of the Lease shall also apply, where applicable, in the Sub-lease;

(6) expressions to which meanings are assigned by clause 1.2 of the Lease shall have the same meanings, unless other meanings are expressly assigned to them, when used in the Sub-lease;

(7) "Date of Review" means each of the dates represented by the same expression in the Lease which falls within the Period of the Sub-lease;

(8) "Revised Rent" means the amount of the rent specified in Clause 3 hereof as increased at each Date of Review in accordance with the provisions contained in Part II of the Schedule to the Lease;

(9) "Date of Expiry" means the date of expiry or sooner termination of the Sub-lease (however the same be determined);

(10) where any matter is expressed to require the consent or approval of the Landlord under the Lease such matter shall also require the consent or approval of the Mid-landlord, but such consent or approval shall not be unreasonably withheld, the consent or approval of the Landlord being a necessary, but not a conclusive, condition for the grant of such consent or approval by the Mid-landlord.[62]

2. *Period of the Sub-lease*
The Mid-landlord hereby sub-lets to the Sub-tenant (but

---

[60]Based on style prepared by Styles Committee of the Law Society of Scotland by permission of the Society. The principal lease to which the style relates is that in para. 29–45 of commercial subjects, and the sub-lease is of the whole premises let under the principal lease.

[61]If recorded in Register of Sasines specify division of Register and date of recording; if mid-landlord's interest registered in Land Register refer to title number.

[62]See para. 31–30 for possible variation.

excluding assignees and sub-under-tenants legal or voluntary and creditors and managers for creditors in any form except where permitted under the Sub-Lease) the Premises subject to the same provisos, conditions and disclaimers in favour of the Mid-landlord and where applicable the Landlord as are created in Part V of the said Schedule in favour of the Landlord and that for the period (the Period of the Sub-Lease) from the [   ] day of [   ] One thousand nine hundred and [   ] ("the Date of Entry") until the [   ] day of [   ] and the Sub-tenant accepts the Premises in their present condition.

3.   *Sub-tenant's monetary obligations*
The Sub-tenant hereby undertakes:
Rent
(1) to pay to the Mid-landlord the yearly rent of [£   ] or from each Date of Review the corresponding Revised Rent by equal quarterly payments in advance at the terms of [   ] clear of all deductions whatsoever, the first of such payments to be made on the Date of Entry, such rent or Revised Rent to be paid without any written demand and, if the Mid-landlord so requires, by Banker's Order;
Reimbursement
(2) to reimburse the Mid-landlord on demand all payments made by way of reimbursement or otherwise by the Mid-landlord to the Landlord under the Lease with the exception of:
(i) the rent and the Revised Rent provided for in the Lease and
(ii) interest on and any expenses incurred by the Landlord in procuring payment of any sum of money payable or reimbursable to the Landlord under the Lease which shall have become due but remain unpaid by the Mid-landlord[63];
Rates and other charges
(3) to pay when due (or reimburse the Mid-landlord on demand any sum paid by the Mid-landlord for) the rates, taxes, duties, charges, assessments, impositions and out-goings for the payment of which the Mid-landlord is responsible under clause 3(3) of the Lease other than taxes arising on the rent payable under the Sub-lease or taxes arising on the disposal or deemed disposal by the Mid-landlord of or other dealing by the Mid-landlord with its interest in the Premises.[63]
Interest on payments in arrears
(4) to pay on demand to the Mid-landlord, without prejudice to any other right, remedy or power available to the Mid-landlord, interest at the Prescribed Rate on any rent or any other sum of money payable or reimbursable to the Mid-landlord under the Sub-lease which shall have become due but remain unpaid for fourteen days, such interest to run (as well after as before any judgment) from the date when the same shall become due until payment thereof.

4.   *Sub-Tenant's further obligations*
The Sub-tenant also undertakes:
Fulfilment of Mid-landlord's obligations

---

[63]See Note 3.

(1) to fulfil the obligations of a non-monetary nature undertaken by the Mid-landlord under the Lease[64];

Entry to Premises
(2) in any case where the Landlord has reserved a right of entry to the Premises under the Lease, to permit such right to be exercised by the Landlord and/or the Mid-landlord subject to any condition in the Lease;

Expenses
(3) to reimburse the Mid-landlord all expenses reasonably incurred by the Mid-landlord:

(a) incidental to the preparation and service of all notices and schedules relating to deficiencies in repair or requiring the Sub-tenant to remedy the breach of any of its obligations under the Sub-lease whether the same be served before or after the Date of Expiry;

(b) in the preparation and service of a schedule of dilapidations before or after the Date of Expiry;

(c) in procuring the remedy of any breach of an obligation or the payment of arrears due by the Sub-tenant under the Sub-lease;

Application for consent or approval
(4) upon making an application for any consent or approval which is required under the Sub-lease to disclose to the Mid-landlord such information as the Mid-landlord may reasonably require and pay the Mid-landlord's proper expenses in connection with such application (including applications where consent or approval is refused or an application is withdrawn);

Alienation
(5) not at any time to assign, sub-underlet or otherwise dispose of or for any purpose or in any way deal with the Sub-tenant's interest in or part with or share possession or occupation of part only of the Premises;

(6) not at any time to sub-underlet the Premises as a whole;

(7) not at any time to assign or otherwise dispose of or for any purpose or in any way deal with the Sub-tenant's interest in or part with or share possession or occupation of the whole of the Premises without the consents of the Landlord and the Mid-landlord (neither of which consents shall be unreasonably withheld).[64a]

5. *Mid-landlord's obligations*
The Mid-landlord hereby undertakes provided that the Sub-tenant indemnifies the Mid-landlord against any costs reasonably incurred by or awarded against the Mid-landlord in the course of the fulfilment of such undertaking:

(1) on the request of the Sub-tenant unless such request is demonstrably unreasonable having regard to the Mid-landlord's interest in the Premises;

(a) to adopt any procedure designed to enforce the fulfilment of the obligations undertaken by the Landlord under the Lease;

(b) to require the Landlord to include any additional risk in the Insured Risks;

---

[64]See Note 4.
[64a]See para. 31–30.

(c) to require the Landlord to adopt a greater sum as "Loss of Rent";

(d) to require the Landlord to adopt a greater amount as "Reinstatement Value";

(2) in relation to Rent Review:

(a) not, without the approval of the Sub-tenant (such approval not to be unreasonably withheld having regard to the Mid-landlord's interest in the Premises), to agree with the Landlord on the Revised Rent nor on the surveyor to be nominated for the purpose of determination of the Revised Rent;

(b) if so required by the Sub-tenant, to request the nomination by the Chairman for the time being of the Scottish Branch of the Royal Institution of Chartered Surveyors of a surveyor for the purpose of such determination.[65]

6. *Mid-landlord's remedies*

The same rights and remedies as are available to the Landlord against the Tenant under the Lease shall be available to the Mid-landlord against the Sub-tenant under the Sub-lease and shall be subject to the same conditions.

7. *Suspension of rent*

If the Premises shall at any time during the Period of the Sub-lease be so damaged or destroyed as to render the Premises unfit for occupation and use in whole or in part in accordance with the terms and provisions of the Sub-lease, then (unless this Sub-lease has been terminated by *rei interitus* in consequence of such damage) the rent or the Revised Rent or a fair proportion thereof according to the nature and extent of the damage sustained shall be suspended (but if such destruction or damage is attributable to an Insured Risk to the extent only that the Insurers meet the Landlord's claim under the policy for the Loss of Rent) until the Premises shall again be rendered fit for occupation and use, or if such destruction or damage is attributable to an Insured Risk until the Loss of Rent insurance effected by the Landlord shall be exhausted, if earlier.

8. *Irritancy*

Subject to the provisions of sections 4, 5 and 6 of the Law Reform (Miscellaneous Provisions) (Scotland) Act 1985, if the rent or the Revised Rent or any part thereof shall at any time be in arrear for fourteen days after the same shall have become due (whether legally demanded or not) and shall remain unpaid for a further period of ten days after demand by the Mid-landlord under threat of irritancy, or if there shall be a breach of any of the obligations undertaken by the Sub-tenant under the Sub-lease which shall not have been remedied by the Sub-tenant within such reasonable period as shall be allowed by the Mid-landlord in a notice requesting the remedy of such breach under threat of irritancy, or if the Sub-tenant shall become apparently insolvent or shall make any arrangement with creditors or shall go into liquidation whether voluntary or compulsory (otherwise than a voluntary liquidation of a solvent company for the purpose of amalgamation or reconstruction) or has an administration order made in relation to it [or being a firm shall be sequestrated,] then

---

[65] The sub-tenant may also be given the right to make representations to the surveyor—see para. 31–31.

and in any such case it shall be lawful for the Mid-landlord by notice to the Sub-tenant to bring the Sub-lease to an end forthwith and to repossess the Premises as if the Sub-lease had not been granted but without prejudice to any right of action or remedy of the Mid-landlord in respect of any previous breach of any of the obligations undertaken by the Sub-tenant under the Sub-lease.[66]

9.   *Notices*

The provisions for notices contained in clause 9 of the Lease shall apply also under the Sub-lease as if "the Mid-landlord" had been substituted for "the Landlord" and "the Sub-tenant" had been substituted for "the Tenant".

10.   *Consent to registration*

The parties consent to registration hereof for preservation and execution.

(To be attested)
(Stamp duty)[67]

NOTES

Clause 1

1. If the sub-lease is of part only of the premises in the principal lease, a definition of the part sub-let will require to be inserted.

2. It is convenient to have the same dates of rent review as in the principal lease. If the first of these dates occurs soon after the date of entry in the sub-lease, it may be desirable to elide a review on that date by modifying the definition of date of review appropriately.

Clause 3(2) and (3)

3. In a sub-lease of part only of the premises in the principal lease, the sub-tenant's responsibility will be restricted to a stated proportion based on the rental value of the sub-let part to the rental value of the whole premises.

Clause 3(1) and (3)

4. In a sub-lease of part only, the obligations of the sub-tenant will be applicable only *quoad* the part sub-let.

Clause 8

5. Consider the insertion of provisions for the benefit of liquidators or receivers or heritable creditors upon insolvency of the sub-tenant—see para. 29–43, cl. 10.

6. Consider negotiation of arrangement with landlord for the granting of a direct lease to the sub-tenant in the event of irritancy of the mid-landlord's right—see para. 31–34. Such an arrangement will be adjusted with landlord and will not appear in the sub-lease.

VARIATION OF LEASES

Variations of formal leases

31–36   Alterations to or variations of the terms of formal written leases may

---

[66]See notes 5 and 6.
[67]See para. 25–44.

be effected (1) by subsequent agreement in probative or holograph writing, (2) by improbative writing followed by homologation or *rei interventus*, (3) by verbal agreement similarly followed or (4) by actings of parties provable by parole evidence which necessarily and unequivocally import acquiescence in alteration of the terms of the formal lease or which constitute waiver of a particular condition.[68]

31–37 **(1) Alteration by probative or holograph agreement.** The proper method of effecting alterations of the provisions of a formal written lease which are intended to be binding upon successors of the parties is by the execution in probative or holograph form of an agreement modifying the terms of the lease. The agreement may be separate or endorsed by way of memorandum on the lease itself. The latter method is preferable in practice in order to ensure that the changes are brought to the notice of parties involved in subsequent dealings with the interest of the landlord or the tenant. If the lease has been recorded in the Register of Sasines or if the tenant's interest has been registered in the Land Register the agreement should likewise be recorded or the variation of its terms registered.

31–38 **(2) Alteration by improbative agreement followed by homologation or rei interventus.** A formal lease may be varied by a subsequent improbative agreement of parties if actings have followed thereon which amount to homologation or *rei interventus*.[69] In general the rule is similar to that relating to the constitution of contracts with regard to heritable property.[70]

31–39 **(3) Alteration by verbal agreement followed by homologation or rei interventus.** The terms of a formal lease may also be varied by a verbal agreement of parties followed by actings amounting to homologation or *rei interventus*.[71] The verbal agreement must be proved by writ or oath, but parole evidence of the actings is competent. In such circumstances, however, there is a further question whether the variations are personal to the parties or are binding on singular successors. A verbal agreement to alteration of the terms of the lease, unsupported by homologation or *rei interventus*, is not enough.[72]

31–40 **(4) Alteration by acquiescence or waiver.** In the absence of any agreement, written or verbal, however, there may be circumstances in which the actings of parties establish an implied agreement to alter the terms of a formal lease if such actings necessarily and unequivocally demonstrate acquiescence in departure from or non-observance of a particular provision of the lease[73] or waiver of a condition of it, and

---

[68]*Carron Co.* v. *Henderson's Trs.* (1896) 23 R. 1042 *per* Lord Ordinary (Kyllachy) at 1048.
[69]*Gowans' Trs.* v. *Carstairs* (1862) 24 D. 1382; *Walker* v. *Flint* (1863) 1 M. 417; *Gibson* v. *Adams* (1875) 3 R. 144 (cases relating to the constitution of a lease but the same rule applies to alterations).
[70]See Vol. II, paras. 15–17 to 15–21.
[71]*Bargaddie Coal Co.* v. *Wark* (1859) 3 Macq. 467.
[72]*Kirkpatrick* v. *Allanshaw Coal Co.* (1880) 8 R. 327.
[73]*Bargaddie Coal Co.* v. *Wark, supra*; *Kirkpatrick* v. *Allanshaw Coal Co., supra*.

such actings may be proved by parole evidence. There is a difference between a plea of acquiescence and one of waiver: the former normally involves the element of personal bar requiring loss or damage to the party concerned, whereas waiver does not require the occurrence of such loss or damage.[74] In general, acquiescence or waiver bars a claim for past contraventions but does not amount to alteration of the contract for the future.[75]

31-41   **(5) Variation by Lands Tribunal for Scotland.** Obligations created in a long lease of duration exceeding 20 years fall within the definition of land obligations in subsection (2) of section 1 of the Conveyancing and Feudal Reform (Scotland) Act 1970 and so may be varied or discharged by the Lands Tribunal for Scotland on any of the grounds specified in subsection (3).[76] But it is incompetent to obtain a variation under that section of a provision in a lease excluding assignees and sub-tenants: the obligations which may be so varied are ones which involve a positive and onerous duty to do or refrain from doing something, not ones which define the persons who may be tenants under the lease.[77]

TERMINATION OF LEASES

Removings

31-42   A lease may be terminated on the expiry of the period of the lease by an action of removing at the instance of the landlord after due notice. If neither party has given due notice of termination the lease will continue by tacit relocation.[78] The topic of removings falls within the field of civil remedies and procedure rather than of conveyancing, and is not treated in detail in this work. Reference may be made to the undernoted texts for fuller accounts of the general law regarding ordinary and extraordinary removings[79] and the special statutory provisions regarding protected and secure tenancies under the Rent (Scotland) Act 1984,[80] tenancies of shops,[80a] agricultural tenancies[81] and small landholdings and crofts.[82]

Rescission by tenant

31-43   If the landlord is in material breach of a condition of the lease[83] or

---

[74]*Banks* v. *Mecca Bookmakers (Scotland) Ltd.*, 1982 S.L.T. 150.
[75]*Carron Co.* v. *Henderson's Trs.*, *supra*; *Earl of Kintore* v. *Pirie & Sons Ltd.* (1903) 5 F. 818 at 849.
[76]*McQuiban* v. *Eagle Star Insurance Co.*, 1972 S.L.T. (Lands Tr.) 39.
[77]*George T. Fraser Ltd.* v. *Aberdeen Harbour Board*, 1985 S.L.T. 384.
[78]See para. 25–29.
[79]Paton and Cameron, *Landlord and Tenant*, Chap. XVII; Walker, *Civil Remedies*, Chap. 12; Walker, *Prin.*, III, 248–257.
[80]D.G. McKerrell, *The Rent Acts*, 120–131.
[80a]Tenancy of Shops (Scotland) Acts 1949 and 1964.
[81]Gill, *Law of Agricultural Holdings in Scotland*, Chap. 21.
[82]Paton and Cameron, *op. cit.*, 437–450.
[83]*Davie* v. *Stark* (1876) 3 R. 1114.

fails to remedy material defects in the condition of the premises having been given a reasonable opportunity of doing so,[84] the tenant is entitled to resile from the contract of lease.

Abandonment by tenant

31–44   If the premises are uninhabitable,[85] or become destroyed or seriously damaged by fire,[86] or rendered unusable by or as the result of supervenient legislation[87] the tenant will be entitled to abandon the lease on the principle of *rei interitu*. Modern leases of commercial or industrial premises, however, normally contain provisions for insurance against the risk of fire, abatement or suspension of rent during the period required for repair or reinstatement and continuance of the lease in such circumstances, thus contractually negativing the right of the tenant to abandon the lease *rei interitu*.[88]

Termination on death of tenant

31–45   Section 16 of the Succession (Scotland) Act 1964[89] entitles the landlord or the executor of the tenant to terminate a lease on specified notice if the executor is satisfied that the interest of the tenant cannot be disposed of according to law and so informs the landlord, or if the interest is not so disposed of within a period of one year from the date of the tenant's death or such longer period thereafter as may be fixed by agreement between the landlord and the executor or, failing agreement, by the sheriff on summary application by the executor. There are special provisions as to the duration of the last-mentioned period in relation to agricultural leases and crofts.[90] The statutory provisions apply notwithstanding any provision in the lease or any enactment or rule of law to the contrary effect.

Where the lease was granted in favour of a partnership the death of a partner terminates the lease,[90a] but the terms of the lease may indicate that the tenancy should continue notwithstanding changes in the personnel of the partners—see paragraph 29–43 *supra*, clause 3.

Resumption

31–46   A lease may be terminated in whole or in part by the exercise by the landlord of a power of resumption expressly reserved in the lease. A power of resumption is frequently reserved in agricultural leases where the landlord may wish to resume possession of the whole or part of a

---

[84] *Scottish Heritable Security Co. Ltd.* v. *Granger* (1881) 8 R. 459.
[85] *Kippen* v. *Oppenheim* (1847) 10 D. 242.
[86] *Duff* v. *Fleming* (1870) 8 M. 769; *Cantors Properties (Scotland) Ltd.* v. *Swears & Wells Ltd.*, 1980 S.L.T. 165.
[87] *Tay Salmon Fisheries Co. Ltd.* v. *Speedie*, 1929 S.C. 593; *Mackeson* v. *Boyd*, 1942 S.C. 56.
[88] See para. 29–43, cll. 5.7 and 11.
[89] s. 16(3) and (4).
[90] For a fuller account see M.C. Meston, *The Succession (Scotland) Act 1964*, 88–90.
[90a] *Jardine-Paterson* v. *Fraser*, 1974 S.L.T. 93.

farm either for personal reasons or for the exploitation of minerals or building development which may yield a greater return.[91] If the clause provides for notice of a specified period being given (which is usual), the landlord should serve notice before the commencement of the period by registered post or recorded delivery which should state the area of land to be resumed.

A power of resumption may also be inserted in leases of residential property in circumstances where the landlord may wish to resume occupation for personal reasons but the precise period when he will require possession is uncertain.

If the clause of resumption specifies the purposes for which land may be resumed followed by general words such as "or for any other purpose," the *ejusdem generis* rule of construction applies to the interpretation of the scope of the general words.[92]

Termination by exercise of break

31–47   Some leases may confer upon either or both parties an option to terminate the lease, usually at specified periods, upon giving notice of the exercise of the right at a stated time prior to the date of break. A break clause in favour of the tenant is often inserted in a mineral lease in order that the tenant may be freed from liability for the fixed rent if the minerals can no longer be worked profitably. A break clause may also be used in leases of dwelling-houses in favour of the landlord or the tenant or either of them; if the clause does not make it clear by which party the right is exercisable the court will determine the question,[93] but the clause should be specific on the matter. The party entitled to break should give notice at the time and by the method stipulated in the lease.[94] In commercial leases the landlord will usually resist the inclusion of a break clause since he wishes a continuing yield from his investment for the whole period of the lease but the tenant may in certain cases be able to negotiate a right to terminate if the revised rent exceeds a stated level upon review,[95] but if a period of notice of intention to exercise the break is stipulated the safe course is to regard time as being of the essence and adhere strictly to the period stated.[96] Where either party has the right to break and one party gives due notice exercising the right, the other party may avail himself of the break without requiring to give notice.[97]

---

[91] See para. 28–02, reservation (C) and para. 28–14.
[92] *The Admiralty* v. *Burns*, 1910 S.C. 531; *Turner* v. *Wilson*, 1954 S.C. 296; *Pigott* v. *Robson*, 1958 S.L.T. 49.
[93] *Grant* v. *Sinclair* (1861) 23 D. 796.
[94] *Guild* v. *McLean* (1897) 25 R. 106; *Fraser's Trs.* v. *Maule & Son* (1904) 6 F. 819.
[95] See Ross and McKichan, *op. cit.*, para. 6.9.
[96] See Ross and McKichan, *op. cit.*, para. 6.13 and authorities there cited.
[97] *Laing* v. *Stephenson* (1848) 11 D. 142.

Styles of break clause

31–48 (1) Mineral lease

If within the period of this Lease the minerals hereby let shall become exhausted or have become unworkable to a profit by reason of any cause not attributable to the actions or neglect of the Tenant, then in any of such cases the Tenant may terminate the tenancy at any term of Whitsunday or Martinmas by giving to the Landlord six months' previous notice to that effect and, provided that the Tenant has made payment of all rents and royalties due up to and including such term and has implemented the whole obligations of the Tenant prestable up to such term or upon termination of the Lease as stipulated therein, the Lease shall cease and determine at the said term, declaring that any dispute as to whether the said minerals have become exhausted or unworkable to a profit shall be determined by arbitration in accordance with Clause   hereof.

(2) Lease of dwelling-house

[The Landlord] [The Tenant] [Either the Landlord or the Tenant] shall be entitled to terminate this Lease on
on giving written notice to the [Tenant] [Landlord] [other party hereto] to that effect not later than [three] months prior to the said date. Such notice, if given, shall be irrevocable. If notice is not given timeously as aforesaid the Lease shall continue for the whole period thereof.

(3) Commercial lease

The Tenant shall be entitled within   days after a revised rent has been determined by a review of rent in accordance with Clause   hereof [Schedule   hereto] and the amount of such revised rent exceeds [£   per annum] [per cent more than the rent paid immediately before such review] to give written notice to the Landlord to terminate the Lease on the next following rental payment date, and the Lease shall then terminate without prejudice to the whole rights and claims of the Landlord in respect of the obligations of the Tenant hereunder prestable prior to and at the termination of the Lease including payment of rent at the revised rate up to the said date of termination.

Insolvency of tenant

31–49 On the insolvency of the tenant the permanent trustee or the liquidator may adopt or disclaim the contract of lease.[98] If the lease is not adopted the landlord may claim damages for his loss.

The legal position as stated above, however, may be and commonly is affected by the terms of the lease itself where the exclusion of

---

[98] *Kirkland* v. *Cadell* (1838) 16 S. 860; *Bidoulac* v. *Sinclair's Tr.* (1889) 17 R. 144; *Asphaltic Limestone Concrete Co. Ltd.* v. *Corporation of Glasgow*, 1907 S.C. 463; Bankruptcy (Scotland) Act 1985, s. 42.

assignees is expressed in a form which expressly or impliedly excludes trustees for creditors or liquidators.[99] An exclusion of "assignees" or of "assignees and subtenants legal and conventional" excludes not only voluntary but also judicial or legal assignees such as trustees in sequestration[99]; if no such exclusion is expressed but is inferred from *delectus personae* only conventional and not judicial assignees such as a trustee in sequestration are excluded.[1]

Renunciation by tenant

31–50   A lease may be brought to an end before its stipulated expiry by the tenant voluntarily renouncing it but, apart from the circumstances in which he is legally entitled to do so,[2] the tenant may renounce the lease only with the agreement of the landlord. Where a tenant renounced a commercial lease before the stipulated date of its expiry it was decided that the landlords were entitled to hold the tenants liable for all their obligations under the lease and were not restricted to a claim for damages, that there must be cogent reasons for the court declining in the exercise of their discretionary power to allow the landlord to enforce his legal rights under the lease and that it was for the tenants to aver the existence of such circumstances.[2a] Where the landlord consents to the tenant giving up the lease, renunciation may be effected either by a bilateral agreement executed by both parties and providing for settlement and discharge of their respective claims[3] or by a unilateral renunciation by the tenant which is accepted by the landlord.[4] A verbal renunciation is ineffective if not followed by *rei interventus*.[4a] Where the lease has been recorded in the Register of Sasines or the tenant's interest has been registered in the Land Register the renunciation should be so recorded or registered.[5] The general rule is that acceptance by the landlord of a renunciation without reservation bars the landlord's right to claim subsequently for loss.[6]

Renunciation without any express agreement may be inferred from the conduct of parties, as by the tenant ceasing to occupy the premises and the landlord taking possession or re-letting,[7] or by the parties entering into a new lease in substantially different terms.[8]

---

[99] *Elliot* v. *Duke of Buccleuch* (1747) Mor. 10329; *Dewar* v. *Ainslie* (1892) 20 R. 203.
[1] Rankine, *Leases*, 177; Bell, *Prin.*, s. 1274.
[2] See paras. 31–43 and 31–44.
[2a] *Salaried Staff London Loan Co. Ltd.* v. *Swears & Wells Ltd.*, 1985 S.L.T. 326.
[3] See, for example, *Encyclopaedia of Scottish Legal Styles*, Vol. 6, No. 164.
[4] *Walker's Trs.* v. *Manson* (1886) 13 R. 1198.
[4a] *Morrison's Exrs.* v. *Rendall*, 1986 S.L.T. 227.
[5] For styles see para. 31–51.
[6] For a fuller discussion, see Paton and Cameron, *op. cit.*, 240.
[7] *Taylor* v. *Maxwell* (1728) Mor. 15310.
[8] Rankine, *Leases*, 524.

Styles of renunciation—recorded or registered leases

31–51 **(1) Renunciation of recorded lease**[9]

I, AB, (*designation*), renounce as from the term of
19   in favour of CD, (*designation*), a Lease granted by the
said CD (*or as the case may be*) in my favour (*or as the case may
be*) of the subjects therein described lying in the county of
, which Lease is dated   and
recorded in the Register of Sasines for the said County of
on   both in the year   :
[10][Which Lease was last vested in GH, (*designation*), whose title
thereto is recorded in the said Register of Sasines on
and from whom I acquired right by (*specify writ
or writs by which AB acquired right from GH*)]   .
(*To be attested*)

(2) Renunciation of tenant's registered interest[11]

I, AB, (*designed*), renounce as from the term of   in
favour of CD, (*designed*), ALL and WHOLE the subjects (*insert
postal address if appropriate* registered under Title Number

(*To be attested*)

Confusio

31–52   Whether a lease is extinguished *confusione* when the landlord
acquires the interest of the tenant or *vice versa* has not been
conclusively decided.[12] The opinion is expressed that where the
landlord acquires the interest of the tenant the lease is almost certainly
extinguished; in the converse situation it is highly probable that the
result is the same.

When the titles of both the debtor (or proprietor) and the creditor in
a heritable security are recorded in the Register of Sasines and
confusio occurs, it has never been thought necessary in practice that
any entry recording the fact should appear in the Register. When a
property and a long lease of the property or part of it are both so
recorded and *confusio* occurs, the position may well be the same. If,
however, the title or interest of the landlord and that of the tenant are
recorded or registered in different registers, *i.e.* one in the Register of
Sasines and the other in the Land Register, the legal result is that the
inferior interest of the tenant is absorbed in the higher interest of the
landlord and the Keeper must be informed so that appropriate entries
may be made in the Registers and any necessary applications made in
appropriate form.[13] Where both interests are registered in the Land

---

[9]Registration of Leases (Scotland) Act 1857, Sched. G, as amended by Conveyancing (Scotland)
Act 1924, s. 24(5) and Conveyancing and Feudal Reform (Scotland) Act 1970, s. 47 and Sched. 11.
[10]Where granter does not have recorded title: no specification of title required if granter has
recorded title.
[11]See R.T.P.B., para. D. 4.22. Application for registration of the renunciation should be made by
the landlord on Form 2.
[12]For a full discussion and references to relevant authorities see Paton and Cameron, *op. cit.*, 102.
[13]See R.T.P.B., paras. D.4.25 to D.4.28.

Register the Keeper should be notified when the Keeper, if satisfied that *confusio* has occurred, will cancel the entry of the tenant's interest.

Irritancy

31–53   A lease may be brought to an end by the landlord exercising a right, legal or conventional, to terminate it consequent upon a breach or non-performance of an obligation of the tenant subject to which his right of tenancy is held. The legal irritancies under common law or statute are now seldom relied upon in practice[14] save for that applicable in leases of agricultural holdings under section 19 of the Agricultural Holdings (Scotland) Act 1949, and even it is normally displaced by a conventional irritancy.[15] Conventional irritancies on the other hand are now found in almost all leases and are a fruitful source of litigation. Once a conventional irritancy has been incurred the landlord has an option to terminate the lease which he normally exercises by formal intimation to the tenant followed by a declarator of the court. Until recently the tenant had no such protection as was available in England under the Common Law Procedure Act 1852 and the Law of Property Act 1925, and once a conventional irritancy had been incurred he was not entitled to purge it by subsequent implement of the obligation of which he had been in breach.[16]

31–54   The law has been significantly altered by the Law Reform (Miscellaneous Provisions) (Scotland) Act 1985[17] in respect of irritancies in leases other than leases of property used wholly or mainly for residential purposes or land comprising an agricultural holding, croft, the subject of a cottar or the holding of a landholder or a statutory small tenant.[18] The Act will apply mainly to commercial and industrial leases.[19]

31–55   **Enforcement of irritancy.** An irritancy may be enforced after the landlord has given notice to the tenant of his intention to terminate the lease,[20] which in the case of leases to which the 1985 Act applies must comply with its requirements.[21] Thereafter an action of declarator of irritancy and extraordinary removing is raised by the landlord in the Court of Session or the appropriate sheriff court.[22] In the case of a recorded or registered lease an extract of the decree should be obtained and recorded in the Register of Sasines or registered in the Land Register as may be appropriate.

---

[14]For a convenient summary of legal irritancies and the kinds of subjects to which they apply, see Paton and Cameron, *op. cit.*, 229, 230.
[15]See para. 28–32.
[16]*Stewart* v. *Watson* (1864) 2 M. 1414; *McDouall's Trs.* v. *MacLeod*, 1949 S.C. 593; *Lucas's Exrs.* v. *Demarco*, 1968 S.L.T. 89; *Dorchester Studios (Glasgow) Ltd.* v. *Stone*, 1975 S.C. (H.L.) 56.
[17]ss. 4–6.
[18]s. 7.
[19]For a summary of its provisions see para. 29–33.
[20]*Waugh* v. *More Nisbett* (1882) 19 S.L.R. 427.
[21]See para. 31–54.
[22]That in which the subjects are situated—Sheriff Courts (Scotland) Act 1907, s. 5, proviso.

31–56 **Defences**. The grounds upon which a tenant may defend an attempt by the landlord to enforce a right of irritancy may be summarised as follows:

(1) *Whether breach of tenant's obligations has occurred*. This may involve construction of the terms of the lease in relation to the facts and will usually be a matter for an arbiter appointed in terms of the lease. If the arbiter determines that there has not been a breach of the tenant's obligations then, subject to any appeal to the court permitted in terms of the arbitration clause, there is no ground for irritancy.

(2) *Oppression and reasonableness*. At common law an irritancy clause is construed in accordance with its terms, subject to a presumption of interpretation *contra proferentem* since the lease is normally framed by the landlord.[23] The courts may, however, decline to enforce an irritancy if the landlord is acting oppressively,[24] but oppression is difficult to establish[25] and it is necessary to show that there has been no oversight on the part of the tenant before the defence of oppression is relevant.[26]

In the case of leases to which the Law Reform (Miscellaneous Provisions) (Scotland) Act 1985 applies,[27] the less exacting test of reasonableness may provide a more readily sustainable ground of defence. If the breach consists in failure to make timeous payment of rent or a monetary obligation, service of a notice requiring payment within a stated period and default in payment within that period is a precondition of enforcement of a conventional irritancy: if the breach is of any other type of obligation a right of irritancy can be relied upon only if a fair and reasonable landlord would so rely and, if the breach is remediable, a reasonable opportunity must have been given to the tenant to remedy it.[28]

(3) *Acquiescence or waiver*. Enforcement of an irritancy may be precluded if it can be demonstrated that the breach on which the irritancy is founded has been acquiesced in or waived by the conduct of the landlord.[29]

---

[23] *Johnston* v. *Gordon* (1805) Hume 822.
[24] *Lucas's Exrs.* v. *Demarco*, 1968 S.L.T. 89, 96; *Dorchester Studios (Glasgow) Ltd.* v. *Stone*, 1975 S.C. (H.L.) 56 at 73.
[25] *H.M.V. Fields Properties Ltd.* v. *Tandem Shoes Ltd.*, 1983 S.L.T. 114.
[26] *H.M.V. Fields Properties Ltd.* v. *Skirt 'n' Slack Centre of London Ltd.*, 1982 S.L.T. 477.
[27] See para. 31–54.
[28] 1985 Act, ss. 4, 5.
[29] See paras. 29–34 and 31–40.

PART II

HERITABLE SECURITIES

CHAPTER 32

HISTORICAL INTRODUCTION

Obsolete and superseded securities and the standard security

32–01   Many of the older forms of heritable security such as wadsets and infeftments of annualrent and the heritable bond are now obsolete, and only a brief indication of their nature is given.[1] Their successors, the bond and disposition in security and the *ex facie* absolute disposition qualified by a relative agreement or back letter, are now superseded since the Conveyancing and Feudal Reform (Scotland) Act 1970[2] provides that a heritable security for debt is only effective in law if it is embodied in a standard security,[3] subject to exception in respect of securities over entailed estates where securities in any of the previous forms may be created.[4] Heritable securities in the form of ground annuals cannot now be created by reason of the provisions of the Land Tenure Reform (Scotland) Act 1974.[5] Accordingly the constitution of securities in the forms of bonds and dispositions in security, *ex facie* absolute dispositions and contracts of ground annual is noticed only briefly, but since many securities in these forms are still encountered in practice their enforcement and assignations, discharges and other dealings with them are dealt with in the text.[6] All aspects of standard securities are treated fully.[7]

Wadset

32–02   The wadset was an early form of security whereby the lands were impledged to a creditor (the wadsetter) until the loan was repaid.

---

[1] See paras. 32–02, 32–03 and 32–04.

[2] Effective from Nov. 29, 1970.

[3] 1970 Act, s. 9(3).

[4] *Ibid.*, s. 9(8)(*b*).

[5] 1974 Act, s. 2 operative from Sep. 1, 1974 subject to a transitional provision applicable to a period which has now expired—s. 7.

[6] See Chaps. 33, 34 and 35.

[7] See Chaps. 37–40.

Later the security came to take the form of an absolute disposition to the wadsetter who granted a separate reversion conferring a right of redemption on the debtor (the reverser). When this later form of deed was used the reverser was exposed to the risk of the wadsetter as *ex facie* proprietor selling to a third party, and so the Reversion Act 1449 entitled the reverser to regain the property on payment of the sum contained in the wadset notwithstanding a sale by the wadsetter. That in turn involved risk to a purchaser, and so the Registration Act 1617 required reversions to be recorded within 60 days on pain of nullity. Thereafter wadsets came to be prepared in the form of a mutual contract containing a conveyance of lands by the debtor and a reversion by the creditor. If the wadsetter accepted the rents of the lands in lieu of interest the wadset was proper; if the wadsetter was entitled to a specified rate of interest and the rents of the lands if less were merely to account of the interest, and if more were *quoad* the surplus treated as repayment of the capital, the wadset was improper.[8]

Infeftment of annualrent and the heritable bond

32–03   Another early type of security, originally adopted as a device to circumvent the pre-Reformation prohibition of taking interest on money lent, was the infeftment of annualrent. The creditor purchased for a price an annualrent out of the debtor's lands which represented an income return on the amount paid and took infeftment in the annualrent purchased. Later, after the laws against usury were relaxed, the deed took the form of a bond by the debtor to repay a principal sum with interest and granted an annualrent out of his lands until the principal sum was repaid. This latter form was the heritable bond.[9] The distinctive feature of the heritable bond was that the obligation to repay had now become the principal element to which the conveyance of the annualrent was accessory, so that on extinction of the personal obligation by repayment the infeftment in the annualrent, being simply an ancillary security, fell with it.[10]

Bond and disposition in security

32–04   The ultimate development from the heritable bond was the bond and disposition in security, which differed in respect that the debtor conveyed to the creditor in security of the sum lent and interest not merely an annualrent but the lands themselves, so that the creditor could recover payment from all the rents of the lands and if need be by sale of the lands or foreclosure. The characteristic of the heritable bond remained that repayment of the principal sum with interest due thereon automatically extinguished the ancillary security.[11]

---

[8] For fuller accounts see Menzies, *Lectures*, 864–867; Wood, *Lectures*, 457, 458.
[9] See Menzies, *Lectures*, 862, 863; Wood, *Lectures*, 458.
[10] *Ranken* v. *Arnot* (1680) 2 R.L.C. 707.
[11] *Cameron* v. *Williamson* (1895) 22 R. 293.

Cash credit bond and disposition in security

32–05   The bond and disposition in security constituted a valid security for a definite sum of money advanced before the creditor took infeftment in the security subjects, but was ineffective to create a heritable security for fluctuating advances made thereafter. That impediment resulted from the rule of the feudal law that a real burden on lands must be definite and the provision of the Bankruptcy Act 1696 that a heritable security was of no effect in relation to a debt contracted after the recording of the security deed. For the convenience of commerce the Debts Securities (Scotland) Act 1856[12] permitted the creation of heritable security for future advances, in the form of a cash credit bond and disposition in security but subject to the qualification that the principal and interest were limited to a definite sum to be specified in the security not exceeding the principal sum and three years' interest at 5 per cent. The operation of this limit, however, could involve difficult legal questions[13] and the more flexible form of security, the *ex facie* absolute disposition qualified by agreement or back letter, was generally preferred in practice, especially as the creditor could much more easily exercise his power of sale.

Ex facie absolute disposition

2–06   The *ex facie* absolute disposition with a qualifying agreement overcame many of the difficulties of providing an adequate security within the constraints of feudal law and, from the point of view of the creditor, was a satisfactory form of security. The debtor granted in favour of the creditor a disposition of the security subjects which on the face of it was an absolute conveyance, the character of the transaction as being one of security being dependent upon a separate agreement of the parties or a unilateral back letter by the creditor which established that the disposition was truly in security of an advance. The loan could be of a fixed amount or of fluctuating advances made before and after the recording of the disposition. Despite its flexibility and utility, however, this form of security had distinct disadvantages. It posed difficult conveyancing problems in effecting subsequent transactions, as when the debtor wished to create a postponed security or the creditor's interest was being assigned to a new lender, and frequently the best solution was to discharge the existing loan and create it afresh. When the loan was repaid a formal reconveyance was required, at least until the Conveyancing and Feudal Reform (Scotland) Act 1970[14] provided a simpler form of discharge. Moreover it imposed initial liability upon the creditor as ostensible

---

[12]s. 7 (now excluded from application to standard securities by Conveyancing and Feudal Reform (Scotland) Act 1970, s. 32 and Sched. 8).
[13]See Burns, 476, 477; *Alston* v. *Nellfield Manure and Chemical Co. Ltd.*, 1915 S.C. 912.
[14]s. 40.

proprietor for certain burdens and payments and it exposed the
creditor to restriction upon the scope of his security if the debtor
recorded the back letter, while the debtor was exposed to the risk of a
fraudulent sale by the creditor to a *bona fide* third party.[15] From the
aspect of public interest, too, the wide use of this form of security
seriously diminished the value of the Register of Sasines as a public
record of ownership of land.

The standard security

32–07   The various limitations and disadvantages of the bond and
disposition in security, the cash credit bond and disposition in security
and the *ex facie* absolute disposition induced the legislature in 1970 to
proscribe for the future these forms of creating heritable security for
debts and to provide a new all-purpose form of heritable security for
debt, the standard security, which would be obligatory. The problems
of creating heritable security for future debts which had led to the use
of the *ex facie* absolute disposition device were surmounted by
disapplying in relation to a standard security the provision of the
feudal law which required precision in a real burden and the
prohibition on the creation of heritable security for advances made
after infeftment imposed by the Bankruptcy Act 1696.[16] Two forms of
standard security were provided, one of which (Form A) consisted of a
single unilateral deed granted by the debtor which contained the
personal obligation and the grant of heritable security and the other
(Form B) which comprised two deeds, the grant in security and a
separate instrument constituting the personal obligation.[17] Form A
resembles in format the former bond and disposition in security; Form
B gives the flexibility of the former *ex facie* absolute disposition in the
creation of more complex personal obligations without the artificiality
of representing the creditor as the apparent proprietor of the security
subjects.

     On the whole the standard security has proved to be a much more
satisfactory form of heritable security than its predecessors and, apart
from the Redemption of Standard Securities (Scotland) Act 1971, has
required only minor statutory amendment.

---

[15]For a full list of the disadvantages to creditor and debtor see Burns. 481. 482.
[16]Conveyancing and Feudal Reform (Scotland) Act 1970, s. 9(6).
[17]*Ibid.*, Sched. 2.

CHAPTER 33

BOND AND DISPOSITION IN SECURITY

Assignation, Transmission, Restriction, Redemption and Discharge

Extinction otherwise than by Express Discharge

CASH CREDIT BOND AND DISPOSITION IN SECURITY

STAMP DUTY

Introduction

33–01
Heritable security for debt cannot now with certain minor exceptions competently be created in the form of a bond and disposition in security,[1] but many pre-1970 bonds and dispositions in security still exist and it may be necessary to consider the validity of their constitution, the rights and powers of creditors and debtors thereunder and the effectiveness of dealings with or the procedure for the enforcement of such securities, which are still governed by the former law.[2] In examining the sufficiency of the constitution of a bond and disposition in security only intrinsic defects matter, since it will have been recorded before November 29, 1970, and will now be fortified by positive prescription. If by inadvertence a heritable security for debt purports to have been created after November 29, 1970 in the form of a bond and disposition in security, the security is void and unenforceable but the personal obligation remains valid, and the creditor may be required by the debtor, or by any other person having an interest, to grant such deed as may be appropriate to clear the Register of Sasines of the security.[3]

Capacity and powers of parties

33–02
As to capacity and powers of various parties to grant, or lend upon, heritable security see Volume I, Chapter 2.

Partnerships. A bond and disposition in security was usually granted by all the partners since a heritable security transaction was not normally part of the ordinary business of the firm for which one

---

[1] Conveyancing and Feudal Reform (Scotland) Act 1970, s. 9(3): as to exceptions, see para. 36–04.
[2] *Ibid.*, s. 31.
[3] *Ibid.*, s. 9(4).

partner had authority to bind the firm under section 5 of the Partnership Act 1890. The personal obligation was granted by the firm and all the partners as such partners and as individuals all jointly and severally. The disposition in security was granted by the partners infeft in the security subjects as trustees for the firm, although often the other partners consented for their interest.

Companies. It will be kept in view that all bonds and dispositions in security by companies will have been granted before the enactment of the European Communities Act 1972, and the relevant paragraph of Volume I is 2–101.[4]

Fiduciary fiars could apply to the Court of Session for power to create heritable securities[5] and power to do so was granted to secure the cost of extraordinary repairs which had become necessary.[6]

Moneylenders. As to technical problems in relation to heritable securities in favour of moneylenders see the undernoted case and text.[7]

The proper title of the granter of the disposition in security was infeftment in the security subjects, since bonds and dispositions in security were not included in the deeds in which deduction of title was competent under section 3 of the Conveyancing (Scotland) Act 1924. Deduction of title was competent in assignations, discharges and deeds of restriction of recorded bonds and dispositions in security, but not in the original bond itself. The want of infeftment could be cured by the operation of accretion if the granter subsequently became infeft.

Form of bond and disposition in security

33–03   A statutory form of bond and disposition in security was provided by the Titles to Land Consolidation (Scotland) Act 1868,[8] and the import of its clauses is defined in section 119 of the 1868 Act as substantially amended by section 25 of the Conveyancing (Scotland) Act 1924. For styles of bonds and dispositions in security appropriate to various circumstances, reference may be made to the undernoted texts.[9]

Bond and assignation in security over recorded lease

33–04   It was competent to create a heritable security over a recorded lease in the form of a bond and assignation in security.[10] Again, the proper title of the granter of the assignation was a recorded title to the lease.[11]

---

[4]See further, Burns, 449, 450.

[5]Trusts (Scotland) Act 1921, s. 8(2)(*a*).

[6]*Pottie* (1902) 4 F. 876 (under the corresponding provision of the Trusts (Scotland) Act 1867).

[7]*Phillips* v. *Blackhurst*, 1912 2 S.L.T. 254; Burns, 451.

[8]s. 118 and Sched. FF No. 1 as amended by Conveyancing (Scotland) Act 1874, Conveyancing (Scotland) Act 1924, s. 9 and Succession (Scotland) Act 1964.

[9]*Encyclopaedia of Scottish Legal Styles*, Vol. 2, Nos. 44 to 84; Burns, 451–459.

[10]Registration of Leases (Scotland) Act 1857, s. 4 and Sched. B as amended by the Conveyancing (Scotland) Act 1924, s. 24 and the Conveyancing and Feudal Reform (Scotland) Act 1970, Sched. 11.

[11]*Russell* v. *Campbell* (1888) 26 S.L.R. 209.

Extent of security

33-05　　As already noted,[12] the Bankruptcy Act 1696 applied to a bond and disposition in security and so the security did not extend to cover advances made after the recording of the bond.[13] Since a real burden on heritage must be precise, lack of specification of the principal sum or the interest has the effect that the security does not cover the obligation to the extent that it is not specific.[14]

Heritable fixtures and fittings attached to the security subjects by the proprietor (the debtor in the bond and disposition in security) fall within the heritable security[15] and the rules for determining whether they are heritable or moveable are the same as those applicable in the case of a sale or purchase of heritable property,[16] the principal criterion being the degree of permanence of the fixture.[17] Where the management of the security subjects has been left in the hands of the debtor and they have been let to a tenant who has installed trade fixtures, the tenant is entitled to remove them in a question with the bondholder.[18] On the other hand, since persons who hire to lessees plant which has been attached to the heritage so as to become a heritable fixture are not tenants they cannot claim as against the proprietor of the land that the plant is a trade fixture which they may remove,[19] and presumably the legal position would be the same in a question with creditors holding a heritable security over the property of the owner.

Rights and powers of debtor

33-06　　The proprietor of land who has granted a bond and disposition in security but remains in possession of the security subjects can perform all acts of ordinary management and such acts are effective in a question with the bondholder. If, however, they are unusual and result in prejudice to the creditor he may challenge them. So the debtor may grant leases of ordinary duration for a fair rent,[20] including leases of minerals so long as they do not contain conditions unusually favourable to the tenant.[21] He may cut timber if that is in the course of proper administration.[22] On the other hand he may not alienate part of

---

[12]para. 32–05.
[13]*Bell's Tr.* v. *Bell* (1884) 12 R. 85; *Smith Sligo* v. *Dunlop & Co.* (1885) 12 R. 907; *Black* v. *Curror & Cowper* (1885) 12 R. 990.
[14]*Forbes* v. *Welsh & Forbes* (1894) 21 R. 630; *Alston* v. *Nellfield Manure and Chemical Co. Ltd.*, 1915 S.C. 912.
[15]*Howie's Trs.* v. *McLay* (1902) 5 F. 214; *Edinburgh and Leith Gas Commissioners* v. *Smart*, 1918 1 S.L.T. 80.
[16]Walker, *Prin.*, III, 14.
[17]*Tod's Trs.* v. *Finlay* (1872) 10 M. 422; *Christie* v. *Smith's Exrx.*, 1949 S.C. 572.
[18]*Richardson's Trs.* v. *Ballachulish Slate Quarries Ltd.*, 1918 1 S.L.T. 413 at 415.
[19]*Cliffplant Ltd.* v. *Kinnaird, Mabey Bridge Co. Ltd.* v. *Kinnaird*, 1982 S.L.T. 2.
[20]*Edinburgh Entertainments Ltd.* v. *Stevenson*, 1926 S.C. 363 (the security was in the form of an *ex facie* absolute disposition but the power is also available where the security is in the form of a bond and disposition in security).
[21]*Reid* v. *McGill*, 1912 2 S.L.T. 246.
[22]*Neilson* v. *McNab* (1903) 11 S.L.T. 387.

the security subjects, *e.g.* fixtures,[23] nor enter into unusual contracts with third parties affecting the security subjects[24] to the effect of making such alienations or contracts binding on the creditor.[25] In a case where the debtor who had reserved the right to grant feus on certain conditions granted feus in contravention of the conditions, the contracts of feu were held not to be binding on a purchaser from the creditor who had sold the lands in the exercise of his power of sale.[26] In practice a debtor who has no reserved power to feu cannot grant feus which will be binding on the creditor except with the consent of the creditor.

ENFORCEMENT OF CREDITOR'S RIGHTS

Rights and powers of creditor

33–07   The creditor has rights to enforce the contract embodied in a bond and disposition in security which stem from the personal obligation in the bond[27] and from the security.[28] The rights under the personal obligation and against the security subjects may be exercised concurrently; a creditor who has served notice calling up the bond may within the period of notice charge the debtor to make payment using his power under the clause of registration for execution[29] or raise an action of maills and duties.[30]

33–08   **Personal diligence**. The creditor may enforce payment of the principal or interest by ordinary action or more expeditiously, when the bond contains a consent to registration for execution as is usual, by summary diligence.[31] As to the competency of summary diligence when a new debtor has undertaken the personal obligation upon purchase of, or succession to, the security subjects, see Volume I, para. 4–74, and as to procedure where there has been a change in the creditor see Volume I, para. 4–72. A judicial factor on the estate of a creditor who is incapax may charge the debtor to make payment.[32]

33–09   **Power to insure**. Upon the granting of a bond and disposition in security the creditor may insure buildings comprised in the security subjects against loss by fire, but only for such sum as may be necessary to cover the creditor's interest.[33] After a creditor has entered into possession of the security subjects[34] he may insure against breakage of

---

[23]*Edinburgh and Leith Gas Commissioners* v. *Smart*, 1918 1 S.L.T. 80.
[24]*Morier* v. *Brownlie & Watson* (1895) 23 R. 67.
[25]*Heron* v. *Martin* (1893) 20 R. 1001.
[26]*Cumming* v. *Stewart*, 1928 S.C. 296.
[27]See para. 33–08.
[28]See paras. 33–09 to 33–43.
[29]*McWhirter* v. *McCulloch's Trs.* (1887) 14 R. 918; *McNab* v. *Clarke* (1889) 16 R. 610.
[30]*McAra* v. *Anderson*, 1913 S.C. 931.
[31]See Vol. I, Chap. 4.
[32]*Yule* v. *Alexander* (1891) 19 R. 167.
[33]Conveyancing (Scotland) Act 1924, s. 25(1)(a).
[34]See para. 33–10.

glass, claims by tenants and third parties and such other incidental risks as a prudent proprietor would reasonably insure against.[33] The premiums may be debited against the rents in accounting with the debtor and so in effect are covered by the security. A bondholder in possession incurs the liability of an owner to third parties[35] and so adequate insurance is necessary.

33–10 **Entering into possession.** The creditor may in certain circumstances enter into possession of the security subjects either with the consent of the debtor or by raising an action of maills and duties,[36] and apply the rents towards the interest and principal payable under the bond and disposition in security. The tenants need not be called in an action of maills and duties and may continue to pay rents to the proprietor until interpelled by notice given to them by the creditor, but after intimation of decree in the action by registered letter or recorded delivery post they are obliged to pay the rents to the creditor.[37]

33–11 An action of maills and duties is competent under the clause of assignation of rents in a bond and disposition in security in any of the following events: (1) default in payment of principal when that has been lawfully required, (2) default in payment of interest (which must be paid punctually[38]), or (3) notour bankruptcy of the proprietor of the security subjects or his granting a trust deed for behoof of his creditors.[39] It may be observed that it is the notour bankruptcy of the proprietor of the security subjects, not that of the debtor in the bond if a different person, which constitutes the ground of action. As regards a proprietor who is subject to the jurisdiction of the courts of England and Wales or Northern Ireland the granting of a receiving order by any of these courts was,[40] and sequestration of his estates or adjudication in bankruptcy in any of these courts is,[41] equivalent to notour bankruptcy in Scotland. Before 1924 there were problems as to the competency of an action of maills and duties where the security subjects were superiorities or ground annuals,[42] but that problem was solved by section 26 of the Conveyancing (Scotland) Act 1924 which authorises the creditor to raise an action of declarator against the superior or the creditor in the ground annual with the same general effect as an action of maills and duties. Where the security is over a recorded lease an action of maills and duties has been held technically incompetent, the appropriate procedure being an application to the sheriff under section 6 of the Registration of Leases (Scotland) Act 1857.[43]

---

[35] *Baillie* v. *Shearer's J.F.* (1894) 21 R. 498.
[36] Heritable Securities (Scotland) Act 1894, s. 3.
[37] *Ibid.*, s. 3.
[38] *Gatty* v. *Maclaine*, 1921 S.C. (H.L.) 1.
[39] Conveyancing (Scotland) Act 1924, s. 25(1)(*a*).
[40] Bankruptcy (Scotland) Act 1913, s. 5.
[41] Bankruptcy (Scotland) Act 1985, ss. 7(1), 75(9).
[42] *Nelson's Trs.* v. *Tod* (1896) 23 R. 1000.
[43] *Dunbar* v. *Gill*, 1908 S.C. 1054.

33–12   *Pari passu* creditors should enter into possession jointly if that course can be agreed: if court procedure is necessary the safe course is that each creditor should raise a separate action of maills and duties.[44] But the holder of a security over only a *pro indiviso* share of security subjects cannot take maills and duties if any joint proprietor or a tenant objects.[45] A prior bondholder may raise an action of maills and duties to which a postponed bondholder cannot object.[46] A postponed bondholder may also raise such an action, but the prior bondholder should insist on an arrangement that his prior claims should be recognised in the accounting for rents received. The right of a bondholder to enforce his bond, including the right to pursue an action of maills and duties, may be lost by the lapse of 20 years after default, but the operation of the negative prescription may be elided if there has been any relevant acknowledgment during that period.[47]

33–13   Forms of initial writ or summons in an action of maills and duties which are still appropriate are given in Burns, *Conveyancing Practice*, pp. 510, 511.

33–14   Where a bondholder wishes to enter into possession of security subjects which are occupied by the proprietor personally he may, if there has been default by the proprietor in punctual payment of interest under the bond or in due payment of the principal after formal requisition, take proceedings to eject him as an occupant without title.[48] The section cannot be used against a liferenter since he is not a proprietor within the meaning of the section[49] nor against a proprietor who is not the debtor in the bond since he is not the person in default, but it is competent against the true proprietor even although he has been technically divested of ownership by an *ex facie* absolute disposition which is in effect merely a security.[50]

33–15   The bondholder in possession may administer the security subjects in accordance with the principles of normal management of the particular kind of property, and may do all things which fall within that description including appropriate repairs and maintenance. He has no power, however, to make improvements or developments. He may factor the property, enforce payment of rents, obtain production and delivery of leases,[51] grant leases for not more than seven years or, with authority of the sheriff, 21 years or 31 years (minerals).[52] He must keep an accurate accounting of the rents received and he should apply these, after deducting proper expenses of collection and outlays on

---

[44] See *Douglas* v. *Tait* (1884) 12 R. 10.
[45] Burns, 507; the case cited does not support the proposition, but it appears sound.
[46] *Graham's Trs.* v. *Dow's Tr.*, 1917 2 S.L.T. 154.
[47] *Marr's Exrx.* v. *Marr's Trs.*, 1936 S.C. 64.
[48] Heritable Securities (Scotland) Act 1894, s. 5.
[49] *Scottish Union and National Insurance Co.* v. *Smeaton* (1904) 7 F. 174.
[50] *Inglis' Trs.* v. *Macpherson*, 1911 2 S.L.T. 176.
[51] *Macrae* v. *Leith*, 1913 S.C. 901.
[52] Heritable Securities (Scotland) Act 1894, ss. 6, 7.

repair, towards arrears of interest[53] and apply any significant surplus in reduction of principal.[54] A tenant is entitled to withhold rent from the creditor in possession if he would have been entitled to do so in a question with the debtor/proprietor.[55]

3–16 **Poinding of the ground.** As a creditor in a *debitum fundi* a bondholder whose bond and disposition in security has been duly recorded may enforce his security by an action of poinding of the ground whereby he makes effectual the preference already secured to him by infeftment in the security.[56] Service of the summons in the action puts a *nexus* on moveable goods belonging to the debtor which are then on the security subjects and interpels the debtor from allowing others to acquire rights over them.[57] Goods belonging to a tenant are poindable only to the extent of arrears of rent due by him and the rent for the current term.[58] The action is competent even after the bondholder has entered into possession.[59]

3–17 Service of the summons does not interpel the tenants from paying rents to the proprietor.[60] The action may be raised by an assignee, even if he has not himself a recorded title, so long as the bond and disposition to which he has right was duly recorded.[61] It may be raised by a prior or postponed bondholder. If raised by the latter the prior bondholder is entitled to have his preference reserved on the face of the decree.[62] Where a prior bondholder poinded the ground and then obtained payment of his loan by realising the security subjects and assigned his preference over the moveables to a postponed bondholder, it was held that the latter had a valid preference against the debtor's trustee in bankruptcy.[63]

3–18 Where the debtor is sequestrated no poinding of the ground executed by the bondholder within the period of 60 days before the date of sequestration is effectual in a question with the permanent trustee, except for interest on the secured debt for the current half-yearly term and arrears of interest for one year immediately before the commencement of that term.[64] The like limitation applies in a question with the liquidator of a company that has been wound up.[65]

3–19 Forms of summons in an action of poinding of the ground which are

---

[53] If there has been conditional agreement to accept a rate lower than that stipulated, *e.g.* on punctual payment, the full rate is chargeable since the debtor has defaulted.

[54] For a more detailed consideration see W.L. McGeachy, "The Bondholder's Final Remedy" (1960) 2 Conv. Rev. 129 at 139, 140.

[55] *Marshall's Trs.* v. *Banks,* 1934 S.C. 405.

[56] *Athole Hydropathic Co. Ltd.* v. *Scottish Provincial Assurance Co.* (1886) 13 R. 818.

[57] *Lyons* v. *Anderson* (1880) 8 R. 24.

[58] Bell, *Comm.,* II, 56.

[59] *Henderson* v. *Wallace* (1875) 2 R. 272.

[60] *Royal Bank of Scotland* v. *Dixon* (1868) 6 M. 995.

[61] *Tweedie* v. *Beattie* (1836) 14 S. 337.

[62] *Young's Trs.* v. *Hill's Tr.* (1893) 1 S.L.T. 357.

[63] *Nicol's Tr.* v. *Hill* (1889) 16 R. 416.

[64] Bankruptcy (Scotland) Act 1985, s. 37(6).

[65] Insolvency Act 1986, s. 185.

still appropriate are given in Burns, *Conveyancing Practice*, pp. 513, 514.

33–20 **Adjudication**. The creditor in a bond and disposition in security may enforce it by an action of adjudication. This remedy is seldom employed, since (1) if the adjudication proceeds on the personal obligation it does not have the same ranking as the heritable security; to obtain that result it must be preceded by an action of poinding of the ground, and (2) in any event it does not give an absolute title until the expiry of the legal 10 years later.[66] For these reasons the remedies of sale and foreclosure are of more practical value.[67]

33–21 **Sale**. The creditor in a bond and disposition in security may require repayment of the principal sum by service of a calling-up notice and on default by the debtor in making payment in compliance with the notice may sell the security subjects by public sale or private bargain.

Calling-up notice

33–22 (1) BY WHOM. The notice should be given by the creditor in the bond and by all joint creditors if more than one. If there are several creditors, each entitled to a separate part of the principal sum, separate notices should be given by each requiring payment of his part.[68] A notice by a *curator bonis* for a minor or an incapax should run in the name of the minor or the ward and by the *curator bonis* for his interest. A notice by a company in liquidation should run in the name of the company and the liquidator. A notice by a factor and commissioner or an attorney should run in the name of the principal whom he represents.

33–23 (2) TO WHOM.[69] The notice must be delivered or sent to the person last infeft in the security subjects and appearing on the record as proprietor. If there are several co-proprietors on the record, notice must be given to each. If the proprietor appearing on the record is an *ex facie* absolute disponee, technically notice to him is all that is required. If the person last infeft in the security subjects or any part thereof is dead, notice must be given to his executor or reputed substitute or the person entitled to succeed to the same in terms of the last recorded title thereto, notwithstanding any alteration of the succession not appearing on the Register of Sasines; if there are no heirs or they are unknown, notice must be given to the Lord Advocate. If the last proprietor was an incorporated company which has been removed from the Register of Companies, notice must be

---

[66] *Watson* v. *Swift & Co.'s J.F.*, 1986 S.L.T. 217.
[67] For a fuller account of adjudication for debt see *Encyclopaedia of the Laws of Scotland*, Vol. I, 117–144; Burns, 533, 534.
[68] See para. 33–24.
[69] Conveyancing (Scotland) Act 1924, s. 33 as amended by Conveyancing and Feudal Reform (Scotland) Act 1970, s. 34.

given to the Lord Advocate. Where the estates of the debtor have been sequestrated, notice must be given to the permanent trustee in sequestration (unless he has been discharged) *and* to the bankrupt. If the proprietor is a body of trustees it is sufficient to give notice to a majority of the trustees infeft in the security subjects. In the case of a bond and disposition in security granted by two persons jointly and severally each of whom disponed property in security, notice must be given to both before either property can be sold.[70]

The foregoing list comprises all the persons to whom in terms of section 33 of the 1924 Act notice *requires* to be given, and the section states that there is no obligation to give notice to any other person unless for the purpose of preserving recourse against him. Clearly the creditor will wish to preserve his right to enforce the personal obligation against any other person or persons who may be liable in payment. Moreover it is advisable to inform any person who may be affected by a subsequent sale of the subjects, since that may lead to an arrangement whereby the creditor's loan will be repaid without the trouble and expense of advertisement and sale. For these reasons it is suggested that notice should be given also to:

(a) all persons (other than the proprietor) who may be liable under the personal obligation, including guarantors;

(b) all known trustees, whether infeft in the security subjects or not, who are proprietors of the security subjects;

(c) the true owner who has granted or consented to an *ex facie* absolute disposition of the security subjects;

(d) both liferenter and fiar where the infeftment in the security subjects was in liferent and fee;

(e) feuars whose feus may be open to reduction at the instance of the bondholder or a purchaser from him on a subsequent sale of the security subjects[71];

(f) tenants under recorded leases (but not other leases) of the security subjects or any part thereof;

(g) the trustee under a trust deed for creditors by the proprietor of the security subjects or by any person liable under the personal obligation as well as the granter of the trust deed himself; and

(h) any firm and all its partners who are proprietors of the security subjects or liable under the personal obligation.

13–24 (3) AMOUNT IN NOTICE. The sum inserted in the notice should be the amount of principal due to the creditor who serves it with interest from the last date to which interest was paid at the rate stipulated in the bond, not any concessionary lower rate or any higher rate subsequently agreed informally.

In the case of a cash credit bond and disposition in security a certificate of the amount due at the date of service of the notice should

---

[70]*Stuart's Exr.* v. *Stuart* (1904) 12 S.L.T. 356.
[71]*Cumming* v. *Stewart*, 1928 S.C. 296.

be prepared and signed in terms of the bond,[72] and the signed certificate should be attached to the notice and a photocopy of it attached to the duplicate notice.

Where the creditor has been in possession the balance due will require to be calculated after accounting for the creditor's intromissions with rents and, to avoid the notice being invalidated by reason of errors or omissions in the accounting statement, it is permissible to state in the notice that the principal sum and interest therein specified is subject to adjustment in amount as calculated in a statement of relevant intromissions. The person on whom the notice is served may request the creditor to furnish such a statement within one month from the date of service of the notice, and failing compliance with that request the notice is ineffectual.[73]

33–25   (4) FORM OF NOTICE. A style of calling-up notice is provided in Form No. 1 of Schedule M to the 1924 Act.[74]

> *Notice*
> To AB (*insert name and last known address of person to whom notice is given*)
> Take notice that CD (*name and design creditor*) requires payment of the principal sum of (*insert sum*) with interest thereon at the rate of   per centum per annum from the   day of   due under a Bond and Disposition in Security by you [*or* by EF (*original debtor*)] in favour of the said CD [*or* of GH (*original creditor*) of which the said CD is now in right] dated (*insert date*) and recorded in (*specify Register of Sasines, and date of recording*): And that failing full payment of the said principal sum, interest and expenses within three months after this demand the subjects held in security may be sold. [The amount of the principal sum and interest specified in this Notice is subject to adjustment as calculated in a statement of relevant intromissions.][75]
> Dated this   day of   (*date of giving notice personally or of posting same*)
> (*To be signed by the creditor, or by his Agent who will add the words "Agent of the said CD"*)

33–26   (5) SERVICE OF NOTICE.[76] The notice may be delivered by personal service to the person to whom it is desired to be given (preferably to his residence) or sent by registered post or recorded delivery service to him at his last known address or in the case of the Lord Advocate at the Crown Office, Edinburgh. An acknowledgment signed by the person to whom notice is given in or as nearly as may be in the terms of Form No. 2 of Schedule M to the 1924 Act or a certificate of posting

---

[72]See Vol. I, para. 4–64.
[73]Conveyancing and Feudal Reform (Scotland) Act 1970, s. 33; see Halliday, *Conveyancing and Feudal Reform (Scotland) Act 1970*, paras. 5–05 to 5–08.
[74]Conveyancing (Scotland) Act 1924, s. 33.
[75]See para. 33–24.
[76]1924 Act, s. 34.

in or as nearly as may be in the terms of Form No. 3 of that Schedule accompanied by the postal receipt is sufficient evidence of service. If the address of the person to whom notice is to be given is not known or if it is not known whether he is still alive, or if the packet containing the notice is returned to the creditor or his solicitor with an intimation that it could not be delivered, the notice should be sent to the Keeper of the Record of Edictal Citations (now the Principal Extractor of the Court of Session), General Register House, Edinburgh, and an acknowledgment by the Keeper is sufficient evidence of service. If posted, notice is held to have been given on the next day after the date of posting.

> *Acknowledgment*
> I, AB above named, hereby acknowledge receipt of the foregoing notice (*or* of the notice of which the foregoing is a copy), [and I agree to the period of notice being dispensed with (*or* shortened to   )].
> Dated this   date of
>
> *Certificate of Posting*
> Notice of which the foregoing is a copy was posted (*or otherwise as the case may be*) to AB above named on the   day of
>
> (*To be signed by the creditor, or by his Agent who will add his designation and the words* "Agent of the said CD"; *and if posted the postal receipt to be attached.*)

A notice ceases to be effective for the purposes of a sale of the security subjects in pursuance of it after five years from its date if no exposure to sale of such subjects or any part of them has followed thereon or otherwise after five years from the date of the last exposure to such sale following upon the notice.[77]

33–27 *Advertisement.* On expiry of the period of three months from the date of the notice or of any shorter period agreed to[78] without payment the creditor may advertise the security subjects for sale, which may be either by public roup or private bargain.[79] A sale by public roup is necessary, however, as a preliminary to an action of foreclosure,[80] and a sale under warrant of the sheriff under section 11 of the Heritable Securities (Scotland) Act 1894 empowering a *pari passu* bondholder to sell must also be made by public roup.[81] The advertisement should specify the property to be sold and in the case of a sale by public roup the day, hour and place of sale and the upset price or prices.[82] In the case of a sale by private bargain it must be for the best price that can be reasonably obtained,[83] thus broadly restating the existing principle

---

[77] 1924 Act, s. 33.
[78] See para. 33–26.
[79] 1924 Act, s. 36; Conveyancing and Feudal Reform (Scotland) Act 1970, s. 35.
[80] Heritable Securities (Scotland) Act 1894, s. 8.
[81] 1970 Act, s. 35(3).
[82] 1924 Act, s. 37.
[83] 1970 Act, s. 35(1).

that a heritable creditor exercising a power of sale is in the position of a quasi-trustee for the debtor.[84] The onus of proving that the price was not the best that could reasonably have been obtained rests on the debtor, but may be displaced if a relationship of interest existed between the creditor and the purchaser.[85] The description of the property in the advertisement should be sufficient to do justice to it, but it is unnecessary to state that the sale is under a bond and disposition in security.[86]

33–28   The minimum periods of advertisement on first exposure or offer or on re-exposure or re-offer are:

Period
(1)   Public exposure, once weekly for three consecutive weeks.
(2)   Private bargain, once weekly for two consecutive weeks.

Newspapers
(1)   Property in Midlothian, one daily newspaper published in Edinburgh.
(2)   Property in Lanarkshire, one daily newspaper published in Glasgow.
(3)   Property elsewhere in Scotland, one daily newspaper published in Scotland circulating in the district where the property or the main part thereof is situated *and* one newspaper (if any) circulating in that district and published in the county where the property is situated or in a county adjacent to that county.[87]

These requirements are the *minima* desiderated by statute: additional advertisement may be desirable. A week means the period between midnight on Saturday and midnight on the succeeding Saturday night.[88] A copy of an advertisement supported by a certificate of publication by the publisher, printer or editor of the newspaper is sufficient evidence of insertion and publication.[89]

33–29   *Exposure and sale.* In the case of a sale by public roup the exposure or re-exposure, as the case may be, must take place within 14 days beginning with the date following the day of publication of the third advertisement[90] and the contract of sale will be made by a minute of enactment and preference annexed to the articles of roup and executed by or on behalf of the exposer and the purchaser.[91] If the sale is by private bargain an enforceable contract of sale must be concluded

---

[84]*Park* v. *Alliance Heritable Security Co.* (1880) 7 R. 546; *Baillie* v. *Drew* (1884) 12 R. 199 at 202; *Aberdeen Trades Council* v. *Shipconstructors and Shipwrights Association*, 1949 S.C. (H.L.) 45 at 65; *Rimmer* v. *Thomas Usher & Son Ltd.*, 1967 S.L.T. 7.
[85]*Davidson* v. *Scott*, 1915 S.C. 924.
[86]1924 Act, s. 37.
[87]1924 Act, s. 38 as substituted by 1970 Act, s. 36.
[88]1924 Act, s. 38(5).
[89]*Ibid.*, s. 38(4).
[90]*Ibid.*, s. 38(1).
[91]See Vol. II, para. 15–147.

within 28 days beginning with the day following the day of publication of the second advertisement.[92] As to practical problems associated with these statutory requirements see the undernoted text.[93] Where there are circumstances in which combined sales may be desirable, as where there are separate bonds over the liferent and fee respectively or securities over *pari passu* shares of the property to be sold, and the problems associated therewith, reference may be made to Burns, *Conveyancing Law and Practice*, pp. 522, 523.

As to procedure on sale by public roup and persons who may bid see Volume II, paragraphs 15–141 to 15–148.

33–30 *Allocation and redemption of feuduty or ground annual on sale by bondholder.* In terms of section 25(1)(d) of the 1924 Act a bondholder when his bond and disposition in security has been called up and there has been failure to comply with the demand for payment may, to the same extent as would have been competent to the debtor, obtain an allocation of any feuduty or ground annual affecting the security subjects "in such proportions and on such terms as to augmentation or otherwise as may be agreed upon between the superior or the holder of the ground annual and the creditor." No amendment of that provision was made by the Conveyancing and Feudal Reform (Scotland) Act 1970 and it may be doubtful if the definition of a "proprietor" in section 5(7) includes a heritable creditor, and so it is uncertain whether the provisions in sections 3 to 5 of the 1970 Act permitting allocation by notice are available in all circumstances to the bondholder, *e.g.* where the debtor in the bond was not the proprietor of the security subjects, so that agreement with the superior or creditor in the ground annual may in certain cases still be required. It is thought that the point is of little practical importance, however, since if necessary the proprietor of the security subjects can require allocation in terms of the 1970 Act.

As regards redemption of feuduty or ground annual required on sale of heritable subjects by section 5 of the Land Tenure Reform (Scotland) Act 1974 there is a similar problem, since the obligation to pay the redemption money is imposed by subsection (4) of that section upon the person who was the proprietor of the subjects immediately before the date of entry under the contract of sale and the definition of "proprietor" in section 7(3) of the Act does not comprehend a creditor selling under power contained in a bond and disposition in security. However, since in practice the purchaser will almost always stipulate for a title which is free from the burden of any allocated feuduty or ground annual, it appears that the selling creditor will pay the redemption money and will be entitled to debit the amount, as a necessary expense of the sale, in an accounting with the debtor.

---

[92]1924 Act, s. 38(2).
[93]Halliday, *op. cit.*, paras. 5–14 and 5–15.

33–31   *Sale in lots.* The security subjects may be exposed or offered for sale
by the bondholder as a whole or in lots. If exposed for sale by public
roup the upset price or prices may be such as the bondholder thinks
proper; if offered for sale by private bargain the price or prices should
be the best that can be reasonably obtained. Where the sale is in lots
the creditor may apportion feuduty, ground annual, stipend, etc., on
the various lots with provisions for relief amongst the purchasers *inter
se* and may create such rights and impose such duties and conditions as
he considers may be reasonably required for the proper management,
maintenance and use of any part of the subjects to be held in common
by the owners of the lots. For that purpose he may execute and record
a deed of declaration of conditions, as a proprietor could do under
section 32 of the Conveyancing (Scotland) Act 1874.[94]

33–32   Since the power of the bondholder to execute a deed of declaration
of conditions rests solely on this statutory provision and is expressed as
exercisable "where there is a sale as aforesaid in lots," it is doubtful
whether he can competently execute and record such a deed before the
sale is made. It was suggested[95] that the safest course would be to
prepare the deed in draft before the sale and execute it and record it
contemporaneously with the dispositions which give effect to the sale.
It should be kept in view that in terms of section 17 of the Land
Registration (Scotland) Act 1979 a deed of declaration of conditions
now makes the burdens and conditions which it creates real on
recording of the deed unless the section is expressly disapplied. This
may create difficult problems. For example, if the security subjects
comprise three lots A, B and C of which A and B are developed and
are sold for sums sufficient to repay the secured debt in full and a deed
of declaration of conditions by the creditor has created a right of access
in favour of lots A and/or B over lot C (which is undeveloped ground),
the result may be that lot C, now unburdened by the bond and
disposition in security, cannot effectively be developed by the
proprietor on account of the impediment of the access right. Since the
creditor is in the position of a quasi-trustee for the debtor he may have
to satisfy the latter that it was impracticable to recover his debt by the
sale of lots A and B without creating the access over lot C.

33–33   As to a style of deed of declaration of conditions by a selling creditor
see the undernoted text,[96] subject to the qualifications that (1) the
inclusion of a clause disapplying section 17 of the 1979 Act should be
considered[97] and (2) recording in the Register of Sasines or registration
of the obligations in the Land Register depends on the position of the
title.[98]

---

[94]1924 Act, s. 40 as amended by 1970 Act, s. 37.
[95]Halliday, *op. cit.*, para. 5–17.
[96]*Ibid.*, para. 5–18.
[97]See Vol. II, para. 19–39.
[98]See Chap. 42.

33–34 *Disposition by selling creditor*

> I, AB, (*designation*), whereas in virtue of a power of sale
> contained in a bond and disposition in security for £ granted
> by CD, (*designation*), [in my favour] *or* [in favour of EF,
> (*designation*), to which I have now right[99]] I advertised the
> subjects hereinafter disponed for sale [and sold the said subjects
> by private contract to GH, (*designation*), at the price of
> £ being the best price that could be reasonably obtained]
> *or* [and exposed the said subjects to public roup at on
> at the upset price of £ and that GH,
> (*designation*), being the [only] *or* [highest] offerer for the subjects
> was by the judge of the roup preferred to the purchase at the
> price of £ ,] all as the [contract of sale dated
>] *or* [articles of roup dated and
> relative minute of enactment and preference dated]
> more fully bear, and whereas the said GH has paid to me the said
> price of £ , therefore I have sold and hereby dispone
> to the said GH heritably and irredeemably ALL and WHOLE
> (*description of subjects*) together with the whole right, title and
> interest of the said CD and myself in and to the said subjects
> (*reference to burdens, if any*): With entry at :
> And I grant warrandice from my own facts and deeds only and
> bind the said CD in absolute warrandice. (*Stamp clause, if
> required*)
>
> (*To be attested*)

As to recording of the disposition in the Register of Sasines or
registration of the purchaser's interest in the Land Register see
Chapter 42 *infra*.

33–35 *Protection of purchaser.* Upon a sale by the bondholder under the
powers conferred in a bond and disposition in security the purchaser is
given certain statutory protections,[1] *viz*.

(1) The sale is valid and effectual notwithstanding that any person
on whom a calling-up notice required to be served was in pupillarity or
minority or subject to any legal incapacity.

(2) Where the disposition by the selling creditor to the purchaser has
been duly recorded in the Register of Sasines and bears to have been
granted in exercise of a power of sale in a bond and disposition in
security, and the exercise of that power was *ex facie* regular, the title of
a *bona fide* purchaser for value is not challengeable on the ground that
the debt had ceased to exist unless that fact appeared on the Register
or was known to the purchaser prior to the payment of the price, or on
the ground of any irregularity relating to the sale or in any procedure
preliminary thereto. As regards the second of these protections it
should be noted that (i) it applies only if the disposition bears that it is
granted in exercise of the creditor's power of sale, (ii) since it is
conditional on the exercise of the power being *ex facie* regular the

---

[99] If the creditor does not have a recorded title to the bond, insert particulars of last recorded title
and specify the links whereby he acquired right.

[1] 1924 Act, s. 41, as amended by Conveyancing and Feudal Reform (Scotland) Act 1970, s. 38.

purchaser must still scrutinise the steps in procedure such as the calling-up notice, advertisements and sale but he is protected against any irregularities in these steps which an examination of the documents would not reveal, and (iii) the purchase must have been made *in bona fide* for value, so that the existence of a business relationship between the creditor and the purchaser[2] or a sale by private bargain at a price which was demonstrably less than its full market value would elide the protection. The protection against the debt having ceased to exist would extend to errors in accounting when the creditor had been in possession (which accounting the purchaser would not be bound to examine). Irregularities in procedure would not extend to cover patent disconformities such as failure to advertise or advertisement for less than the statutorily-required periods although the latter might be excusable so long as there was advertisement which the court considered to have given broadly adequate publicity to the exposure or offer for sale.

33–36   *Consignation of surplus and disburdenment of security subjects.* Upon receipt of the price by the creditor who has sold the security subjects in exercise of his power of sale any surplus must be consigned in bank "for behoof of the party or parties having best right thereto."[3] If the sale is by public roup the particular bank must be specified in the articles of roup. Before the surplus is ascertained the creditor may deduct (1) his debt and interest due thereon, (2) expenses incurred if he has been in possession of the security subjects including expenses of insurance, repairs and management, (3) the expenses of the calling-up and sale, and (4) all previous incumbrances and the expenses of discharging them. Whether there is a surplus or not a solicitor or notary public executes a certificate to the effect that a specified surplus has been consigned on deposit receipt in a particular bank, or that no surplus remains for consignation, as the case may be, in the form of Schedule N to the Conveyancing (Scotland) Act 1924. Upon the disposition by the creditor to the purchaser and the certificate of surplus or no surplus being recorded in the Register of Sasines, the security subjects are disencumbered of the security and diligence of the selling creditor and also of all securities and diligences posterior to the security of the selling creditor, except when the security and diligence of the selling creditor and any prior securities and diligences are assigned by way of further or collateral security to the purchaser.[4]

33–37   *Certificate of no surplus or surplus*

I, AB, (*designation*), solicitor, with reference to the sale of the subjects contained in the bond and disposition in security aftermentioned, which sale took place at   upon

---

[2]*Davidson* v. *Scott*, 1915 S.C. 924; *Rimmer* v. *Thomas Usher & Son Ltd.*, 1967 S.L.T. 7.
[3]Titles to Land Consolidation (Scotland) Act 1868, s. 122.
[4]Conveyancing (Scotland) Act 1924, s. 42.

the (*insert date*) at the instance of CD, (*designation*), in virtue of the power of sale contained in a bond and disposition in security for the sum of £   granted by EF, (*designation*), in favour of [the said CD] *or* [GH, (*designation*),] dated   and recorded in the Register of Sasines for the County of on   [to which bond and disposition in security (to the extent of £   ) the said CD acquired right by (succession) *or* (transmission)] do hereby certify that there has been submitted to me a statement of the intromissions of the said CD with the price of the said subjects subscribed by [the said CD] *or* [JK, (*designed*), agent of the said CD on his behalf] from which it appears that [5][no surplus remains for consignation in terms of section 122 of the Titles to Land Consolidation (Scotland) Act 1868] *or* [6][a surplus of £   remains for consignation in terms of section 122 of the Titles to Land Consolidation (Scotland) Act 1868, and I further certify that such surplus has been so consigned in (*specify bank or branch of bank in which money consigned*) conform to deposit receipt dated (*insert date*) by said bank for said amount in the joint names of the said CD and of LM, (*designation of purchaser of subjects*), which deposit receipt has been presented to me.]

(*To be attested*)

33–38 *Consignation receipt*

Received from CD, (*designation*), the sum of £   being the surplus remaining from the sale of the property (*describe by postal address*) under bond and disposition in security by EF, (*designation*), in favour of the said CD (*or other person as the case may be*) for the sum of £   dated and recorded in the Register of Sasines for the County of   on   , which sum is, in terms of section 122 of the Titles to Land Consolidation (Scotland) Act 1868, consigned in joint names of the said CD and LM, (*designation of purchaser*), for behoof of the parties having best right thereto, with all of which the bank has no concern.

33–39 **Foreclosure.** Where the creditor in a bond and disposition in security has exposed the security subjects for sale by public roup under his power of sale at a price not exceeding the amount due under his security and under any prior or *pari passu* security (exclusive of the expenses attending the exposure or prior exposures) and has failed to find a purchaser he may apply to the sheriff for decree in terms of Schedule D to the Heritable Securities (Scotland) Act 1894 with the effect that the creditor becomes absolute proprietor of the security subjects. That effect occurs when an extract of the decree containing a description of the lands, full or by reference, is recorded in the Register of Sasines. As from the date of such recording the creditor has right to the security subjects as if the disposition in security had been irredeemable as from that date and the security subjects are disburdened of all securities and diligences posterior to his security.

[5]Where no surplus.
[6]Where surplus.

The sheriff may instead of granting such decree order re-exposure of the subjects at a price fixed by him when the creditor may bid for and purchase the subjects and, if he does so, either the sheriff may pronounce decree as above or the creditor may grant a disposition of the lands in his own favour.[7]

33–40　　*Pari passu bondholder.* Prior to 1894 there were difficult problems if one *pari passu* bondholder wished to call up his security and proceed to sale but the other *pari passu* bondholder refused to co-operate. In such circumstances although either of the bondholders could sell he could not compel the other to discharge his security for less than full payment,[8] so that sale was only practicable if the price obtained was sufficient to pay off both creditors in full. Section 11 of the Heritable Securities (Scotland) Act 1894 provides that in such circumstances the creditor who desires to sell may apply to the sheriff for warrant to sell, calling the other *pari passu* bondholder as defender, and the sheriff may order a sale of the security subjects if he thinks fit and may fix the price and authorise either party or some other person to carry through the sale, and upon payment or consignation of the price to grant a conveyance and disencumber the lands of both securities as if the two creditors were carrying through the sale by agreement. The expenses of the sale are a first charge on the proceeds and the balance of the proceeds "shall be paid to the creditors in the securities charged upon the lands according to their just rights and preferences." If the proceeds of sale are sufficient to satisfy the amounts due to both *pari passu* creditors there is no problem, but if not there can be a question, not satisfactorily resolved by the statute, as to the right to foreclose.[9] In effect the section gives an opportunity to the bondholder who wishes to sell to test the market; if the best price available is insufficient to satisfy both *pari passu* bondholders, they will probably require to reach agreement as to foreclosure.

33–41　　*Action of foreclosure.* A style of initial writ in an action of foreclosure is given in Burns, *Conveyancing Practice*, pages 541 to 544, including variations required in particular circumstances. This style is still appropriate with minor amendments to take account of the amending provisions in the Conveyancing and Feudal Reform (Scotland) Act 1970, s. 39, *e.g.* the crave should refer to the date of recording of the extract of the decree to follow hereon, not the date of the decree.

33–42　　In relation to foreclosure proceedings:

(1) The title of the creditor to the bond and disposition in security should have been recorded. In terms of section 8 of the 1894 Act the effect of the recorded extract decree of foreclosure is to make the

---

[7]Heritable Securities (Scotland) Act 1894, s. 8 as amended by the Conveyancing and Feudal Reform (Scotland) Act 1970, s. 39.

[8]*Nicholson's Trs.* v. *McLaughlin* (1891) 19 R. 49.

[9]See Burns, 537.

creditor's right to the security subjects "to the same effect as if the disposition in security had been an irredeemable disposition." On strict construction that provision does no more than alter the quality of an unrecorded disposition in security by making it equivalent to an irredeemable disposition, not a *recorded* disposition.

(2) Trustees, executors, tutors, curators and judicial factors may exercise a right of foreclosure.[10] At least one of the trustees or executors should have a recorded title to the bond and disposition in security.

(3) The security subjects must have been exposed as a whole.[11] If that has been done, however, without a price having been offered which is sufficient to repay the amount due to the creditor and there has been a subsequent exposure in lots when some were sold for a total less than that amount but the others attracted no offer, the creditor would probably be entitled to foreclose on the unsold lots.

(4) A decree of foreclosure or a disposition by the creditor to himself under section 11 of the 1894 Act must contain a description of the security subjects and a reference to burdens, whether the latter is contained in the bond and disposition in security or not.[12]

(5) After foreclosure the debtor in the bond remains personally liable for any balance of the debt after deduction of the price stated in the decree of foreclosure.[13]

(6) Any destination in the bond remains applicable in the deemed irredeemable disposition in the decree of foreclosure.

(7) As to recording in the Register of Sasines or registration in the Land Register of the extract decree of foreclosure or the disposition by the heritable creditor in his own favour, see Chapter 42 *infra*.

33–43 *Irregularities in procedure.* Since foreclosure is a statutory remedy it is essential that the whole antecedent procedures and that of the action itself conform in all respects to the statutorily prescribed conditions. Inevitably there has been considerable litigation with regard to irregularities: for a summary of the relevant decisions reference may be made to the undernoted article.[14] A purchaser who has acquired the security subjects from a creditor who has foreclosed and any successor in title from such purchaser is not affected by any irregularity in the proceedings whereby the creditor acquired right to the subjects, but without prejudice to any competent claim of damages, *e.g.* by the debtor against the creditor.[15]

---

[10]1894 Act, s. 13.
[11]*Webb's Exrs.* v. *Reid* (1906) 14 S.L.T. 323.
[12]Conveyancing (Scotland) Act 1924, s. 9(1).
[13]1894 Act, s. 9.
[14]W.L. McGeachy, "The Bondholder's Final Remedy" (1960), 2 Conv. Rev. 129–141.
[15]1894 Act, s. 10.

ASSIGNATION, TRANSMISSION, RESTRICTION, REDEMPTION
AND DISCHARGE

Forms

33–44   The Conveyancing and Feudal Reform (Scotland) Act 1970 provides that any existing security in the older forms may be dealt with as formerly[16] and assignations, deeds of restriction, and discharges of bonds and dispositions in security may be framed in the forms previously in use.

(1) Assignations

33–45   **Policy.** An assignation of a bond and disposition in security has the advantages of (i) retaining the original ranking of the bond and (ii) being less expensive than a discharge and the grant of a standard security in favour of the new lender. On the other hand it has the disadvantages that (i) there is the risk that the debtor's obligation may have been extinguished by payment without a discharge having been recorded, but the facts should be verified by inquiry of the debtor; (ii) if the ownership of the security subjects has changed the assignee may not have the personal obligation of the present proprietor, but a bond of corroboration may be requested in such a case; (iii) the assignee is accepting responsibility for the validity of the assignation in a question with the debtor, who is entitled on repayment to a valid discharge; and (iv) the assignor, on the principle of *debitum subesse*, is warranting to the assignee that there has been no change in the personal obligation or the extent of the security,[17] and also, if there have been previous assignations, that these are valid. For example, there may have been payments to account or alterations of the amount due under the bond by a course of accounting between creditor and debtor[18] which are not disclosed on the Register of Sasines, or implied discharge, by actings, of a co-obligant under the bond who was truly a guarantor,[19] or reduction by informal agreement of the rate of interest stipulated in the bond conditional on punctual payment. There is much to be said for the view that a creditor, when payment of his debt is tendered by the debtor or a third party, is not bound to grant an assignation with those attendant risks. Burns[20] discusses the point at some length, but much depends on circumstances. Briefly:

(1) If the creditor is simply realising his investment of his own volition, an assignation is appropriate: he cannot require the debtor to accept a discharge and grant a standard security to the new lender but he may be able to achieve that result by threatening to call up the bond.

---

[16]s. 31.
[17]*Reid* v. *Barclay* (1879) 6 R. 1007.
[18]*Jackson* v. *Nicoll* (1870) 8 M. 408.
[19]See Vol. I, para. 6–20.
[20]pp. 557, 558.

(2) If the creditor seeks repayment and the debtor finds a new lender, the creditor cannot be required to grant an assignation if his position may be prejudiced thereby[20a]; the debtor's only statutory right on redemption is to obtain a discharge.[21]

(3) If the transaction is effected by an assignation, both the assignor and the assignee should be satisfied by appropriate inquiries that none of the risks above-mentioned exists.

(4) If the transaction is effected by discharge of the bond and the granting of a standard security, the new lender should see searches in the property and personal registers to ensure that no incumbrances or diligences have been created since the recording of the bond which would result in the standard security having a less favourable ranking and that the debtor's financial position is such that there is no danger of reduction of the standard security under section 36 of the Bankruptcy (Scotland) Act 1985.

As to assignations to cautioners on making partial payment, assignations to prevent extinction of the bond *confusione* and assignations where catholic and secondary securities are involved, reference may be made to the undernoted text.[22]

33–46   Terms of assignations. As regards the terms of an assignation of a bond and disposition in security in statutory form:

(1) It is unnecessary to describe or refer to the security subjects or any burdens thereon.[23] If there is collateral moveable security, however, that must be specifically assigned.

(2) The assignation impliedly carries (i) the assignor's right to the writs, (ii) the benefit of all corroborative or substitutional obligations for the debt or any part thereof, whether in bonds or clauses of corroboration or agreements *in gremio* of conveyances or by operation of law or otherwise, (iii) the right to recover payment from the debtor of all expenses properly incurred by the creditor in connection with the security, and (iv) the benefit of any notices which have been served calling up the security and all procedure that may have followed thereon.[24]

(3) Deduction of title is competent where the assignor, although not the original creditor, has right to the bond but not a recorded title to it[25]: if he has a recorded title to the bond no specification of that title is required.[26]

[20a]*Guthrie and McConnachy* v. *Smith* (1880) 8 R. 107 at 111.

[21]Conveyancing (Scotland) Act 1924, s. 32. The position may be otherwise if the debtor has sold the security subjects under burden of the bond and the debtor tenders repayment: he is then entitled to an assignation (*North Albion Property Investment Co. Ltd.* v. *MacBean's C.B.* (1893) 21 R. 90).

[22]Burns, 558–560.

[23]Conveyancing (Scotland) Act 1924, ss. 9(1), 31.

[24]*Ibid.*, s. 28.

[25]*Ibid.*, s. 3.

[26]Conveyancing and Feudal Reform (Scotland) Act 1970, s. 47 and Sched. 10, para. 3.

33–47   *Assignation by infeft creditor, whether original creditor or not*[27]

I, AB, (*designation*), in consideration of the sum of £   paid to me by CD, (*designation*), hereby assign to the said CD a bond and disposition in security for the sum of £   granted by EF, (*designation of original debtor*), in [my favour] *or* [favour of GH, (*designation of original creditor*),] dated   and recorded in the Register of Sasines for the County of   on   : With interest from 19   .

(To be attested)

33–48   *Assignation by uninfeft creditor*[27]

I, AB, (*designation*), in consideration of the sum of £   paid to me by CD, (*designation*), hereby assign to the said CD a bond and disposition in security for the sum of £   granted by EF, (*designation of original debtor*), in favour of GH, (*designation of original creditor*), dated   and recorded in the Register of Sasines for the County of   on   : With interest from   19   : Which bond and disposition in security was last vested in [the said GH as aforesaid] [LM, (*designation*),] whose title thereto was recorded in the said Register of Sasines on   and from whom I acquired right by (*specify writ or writs whereby right acquired by granter of assignation*).

(To be attested)

33–49   *Partial assignation*. As in paragraph 33–47 (where assignor infeft) or paragraph 33–48 (where assignor not infeft) subject to the following insertion before "With interest":

"but only to the extent of £   of principal"

and, in a case where the assignor is not infeft and has right to the bond only to a partial extent, the insertion in the deduction of title clause of specification of the extent to which the assignor and/or the person last infeft, as the case may be, had right to the bond.

33–50   *Combined partial assignation and partial discharge*[28]

I, AB, (*designation*), (First) in consideration of the sum of £2,000 paid to me by CD, (*designation*), hereby assign to the said CD a bond and disposition in security for the sum of £3,000 granted by EF, (*designation of original debtor*), in [my favour] *or* [favour of GH, (*designation of original creditor*)], dated   and recorded in the Register of Sasines for the County of   on   , but only to the extent of £2,000 of principal, with interest from   19   : and (Second) in consideration of the sum of £1,000 paid to me by [the said EF] *or* [JK, (*designation*), the present proprietor of the subjects conveyed by the said bond and disposition in security,] hereby discharge the said bond and disposition in security to the extent of the balance of £1,000 of principal: (*Continue with clause*

---

of deduction of title as in para. 33–48 where granter not infeft).
                                                                    (*To be attested*)

33–51   **Variations.** The styles in paragraphs 33–47 to 33–50 *supra* are basic
statutory styles applicable in circumstances which may still occur
relatively often. Variations and additional clauses may be required in
special cases which are now encountered less frequently since the bond
and disposition in security is obsolescent. Styles of many such
variations may be found in Burns, *Conveyancing Practice*, pages 562 to
577, but practitioners in using them should keep in view that (1)
specification of the title of an infeft assignor is no longer required[29] and
(2) assignations of unrecorded bonds and dispositions in security are
no longer competent.[30]

(2) Transmissions

33–52   **Transmission of creditor's right.** As to transmission of the creditor's
right to a bond and disposition in security, see Volume IV.

33–53   **Transmission of personal obligation of debtor.** In terms of section 47 of
the Conveyancing (Scotland) Act 1874 a heritable security upon an
estate in land and any personal obligation therein transmitted against
any person taking such estate by succession, gift or bequest, or by
conveyance, where an agreement to that effect appeared *in gremio* of
the conveyance, without the necessity of a bond of corroboration, and
the personal obligation could be enforced against that person by
summary diligence in the same manner as against the original debtor.
That provision was modified by section 15 of the Conveyancing
(Scotland) Act 1924 to the effect that (1) in the case of a person taking
the estate by conveyance the personal obligation would not so transmit
against him unless he signed the conveyance, and (2) in the case of a
person whose obligation was created by succession, gift or bequest
summary diligence would not be competent against him unless there
was an agreement to the transmission of the obligation executed by
him.

33–54   (1) *By succession, gift or bequest.* Before 1964 the personal obligation
did not transmit against the heir entitled to succeed to the security
subjects merely by his surviving the debtor; it was necessary that he
had accepted the succession by making up title or taking benefit from
the estate.[31] This question is now of less frequent occurrence since the
whole estate, heritable and moveable, of the deceased vests in his
executor for the purposes of administration[32] but the executor incurs
liability for the deceased's debts only in his capacity as executor and so

---

[29]Conveyancing and Feudal Reform (Scotland) Act 1970, s. 47 and Sched. 10, para. 3.
[30]*Ibid.*, s. 48 and Sched. 11, Pt. II.
[31]*Fenton Livingstone* v. *Crichton's Trs.*, 1908 S.C. 1208.
[32]Succession (Scotland) Act 1964, s. 14.

not beyond the value of the estate.[33] Accordingly, if the debtor's estate is solvent the creditor will be paid in full; if it is not, then the estate will be sequestrated, the creditor may recover what he can from sale of the security subjects and rank for the balance of his debt on the sequestrated estate. Exceptionally, where the title to the security subjects contains a special destination to an identified person so that they do not form part of the estate which vests in the executor[34] with the result that the person entitled to succeed under the destination has on survivance a title to the security subjects which, without any procedure, is complete, he may be liable for the heritable security, but it is thought that if he renounces his right to the subjects without taking any benefit from them he may avoid that liability. If the special destination is in favour of an unidentified person so that the intervention of the executor is necessary for completion of the title of the person entitled to succeed,[35] the successor should refuse to accept a conveyance or transfer by docket of the subjects from the executor if he wishes to avoid personal liability under the heritable security. In all cases of succession, gift or bequest, liability to summary diligence is incurred only if the person entitled to the subjects has executed an agreement to the transmission of the personal obligation.[36]

33–55   (2) *By conveyance.* Where the security subjects are conveyed under burden of the security, the grantee incurs liability for the personal obligation and summary diligence upon it only if there is an agreement to its transmission contained *in gremio* of the conveyance *and* the conveyance is signed by the grantee.[37] As to the terms of dispositions which were or were not agreements to the transmission of the personal obligation against the disponee, see the undernoted cases.[38] As regards transmission of the personal obligation by conveyance it should be noted that (1) the obligation which transmits by agreement in terms of the 1874 and 1924 Acts is only that contained in the deed which constituted the heritable security so that, if it is desired that a disponee should incur liability for an obligation constituted by some other separate deed, *e.g.* an agreement for increase of the rate of interest, a bond of corroboration will be required; (2) transmission of the personal obligation against the disponee does not of itself terminate the personal liability of the original debtor[39]: an express discharge of that is necessary; (3) where the personal obligation has been transmitted against a disponee a discharge of the personal obligation of

---

[33]*Cullen* v. *Baillie* (1846) 8 D. 511 at 522.
[34]1964 Act, s. 36(2)(*a*).
[35]*Ibid.*, s. 18(2) and (4).
[36]1924 Act, s. 15(2).
[37]1924 Act, s. 15(1).
[38]No transmission: *Ritchie and Sturrock* v. *Dullatur Feuing Co.* (1881) 9 R. 358; *Carrick* v. *Rodger, Watt & Paul* (1881) 9 R. 242; *Sherry* v. *Sherry's Trs.*, 1918 1 S.L.T. 31. *Contra: Wright's Trs.* v. *McLaren* (1891) 18 R. 841.
[39]*University of Glasgow* v. *Yuill's Tr.* (1882) 9 R. 643.

the original or any subsequent debtor does not prejudice the security
or the obligation as so transmitted against the disponee "where the
debt still exists"[40]; in such a transaction the discharge of the obligation
of the former debtor should for safety be made after and not before
the execution of the disposition by the granter and grantee; (4) where
there has been a series of conveyances a bond of corroboration granted
on the occasion of an earlier conveyance will be extinguished by the
operation of negative prescription after 20 years from its date
notwithstanding that the personal obligation in the heritable security
has been kept alive by subsequent payments of interest by succeeding
proprietors of the security subjects,[41] but it is thought that the same
result would not follow if the obligation had been transmitted under
section 47 of the 1874 Act in the earlier conveyance since it was an
obligation to pay the original advance constituted by the heritable
security, not a new and independent obligation[42]; and (5) if a
disposition of the security subjects has been granted in which the
personal obligation under the heritable security which burdens them
has transmitted against the disponee but the personal obligation of the
disponer has not been discharged, the creditor may sue the disponer
for payment but the disponer may claim relief against the disponee to
the extent of the value of the subjects.[43]

33–56   *Agreement by successor to transmission of personal obligation*

I, AB, (*designation*), in respect that I have acquired by
[succession to] *or* [gift or bequest by] CD, (*designation*), the
heritable property (*brief description*) which property is burdened
by a bond and disposition in security for the sum of £   [now
outstanding to the extent of £   ] granted by the said CD (*or
otherwise as the case may be*) in favour of EF, (*designation*),
dated   and recorded in the Register of Sasines for
the County of   on   , hereby agree
that the personal obligation in the said bond and disposition in
security for repayment of the said sum of £   [but only to the
extent of £   ] with interest and other obligations contained
therein shall transmit against me from and after the term of

(*To be attested*)

33–57   *Clause in disposition transmitting liability under heritable security*[44]

(*To be inserted after statement of cash consideration*)
and in consideration also of the said [CD (*disponee*) undertaking
as by his signature hereto he undertakes] *or* [CD and EF (*joint
disponees*) undertaking as by their signatures hereto they jointly

[40] 1874 Act, s. 47.
[41] *Yuill's Trs.* v. *Maclachlan's Trs.*, 1939 S.C. (H.L.) 40.
[42] *Ibid.*, *per* Lord Macmillan at 48.
[43] For somewhat complex cases see *McWhirter* v. *Caird* (1884) 12 R. 48; *Todd* v. *Millen &
Somerville*, 1911 S.C. 1189.
[44] 1924 Act, Sched. A, Form No. 2.

and severally undertake] the personal obligation contained in a bond and disposition in security for the sum of £   granted by [me] [PQ, (*designation*),] in favour of RS, (*designation*), dated and recorded in the Register of Sasines for the County of   on   with interest on the said sum of £   from the term of   and the other obligations contained in the said bond and disposition in security also from that term Therefore I have sold and hereby dispone, etc.

NOTES

1. The disponee(s) *must* sign the disposition.
2. The bond and disposition in security will be excepted from warrandice.

(3) Restriction of Security Subjects

Deed of restriction

33–58   The security constituted by a recorded bond and disposition in security may be restricted as regards part of the security subjects by a deed of restriction granted by the creditor in or as nearly as may be in the terms of Form No. 5 of Schedule K to the Conveyancing (Scotland) Act 1924. The restriction may be combined with a partial discharge in or as nearly as may be in the terms of Form No. 6 of said Schedule K.[45] An uninfeft creditor may deduce his title but, if not the original creditor and he has a recorded title, specification of that title is unnecessary.[45a]

33–59   **Consents of all obligants**. Before granting any restriction of the security the creditor should have the consents of all persons who are at the time obligants under the personal obligation in the bond, *e.g.* guarantors, or all joint, or joint and several, obligants, since giving up part of the security may release any obligant whose obligation is of a cautionary character.[46]

33–60   **Description of subjects released and apportionment of ground burdens**. The subjects released must be described with the necessary precision in the deed of restriction and if there is a *cumulo* feuduty or ground annual over both the part released and the remainder of the security subjects it should be apportioned in the deed.[47]

Style—deed of restriction

33–61   I, AB, (*designation of creditor*), [in consideration of the sum of £   paid to me by CD, (*designation of debtor*),] *or* [at the request of CD, (*designation of debtor*), but without any payment being made to me] hereby disburden of a bond and disposition in security for the sum of £   granted by the said CD (*or*

---

[45] 1924 Act, s. 30.
[45a] 1924 Act, s. 3; Conveyancing and Feudal Reform (Scotland) Act 1970, s. 47.
[46] See Vol. I, para. 6–26.
[47] See Burns, 590, 591.

otherwise as the case may be) in my favour (*or otherwise as the case may be*) dated   and recorded in the Register of Sasines for the County of   on
[but only to the extent of £   of principal] ALL and WHOLE (*description of disburdened land, full or by reference*).[47a]
(*Deduction of title, if required*).

(To be attested)

Style—combined partial discharge and deed of restriction

33–62 I, AB, (*designation of creditor*), in consideration of the sum of £   paid to me by CD, (*designation of debtor*), discharge a bond and disposition in security for the sum of £   granted by the said CD (*or otherwise as the case may be*), in my favour (*or otherwise as the case may be*) dated   and recorded in the Register of Sasines for the County of   on   , but only to the extent of £   of principal; And I disburden of the said bond and disposition in security [*adding if necessary* but only to the extent of £   of principal] ALL and WHOLE (*description of disburdened land, full or by reference*)[47a]; (*Deduction of title, if required*).

(To be attested)

(4) Redemption

Persons who may redeem

33–63 In terms of section 32 of the Conveyancing (Scotland) Act 1924 a bond and disposition in security may be redeemed by the debtor or his successors[48] or by the proprietor of the security subjects. A postponed bondholder may give notice of redemption of prior securities,[49] and may seek an assignation of a prior security redeemed instead of a discharge but the creditor may decline the request if prejudice to him could result.[50]

Conditions of right to redeem

33–64 Three months' notice must be given before the term of payment stated in the bond or before any term of Whitsunday or Martinmas thereafter. The payment must be in full and the creditor is entitled to refuse to discharge the security until all questions as to the amount due are settled.[51] If the debt has been split by partial assignations the creditor in any part may be required to accept payment of the amount due to him, although payment of the remainder of the sum due is not

---

[47a] As to description in cases where registration of title is involved see Chap. 42.
[48] Titles to Land Consolidation (Scotland) Act 1868, s. 3. "Successors" includes disponees, executors and representatives.
[49] *Adair's Tr.* v. *Rankin* (1895) 22 R. 975; *Reis* v. *Mackay* (1899) 6 S.L.T. 331.
[50] *Guthrie and McConnachy* v. *Smith* (1880) 8 R. 107 at 111.
[51] *Bruce* v. *Scottish Amicable Life Assurance Society*, 1907 S.C. 637.

tendered to the other partial creditors. On the other hand if the same creditor has obtained several partial assignations, he is entitled to require payment of the total amount due to him and need not accept payment of any part of the debt which has been assigned by one of the partial assignations.

Notice

33–65   Premonition of repayment may be given by or on behalf of the debtor or the proprietor to the person appearing on the record as having the last recorded title to the bond or, if that person is dead, the executor or reputed substitute or person entitled to succeed thereto in terms of the bond or any recorded transmission thereof, notwithstanding any alteration of the succession not appearing on the Register of Sasines. The notice or premonition should be in or as nearly as may be in terms of Form No. 1 of Schedule L to the 1924 Act, it should be delivered or sent by registered post or recorded delivery service to the creditor at his last known address, and either an acknowledgment of receipt by the creditor (Form No. 2 of Schedule L) or a certificate of posting (Form No. 3 of said Schedule) is sufficient evidence of service. If the address of the creditor is not known or the packet containing the notice is returned with intimation that it could not be delivered, premonition should be given to the Keeper of the Record of Edictal Citations (now the Principal Extractor of the Court of Session).[52]

Consignation

33–66   Where the creditor is dead or absent or for any other cause the debtor or proprietor cannot obtain a discharge of the bond he may consign the amount due, including interest and expenses, in a bank in Scotland incorporated by or under Act of Parliament or Royal Charter in the name of the creditor or his representatives, and a certificate of consignation in or as nearly as may be in terms of Form No. 4 of Schedule L to the 1924 Act, when recorded in the Register of Sasines, disencumbers the security subjects to the extent of the amount consigned.[53] The warrant of registration on the certificate should be on behalf of the person for whose benefit the money is consigned. Disburdenment by consignation cannot be effective, however, if there is a dispute as to the amount of the sum due under the security.[54]

(5) Discharge

Express discharge

33–67 A bond and disposition in security may be discharged, and the

---

[52]1924 Act, s. 32.
[53]1924 Act, s. 32.
[54]*Bruce* v. *Scottish Amicable Life Assurance Society, supra.*

security subjects disburdened of it, by an express discharge in or as nearly as may be in terms of Form No. 3 of Schedule K to the Conveyancing (Scotland) Act 1924 duly recorded in the appropriate Register of Sasines.[55] If the personal obligation has been altered, *e.g.* by an agreement for conditional restriction or increase of the rate of interest, or has been supplemented by a guarantee or bond of corroboration, or if an addition has been made to the security subjects, by an agreement or deed separate from the original bond and disposition in security which is being discharged, it is recommended that such separate deed should be mentioned and included in the discharge. The creditor need not be infeft in the bond provided that he deduces his title to it.[56] If the creditor is not the original grantee of the bond but has a recorded title, no specification of that title is required.[57] Strictly a recorded discharge is not necessary to extinguish the debt and disburden the security subjects; a receipt by the creditor for the amount due extinguishes the debtor's personal obligation and the security, which is merely ancillary to the obligation, falls with it,[58] so that a recorded discharge is required only to clear the record. It follows that technical irregularities in the progress of titles whereby a creditor has acquired right to the bond are less important provided that *de facto* he is entitled to the amount due under it.[59]

Discharge[60]

33–68

I, AB, (*designation*), in consideration of the sum of £   paid to me by CD, (*designation*), hereby discharge a bond and disposition in security for the sum of £   granted by [the said CD] *or* [by EF, (*designation of original debtor*),] in [my favour] *or* [favour of GH (*designation of original creditor*),] dated   and recorded in the Register of Sasines for the County of   on   [(*where partial discharge*) but only to the extent of £   of principal]; [(*where creditor uninfeft*) Which bond and disposition in security (to the extent foresaid) was last vested in [the said GH as aforesaid] *or* [in JK, (*designation of creditor having last recorded title*), and from whom I acquired right by (*specify writs whereby granter acquired right*).]]

(*To be attested*)

Extinction otherwise than by Express Discharge

Confusio

33–69

A bond and disposition in security may be extinguished where the

---

[55] 1924 Act, s. 29.
[56] *Ibid.*, s. 3.
[57] Conveyancing and Feudal Reform (Scotland) Act 1970. s. 47.
[58] *Cameron* v. *Williamson* (1895) 22 R. 293; *Niven* v. *Burgh of Ayr* (1899) 1 F. 400.
[59] *Macrae* v. *Gregory* (1903) 11 S.L.T. 102. See Conveyancing and Feudal Reform (Scotland) Act 1970. s. 41(1).
[60] 1924 Act, Sched. K, Form No. 3.

same person becomes both creditor and debtor in the personal obligation. Where the debtor acquires the bond, even if he takes an assignation rather than a discharge, *confusio* operates,[61] unless there is a special interest to keep up the debt.[62] But the opinion has been expressed judicially that where the proprietor of one-half *pro indiviso* of the security subjects subsequently acquired right to the bond it was not *pro rata* extinguished *confusione*.[63]

Prescription

33–70   A bond and disposition in security may be extinguished by negative prescription if no payments of interest or to account of principal have been made for a continuous period of 20 years and there has been no relevant claim by the creditor or relevant acknowledgment by the debtor.[64] In *Marr's Exrx.* v. *Marr's Trs.*[65] it was held that inclusion of a bond and disposition in security as a debt in an inventory of the estate of the deceased debtor and admission of the debt in correspondence by one of the testamentary trustees of the debtor constituted an acknowledgment sufficient to interrupt prescription, but *quaere* whether such facts would now be within the statutory definition of a relevant acknowledgment in section 10(1) of the 1973 Act? Payment of interest on the bond does not preclude the extinction by negative prescription of a separate bond of corroboration.[66]

Payment

33–71   As already noted,[67] payment of the full amount due under the bond evidenced by a receipt extinguishes the personal obligation and disencumbers the land of the security. It was decided that a bond and disposition in security was extinguished by the creditor applying indefinite payments by the debtor as evidenced by an account current in the creditor's ledger.[68]

CASH CREDIT BOND AND DISPOSITION IN SECURITY

Constitution

33–72   Prior to November 29, 1970, it was competent to provide heritable security for fluctuating advances past and future by a bond of cash credit and disposition in security as authorised by and subject to the

---

[61]*Murray* v. *Parlane's Tr.* (1890) 18 R. 287; *Balfour-Melville's M.C. Trs.* v. *Gowans* (1896) 4 S.L.T. 111.
[62]*Fleming* v. *Imrie* (1868) 6 M. 363; *MacBean's C.B.* (1890) 28 S.L.R. 8; *McInnes* v. *Hill*, 1912 1 S.L.T. 80.
[63]*Sherry* v. *Sherry's Trs.*, 1918 1 S.L.T. 31.
[64]Prescription and Limitation (Scotland) Act 1973, ss. 7, 10.
[65]1936 S.C. 64.
[66]*Yuill's Trs.* v. *Maclachlan's Trs.*, 1938 S.C. 52.
[67]para. 33–67.
[68]*Jackson* v. *Nicoll* (1870) 8 M. 408.

limitations prescribed in section 7 of the Debts Securities (Scotland) Act 1856.[69] Styles of a cash credit bond and disposition in security formerly in use may be found in the undernoted texts.[70] Such bonds were normally used for securing advances made by banks or financial houses on running accounts.

Enforcement

33–73   The creditor's remedies for enforcement of the personal obligation or the security were similar to those applicable to a bond and disposition in security save that for registration for execution or a calling-up notice a certificate was required of the amount outstanding at the time.[71]

Assignation

33–74   A cash credit bond and disposition in security is assignable, but only to the extent of the balance due at the time, and does not authorise or create security for subsequent advances by the assignee. The assignation specifies the amount outstanding and assigns the bond only to that extent, but otherwise generally is in the form of an assignation of a bond and disposition in security.[72]If it is intended that further advances will be made by the assignee, the proper method is a discharge of the existing bond and the execution of a standard security in favour of the new lender after a search has been obtained which discloses no other existing securities or diligences.

Restriction and discharge

33–75   Deeds of restriction or discharge of a cash credit bond and disposition in security are in similar form to those in respect of a bond and disposition in security.

Notification of subsequent securities or conveyances

33–76   As to the effect of notification of subsequent recorded securities or conveyances, the principles in relation to the effect of such notification where the security is in the form of an *ex facie* absolute disposition apply.[73]

STAMP DUTY

33–77   Stamp duties on assignations, deeds of restriction and discharges of heritable securities have now been abolished.[74]

---

[69]See Vol. I, para. 5–62 and para. 32–05.
[70]*Encyclopaedia of Scottish Legal Styles*, Vol. 2, No. 201; Burns, 478.
[71]See Vol. I, para. 4–64 and para. 33–24.
[72]For a style, see Burns, 576.
[73]See para. 34–04.
[74]Finance Act 1971, s. 64.

CHAPTER 34

EX FACIE ABSOLUTE DISPOSITIONS

Constitution of security

34–01 Prior to November 29, 1970, the most favoured form of heritable security for debt was the *ex facie* absolute disposition qualified by an unrecorded bilateral agreement executed by both parties or a unilateral back letter granted by the creditor which established that the disposition, although in its terms *ex facie* absolute, was truly granted in security of a fixed amount, or of advances present and future, made or to be made by the creditor or disponee to the debtor. This type of security was particularly useful to secure fluctuating advances.[1]

---

[1]See para. 32–06.

The disposition could be granted by the proprietor of the property "for certain good and onerous causes and considerations"; the granter, if not infeft, would deduce title in accordance with section 3 of the Conveyancing (Scotland) Act 1924. Alternatively, when the advance was made on the occasion of a purchase of the property, the disposition would be granted by the seller with the consent of the purchaser in favour of the lender to the purchaser. In earlier practice the fact that the conveyance was truly in security was evidenced by a back letter by the creditor but later usually, and in the case of advances by a building society almost always, by an unrecorded agreement. The back letter or agreement specified the amount of the loan, if fixed, or that it was for fluctuating advances, with or without a limit of total amount, and set out the terms of the loan as to interest and other conditions.

Proof of security transaction

4-02   If there is no written agreement or back letter which establishes that the *ex facie* absolute disposition is truly in security, an averment by the debtor/granter to that effect can be proved only by the writ or oath of the disponee. If, however, the disponee admits that the disposition was not an absolute conveyance, proof of the true nature of the transaction is not so limited.[2]

Extent of security

4-03   Where the back letter or agreement is not recorded and specifies a loan of fixed amount the security extends also to subsequent advances,[3] since specification of the amount of the loan for which the security was originally advanced does not debar the creditor holding an *ex facie* absolute title from taking the benefit of it until all that he has advanced is repaid. If the unrecorded back letter or agreement bears that the security is for future advances without limit clearly it extends to cover all future advances, but if a limit of credit is expressed then there can be an argument that in a question with the debtor the creditor cannot use the security for advances beyond the amount of the specified limit and interest thereon.[3a]

4-04   **Notification of subsequent securities or conveyances.** Where the creditor receives notice of the creation of a subsequent security over, or a recorded assignation or conveyance of, the whole or part of the property, his preference is restricted to security for his existing advances and any future advances which he may be required to make under the contract to which the security relates, plus interest present or future due thereon and expenses or outlays (with interest thereon)

[2]*Grant's Trs.* v. *Morison* (1875) 2 R. 377; *Grant* v. *Grant* (1898) 6 S.L.T. 203.
[3]*Nelson* v. *Gordon* (1874) 1 R. 1093.
[3a]See *Scottish and Newcastle Breweries Ltd.* v. *Liqdr. of Rathburne Hotel Ltd.*, 1970 S.L.T. 313.

reasonably incurred in the exercise of any power conferred on him by the back letter or agreement.[4] The proper construction and implications of the provisions of the 1970 Act, which are applicable both to standard securities and securities created by *ex facie* absolute dispositions, are considered more fully later.[5] It is sufficient in this chapter to point out that their effect is not to restrict the *security* of the original creditor but merely to regulate the *ranking* upon the security subjects of the original creditor and the person who subsequently obtains a security or conveyance express or implied by law.

34–05   **Publication of security on record**. The security of the creditor may be limited by the publication on the Register of Sasines of the fact that the *ex facie* absolute disposition was truly a security, which can happen either by a reference in any subsequent recorded deed which publishes the fact or by the recording of the back letter or qualifying agreement. The decisions of the courts are not wholly reconcilable and are discussed in the undernoted work,[6] but as regards limitation of the security of the creditor it appears that if the back letter or agreement provided that (1) the security was for a fixed sum any greater amount advanced is not secured, (2) the security was for fluctuating advances without limit or subject to a limit which has not been reached, the security is restricted to the sums advanced at the date of publication, and (3) the security was for fluctuating advances subject to a limit which has been exceeded, the security extends only to the amount of the specified limit, with in all cases interest on these amounts. Otherwise the rights of the *ex facie* absolute disponee are restricted to those which he would have had if the disposition had been *ex facie* in security so that persons transacting with him, *e.g.* a purchaser of the security subjects, must be satisfied that the transaction is within the powers of the creditor in terms of the qualifying back letter or agreement.

34–06   **Death of debtor**. Where the qualifying agreement covers only transactions between the creditor and the debtor the security does not extend to advances made after the debtor's death to his executors or testamentary trustees, but does extend to expenses of management and realisation of the security subjects incurred after the death.[7]

34–07   **Insolvency of debtor**. Where the debtor is sequestrated or, being a company, is wound up by the court or by creditors' voluntary liquidation and the qualifying agreement, whether unrecorded or not, provided that the *ex facie* absolute disposition covered future advances, any subsequent advances made to the trustee in sequestration or the liquidator are not covered by the security.[8] Since

---

[4]Conveyancing and Feudal Reform (Scotland) Act 1970, ss. 13, 42.
[5]See para. 36–19.
[6]Gloag and Irvine, *Law of Rights in Security*, 155–157.
[7]*Morton's Tr.* v. *Kirkhope & Gilmour* (1907) 15 S.L.T. 203.
[8]*Callum* v. *Goldie* (1885) 12 R. 1137.

sequestration or liquidation is a public fact the effect is that, without the need of notification to the creditor, the preference of the creditor is restricted to advances made prior thereto and future advances which he is required to make in terms of the agreement,[9] plus interest and expenses or outlays (with interest thereon) reasonably incurred in the exercise of any power conferred on him by the agreement.[10] It was decided in *Campbell's Judicial Factor* v. *National Bank of Scotland Ltd.*[11] that when the debtor died insolvent the creditor bank was entitled to claim interest on its advances only down to the date of appointment of the judicial factor on the debtor's bankrupt estate, but that decision is now superseded by the provisions of sections 13 and 42 of the Conveyancing and Feudal Reform (Scotland) Act 1970 which make it clear that the creditor may claim interest present and future on advances already made including interest which may accrue.

4–08 **Insolvency of creditor**. Upon the bankruptcy of a creditor in whose favour an *ex facie* absolute disposition has been granted, with a separate deed acknowledging that the property conveyed was held in trust or in security, the property does not form part of his sequestrated estate.[12]

Rights of debtor

4–09 **(1) Postponed securities**. If the debtor was previously infeft in the property (as where an infeft proprietor has granted the *ex facie* absolute disposition to the creditor, but not where he has simply consented to a disposition by a seller to the creditor) he may grant a postponed security in virtue of his radical right.[13,14] The second security over the reversionary right must now be in the form of a standard security granted subject to the first disposition, and usually contains also an assignation of the reversionary right and the right to claim a reconveyance or discharge from the first creditor on payment of the amount due to him.[15] It should be notified to the first creditor in order to restrict his preference.[16] The inclusion of the assignation of the reversionary right and the provision that the standard security is subject to the previous disposition publishes on record the security character of that disposition, but the original creditor still has a

---

[9]It is extremely unlikely that an agreement would provide for the making of future advances after sequestration or liquidation of the debtor.

[10]Conveyancing and Feudal Reform (Scotland) Act 1970. ss. 13, 42.

[11]1944 S.C. 495.

[12]*Heritable Reversionary Co. Ltd.* v. *Millar* (1892) 19 R. (H.L.) 43; Bankruptcy (Scotland) Act 1985, s. 33(1)(*b*).

[13]So may also a debtor who has granted the *ex facie* absolute disposition with a clause of deduction of title—he may grant a standard security if he deduces title from his original infeft author—Conveyancing and Feudal Reform (Scotland) Act 1970, s. 12(2).

[14]*Ritchie* v. *Scott* (1899) 1 F. 728 *per* Lord Kinnear at 736.

[15]For a style see para. 37–15.

[16]See para. 34–04.

preference for existing advances and any future advances which he is required to make in terms of the security.

34–10   If the debtor has never had a title to the property the legal position is notably different. Lord Kinnear in the case cited[17] drew a clear distinction between a debtor who was originally infeft and one who had not been, the latter having only a *jus crediti*. No doubt that reversionary right may be made a fund of credit by assignation to a second lender duly intimated to the first creditor, but the respective preferences of the two creditors would not be regulated by section 42 of the 1970 Act which relates only to a subsequent *recorded* security or conveyance and the rules laid down in the case of *Union Bank* v. *National Bank*[18] would apply. If the debtor had simply consented to the *ex facie* absolute disposition it is at least doubtful whether a standard security granted by him in favour of a second lender would create a valid security, since the granter had not been infeft and could not competently deduce title. If the second lender wishes to obtain a valid heritable security the proper course, if it can be arranged, would be to extinguish the existing security of the original creditor by reconveyance or discharge and for the debtor to grant standard securities to both lenders containing appropriate ranking clauses: any such arrangement would be practicable only if clear searches were available and there was no question that the debtor was solvent at the time.

34–11   **(2) Leases.** A debtor who has granted an *ex facie* absolute disposition but remains in possession of the property may grant leases, at least if they are of a kind normal in relation to the type of property and contain no extraordinary conditions. His right to do so may rest on two separate grounds:

(a) *Mandate*, express or implied. The qualifying agreement may confer on the debtor an express right to grant leases. Even if the agreement is silent on the matter, the fact that the property remains under his administration implies that he has a right to perform ordinary acts of management of the property including the granting of leases.[19] The mandate is personal to the debtor and not transmissible and may be revoked by the creditor.

(b) *Infeftment*. Where the debtor has been infeft in the property, but only in that case, he may be entitled to grant leases by virtue of his radical right.[20]

Rights of creditor

34–12   **(1) Personal obligation.** Any right which the creditor may have to

---

[17] *Ritchie* v. *Scott, supra.*
[18] (1886) 14 R. (H.L.) 1.
[19] *Abbott* v. *Mitchell* (1870) 8 M. 791; *Ritchie* v. *Scott, supra*; *Edinburgh Entertainments Ltd.* v. *Stevenson,* 1926 S.C. 363.
[20] *Ritchie* v. *Scott, supra*; *Edinburgh Entertainments Ltd.* v. *Stevenson, supra.*

enforce repayment of the secured advance by proceedings against the debtor personally depends upon the terms of the qualifying agreement. If it contains an acknowledgment of the debt the creditor may enforce repayment by personal action, subject to any provision as to a minimum period of duration of the loan; if it contains a personal bond by the debtor with a clause of consent to registration for execution, summary diligence may be competent. Where the security is in respect of fluctuating advances by a bank or financial institution the bond will normally have provided for ascertainment of the amount due by a certificate of an officer of the lender which will be a necessary preliminary step to enforcement of the personal obligation.[21]

34–13 (2) **Entering into possession**. In contrast to the position of the creditor in a bond and disposition in security whose right to enter into possession and draw rents depends upon the clause of assignation of rents in the bond and, if the debtor objects, requires to be enforced by an action of maills and duties, an *ex facie* absolute disponee has the right to assume management of the property as proprietor which he may enforce, if need be, by a declarator of the court which may ordain the debtor to remove.[22] An action of summary ejection, however, is incompetent.[23]

34–14 (3) **Poinding of the ground**. The creditor cannot competently raise an action of poinding of the ground since, as *ex facie* proprietor, he cannot be the holder of a *debitum fundi*.[24] This may be a serious disadvantage in circumstances where the property is a factory or hotel and the right to attach the moveables may be a valuable addition to the security.

34–15 (4) **Sale**. The most effective remedy available to the creditor is to sell the security subjects. If there is no back letter or qualifying agreement, or if any such document does not impose conditions as regards the creditor's right of sale, the creditor may sell by private bargain and he does not require the consent of the debtor.[25] If the creditor's powers of sale are expressed in a qualifying document the creditor should sell in accordance with the conditions of the contractual bargain. In all cases, however, the creditor as quasi-trustee for the debtor must have due regard to the debtor's interests and must not act in disregard of them. Sale must be after adequate advertisement in an arm's-length transaction.[26] A building society creditor must sell at the best price that can reasonably be obtained.[27]

---

[21]See Vol. I, para. 4–64.
[22]*Rankin* v. *Russell* (1868) 7 M. 126.
[23]*Scottish Property Investment Co. Bldg. Soc.* v. *Horne* (1881) 8 R. 737.
[24]*Scottish Heritable Security Co.* v. *Allan, Campbell & Co.* (1876) 3 R. 333.
[25]*Baillie* v. *Drew* (1884) 12 R. 199; *Duncan* v. *Mitchell & Co.* (1893) 21 R. 37; *Shrubb* v. *Clark* (1897) 5 S.L.T. 125; *Aberdeen Trades Council* v. *Shipconstructors and Shipwrights Association*, 1949 S.C. (H.L.) 45.
[26]*Shrubb* v. *Clark, supra; Rimmer* v. *Thomas Usher & Son Ltd.*, 1967 S.L.T. 7.
[27]Building Societies Act 1962, s. 36. (The 1962 Act is repealed by the Building Societies Act 1986 but the like requirement is contained in the 1986 Act, Sched. 4, para. 1.)

The purchaser, if he is aware that the seller's title was truly in security, either because the qualifying back letter or agreement has been recorded or has been disclosed otherwise, should examine the relevant provisions of the qualifying deed and is entitled to be satisfied that the circumstances have occurred in which the creditor has right to sell and that the sale procedure has been in accordance with any conditions imposed. On the other hand if the purchaser has no such knowledge and transacts in the *bona fide* belief that the seller is absolute proprietor, his title is not challengeable by the debtor who is the true owner. In practice it is comparatively seldom that the purchaser will not suspect from the nature of the seller's business and the type of property that the seller is really a secured creditor. It can be a difficult decision whether the purchaser should make inquiry on the matter: in general if he does make such inquiry and the seller declines to give any information, it is thought that the purchaser may safely accept a disposition from the seller. The disposition should be a simple absolute disposition in consideration of the price: even if the purchaser is aware that the seller is truly a secured creditor who is selling in accordance with his powers under an unrecorded security agreement, it is unnecessary to narrate that in the disposition. If the fact that the seller is a secured creditor is not disclosed, warrandice should be absolute: if the transaction proceeds on the basis that the purchaser has knowledge of the true position, the seller should grant warrandice from fact and deed only and assign the debtor's warrandice.

Assignation

34–16   Assignation of a security constituted by way of *ex facie* absolute disposition and qualifying agreement presents difficulties because of the inconsistency between the substance of the transaction and the form of the documentation. In theory the creditor may grant an absolute disposition to the new lender and an unrecorded assignation of his rights under the agreement,[28] but the new lender will usually wish a direct personal obligation from the debtor with a consent to registration for execution and there is no such facility for transmission of the personal obligation as is available by statute in the case of a true security.[28a] Participation by the debtor in the documentation is usually necessary, and the more satisfactory solution is to discharge the existing security and constitute it afresh in favour of the new lender with the attendant problems of loss of ranking and expense.

Discharge

34–17   Before 1970 when a loan secured by an *ex facie* absolute disposition

---

[28] It is usually accepted that the assignation can only be of the amount of the advance then outstanding.
[28a] See paras. 33–52 to 33–57.

was repaid it was necessary to prepare and record a reconveyance, although in many cases in practice the need for a separate reconveyance or discharge was elided by a disposition on sale granted by the creditor and the debtor to a new purchaser. Section 40 of the Conveyancing and Feudal Reform (Scotland) Act 1970 permits the discharge to be effected by a document of discharge, separate or endorsed on the original disposition, which, when duly recorded, disburdens the security subjects and vests them in the person entitled to them to the same effect as if a conveyance containing a clause of warrandice from fact and deed only and all other usual and necessary clauses had been granted by the creditor to that person and duly recorded. A style of discharge is provided in Schedule 9 to the Act, deduction of title being necessary where the creditor does not have a recorded title, but no specification of his title is required if the granter of the discharge, although not the original creditor, has a recorded title.[29] If the granter is not the original creditor, the separate form of discharge must be used.[30]

The statutory discharge is not obligatory: it is still competent to use a reconveyance.[31] In the normal case where the loan is repaid by the original debtor to the original creditor the statutory form of discharge may be used: there is then no doubt that the debtor is the person in whose favour the deemed reconveyance is granted. Where there has been alienation or devolution of the debtor's right during the subsistence of the loan, however, it may be more satisfactory to use a reconveyance containing a narrative of the change in beneficial ownership of the property. Also if there has been collateral moveable security, *e.g.* a life policy, a retrocession will be required in conjunction with either a reconveyance or discharge.

Succession of debtor and creditor

34–18   The rights of succession to the interests of the debtor and creditor under a security constituted by *ex facie* absolute disposition are treated in Volume IV.

Effect of intervening diligence against debtor or creditor

34–19   The reversionary right of the debtor may be attached during the subsistence of the security by adjudication at the instance of a third party.[32] An inhibition used against the debtor during the subsistence of the security will preclude any subsequent alteration of its terms which is more favourable to the creditor and in prejudice of the inhibitor or the subsequent granting of a standard security as part of a process of

---

[29] 1970 Act, Sched. 9, Note 3.
[30] *Ibid.*, Sched. 9, Note 2.
[31] *Ibid.*, s. 40(2).
[32] *Jackson* v. *Halliday* (1758) Mor. 2769, 5 Br.Sup. 362; *Paul* v. *Boyd* (1829) 7 S. 621; *Herries, Farquhar & Co.* v. *Burnett* (1846) 9 D. 111.

reconstitution of the security, *e.g.* on the occasion of granting a postponed security[33] or assignation of the security to a new lender.[34] An inhibition also, of course, strikes at the subsequent granting of any postponed security to a second lender. It was decided in *Campbells' Tr.* v. *De Lisle's Executors*[35] that an inhibition against a debtor in a cash credit bond and disposition in security did not destroy the effect of the bond recorded prior to the inhibition as a security for advances made after the date of the inhibition and the Lord Justice-Clerk expressed the opinion that there was no difference if the security had been constituted by absolute disposition. The *ratio* was that the heritable security for future advances was created before the inhibition and so was unaffected by it while the debt contracted by subsequent operations was not, so far as personal, affected by the inhibition. Graham Stewart in the *Law of Diligence*[36] expresses a contrary opinion, but it is based on the decision in the *Union Bank* case[37] relating to an assignation of the debtor's reversionary interest which carries rights much more extensive than those resulting from a prohibitory diligence affecting only heritable property. If the further advance is made under a new and special arrangement neither required nor contemplated when the absolute disposition was granted, the effect of an intervening inhibition is more dubious and the creditor may not be able to rely on the disposition as an effective security for the further advance.

34–20   The right of the disponee under an *ex facie* absolute disposition, *i.e.* the creditor, may be attached by adjudication at the instance of a third party but subject to the reversionary right of the debtor.[38] An inhibition used against the creditor does not affect the right of the debtor to redeem nor the right of the creditor to grant a reconveyance or discharge which the debtor can demand upon repayment.[39] If the inhibitor wishes to restrain discharge of the security without his being consulted, he must intimate the inhibition to the debtor notarially.[40] An inhibition against the creditor, however, affects his right to realise his security by transfer to a third party as being a voluntary transaction, not instigated by the debtor, which is prejudicial to the inhibitor.

Liabilities of creditor to third parties

34–21   Since the creditor is feudally vested in ownership by the absolute

---

[33]See para. 34–10.
[34]See para. 34–16.
[35](1870) 9 M. 252.
[36]at 565.
[37]*Union Bank* v. *National Bank* (1885) 13 R. 380, rev. (1886) 14 R. (H.L.) 1.
[38]*Thomson* v. *Douglas, Heron & Co.* (1784) Mor. 10229; *Heritable Reversionary Co.* v. *Millar* (1892) 19 R. (H.L.) 43 at 48.
[39]*Mackintosh's Trs.* v. *Davidson & Garden* (1898) 25 R. 554 (relating to a bond and disposition in security, but the principle applies to a security by way of absolute disposition).
[40]Act of Sederunt, Feb. 19, 1680.

disposition he is liable to the superior in payment of feuduty, a liability which is terminated only upon reconveyance or discharge,[41] but the creditor is entitled to relief from the debtor.[42] It is less clear whether the creditor is liable to the superior for implement of other prestations of the feu which have been made real burdens, and there are authorities which are difficult to reconcile.[43] It would appear that the right of the superior to enforce such other conditions of the feu against a creditor who has not entered into possession of the property, without attempting to enforce liability against the debtor who is the true proprietor, is at least doubtful. Liability for stipend is not incurred by the creditor unless he has entered into possession.[44] Local rates are now the responsibility of the occupier so that unless the creditor has taken possession of the property, has occupied it personally and been entered as occupier on the valuation roll, he is not liable to the local authority for payment of rates. Responsibility for the making up and maintenance of a private road is now placed upon the frontagers,[45] who are defined as owners of land fronting or abutting it, but "owners" are the persons entitled to receive the rents of the property,[46] so that the creditor would incur liability only if he had entered into possession and was drawing the rents. The creditor may avoid any possible liabilities which he may incur as *ex facie* proprietor by divesting himself of the security by reconveyance or discharge, to which the debtor cannot object.

Documentation

34–22 Since heritable securities for debt can no longer be created by *ex facie* absolute disposition, the framing of the constituting documents is no longer a matter of practice. Styles of disposition and qualifying agreement may be found in the undernoted texts.[47] Assignations to new lenders, always difficult documents, will now seldom be granted; reconstitution of the security by a standard security will usually be preferred. The only type of document in the older form which may occasionally be used is a reconveyance,[48] a style of which is offered in the following paragraph.

Reconveyance[49]

34–23 I, AB, (*designation*), [for certain good causes and considera-

[41] *Trustees for Debenture Holders of Eastern Counties Properties Ltd.* v. *Prudential Investment Bldg. Soc.*, 1943 S.L.T. (Sh.Ct.) 30.
[42] *Liqdrs. of City of Glasgow Bank* v. *Nicolson's Trs.* (1882) 9 R. 689.
[43] *Clark* v. *City of Glasgow Life Assce. Co.* (1854) 1 Macq. 668. *Cf. Patterson* v. *Robertson*, 1912 2 S.L.T. 494.
[44] *Jackson* v. *Cochrane* (1873) 11 M. 475.
[45] Roads (Scotland) Act 1984, s. 13.
[46] *Ibid.*, s. 151.
[47] *Encyclopaedia of Scottish Legal Styles*, Vol. 1, Nos. 1–15; Burns, 488–491.
[48] See para. 34–17.
[49] Appropriate where there has been devolution or transmission of debtor's right.

tions] *or* [considering that CD, (*designation*), conveyed the subjects hereinafter disponed to me by disposition dated   and recorded in the Register of Sasines for the County of   on   and that the said disposition although ex facie absolute was truly granted in security of (a loan of £   ) (advances on current account made and to be made by me to the said CD) and further considering that EF, (*designation*), has now right to the reversionary right of the said CD to the said subjects by virtue of (*narrate shortly the devolution or transmission of the right*)] and now seeing that [the said loan] [the whole amount of said advances which did not in total exceed £   ] has now been repaid with all interest due thereon Therefore I hereby dispone to the said EF heritably and irredeemably ALL and WHOLE (*description of subjects exactly as conveyed in original disposition*) but always with and under (*reference to deeds creating burdens*): With entry at   : Declaring that the said EF and his successors shall be bound, as by acceptance (*execution*) hereof he binds himself and his executors and representatives whomsoever to free and relieve me and my successors of all feu-duties [ground annuals] and public burdens and of all other liability and responsibility in connection with the said subjects as well before as after the said date of entry: And I grant warrandice from fact and deed only.

(To be attested)
(Stamp duty nil)

Discharge (separate)[50]

34–24   I, AB, (*designation*) hereby acknowledge that the [disposition] [assignation[51]] granted [by CD, (*designation*),] [by EF, (*designation*), with consent of CD, (*designation*),] in my favour [in favour of GH, (*designation of original creditor*),] recorded in the Register of Sasines for the County of   on   , although in its terms *ex facie* absolute, was truly in security of an advance of £   , and that all moneys intended to be secured thereby have been fully paid.

(To be attested)

NOTES

1. This style is appropriate whether or not the granter is the original creditor so long as he has a recorded title.

2. Where the granter is not the original creditor and has not a recorded title insert at the end a clause of deduction of title thus:

The subjects conveyed by the said disposition (*or otherwise as the case may be*) were last vested in the said GH as aforesaid (*or where the last recorded title to the subjects was in favour of a person other than the original creditor*) in JK, (*designation*), whose title thereto was recorded in the said Register of Sasines on   ) and from whom I acquired right by (*specify shortly the writ or writs by which right was acquired*).

—Sched. 9, Note 3.

---

[50]Statutory form—1970 Act, Sched. 9.
[51]Where recorded lease was assigned.

3. Where the security was for an advance of a maximum amount for "an advance" substitute "a maximum sum".

4. Where the security was for fluctuating advances of uncertain amount for "an advance of £   " substitute "all sums due or that might become due by the said CD and the total amount of which did not actually exceed £   " (*or otherwise as the case may be, specifying shortly the nature of the obligation*).

Discharge (endorsed)

34-25   I, AB, (*designation*), hereby acknowledge that the foregoing [disposition] [assignation[52]] granted by CD, (*designation*), in my favour recorded in the Register of Sasines for the County of   on   although in its terms *ex facie* absolute, was truly granted in security of an advance of £   , and that all moneys intended to be secured thereby have been fully paid.

(*To be attested*)

NOTES

1. This style can be used *only* where the granter is the original creditor.—Sched. 9, Note 2.

2. Where the security was for a maximum amount or for fluctuating advances of uncertain amount substitute for reference to "an advance of £   " the alternative wording in Note 3 or 4 to style in para. 34-24.

Registration

34-26   The reconveyance or discharge should be recorded in the Register of Sasines with a warrant of registration on behalf of the person entitled to the security subjects.[53]

Stamp duty

34-27   Stamp duty on assignations, restrictions, reconveyances and discharges of heritable securities has now been abolished.[54]

---

[52]Where recorded lease was assigned.

[53]If the reconveyance or discharge is granted as part of a transaction which induces first registration in the Land Register, a warrant of registration is not required—see R.T.P.B., para. D.2.22.

[54]Finance Act 1971, s. 64.

CHAPTER 35

REAL BURDENS FOR MONEY, GROUND ANNUALS AND STATUTORY CHARGES ON LAND

Introduction

35–01   Before the reforms made by the Conveyancing and Feudal Reform (Scotland) Act 1970 and the Land Tenure Reform (Scotland) Act 1974 it was competent to create real burdens for money, either in the form of a lump sum or continuing periodic payments, secured over land. So far as the security is for debt as defined in section 9(8)(c) of the 1970 Act that can now be effected only by a standard security[1] and the creation of periodical payments secured over land, *e.g.* ground annuals, is now prohibited by section 2 of the 1974 Act. Some real burdens and ground annuals created before the enactment of these statutes still exist: this chapter deals only with the legal principles of such earlier burdens and with their enforcement, assignation and discharge, which may still be relevant matters although in a diminishing number of cases. Certain statutory charges may be imposed on land which form real burdens upon it: some of these which may be encountered in practice are noticed in Part III of this chapter.[1a]

I. REAL BURDENS FOR MONEY

Constitution

35–02   Real burdens for money could be created either by reservation or constitution in conveyances of land. If A conveyed property to B, he might do so under the real burden of a sum or periodic payments of an annual amount payable to himself (creation by reservation). If A conveyed property to B he might do so under burden of such a payment to C (creation by constitution). Whatever the form of its creation an effective real burden had to satisfy the requisites already mentioned in the case of a valid real burden, *viz.* (1) it had to be definite both as to the amount and the time of payment,[2] (2) the creditor had to be identified,[3] (3) the intention had to be clearly expressed to burden the property as distinct from the grantee of the conveyance personally,[4] (4) the burden had to appear in the dispositive clause of the conveyance,[5] and (5) the burden had to enter the record by the conveyance or a notarial instrument or notice of title following upon it being recorded in the Register of Sasines.[6,7]

---

[1] 1970 Act, s. 9(3).

[1a] Certain statutes enacted but not fully in force at Dec. 31, 1986, or currently in course of preparation may affect conveyancing practice or impose charges on land, *e.g.* the Building Societies Act 1986 and the Telecommunications Bill.

[2] *Ewing's Trs.* v. *Crum Ewing*, 1923 S.C. 569.

[3] But a real burden in favour of unnamed children of named persons was sustained—*Erskine* v. *Wright* (1846) 8 D. 863.

[4] *Tailors of Aberdeen* v. *Coutts* (1840) 1 Rob.App. 296; *Davidson* v. *Dalziel* (1881) 8 R. 990; *Buchanan* v. *Eaton*, 1911 S.C. (H.L.) 40.

[5] Bell, *Prin.*, s. 920; *Kemp* v. *Magistrates of Largs*, 1939 S.C. (H.L.) 6.

[6] *Tailors of Aberdeen* v. *Coutts, supra*; *Cowie* v. *Muirden* (1893) 20 R. (H.L.) 81.

[7] See Vol. II, Chap. 19.

Enforcement

35–03   There was no infeftment of the creditor in the real burden: it was merely a burden on the land and the infeftment therein completed the creditor's title to the burden. In the absence of a personal obligation of the proprietor of the burdened land the creditor in the burden has no right of personal action, and his right can be enforced only by the remedies competent in law to the holder of a *debitum fundi*. He may poind the ground subject to the limitation already mentioned in a question with a trustee in sequestration or a liquidator.[8] He may adjudge the land, but that merely gives a right to possess it and he obtains an absolute title only on expiry of the legal; as regards ranking in competition with other adjudgers he may obtain a preference based on the date of creation of the burden only if his adjudication is preceded by a poinding of the ground. He cannot attach the rents by an action of maills and duties since that depends upon a clause of assignation of rents, nor has he a power to sell the burdened land unless expressly conferred.[9]

Assignation

35–04   A real burden may be assigned in Form No. 1 of Schedule K to the Conveyancing (Scotland) Act 1924[10] with appropriate adaptation in terms of Note 4 to that Schedule.[11] Assignations of real burdens are now relatively uncommon in practice, but forms appropriate to various circumstances are provided in the undernoted text.[12]

Restriction and discharge

35–05   The release of the burdened property or part of it from the burden or the discharge of the burden may be in Form No. 5 or in Form No. 4 of Schedule K to the 1924 Act,[10] appropriately adapted in terms of Note 4 thereto.[11]

Succession

35–06   The succession of the creditor and the debtor in a real burden is treated in Volume IV.

Preference in competition with third parties

35–07   The criterion of preference of a real burden in a competition with other securities or diligences was and is determined by the date when

---

[8]See para. 33–18.

[9]See *Fraser* v. *Wilson* (1824) 2 Sh.App. 162.

[10]s. 43.

[11]Forms in Sched. K now amended—Conveyancing and Feudal Reform (Scotland) Act 1970, s. 47 and Sched. 10, para. 3.

[12]Burns, 503 (stamp duties are now abolished—Finance Act 1971, s. 64).

the deed creating the real burden was recorded in the Register of Sasines. Before 1874, however, the assignee of a real burden completed his title by intimation of the assignation to the proprietor of the burdened lands, but section 30 of the Conveyancing (Scotland) Act 1874 provided that intimation would be unnecessary when the assignation was so recorded, and the date of recording was made the criterion of the assignee's preference in competition with third parties.

II. GROUND ANNUALS

Origins, development and prohibition in future

35–08   Ground annuals were originally created over burgage lands or feudal holdings where subinfeudation had been prohibited. The Conveyancing (Scotland) Act 1874 abolished the distinction between feudal and burgage property for conveyancing purposes[13] and provided that prohibitions of subinfeudation would be null and void,[14] and thereafter ground annuals were created to provide an annual income from land to persons who were not superiors, often with the addition of further building or other conditions imposed by the creditor in the ground annual. The Land Tenure Reform (Scotland) Act 1974, subject to certain transitional provisions that are now spent,[15] prohibited the creation of ground annuals after September 1, 1974,[16] and of any increase in the total amount of any existing ground annual.[17]

Nature and characteristics

35–09   A ground annual has been described judicially as "a perpetual rentcharge secured in some effectual fashion as a real burden on land."[18] Although perpetual,[19] it is redeemable by the proprietor of the burdened land.[20] There is a clear distinction in legal principle between a ground annual right and a feu or sub-feu. A contract of ground annual in its modern form[21] created the relationship of creditor and debtor in a real burden with a personal obligation adjected to it and the rights of parties depended on contract and the law of real burdens, whereas a feu or sub-feu created a relationship of superior and vassal in a feudal estate and the right to feuduty depended upon a contract by tenure with implied renewal of the contract as between

---

[13]s. 25.
[14]s. 22, as extended by Conveyancing Amendment (Scotland) Act 1939, s. 8.
[15]s. 7.
[16]s. 2.
[17]s. 3(2).
[18]*Church of Scotland Endowment Committee* v. *Provident Association of London Ltd.*, 1914 S.C. 165 at 172.
[19]See *Healy & Young's Tr.* v. *Mair's Trs.*, 1914 S.C. 893.
[20]Conveyancing (Scotland) Act 1924, s. 2(1)(b) expressly includes ground annuals within the definition of heritable securities, and s. 23(2) provides for their discharge.
[21]See para. 35–10.

each successive superior and vassal. This fundamental distinction has a number of important practical effects:

(1) It is the proprietor of the property, not the holder of the ground annual, who is liable to implement the obligations of the feu, so that a ground annual was a more attractive proposition for an investor.

(2) A ground annual being simply a special example of creditor-debtor relationship with real security could be extinguished entirely, not only as to arrears but also as to future payments, by non-payment and the absence of any acknowledgment by omission of any reference to the burden from the title deeds, both for a continuous period of 20 years.[22] In the case of a feuduty, however, although the right to claim arrears is lost after non-payment and without judicial interruption for a period of five years,[23] the right to claim subsequent payments being a real right of ownership in land (the superiority) is imprescriptible.[24]

(3) The original debtor in a contract of ground annual who was personally liable does not cease to be so when he has parted with the ownership of the burdened property.[25] On the other hand the liability of the original feuar for payment of future feuduties ceased when he conveyed the property to another and the disponee recorded his title and notice of change of ownership was served on the superior unless there was some specialty in the personal obligation in the feu contract which had the effect of binding the original feuar and his heirs, executors and successors jointly and severally.[26] Consistently with that principle a subsequent owner of a property burdened with a ground annual had no contractual relationship with the creditor in the ground annual and was not personally liable in payment of it. In order to protect his property from real diligence if the ground annual was not paid he might, and normally did, ensure that it was paid but there was no obligation to do so which the creditor could enforce against him by personal action.[27] On the other hand each successive feuar when he recorded his title became personally liable to the superior for payment of the feuduty. The practical importance of this distinction is now less, since an allocated ground annual or feuduty is compulsorily redeemable on sale or compulsory acquisition of the property.[28]

(4) Likewise, building or other conditions *ad factum praestandum* contained in a contract of ground annual are not enforceable personally against a singular successor in ownership of the property,[29] whereas a successor of a feuar upon recording his title becomes personally liable for implement of the whole conditions of the contract of feu unless there is some specialty in the terms of the contract which

---

[22]Prescription and Limitation (Scotland) Act 1973, s. 8.
[23]*Ibid.*, s. 6 and Sched. 1, para. 1.
[24]*Ibid.*, s. 8(2) and Sched. 3.
[25]*Millar* v. *Small* (1853) 15 D.(H.L.) 38.
[26]*e.g.* as in *Police Commissioners of Dundee* v. *Straton* (1884) 11 R. 586.
[27]*Royal Bank* v. *Gardyne* (1853) 15 D.(H.L.) 45.
[28]Land Tenure Reform (Scotland) Act 1974, ss. 5 and 6.
[29]*Marshall's Tr.* v. *Macneill & Co.* (1888) 15 R. 762.

demonstrates that the obligation was not a continuing one but part of a bargain between the superior and the original feuar.[30]

Constitution and form of contract

35–10   A contract of ground annual must be made between two separate persons since that is necessary to constitute a debtor-creditor relationship.[31] In the modern form in use before 1974 the deed comprised (1) a disposition of the property to a purchaser under the reserved real burden of the ground annual, (2) a personal obligation of the purchaser for payment of the ground annual, (3) a disposition by the purchaser to the seller of both the ground annual and the property in security for the ground annual, and (4) a consent to registration for preservation and execution. In addition it might impose conditions as to buildings and their maintenance and insurance, the creation of those as real burdens, the burden of payment of feuduty and implement of any existing feuing conditions and a conventional irritancy in the event of non-payment of the ground annual or non-implement of the other conditions of the contract.[32] Clause (2) above founded a right of personal action and clause (3) gave an active title to enforce the security. The personal obligation in ordinary form would, for the reasons already given,[33] bind only the original debtor and his executors and representatives but not singular successors in the ownership of the burdened property, but the irritancy clause created an effective compulsitor upon any successor to implement the conditions of the contract, and indeed even without the inclusion of a conventional irritancy the creditor has a statutory right of irritancy under section 23(5) of the Conveyancing (Scotland) Act 1924.

The deed was recorded in the Register of Sasines with two warrants, one on behalf of the purchaser for preservation as well as for publication and one on behalf of the seller (the creditor in the ground annual) for preservation and execution as well as for publication.

Allocation

35–11   A ground annual may be allocated by agreement or by using the statutory right of allocation by notice conferred by sections 3 to 6 of the Conveyancing and Feudal Reform (Scotland) Act 1970 which is available in respect of ground annuals as well as feuduties.[34]

Enforcement

35–12   Payment of a ground annual may be enforced against the original

---

[30] e.g. as in Magistrates of Edinburgh v. Begg (1883) 11 R. 352.
[31] Church of Scotland Endowment Committee v. Provident Association of London Ltd., 1914 S.C. 165.
[32] For styles see Encyclopaedia of Scottish Legal Styles, Vol. 5, No. 234; Burns, 281.
[33] In para. 35–09.
[34] For particulars of procedure, see Vol. II, paras. 17–39, 17–40.

debtor by personal action or, if the contract contained a consent to registration for execution, by summary diligence. Since the disposition in security incorporated in the contract in its modern form contains an assignation of rents an action of mails and duties is competent,[35] and the provisions of the Heritable Securities (Scotland) Act 1894 apply.[36] As creditor in a *debitum fundi* the holder of the ground annual may poind the ground subject to the limitation in a question with a trustee in sequestration or a liquidator[37] and he may adjudge.[37a] An action of declarator of irritancy is also competent based either upon a conventional irritancy in the contract or upon the statutory right of irritancy under section 23(5) of the Conveyancing (Scotland) Act 1924.

Assignation

35–13   A statutory form of assignation is provided in the Conveyancing (Scotland) Act 1924,[38] and its implications are explained therein. As regards these:

(1) The implied destination to heirs and assignees whomsoever[39] now requires consideration. Ground annuals were and are heritable in the succession of the debtor, but in the succession of the creditor they are moveable except *quoad* the fisc and legal rights for which purposes they are heritable.[40] Paragraph 1 of Schedule 2 to the Succession (Scotland) Act 1964 provides that references in any enactment to the heir-at-law of a deceased person "in relation to any heritable property" shall be construed as references to the persons entitled to succeed by virtue of the 1964 Act, and paragraph 2 of the same Schedule provides that references in general terms to the heirs of a deceased person include persons entitled to succeed on intestacy to any part of the estate of the deceased and so far as necessary for the purposes of Part III of the 1964 Act to the executor of the deceased. Although the matter is not altogether free from doubt it would appear that the destination implied in the 1924 Act will now be construed as in favour of executors and assignees whomsoever. If the assignee wishes the ground annual to be moveable except *quoad* the fisc and legal rights, the assignation should be taken in name of the assignee *simpliciter*; if he wishes the ground annual to be moveable in his succession for all purposes, including legal rights, he should insert a declaration to that effect.

(2) If there has been any alteration in the amount of the ground

---

[35] *Somerville* v. *Johnston* (1899) 1 F. 726.
[36] Conveyancing (Scotland) Act 1924, s. 23(4).
[37] See para. 33–18.
[37a] For a form of decree of adjudication, see the Conveyancing (Scotland) Act 1924, Sched. K, Form No. 8.
[38] s. 23(1) and Form No. 2 of Sched. K.
[39] *Ibid.*, s. 23(1)(*a*).
[40] For an account of how this result arises from various statutory provisions see Meston, *The Succession (Scotland) Act 1964*, 46.

annual from that in the original contract, as by previous commutation of duplicands or augmentation on allocation, that should be expressly mentioned.[41]

(3) The property from which the ground annual is payable must be described. That can involve complications. If the ground annual has been allocated over several parts of the original property, the proper course would be to assign each allocated part of the ground annual as currently payable including any augmentation with a description of the part of the property over which it is now secured.

(4) Reference to burdens or conditions of the title to the burdened property is unnecessary.[42]

Specification or deduction of title

35–14 If the granter of the assignation, whether or not the original creditor, has a recorded title to the ground annual, specification of his title is now unnecessary.[43] If he does not have such a recorded title he may deduce title.[44]

Examination of title

35–15 In a sale of a ground annual the purchaser should examine the title to the property over which it is secured in order to be satisfied that (1) the ground annual has been constituted by a proprietor of the property who had a title to do so, (2) the ground annual has been referred to in subsequent conveyances of the property and (3) where there has been any augmentation or alteration affecting the ground annual, it was effected by agreement with a proprietor of the property who at the time had a valid title. In cases (1) and (3) he should confirm that any necessary consents, *e.g.* of heritable creditors, have been taken. As regards the title to the ground annual itself he should ensure that there is a valid prescriptive progress of the title to it. Searches in the property register should be examined against the title to the ground annual for 40 years back or the date when it was constituted, whichever is the lesser, and against the title to the burdened property for 20 years back,[44a] although in certain circumstances a lesser period may be acceptable. A search in the personal register for five years preceding the date of the current transaction is usually sufficient.

---

[41]s. 23(1)(*b*) and (*c*) imply the assignation of additional payments and any agreement constituting them, but in the interests of clarity it is preferable to make express mention of them.

[42]Conveyancing (Scotland) Act 1924, ss. 9(1) and 2(1)(*b*).

[43]Conveyancing and Feudal Reform (Scotland) Act 1970, s. 47 and Sched. 10, para. 3.

[44]1924 Act, Sched. K, Note 2 as amended by 1970 Act, Sched. 10, para. 3.

[44a]The search against the ground annual is to ensure that there has been no security over it which has been kept alive by payment of interest: the search against the property is to ensure that the right to the ground annual has not been extinguished by negative prescription if reference to it has been omitted from the title to the property and it has been unpaid for 20 years.

Assignation—granter having recorded title

35–16   I, AB, (*designation*), in consideration of the sum of £
paid to me by CD, (*designation*), hereby assign to the said CD a
ground annual of £   exigible [in each year] [in equal
portions half-yearly] at (*state term or terms of payment*) in each
year constituted by a contract of ground annual entered into
between EF, (*designation*), and GH, (*designation*), recorded in
the Register of Sasines for the County of   on
               , [and also the additional ground annual of
£   exigible at the same [term] [terms] in each year [in lieu
and commutation of casual payments constituted by memorandum
of commutation between (*state parties and designations*) recorded
in the said Register of Sasines on   ] *and/or* [and
also an additional ground annual of £   constituted by
minute of allocation between (*state parties and designations*)
recorded in the said Register of Sasines on   ], all
[now] payable from ALL and WHOLE (*describe burdened
property by short statutory description by reference*): with right to
the said ground annual [and others] from and after   .
                                                    (*To be attested*)

Assignation by granter without a recorded title

35–17   [*As in style in paragraph 35–16, adding at the end*] which ground
annual(s) [is] [are] last vested in (*name and designation of person
having last recorded title*) whose title thereto was recorded in the
said Register of Sasines on   , and from whom I
acquired right conform to (*specify writ or series of writs by which
right was so acquired*).
                                                    (*To be attested*)

Deed of restriction

35–18   The property from which a ground annual is exigible may be
restricted by release of a part thereof from the burden of the ground
annual.[45] The statutory style is:

I, AB, (*designation of creditor*), in consideration of (*specify
consideration, if any*) hereby disburden of the ground annual of
£   constituted by a contract of ground annual between
(*names and designations of parties*) recorded in the Register of
Sasines for the County of   on
[and also of the additional ground annual of £   in lieu and
commutation of casual payments constituted by memorandum of
commutation between (*state parties and designations*) recorded in
the said Register of Sasines on   ] *and/or* [and also
of an additional ground annual of £   constituted by minute
of allocation between (*state parties and designations*) recorded in
the said Register of Sasines on   ], ALL and
WHOLE (*describe disburdened property by description, full or by
reference*), which subjects hereby disburdened are part of ALL
and WHOLE (*describe the whole subjects out of which ground

---

[45]Conveyancing (Scotland) Act 1924, s. 23(3) and Sched. K, No. 7.

annual was payable by short statutory description by reference) being the subjects out of which the said ground annual [and others] [is] [are] payable (if granter does not have a recorded title, deduce title as in style in paragraph 35–17).

(To be attested)

Succession

35–19 As to succession of the debtor and creditor in a ground annual, see Volume IV.

Redemption

35–20 A ground annual may be redeemed voluntarily by the debtor either in accordance with the terms of a power to redeem contained in the contract of ground annual or under the statutory power conferred by section 4 of the Land Tenure Reform (Scotland) Act 1974 of which it is not permissible to contract out.[46] A conventional power of redemption contained in the original contract almost always provides that redemption shall not affect the other conditions of the contract, e.g. as to maintenance of buildings, and the statutory right likewise does not affect the other conditions of the contract which continue in force.[47]

An allocated ground annual is redeemable compulsorily upon sale or compulsory acquisition of the burdened property in terms of section 5 or 6 of the 1974 Act. Again, the other conditions of the contract continue in force.[48]

The detailed procedure and the legal effects of voluntary or compulsory redemption in terms of the 1974 Act are the same mutatis mutandis as in the case of redemption of feuduties.[49]

Receipt

35–21 Upon voluntary redemption of a ground annual in accordance with section 4 of the 1974 Act the holder of the ground annual is required at his expense to grant a receipt in the form contained in Form 2 of Schedule 1 to the Act.[50] The receipt runs:

I hereby acknowledge to have received from (name of proprietor) the sum of £   in redemption (in terms of section 4 of the Land Tenure Reform (Scotland) Act 1974) of the ground annual at £   per annum exigible as at (give date of notice of redemption) in respect of (give sufficient identification of the land in respect of which the payment being redeemed is exigible).

Dated this   day of
19
(Signed) XY
or WZ
Agent for XY.

---

[46]1974 Act, s. 21.
[47]Ibid., s. 4(3).
[48]Ibid., ss. 5(3) and 6(2)(b), subject in the case of a compulsory acquisition to the terms of the statute conferring the right.
[49]See Vol. II, paras. 17–42 to 17–62.
[50]1974 Act, s. 4(4).

It is thought that the provision that the receipt is to be granted at the expense of the holder of the ground annual extends only to the expense incurred by him or his agent in preparing and signing the receipt: it does not impose upon him liability for the expense of the debtor's solicitor in checking its terms. The Act does not require the receipt to be recorded in the Register of Sasines, so the fact that the ground annual has been redeemed will not appear on the record, but it is suggested in the Act that the receipt be endorsed on or attached to the contract of ground annual.[51]

Where redemption under the 1974 Act is compulsory there is no provision in the Act for the granting of a receipt since the scheme of the statute in relation to compulsory redemption is different. In terms of section 5 or 6 redemption is deemed to have taken place when entry has been taken under a contract for sale of the burdened property which is complete and binding or when the deed conveying the property is executed or, in the case of compulsory acquisition, when a notice to treat or deemed notice to treat has been given by the acquiring authority. In practice, however, a receipt should be obtained as the readiest evidence of redemption for the purpose of future transactions, and in particular to satisfy the Keeper on an application for first registration of the title to the burdened subjects in the Land Register.

Discharge

35–22   Since redemption of a ground annual will now in almost all cases be effected voluntarily or compulsorily under the 1974 Act a formal recorded discharge will seldom now be used. If for any reason such a discharge is desired, the style in Form No. 4 of Schedule K to the Conveyancing (Scotland) Act 1924 may be adopted.

Prescription

35–23   The period of positive prescription applicable to a ground annual constituted by a recorded contract is now 10 years.[52]

As already mentioned,[53] the right to a ground annual may be extinguished by negative prescription if for a continuous period of 20 years there is neither payment of it nor acknowledgment by reference to it in the title deeds of the burdened property.

Confusio

35–24   It was decided in *Healy & Young's Tr.* v. *Mair's Trs.*[54] that a ground annual could not be extinguished *confusione*. Although some weight

---

[51] 1974 Act, Note to Sched. 1.
[52] Prescription and Limitation (Scotland) Act 1973, s. 1.
[53] para. 35–09.
[54] 1914 S.C. 893, following opinions in *Murray* v. *Parlane's Tr.* (1890) 18 R. 287.

was attached to the fact that the ground annual in that case was expressed as irredeemable (and now all ground annuals are redeemable since it is not permissible to contract out of the statutory right of redemption), there were other grounds of decision and the court was clearly disinclined to extend the doctrine of *confusio* to any case to which it had not hitherto applied. When the creditor in a ground annual becomes the proprietor of the subjects burdened or *vice versa* the result is that the termly payments are extinguished so long as that coincidence of debtor and creditor subsists, but the ground annual and any conditions which are inserted in the grant continue, at least until they are extinguished by the negative prescription in 20 years where they are not referred to in subsequent conveyances of the subjects.

III. STATUTORY CHARGES ON LAND

35–25 Charges may be imposed on land in various circumstances and form real burdens upon it. Their effect and ranking in relation to heritable securities and other real burdens may be defined by the particular statute. Some of these charges which may be encountered in practice are noticed in the following paragraphs.

Standard charge

35–26 The standard value of stipend exigible from the teinds of any lands when the teind roll becomes final is constituted as a real burden, the standard charge, on the lands from the teinds of which it is exigible, and is preferable to all other securities or burdens which are not incidents of tenure. The standard charge is payable half-yearly at Whitsunday and Martinmas.[55] It may be allocated on parts of the lands which are separately disponed and the allocation must be intimated in terms of the 1925 Act.[56] If the portion so allocated does not exceed £1 the disponer must redeem it at 20 years' purchase: if the portion allocated exceeds £1 but is less than £15 the amount allocated is augmented by 5 per cent per annum. Standard charge may be redeemed by the heritor,[57] and is redeemable compulsorily on sale or compulsory acquisition of the burdened lands.[58]

Charging orders by local authorities

35–27 Under various statutes[59] local authorities who have carried out repairs on or demolished buildings may make a charging order in their own favour in respect of the expenses thereby incurred, which is

---

[55]Church of Scotland (Property and Endowments) Act 1925, s. 12.
[56]*Ibid.*, s. 13.
[57]*Ibid.*, s. 12(3).
[58]Land Tenure Reform (Scotland) Act 1974, ss. 5(12) and 6(7).
[59]Building (Scotland) Act 1959, ss. 10, 11 and 13 and Sched. 6 as amended by Local Government (Scotland) Act 1973, Sched. 15; Housing (Scotland) Act 1966, ss. 30, 109; Housing (Scotland) Act 1969, s. 25 and Sched. 2.

recorded in the Register of Sasines and forms a burden on the property. The charge created is for an annuity at a rate specified or prescribed in pursuance of the relevant statute for a period of 30 years. It ranks prior to all future burdens and incumbrances on the property and to all existing burdens and incumbrances except feuduties, teinds, ground annuals, stipends and standard charges and any other specified statutory charges and may be recovered by the same means and in like manner as if it were a feuduty. There are decisions to the effect that such charges, being imposed in the public interest, continue to burden the property notwithstanding bankruptcy of the owner or irritancy of the owner's right by the superior,[60] but much depends upon the wording of the relevant statute.[61]

Unpaid compensation—agricultural holdings

35–28   Where any compensation or a reorganisation payment due by a landlord has not been paid to the tenant of an agricultural holding the tenant may apply to the Secretary of State to create a charge on the holding or on the landlord's recorded lease, as the case may be, in the form of an annuity payable over a period not exceeding 30 years, and the charging order when recorded in the Register of Sasines makes the annuity a charge on the lands or lease, with specific provisions as to its ranking in relation to other real rights and burdens.[62]

Supply of water—houses

35–29   In cases where a local authority incurs expense in providing a supply of water in pipes within the house (which is primarily the responsibility of the owner) it may make a charging order imposing a charge in the form of an annuity for 30 years which, when recorded in the Register of Sasines, is a charge upon the property ranking in accordance with a specified order of priority.[63]

---

[60]*Macknight* v. *Oman's Tr.* (1872) 11 M. 154; *Pickard* v. *Glasgow Corporation*, 1970 S.L.T. (Sh.Ct.) 63.
[61]See *Sowman* v. *City of Glasgow District Council*, 1983 S.L.T. 132.
[62]Agricultural Holdings (Scotland) Act 1949, s. 70 as extended by Agriculture (Miscellaneous Provisions) Act 1968, s. 11(5) and amended by Water (Scotland) Act 1980, Sched. 10, Pt. II.
[63]Water (Scotland) Act 1980, s. 65.

THE STANDARD SECURITY

CHAPTER 36

LEGAL BASIS AND STATUTORY PROVISIONS

Introduction

36–01   As has already been explained,[1] the Conveyancing and Feudal Reform (Scotland) Act 1970[2] introduced a new form of heritable security, the standard security, the use of which is obligatory for the creation of a heritable security for debt over an interest in land (other than an entailed estate). Maximum flexibility is secured by provisions that (1) the rule of feudal law that burdens on land must be precise and

---

[1] para. 32–07.
[2] s. 9.

the prohibition imposed by the Bankruptcy Act 1696 (c. 5) against the creation of a heritable security for a debt contracted after infeftment of the creditor are inapplicable to a standard security,[3] and (2) the forms prescribed may be used whether the debt is fixed or fluctuating, already due when the security is granted or may become due by future advances.

The debt

36–02   "Debt" is defined in the 1970 Act[4] as meaning any obligation due, or which will or may become due, to repay or pay money, including any such obligation arising from a transaction or part of a transaction in the course of any trade, business or profession, and any obligation to pay an annuity or *ad factum praestandum*, but excluding an obligation to pay any feuduty, ground annual, rent or other periodical sum payable in respect of land. The definition embraces all loans or advances of money, present or future, of fixed or fluctuating amount, and also cautionary obligations under which money may become due. By reason of the wide scope of the definition, care must be taken in framing a composite agreement to ensure that if any obligation within the statutory definition of "debt" is included and heritable security for it is provided, the appropriate form of standard security is used. Periodical payments in respect of land such as feuduties or ground annuals are excluded from the definition of "debt" (these cannot now be created[5]), but obligations to pay rent may still be constituted by leases. A heritably-secured obligation to pay interest on a loan, however, is not excluded since it is a periodical payment, not in respect of land, but in respect of the loan.

Creditor and debtor

36–03   These terms are defined in relation to a standard security by reference to the definition of "debt."[6] Throughout the 1970 Act the terms "grantor" and "grantee" are used to denote the original parties to a standard security, but the terms "debtor" and "creditor" comprehend not only the original parties but also any of their respective successors in title, assignees or representatives.[7]

Heritable security and interest in land

36–04   A "heritable security" is defined as any security capable of being constituted over any interest in land by disposition or assignation of that interest in security of any debt and of being recorded in the

---

[3] s. 9(6).
[4] s. 9(8)(c).
[5] Land Tenure Reform (Scotland) Act 1974, ss. 1 and 2.
[6] 1970 Act, s. 9(8)(c).
[7] *Ibid.*, s. 30(1).

Register of Sasines.[8,9] An "interest in land" means any estate or interest in land, other than an entailed estate or any interest therein, which is capable of being owned or held as a separate interest and to which a title may be recorded in the Register of Sasines. The definition includes:

(1) Ownership of land held on feudal tenure, whether superiority or *dominium utile*, and any more limited interest therein, *e.g.* a proper liferent, to which a title as a separate interest may be recorded in the Register of Sasines.

(2) Registrable leases, whether actually recorded or not, since the interests which they create are capable of being recorded.

(3) Servitude rights created by deed, whether recorded or not, since the deed could be recorded, although a heritable security could not in practice be created over a servitude separately from the subjects affected.

(4) The reversionary interest of a person who has granted an *ex facie* absolute disposition or assignation which is truly in security since (a) if the granter was formerly infeft his title remains entire subject to the security[10] or (b) even if he was not formerly infeft, as where he had simply consented to a disposition by a former proprietor to the *ex facie* absolute disponee and so he has only a *jus actionis* which is a personal rather than a real right, it relates to heritable property and is a separate interest in land which in practice could be transferred by disposition or assignation which could be recorded in the Register of Sasines, usually combined with an assignation of the reversionary right.

(5) A heritable security, *e.g.* another standard security, since the creditor in the original security has an interest in land which is capable of being owned or held as a separate interest to which a title may be recorded in the Register of Sasines. In practice a standard security over another standard security is undesirable because of the problems of monitoring insurance and calling-up. An assignation of the existing standard security will be preferable and avoids the need for a further standard security.

The following are outwith the statutory definition:

(1) A right to shootings or fishings (other than salmon fishings) enjoyed separately from ownership of the land or water over which it is exercisable, since such a right is not a separate *praedium*,[11] although a lease of fishings for consideration for a period exceeding 20 years may now be included in the definition.[12]

---

[8] *Ibid.*, s. 9(8)(*a*).

[9] For the purposes of registration of title "heritable security" has the same meaning—Land Registration (Scotland) Act 1979, s. 28(1).

[10] *Ritchie* v. *Scott* (1899) 1 F. 728 at 736; *Edinburgh Entertainments Ltd.* v. *Stevenson*, 1926 S.C. 363.

[11] *Patrick* v. *Napier* (1867) 5 M. 683; *Earl of Galloway* v. *Duke of Bedford* (1902) 4 F. 851; *Beckett* v. *Bisset*, 1921 2 S.L.T. 33.

[12] Freshwater and Salmon Fisheries (Scotland) Act 1976, s. 4.

(2) Leases for a period not exceeding 20 years, since they cannot be recorded in the Register of Sasines.

(3) A right to a liferent or annuity which is protected by a trust, since the liferenter or annuitant does not have a separate title which is capable of being recorded.

(4) An entailed estate and any interest therein,[13] so that securities over them may be created in the forms previously competent.

Small dwellings under the Small Dwellings Acquisition (Scotland) Acts 1899 to 1923 were originally excluded from the definition subject to the qualification that it was not permissible for a local authority to create a security for an advance under those Acts in the form of an *ex facie* absolute disposition, whether qualified by a back letter or not, but the provision to that effect in subsection 9(7) of the 1970 Act has now been repealed.[14]

Invalidation of heritable securities in any other form

36–05 As from November 29, 1970, the grant of any right over an interest in land[15] for the purpose of securing any debt[16] by way of a heritable security[17] is only capable of being effected at law if it is embodied in a standard security.[18] Where for that purpose any deed is granted which is not in that form but contains a disposition or assignation of an interest in land it is *to that extent* void and unenforceable, *i.e.* the creditor will not have a valid heritable security but the other provisions of the deed, *e.g.* the personal obligation to repay the debt, will not be affected. In order to rectify the Register of Sasines where the deed which purported to create a heritable security is thus ineffective for that purpose, the creditor may be required by any other person having an interest to grant any deed which may be appropriate to clear the Register of Sasines of the purported security.[19]

Statutory forms

36–06 A standard security may be in one or other of two forms contained in Schedule 2 to the 1970 Act.[20] Form A is appropriate where both the personal obligation and the grant of security are included in a single deed. Form B should be used where the personal obligation is contained in a separate instrument or instruments.[21]

---

[13] 1970 Act, s. 9(8)(*b*).
[14] Tenants' Rights, Etc. (Scotland) Act 1980, s. 84 and Sched. 5.
[15] See para. 36–04.
[16] See para. 36–02.
[17] See para. 36–04.
[18] 1970 Act, s. 9(3).
[19] *Ibid.*, s. 9(4).
[20] s. 9(2).
[21] As to selection of the appropriate form, see para. 37–10.

Personal obligation (Form A)

36–07   The style of personal obligation contained in Form A is commendably brief and its import is defined more fully in section 10 of the 1970 Act. It is not essential that the precise words of Form A be adhered to, so long as the deed conforms as closely as may be to the statutory style, and any relevant additional matter may be included.[22] The legal effect of the personal obligation as stated in section 10, unless specially qualified, is outlined below.

36–08   **(1) Obligation of repayment.** If the security is for a fixed amount advanced or payable at or prior to delivery of the deed, the clause undertaking payment to the creditor imports (a) an acknowledgment of receipt by the debtor of the principal sum advanced or an acknowledgment by the debtor of liability to pay that sum, as the case may be, and (b) a personal obligation by the debtor to repay or pay to the creditor on demand in writing at any time after the date of delivery of the deed (i) the sum itself, (ii) interest at the rate stated payable on the dates specified in the deed, and (iii) all expenses for which the debtor is liable by virtue of the deed or of Part II of the Act. If the security is for a fluctuating amount, whether subject to a maximum or not and whether advanced or due partly before and partly after delivery of the deed or whether advanced or to become due wholly after such delivery, the clause imports a personal obligation by the debtor to repay or pay to the creditor on demand in writing (i) the amount, subject to any maximum specified in the deed, advanced or due and outstanding at the time of demand, (ii) interest on each advance from the date when it was made until repayment, or on each sum payable from the date when it became due until payment thereof, at the rate and on the dates specified, and (iii) all expenses for which the debtor is liable by virtue of the deed or of Part II of the Act.

36–09   **(2) Liability on demand.** The provision that the obligation of the debtor is prestable on demand by the creditor preserves in a standard security the independence of the remedies available to the creditor under the personal obligation and the grant of security on the same principle as applied in the case of a bond and disposition in security.[23] He may enforce his security by serving a calling-up notice or a notice of default, and a sale may follow on expiry of the appropriate period of notice, but at the same time he may enforce payment under the personal obligation by registering the standard security for execution.

36–10   **(3) Interest.** Simple interest is due under a standard security at the rate stated in the deed either from the date specified (where the amount is fixed) or from the respective dates of advance or the dates when the sum became payable (where the amount is fluctuating). When Form A

---

[22] 1970 Act, s. 53(1).
[23] *McWhirter* v. *McCulloch's Trs.* (1887) 14 R. 918; *McNab* v. *Clarke* (1889) 16 R. 610.

is used, both the rate of interest and the commencing date must be stated in the deed. When Form B is used these particulars should be specified in the separate instrument containing the personal obligation, but *quaere* whether an omission to do so would now invalidate the security for interest if an obligation to pay interest is undertaken or implied by law?[24] Compound interest, if it is to be exigible, would require to be specially stipulated in accordance with the ordinary rule to that effect. Compound interest may become payable on the occurrence of certain events, and presumably the rules already established in that matter for heritable securities in their previous forms will apply to a standard security.[25]

36–11 **(4) Expenses**. The standard security contains no penalty clause, nor is a penalty clause in the present form implied by section 10(1). The personal obligation, however, will cover all expenses for which the debtor is liable by virtue of the deed or Part II of the Act. It is permissible to insert a more detailed stipulation for expenses in the deed, but in most cases this will be unnecessary. The standard conditions imported into a standard security by the Act[26] impose liability upon the debtor for expenses in comprehensive terms.[27]

36–12 **(5) Registration for execution**. A standard security in Form A contains a clause of consent to registration for execution. The import of the clause is defined in section 10(3) of the Act.[28] The clause does not appear in Form B (since that form does not contain the personal obligation), so that, if Form B is used, the clause should be incorporated in the separate instrument containing the personal obligation.

Grant of security (Forms A and B)

36–13   Both forms contain in similar terms a grant to the creditor of the interest in land upon which the debt is to be secured. It consists of a grant of a standard security over subjects described as indicated in note 1 to Schedule 2, a statement that the standard conditions in Schedule 3 to the Act, with any lawful variation thereof, will apply and a clause of warrandice. The standard conditions contain detailed provisions as to the obligations of the debtor and the rights and powers of the creditor in relation to the security subjects, and may, except on certain matters,

---

[24] The basis of the rule that the rate of interest and the commencing date must be specified if the heritable security is to cover the interest (see *Alston* v. *Nellfield Manure and Chemical Co. Ltd.*, 1915 S.C. 912; 1915 2 S.L.T. 50) is that a real burden for money must be precise, and that rule does not apply to a standard security (s. 9(6)).

[25] For a convenient summary of these rules, see Burns, *Handbook of Conveyancing* (5th ed.), 46, 47.

[26] s. 11(2).

[27] Sched. 3, s.c. 7(3) and 12; see para. 38–26.

[28] The subsection departs from the somewhat archaic wording of s. 138 of the Titles to Land Consolidation (Scotland) Act 1868 by substituting a definition of the import of the clause which is a "non-definition." In effect it merely states that a clause of consent to registration for execution imports a consent to registration in certain court books for execution. The legal effect of such a clause is so well-established, however, that there can be no doubt on the matter.

be varied as the parties may agree.[29] The standard conditions are treated in Chapter 38 *infra*.

36–14 **(1) Legal effect**. When a standard security is duly recorded it will operate to vest the interest over which it is granted in the grantee as a security for the performance of the contract to which it relates.[30] When the Form B style is used, the separate instrument will be the contract to which the security relates and will normally include all obligations of the debtor which are to be covered by the security. When Form A is used, however, the contract to which the security relates will be that expressed in the personal obligation section of the standard security. So, if in a Form A type of security, reference is made to a separate document only as varying the standard conditions and that document also contains provisions relevant to the personal obligation, there may be doubt whether these provisions are effectively covered by the security: in such cases either the expression of the personal obligation in the standard security should be wide enough to embrace the provisions in the separate document or the separate document should be referred to in the personal obligation section of the standard security as well as in the clause varying the standard conditions.

The title of the grantee is a limited title; in feudal terminology it is an infeftment in security. It is ancillary to the personal obligation in respect of which it is granted, even when Form B is used and the personal obligation is created in a separate deed. Where the debt is an advance of fixed amount, full repayment of the advance automatically extinguishes the security,[31] although a discharge will be required to clear the record.

36–15 **(2) Warrandice: prior securities**. The import of the clause of warrandice is unchanged in the new security,[32] absolute warrandice as regards the security subjects and the titles and warrandice from fact and deed as regards the rents. Prior securities should be excepted from warrandice: if that is not done the grantor will be liable to indemnify the grantee against them.[33] A rather more elaborate reference to prior securities than a simple exception from warrandice is required in Note 5 to Schedule 2 to the Act. The grant in the standard security should be expressed as subject to any prior security or securities and the warrandice is made subject to them also.[34]

36–16 **(3) Assignation of writs**. No clause of assignation of writs is contained in either of the statutory forms, but there is implied an assignation to the creditor of the title deeds (including searches and unrecorded

---

[29]s. 11(2) and (3) as amended by the Redemption of Standard Securities (Scotland) Act 1971.
[30]s. 11(1).
[31]As in the case of a bond and disposition in security—*Cameron* v. *Williamson* (1895) 22 R. 293, *per* Lord Kinnear at 298.
[32]s. 10(2): *cf.* Titles to Land Consolidation (Scotland) Act 1868, s. 119.
[33]*Horsbrugh's Trs.* v. *Welch* (1886) 14 R. 67.
[34]See para. 37–14.

conveyances) affecting the security subjects, with power to the creditor in the event of the exercise of his power of sale to deliver them to the purchaser and to assign to the purchaser his right to have them made forthcoming.[35] Section 27 of the Conveyancing (Scotland) Act 1924 applies to a standard security and so, after the security is recorded, the solicitor for the proprietor or creditors or others whose rights over the security subjects are postponed to those of the creditor in the standard security cannot acquire a lien over the titles which will be effective against him. The existing law as regards liens acquired before the security is recorded and against other parties remains unchanged.[36]

36–17 **(4) Assignation of rents**. Neither Form A nor Form B contains a clause of assignation of rents and no such clause is imported by the Act. The standard conditions, however, confer powers on the creditor, where the debtor is in default, to enter into possession of the security subjects and to let, manage, maintain, repair, reconstruct and improve them.[37] He may also insure them.[38] Thus the creditor has under the standard conditions the material powers conferred by a clause of assignation of rents.[39] There is old authority to the effect that the recording of a heritable security containing a clause of assignation of rents constituted public notice of the security right and that the creditor could interpel tenants, by mere intimation, from paying rents to the proprietor.[40] In a later case,[41] however, that principle was not applied although the judgment proceeded rather on the right of retention in bankruptcy than by negativing the principle. In the absence of a clause of assignation of rents, the principle would appear to be inapplicable to a standard security. The scheme of the Act is that, so long as the debtor implements his obligations under the security and is not in default, the security subjects remain under his control. If the debtor is in default, however, he may lose possession after formal notice duly given to him.

36–18 **(5) Ranking clauses**. A clause of ranking, whether in relation to prior, *pari passu* or postponed securities, may be inserted in a standard security immediately prior to the warrandice clause.[42] The statutory wording makes clear the intention that the provisions of the ranking clause qualify the security and not merely the contractual bargain between the debtor and creditor, as would be the case if the ranking provision were expressed merely as a qualification of warrandice.[43]

36–19 **(6) Notice of subsequent securities or conveyances**. Where the creditor in a standard security duly recorded receives notice of the creation of a

---

[35]s. 10(4).
[36]See Burns, 442.
[37]Sched. 3, s.c. 10(3)–(6) and s. 20(3) of the Act.
[38]Sched. 3, s.c. 5 and 7.
[39]Conveyancing (Scotland) Act 1924, s. 25(1)(a).
[40]*Webster* v. *Donaldson* (1780) Mor. 2902.
[41]*Stevenson, Lauder & Gilchrist* v. *Dawson* (1896) 23 R. 496.
[42]Sched. 2, Note 5. For styles see paras. 37–54 and 37–55.
[43]See Burns, 446: *Leslie* v. *McIndoe's Trs.* (1824) 3 S. 48.

subsequent standard security over, or of a subsequent assignation or conveyance of, the same interest in land or any part thereof, being a security, assignation or conveyance so recorded, the preference in ranking of the security of that creditor is restricted to the security for his present advances and future advances which he may be required to make under the contract to which the security relates and interest present or future due thereon (including any such interest which has accrued or may accrue) and for any expenses or outlays (including interest thereon) which may be, or may have been, reasonably incurred in the exercise of any power conferred on any creditor by the deed expressing the security.[44]

16–20 As to the interpretation and legal effect of this provision the following points may be noted:

(1) Section 13 applies to a security which has been *recorded* in the Register of Sasines and a subsequent security, assignation or conveyance which has been so *recorded*. Although the section applies in terms to deeds recorded in the Register of Sasines, which was the only general register of land rights operative when the 1970 Act was passed, it seems logical that the rules embodied in it would now apply also to interests registered in the Land Register in circumstances where registration of an interest therein superseded recording in the Register of Sasines and recording in the latter register became incompetent or inappropriate.[45] Where there has been an assignation or conveyance of the debtor's reversionary right or his right to the property which has not been either recorded or registered but has been intimated to the first creditor the section has no application, but it would seem that the rule established in *Union Bank* v. *National Bank*[46] would apply with the result that the first creditor's security, and not merely his preference, would be limited to the amounts previously advanced by him.

(2) The preference of the prior creditor is restricted only when he has received notice of the subsequent transaction. The recording or registration of the deed creating the subsequent interest is not enough to constitute notice to the prior creditor; there must be intimation.[47] If, however, the subsequent interest arises from an assignation, conveyance or vesting in another person resulting from a judicial decree, that is sufficient notice to the prior creditor, without intimation. Similarly, where the subsequent interest is created by operation of law, as when a floating charge granted by a debtor which is an incorporated company over all assets crystallises, notice to the prior creditor is not required.[48]

---

[44]1970 Act, s. 13.

[45]This view is obliquely supported by the terms of s. 7 of the Land Registration (Scotland) Act 1979 which regulates ranking as between registered interests and recorded titles "without prejudice to any express provision as to ranking in any enactment"—s. 7(1).

[46](1886) 14 R.(H.L.) 1.

[47]1970 Act, s. 13(2)(*a*).

[48]*Ibid.*, s. 13(2)(*b*).

(3) It is thought that on a proper construction of the sections the creation and notification of a subsequent security results only in the restriction of the first creditor's *preference* in a question with the notifying creditor, not the restriction of the first creditor's *security*. So, if a first creditor holding a security for advances on current account continues to make advances which he is not required to make after receiving notice of the creation of a subsequent security, he still has security for these further advances postponed to the security of the second creditor, with the result that if the second security is redeemed or discharged the first creditor's security for all advances is valid.

(4) The first creditor's preference over that of the subsequent notifying creditor is for (a) his existing advances at the time when he receives notification, (b) any future advances which he is required to make under the contract to which the security relates (not, it would seem, any future advances which he has agreed to make under a subsequent separate document), (c) interest present or future thereon (accrued or yet to accrue) and not limited to cease on bankruptcy or liquidation of the debtor,[49] and (d) any expenses or outlays, with interest thereon, reasonably incurred in exercise of any power conferred in the deed expressing the security (not expenses authorised by some separate agreement between the creditor and debtor).

(5) The restriction of the first creditor's preference occurs upon notice being received of the subsequent security, assignation or conveyance even although the latter affects only part of the subjects of the original security. Since there is a competition of preference only as regards that part, probably the first creditor's preference is not restricted as regards the remainder, but for the avoidance of doubt it is suggested that there should be a ranking agreement amongst the debtor and the two creditors, recorded in the Register of Sasines or entered in the Land Register as may be appropriate, expressing that result.

(6) It should be noted that subsection (3)(b) of section 13 is without prejudice to any powers of the creditor and debtor to regulate the preference to be enjoyed by creditors. The creditor and debtor have power to make the standard security postponed to an existing security but do not have power to make it prior to or *pari passu* with an existing security. In practice the debtor and the creditor may be parties to a ranking agreement which makes the security postponed to an existing security, but the debtor and both creditors should be parties to an agreement which makes the security prior to or *pari passu* with existing security. It should be further noted that the debtor should be a party: an agreement between the two creditors only is not within the terms of the subsection and would merely regulate the contractual rights of the creditors *inter se*. Further, if the two standard securities are created at different times, the normal circumstances in which the

---

[49]Contrary to the previous law—*Campbell's J.F.* v. *National Bank of Scotland Ltd.*, 1944 S.C. 495.

section applies, the ranking agreement should be made and recorded in the Register of Sasines or entered in the Land Register before or contemporaneously with the recording or registration of the new security so that the agreement will exclude the application of section 13(1). If the ranking agreement is made after the new security has been recorded or the interest of the second creditor registered in the Land Register and notified to the first creditor, then section 13(1) will already have restricted the preference of the first creditor and the ranking agreement, although it may competently vary the relative preferences under section 13(3)(*b*), may well be a variation of the recorded or registered particulars of the first security and, in compliance with the requirements of section 16 of the 1970 Act, must be recorded or registered.

(7) Some doubt must attach to the effectiveness of a prohibition contained in a standard security against the creation of a subsequent security over the same subjects. Section 13(1) is unqualified in its application save for the reserved power with regard to ranking agreements in section 13(3)(*b*). It would appear therefore that, if a second creditor made advances under a subsequent standard security duly recorded in the Register of Sasines or entered in the Land Register and notified to the first creditor, the preference of the first creditor would be restricted in accordance with section 13(1). The original creditor would have the remedies available to him for breach of the contractual prohibition, which in a properly-drawn document would constitute default by the debtor, but his preference over the security subjects might be restricted in accordance with the Act, subject to the argument that, since the original security was recorded, the second creditor might not have been acting in good faith.

Deduction of title

6–21 Section 12 of the 1970 Act authorises the granting of a standard security by a person having right to the interest in land which forms the subject of the security but whose title to it has not been completed by recording. He may insert in the standard security a deduction of his title in the form prescribed in Note 2 or 3 of Schedule 2 to the Act. Upon the deed being recorded the title of the grantee will be as effective as if the granter's title to the security subjects had been duly completed, *but only* for the purposes of the rights and obligations between the grantor and the grantee and those deriving right from them, and for no other purpose. The provisions of section 5 of the Conveyancing (Scotland) Act 1924 are adopted for defining the writings which it will be competent to specify as titles, midcouples or links.

6–22 **(1) Limitation in effect**. In order to be consistent with feudal theory it is necessary that the title of the granter of a heritable security has been completed. The 1970 Act enables an uninfeft debtor to grant a standard security by a legal fiction that, for the purposes of the rights and obligations created by the security, the granter's title to the security subjects will be deemed to have been completed. The deemed infeftment is restricted in its effect to that purpose, and for all other purposes, *e.g.* completion of title to or conveyance of the security subjects, the title of the owner of the security subjects remains uncompleted. The effect extends to those deriving right from either of the parties to the standard security, so that creditors who subsequently adjudged the property of the grantor would require to recognise the validity of a standard security completed before adjudication.

36–23   **(2) Persons who may deduce title**. The persons who may grant a standard security containing a clause of deduction of title are those who have a right to the interest in land which is to be the subject of the security but whose title thereto has not been completed by being recorded. The Act adopts the phraseology of section 3 of the Conveyancing (Scotland) Act 1924 and the persons who may use the facility of deducing title in granting a standard security are those who could have granted a disposition or assignation of the interest containing a deduction of title by virtue of the 1924 Act. They include persons who could have completed title to the security subjects by notice of title such as (1) executors of a deceased infeft proprietor who have obtained confirmation which includes the subjects in terms of section 14 of the Succession (Scotland) Act 1964, (2) the grantee of a special conveyance which has not been recorded, and (3) trustees assumed by deed of assumption. Persons who do not have the right include (1) a purchaser under missives and (2) a legatee to whom trustees have been directed to convey the subjects in terms of a trust disposition and settlement.

36–24   **(3) Securities granted upon purchase of subjects**. Doubts were expressed whether a purchaser under missives could effectually grant a standard security before his title to the security subjects was completed by recording of the conveyance in his favour, since he had no recorded title to the subjects and could not deduce title. Senior counsel has advised that there is no impediment to such a person granting a standard security without a clause of deduction of title since in that context granting is effective upon delivery and recording of the security, which normally follows recording of the granter's title, and the standard security would in any event be validated by accretion even if the granter's title was recorded subsequently.

36–25   **(4) Grantor of ex facie absolute disposition**. The situation which occasions most problems in practice is that in which a disposition of the security subjects has been granted *ex facie* absolutely but truly in security and it is desired to grant either a security for a further loan from the original creditor or a postponed security to a second creditor.

36–26   (a) *Where the grantor has previously been infeft*. In this case a standard security may be granted and recorded: no deduction of title is required.[50] The *ex facie* absolute disposition being truly a security has not divested the owner of the security subjects and his title is entire subject to the security.[51]

36–27 (b) *Where the grantor has not previously been infeft but has right to the security subjects by a title which has not been completed by being recorded*. In this case a standard security may be granted with a clause of deduction of title.[52] Illustrations are (i) where testamentary trustees have granted the existing *ex facie* absolute disposition deducing their title from the testator who was infeft or (ii) where an infeft owner of the subjects has granted the *ex facie* absolute disposition and his executor now wishes to grant a standard security.

36–28 (c) *Where the grantor has not previously been infeft and does not have a right to the security subjects which can be completed by being recorded*. This is the common situation where A (seller) has granted a disposition *ex facie* absolute with consent of B (purchaser) to C (lender to B). B is not a person who has right to land and so the facility of deducing title in a subsequent standard security is not available to him. He may nevertheless grant a standard security without deducing title[53] and incorporate in it an assignation of his reversionary interest[54] which, if the grantee is a new lender, will be intimated to C. The grantee will not have a real security but he will have an inchoate security which will be validated by accretion on discharge of the security constituted by the *ex facie* absolute disposition with retrospective effect to the date of recording of the standard security, and meantime he has an effective assignation of B's reversionary interest.

36–29 (d) *Additional advance by original creditor*. Where an *ex facie* absolute disposition has been granted and a further advance is being made by the same creditor, it is probably the law that the transaction can be effected by a further agreement without the need of a standard security.[55] (i) Where the *ex facie* absolute disposition has been granted in security of advances unlimited in amount, it is thought that a standard security is unnecessary and that a supplementary agreement will suffice. The original grant of land in security was *ex facie* exhaustive of the grantor's interest and the personal obligation in the agreement was not restricted to any particular amount. The further

---

[50]Sched. 2, Note 3(a).

[51]*Ritchie* v. *Scott* (1899) 1 F. 728, *per* Lord Kinnear at 736.

[52]Sched. 2, Note 3(b).

[53]s. 12 is enabling, not mandatory in every case where the granter does not have a recorded title.

[54]It is arguable, since a reversionary interest in land is an interest to which a title can be completed by registration in the Register of Sasines, that an assignation of it in security must be in the form of a standard security. Hence it is incorporated in the security subjects and also assigned in Styles 4, 5 and 6 in paras. 37–15, 37–16 and 37–17.

[55]Where the grantor is an incorporated company the agreement will be an instrument of alteration which requires registration in the register of charges within 21 days of its execution: Companies Act 1985, s. 466(5).

advance requires no grant over an interest in land for securing it within the meaning of section 9(3) of the 1970 Act, since the original grant in security was unqualified in form and in fact related to an advance of unrestricted amount. The subsequent advance is simply a further dealing within the scope of the existing security. (ii) Where the absolute disposition was truly in security of a fixed or maximum amount, however, the position is slightly less clear. One possible view is that the grant in the *ex facie* absolute conveyance is in form unlimited, that the debt is distinct from the security and that a subsequent agreement which extends the availability of the security to cover a further advance is merely a dealing with an unlimited security which alters the amount of the debt as between the creditor and the debtor. On that view it may be effected under section 31 of the 1970 Act by the present method of a supplementary unrecorded deed. There is, however, an alternative view that, since in substance the original transaction was simply a security for the amount originally advanced, any subsequent advance is in effect a new security.[56] On that view a new standard security would be the proper method, and for the avoidance of doubt is recommended.

36–30   (e) *Advance by new lender.* In all cases, whether the original loan was for a fixed, maximum or unlimited amount, a standard security will be required. It will include the debtor's reversionary interest in the description of the security subjects and will incorporate also an express assignation of that interest. In addition to registration, it should be intimated immediately to the first creditor.[57]

The preference of the first creditor will be restricted as from the date of intimation in accordance with section 42 of the 1970 Act.[58]

Recording or registration

36–31   The right of the creditor is made real by recording the standard security in the Register of Sasines with a warrant of registration on behalf of the creditor[59] or by registration of the interest of the creditor in the Land Register.[60]

---

[56]This view is based upon Lord Kinnear's *obiter dictum*: "The doctrine is that a security in the form of an absolute disposition but qualified by a back-bond declaring the title to be limited to a definite security is neither more nor less than a heritable security" (*Ritchie* v. *Scott* (1899) 1 F. 728 at 736), subsequently approved by the court in *Edinburgh Entertainments Ltd.* v. *Stevenson*, 1926 S.C. 363. This alternative view also derives support from the decision in *Scottish & Newcastle Breweries Ltd.* v. *Liquidator of Rathburne Hotel Co. Ltd.*, 1970 S:L.T. 313.

[57]For a style, see para. 37–17.

[58]See para. 36–19.

[59]Conveyancing (Scotland) Act 1924, s. 10 and Sched. F.

[60]As to the circumstances in which recording in the Register of Sasines or registration in the Land Register is appropriate, see Chap. 42.

CHAPTER 37

STANDARD SECURITY—PRACTICE AND PRECEDENTS

PRELIMINARY MATTERS

DOCUMENTATION

General Styles

Particular Parties

Particular Subjects and Transactions

Ranking Clauses

PRELIMINARY MATTERS

Contract

37–01   The rules for conclusion and execution of a valid contract for the granting and accepting of a heritable security are those applicable to any contract relating to heritage.[1] The important matters are (1) the representations on which the lender proceeds; (2) the amount to be lent, whether a fixed sum or fluctuating on current accounting and if so whether any limit is imposed; (3) a valuation of the security subjects; (4) rate of interest and periods of payment; (5) any arrangements as to periodical repayments; (6) production of a valid title by the borrower; and (7) any special conditions or reservations, *e.g.* reduced rate of interest conditional on punctual payment, reserved right to feu, conditions as to erection of buildings and advances by instalments as buildings are completed or at stages of completion. It should be noted, however, that a contract to lend money will not be enforced: the remedy is damages,[2] except in a contract to take debentures from a limited company.[3] The documentation of advances by building societies normally comprises an application by the borrower with particulars of matters specified in the form of application and an offer to lend by the society subject to or after a satisfactory valuation of the security subjects: the offer will not be withdrawn or the amount reduced unless the valuer's report is unsatisfactory or there have been

---

[1] See Vol. I, paras. 3–02 to 3–04.
[2] Gloag, *Contract*,.655; *South African Territories* v. *Wallington* [1898] A.C. 309; *Re Smelting Corporation* [1915] 1 Ch. 472.
[3] Companies Act 1985, s. 195.

alterations or mis-statements in the particulars furnished in the application form.

Specialties as to particular parties and subjects

37–02   Standard securities by or in favour of particular parties or over certain types of property require special consideration and are treated separately in paragraphs 37–20 to 37–41 *infra*, with illustrations of appropriate styles.

Examination of title

37–03   As a preliminary step to the granting of a standard security the debtor's title should be examined in the way and to the extent required in respect of sasine titles or titles to an interest already registered in the Land Register[4] and inquiries made on any relevant matters which should be investigated,[5] including the financial status and income of the borrower, in order to ensure that he will be in a position to meet the payments of interest and (where appropriate) periodical payments to account of capital. Where the security is granted over a long lease see paragraphs 31–04 to 31–12, *supra*.

Valuation

37–04   Building societies and other institutional lenders, subject to certain exceptions, normally require an independent professional valuation of the security property before making an advance. Other lenders, if prudent, should also do so. Trustees who wish to avoid the risk of personal liability should instruct an independent valuation and restrict the amount lent to two-thirds of the value of the property, taking into account any prior and *pari passu* loans.[6] Loans on the security of heritable property are narrower-range investments for the purposes of the Trustee Investments Act 1961 and, subject to valuation as above mentioned, advice on the suitability of such a loan is not required.[7]

Income tax

37–05   Income tax on interest on money borrowed will be allowed as a deduction from income for tax purposes if it is borrowed in order to finance the purchase or improvement of certain kinds of land or buildings or to replace a loan obtained to finance the original purchase thereof. To qualify for this relief the land or buildings must be (a) in use as the only or main residence of the borrower or a dependent relative or former or separated spouse of his or to be so used within 12 months of the time of the loan, or (b) let at a commercial rent for

---

[4]See Vol. II, Chap. 21.
[5]See Vol. II, paras. 23–36 to 23–51.
[6]Trusts (Scotland) Act 1921, s. 30.
[7]s. 6(7).

more than 26 weeks out of any period of 52 weeks or is available for such letting or used as in (a) above. As regards a loan made for the purchase of an only or main residence the relief is available only up to a maximum of £30,000.[8]

In the case of loans from building societies the relief is effectively given to the borrowers by deduction from the interest payable to the societies under the MIRAS scheme as part of the composite arrangement with the Inland Revenue.

Matrimonial homes

37–06   The grant of a heritable security over a matrimonial home is a dealing within the meaning of that term as defined in the Matrimonial Homes (Family Protection) (Scotland) Act 1981,[9] and so, in order that the creditor shall have an enforceable security which will not be prejudiced by the occupancy rights of a non-entitled spouse, it is necessary that (1) the creditor in making the loan has acted in good faith and (2) at or before the delivery of the standard security there was produced to the creditor a consent to the granting of the standard security or a renunciation of occupancy rights by the non-entitled spouse or an affidavit sworn or affirmed by the granter of the standard security that the security subjects are not a matrimonial home in relation to which a spouse of the granter has occupancy rights.[10] The forms of consent, renunciation or affidavit are contained in Volume II, paragraphs 21–29, 21–30 and 21–31 *supra*. The provisions of the 1981 Act as originally enacted caused problems in circumstances where the standard security was granted in respect of previous advances since the consent, renunciation or affidavit had to be made "before the granting of the loan," *i.e.* when the loan was made, so that if made only when the standard security was later granted that did not constitute compliance with the statute. The amendment made by the 1985 Act (applicable to standard securities granted on or after December 30, 1985) provides that the relevant point of time when the consent, renunciation or affidavit is required is the granting, *i.e.* the delivery, of the security. The 1985 amendments also clarify the position as to subsequent advances upon a current account secured by a standard security: the consent, renunciation or affidavit made at or before the grant of the standard security is sufficient provided that no further standard security is required.[11] It is recommended that the consent of a non-entitled spouse should be incorporated in the standard security

---

[8]F.A. 1972, s. 75 and Sched. 9 as amended by F.A. 1974, s. 19 and Sched. 1 and F.A. 1985, s. 37(1).

[9]s. 6(2).

[10]s. 8(2A) as inserted by the Law Reform (Miscellaneous Provisions) (Scotland) Act 1985, s. 13(8).

[11]See Vol. II, para. 21–28. The discussion in the second subparagraph relates to securities granted before December 30, 1985: the problem is now simplified in the case of standard securities granted on or after that date.

itself. If a separate consent or renunciation or an affidavit is made it should be carefully preserved by the creditor or registered in the Books of Council and Session.

Period of loan

37–07   As originally enacted the Conveyancing and Feudal Reform (Scotland) Act 1970 conferred upon the debtor in a standard security power, which could not be varied by agreement, to redeem the security at any time upon giving two months' notice. That provision was amended by the Redemption of Standard Securities (Scotland) Act 1971 which permits alteration of the debtor's absolute right to redeem by agreement to the contrary, although the statutory procedure on redemption remains applicable in all cases.[12] Perpetual debentures issued by companies are still competent.[13] The debtor's power of redemption under a standard security granted before July 1, 1971 may be varied, but only by a recorded agreement[14]; agreements varying the debtor's power of redemption contained in a standard security after that date may be made by unrecorded or recorded agreement as may be appropriate.[15]

Pre-settlement procedure

37–08   The pre-settlement procedure in a transaction of secured loan is illustrated in the case of a transaction of contemporaneous purchase and loan in Volume II, Chapter 23 with searches of the sasine register or Reports from the Land Register as explained in Chapters 21 and 23 *supra*.

DOCUMENTATION

Framing the standard security—selection of form

37–09   It must be kept in view that the heritable security will cover only the amounts due under the personal obligation, whether that is incorporated in a standard security in Form A or in the separate instrument related to Form B. It follows that, if Form A is used, the personal obligation should be expressed in terms wide enough to embrace not only the principal sum advanced and interest at a stipulated or ascertainable rate but also any further advances and any variations in the rate of interest that may be contemplated: if that is done the security will cover these, but if not it will be necessary to have a deed of variation executed and recorded.[16] The same principle is applicable

---

[12] 1971 Act, s. 1.
[13] *Ibid.*, s. 2; Companies Act 1985, s. 193.
[14] *Ibid.*, s. 3.
[15] See paras. 40–02 and 40–03.
[16] Conveyancing and Feudal Reform (Scotland) Act 1970, s. 16(1).

to a standard security in Form B: if the separate related document which constitutes the personal obligation is not in terms sufficiently comprehensive to include subsequent changes therein, any additional obligation will require to be expressed in a further deed of variation which provides that it will be covered by the existing standard security, although such further deed does not require to be recorded.[17]

37–10 Form A may be used for an advance of fixed amount at a stated rate of interest where it is improbable that there will be further advances or alteration in the rate of interest or other conditions of the advance. It may also be used in respect of an advance by a building society and will extend to further advances or re-advances if that is stated and to variations in the rate of interest ascertainable by reference to the rules or practice of the society. It should be used only where neither of the parties object to the publication of the terms of the transaction, since these will appear on record when the standard security is recorded or the interest of the creditor registered in the appropriate register.

Form B may be used where the parties do not desire that the terms of the contract should be so published. It is convenient where the obligation secured is complex or is *ad factum praestandum* or where there is other security, so that the separate instrument can be used to express an obligation which can be secured by a standard security *quoad* heritable property and an appropriate document or documents of transfer executed to cover any moveable security.

Conformity with statutory forms

37–11 Section 53(1) of the 1970 Act makes it clear that precise adherence to the actual words of the prescribed forms is not essential so long as the deed conforms as closely as may be to them, and it is permissible to include any additional matter which may be relevant. It would appear that the requirement that a valid heritable security for debt must be "embodied in a standard security"[18] is one which relates to the form and structure of the deed rather than to the *ipsissima verba* of the statutory forms. The deed must contain all the essential clauses of the statutory form used and the omission of any of them which is relevant will render the validity of the security dubious, and in practice the essential parts of the statutory forms should be used in the words prescribed although minor variations in wording are permissible. Subject to observance of these basic requirements, however, the general presentation and layout of the deed may be in any convenient style, and it may include other provisions as to related matters which the parties desire to incorporate.

---

[17]*Ibid.*, s. 16(2).
[18]1970 Act, s. 9(3).

General Styles

Note. The following styles of standard security Nos. 1 to 18 and 22 are appropriate where the standard security is to be recorded in the Register of Sasines. For variations where the interest of the creditor is to be registered in the Land Register see paragraph 37–41A *infra*.

Style 1

Standard security—simple form—fixed amount—Form A

37–12   I, AB, (*designation*), hereby undertake to pay to CD, (*designation*), the sum of £   with interest from [19]   at   per centum per annum (or other rate as may be agreed in writing)[20] half-yearly on [21]   and   in each year (*adjust appropriately for monthly or other terms of payment*) commencing on [22]   ; For which I (*consent of non-entitled spouse, where appropriate*) grant a standard security in favour of the said CD over ALL and WHOLE (*description of security subjects*)[23]: (*Clause of deduction of title, if required*)[24]: The standard conditions specified in Schedule 3 to the Conveyancing and Feudal Reform (Scotland) Act 1970, and any lawful variation thereof operative for the time being, shall apply (*clause varying standard conditions or reference to document containing such variations, if required*): And I grant warrandice: And I consent to registration for execution.

(*To be attested*)

Style 2

Standard security—fluctuating amount on current account—Form A

37–13   I, AB, (*designation*), hereby undertake to pay to (*name and address of bank*) (hereinafter called "the Bank") all sums of principal and interest which are now and which may at any time hereafter become due to the Bank in any manner of way by me, either solely or jointly with any person or persons or corporation or other body and whether as principal or surety, [but not exceeding in total the sum of £   of principal] with interest on such sums severally from the respective dates of advance or becoming due until payment at   per centum per annum or at such higher or lower rate as shall be charged by the Bank for overdrafts on current or cash accounts for the time (the Bank being entitled to fix such rate of interest from time to time without notice) which interest may be debited to my account or accounts with the Bank half yearly on   and   in each year (*or otherwise as the practice of the Bank may be*), declaring

---

[19]Normally date of payment of advance, whether earlier than date of deed or later, *i.e.* at settlement.

[20]To allow for alteration in rate of interest without the need of a recorded variation.

[21]Usually six months after payment of advance, but may be varied according to the bargain.

[22]Even if the first payment of interest is for a broken period between terms it is unnecessary to state "for the period preceding." Interest will be payable for the broken period at the rate stated.

[23]As to description of subjects see Vol. II, Chap. 18.

[24]See 1970 Act, Sched. 2, Note 2.

that (1) a certificate signed by the (*specify official or officials of the Bank having authority to sign*) or any other signing official authorised by the Bank at any of its offices shall ascertain and constitute the amount or balance of principal and interest due to the Bank by me at the date of such certificate,[25] (2) to (7) (*insert such of the provisions in clauses FIRST to SIXTH of bond of cash credit in paragraph 5–44 of Volume I supra as may be desired*): For all which sums I (*consent of non-entitled spouse where appropriate*) grant a standard security in favour of the Bank over ALL and WHOLE (*description of security subjects*): (*clause of deduction of title if required*): The standard conditions specified in Schedule 3 to the Conveyancing and Feudal Reform (Scotland) Act 1970, varied as hereinafter provided, and any lawful variation thereof operative for the time being, shall apply: And I agree that the said standard conditions shall be varied to the effect that (1) the insurance to be effected in terms of standard condition 5(a) shall provide cover to the extent of the full reinstatement value of the security subjects and not the market value thereof, (2) all policies of insurance effected by the debtor which afford cover in respect of the security subjects against fire and other risks within the terms of standard condition 5(a) shall be disclosed to the Bank by the debtor in order that they may be written or endorsed for the interest of the Bank and the debtor and shall in other respects be deemed for the purpose of this standard security to have been effected under standard condition 5(a), (3) it shall be an obligation on the debtor not to create or agree to create a subsequent security over the said subjects or any part thereof, nor to assign or convey the said subjects or any part thereof to any person (otherwise than by *mortis causa* deed) without the prior consent in writing of the Bank, which consent, if granted, may be so granted subject to such conditions as the Bank may impose[26] and (4) in the event of the Bank entering into possession of the said subjects it shall be entitled as agent for the debtor to remove, store, sell or otherwise deal with any goods, furniture and fittings and fixtures which the debtor shall fail to remove from the said subjects within fourteen days of being requested to do so by written notice from the Bank, and the Bank shall not be liable for any loss or damage occasioned to the debtor who shall indemnify the Bank against all expenses incurred by the Bank in relation to such goods, furniture, fittings and fixtures, provided always that the Bank shall account to the debtor for the proceeds of any such sale after deducting any such expenses; Declaring that words or expressions which are incorporated in the foregoing variation and which are defined in the said Act or the said Schedule shall be deemed to be so defined for the purpose of these presents: And I grant warrandice; And I consent to registration hereof and of any such certificate as aforesaid for execution.

(*To be attested*)

---

[25] 1970 Act, Sched. 2, Note 6.
[26] The effectiveness of this prohibition operating so as to exclude the application of s. 13 of the 1970 Act may be doubtful—see para. 36–20(7)—but its contravention by the debtor would be a breach of contract.

Style 3

Standard security postponed to existing standard security—Form A[27]

37-14
(*Personal obligation and grant of security as in Style 1 or Style 2
so far as appropriate to beginning of warrandice clause*); But the
security hereby granted is subject to a standard security [for
£   ] [all sums due or to become due by me] granted by me in
favour of EF, (*designation*), recorded in the Register for[28] the
County of   (*or if already mentioned* the said
Register of Sasines) on   , (*in the case of a fixed
amount which has been partly repaid, and in all cases where the
amount is a maximum sum or is indefinite, add* the amount of
principal now due thereunder being £   )[29]: And, subject as
aforesaid, I grant warrandice: And I consent to registration for
execution.

(*To be attested*)

Style 4

*Standard security postponed to ex facie absolute disposition, with
assignation of reversionary interest—grantor previously infeft*[30]

37-15
(*Personal obligation as in Style 1 or Style 2 so far as appropriate*):
For which I (*consent of non-entitled spouse, where appropriate*)
grant a standard security in favour of the [said CD] [Bank] over
ALL and WHOLE (*description of security subjects*) and my
whole right, title and interest in the said subjects including
without prejudice to the foregoing generality my whole reversionary right in the said subjects and all rights relating thereto as
hereinafter specially assigned[31]: The standard conditions specified
in Schedule 3 to the Conveyancing and Feudal Reform (Scotland)
Act 1970, and any lawful variation thereof operative for the time
being, shall apply: (*clause varying standard conditions, if
required*): But the security hereby granted is subject to a
disposition of the said subjects [*or* inter alia the said subjects]
granted by me in favour of GH, (*designation*), recorded in the
Register for[32] the County of [*or if already mentioned*, the said
Register of Sasines) on   : And I assign to the said
[CD] [Bank] my said reversionary right and all such other right,
title and interest as I may have in the said subjects and the rents
thereof and any property or funds which may hereafter represent

---

[27] See 1970 Act, Sched. 2, Note 5.

[28] *Ibid.*, s. 53(2).

[29] Specification of the amount outstanding is useful but not essential and may be misleading if the
prior creditor is under obligation to make future advances—1970 Act, s. 13(1). If the amount is
inserted the agreement of the prior creditor to the figure should be obtained.

[30] 1970 Act, Sched. 2, Notes 3 and 5.

[31] The reversionary right to land is an interest a title to which can be recorded so that a security
over it must be in the form of a standard security. The inclusion of the description of the subjects
with a grant of absolute warrandice would effectively bring the reversionary right within the security
but, in order to ensure that any rights arising from the reversion are included, it is specially
incorporated in the description as well as being assigned later since the later assignation may not be
technically in the form of a standard security.

[32] 1970 Act, s. 53(2).

the same and my right to claim from the said GH a reconveyance of the said subjects or a discharge of the said disposition in favour of the said GH and an accounting for the rents and profits thereof and payment of any balance due or that may become due thereon and my whole right, title and interest present and future under the said last mentioned disposition[33,34]: And subject as aforesaid, I grant warrandice: And I consent to registration for execution.

(*To be attested*)

Style 5

Standard security postponed to ex facie absolute disposition by infeft proprietor with assignation of reversionary interest—uninfeft grantor having right to subjects[34a]

37–16   (*Personal obligation and grant of security as in Style 4 to end of description of subjects including security over reversionary right*); Which subjects were formerly vested in EF, (*designation*), whose title thereto was recorded in the Register for the County of   (*or if already mentioned*, the said Register of Sasines) on   (*or if the infeftment of EF has already been mentioned*, the said EF as aforesaid) and from whom I acquired right by (one) confirmation by the sheriff of   at   in favour of JK as executor of the said EF dated   and (two) docket on a certificate of said confirmation by the said JK in favour of me the said AB dated   : The standard conditions specified in Schedule 3 to the Conveyancing and Feudal Reform (Scotland) Act 1970, and any lawful variation thereof operative for the time being, shall apply; (*clause varying standard conditions, if required*): But the security hereby granted is subject to a disposition of the said subjects granted by the said EF in favour of GH, (*designation*), recorded in the said Register of Sasines on   : And I assign (*as in Style 4 to the end*).[35]

(*To be attested*)

Style 6[36]

Standard security by uninfeft grantor who has consented to ex facie absolute disposition, with assignation of reversionary interest

37–17   (*Personal obligation and grant of security as in Style 4 to end of clause applying standard conditions*): But the security hereby

---

[33]The inclusion in the recorded standard security of an assignation of the reversionary right with a reference to the absolute disposition raises the question of publication of the security character of the disposition. But the postponed creditor will wish to have a clear assignation and s. 42 of the 1970 Act now gives protection to the first lender except for new advances.

[34]The standard security should be intimated to the prior creditor as well as being recorded. Recording alone does not satisfy the conditions of s. 13 or s. 42 of the 1970 Act.

[34a]The history of the title is (i) disposition *ex facie* absolute by EF (infeft proprietor) to GH (ii) on death of EF his executor JK acquired right by confirmation and (iii) JK transferred subjects by docket to AB, who is granting the present standard security, without completing title, in favour of CD or the bank.

[35]See nn. 33 and 34 to Style 4.

[36]This deed does not give a valid heritable security. For its effect see para. 36–28.

granted is subject to a disposition of the said subjects granted by EF, (*designation*), with my consent in favour of GH recorded (*as in Style 4 to the end except that the reference is to "conveyance" instead of "reconveyance"*).

(*To be attested*)

Style 7[37]

Standard security by two persons over property belonging to one of them—fixed amount

37–18   We, AB, (*designation*), and CD, (*designation*), hereby jointly and severally undertake to pay to EF, (*designation*), the sum of £   (*as in Style 1 to end of personal obligation*): For which I the said AB[37a] (*consent of non-entitled spouse, where appropriate*) grant a standard security in favour of the said EF over ALL and WHOLE   (*Clause of deduction of title, if required*)[38]: The standard conditions specified in Schedule 3 to the Conveyancing and Feudal Reform (Scotland) Act 1970, and any lawful variation thereof operative for the time being, shall apply (*clause varying standard conditions, if required*): And I the said AB grant warrandice: And we the said AB and CD consent to registration for execution.

(*To be attested*)

Style 8

Standard security—fixed amount—recorded lease—Form A

37–19   (*Personal obligation as in Style 1*)[38a]: For which I (*consent of non-entitled spouse, where appropriate*) grant a standard security in favour of the said CD over a Lease granted by EF, (*designation*), in [my favour] [favour of GH, (*designation*), to which I have now right] of the subjects therein described lying in [the County of   ] [Burgh of   and County of   ] dated   and recorded in the Register for the County of   on (*adding, if only part of the original subjects leased*, but only to the extent of (*description of part*): (*clause of deduction of title, if required*): The standard conditions (*continue as in Style 1 to the end*).

(*To be attested*)

Particular Parties

Building societies

37–20   Most building societies elect to use a standard security in the style of Form A along with a deed of variations or conditions of lending which

---

[37]This traditional style involving the debtor and the guarantor being bound as co-obligants is now less desirable for reasons relating to prescription of the guarantor's obligation—see para. 37–57.
[37a]Person to whom security subjects belong.
[38]As to form of deduction of title, see 1970 Act, Sched. 2, Note 2.
[38a]For special matters to be considered see para. 37–43, in particular the consent of the landlord.

is applicable to all or most of the society's loans and is registered in the Books of Council and Session and incorporated by reference in the standard security. The standard security is framed so as to permit of flexibility in such matters as the amounts of the monthly repayments and the rate of interest, and covers further advances and re-advances. Provision is made in the standard security for ascertainment of the amount due at any time by a certificate under the hand of an officer of the society. The standard conditions are varied by reference to the registered deed of variations and the rules of the society.[39] The adoption of Form A is convenient in respect that only one document is necessary to constitute the loan and the security, thus simplifying execution by the borrower and economising on the storage accommodation required by the society.

Style 9

Standard security—building society

37–21

.... Building Society

STANDARD SECURITY   Account No.

_____

I, the Borrower hereinafter designed, whereas the expressions set out below shall have the meanings and effect respectively set opposite them:

_____

The Borrower:

The Guarantor (if any):

Where the Borrower or the Guarantor is more than one person the singular includes the plural and all obligations of the Borrower and the Guarantor are undertaken jointly and severally

_____

The Society: .... Building Society,
                      (*address*)

_____

Advance   £   Advance Date   19

_____

Property: (*Postal address*)

Being the subjects hereinafter described

_____

[39]For an example see para. 38–28 related to the standard security in Style 9.

Hereby undertake to pay the Society the Advance made or about to be made by the Society to me and all other sums due and that may become due by me to the Society in respect of any Further Advances and re-advances that may be made by the Society to me with interest computed in accordance with the practice of the Society at the Interest Rate by the Monthly Payment (or where applicable the Reduced Monthly Payment), the first payment to be made on the date specified for such purpose in the notice of completion issued by the Society and each subsequent payment at successive intervals of one calendar month until the whole sums hereby secured are paid and satisfied; and I agree that a Certificate signed by an Official of the Society duly authorised for that purpose shall be sufficient to ascertain and constitute conclusively the amount due by me to the Society at the date of the Certificate: For which I grant a Standard Security in favour of the Society over the property being ALL and WHOLE (*short conveyancing description*):

The Standard Conditions specified in Schedule 3 to the Conveyancing and Feudal Reform (Scotland) Act 1970 as varied by the Rules of the Society and the Deed of Variation[40] made by the Society dated   and registered in the Books of Council and Session on   (a copy of which I hereby acknowledge to have received) and any lawful variation thereof operative for the time being shall apply: And I grant warrandice: And I consent to the registration hereof and of any such Certificate as aforesaid for execution: IN WITNESS WHEREOF these presents consisting of this and the preceding pages are executed by the Borrower at

on the   day of
Nineteen hundred and   before these witnesses

(*To be attested*)

NOTE

This style does not incorporate the consent of a non-entitled spouse. The necessary consent, renunciation or affidavit required for the purposes of the Matrimonial Homes (Family Protection) (Scotland) Act 1981 in a separate document should be executed and delivered at or before settlement—see paragraph 37–06 *supra*.

Banks

37–22   Banks usually elect to take a standard security in Form B, the personal obligation being constituted by a bond of cash credit[41] which can be used as the basic document of obligation and referred to in the

---

[40]For deed of variation see para. 38–28.
[41]For a style of bond of cash credit see Vol. I, para. 5–44.

standard security as the separate instrument to which the security relates. The practical advantages of the method are that the privacy of the loan arrangement is preserved and additional securities over moveable assets can be granted in relation to the general obligation constituted by the bond. Variations in the standard conditions may be made in a separate schedule of conditions executed by the bank and incorporated by reference in the standard security. An alternative method, illustrated by Style 2 in paragraph 37–13 *supra*, incorporates both the personal obligation and variations of the standard conditions in a standard security in Form A.

Style 10

Standard security—bank—Form B

37–23   I, AB, (*designation*), hereby (*consent of non-entitled spouse, if appropriate*) in security of the whole obligations to pay all sums of principal and interest which are now and which may hereafter become due by me to (*name and address of bank*) (hereinafter called "the Bank") by virtue of a Bond granted by me in favour of the Bank dated   grant a standard security in favour of the Bank over ALL and WHOLE (*description of security subjects*): The standard conditions specified in Schedule 3 to the Conveyancing and Feudal Reform (Scotland) Act 1970 as varied by the Schedule of Conditions of Lending[42] executed by the Bank dated   (a copy of which I hereby acknowledge to have received), and any lawful variation thereof operative for the time being, shall apply: And I grant warrandice.[43]

(To be attested)

Commercial lenders

37–24   The form of documentation used in commercial lending on heritable security varies according to the nature of the transaction and the practice of the lender.

Form A may be used for an advance of fixed amount for a specific project where no additional advances are contemplated (although Form A may and usually should provide for additional advances which will be covered by the security). It will usually be desirable to make alterations in the standard conditions appropriate to the circumstances of the transaction so that a separate deed of variations will also be executed by the parties and incorporated by reference in the standard security. An illustration of documentation of this kind is offered in Style 11 in paragraph 37–25 and Style 2 in paragraph 38–29 *infra*.

In most cases, however, Form B will be found more suitable, *e.g.* where the loan is of fluctuating amount and repayments are to be made

---

[42]The terms of the schedule vary according to the practice of the bank.
[43]No consent to registration for execution: that will be incorporated in the bond.

by instalments as the borrower receives payment for properties constructed or reconstructed and sold. In such cases the documentation may comprise (1) a bond or loan agreement setting out the terms of the lending arrangement including the personal obligation of the borrower to repay with stipulated interest, (2) a standard security in Form B, and also perhaps (3) a deed of variation of the standard conditions. It is permissible for the loan agreement to incorporate the variations of the standard conditions—what may not be technically permissible in terms of the 1970 Act is to include the variations only by reference to a schedule annexed to the standard security.[44]

A specimen of a commercial security over heritable property using Form B is offered in Styles 12 and 12A in paragraphs 37–26 and 37–27 *infra*.

Style 11

Standard security—fixed amount with possible further advances in security of commercial transaction—building development—Form A

37–25   We A Limited, (*designation*), whereas C Finance Company Limited, (*designation*), (hereinafter called "C") has agreed to provide a loan of £   to us in connection with a building development on the subjects hereinafter described at (*postal address*) and may provide further sums on loan in connection with the said development, all to be secured over the said subjects, therefore we hereby undertake to repay to C the said sum of £   and all other sums that may become due by us to C in respect of moneys advanced or to be advanced to us by C in connection with the said development [or otherwise in any manner of way][45] with interest on the said sum of £   and any such other sums severally from the respective dates of advance until payment at the rate of [per centum per annum] [per centum per annum above the base rate of the   Bank from time to time] applied quarterly on   ,   ,   and   in each year, the whole amounts advanced and outstanding with all interest due thereon to be repaid by us on   19   but without prejudice to the right of C to require such repayment on any earlier date if C in its sole discretion so decides, declaring that a certificate [subscribed by a director or the secretary of C] [signed by EF & Co., Chartered Accountants, Glasgow, or any other firm who may be the auditors of C for the time being] shall ascertain, constitute and be sufficient and conclusive evidence of the amount of principal and interest due at the date of such certificate: For all which sums we grant a standard security in favour of C over ALL and WHOLE (*description of security subjects*); (*clause of deduction of title, if*

---

[44]Since Note 4 to Sched. 2 to the Act provides for variations of the standard conditions to be effected by an instrument or instruments *other than the standard security* or by the insertion of the variations in the body of the standard security itself.

[45]To avoid argument that any further advance was wholly in connection with the particular development.

required): The standard conditions specified in Schedule 3 to the Conveyancing and Feudal Reform (Scotland) Act 1970, and any lawful variation thereof operative for the time being, as varied by the Deed of Variations after mentioned, shall apply: And we agree that the standard conditions shall be varied to the effect specified in the Deed of Variations between us and C dated 19 [46]: And we certify that this standard security does not contravene any of the provisions of our Memorandum and Articles of Association[47]: And we grant warrandice: And we consent to registration hereof and of any such certificate for execution.

(*To be attested*)

Style 12

Standard security—fluctuating advances—building development—Form B

37–26   We, A Limited, (*designation*),[48] hereby in security of advances made and to be made to us by C Finance Company Limited, (*designation*), (hereinafter called "C") and the whole obligations undertaken by us in terms of Loan Agreement between us and C dated 19 [49] in connection with a building development on the subjects hereinafter described at (*postal address*) grant a standard security in favour of C over ALL and WHOLE (*description of subjects*); (*clause of deduction of title, if required*): The standard conditions specified in Schedule 3 to the Conveyancing and Feudal Reform (Scotland) Act 1970, and any lawful variation thereof operative for the time being, shall apply; And we agree that the standard conditions shall be varied in accordance with the said Loan Agreement: And we certify that this standard security does not contravene any of the provisions of our Memorandum and Articles of Association[50]: And we grant warrandice.

(*To be attested*)

Style 12A

Loan agreement containing personal obligation and variations of standard conditions relative to Style 12

37–27

LOAN AGREEMENT
between
A Limited (*designation*)
(hereinafter called "A")
and
C Finance Company Limited
(*designation*) (hereinafter
called "C").

---

[46]For deed of variations see Style 2, para. 38–29.
[47]As to reasons for this clause, see para. 37–37.
[48]As to standard securities by a company, see paras. 37–37 and 37–38.
[49]For loan agreement, see Style 12A, para. 37–27.
[50]For the reasons for this clause, see para. 37–37.

WHEREAS C has agreed to advance certain moneys to A on the terms herein contained THEREFORE the parties AGREE as follows:—

1. In this deed the following expressions have the meanings underwritten:—

   (a) "Initial Advance" means all sums advanced by C to A and debited to A's loan account with C in accordance with Clause 2 hereof.

   (b) "Special Addition" means the sum of £   specified in Clause 3 hereof.

   (c) "Lending Rate" means   per centum per annum or a rate of interest which is   per centum per annum above the base rate of the (*Bank*) from time to time, whichever is the greater, to be charged (except as aftermentioned) on the balance of the Total Advance for the time being outstanding and applied on the last day of each calendar month.

   (d) "Total Advance" means the Initial Advance, the Special Addition and all payments made and expenses incurred by C in terms hereof, and all interest at the Lending Rate accruing due on all these items.

   (e) "Subjects" means the terraced villa forming (*postal address*), the ground effeiring thereto and any other buildings erected thereon and all property and rights held in connection therewith.

   (f) "Development Work" means the renovation of the Subjects and the conversion thereof into four separate flats and all further works necessary to comply with the relevant consents or permissions.

   (g) "Completion Date" means 30th June, 1989.

2. A shall be entitled to draw (a) on fulfilment to the satisfaction of C of the conditions contained in Clause 7 hereof such sum as C shall approve, not exceeding £   , and (b) thereafter, such further sums at such times as shall be agreed between A and C, and the sums so drawn shall be debited to A's loan account with C.

3. In respect that C is to be entitled to receive payment of an additional sum of £   by way of a share of profit, C shall debit the said sum of £   to A's loan account on the last date of this Agreement.

4. Interest at the Lending Rate shall be charged and applied to A's loan account as aforesaid on the amount of the Total Advance for the time being (other than the Special Addition upon which interest at the Lending Rate shall be charged only from and after the Completion Date).

5. The Total Advance shall be repayable by A to C on the Completion Date but without prejudice to the right of C to require repayment by A in terms of Clause 10(c) hereof.

6. The Initial Advance shall be used by A solely to enable A to complete the purchase of the Subjects and A shall be obliged to

meet and defray from its own resources the whole costs of the Development Work and the procuring of all necessary consents and permissions in terms of clause 7(2) hereof unless with the prior written consent of C.

7. Before C shall be required to make any payment hereunder A shall (1) in security of A's obligations herein contained (a) deliver to C a first Standard Security over the Subjects duly executed and will deliver or exhibit a good marketable title to the Subjects with clear searches in the Property and Personal Registers and in the Companies Register of Charges and A's company file [and (b) procure and deliver to C a Guarantee in terms satisfactory to C by CD, (*designation*), in favour of C of fulfilment of the obligations of A under this Agreement] and (2) obtain and exhibit to C planning permission, [listed building consent] and a building warrant and all other necessary consents of the superior, other proprietors and all other persons having an interest, for the carrying out of the Development Work, all in terms satisfactory to C.

8. A shall carry out the Development Work in accordance with the said planning permission and building warrant and shall complete the same not later than the Completion Date.

9. A shall not without the consent of C (1) sell the Subjects or any part thereof or (2) grant any other security over the Subjects.

10. The Standard Conditions in Schedule 3 to the Conveyancing and Feudal Reform (Scotland) Act 1970 shall apply subject to the following variations:—

(a) In Standard Condition 2 the expression "unfinished buildings or works" shall include the Development Work and every part thereof whether commenced or not and A shall in addition be bound to have the Development Work carried out and completed under the supervision of a qualified architect and, where appropriate, a structural engineer, who will each grant such interim certificates as C may require and a final completion certificate.

(b) The Subjects and the Development Work shall be insured for their full reinstatement value as completed in names of A and C through the agency of C against loss or damage by fire and such other risks as C may require: A shall be liable for payment on demand of the premiums payable for such insurance but, in the event of failure by A to pay such premiums punctually on demand, C shall be entitled, but not bound, to pay the same and treat them as part of the Total Advance, and Standard Condition 5 shall be varied to that extent only.

(c) Notwithstanding anything contained herein or in Standard Condition 8, C reserves power to require repayment of the Total Advance and to serve a calling-up notice at any time

C thinks fit and on receipt of such notice the Total Advance shall become immediately due and payable.

11. In the event of A failing to make due payment when demanded by C of any sums payable in terms hereof or failing to implement any of its obligations hereunder or of the said Standard Conditions as hereby varied, A shall be in default in terms of Standard Condition 9(1)(b) of said Schedule and the Total Advance shall thereupon become immediately due and payable by A.

12. A undertakes to pay the whole fees and outlays (whether of solicitors, surveyors, architects, engineers or other professional advisers) incurred or that may be incurred by C in connection with the Total Advance, these presents and the said security [securities] and the discharge thereof and any proceedings for the enforcement of C's remedies.

13. A statement or certificate subscribed by a director, the secretary, cashier, accountant or other signing official of C shall ascertain and constitute the amount due to C, whether capital or interest, at any time in terms of this Agreement.

14. A consents to the registration hereof and of any statement or certificate under Clause 13 hereof for execution.

(To be attested)

Trustees

37–28 **(1) Grantors**. Trustees may borrow on the security of the heritable property of the trust by virtue of powers expressed in the deed of trust or, even without express power, if the borrowing is not at variance with the terms or purposes of the trust.[51] If there is doubt as to the powers of the trustees, the court may authorise the transaction if satisfied that it is expedient for execution of the trust.[52] Even if the transaction is at variance with the terms or purposes of the trust, the lender is protected both as to the validity of the transaction and the security title which he acquires.[53] As to exclusion of personal liability and limitation of warrandice see Style 13, paragraph 37–31 *infra*.

37–29 **(2) Grantees**. As to power to lend on the security of heritable property see Volume I, paragraphs 2–63 to 2–74. As to valuation see Volume I, paragraph 2–68 and paragraph 37–04 *supra*. As to the form of the standard security see paragraph 37–32 *infra*.

---

[51]Trusts (Scotland) Act 1921, s. 4.
[52]*Ibid.*, s. 5.
[53]Trusts (Scotland) Act 1961, s. 2.

Executors

37–30   An executor, whether nominate[54] or dative,[55] has the same powers
           as a trustee *quoad* transactions in heritable securities.

Style 13

Standard security by trustees—fixed amount—one trustee infeft

37–31   We, AB, (*designation*), CD, (*designation*), and EF, (*designa-
           tion*), the trustees acting under trust disposition and settlement by
           GH, (*designation*), dated   and registered in the
           Books of Council and Session on   hereby
           undertake that we and our successors in office but only as
           trustees foresaid and not personally nor as individuals and the
           trust estate under our charge will pay to JK, (*designation*), the
           sum of £   [*as in Style 1 to end of personal obligation*]: For
           which I the said AB as trustee foresaid heritably vest in the
           subjects hereinafter described with consent of us the said CD and
           EF as trustees foresaid for all right, title and interest competent
           to us as trustees foresaid and we the said AB, CD and EF as
           trustees foresaid[55a] grant a standard security in favour of the said
           JK over ALL and WHOLE   (*description of security
           subjects*)[56]: The standard conditions specified in Schedule 3 to the
           Conveyancing and Feudal Reform (Scotland) Act 1970, and any
           lawful variation thereof operative for the time being, shall apply
           (*clause varying standard conditions, if required*): And we the said
           AB, CD and EF as trustees foresaid grant warrandice from our
           own facts and deeds only and we bind the trust estate under our
           charge in absolute warrandice: And we as trustees foresaid
           consent to registration for execution.

                                                              (*To be attested*)

Style 14

Standard security in favour of trustees—fixed amount

37–32   I, AB, (*designation*), hereby undertake to pay to CD, (*designa-
           tion*), EF, (*designation*), and GH, (*designation*), the trustees now
           acting under trust disposition and settlement by JK, (*designa-
           tion*), dated   and registered in the Books of
           Council and Session on   and the survivors and
           survivor of them as trustees and trustee foresaid the sum of
           £   (*as in Style 1 to end of personal obligation*); For which I
           (*consent of non-entitled spouse, where appropriate*) grant a
           standard security in favour of the said CD, EF and GH and the
           survivors and survivor of them as trustees foresaid over ALL and
           WHOLE (*description of security subjects*) (*clause of deduction of
           title, if required*): (*As in Style 1 to the end*).

                                                              (*To be attested*)

---

[54]Trusts (Scotland) Act 1921, ss. 2, 4 and 5.
[55]Succession (Scotland) Act 1964, s. 20.
[55a]If the trustees hold the security subjects for the benefit of a liferenter the consent of the spouse
of the liferenter or an affidavit by the liferenter as in Vol. II, para. 21–29 or para. 21–31 will be
required.
[56]No deduction of title required, since one trustee infeft.

Pupils and minors

37–33   As to the power of the tutor of a pupil or a minor with or without a curator to borrow or lend on the security of heritable property see Volume I, paragraphs 2–13, 2–14 and 2–25. Since such transactions may be vulnerable to reduction within the *quadriennium utile*, they should in general be avoided.

A standard security granted on behalf of a pupil runs in name of the tutor on behalf of his ward but the tutor does not connect himself with the title: if the pupil has a recorded title, no deduction of title is required.[57] Money lent by the tutor from the funds of the pupil is a narrower-range trustee investment which does not require special advice,[58] but there should be an independent valuation and limitation of amount lent as in the case of trustees.[59] The standard security should be granted in favour of the pupil.

A standard security by a minor who has a curator will be granted by the minor with consent of the curator: when money is lent by a minor on heritable security the standard security will be granted in favour of the minor.

Partnerships

37–34   **(1) Grantors**. The title to the heritable property of the partnership is a trust title, the deed of trust normally being a disposition to the partners as trustees for the firm. Subsequent contracts of partnership, whether between the same or new partners, merely affect the devolution of the beneficial interest in the trust for the partners of the firm, present and future, created in the title deeds: they are not links in the title. For devolution of the title, conveyances, general or special, are required. If any of the partners originally infeft remains no deduction of title is necessary, but all partners should sign the standard security and the personal obligation should be granted by the firm and all the partners, jointly and severally. See Style 15, paragraph 37–36 *infra*.

37–35   **(2) Grantees**. The personal obligation should be expressed in favour of the firm, but the grant of security should be in favour of all the partners and the survivors and survivor as trustees and trustee for the firm.

Style 15

Standard security by firm and partners over the partnership's property-fixed amount

37–36   We AB and Company, (*designation*), and we CD, (*designation*), EF, (*designation*), and GH, (*designation*), the individual partners

---

[57]*Scott* (1856) 18 D. 624.
[58]Trustee Investments Act 1961, Sched. 1, para. 13 and s. 6(7).
[59]Trusts (Scotland) Act 1921, s. 30.

of the said AB and Company, as such partners and as individuals, jointly and severally undertake to pay to JK, (*designation*), the sum of £ (*as in Style 1 to end of personal obligation*); For which we the said CD, EF and GH as trustees for the said AB and Company grant a standard security in favour of the said JK over ALL and WHOLE (*description of security subjects*) (*clause of deduction of title, if required*): The standard conditions specified in Schedule 3 to the Conveyancing and Feudal Reform (Scotland) Act 1970, and any lawful variation thereof operative for the time being, shall apply; (*clause varying standard conditions, if required*): And we all jointly and severally grant warrandice: And we all consent to registration for execution.

(*To be attested*)

Companies

7–37   In favour of a person dealing with a company in good faith any transaction of borrowing or lending on heritable security entered into by the directors of a company is deemed to be one which it is within the capacity of the company to enter into, and the power of the directors to bind the company shall be deemed to be free of any limitation under the memorandum or articles of association.[60] A party transacting with a company is not bound to inquire as to the capacity of the company to enter into the transaction nor as to any such limitation of the powers of the directors.[60] Although good faith is thus presumed by statute there may be a question whether the presumption is displaced if the other party to the transaction is put on his inquiry, and so it may be advisable to insert in a standard security by a company an express statement that the transaction does not contravene any of the provisions of the memorandum or articles of association of the company.[61]

7–38   Matters which require attention include:

(1) The existence of any prior floating charge or fixed security containing a prohibition against or restrictions upon the creation of any fixed security having priority over or ranking *pari passu* with any such floating charge or fixed security or making provision as to ranking which may affect the preference obtained by a fixed security subsequently created.[62]

(2) Registration of the charge created by the standard security in the company's register of charges.[63]

(3) Registration of the charge created by the standard security in the Register of Charges kept by the Registrar of Companies within 21 days after the date of its creation, *i.e.* after the date of recording the standard security in the Register of Sasines or of registration of the creditor's interest in the Land Register.[64]

---

[60]Companies Act 1985, s. 35.
[61]See Style 12, para. 37–26.
[62]Companies Act 1985, s. 464.
[63]*Ibid.*, s. 422.
[64]*Ibid.*, ss. 410, 415.

Local authorities

37–39   Standard securities are frequently granted in favour of local authorities for the purposes of securing (1) housing loans provided under the Housing (Scotland) Act 1966 and the Housing (Financial Provisions) (Scotland) Act 1968 and the Finance Act 1982 and (2) the liability to repay discount or a part thereof where a dwelling-house, having been purchased at the discount under the Tenants' Rights, Etc. (Scotland) Act 1980, is sold by the purchasing tenant within three years. Illustrations of standard securities for those purposes are given in paragraphs 37–40 and 37–41 *infra*.[65]

Style 16

Standard security—local authority housing loan

37–40   The Debtor, being (*name and designation of grantor*)[66]

hereby undertakes to pay to the City of Glasgow District Council as the Local Authority for the said District for the purposes of the Housing (Scotland) Act 1966, and the Housing (Financial Provisions) (Scotland) Act 1968 and the Finance Act 1982 and Acts amending the same ("the Council") the sum of £   , together with all other sums that may become due by the Debtor to the Council in respect of any other advance or advances that may be made by the Council to the Debtor,[67] with interest from the date or respective dates of advance at the ruling rate as defined in the City of Glasgow District Council Home Loans Scheme Clauses 1975 Edition dated sixteenth and registered in the Books of Council and Session for preservation on nineteenth both days of May Nineteen hundred and Seventy-five a copy of which the Debtor hereby acknowledges to have received and which it is agreed shall be incorporated in and shall form part of these presents subject to the following amendment, namely, that the period of notice referred to in Clause 4(D)(iii)[68] thereof is hereby declared to be one month instead of three months (the initial rate of interest being   per centum per annum) by monthly instalments of such amount as may be decided by the Council from time to time (the initial monthly instalment being £   ) payable said instalments as provided in the said Home Loans Scheme Clauses; and the Debtor agrees that a Certificate by the Director of Finance of the Council as to the amount due to the Council at any time by the Debtor shall be final, conclusive and unchallengeable[69]; For which the Debtor (*consent of non-entitled spouse, where appropriate*) grants a standard security in

---

[65]Styles provided by courtesy of City of Glasgow District Council.

[66]Where more than one grantor, incorporate joint and several obligation.

[67]Any additional advances are brought within the personal obligation and the security—no recorded variation will be required in respect of them.

[68]Notice altering rate of interest to provide flexibility for change in lending rates.

[69]Required to fix amount due at any time, *e.g.* for registration for execution—see 1970 Act, Sched. 2, Note 6.

favour of the Council over ALL and WHOLE (*description of security subjects*); (*clause of deduction of title, if required*[70]): The standard conditions specified in Schedule 3 to the Conveyancing and Feudal Reform (Scotland) Act 1970 as varied by the said Glasgow Home Loans Scheme Clauses 1975 Edition shall apply; And the Debtor grants warrandice: And the Debtor consents to registration for execution: IN WITNESS WHEREOF these presents are executed by the Debtor on the   day of   Nineteen hundred and   before the witnesses hereto subscribing:—

Signature of Debtor   *Signatures, occupations and addresses of witnesses*

Style 17

Standard security—repayment of discount—purchase under Tenants' Rights, Etc. (Scotland) Act 1980[70a]

37–41 I/We (*name(s) and designation(s)*)[71]

(hereinafter referred to as "the Debtor") Whereas THE CITY OF GLASGOW DISTRICT COUNCIL, as the Local Authority for the said District under the Housing (Scotland) Acts, and Acts amending the same, (hereinafter referred to as "the Council") have sold to the Debtor the subjects aftermentioned and Whereas the Council, in calculating the price of the said subjects, have given to the Debtor a discount in terms of Section 1(5)(*b*) of the Tenants' Rights, Etc. (Scotland) Act 1980, as amended by Section 1(1) of the Tenants' Rights, Etc. (Scotland) Amendment Act 1984 and Section 2(1) of the Housing (Scotland) Act 1986 amounting to £

and Whereas it has been agreed between the Debtor and the Council that in the event of the subjects being sold or otherwise disposed of by the Debtor within the period of three years from

(hereinafter referred to as "the discount period") the said discount, or a part thereof, shall be repaid by the Debtor to the Council, Therefore the Debtor undertakes that, in the event of the said subjects being sold or otherwise disposed of by the Debtor within the discount period, the Debtor shall repay the said discount, or a part thereof, as follows:—

---

[70]As to form of clause, see 1970 Act, Sched. 2, Note 2.
[70a]See Vol. II, para. 15–129.
[71]Where more than one debtor, obligation should be joint and several.

Date of sale or disposal	*Amount of discount repayable*
Within one year of said date	— the whole discount
On or after the first but before the second anniversary of said date	— 66% of the discount
on or after the second but before the third anniversary of said date	— 33% of the discount

Declaring that for the aforesaid purpose the date of sale or disposal shall be the date of conclusion of Missives whereby the subjects are agreed to be sold or disposed of by the Debtor, or if there be no Missives, the date of entry in the Disposition or other deed conveying the subjects granted by the Debtor. The Debtor further undertakes to make payment to the Council of such discount, or part thereof, as may be due as aforesaid not later than the date of entry in terms of any agreement for the sale or disposal of the said subjects by the Debtor to a third party and to pay interest thereon at the rate laid down from time to time by the Acquisition of Land (Rate of Interest after Entry) (Scotland) Regulations ("statutory rate") from the said last mentioned date of entry until payment: Declaring that a certificate under the hand of the Council's Director of Finance for the time being shall ascertain and constitute the whole amount of discount or part thereof and interest and expenses due by the Debtor to the Council at the date of such certificate; For all which sums the Debtor (*consent of non-entitled spouse, where appropriate*) grants a Standard Security in favour of the Council over ALL and WHOLE (*description of subjects*)

The Standard Conditions specified in Schedule 3 to the Conveyancing and Feudal Reform (Scotland) Act 1970, as hereinafter varied by these presents and any lawful variation thereof operative for the time being, shall apply; Declaring, however, that in respect of Standard Condition 5 of the said Standard Conditions, the extent of the insurance cover shall be such sum as is determined in terms of the Debtor's title and not the market value and that the Council will not exercise its option to insure the subjects in terms of the said Standard Condition provided always that there is in force a valid Policy of Insurance covering the subjects for the aforesaid sum.[72] Further Declaring that Standard Condition 6 of the said Standard Conditions shall be deleted and the following substituted therefor:— "6. It shall be an obligation on the Debtor not, without the prior written consent of the Creditor, at any time during the continuance of the security (1) to make any alteration in the use of the security subjects, (2) in any way to part with the occupation of the security subjects or any part thereof, or (3) to create a subsequent security over the security subjects or any part thereof." Further Declaring that Standard Condition 12 of the said Standard Conditions shall be deleted and the following substituted therefor:— "12. The Debtor shall keep the Creditor indemnified from and against all actions, proceedings, claims,

---

[72]Where there is a prior security, *e.g.* to a building society, the prior creditor will normally require insurance to the extent of the market value or full reinstatement value, but for the purposes of securing the repayment of discount the lower value based on the price paid by the debtor is sufficient.

expenses and damages occasioned by any breach of any undertaking, obligation or stipulation, or the non-payment of any outgoing, and will pay on demand to the Creditor all fees, expenses and outlays and other moneys due to the Creditor, or incurred by the Creditor, or any of its officers, solicitors, surveyors or agents in connection with the Standard Security, or the collection of any money due thereunder, together with interest thereon and, until paid by the Debtor, such fees, expenses, outlays and other moneys shall be part of the moneys secured by the Standard Security." Further Declaring that the Council shall, if requested, discharge this Standard Security after the expiry of the discount period subject to the whole expenses of the Discharge being paid by the Debtor: And the Debtor grants warrandice[72a]; And the Debtor consents to registration hereof and of the aforesaid certificate for execution.

(To be attested)

Particular Subjects and Transactions

Registered interests

37–41A Where a standard security is granted over an interest registered in the Land Register of Scotland, the security subjects should be described by reference to the title number of that interest (Land Registration (Scotland) Act 1979, s. 15(1) and rule 25 and Schedule B of the Land Registration (Scotland) Rules 1980). If the interest of the proprietor or tenant of the security subjects has already been registered in the Land Register the description of the security subjects in the standard security may be in the form in paragraph 18–75 of Volume II (security over whole registered interest) or in paragraph 18–77 of Volume II (security over part of registered interest) or in paragraph 26–12 *supra* (registered leases). If the standard security is being granted over subjects where the interest of the proprietor or tenant is about to be registered in the Land Register but has not yet been so registered (as when there is a disposition for value or a long lease, with a new loan over the interest being registered) with the result that a title number is not available when the standard security is being prepared, the description to be inserted in the standard security should repeat that in the disposition or lease and any relative plan should be prepared in duplicate and one copy annexed to the standard security.

Where the grantor of the standard security is the uninfeft proprietor of an interest registered in the Land Register a clause of deduction of title need not be inserted in the standard security, but the necessary links in title must be produced to the Keeper with the application for registration of the interest of the creditor in the standard security.

[72a]If there is a prior security—see Vol. II, para. 15–129—it should be referred to as in Sched. 2, Note 5 to the 1970 Act and excepted from warrandice.

Feudal property

37–42   As to the description of the security subjects see Volume II, Chapter 18. A short conveyancing description including a postal address is sufficient. A reference to fixtures and fittings and parts, privileges and pertinents should be added. No reference to burdens is required.[73]

Long leases

37–43   Certain conditions of a long lease which is offered as security are of special concern to the lender, *viz.*—(1) The tenant's right to assign the lease should be unrestricted or at least assignable with the consent of the landlord which shall not be unreasonably withheld. If otherwise, the creditor, if he seeks to enforce the standard security, may be prevented or restricted in assigning the lease on sale. (2) The limitations on use of the subjects should not be unduly restrictive, so that, if the security has to be enforced by sale of the lease, the market is not too limited. (3) Despite the limited protection given by sections 3 to 6 of the Law Reform (Miscellaneous Provisions) (Scotland) Act 1985 in leases to which they apply an irritancy may still be incurred on failure to pay rent after due notice or breach of other obligation or upon insolvency, bankruptcy or winding-up of the tenant, with the result effectively of destroying the security. The lender should check that the lease in such circumstances confers upon a heritable creditor, or in the case of insolvency, bankruptcy or winding-up of the tenant upon the trustee in bankruptcy or liquidator, a period of grace within which he may, subject to implement of the tenant's obligations, sell the tenant's interest.[74] (4) Potentially onerous obligations of the tenant, *e.g.* to rebuild on destruction of or serious damage to the subjects through the occurrence of an uninsurable risk, should be evaluated as a risk factor.

Advances on the security of a sub-lease involve most of the foregoing considerations *mutatis mutandis* and also some additional ones. It is necessary to verify that the sub-lease is consistent with the terms of the head lease. Irritancy of the head lease will destroy also the sub-lease, so that the existence of protective provisions in irritancy clauses in both the head lease and the sub-lease is of importance.

Where the security is to be granted over let premises in a multiple-tenancy building, whether held on sub-lease or by assignation of part of a lease, the valuer instructed by the potential lender should be asked to report also on the general condition of the whole building.

The right of the debtor to grant interposed leases should be made subject to the consent of the heritable creditor.

Confirmation by the landlord as to implement of the obligations of the tenant or sub-tenant to date should, if practicable, be obtained.

---

[73]Conveyancing (Scotland) Act 1924, s. 9(1).
[74]See paras. 29–33 and 29–43, cl. 10.

Where the security is over a head lease the borrower should certify that the obligations of all sub-tenants have been implemented to date.

A style of standard security over leasehold subjects is given in paragraph 37–19 *supra*, but it may be necessary to incorporate special provisions to cater for some of the above suggestions and any other special provisions appropriate to the circumstances of the transaction.

Licensed premises

37–44   Standard securities over licensed premises are frequently taken in favour of suppliers of liquor to the proprietor in combination with a solus agreement creating a trade tie. Normally the documentation comprises:

(1) A standard security in Form B.

(2) A separate agreement creating the personal obligation and specifying the other terms of the bargain.

(3) A separate solus agreement regarding supplies of beers and other drinks which complies with the EEC Regulations as regards maximum duration (see Volume I, paragraph 8–52 *supra*).

If the loan made does not exceed £15,000 the procedure required by the Consumer Credit Act 1974 must be followed—see paragraph 37–47 *infra*.

If the borrower is a company, consideration should be given to guarantees by directors, restrictions on share dealings, appointment of new directors, etc.

Style 18

Standard security by owner of licensed premises—personal obligation in separate instrument—Form B—grantor uninfeft

37–45   I, AB, (*designation*), hereby in security of all advances and other sums due and that may become due by me to C and Company Limited, (*designation*), in connection with the property belonging to me at   in terms of Agreement between the said C and Company Limited and me dated of even date with these presents (hereinafter called "the Agreement") (*if premises include a dwelling-house consent of non-entitled spouse, if appropriate*) grant a standard security in favour of the said C and Company Limited over ALL and WHOLE (*include fittings, fixtures and goodwill of business*): which subjects were last vested in EF, (*designation*), whose title thereto was recorded in the Register for the County of   [*or, if already mentioned*, the said Register of Sasines] on   [*or, if the infeftment of EF has already been mentioned*, the said EF as aforesaid] and from whom I acquired right by (one) confirmation by the Sheriff of   at   in favour of me the said AB as executor of the said EF dated and (two) docket on a certificate of said confirmation by me as executor foresaid in favour of myself as an individual dated : The standard conditions specified in Schedule 3 to the Conveyancing and Feudal Reform (Scotland) Act 1970, and any lawful variation thereof operative for the time being, shall apply: and I agree that the standard conditions shall be varied in accordance with the Agreement[75]: And I grant warrandice.

(To be attested)

Style 18A

Separate agreement constituting personal obligation relative to Style 18

37–46
AGREEMENT
between

C and Company Limited (*designation*), (hereinafter called "the Company") and AB, (*designation*), (hereinafter called "the Second Party").

WHEREAS by Standard Security granted by the Second Party of even date with his execution of these presents a heritable security was created by the Second Party in favour of the Company over the subjects known as   , with the goodwill of the licensed business carried on therein and the whole fittings and fixtures in and upon the same so far as heritable and all trade and working utensils and furniture and furnishings (all hereinafter collectively referred to as "the Security Subjects") and it is proper that the debt and the whole obligations of the Second Party secured by the said Standard Security and the conditions applicable thereto should be reduced to writing

THEREFORE the parties hereby agree as follows:

1. In construing these presents the following expressions shall have the meanings hereby assigned to them respectively, videlicet:

"The Company" shall include their successors and assignees whomsoever.

"The Second Party" shall whenever used herein in relation to individual persons and unless otherwise specifically provided include the respective executors and representatives whomsoever of such individual persons to the effect in particular that all obligations undertaken shall be held to have been so undertaken by such individual persons to bind themselves and their respective executors and representatives whomsoever jointly and severally without the benefit of discussion and that where two or more parties (whether individual persons or not) are hereinbefore defined as the Second Party all obligations herein undertaken by the Second Party shall bind all such parties jointly and severally.[76]

Words importing the masculine gender shall include the feminine gender and a corporate or unincorporated body. Words importing the singular number shall include the plural number and vice versa.

2. The Company hereby admit and declare and the Second Party hereby agrees that the said Standard Security is and shall

---

[75]Agreement: Style 18A, para. 37–46.
[76]The style is framed so as to be appropriate for individual or several borrowers.

be held by the Company and their assignees in security of payment of all sums due and that may become due by the Second Party to the Company in any manner of way including all sums advanced and to be advanced by the Company to the Second Party, or on his account, and all trade accounts and accounts for services incurred and to be incurred by the Second Party to the Company, [or to any of the Company's associated or subsidiary trading companies acting as agents for the Company which sums are for the purposes of these presents sums due to the Company,] and of payment of, and relief from, all obligations undertaken or that may be undertaken by the Company on behalf of the Second Party, and of and from all feuduties, ground annuals, additional payments, rates, taxes, premiums of insurance against loss by fire and other perils, loss of licence, damage to plate glass, or otherwise, repairs, improvements, expenses of management and all other outgoings and expenses, and in security of all obligations undertaken by the Second Party under these presents or otherwise in favour of the Company, with interest at the rate aftermentioned from the respective dates of advance or disbursement until repaid and for relief of all liabilities in respect of the Security Subjects, and further and generally in security of all claims present and future, whether actual or contingent of whatever nature, at the instance of the Company or their foresaids against the Second Party.

3. The Second Party grants him to have instantly borrowed and received from the Company the sum of £   which sum, together with all other sums due or which may become due by the Second Party to the Company [whether directly or through their associated or subsidiary trading companies acting as their agents as aforesaid] including any further sums which may be advanced by the Company to the Second Party or which may become due by the Second Party to the Company in any manner of way, the Second Party binds himself and his executors and representatives whomsoever, all jointly and severally and without the necessity of discussing them in their order, to make payment on demand to the Company or their assignees, with interest on the said sum or sums or on such part or parts thereof as shall be due for the time, at the rate of   *per centum per annum* (or such other higher or lower rate as may from time to time be fixed by the Company by notice in writing to the Second Party or to his successors): And that at   and in each year by equal portions, beginning the first payment of the said interest at   next for the interest due preceding that date and the next payment thereof at the succeeding   and so forth half yearly and proportionally thereafter during the non payment of the said principal sums, with a fifth part more of the interest due at each term as liquidate damages in case of failure in the punctual payment thereof: And it is hereby provided and declared that a Certificate under the hand of the Secretary or any Director of the Company for the time being of the amount due at any time under these presents shall be sufficient to constitute and ascertain the sum or balance due and to charge same against the Second Party and his foresaids under these presents.

4. Standard Condition 5 of Schedule 3 to the Conveyancing and Feudal Reform (Scotland) Act 1970 shall be and the same is

hereby varied to the following effect viz.:—

During the continuance of this security the Company may require the Second Party to, or (at the Company's option) the Company may themselves (a) insure the Security Subjects against loss or damage by fire and such other risks as the Company may deem necessary, to the extent of the full Market Value thereof, in the name of the Company, and (b) keep the licence of the business carried on by the Second Party insured in the name of the Company against loss for such amount as the Company shall deem right: And such insurances shall be with such insurers, and through the Company's agency or such other agency as the Company may from time to time think fit; And the Second Party binds himself and his foresaids to pay or repay to the Company the premiums of said insurances with interest thereon at   *per centum per annum* (or such other rate as may be fixed aforesaid) from the date of the respective payments till repaid. The said insurances shall be held by the Company for their rights and interests in the Security Subjects but the Company shall be under no liability whatsoever to effect, or to see that the said insurances or any of them have been effected, or are kept in force, or as to the validity or effect of the policy or policies of insurance, and they shall incur no liability or responsibility whatever in connection therewith, the Second Party being bound to satisfy himself in regard thereto; The Second Party also binds himself to exhibit to the Company when required so to do, any Fire or Licence or other Policies effected by him and also the receipts for the premiums as they fall due.

5. The Second Party undertakes during the continuance of this security to carry on the said licensed business in the Security Subjects in a proper and businesslike manner and that he will not knowingly do, or permit, or suffer anything to be done, whereby the goodwill of the said business may be liable to be prejudicially affected: And further, that he will not do, or suffer to be done anything whereby the Licence Certificate held in connection with the said business shall become forfeited, and that as and when the said Licence Certificate shall become renewable, he will apply for renewal thereof, and will use his best endeavours, and do everything in his power, to have the same renewed, and in the event of the application being refused by the Licensing Board, and if required by the Company to do so, will appeal said decision, and prosecute such appeal to a conclusion, and use his best endeavours to procure by means of such appeal the necessary Licence Certificate: And Further, that in the event of any charge being brought against the Licence holder for a breach of the Licence Certificate or in the event of the Licensing Board seeking to suspend the Licence Certificate the Second Party shall inform the Company immediately on receipt of the charges and take any such action as is necessary to preserve the said Licence Certificate: And in the event of the Company entering into possession of or selling the Security Subjects, or part thereof, in virtue of the powers herein contained, the Company, or their nominees, or the purchaser, shall be entitled to apply for a transfer or renewal of the Licence for the Security Subjects, and the Second Party and his foresaids undertake not to oppose, directly or indirectly, the granting of such transfer or renewal, but to assist in every way in obtaining the same.

6. The Second Party shall keep regular, correct and distinct books and accounts showing the drawings, expenses and whole transactions in connection with the said licensed business, and such books shall be open at all times to the inspection of the Company or anyone authorised by them. The Second Party shall, if called upon by the Company so to do, furnish to the Company, free of expense at the conclusion of the Second Party's business year, and in any event not later than 90 days thereafter, a true and correct Profit and Loss Account and Balance Sheet for such year, duly audited by a professional accountant. The Second Party shall also allow stock to be taken and accounts to be made up by the Company, or anyone authorised by them, quarterly or at such other periods as may be required by the Company.

7. Standard Condition 10 of Schedule 3 to the Conveyancing and Feudal Reform (Scotland) Act 1970 shall be and the same is hereby varied to the effect that on default by the Second Party or his foresaids he or they shall vacate the Security Subjects in so far as occupied by him or them or others for whom he or they are responsible, and give the Company immediate vacant possession of the Security Subjects on the expiry of a period of seven days after being given written notice by the Company so to do. And except as so varied or as herein otherwise varied Standard Condition 10 shall in all other respects apply. The Second Party agrees that a warrant of summary ejection may competently proceed against him in the Sheriff Court of the County in which the Security Subjects are situated at the instance of the Company.

8. The security constituted by the said Standard Security and these presents shall not be prejudiced or affected in any way by any bills of exchange or promissory notes which shall have been, or shall be granted, accepted, negotiated, renewed, cancelled or otherwise dealt with, but the said security and the rights of the Company shall subsist in full force so long as any sums remain due by the Second Party to the Company, and shall apply to such sums: And declaring also that notwithstanding the existence of the security constituted by the said Standard Security or the exercise by the Company of any of their statutory rights and remedies, the Company shall always be entitled to recover from the Second Party, when due, any of the sums payable by him under these presents, or under any other obligation or document of debt granted by the Second Party in favour of the Company, and in particular the Company shall be entitled, at any time they think fit, to enforce payment of the sum contained in any bill of exchange or promissory note granted by the Second Party in favour of the Company.

9. Unless repayment of the advances and other sums secured by the said Standard Security and these presents as aforesaid shall be sooner demanded by the Company (full power to demand repayment thereof at any time being reserved to the Company) the Second Party shall repay the said advances and other sums to the Company by   instalments of £   (or such other sums as the Company may from time to time determine) the first   payment being made on the   day of   : And without prejudice to the foregoing obligation the Second Party authorises and empowers the Company at the Company's sole discretion (a) to

debit the said   payments in the trading accounts incurred by the Second Party to the Company [or to any of the Company's associated or subsidiary trading companies acting as agents for the Company] (b) to credit sums paid by the Second Party to the Company to whichever of the accounts of the Second Party with the Company [or with any of the Company's associated or subsidiary trading companies acting as agents for the Company] as the Company shall choose and (c) to transfer any balance or part thereof at debit or credit in any of the accounts of the Second Party with the Company [or with any of the Company's associated or subsidiary trading companies acting as agents for the Company] to any other of the accounts of the Second Party with the Company [or with any of the Company's associated or subsidiary trading companies acting as agents for the Company]. No extraordinary expenditure shall be incurred by the Second Party without the prior knowledge and approval of the Company.

10. In the event of the Second Party or his foresaids deciding to sell or otherwise dispose of the Security Subjects or any part thereof at any time either when any sum remains due by the Second Party or his foresaids to the Company under this Agreement or any Supplementary Agreement to follow hereon or within two years from the date of repayment of all sums due by the Second Party or his foresaids to the Company under this Agreement or any Supplementary Agreement to follow hereon, the Second Party or his foresaids shall in the first instance notify the Company and the Company shall have the option of purchasing the Security Subjects or such part thereof as the Second Party or his foresaids shall have decided to sell or otherwise dispose of as aforesaid, (a) in the case of sale, at a price equivalent to the highest offer made by any other party for the same, and immediately on receipt of such highest offer the Second Party or his foresaids shall notify the Company by sending them a copy of such highest offer, and in the event that the Company do not exercise their option under this Clause the Second Party may accept only the said highest offer and no other and (b) in the case of disposal otherwise than by sale, at a price failing agreement to be fixed by a Valuer to be mutually chosen by the parties. The said option shall be exercised by the Company giving notice in writing to the Second Party or his foresaids within seven days from (a) in the case of sale, the date of receipt by the Company of a copy of the highest offer as aforesaid, or (b) in the case of disposal otherwise than by sale, the date on which the Company receive notice in writing from the Second Party or his foresaids of the decision to dispose of the Security Subjects or any part thereof otherwise than by sale. In the event of a sale of the Security Subjects or any part thereof to the Company, the Second Party or his foresaids shall, if desired by the Company, apply or concur in or support an application to the Licensing Board for a transfer of the Licence Certificate for the Security Subjects to the Company or any nominees or nominee of the Company.

11. The Second Party hereby undertakes that he will not, while and so long as the said advances and other sums secured by the said Standard Security and these presents as aforesaid or any part thereof shall remain due and outstanding except with the prior written consent of the Company (a) create a subsequent security

by way of a fixed or floating charge over the Security Subjects or any part thereof or (b) transfer the Security Subjects or any part thereof under burden of the Standard Security.

[11A. The rate of the total charge for credit (as the same is defined in Section 20 of the Consumer Credit Act 1974 and the regulations made thereunder as the same may be amended or re-enacted from time to time) under this Agreement and the said Standard Security shall not exceed the higher of the following, that is to say:—

(a) The sum of One *per cent* and the base rate of the Bank of Scotland as at the date twenty-eight days before the date on which this Agreement is made: and

(b) Thirteen *per cent*: And the right of the Company to fix the rate of interest under this Agreement, as specified in Clause 3 hereof, shall be circumscribed accordingly.][77]

12. The standard conditions contained in Schedule 3 to the Conveyancing and Feudal Reform (Scotland) Act 1970, shall, except in so far as they have been varied by these presents, apply to this security to the same force and effect as if they had been inserted herein at length and had formed part of these presents: And both parties consent to registration hereof for preservation and execution.

(To be attested)

Loans not exceeding £15,000—consumer credit

37–47   A loan not exceeding £15,000 secured by a standard security is (unless the creditor is an exempt body as aftermentioned) a regulated debtor-creditor agreement in terms of the Consumer Credit Act 1974 and the documentation must comply with the provisions of the Consumer Credit (Agreements) Regulations 1983[78] and the procedure required by the 1974 Act with regard to mortgages[79] must be followed. Local authorities and building societies are exempt from these provisions,[80] but banks are not. The Secretary of State may by order exempt other specified bodies of certain kinds. Accordingly creditors who are local authorities or building societies need not observe the statutory provisions as to documentation and procedure, but banks and other non-exempt creditors must do so. As regards advances on current account by banks (1) overdraft facilities provided by a bank on current account in the ordinary course of business without any special written agreement are exempt from the requirements of the 1974 Act,[81] but (2) if there is a written agreement regulating advances on current account which do not exceed £15,000, the Act applies to them and the documentation and procedure for a loan of fixed amount not exceeding £15,000 required by the Act must comply with the provisions of the statute.

---

[77]Required where loan does not exceed £15,000.
[78]S.I. 1983 No. 1553.
[79]Principally s. 58(1).
[80]1974 Act, s. 16(1).
[81]s. 74(1)(*b*).

37–48   On account of the difficulties in relation to the creation and registration of heritable securities, these transactions are exempt from the cancellation provisions of the 1974 Act. Instead the creditor is required to give the debtor an advance copy of the unexecuted agreement containing a notice in prescribed form indicating the right of the debtor to withdraw from the proposed agreement and how and when he may do so, and the executed copy contains a brief reminder that the debtor should have received such a notice at least seven days before.[82] Both the advance and principal copies are otherwise identical and contain the statutory information required in a regulated debtor-creditor agreement including statements of the amount of the loan, rate of interest, any additional charges, the annual percentage rate, the total amount payable and the timing and amount of any instalment repayments or if there are none a statement that the creditor will be entitled to require immediate repayment after any notice required by law, a brief identifying description of the security subjects, a statement of the debtor's right to have received a copy of the agreement at least seven days before and his right to withdraw, the rights of the creditor to terminate the agreement in certain specified circumstances, *e.g.* failure to implement any conditions of the agreement or to maintain the value of the security subjects, the rights of the debtor under the Consumer Credit Act 1974, the right to terminate the agreement on repayment and to a rebate on early settlement and advice to consult the local Trading Standards Department or the nearest Citizens' Advice Bureau as to the remedies and protection provided under the 1974 Act. The documentation normally comprises:

(1) An advance copy of the loan agreement—see Style 19, paragraph 37–49.

(2) The principal copy of the loan agreement—see Style 19A in paragraph 37–50.

(To each of the above General Conditions are appended—see paragraph 37–51.)

(3) Standard security—see paragraph 37–52.

These styles are appropriate to a fluctuating loan on current account, but are suitable with appropriate alteration to loans of fixed amount not exceeding £15,000.

---

[82] 1974 Act, s. 58(1).

37–50

Style 19

CURRENT ACCOUNT LOAN AGREEMENT FORM SECURED BY LAND ADVANCE COPY

Copy of proposed credit agreement containing notice of your right to withdraw
Do NOT sign or return this copy

——————————— Bank Public Limited Company

Name(s) in full ———————

Full Branch Address ———————

Address(es) ———————

———————

In consideration of the Bank granting to me/us a loan I/we undertake to repay the loan and charges in accordance with the terms set out below and subject to the General Conditions printed on the reverse of this Form (which I/we have read and understand).

Amount of loan £

Rate of interest-per annum %

Interest will be charged quarterly in arrears or on the repayment date on the daily debit balance outstanding at %
over the current ——————— Bank Base Rate of %
which is variable.

Additional charges*

Security
This agreement is secured by an effective security over the property known as:

*Delete if not applicable.

Annual percentage rate

	%

subject to changes in the interest rate by the Bank by notices exhibited in its Branches and in the Press. No account has been taken of any variation of the rate which may occur.

Repayment

The Bank may require immediate repayment at any time after giving the notice required by law, but subject to this the Bank envisage that the loan will be repaid by:

IMPORTANT—YOU SHOULD READ THIS CAREFULLY YOUR RIGHTS

The Consumer Credit Act 1974 covers this agreement and lays down certain requirements for your protection which must be satisfied when the agreement is made. If they are not, the Bank cannot enforce the agreement against you without a court order.

The Act also gives you a number of rights. You have a right to settle this agreement at any time by giving notice in writing and paying off all amounts payable under the agreement.

If you would like to know more about the protection and remedies provided under the Act, you should contact either your local Trading Standards Department or your nearest Citizens' Advice Bureau.

YOUR RIGHT TO WITHDRAW

This is a copy of your proposed credit agreement which is to be secured on land. It has been given to you now so that you may have at least a week to consider its terms before the actual agreement is sent to you for signature. You should read it carefully. If you do not understand it, you may need to seek professional advice. If you do not wish to go ahead with it, you need not do so.

If you decide NOT to go ahead with the agreement, you should inform ———— BANK PLC or, if you prefer, any supplier or broker involved in the negotiations. You can do this in writing or orally for example by telephone. If the agreement arrives for signature and you have decided NOT to go ahead, DO NOT SIGN IT. Then you will not be legally bound by the agreement.

For ———— Bank PLC

Date approved ———— Manager

PLEASE READ THE GENERAL CONDITIONS OVERLEAF. WE SHALL BE PLEASED TO EXPLAIN ANYTHING YOU DO NOT UNDERSTAND.

Style 19A

37–49

CURRENT ACCOUNT LOAN AGREEMENT FORM SECURED BY LAND

Credit Agreement regulated by the Consumer Credit Act 1974

———— Bank Public Limited Company

Full Branch Address ————

Name(s) in full ————

Address(es) ————

In consideration of the Bank granting to me/us a loan I/we undertake to repay the loan and charges in accordance with the terms set out below and subject to the General Conditions printed on the reverse of this Form (which I/we have read and understand).

Amount of loan   £

Rate of interest-per annum   %

Additional charges*

*Delete if not applicable.

Annual percentage rate   %

subject to changes in the interest rate by the Bank by notices exhibited in its Branches and in the Press. No account has been taken of any variation of the rate which may occur.

Repayment
The Bank may require immediate repayment at any time after giving the notice required by law, but subject to this the Bank envisage that the loan will be repaid by:

IMPORTANT—YOU SHOULD READ THIS CAREFULLY YOUR RIGHTS

The Consumer Credit Act 1974 covers this agreement and lays down certain requirements for your protection which must be

Interest will be charged quarterly in arrears or on the repayment date on the daily debit balance outstanding at   % over the current ——— Bank Base Rate of   % which is variable.

Security
This agreement is secured by an effective security over the property known as:

satisfied when the agreement is made. If they are not, the Bank cannot enforce the agreement against you without a court order.

The Act also gives you a number of rights. You have a right to settle this agreement at any time by giving notice in writing and paying off all amounts payable under the agreement.

If you would like to know more about the protection and remedies provided under the Act, you should contact either your local Trading Standards Department or your nearest Citizens' Advice Bureau.

YOUR RIGHTS

Under the Consumer Credit Act 1974, the Bank should have given you a copy of this agreement at least seven days ago to allow you time to consider whether to go ahead. If the Bank did not, the agreement cannot be enforced without a court order.

For ——— Bank PLC

Date approved ——— Manager

> This is a Credit Agreement regulated by the Consumer Credit Act 1974. Sign it only if you want to be legally bound by its terms.
>
> Signature(s) ———
> of Customer(s)
> Date(s) of Signature(s) ———

Witness ———

Occupation ———

Address ———

Witness ———

Occupation ———

Address ———

PLEASE READ THE GENERAL CONDITIONS OVERLEAF. WE SHALL BE PLEASED TO EXPLAIN ANYTHING YOU DO NOT UNDERSTAND.

General conditions annexed to Styles 19 and 19A

37–51   1. *Our right to end the agreement.* We may end the agreement and demand immediate repayment of all sums due in respect of the agreement, after giving any written notice required by law, if:—

(i)   You fail to keep to any part of this agreement;

(ii)   You fail to keep in force or maintain in value any security given to the Bank;

(iii)   You fail to keep to the terms of any other credit agreement with the Bank;

(iv)   You have given false information in connection with this agreement or any other credit agreement between you and the Bank;

(v)   You become unable to pay your debts;

(vi)   You are the subject of a court action which has the effect of taking control of any of your assets away from you;

(vii)   You become incapable of managing your affairs;

(viii) Any person (including yourself) providing security for any debt you have to the Bank advises us of his intention to withdraw the security;

(ix)   We are advised of the death of any person who has provided security for any debt you have to the Bank.

2. *Security.* Unless the contrary is stated, no other security is required for this agreement and any security which we hold to secure other borrowing from us is not available as security for this agreement.

3. *Our right to amalgamate balances.* If we end the agreement and demand repayment of the whole sum due under the agreement we may retain any money in any of your accounts and apply it in or towards repayment of the agreement.

4. *Our expenses.* You may be asked to repay our legal expenses if we require to take court action to obtain repayment of the whole sum due under the agreement from you.

5. *Partnership.* Where the customer named is a Scottish partnership the liability to implement the terms of this agreement shall be the joint and several liability of the firm and partners.

Where the customer named is an English partnership the liability to implement the terms of this agreement shall be the joint and several liability of the partners.

Joint and several liability means that each partner can be held fully responsible for all the terms and conditions of the agreement including the obligation to repay the whole sum due under the agreement.

6. *More than one borrower.* If two or more people are named as the customer the liability of each shall be joint and several. This means that each person can be held fully responsible for all the terms and conditions of the agreement including the obligation to repay the whole sum due under the agreement.

7. *Information.* We may make such inquiries about your financial affairs as we may think fit.

NOTE

Other appropriate conditions may be added. If the loan agreement is also used in conjunction with a standard security in Form B (see paragraph 37–52) any desired variations in the standard conditions will also be incorporated.

Standard security relative to loan agreement Style 19A

37–52   The standard security used in connection with a regulated consumer credit loan may be in Form B using the loan agreement (Style 19A) as the separate instrument constituting the personal obligation, in which case the general conditions will also incorporate any variations in the standard conditions.

Procedure

37–53   The procedure is:

(1) Before settlement of the transaction the creditor will have examined the title, obtained searches or reports from the Land Register, as the case may be, and made all necessary inquiries.

(2) At least seven days before signature of the principal copy of the agreement and the relative standard security the creditor will send to the debtor an advance copy of the agreement containing the necessary notice as to his right to withdraw together with a copy of the standard security.

(3) At least seven days thereafter the principal signing copy of the agreement and the relative standard security will be signed by or sent for signature to the debtor (if he has not withdrawn). If presented for signature to the debtor and the creditor also executes it, a copy of the agreement and standard security will be delivered to the debtor there and then. If sent to the debtor unexecuted a copy of the agreement and standard security must be sent to him at the same time and after execution of these documents copies of the executed documents must be sent to the debtor within seven days after execution of the document is complete.[83]

(4) The standard security will be sent for recording in the Register of Sasines or sent, with any other documents required by the Keeper, for registration in the Land Register, as the case may be.

(5) When received, check the certificate of recording on the standard security or the charge certificate.

Ranking Clauses[84,85]

(A) Prior or postponed

37–54   Provided that the said sum of £   [or] [the whole amount hereby secured] with interest thereon and all expenses for which I am liable in connection with the standard security hereby granted

[83] 1974 Act, ss. 62, 63.
[84] 1970 Act, Sched. 2, Note 5.
[85] As to ranking of heritable securities, see Chap. 42.

shall be ranked and preferred on the said subjects and on the
rents thereof and on the proceeds thereof or of any part thereof
in the event of a sale of the same [prior and preferably] [*or* after
and postponed] to the sum of £   [*or* the whole amount]
secured or to be secured by a standard security granted or about
to be granted by me in favour of XY, (*designation*), and all
interest and expenses secured or that may be secured thereby and
that without regard to the order in which the last mentioned
standard security and these presents have been or shall be
[registered] [recorded]. [And the said (*creditor*) and the said XY
hereby for their respective rights and interests agree as by their
execution hereof they hereby agree to the provisions of this
ranking clause.][85a]

Warrandice[86] *(where postponed).* And I grant warrandice
excepting therefrom the said standard security for the sum of
£   (*or otherwise as the case may be*) in favour of the said
XY.

(B) *Pari passu*

37–55   Provided that the said sum of £   [*or* the whole amount]
hereby secured and the further sum of £   [*or* the further
amount] borrowed and secured or about to be borrowed and
secured by me in terms of a standard security granted or to be
granted by me in favour of XY, (*designation*), over the said
subjects with interest on the said two sums (*or as the case may be*)
and all expenses secured or that may be secured by these presents
and the said standard security in favour of the said XY shall be
ranked and preferred *pari passu* on the said subjects and the
rents thereof and on the proceeds thereof or of any part thereof
in the event of a sale of the same and that without regard to the
order in which these presents and the said standard security in
favour of the said XY have been or shall be [registered]
[recorded]. And the said (*creditor*) and the said XY hereby for
their respective rights and interests agree as by their execution
hereof they hereby agree to the provisions of this ranking clause.

Warrandice. And, subject to the foregoing provision as to *pari
passu* ranking, I grant warrandice.

Guarantees and Collateral Securities

Guarantees

37–56   A guarantee of the debtor's obligations under a standard security
may be effected by a joint and several personal obligation undertaken

---

[85a]In terms of s. 13 of the 1970 Act a subsequent standard security, when recorded and notified to
the creditor in an existing standard security, will restrict the preference of the earlier creditor in
accordance with the section, but subs. 13(3)(*b*) provides that that does not affect any powers of the
creditor and debtor in any standard security to regulate the preference to be enjoyed by creditors
under a ranking agreement. If the second security is postponed to the first security the grantor
(debtor) and the grantee (new creditor) have power so to provide (unless the first security has
contained a prohibition against granting of any other security), but if the second security is to rank
prior to or *pari passu* with the first security the debtor and the second creditor do not have power so
to provide without the consent of the first creditor and the bracketed clause in the Style (A) or a
separate agreement between the debtor and both creditors is required.
[86]1970 Act, Sched. 2, Note 5.

by the principal debtor and the guarantor in the standard security itself—see Style 7, paragraph 37–18 *supra*. A separate, unrecorded agreement between the principal debtor and the guarantor will regulate the arrangements between them and will include an obligation of relief by the principal debtor.[87]

Alternatively, the standard security may be granted by the debtor only and a separate guarantee granted by the guarantor to the creditor.

Prescription of guarantees

37–57   Where a separate guarantee is granted and the guarantor's obligation becomes prestable upon default by the principal debtor, the position on and after July 25, 1976 is that the short prescription of five years will commence to run in favour of the guarantor only upon that default, since only then does the guarantor's obligation become enforceable.[88] It is thought that the same result is reached in the case where the guarantor is bound jointly and severally as a co-obligant with the person who is truly the principal debtor, although the position is somewhat less clear since it depends upon construction of the interrelated provisions cited.[89] In practice it is suggested that it will now be preferable to have a separate guarantee rather than the style in which the guarantor is bound as a co-obligant.

Style 20

Guarantee (separate)[90,90a]

37–58   I, EF, (*designation*), WHEREAS AB, (*designation*), has granted or is about to grant a standard security in favour of CD, (*designation*), for payment of the sum of £   (*or otherwise as the case may be*) over the subjects known as   and also for payment of all interest and other moneys which may become due by the said AB in terms of the said standard security:

1. I hereby bind and oblige myself and my executors and representatives whomsoever all jointly and severally in the event of the said AB at any time making default in the performance of any of the obligations on his part under any of the conditions or provisions of the said standard security to pay on demand to the said CD or his executors or representatives all moneys that may be due and payable or that may thereafter become due and payable to the said CD or his foresaids under the said standard security.

2. I hereby agree that neither the giving of time to the said AB

---

[87]See Vol. I, para. 6–50.

[88]Prescription and Limitation (Scotland) Act 1973, s. 6(3); *Royal Bank of Scotland Ltd.* v. *Brown*, 1983 S.L.T. 122.

[89]*Ibid.*, s. 6(3) and Sched. 1, paras. 2(*c*) and 3.

[90]This is a simple basic style. More sophisticated and complex forms of guarantee used in commercial lending are outwith the scope of this book.

[90a]As to a special style of guarantee where the guarantor was held liable beyond the amount originally guaranteed, see *Bank of Scotland* v. *MacLeod*, 1986 S.L.T. 504.

nor the suspension of any payments due by the said AB under the said standard security nor any other indulgences shown by the said CD or his foresaids to the said AB shall in any way release or discharge me or my foresaids from liability hereunder nor shall the obligation hereby undertaken by me be in any way affected through the said CD or his foresaids exercising or refraining from exercising all or any of the powers conferred upon him or them under the said standard security.

(*To be attested*)

Collateral securities

37–59   (a) **Provided by debtor.** Where the collateral security is other heritable property the simplest method is to include it, along with the principal subjects, in the grant of security contained in the standard security itself. If the collateral security over heritable property is provided later, a further standard security will be necessary with an appropriate narrative. Where the collateral security consists of moveable property it is permissible to include an assignation of it in the standard security,[91] but it will generally be more convenient to grant a separate assignation since the subsequent release of or other dealing with the collateral security will be simplified.

Style 21

Assignation of life policy as collateral security to standard security[92]

37–60   I, AB, (*designation*), WHEREAS I have granted or am about to grant a standard security in favour of CD, (*designation*), for payment of the sum of £   (*or otherwise as the case may be*) over the subjects known as   and also for payment of all interest and other moneys which may become due by me in terms of the said standard security:

1. I hereby assign to the said CD the Policy of Assurance (hereinafter called "the Policy") short particulars of which are:

Company	Number	Date	Life Assured	Sum Assured

and all moneys which may become payable thereunder and the full benefit of all powers and remedies for enforcing my rights under the Policy.

---

[91] 1970 Act, s. 53(1).
[92] This is a very simple basic style. More detailed powers may be included if desired.

2. The Policy shall be held by the said CD as security for all sums due and that may become due under the said standard security and the said CD shall have full power to deal with the Policy as absolute owner thereof subject only to the provision for retrocession after mentioned.

3. I shall pay all premiums due and that may become due in respect of the Policy but in case of default by me in doing so timeously the said CD may pay the same and all moneys so expended by the said CD and all costs and expenses incurred by the said CD in keeping in force the Policy or restoring it should it be or become voidable or effecting a new policy to replace it in the event of its lapse shall be secured on the Policy and upon any other policy which shall replace it.

4. Upon repayment to the said CD of all moneys due by me under the said standard security or under these presents the said CD shall at the request and at the expense of me or my executors retrocess or assign the Policy to the person entitled to it with warrandice from fact and deed only.

(To be attested)

37–61 (b) **Provided by a guarantor**. Where a guarantor is providing collateral security of his guarantee then, if it consists of heritable property, a standard security will be required. The most suitable form of standard security to be used will depend on the circumstances. (1) If the guarantor is bound as a co-obligant with the debtor in the principal standard security (i) the collateral security, if it is being provided at the outset, may simply be included by way of a grant of security over it by the guarantor as a co-obligant in the original standard security, or (ii) alternatively, or if the collateral security is being provided subsequently, the guarantor may grant a standard security using Form B and referring to the original standard security as the document containing the personal obligation. (2) If the guarantor is bound in a separate document, the collateral security may be provided either (i) in the original document of guarantee which will then be in the form of a standard security, the guarantee constituting the personal obligation, or (ii) alternatively, or if the collateral security is being provided subsequently, a standard security using Form B may be granted with a reference to the guarantee as constituting the personal obligation. For the reasons explained in para. 37–57 *supra*, it is probable that the separate document form of guarantee will now usually be preferred.

Style 22

Standard security for guarantee (separate)—Form B[93]

37–62 I, EF, (*designation*), hereby in security of the whole obligations undertaken by me under Guarantee granted by me in favour of the C Bank, (*designation*), (hereinafter called "the Bank") dated

---

[93]This style is relative to a guarantee of a current account, the document of guarantee being separate from the document creating the principal debtor's obligation. It has been framed as related to Style 2, para. 37–13.

of even date with my subscription hereto [*or* dated   ]
grant a standard security in favour of the Bank over ALL and
WHOLE   (*clause of deduction of title, if
required*)[94]: The standard conditions specified in Schedule 3 to
the Conveyancing and Feudal Reform (Scotland) Act 1970, and
any lawful variation thereof operative for the time being shall
apply: (*Insert any of the special conditions as in Style 2, para.
37–13 which may be desired with appropriate adaptation*): And I
grant warrandice.

(*To be attested*)

37–63   If the collateral security provided by the guarantor is moveable, a
separate assignation will generally be preferable, since its use will
facilitate the release of the collateral security in circumstances where
the personal obligation of the guarantor is not being discharged.

Style 23

*Assignation of building society account in security of guarantee to the
society*

37–64   I, EF, (*designation*), WHEREAS AB, (*designation*), has granted
or is about to grant a standard security in favour of the C
Building Society (*designation*), (hereinafter called "the Society")
for payment of the sum of £   and all other sums due and
that may become due by the said AB to the Society over the
property known as   AND WHEREAS I am the
holder of a (*describe the account by reference to its class and
number*) with the Society for the sum of £   (the expression
"the Account" in this deed being inclusive of all moneys from
time to time standing to the credit thereof and all interest
thereon):
    1. I hereby assign the Account to the Society in security of all
sums due and that may become due by the said AB to the Society
secured by the said standard security.
    2. If the Society's power of sale under the said standard
security shall become exercisable the Account or any part of it
may be applied by the Society in reduction of the moneys secured
by the said standard security.
    3. The Account shall be released from all liability under this
assignation when the total amount secured by the said standard
security shall have been reduced to such sum as the Society shall
consider to be the normal lending limit on the security of the
property which is the subject of the said standard security [and
for that purpose the Society may at the expense of the said AB or
me the said EF re-value the said property].
    4. Neither the giving of time to the said AB for the payment of
any moneys secured by the said standard security nor the
suspension of monthly payments due thereunder nor any other
indulgence which may be shown to the said AB by the Society
shall in any way release the Account or any part of it from this
assignation.

(*To be attested*)

---

[94] As to form of deduction of title, see 1970 Act, Sched. 2, Note 2.

CHAPTER 38

THE STANDARD CONDITIONS

THE STATUTORY PROVISIONS

Deed of variations—commercial transactions—
building development   38–29

THE STATUTORY PROVISIONS

The statutory objectives

38–01   Before the enactment of the Conveyancing and Feudal Reform
(Scotland) Act 1970 the most favoured form of heritable security for
debt was the *ex facie* absolute disposition qualified by an agreement
which set out at length the conditions of the loan arrangement. The
terms of these agreements varied widely according to the nature of the
transaction and the policy of the lenders, but they included conditions
which were common to almost all of them such as obligations of
maintenance and insurance of the security subjects, restriction on
letting, etc. One of the objectives of the legislature in prescribing the
standard conditions in Schedule 3 to the Act was to simplify
documentation by setting out conditions which were normally applicable
to all heritable securities, thus obviating the need to express them at
length in the documents. It was recognised, however, that in certain
cases the statutory conditions would not in terms be appropriate and so
it was permissible to vary them contractually. Very broadly, standard
conditions 1 to 7 inclusive of Schedule 3 are in that category.

Nevertheless it was evident that an all-purpose obligatory form of
heritable security for debt should provide a measure of protection for
the debtor in a situation where the creditor was normally in a position
of superior negotiating strength and so certain of the standard
conditions, *e.g.* those relating to procedure on redemption and powers
of sale and foreclosure, are not variable contractually.

Accordingly the result of the 1970 Act is that the standard conditions
in Schedule 3 regulate every standard security except to the extent that
they had been varied, so far as permissible, by agreement of the
parties.[1]

Non-variable conditions

38–02   The standard conditions which cannot be varied are standard
condition 11 (procedure on redemption) and those relating to the
powers of sale and foreclosure.[2] As originally enacted the 1970 Act
provided that the standard conditions relating to the debtor's power of
redemption at any time also were non-variable, but that imposed an
unacceptable restriction on fixed-term loans and the Redemption of
Standard Securities (Scotland) Act 1971 amended the 1970 Act by
permitting alteration of the debtor's right to redeem by agreement to

---

[1] 1970 Act, s. 11.
[2] *Ibid.*, s. 11(3).

the contrary, although the statutory procedure on redemption remains applicable in all cases.[3] As to transitional provisions to enable amendments to standard securities granted before July 1, 1971, reference may be made to the undernoted text.[4]

38–03 **(1) Procedure on redemption**. The parties may agree as to the time for which a loan may subsist,[5] the period of notice of redemption and any additional payments if redemption is made before a stipulated period of endurance of the loan, but the provisions of paragraphs (3) to (5) of standard condition 11 relating to procedure on redemption cannot be varied.

38–04 **(2) Sale**. Section 11(3) of the 1970 Act as amended by the 1971 Act provides that the provisions of Schedule 3 relating to the powers of sale and the exercise of those powers are not variable. Standard condition 10(1) provides that where the debtor is in default the creditor may, without prejudice to any other remedy arising from the contract to which the standard security relates, exercise, in accordance with the provisions of Part II of the 1970 Act and of any other enactment applying to standard securities, such of the remedies specified in the following sub-paragraphs of standard condition 10 as he may consider appropriate, and sub-paragraph (2) provides that the creditor may proceed to sell the security subjects or any part thereof. It is clear that the provisions of sections 25 and 27 of the Act cannot be altered by agreement and the safe course is to regard the provisions as to calling-up and notice of default, which form part of the procedure antecedent to a sale, also as being non-variable. On the other hand it would appear that it is permissible to stipulate for additional rights exercisable in relation to a sale where the debtor is in default such as that of removing goods, furniture and effects in the subjects so that they will be available, cleared of such items, to a purchaser.

38–05 **(3) Foreclosure**. The ambit of the term of foreclosure is reasonably clear: the provisions of sections 28 and 29 of the 1970 Act plainly cannot be altered by contract.

Construction and effect of purported variations of non-variable conditions

38–06 Since the object of making certain conditions non-variable is the protection of the debtor, it would seem that purported variations of those conditions which are more favourable to the debtor are enforceable in accordance with a contractual bargain having that effect. If otherwise, any purported variation will be ineffective but it is

---

[3] 1971 Act, s. 1.

[4] Halliday, *Conveyancing and Feudal Reform (Scotland) Act 1970*, para. 7–09.

[5] The power of a company to issue perpetual debentures under s. 89 of the Companies Act 1948 (now s. 193 of the Companies Act 1985) was expressly preserved—1971 Act, s. 2.

thought that the validity of the security is not affected save that the variation so far as impermissible will be replaced by the terms of the standard condition which it purported to alter.

PRACTICE

Variations of standard conditions

38–07   The standard conditions in Schedule 3 to the Act relate primarily to the security subjects rather than to the debt. Accordingly, as a matter of tidy draftmanship, particulars of the contract which relate to the constitution and conditions of the debt should be expressed in the standard security itself (if Form A is used) or in the separate instrument constituting the personal obligation (if Form B is used), whereas details of the contract which relate to the security should, so far as not sufficiently regulated by the standard conditions, be expressed as variations of the standard conditions. There is no rule of law, however, that requires the adoption of any such rigid technique. The personal obligation and the security constitute a single contract, and the continuance of the security right is dependent on the existence of the personal obligation to which it is ancillary. So, if it is convenient to express in a single schedule or deed of variation of the standard conditions details relating primarily to the personal obligation as well as conditions affecting the security, there is no reason in law why that should not be done. If, however, the personal obligation is contained in the standard security and provisions which may alter the amount of the debt are contained in a deed of variation of the standard conditions, the recorded standard security, which is the measure of the real security, should contain a personal obligation expressed in terms sufficiently wide to comprehend alterations of the debt which may result from the provisions of the unrecorded document.[6]

The variations treated in this chapter are variations in standard conditions made contemporaneously with the granting of the security; for variations in existing standard securities and/or the relative standard conditions see Chapter 40 *infra*.

Methods of effecting variations

38–08   Variations of the standard conditions may be effected either (i) by an instrument or deed other than the standard security, in which case it is unnecessary to record the separate instrument or deed in the Register of Sasines or register the variation in the Land Register, as the case may be, or (ii) by inserting the variations in the standard security itself after the description of the security subjects.[7]

---

[6]For illustrations of a comprehensive deed of variation of standard conditions linked with a standard security expressed so as to cover additions to the debt, see styles in paras. 37–21 and 38–28.
[7]1970 Act, Sched. 2, Note 4.

38–09   **(1) Separate deed of variations**. Where the creditor is an institutional lender or a building society, or is a local authority, large numbers of loans are made to different borrowers but the variations desired in the standard conditions are common to all loans. In such cases it is convenient for the creditor to execute a separate deed of variations of the standard conditions and to have it registered in the Books of Council and Session.[8] The separate deed is then incorporated by reference in a single deed, the standard security, and a print of the separate deed of variations can be furnished to each debtor.[9] Also, where the variations impose obligations on the creditor, it may be desirable to incorporate them in a separate bilateral deed executed by both parties.[10]

38–10   **(2) Variations incorporated in standard security**. The variations may be incorporated in the standard security itself, thus:

> And I agree that the standard conditions shall be varied to the effect that (*specify variations*).

Since Note 4 to Schedule 2 to the 1970 Act permits variations to be effected "either by an instrument or instruments other than the standard security . . . or by inserting in the standard security after the description of the security subjects," some doubt attaches to the competency of effecting variations in a schedule attached to the standard security where the schedule is not recorded as part of the standard security, since it is neither an instrument other than the standard security nor inserted in the recorded standard security.

Recorded or unrecorded variations—choice of method

38–11   Where relatively few alterations are desired, and it is improbable that these will be changed during the currency of the security transaction, they may conveniently be made in the standard security itself. If that method is adopted it should be kept in view that, should for any reason the alterations be subsequently changed or new variations introduced, the document by which that is effected will require to be recorded.[11] Institutional lenders, building societies and local authorities for the reasons already mentioned prefer to have special provisions varying the standard conditions incorporated in a separate document in standard form which is not recorded in the Register of Sasines. That method has the advantage, in addition to the reasons of practical convenience explained in para. 38–09, that if alterations in the special provisions are subsequently made, these

---

[8] See Style 16, para. 37–40.
[9] If the separate deed of variations is registered in the Books of Council and Session, prints of it should be plainly marked as copies to avoid any question of their purporting to be official extracts.
[10] See for example Style 12A, para. 37–27.
[11] 1970 Act, s. 16(1).

alterations can be effected by a further unrecorded document.[12] The provisions, as subsequently altered, will apply to all future standard securities, and, if power has been reserved to the creditor to make subsequent alterations in the original deed of variations, either generally as in the case of rules of a building society or specifically in relation to particular conditions, the altered provisions will apply to existing standard securities.[13]

Documents effecting variations—drafting

38–12   Conveyancers have now evolved their own drafting techniques in documents effecting variations of standard conditions. The following suggestions are offered by way of general guidance:

(1) Care should be taken that none of the variations has the effect of altering, or purporting to alter, directly or indirectly, any of the non-variable conditions as to powers of sale (including procedures preliminary to exercising these powers), foreclosure or procedure on redemption.

(2) Minor changes of wording of the standard conditions, unless they are of significant value, should be avoided. The standard conditions are familiar to practitioners, and it will simplify practice if they are adopted unchanged in circumstances where they are reasonably adequate.

(3) If a standard condition, or a paragraph of it, is being changed, it will save the reader the task of referring to two documents if the whole condition or paragraph, as altered, is reproduced in the document effecting the variation, followed by a statement that the standard condition or its paragraph will not apply. The interpolation of different words or phrases by way of amendment of the standard condition is a less desirable method.

(4) It will often be convenient to include, in a document which effects variations in the standard conditions, special provisions relating to the personal obligation or the debt. In any such document it will be helpful to arrange the contents to deal with (a) provisions which refer to matters relating only to the personal obligation and (b) provisions which alter parts of the standard conditions. The former group are self-contained, whereas the latter group may require to be construed along with the particular standard conditions which they alter.

(5) Where substantial additions to or alterations of the standard conditions are required, as in the case of building societies where there are special rules and repayment conditions to be incorporated, the document should be arranged broadly so as to deal first with the special features affecting the debt and thereafter with the conditions which relate to the security.

---

[12]*Ibid.*, s. 16(2).
[13]See Style 1, cll. 1(2)(xv) (Rules) and 5 (Interest), para. 38–28.

Particular variations

38–13 **(1) Personal obligation**. There are an infinite number of possible variations of the personal obligation, but some of more common occurrence are given or referred to in this paragraph.

(i) *Reduced rate of interest*

> If interest is paid punctually when due [or within [7] [14] days thereafter] at the rate of   % per annum (*the reduced rate*) and the debtor is not in default under any of the conditions of the standard security, the creditor will accept interest at that rate in lieu of interest at the rate specified in the standard security.

(ii) *Restriction on calling-up – period loan*

> If interest is paid punctually when due [or within [7] [14] days thereafter] and the debtor is not in default under any of the conditions of the standard security, the creditor shall not be entitled to require repayment of the principal sum due under the standard security before (*expiry of minimum period of endurance of loan*).

(iii) *Repayment by periodical instalments of principal and interest*. See Style 1, para. 38–28, clause 6.

(iv) *Compound interest on default*

> If the debtor makes default in payment of any interest payable under the standard security when due [or within [7] [14] days thereafter] the interest or any part thereof so unpaid shall from the date of such default be converted into principal and shall bear interest at the rate from time to time payable in terms of the standard security, and the whole provisions of the standard security shall apply to the sum so converted as if it were principal money thereby secured.

38–14 **(2) Standard conditions**. The standard conditions specified in Schedule 3 to the 1970 Act (other than those relating primarily to redemption which are treated in Chapter 40) are reproduced for convenient reference with suggestions as to possible variations.

38–15 *Maintenance and repair*

> STANDARD CONDITION 1
> It shall be an obligation on the debtor—
> (a)   to maintain the security subjects in good and sufficient repair to the reasonable satisfaction of the creditor;
> (b)   to permit, after seven clear days' notice in writing, the creditor or his agent to enter upon the security subjects at all reasonable times to examine the condition thereof;
> (c)   to make all necessary repairs and make good all defects in pursuance of his obligation under head (a) of this condition within such reasonable period as the creditor may require by notice in writing.

If specified repairs or improvements are to be made as a condition of the advance, it is suggested that part of the advance should be withheld until the work is done, and it will be unnecessary to alter the standard condition to provide for this temporary situation.

38–16 *Completion of buildings and prohibition of alterations*

STANDARD CONDITION 2
It shall be an obligation on the debtor—
(a)   to complete, as soon as may be practicable, any unfinished buildings and works forming part of the security subjects to the reasonable satisfaction of the creditor;
(b)   not to demolish, alter or add to any buildings or works forming part of the security subjects, except in accordance with the terms of a prior written consent of the creditor and in compliance with any consent, licence or approval required by law;
(c)   to exhibit to the creditor at his request evidence of that consent, licence or approval.

Where a building loan is being made by instalments the arrangements may be regulated by correspondence between the parties and the lender is safeguarded by making payments in accordance with a surveyor's report on the progress of the building. The bargain on this matter can usually be left on the basis of the correspondence without special provision in the standard security or the standard conditions. The standard security will be framed to cover the full amount of the advance. For loans for a building project made by instalments see Styles 12 and 12A, paragraphs 37–26 and 37–27.

38–17 *Title conditions, payment of charges and compliance with legal requirements relating to property*

STANDARD CONDITION 3
It shall be an obligation on the debtor—
(a)   to observe any condition or perform any obligation in respect of the security subjects lawfully binding on him in relation to the security subjects;
(b)   to make due and punctual payment of any ground burden, teind, stipend, or standard charge, and any rates, taxes and other public burdens, and any other payments exigible in respect of the security subjects;
(c)   to comply with any requirement imposed upon him in relation to the security subjects by virtue of any enactment.

This condition is comprehensively expressed and it will seldom require expansion.

38–18 *Planning notices*

STANDARD CONDITION 4
It shall be an obligation on the debtor—
(a)   where he has received any notice or order, issued or made by virtue of the Town and Country Planning (Scotland) Acts 1947 to 1969 or any amendment thereof, or any proposal so made for the making or issuing of any such

notice or order, or any other notice or document affecting or likely to affect the security subjects, to give to the creditor, within fourteen days of the receipt of that notice, order or proposal, full particulars thereof;

(b) to take, as soon as practicable, all reasonable or necessary steps to comply with such a notice or order or, as the case may be, duly to object thereto;

(c) in the event of the creditor so requiring, to object or to join with the creditor in objecting to any such notice or order or in making representations against any proposal therefor.

For a clause assigning to the creditor the benefit of rights to claim payment for *inter alia* withdrawal or modification of planning permission, see Style 1, clause 7, paragraph 38–28.

38–19 *Insurance*

STANDARD CONDITION 5

It shall be an obligation on the debtor—

(a) to insure the security subjects or, at the option of the creditor, to permit the creditor to insure the security subjects in the names of the creditor and the debtor to the extent of the market value thereof against the risk of fire and such other risks as the creditor may reasonably require;

(b) to deposit any policy of insurance effected by the debtor for the aforesaid purpose with the creditor;

(c) to pay any premium due in respect of any such policy, and, where the creditor so requests, to exhibit a receipt therefor not later than the fourteenth day after the renewal date of the policy;

(d) to intimate to the creditor, within fourteen days of the occurrence, any occurrence which may give rise to a claim under the policy, and to authorise the creditor to negotiate the settlement of the claim;

(e) without prejudice to any obligation to the contrary enforceable against him, to comply with any reasonable requirement of the creditor as to the application of any sum received in respect of such a claim;

(f) to refrain from any act or omission which would invalidate the policy.

For a fuller insurance clause, see Style 1, clause 11, paragraph 38–28. In many cases the creditor will desire insurance to the extent of the replacement value of the subjects.

38–20 *Restriction on letting*

STANDARD CONDITION 6

It shall be an obligation on the debtor not to let, or agree to let, the security subjects, or any part thereof, without the prior consent in writing of the creditor, and "to let" in this condition includes to sub-let.

For prohibitions against parting with occupation of the property or transfer of the property under burden of the security, see Style 1, clause 8, paragraph 38–28.

38–21 *Power of creditor to perform obligations on failure of debtor and charge expenses*

STANDARD CONDITION 7

(1) The creditor shall be entitled to perform any obligation imposed by the standard conditions on the debtor, which the debtor has failed to perform.

(2) Where it is necessary for the performance of any obligation as aforesaid, the creditor may, after giving seven clear days notice in writing to the debtor, enter upon the security subjects at all reasonable times.

(3) All expenses and charges (including any interest thereon), reasonably incurred by the creditor in the exercise of a right conferred by this condition, shall be recoverable from the debtor and shall be deemed to be secured by the security subjects under the standard security, and the rate of any such interest shall be the rate in force at the relevant time in respect of advances secured by the security, or, where no such rate is prescribed, shall be the bank rate in force at the relevant time.

The power conferred on the creditor applies to obligations imposed by the statutory conditions and also obligations imposed by any agreed variation of them.[14] All expenses and charges reasonably incurred by the creditor, with interest, are recoverable from the debtor and are included in the security.

38–22 *Calling-up*

STANDARD CONDITION 8

The creditor shall be entitled, subject to the terms of the security and to any requirement of law, to call-up a standard security in the manner prescribed by section 19 of this Act.

The right to call-up is subject to the terms of the standard security. If the standard security provides for payment only by instalments and the creditor wishes to reserve the right to call-up, even if the debtor is not in default, a special power to do so is required. See Style 12A, clause 10(c), paragraph 37–27.

38–23 *Default*

STANDARD CONDITION 9

(1) The debtor shall be held to be in default in any of the following circumstances, that is to say—

(a) where a calling-up notice in respect of the security has been served and has not been complied with;

(b) where there has been a failure to comply with any other requirement arising out of the security;

(c) where the proprietor of the security subjects has become insolvent.

(2) For the purposes of this condition, the proprietor shall be taken to be insolvent if—

(a) he has become apparently insolvent, or he has executed a

---

[14] 1970 Act, s. 11(2).

trust deed for behoof of, or has made a composition contract or arrangement with, his creditors;

(b)   he has died and a judicial factor has been appointed under section 11A of the Judicial Factors (Scotland) Act 1889 to divide his insolvent estate among his creditors, or an order has been made for the administration of his estate according to the law of bankruptcy under section 421 of the Insolvency Act 1986;

(c)   where the proprietor is a company, a winding-up order has been made with respect to it, or a resolution for voluntary winding-up (other than a members' voluntary winding-up) has been passed with respect to it, or a receiver or manager of its undertaking has been duly appointed, or possession has been taken, by or on behalf of the holders of any debentures secured by a floating charge, of any property of the company comprised in or subject to the charge.

It is the apparent insolvency of the proprietor of the security subjects, not the apparent insolvency of the debtor (if different), which constitutes default under standard condition 9(1)(c). If the debtor is insolvent, he will normally be in default under standard condition 9(1)(b).

38–24   *Rights of creditor on default*

STANDARD CONDITION 10

(1) Where the debtor is in default, the creditor may, without prejudice to his exercising any other remedy arising from the contract to which the standard security relates, exercise, in accordance with the provisions of Part II of this Act and of any other enactment applying to standard securities, such of the remedies specified in the following sub-paragraphs of this standard condition as he may consider appropriate.

(2) He may proceed to sell the security subjects or any part thereof.

(3) He may enter into possession of the security subjects and may receive or recover feuduties, ground annuals or, as the case may be, the rents of those subjects or any part thereof.

(4) Where he has entered into possession as aforesaid, he may let the security subjects or any part thereof.

(5) Where he has entered into possession as aforesaid there shall be transferred to him all the rights of the debtor in relation to the granting of leases or rights of occupancy over the security subjects and to the management and maintenance of those subjects.

(6) He may effect all such repairs and may make good such defects as are necessary to maintain the security subjects in good and sufficient repair, and may effect such reconstruction, alteration and improvement on the subjects as would be expected of a prudent proprietor to maintain the market value of the subjects, and for the aforesaid purposes may enter on the subjects at all reasonable times.

(7) He may apply to the court for a decree of foreclosure.

The rights of the creditor under this standard condition are considered more fully later.[15]

The provisions of the standard condition may require elaboration, *e.g.* by imposing on the debtor a specific obligation to vacate the property, by incorporating a consent to a warrant of summary ejection and by conferring rights on the creditor as to furniture and effects in the property. See Style 1, clause 12, paragraph 38–28.

38–25 *Exercise of right of redemption*

STANDARD CONDITION 11. This condition is considered more fully in Chapter 40, paragraphs 40–50 to 40–62 *infra*.

38–26 *Expenses*

STANDARD CONDITION 12
The debtor shall be personally liable to the creditor for the whole expenses of the preparation and execution of the standard security and any variation, restriction and discharge thereof and, where any of those deeds are recorded, the recording thereof, and all expenses reasonably incurred by the creditor in calling-up the security and realising or attempting to realise the security subjects, or any part thereof, and exercising any other powers conferred upon him by the security.

For a fuller clause see Style 1, clause 16, paragraph 38–28.

SPECIMEN STYLES—DEED OF VARIATIONS

38–27 It is impracticable to provide a representative selection of styles of deeds of variation used by institutional and commercial lenders within the constraints of space in a general textbook. Two specimen styles are offered: (1) a deed of variations, based with permission upon that adopted by Alliance & Leicester Building Society, which is a comprehensive style incorporating many conditions which are applicable to heritable securities by institutional lenders; and (2) a deed of variations relative to a commercial lending in respect of a building development.

Style 1

Deed of variation—building society[16]

38–28 We   Building Society (*address*) (hereinafter referred to as "the Society") Whereas we make advances in accordance with our Rules which are secured by Standard Securities granted in our favour over heritable property in Scotland have resolved and hereby declare that the said Standard Securities shall be regulated by the standard conditions specified in Schedule 3 to the Conveyancing and Feudal Reform (Scotland) Act, 1970 as amended by the Redemption of Standard Securities

---

[15]See Chap. 39.
[16]Relative to Style 9, para. 37–21. Based on style used by Alliance & Leicester Building Society.

(Scotland) Act, 1971 and, where so specified, by the following conditions, videlicet:—

Interpretation

1. In this Deed and in the Security where the context permits the following rules of construction shall apply—

(1)   (i)   "Society" means the   Building Society of   and includes its successors and assignees.

(ii)   "Borrower" means the person to whom an Advance has been made and his successors, executors and representatives whomsoever all jointly and severally renouncing the benefit of discussion and persons deriving title from the Borrower and includes any guarantors and their respective executors and representatives all jointly and severally.

(2)   (i)   "Policy Owner" means the Borrower if the Borrower provided the security of a policy or policies of life assurance under Condition 15 but if not then the person who provided such security (whether or not including the Borrower or any guarantor) and includes the persons deriving title under the Policy Owner.

(ii)   "Security" means the particular Standard Security or other document in which these Conditions are incorporated granted by a Borrower in favour of the Society and any security deeds supplemental or collateral thereto or substituted therefor.

(iii)   "Security Subjects" means the heritable subjects over which the security is granted and all other property (if any) at any time or times subject to the Security.

(iv)   "Advance" means the sum originally advanced under the Security and in relation thereto "Offer of Advance" means the Society's offer of the Advance as amended (if at all) prior to the making of the Security.

(v)   "Further Advance" means all or any further sum or sums which the Society may advance to the Borrower in addition to the Advance during the continuance of the Security, and "re-advance" means all or any sum re-advanced to the Borrower by the Society during the continuance of the Security, and in relation to a Further Advance or re-advance the "Offer of Advance" means the Society's offer of the Further Advance or re-advance as amended (if at all) prior to the making of the Further Advance or re-advance.

(vi)   "Payment Day" means the first day in every month (beginning with the month immediately following the date of the Security) or such later day in every month as the Society shall specify whether before or after the commencement of the Security.

(vii)   The "Basic Rate" the "Differential Rate" and the "Interest Rate" (which comprises the Basic Rate and the Differential Rate) mean the rates of interest (subject to variation) specified as such in the Offer of Advance.

(viii) The "Differential Rate" of interest includes any rate subsequently agreed by the Borrower in writing to be or become the "Differential Rate."

(ix) "Combined payment" means one of a number of regular payments which are attributable in part to repayment of capital and in part to payment of interest (whether or not on particular occasions in events which happen the payment is attributed wholly to interest or wholly to capital).

(x) "The Monthly Payment" and the "Reduced Monthly Payment" (where applicable) mean the amounts (subject to variation) specified as such in the Offer of Advance.

(xi) The "Repayment Table" means the period of time specified as such in the Offer of Advance.

(xii) "Relevant loan interest" has the meaning given by Part I of Schedule 7 to the Finance Act 1982 and references to relevant loan interest are references to relevant loan interest to which section 26 of that Act applies.

(xiii) "Related Rights" means and includes

(a) the benefit of any covenant agreement option guarantee undertaking charge right indemnity or remedy relating to the Security Subjects or to any road on which it abuts or to the services to it,

(b) the benefit of any compensation of any kind whatsoever available to the Borrower in respect of the Security Subjects,

(c) all rights whether or not in being at the date of the Advance which may be or become exercisable by the Borrower and any sums which (under any statute or law or contract and whether as of right or ex gratia or otherwise) may be or become payable in respect of the Security Subjects or any damage or injury to it or depreciation of it, and

(d) the benefit of any other obligation or security affecting or concerning the Security Subjects, But "Related Rights" does not include any sum which may become payable to the Borrower by statute because he has well-maintained the Security Subjects or the benefit of any insurance which (as between the Borrower and the Society) is otherwise provided for.

(xiv) "Whole Debt" means the whole of the moneys outstanding for the time being together with all interest fines subscriptions legal expenses and other sums due from the Borrower to the Society under the Security or the Rules or otherwise.

(xv) "Rules" means the Rules of the Society in force from time to time including Rules adopted and amendments made after the date of the Security.

(xvi) "Year" means year from 1 January to 31 December.

(xvii) Obligations undertaken by more than a single person are joint and several obligations.

(xviii) The "Board" means the Board of Directors for the time being of the Society.

(3) In case of conflict between the Rules and the Security (including these Conditions) the Security shall prevail. In case of conflict between the Security and these Conditions the Security prevails.

(4) The headings to these Conditions do not form part of these Conditions.

Security

2. The Security Subjects shall be held by the Society as security not only for the Advance but also for any Further Advance or re-advance and all money which may become owing by the Borrower to the Society on any account and the Security Subjects shall not be released by the Society until all moneys owing by the Borrower to the Society whether under the Security the Rules or otherwise shall have been paid.

Payments

3.

(1) The Security is intended to provide for repayment of capital and payment of interest primarily by combined payments at monthly intervals.

(2) The Borrower will in accordance and consistently with the terms of the Security (including these Conditions)—

(i) repay to the Society the Loan and all Further Advances which may be made to the Borrower under the Security,

(ii) pay to the Society all such fines fees and moneys as according to the Rules or the Security or these Conditions (whichever in the case of difference be the greatest) may become payable by the Borrower to the Society at any time before the Whole Debt has been fully discharged, and

(iii) pay interest on the Whole Debt (without any deduction except for sums equal to income tax at the basic rate on payments of Relevant loan interest).

(3) On the expiration of six months' notice in writing to that effect from the Society the Borrower will pay the Whole Debt and on default will pay to the Society interest on the Whole Debt from the expiration of the notice until the Whole Debt shall be paid and satisfied.

(4) If on realisation of the Security by the Society the net proceeds shall be insufficient to repay the Whole Debt the Borrower will immediately pay the amount of the deficiency with interest at the Interest Rate until payment.

(5) On the balancing date (which shall be the 31st December in the first year of the Security or such earlier day in that year as the Society shall specify for the purpose whether before or after the date of the Security) the Borrower shall pay to the Society a sum representing the interest charged under Condition 5 up to the balancing date and any premiums in

respect of any insurance effected by the Society under Condition 11 to the extent that the same have not been paid as part of a Monthly Payment or Reduced Monthly Payment made prior to the balancing date.

Suspension of combined payments

4. Notwithstanding the provisions of paragraphs (1) and (2) of Condition 3 and paragraphs (2) and (3) of Condition 6 the Society will not require repayments of capital to be made—

(1) where the security is to finance building works so long as there are one or more stage or progress payments which remain to be made and the Society has not either stipulated in the Offer of Advance or given at least twenty-one days notice that repayments of capital are to be started, or

(2) in respect of any amount which a subsisting policy of assurance included in the Society's security is intended to cover by means of endowment.

Interest

5.

(1) For the purposes of calculating interest under the Standard Security percentages shall not be taken beyond three places of decimals.

(2) Interest (including interest on any capitalised arrears of interest) will be charged by the Society at the Interest Rate (appropriate to the Whole Debt or to the relevant part of it as the case may be) as well after as before any judgment.

(3) The Society shall be entitled in any year

    (i) to charge interest on the amount of the Whole Debt on the thirty-first day of December in the immediately preceding year and on the full amount of any money advanced to or becoming owing by the Borrower during the year as from and including the date on which it was advanced or became owing, and

    (ii) to enter (prospectively and provisionally) interest for the year in the account of the Borrower on the first or any subsequent day in the year.

(4) Interest shall accrue from day to day but shall be payable partly in advance (if appropriate having regard to the Payment Day) by equal monthly instalments during the year (each month being treated for this purpose as a twelfth of the year) and on redemption interest shall be chargeable up to and including the date on which redemption takes place.

(5) As between capital and interest (other than Relevant loan interest) payments made by the Borrower in any year may be credited in the first instance against interest and any balance carried over to reduce the Whole Debt at the end of the year.

(6) Where part only of an intended advance has been made interest shall not be charged against the Borrower on more principal money than has actually been advanced.

(7) The Society may at any time vary the Interest Rate by varying the Basic Rate subject to the following paragraphs of this Condition.

(8) If the variation is by way of increase then (unless the variation is expressly notified to the Borrower) the variation shall be published as follows:

(i) by advertisement in two or more national daily newspapers selected by the Society (one of which shall circulate generally in Scotland). Provided that so long as at least two selected newspapers are available for advertising it shall not be necessary hereunder to advertise in any selected newspaper which for reasons outside the control of the Society is (when required) not available for advertising, or

(ii) by notices exhibited at the Chief and Branch Offices of the Society but so that such notices need not be exhibited at Agency or Local Offices which are not staffed exclusively by employees of the Society and the accidental omission by the Society to exhibit such a notice at a Branch Office shall not invalidate the publishing of such notice.

(9) The variation shall take effect on such date as the Society shall determine but (in case of a variation by way of increase which is published under Paragraph (8) of this Condition) not earlier than the date notice of it is so published.

(10) The Borrower may by notice given to the Society within one month from the date upon which any increase is to take effect in respect of the Security and referring to this provision be entitled to redeem the Security without paying the additional interest resulting from the increase provided that such redemption is effected within three months of the said date.

(11) In case at the time of a variation in the Interest Rate (whether or not such variation is attended or followed by a related variation in the Monthly Payment or Reduced Monthly Payment) the Borrower shall be in arrear with payments to the Society then such variation or variations shall be without prejudice to the arrears and the Borrower shall not by any such variation be relieved from the obligation to pay such arrears to the Society whether or not arrears are mentioned in the notices notifications or advertisements of the variation or variations.

The Monthly Payment and the Reduced Monthly Payment
6.
(1) The method of
   (i) calculating as at the date of the Security the Monthly Payment and any Reduced Monthly Payment has been based on the Advance the Interest Rate and the Repayment Table,

   (ii) calculating or re-calculating as at any subsequent date the Monthly Payment or a Reduced Monthly Payment may be based on the Whole Debt and the rate of interest relevant to the calculation and either the Repayment Table or the Repayment Table and the extent to which the period of it has expired,

and calculation or re-calculation has been and may be made by the Society by reference to tables either written out or programmed in a computer.

(2) The Borrower will discharge the primary obligations of the Borrower under paragraphs (1) and (2) of Condition 3 by

making to the Society on the Payment Day in every month a combined payment comprising separate components (so far as applicable and if any in each case) in the following order of priority but subject as between component (iii) and component (iv) to paragraph (5) of Condition 5—

Component (i): Relevant loan interest after deducting thereout a sum equal to income tax thereon at the basic rate

Component (ii): Relevant loan interest of which the Borrower is acquitted and discharged by section 26(2)(b) of the Finance Act 1982

Component (iii): interest (other than Relevant loan interest)

Component (iv): a component of capital which when added to components (i) and (iii) will make up the Monthly Payment or (in case paragraph (3) of this Condition is applied) the Reduced Monthly Payment.

(3) If and when

    (i) the combined payment includes Relevant loan interest but no interest (other than Relevant loan interest) then for so long thereafter as there is no variation or further variation in the Interest Rate or change or further change in the basic rate of income tax the Borrower may pay to the Society on the Payment Day in every month instead of the Monthly Payment a Reduced Monthly Payment of an amount calculated as if interest so far as it is Relevant loan interest were chargeable not at the Interest Rate but at a rate less than the Interest Rate by a percentage of the basic rate of income tax;

    (ii) the combined payment includes both Relevant loan interest and interest (other than Relevant loan interest) then by operation of paragraphs (2) and (3) of this Condition the Borrower may pay partly a Monthly Payment and partly a Reduced Monthly Payment

(4) Subject to the provisions of this Condition the Monthly Payment and any Reduced Monthly Payment may be varied at any time and from time to time by written notice to the Borrower from the Society so as—

    (i) to take account of and provide for any variation in the Interest Rate or any change in the basic rate of income tax,

    (ii) to include any increased or additional amount which the Society may require to be paid in respect of a Further Advance or expenses,

    (iii) to provide for the discharge of the Whole Debt by such time (not being earlier than the end of the period of the Repayment Table save in respect of a Further Advance to which a shorter period of repayment is applicable) as shall be specified in the notice,

    (iv) to provide for the Whole Debt or any part of it to be reduced by the end of any year or number of years to such amount (not being less than it would then have been if none of the Interest Rate the Monthly Payment and the Reduced Monthly

Payment had ever been varied and no payments by way of expenses or otherwise in relation to the Borrower or the Security Subjects or its contents had ever been made by the Society) as shall be specified in the notice,

(v) to bring the Monthly Payment or the Reduced Monthly Payment up to the nearest round sum which is 5p or a multiple of 5p up to a pound.

(5) Without prejudice to the powers of the Society under this Condition the Borrower may on receipt of a notice under paragraph (4) of this Condition elect to increase or reduce the Monthly Payment or Reduced Monthly Payment to any amount which is sufficient to discharge the Whole Debt within the period of the Repayment Table and any Further Advance to which a shorter period is applicable within such shorter period.

(6) Notwithstanding anything contained in this Condition the Monthly Payment or the Reduced Monthly Payment may be varied at any time by written agreement signed by the Borrower and by or on behalf of the Society.

(7) Notwithstanding anything contained in this Condition the Society may defer the giving of notice of variation under paragraph (4) of this Condition or the effective date of any variation under such paragraph (4) for a period not exceeding twelve months after the change or changes in the Interest Rate to which such variation relates without being deemed to have waived the right to make the variation and in the event of a variation being so deferred the variation shall take effect on the date specified in the notice of variation.

Related Rights

7.

(1) So far as he is able (but subject to redemption) the Borrower

    (i) assigns all Related Rights to the Society,

    (ii) declares and agrees that he will hold all Related Rights in trust for the Society, and

    (iii) irrevocably appoints the Society to be his attorney to claim assess agree enforce recover and receive all Related Rights and also to give any notice or counter-notice and exercise any right in respect of the Security Subjects which under any statute or otherwise the Borrower may be or become entitled to give or exercise to or against any local or other authority or body.

(2) Money arising in respect of Related Rights (unless laid out to the satisfaction of the Society in restoring or improving the security) shall be applicable by the Society in reduction of the Whole Debt.

Prohibitions

8. The Borrower shall not unless the Society shall have given prior agreement in writing (which agreement the Society shall be entitled to refuse without assigning any reason for such refusal)

(1) part with the occupation of the Security Subjects or any part thereof,

(2) apply under the Housing (Scotland) Act 1950 or any

amendment thereof or any other like enactment for any improvement grant in respect of the Security Subjects, or

(3) sell or transfer or purport to sell or transfer the Security Subjects under burden of the Security.

Rules

9. The Borrower has been granted membership of the Society from the date on which the Society's cheque for the Advance was encashed and undertakes to observe and be bound by the Rules (so far as applicable).

Security Subjects

10. The Borrower undertakes without prejudice to the obligations imposed by the said Standard Conditions

(1) to indemnify the Society from and against all actions proceedings claims for damage and expenses which may be brought against the Society in connection with the Security Subjects including all claims by third parties and the costs thereof,

(2) to duly pay any charges in connection with road making or paving which may become chargeable on the Security Subjects,

(3) that any sums received by the Borrower under any statutory provision as a result of his interest in the Security Subjects shall be paid to the Society who shall apply the sum in reduction of the Whole Debt,

(4) to deliver to the Society within fourteen days of receipt a copy of any notice order regulation or proceedings notified to him under any Act or regulation relating to or affecting the Security Subjects and to notify the Society in writing of all steps taken or proposed to be taken by him,

(5) to keep the Security Subjects in good and substantial repair and also without delay and in a proper manner to the satisfaction of the Society to complete any buildings in course of erection on the Property, and

(6) to pay any rent and other sums payable under a lease under which the Property is held by the Borrower immediately the same shall become due and to perform and observe all the undertakings and agreements on the part of the lessee and the conditions contained in every such lease and if requested to produce to the Society within fourteen days after payment the receipt for every such payment.

Insurance

11.

(1) The Society may either itself insure or (at the Society's option) require the Borrower to insure the Security Subjects against fire and such other risks in such names and for such amounts with such insurers and through such agency as the Society may from time to time think fit and the Borrower shall not except at the request of the Society effect or keep on foot any insurance in respect of the Security Subjects or any part thereof where the Society effects and keeps on foot such an insurance. The Borrower shall give to the Society such particulars relating to the Security Subjects as may be required and shall within seven days of the event inform the Society in writing of any circumstances which would be likely to affect the validity of any policy.

(2) Such insurance may be effected through the agency of the

Society who shall not be liable to account to the Borrower for any commission received on any fire life or other insurance whatsoever effected through the Society's agency.

(3)   The Society shall have power to settle and adjust with the insurers all questions with respect to the amount of the moneys payable under any policy and to the liability of the insurers.

(4)   Any moneys received on any insurance of the Security Subjects whether effected by the Society or the Borrower shall be applied at the Society's option either in or towards making good the loss or damage in respect of which the moneys are received or in or towards the repayment of the moneys secured by the Security and the Borrower shall hold any moneys received by him on any such insurance upon trust for the Society.

(5)   The Borrower will pay all premiums payable in respect of any insurance of the Security Subjects effected by him with the Society's consent within seven days after the premiums become due and will produce to the Society on demand the receipt for every such premium and also will deliver to the Society on demand every policy of such insurance.

(6)   The Borrower will pay to the Society all premiums and other expenses incurred by the Society in connection both with any insurance of the Security Subjects under the provisions of the Security and with any other policies of insurance or assurance (including but not limited to contents and mortgage protection insurances) at the request of the Borrower with interest thereon at the Interest Rate in any such case either upon demand or (at the option of the Society in respect of any annual premium) by an addition to the Monthly Payment or Reduced Monthly Payment of an amount not less than one twelfth of the annual premium.

Default

12.

(1)   In the event of the Borrower being in default for a period of two months in making a payment of money under the Security or of his being in breach at any time of any obligation imposed upon him by these presents or the Rules or if the Security Subjects or any part of it is purchased compulsorily or requisitioned the Whole Debt shall become due and the Society shall be entitled to exercise the rights conferred upon a Creditor by the Security as set out in Schedule Three to the Conveyancing and Feudal Reform (Scotland) Act 1970 or any later amendment thereof and also all other remedies competent to the Society under the Rules or these Conditions or by Statute or at Common Law.

(2)   The Borrower agrees to have the Security Subjects vacated and to give the Society immediate possession thereof on the expiry of a period of seven days after the posting of a notice given by or on behalf of the Society and addressed to the Borrower at his latest address in the Society's records or at the Security Subjects at any time after the Society shall have become entitled to enter into possession of the Security Subjects; and the Borrower agrees that a warrant of summary ejection may competently proceed against him in

the Sheriff Court of the County in which the Security
Subjects are situated at the instance of the Society.

(3) Without prejudice to the foregoing provision the Borrower
agrees and hereby authorises the Society that should he fail
in any one of the obligations hereby undertaken by him or
for which he is liable under the Rules of the Society or in
payment of any sum due by him to the Society under or in
consequence of these presents the Society shall be entitled
and shall have full power to charge any such sums whether
principal interest expenses or penalties or sums advanced by
the Society or subscriptions or fines against any sums of
money shares deposits or securities which may be in the
Society's possession or standing in its books as due to the
Borrower.

(4) At any time after its power of sale has become exercisable
the Society may:—

    (i) enter on the Security Subjects and execute and
contract for the execution of any alteration to the
building or other works thereon,

    (ii) dedicate any part or parts of the Security Subjects
for highways, and

    (iii) make any exchange or arrangement as to boun-
daries with neighbours.

(5) (i) On or after taking possession of the Security
Subjects the Society may as agent of the Borrower
(the Society being hereby irrevocably appointed the
agent of the Borrower for the purpose) and at his
expense remove store sell or otherwise deal with
any furniture goods or livestock which the
Borrower shall fail or refuse to remove and the
Society shall not be liable for any loss or damage
thus occasioned to the Borrower.

    (ii) If at the time of entry into possession or receipt of
the rents and profits of the Security Subjects by the
Society or by any receiver appointed by the Society
the Security Subjects or any part thereof shall be let
furnished under a tenancy which is or becomes
binding on the Society then and in any and every
such case the Society shall be entitled to receive
and apply the whole of the rent reserved by such
tenancy as if it were rent of the Security Subjects
and the Society shall neither be required nor bound
to make any apportionment of such rent in respect
of any furniture or chattels of the Borrower
comprised in the tenancy.

(6) At any time after taking possession the Society may give up
possession on giving notice to the Borrower.

(7) The powers hereby conferred on the Society are in addition
and without prejudice to all other powers and remedies
competent to the Society under the Rules or by Statute or
at Common Law or otherwise for recovering or enforcing
payment of any money due to the Society.

(8) If the Security Subjects or any part thereof are let serve any
landlords notice (statutory or otherwise) to terminate such
tenancy the Society being hereby irrevocably appointed the
attorney of the Borrower for the purpose of service of any

such notice and with power to sign execute seal and deliver any notice deed or document necessary to give effect thereto.

Power to Transfer

13.

(1) The Society shall at any time have power to transfer the Security to any person Society or Corporation.

(2) On any such transfer the Whole Debt at the time shall be treated as principal money and become due to the transferee at the end of six months with interest in the meantime at the Interest Rate in force at the time of the transfer.

(3) After the execution of any such transfer the Rules and these Conditions shall cease to apply to the Security but all powers and discretions conferred on a creditor by the Conveyancing and Feudal Reform (Scotland) Act 1970 shall be exercisable by the transferee.

(4) Every statement of fact made in good faith and contained in such transfer shall as against the Borrower be conclusive and binding.

(5) This Condition does not apply to a transfer of the Security on a union of building societies or a transfer of engagements from one building society to another.

Consolidation and Redemption

14.

(1) Except on such terms as the Society may determine the Borrower may not:—

    (i) redeem the Security without at the same time redeeming any other Security on other property which may be secured to the Society, or

    (ii) redeem any other Security without redeeming this Security.

(2) The execution and delivery by the Society of a discharge of the Standard Security shall not discharge the Borrower or the Guarantor (if any) from personal liability in case it shall subsequently appear that on redemption the amount of the Whole Debt was undercalculated or understated by mistake. But (unless the Borrower or the Guarantor as the case may be was party or privy to this mistake) the Society will not rely on this paragraph to sustain a claim against him unless it is made in writing within three months after the date of the redemption.

Endowment Loans

15. This Condition applies to every policy of life assurance or certificate of assurance from time to time included in the Society's security and the expression "the policy" shall include any certificate of assurance and any new or exchange or replacement policy. Where the policy shall be assigned to the Society in further Security of any Advance the following conditions shall apply:—

(1) The Society shall receive the benefit of the policy together with the sum thereby assured and all bonuses and other additions thereto and all claims advantages and benefits which have accrued or which may thereafter accrue and all the Policy Owner's right title and interest present and future in and to the same to be held by the Society absolutely.

(2)   On payment to the Society according to the Rules and this Security of all sums which shall from time to time be due by the Borrower to the Society the Policy shall be retrocessed at the expense of the Borrower.

(3)   The Borrower and the Policy Owner are to be held as agreeing and warranting to the Society that:—

    (i)   The policy is valid and nothing shall be done or suffered to be done whereby the Society may be prevented from receiving the sums payable thereunder or any part thereof.

    (ii)   If the policy shall become voidable or void the Borrower or the Policy Owner will forthwith at their own expense do all that may be necessary for keeping the same in force (if only voidable) or for effecting or for enabling the Society to effect (as the Society is authorised to do) a new policy or new policies on the life of the Borrower or Policy Owner (if it or any of them shall become void) for such sum or sums as would have been payable under the void policy if the life assured had ceased immediately before the same became void and maturing on the date on which the void policy would have matured if it had been kept in force such policy or policies to be effected in the name of the Society or in such other name or names and in such Insurance Company as the Society may direct.

    (iii)   Every such new policy and the sums to be assured thereby shall be subject to security of the Society and to the powers and provisions of the Society relating to the Advance whether under these presents or otherwise as fully to all intents as the policy originally assigned.

    (iv)   The Borrower and/or the Policy Owner will during the continuance of the Security punctually pay all premiums for keeping in force the policy or any such new and substituted policy as aforesaid.

    (v)   If there shall be at any time any default in payment of any of the premiums it shall be lawful for the Society to pay the same.

    (vi)   Any sums so paid and any sums expended by the Society in keeping in force the policy or in effecting any new policy in place of any policy which may become void shall be added to the amount then due to the Society by the Borrower and shall bear interest accordingly from the time of payment and shall be secured by the Security.

(4)   Subject and without prejudice to the other conditions imposed upon the Borrower so long as the Borrower shall punctually pay to the Insurance Company direct the premiums payable for keeping in force the policy or any new policy substituted therefor as herein provided and shall in all other respects observe and perform the obligations and stipulations imposed upon the Borrower in respect of the Advance the Society shall accept upon each of the Payment Days specified by the Society in place of the monthly instalment of combined principal and interest

thereby provided for a monthly payment of interest only as may be appropriate for the time being to cover interest at the Interest Rate.

(5) In the event of the Borrower being in default the Society shall be entitled to sell the policy or to assign transfer surrender or otherwise deal therewith and to collect the policy moneys which when received shall be immediately applied by the Society in discharging or reducing the Whole Debt it being specially provided that in case of default for ten days in payment to the Insurance Company of any premium for keeping in force the said policy or any new policy substituted therefor the said power of sale and others shall arise and take effect.

(6) Exercise by the Society of any rights hereinbefore conferred in respect of the policy assigned shall be without prejudice to the Society's rights under the Security.

Expenses

16.

(1) The Society shall be entitled to all expenses upon a basis of indemnity and expenses shall be chargeable with interest at the Interest Rate from the date of expenditure.

(2) Expenses with interest shall be payable by the Borrower on demand and until repaid shall be a charge on the Security.

(3) "Expenses" include all payments made or to be made by the Society in respect of:

    (i) works (whether of construction alteration or removal or of repair maintenance or improvement) carried out to the Security Subjects or the building thereon or the garden or grounds or the boundary walls or fences thereof,

    (ii) the discharge of any tax rate assessment feuduty rent or maintenance charge or other outgoing in relation to the Security Subjects,

    (iii) taking out and maintaining any policy on the life of the Borrower or any policy guaranteeing the repayment of the money secured by the Security,

    (iv) any work in or in connection with the maintenance or improvement of any private road or street,

    (v) any compliance with a notice relating to dilapidations or any notice or requirement of a like nature affecting the Security Subjects,

    (vi) all costs and expenses (legal or otherwise) incurred or paid by the Society in connection with the Security or with the recovery of moneys due thereunder or with the Security Subjects or with the protection enforcement transfer release discharge or repayment of the Security whether in whole or part, and

    (vii) all costs and expenses (legal or otherwise) incurred or paid by the Society where such costs and expenses have been incurred at the request of the Borrower.

(4) The Society shall also be entitled to recover from the Borrower a reasonable sum in respect of the expense to the Society of producing or supplying deeds and documents or copies thereof to the Borrower or the Borrower's Solicitor

or other agent or the provision of any assistance or information in connection with the Security Subjects or the mortgage account including a fee to be decided from time to time by the Society in connection with the sealing of the discharge of the Standard Security and the return of the title deeds to the Borrower or as he shall direct or to any third party entitled thereto.

(5) On any application by the Borrower for a Further Advance under the Security or for a variation of the terms of the Security the Borrower may be required to pay to the Society or there may be debited to the Borrower such reasonable fee by way of administration charge as the Society may prescribe from time to time but so that in case on the application the Society shall not make any Further Advance or agree to any variation then (without prejudice to any entitlement of the Society to expenses) the amount of the fee shall be refunded or re-credited to the Borrower.

Concessions

17. The Society may from time to time in writing at its absolute discretion authorise the Borrower to repay money by instalments other than those agreed to be made or may remit any instalment or give further time for the payment of any money secured or generally make such other arrangements with the Borrower as to the mode and time for payment of any money (whether in the nature of capital interest or otherwise) as the Society may think fit. But no such authority or arrangement shall affect the power of sale or other powers conferred on the Society or render the Society liable in damages or otherwise for the exercise of any such power where if the arrangement had not been made no such liability would have arisen.

Guarantor

18. If there is a Guarantor to the Security then:

(1) The Guarantor shall as between himself and the Society be deemed a principal debtor and not just a guarantor and accordingly the Guarantor shall not be discharged nor shall his liability be affected by any act thing omission or means by which his liability would not have been discharged if he had been principal debtor.

(2) The Guarantor waives all rights to participate in the proceeds of any security held or acquired by the Society or in any money which may be received by the Society whether from the Borrower or any other source in or towards reduction of the money secured by the Security unless and until all money secured by the Security has been received by the Society in full.

(3) The Guarantor shall not be liable in respect of any Further Advance or interest thereon unless the Further Advance is made with the consent of the Guarantor.

Notices

19. Any Notice given to the Borrower in writing (whether for varying the Interest Rate or the Monthly Payment or the Reduced Monthly Payment or otherwise) shall be sufficiently given if sent by prepaid letter post addressed to the Borrower at the last known address of the Borrower or at the Security Subjects and any such notice shall be deemed to have been served at the expiration of forty-eight hours from the time of the posting.   (*To be executed formally by the Society*)

Deed of variations—commercial transaction—building development

38–29   A deed of variations in the following style is relative to the standard security (Form A), Style 11, in paragraph 37–25 *supra*.

Style 2

Deed of variation of standard conditions—advances for building development

DEED OF VARIATION OF STANDARD CONDITIONS
between

A Limited, [*designation*], (hereinafter called "A") and C Finance Company Limited, [*designation*], (hereinafter called "C") WHEREAS A has granted or is about to grant a standard security in favour of C over   (hereinafter called "the property") [*dated of even date with the execution by A of these presents*] and it has been agreed that the standard conditions applicable to the said standard security shall be varied as hereinafter written, THEREFORE the parties AGREE—

Development of Property	1. A shall with due expedition lay out the property as a building estate and erect to the satisfaction of the Local Authority and C not less than bungalows to be completed before 19 .
	2. A shall construct a service road to enable said bungalows to be erected and complete all fencing of the ground and other preparatory work required under the conditions of title to the property or by the Local Authority and obtain all necessary consents or permissions for the erection of all buildings to be erected on the property.
	3. A shall form and complete to the satisfaction of the Local Authority and C proper roads and sewers necessary or convenient for the development of the property as a building estate.
Advances	4. C has advanced to A on 19 the sum of £ of which sum A acknowledges receipt.
	5. A may from time to time request further advances as the building development proceeds. Each such request shall be accompanied by a certificate from Architects, or such other architects or surveyors as may be approved by C, stating the amount expended on materials and labour in erecting and completing said bungalows as at the date of the certificate. Such certificate shall be conclu-

sive of the amount so expended at the time of the request.

6. Provided A shall not be in default under any of the conditions of the said standard security as hereby varied C shall within 21 days of receipt of each such request and relative certificate make a further advance to A subject to the provisions of Clause 7 hereof.

7. The aggregate amount of such further advances shall not exceed (a) the sum of £   paid for the property by A plus 75 per centum of the total amount certified to have been expended in all the certificates furnished at or before the time when the advance is requested or (b) the sum of £   , whichever shall be the less.

Restrictions

8. So long as any sums remain due by A to C under the standard security A shall not without the prior written consent of C (a) grant a conveyance of the property or any part thereof to any person, (b) create a security over the property in favour of any person or (c) grant leases or part with the occupation of the property or any part thereof.

Partial Release of Security

9. C shall release parts of the property from the security created by the said standard security on such terms as to repayment to account of the sums advanced as C may consider reasonable.

Repayment

10. The whole sums advanced by C to A shall, with all interest thereon and all other sums due to C by A under the said standard security and these presents be repaid by A not later than 19   .

Registration

11. A shall duly register the charge created by the standard security so as to comply with all the relevant provisions of the Companies Act 1985 or Acts amending the same.

General

12. Save as hereby varied the standard conditions specified in Schedule 3 to the Conveyancing and Feudal Reform (Scotland) Act 1970 as amended shall apply to the said standard security.

CHAPTER 39

ENFORCEMENT OF STANDARD SECURITIES

Introduction—scheme of legislation

39–01   The scheme of the legislation in the Conveyancing and Feudal Reform (Scotland) Act 1970, which introduced the standard security, was to prescribe most of the principal remedies available to the creditor for enforcing his rights under a standard security, but to retain some of the former remedies available to the creditor in a bond and disposition in security, namely, those which were not inconsistent with or effectively superseded by the 1970 Act and were not specifically excluded in Schedule 8.[1] Further, on default by the debtor the creditor's rights under contract or any enactment or rule of law remain available.[2] In effect therefore the remedies available to the creditor in a standard security are to be found:

(i) **In the 1970 Act**. Sections 10 and 11 (relating mainly to the personal obligation) and sections 19 to 29 inclusive and the standard conditions, particularly conditions 8, 9 and 10 (relating mainly to rights under the security).

(ii) **At common law or under earlier statutes**. The right to poind the ground available at common law to the creditor in a *debitum fundi* remains. Of the rights under earlier statutes the most important which

---

[1] 1970 Act, s. 32 and Sched. 8.
[2] *Ibid.*, s. 20(1).

remain are (a) the provisions relating to transmission of the personal obligation of the debtor on sale by, or on the death of, the debtor in section 47 of the Conveyancing (Scotland) Act 1874 as amended by section 15 of the Conveyancing (Scotland) Act 1924, (b) the right of the creditor to enter into possession by an action of maills and duties under sections 3 and 4 and the right to eject a debtor in personal occupation under section 5 of the Heritable Securities (Scotland) Act 1894, (c) the right to raise an action of declarator enabling the creditor in a security over superiorities or ground annuals to obtain payment of them under section 26 of the 1924 Act, (d) the right of an adjudger of a security over a lease to obtain a completed title to the lease by recording the extract decree under section 24(7) of the 1924 Act, (e) the right to sell the security subjects in lots under section 40 of the 1924 Act as subsequently amended by section 37 of the 1970 Act, and (f) the provisions for protection of purchasers under section 41 of the 1924 Act as amended by section 38 of the 1970 Act.

PERSONAL OBLIGATION

Personal diligence

39–02   The personal obligation of the debtor under a standard security in Form A may, unless the deed otherwise provides, be enforced on demand,[3] notwithstanding that particular periods of notice are required for enforcing the security.[4] There is no such statutory provision in relation to the personal obligation contained in the separate instrument when Form B is used: care should be taken to express the obligation appropriately in the separate instrument.[5] The powers are in addition to any other remedy of the creditor arising from the contract to which the security relates or available to him under statute or any rule of law.[6] Where the standard security or the separate instrument constituting the personal obligation contains a consent to registration for execution, or where a successor of the original debtor has agreed to transmission of the personal obligation or to accept liability to summary diligence,[7] summary diligence on a charge of six days is competent. If the debt is for a fluctuating or uncertain amount a certificate ascertaining the amount due by a person authorised in terms of the standard security or the separate instrument to grant it will determine the sum due for the purposes of registration for execution. If a consent to registration for execution has not been included in the relevant deed, or if the debt or obligation is insufficiently precise to enable a warrant for summary diligence to be issued,[8] the obligation

---

[3] 1970 Act, s. 10(1).
[4] *Ibid.*, ss. 19, 21.
[5] See, for example, Style 12A, cll. 10(c) and 11, para. 37–27.
[6] 1970 Act, ss. 20(1) and 21(1).
[7] Conveyancing (Scotland) Act 1874, s. 47 as amended by Conveyancing (Scotland) Act 1924, s. 15.
[8] See Vol. I, para. 4–65.

may be enforced by ordinary action and diligence done upon the
extract decree.

CALLING-UP

When competent

39–03   Where a creditor in a standard security intends to require repayment
of the debt thereby secured and, failing such repayment, to exercise
any of his powers in respect of the security, he may serve a calling-up
notice.[9] He may be precluded from doing so, however, by the terms of
the standard security or any requirement of law.[10] For example, the
standard security or the relevant separate instrument creating the
personal obligation may require the debtor to make payment only by
instalments,[11] or the permanent trustee in a sequestration of the debtor
may have intimated to the creditor that he intends to sell the security
subjects.[12] If the standard security was made before September 1, 1982
or, if later, the appropriate consent or renunciation by a non-entitled
spouse or an affidavit by the grantor of the standard security was
obtained thereto, the occupational rights of a non-entitled spouse of
the debtor do not affect the creditor's right to enforce the security.

Calling-up notice

39–04   A calling-up notice should be in Form A of Schedule 6 to the 1970
Act. The statutory form is:

> To AB, (*address*).
> TAKE NOTICE that CD, (*designation*), requires payment of
> £   with interest thereon at the rate of   per centum
> per annum from the   day of
> (*adding if necessary* subject to such adjustment of the principal
> sum and the amount of interest as may subsequently be
> determined) secured by a standard security by you[*or* by EF] in
> favour of the said CD [*or* of GH to which the said CD has now
> right] recorded in the Register for the County of
> on   ; And that failing full payment of the said sum
> and interest thereon (*adding if necessary* subject to any
> adjustment as aforesaid), and expenses within two months after
> the date of service of this demand, the subjects of the security
> may be sold.
> Dated this   day of   .

The notice should be signed by the creditor, or by his agent, the
latter adding his designation and the words "Agent of the said CD."

---

[9]1970 Act, s. 19(1).
[10]*Ibid.*, Sched. 3, s.c. 8.
[11]As in Style 9, para. 37–21, but the power to call-up may be reserved as in Style 12A, cl. 10(c),
para. 37–27.
[12]Bankruptcy (Scotland) Act 1985, s. 39(4)(*b*).

39–05   Sum in notice. Section 19(1) of the 1970 Act refers to "the debt thereby secured," *i.e.* the sum in the notice should be the whole amount secured by the heritable security. It should not include any sum which is not heritably secured, since the creditor is not entitled to exercise his power of sale in relation to a debt which has not been secured under the standard security. So if there has been any alteration in the contract made by informal agreement but not rendered subject to the security by a variation made in appropriate form under section 16 of the Act, *e.g.* an alteration in the rate of interest, that should be disregarded in computing the amount stated in the notice. If there is any doubt as to the amount heritably secured, the qualification as to adjustment may be inserted. Where there are sums due by the debtor to the creditor under two or more separate standard securities, the safest course is to serve a separate notice for the amount due under each security.

39–06   Debt of fluctuating or uncertain amount. Before a standard security for a fluctuating or uncertain amount can be called up it is necessary to have a certificate of the amount due as at the date when the calling-up notice is served. The certificate should be signed by a person authorised to do so in terms of the standard security or the separate instrument creating the personal obligation. A copy of the certificate should be annexed to the notice and each copy of it. In such a case no reference need be made to any subsequent adjustment, since the certificate will normally be conclusive of the amount due in terms of the standard security or separate instrument. Reductions or increases in the amount due occasioned by repayments or further advances made after the date of the notice will not invalidate the notice: it will have been correct when served. If the amount due is thereby increased, the security still extends to the increased amount, since the issue of the certificate and the service of the notice do not affect the contract.

39–07   Non-monetary obligation. If the obligation is not for payment of money the notice may run:

> To AB (*address*).
> TAKE NOTICE that CD, (*designation*), requires fulfilment of the obligation to erect and complete a bungalow to the value of not less than £   on the subjects known as
> as such obligation is contained in and secured by a standard security by you [*or* by EF] in favour of the said CD [*or* of GH to which the said CD has now right] recorded in the Register for the County of   on   ; And that failing fulfilment of the said obligation within two months [*or longer period*] after the date of service of this demand, the subjects of the security may be sold.

The notice should be signed in the same way as in the case of a notice requiring payment.

39–08 **Persons by whom notice served**

Trustees are joint proprietors; notice should be served by or on behalf of all of them.

Several creditors. If the creditors are joint or common owners of the security, all must concur and the notice should be given by or on behalf of all. If each of several creditors is entitled to a specified part of the moneys secured, the notice should bear that each requires payment to him of his own share, and separate notices by each for his own share may be preferable.

Minor. The notice should be on behalf of the minor and his curator.

Incapax. The notice should be by the ward acting through the *curator bonis* and by the curator for his interest.

Trustee in sequestration. The notice should be by or on behalf of the trustee.

Liquidator. The notice should be by the company (in liquidation) and the liquidator.

Attorney. The notice should be by the constituent and signed by the attorney on his behalf.

It is thought that it is unnecessary for the creditor who serves a calling-up notice to have a recorded title to the standard security. That was probably the position in relation to a creditor under a bond and disposition in security on the ground that he was selling, not as owner, what was vested in him, but under a mandate, what was vested in the mandant.[13] Since the grantor of a bond and disposition in security required to be infeft, the creditor was accordingly selling as mandatory of an infeft proprietor. It is thought that the provisions of section 12(2) of the 1970 Act effectively preserve that argument since, even where a standard security is granted by an uninfeft proprietor, the effect of the clause of deduction of title is that the title of the creditor is in all respects the same as if the grantor of the standard security had been infeft for the purposes of the rights and obligations of the grantor and grantee of the standard security and those deriving right from them, and the disponee on a sale by the creditor is a person deriving right from the creditor. The same argument applies where a standard security has been granted over a registered interest and deduction of title has not been required by virtue of section 15(3) of the Land Registration (Scotland) Act 1979.

39–09 **Persons on whom notice served**

Person last infeft and appearing on record as proprietor. Notice must be given to the person last infeft and appearing on record as

---

[13]Burns, 515.

proprietor.[14] An up-to-date search of the sasine register or report from the Land Register will be required, continued as nearly as possible to the actual date of service of the notice. If there is an *ex facie* absolute disponee, service on him is necessary since he appears on the record as proprietor. If it is suspected that the person last appearing on record as proprietor is only an *ex facie* absolute disponee, inquiry should be made as to the true owner (although the creditor will normally know that) and service should be made on him also.

Deceased. If the person last appearing on record as proprietor is dead, service should be made on his representative or the person entitled to the subjects in terms of the last recorded title, notwithstanding any alteration of the succession not appearing on the Register of Sasines or the Land Register.[15] Normally that will now be the executor or the person entitled to succeed under a special destination in the recorded or registered title.

Deceased leaving no representatives. Notice should be served on the Lord Advocate.[16]

If not known whether alive. Notice should be sent to the Extractor of the Court of Session.[17]

Company removed from register of companies. Notice should be served on the Lord Advocate.[18]

Bankrupt. Notice should be served on the bankrupt and his trustee in sequestration (unless the trustee has been discharged).

Trust deed for creditors. Notice should be served on the grantor and the trustee.

Trustees. It is sufficient to serve the notice on a majority of the infeft trustees.[19]

Superior or proprietor of mixed estate. If the standard security is over an estate of superiority or a mixed estate, notice should be served on the owner last infeft in the superiority of the estate and appearing on record as proprietor and also on any feuars whose feu rights are not valid against the security, since their property may be sold by the creditor.

Partnership. Notice is required only to the trustees for the firm infeft and appearing as proprietors on record. Notice to a majority of the trustees infeft will probably suffice, but in practice should be given to

---

[14]1970 Act, s. 19(2).
[15]*Ibid.*, s. 19(2).
[16]*Ibid.*, s. 19(3).
[17]*Ibid.*, s. 19(6).
[18]*Ibid.*, s. 19(3).
[19]*Ibid.*, s. 19(4).

all. Notice should also be given (although it is probably not strictly necessary) to the firm and to all its partners at the time.

True proprietor. Where it is known to the creditor that for any reason the person appearing on record as proprietor is not the real owner of the subjects, notice should be given to the true proprietor also.

Non-entitled spouse. Any non-entitled spouse who may have occupancy rights—but see paragraph 39–03 *supra*.

39–10 **Preserving recourse**. If the creditor wishes to preserve recourse against any other person, *i.e.* if he wishes to retain the right to require payment of the secured debt from any person other than the proprietor, notice must also be served on that person.[20] The Act requires service on the *proprietor* of the security subjects, who may not be the debtor in the personal obligation. In such a case service plainly should be made on the debtor also. In addition notice should be given to co-obligants, guarantors, former owners of the property whose personal obligations for the standard security have not been discharged and owners of all other property, heritable or moveable, over which security for the debt called-up has been given.[21]

39–11 **Procedure on service**. Service of a calling-up notice may be made:
(1) by delivery to the person,[22] or
(2) by registered post or recorded delivery service to him at his last known address or, in the case of the Lord Advocate, at the Crown Office, Edinburgh,[22] or
(3) if the address of the person is not known, or if it is not known whether he is still alive, or if the packet containing the notice is returned to the creditor with an intimation that it could not be delivered, by sending it to the Extractor of the Court of Session.[22]
A calling-up notice served by post will be deemed to have been served on the next day after the day of posting.[23]

39–12 **Evidence of service**. Service of a calling-up notice may be evidenced:
(1) by an acknowledgment of receipt[24] by the person on whom service has been made in the following form[25]:

> I, AB, above named, hereby acknowledge receipt of the foregoing Notice of Calling-up of which the foregoing is a copy of the notice.
> Dated this   day of   .

signed by the person on whom notice is served, or by his agent who

---

[20]*Ibid.*, s. 19(5).
[21]*Stuart's Exr.* v. *Stuart* (1904) 12 S.L.T. 356.
[22]1970 Act, s. 19(6).
[23]*Ibid.*, s. 19(8).
[24]*Ibid.*, s. 19(6).
[25]*Ibid.*, Sched. 6, Form C.

will add his designation and the words "Agent of the said AB," or
(2) by a certificate[26] by the person making the service in the
following form[26a]:

> Notice of Calling-up, of which the foregoing is a copy, was posted
> [*or otherwise, as the case may be*] to AB above named on the
> day of   .

signed by the creditor, or by his agent who will add his designation and
the words "Agent of the said CD," and having attached to it (if
posted) the postal receipt.[27]

In practice three copies of a calling-up notice will be prepared, the
principal and one duplicate copy being delivered or posted and the
remaining copy retained by the person making service. The duplicate
sent may be used for endorsement of an acknowledgment of receipt;
the duplicate retained may be used for endorsement of a certificate of
delivery or posting.

39–13   Adjustment of amount stated in notice. Section 19(9) of the 1970 Act
provides that, where the creditor has indicated in a calling-up notice
that any sum and any interest thereon due may be subject to
adjustment in amount, he shall, if so requested by the person on whom
the notice has been served, furnish the debtor with a statement of the
amount as finally determined within a period of one month from the
date of service of the calling-up notice. Failure to do so will render the
calling-up notice ineffective.[28] The right to serve a calling-up notice in
respect of a sum due under a standard security subject to adjustment is
available whether the creditor has been in possession of the security
subjects or not.[29] Any person on whom the notice has been served may
request that a statement of the amount as finally determined be
furnished within the period of one month, but the obligation of the
creditor is to furnish the statement to the debtor. Since, however, the
term "debtor" includes any successor in title, assignee or representative,[30] the safe course of action, if a request for such a statement is
made by any person on whom notice has been served, will be to
furnish the statement to the debtor and to all other persons on whom
the notice has been served. The request may be made at any time, but
the statement must be furnished within one month from the date of
service of the notice, *i.e.* the day next after the date of posting or
delivery. Accordingly the creditor should prepare the statement
without delay immediately after serving the notice so that he is in a

---

[26]*Ibid.*, s. 19(6).

[26a]*Ibid.*, Sched. 6, Form D.

[27]When notice is sent to the Extractor of the Court of Session the proper evidence of service is the
acknowledgment of the Extractor.

[28]1970 Act, s. 19(9).

[29]*Cf.* s. 33 of the 1970 Act whereby the corresponding procedure under a bond and disposition in
security is available only if the creditor has been in possession.

[30]1970 Act, s. 30(1).

position to furnish it within the 30-day period, even if it is requested only a day or two before the expiry of the period. If the creditor fails to furnish the statement timeously when requested to do so, he must start afresh by serving a calling-up notice, since the notice originally served will have become ineffective.

9–14 *Evidence of request and furnishing of statement.* Since the continuing validity of a calling-up notice may depend upon a request for a statement having been made and upon the statement having been timeously furnished, it is recommended that the request should be made and the statement furnished by registered post or recorded delivery service. A copy of the letter of request, and a copy of the letter furnishing the statement along with a copy of the statement itself, in either case having the postal receipt attached, should be retained as evidence.

9–15 **Dispensing with or shortening period of notice**. The period mentioned in the calling-up notice (normally two months) may be dispensed with or shortened by the person on whom it is served by a minute written or endorsed on the notice or a copy of it.[31] The form of the minute[32] is:

> And I agree to the period of notice being dispensed with [*or* shortened to   ].

There are two important qualifications. (1) In terms of the Act[31] the consent of creditors holding securities *pari passu* with, or postponed to, the security held by the creditor who is calling-up is required to an agreement to dispense with or shorten the period of notice. These other creditors may not wish the security subjects to be sold, and the time available to them to arrange for replacement of the security which is being called-up cannot be reduced without their consent. (2) The agreement to dispense with or shorten the period by one recipient of a calling-up notice will not bind any other persons on whom the notice may have been served. If notice has been served on more than one person, the consent of all should be obtained to any restriction of the period.

9–16 **Life of notice**. A calling-up notice will cease to have effect for the purpose of a sale in the exercise of any power contained in the security on the expiration of five years from (a) the date of the notice, if no offer for or exposure to sale of the security subjects or any part of them has followed or (b) from the date of the last offer or exposure, where there has been offer or exposure.[33] The date of the last offer is presumably the date when the last advertisement of the security subjects was published. Evidence of that should be preserved.[34]

---

[31] *Ibid.*, s. 19(10).
[32] *Ibid.*, Sched. 6, Form C.
[33] *Ibid.*, s. 19(11).
[34] See para. 39–41.

Powers exercisable on non-compliance

39–17   Where the debtor fails to comply with a calling-up notice the creditor may exercise any of the rights under the security which he may consider appropriate.[35] If the standard conditions have been adopted unchanged in the contract which regulates the security the creditor may exercise any of the remedies available to him under sub-paragraphs (2) to (7) of standard condition 10, *viz.* (i) to sell the security subjects, (ii) to enter into possession of the security subjects and receive feuduties, ground annuals or rents, (iii) after he has entered into possession, to let the security subjects or any part of them and to exercise all the rights of the debtor as regards granting leases or rights of occupancy and management and maintenance, (iv) to effect maintenance and repairs on and to reconstruct, alter and improve the security subjects so as to maintain their market value and (v) to apply for a decree of foreclosure. In addition the creditor may exercise any other remedy arising from the contract constituting the standard security and also any other right conferred by statute or at common law on the creditor in a heritable security.[36]

39–18   The various remedies available to the creditor are considered more fully later.[37] When they are exercised upon failure to comply with a calling-up notice the principal relevant statutory provisions which regulate the rights are:

(1) Power of sale.	1970 Act, ss. 20(1) and (2) and 25, 26 and 27.
	s.c. 10(1) and (2).
(2) Powers of entering into possession and rights relating thereto.	1970 Act, s. 20(1), (3), (4) and (5).
	s.c. 10(1), (3), (4) and (5).
	1894 Act, ss. 3 and 5.
(3) Power to effect repairs, maintenance, reconstruction and improvement.	1970 Act, s. 20(1).
	s.c. 10(1) and (6).
(4) Foreclosure.	1970 Act, ss. 20(1) and 28.
	s.c. 10(1) and (7).

NOTICE OF DEFAULT

When competent

39–19   The 1970 Act introduced a new form of remedy which is available to a creditor in a standard security in certain circumstances, namely, to

---

[35] 1970 Act, s. 20(1).
[36] *Ibid.*, s. 20(1).
[37] In paras. 39–38 to 39–85.

serve a notice of default. The remedy is available where the debtor has failed to comply with any requirement arising out of the security (other than failure to pay the amount due after service of a calling-up notice) and the default is remediable.[38] Any failure by the debtor to implement an obligation enforceable under a standard security will entitle the creditor to serve a notice of default. Default in payment of interest or of a periodic instalment of capital and interest, or breach of an obligation under standard condition 1, 2, 3 or 5, or failure to implement an obligation undertaken in the personal obligation or in a variation of the standard conditions, are obvious examples. The only qualification is that the failure should be remediable. So, if the debtor has failed to notify the creditor of a notice under the Town and Country Planning Acts and the time for objecting has expired, a notice of default would not be competent since objection could no longer be made timeously. In such circumstances the creditor, if he considers that his position has been prejudiced, would serve a calling-up notice.

Calling-up notice or notice of default

39–20   The remedies of serving a calling-up notice and serving a notice of default are not mutually exclusive[39] and there may be situations in which the creditor will exercise both rights contemporaneously. Where the default is in some relatively minor matter, *e.g.* failure to execute necessary repairs to the security subjects, but the security is not seriously jeopardised, the creditor may serve a notice of default rather than use the sledgehammer of calling-up. Where interest on or instalments of capital are in arrear, although not seriously, the service of a notice of default may be used as a warning shot across the debtor's bows and may prove effective. Where there is serious default in payment of interest or principal and the debtor has abandoned the security subjects, which are deteriorating, service of a notice of default may be the quickest method of approach to a sale of the security subjects. The period of notice is only one month instead of the period of two months required in a calling-up notice and it is improbable in the circumstances that the debtor will object to the notice of default. If the debtor has been consistently in arrear with payments or his conduct in other respects is so unsatisfactory that the creditor wishes repayment, service of a calling-up notice will be the proper method. If a notice of default is served the debtor may purge the particular default or use his right of objection to the notice as a delaying tactic, and a calling-up notice, despite the longer period of notice, may be the speediest route to repayment or sale of the security subjects.

---

[38] 1970 Act, s. 21(1) and Sched. 3, s.c. 9(1)(*b*).
[39] *Ibid.*, s. 21(1).

Notice

39–21   A notice of default should follow the form contained in form B of
Schedule 6 to the Act. It runs:

> To AB, (*address*).
> TAKE NOTICE that CD, (*designation*), the creditor in a
> standard security by you [*or* by EF] in favour of the said CD [*or*
> of GH to which the said CD has now right] recorded in the
> Register for the County of   on
> requires fulfilment of the obligation(s) specified in the schedule
> hereto in respect of which there is default; And that failing such
> fulfilment within one month after the date of service of this
> notice, the powers competent to the said CD on default may be
> exercised.
> Dated this   day of   .

The notice should be signed by the creditor, or his agent who will add
his designation and the words "Agent of the said CD." To the notice
there is annexed a schedule headed "Schedule of Obligation(s) in
respect of which there is default," and the obligation(s) in respect of
which default has occurred will be specified in the schedule. It is
suggested that the particular obligation should be identified in relation
to the provision of the standard conditions or of the contract which has
not been fulfilled and that the respects in which there has been failure
to do so should be particularised in reasonably precise terms, *e.g.*

> The obligation of the debtor to maintain the security subjects in
> good and sufficient repair to the reasonable satisfaction of the
> said CD in respect that (1) a crack has developed extending from
> the roof eaves to the top of the doorway in the rear wall, (2) a
> considerable number of roof tiles are cracked or missing and (3)
> the external woodwork of all windows requires repainting.

Where the default has been in payment of money the precise amount
of the arrears should be stated. Since the debtor is being called upon to
fulfil the obligations, it is proper that he should be informed
specifically of what is required of him.

39–22   **Persons by whom notice served**. The notice may be served by or on
behalf of the creditor. The persons in whose names it should run will
be the same as in the case of a calling-up notice.[40]

39–23   **Persons on whom notice served**. The creditor is entitled to call on the
debtor and on the proprietor, where he is not the debtor, to purge the
default.[41] Accordingly the notice should be served on the debtor and,
as the case may be, the proprietor.[42] It appears that the only persons
on whom notice must be served are the debtor and (if a different

---

[40]See para. 39–08.
[41]1970 Act, s. 21(1).
[42]*Ibid.*, s. 21(2).

person) the proprietor. The general principles already stated[43] as to identifying the proprietor where a calling-up notice is being served will apply.

39–24 *Co-obligants and guarantors.* In relation to a notice of default the Act contains no provision corresponding to section 19(5) in the case of calling-up as to serving a copy of the notice on persons against whom the creditor wishes to preserve recourse. Accordingly failure to serve a copy of a notice of default upon a co-obligant or guarantor would not in terms of the Act affect his liability for the debt. Whether it would have that result on equitable principles is a matter which the courts will have to determine, and it may depend upon the terms of the contract. It is suggested, however, that, at least if the creditor contemplates exercising his power of sale on failure to purge the default, notice should be given to co-obligants or guarantors. Even if it is not strictly necessary, it is probably advisable as a matter of fair dealing between the creditor and a co-obligant that the latter should know of the debtor's failure to fulfil part of the obligation for which the co-obligant may ultimately be liable.

39–25 **Service of notice and evidence of service.** The Act provides that a notice of default shall be served in the like manner and with like requirements as to proof of service as a calling-up notice.[44] The forms of acknowledgment of service (form C) and of certificate of postage (form D) contained in Schedule 6 to the Act are applicable also in the case of a notice of default.[45]

39–26 **Dispensing with or shortening period of notice.** The provisions as to dispensing with or shortening the period of notice in relation to a calling-up notice apply also in relation to a notice of default.[46]

39–27 **Life of notice.** Even although there is failure to comply with any requirement contained in a notice of default, the notice will cease to be authority for the exercise of certain rights of the creditor on the expiration of five years from the date of the notice.[47] The rights affected are those under standard condition 10(2), (6) and (7) (sale, repair and reconstruction and alteration of the security subjects).[48]

39–28 **Objections to notice.** Where a person on whom a notice of default has been served considers himself aggrieved by any requirement in it, he may, within 14 days of the service of the notice, object to the notice by way of an application to the sheriff having jurisdiction over the security subjects.[49] Not later than the lodging of the application a copy of it

---

[43]See para. 39–09.
[44]1970 Act, s. 21(2). See paras. 39–11 and 39–12.
[45]See para. 39–12.
[46]1970 Act, s. 21(3). See para. 39–15.
[47]*Ibid.*, s. 21(4).
[48]*Ibid.*, s. 23(2).
[49]*Ibid.*, ss. 22(1) and 29(1).

must be served by the applicant on the creditor and any other party on whom the notice of default has been served by the creditor.[49] The court, after hearing the parties and making such inquiry as it thinks fit, may order the notice to be set aside, in whole or in part, or otherwise to be varied, or it may uphold the notice.[50]

39–29   The right to object to a notice of default is a proper safeguard for the debtor since it will prevent the rights of the creditor on default being exercisable on a mere notice given by the creditor when the occurrence of the default alleged may be a matter of dispute. From the point of view of the creditor, however, it is a disadvantage of proceeding by way of notice of default that the right to exercise certain powers arising on default may be considerably delayed, even if the notice is ultimately upheld. On the other hand the process of objection to a notice of default is not without hazards to the debtor. There are certain remedies of the creditor arising from a notice of default the exercise of which require the authority of the court,[51] and an application by the debtor objecting to a notice of default may enable the creditor by counter-application in the same process to obtain that authority and so widen the range of remedies available to him.[52] Any such counter-application may be accompanied by a certificate in the form of Schedule 7 to the 1970 Act which is *prima facie* evidence of the facts stated therein.[52a]

Powers exercisable by creditor on default

39–30   Where there has been failure to comply with a notice of default, or a notice of default as varied by the court, the creditor may exercise the rights which arise on default. In general the creditor should make a summary application to the court under section 24 of the 1970 Act to exercise such of these rights as he proposes to enforce (unless he has already obtained the authority of the court in a counter-application under section 22 of the Act).[53] The ultimate remedy of applying for a decree of foreclosure may be exercised when an exposure to sale has not yielded an amount sufficient to satisfy the debt and expenses.[54] These rights and the procedure for exercising them (except *quoad* sale and foreclosure) may, of course, have been altered by the contract relating to the standard security.

39–31   **Non-possessory remedies**. The remedies of sale of the security subjects and repairing, reconstructing, altering and improving the security subjects to maintain their market value, which may be exercised immediately, are considered more fully later.[55] When they are

---

[50]*Ibid.*, s. 22(2).
[51]See para. 39–30.
[52]1970 Act, s. 22(3) and (4).
[52a]*Ibid.*, s. 22(4).
[53]See paras. 39–35 and 39–61.
[54]1970 Act, Sched. 3, s.c. 10(7). See paras. 39–70 to 39–85.
[55]See paras. 39–38 to 39–52 and 39–66, 39–67.

exercised upon failure to comply with a notice of default the principal relevant statutory provisions are:

(1) Power of sale.	1970 Act, ss. 23(2), 25, 26 and 27.
	s.c. 10(1) and (2).
(2) Power to effect repairs, maintenance, reconstruction and improvement.	1970 Act, s. 23(2). s.c. 10(1) and (6).

Rights of debtor in default

39–32   A debtor under a standard security who is in default may purge the default at any time within the period stated in the notice of default. After that period has elapsed without compliance, however, the creditor may proceed to exercise his power of sale[56] but the debtor or the proprietor may redeem the security without notice at any time before the conclusion of an enforceable contract of sale.[57] It is not enough at that stage for the debtor or proprietor merely to purge the default; the security must be redeemed. On the other hand if the creditor does not propose to proceed to sale but elects to apply for a warrant to exercise the right to enter into possession,[58] it is probable that the warrant will be refused if at any time before decree has been pronounced the default has in fact been purged.

APPLICATION BY CREDITOR TO COURT

Section 24 applications

39–33   Without prejudice to the right of the creditor to proceed by way of notice of default, he may make a direct application to the court for a warrant to exercise any of the remedies which he is entitled to exercise on a default within the meaning of standard condition 9(1)(a). In terms of section 29(2) of the 1970 Act any such application must be by way of summary application. In making such an application the solicitor for the creditor should consider (1) the circumstances in which the application may be made, and (2) the extent of the remedies which may be sought and the appropriate form of action to enforce them.

39–34   **(1) Circumstances in which application may be made.** In terms of section 24(1) the application may be made either (i) where the debtor is in default within the meaning of standard condition 9(1)(b) or (ii) where the debtor is in default within the meaning of standard condition 9(1)(c).

39–35   In terms of standard condition 9(1)(b) there is default "where there

---

[56] 1970 Act, s. 23(2).
[57] Ibid., s. 23(3).
[58] Ibid., s. 24(1).

has been a failure to comply with any other [*i.e.* other than non-compliance with a calling-up notice] requirement arising out of the security." The creditor may apply to the court without first having served a notice of default, and a certificate in the form of Schedule 7 to the 1970 Act is *prima facie* evidence of the facts stated in the certificate. Nevertheless in practice it is suggested that in cases where the default is remediable it is preferable that the application to the court is preceded by a notice of default, for the reasons that (1) the applicant will then be in a stronger position since the fact that a notice of default has been served and there has been failure to comply with its requirements is more than merely *prima facie* evidence of default and (2) it is not unreasonable that the debtor or proprietor should have been given an opportunity to remedy the default without being involved in the expense of defending an application to the court. If the default is not remediable the creditor will usually prefer to proceed by way of a calling-up notice so that he may more quickly proceed to sell the subjects and their site for what they may realise.

39–36   The other circumstance in which application may be made to the court under section 24(1) is that there has been default by the debtor within the meaning of standard condition 9(1)(*c*), *i.e.* where the proprietor of the security subjects has become insolvent. What constitutes insolvency for this purpose is defined in detail in standard condition 9(2).[59] It should be noted that it is apparent insolvency of the *proprietor* of the security subjects, not that of the debtor, which constitutes default. Usually the proprietor and the debtor will be the same person. If the debtor is not the proprietor and becomes insolvent, he will normally have failed to make payments of interest or instalments of capital, or have failed to comply with a calling-up notice, so that default will have occurred on other grounds. If, however, the proprietor of the security subjects is not the debtor and becomes insolvent there may have been no default by the debtor but the creditor's security may be liable to realisation by other creditors of the proprietor, and in these circumstances the creditor in the standard security should have the right to realise the security subjects in accordance with the preference which his security confers.

39–37   **(2) Extent of remedies which may be sought by a summary application under section 24.** For the purpose of determining the form of action by which a creditor in a standard security may enforce the security by remedies available to him the remedies may be classified as follows:

(A) *Remedies specified by the 1970 Act.* These include the remedies specified in standard condition 10(3) to (7) inclusive and should be enforced by summary application in terms of sections 24(1) and 29(2) of the Act.

---

[59]For the reference in s.c. 9(2) to s. 163 of the Bankruptcy (Scotland) Act 1913 now substitute a reference to s. 11A of the Judicial Factors (Scotland) Act 1889 (Bankruptcy (Scotland) Act 1985, Sched. 7, para. 8), and for the reference to notour bankruptcy substitute a reference to apparent insolvency.

(B) *Additional remedies stipulated in the contract to which the standard security relates*. An example is a condition that the creditor may eject a proprietor who is in occupation of the security subjects, a right frequently contained in securities in favour of a building society. In terms of standard condition 10(1) the statutory rights of the creditor are "Without prejudice to his exercising any other remedy arising from the contract to which the standard security relates." It is thought that on strict construction that phrase simply preserves the right of the creditor to enforce any contractual remedies available to him by any appropriate process but does not make them remedies under Part II of the 1970 Act, so that procedure by way of summary application under section 29(2) is incompetent.[60]

Additional non-statutory and non-contractual remedies. It is clearly incompetent to include in a summary application remedies which are neither given by the 1970 Act nor by the contract relating to the security, *e.g.* interdict against the debtor interfering with the creditor's possession of the security subjects.[60a]

REMEDIES AGAINST SECURITY SUBJECTS

1. Sale

When exercisable

39–38   The power of the creditor to sell the security subjects, or any part of them, may be exercised:

(1) where a calling-up notice has been served and has not been complied with, normally on the expiration of the two months' period without payment,[61] or

(2) where a notice of default has been served and either not objected to or upheld or varied after objection and there has been failure to comply with any requirement in the notice (or the notice as varied),[62] or

(3) where the proprietor of the security subjects is insolvent and the court has granted a warrant to the creditor to sell.[63]

There have been several decisions, not altogether consistent, as to the circumstances in which a creditor may exercise the power of sale.[63a] The opinion is expressed that:

(i) Where there has been failure to comply with a calling-up notice the creditor may proceed to advertise and sell the security subjects.

---

[60]*Provincial Building Society* v. *Menzies*, 1984 S.L.T. (Sh.Ct.) 81; *Mountstar Metal Corporation v. Cameron*, 1987 S.L.T. (Sh.Ct.) 106; *Bradford and Bingley Building Society v. Roddy*, 1987 S.L.T. (Sh.Ct.) 109; Contra *National & Provincial Building Society* v. *Riddell*, 1986 S.L.T. (Sh.Ct.) 6.

[60a]*National & Provincial Building Society* v. *Riddell*, *supra*.

[61]1970 Act, s. 20(1) and (2).

[62]*Ibid.*, s. 23(2).

[63]*Ibid.*, s. 24(1).

[63a]*United Dominions Trust Ltd.*, *Noters*, 1977 S.L.T. (Notes) 56; *United Dominions Trust Ltd.* v. *Site Preparations Ltd.* *(No. 1)*, 1978 S.L.T. (Sh.Ct.) 14; *United Dominions Trust Ltd.* v. *Site Preparations Ltd.* *(No. 2)*, 1978 S.L.T. (Sh.Ct.) 21.

His right to do so is express in terms of section 20(2) of the 1970 Act.

(ii) Where there has been failure to comply with a notice of default the creditor should make a summary application to the court for a warrant to sell under section 24 of the 1970 Act.

(iii) Where the proprietor of the security subjects is apparently insolvent the creditor should likewise make a summary application to the court for warrant to sell. If the proprietor is a company the creditor may obtain such a warrant notwithstanding liquidation of the company or the provisions of section 127 of the Insolvency Act 1986.[63b]

Prior, pari passu and postponed heritable creditors

39–39 **(1) Prior.** The existence of a heritable security ranking prior to the security of the creditor under the standard security does not preclude the latter from selling, but he cannot give an unencumbered title. The disposition to the purchaser remains subject to the prior security, but the postponed creditor who is selling has the same right as the debtor to redeem it.[64]

(2) Pari passu. The creditor in a standard security may exercise the power of sale notwithstanding that there is a *pari passu* heritable creditor who does not concur in the sale. It is still competent to apply to the sheriff for an order of sale under section 11 of the Heritable Securities (Scotland) Act 1894, but it would not appear to be a necessary preliminary to a sale by one of the *pari passu* creditors.[65] The disposition on sale, when recorded, will disburden the security subjects of a *pari passu* security and the selling creditor must apply the proceeds giving due ranking to the *pari passu* security in the distribution.[66]

(3) Postponed. The creditor may sell notwithstanding the existence of postponed securities. The recorded or registered disposition will disburden the security subjects of any postponed security and the proceeds of sale will be distributed giving effect to the rights of the postponed creditor.[67]

Exercise of the power

39–40 One of the most valuable features of the standard security from the creditor's point of view is the simplicity of the procedure for bringing the security subjects to sale when the right to do so has emerged. The requirements of public exposure, advertisement for stated periods in particular newspapers and the times within which exposure must follow

---

[63b] *United Dominions Trust Ltd., Noters, supra* (relating to the corresponding s. 227 of the Companies Act 1948).
[64] 1970 Act, s. 26(2).
[65] *Ibid.*, s. 26(1).
[66] *Ibid.*, s. 27(1).
[67] *Ibid.*, ss. 26(1) and 27(1).

advertisement have no application to the exercise of a power of sale under a standard security. The Act simply imposes a duty on the creditor (1) to advertise the sale and (2) to take all reasonable steps to ensure that the price at which all or any part of the security subjects are sold is the best that can be reasonably obtained.[68] The sale may be effected by private bargain or public exposure.[69]

39–41 **Advertisement.** The duty imposed on the creditor by the Act is simply "to advertise the sale," but that must be read along with the duty to take all reasonable steps to ensure that the price is the best that can be reasonably obtained. That implies that the advertisement must be reasonably adequate, both as to the period of it and the journals in which it appears, regard being had to the nature and location of the property and the market for it. There is no need to adopt the conditions as to advertisement which the Act imposes in sales under powers contained in a bond and disposition in security, but it would be difficult to challenge the adequacy of advertisement which complied with statutory requirements in the case of a comparable heritable security. Conveyancers, who are a cautious race, may tend to adopt that criterion. Certificates of advertisement by the publishers of the newspapers should be obtained and preserved.

39–42 **Best price.** The duty of the creditor to obtain the best price has already been considered in relation to sale under the powers contained in a bond and disposition in security,[70] and the same principles apply to a sale under the powers contained in a standard security but in the different circumstances that in the latter case there is no limit of time within which a sale may be effected. One of the more difficult problems is whether a conditional offer of the highest amount must necessarily be accepted in preference to a slightly lower offer which is unqualified. When a heritable property is being sold and the debtor has either left the property unoccupied or is not in a financial position to maintain it properly the result of accepting an offer subject to a condition which is not ultimately purified may be that the creditor has again to advertise and sell when the condition of the property may have deteriorated and the price originally offered without qualification may be unobtainable. In such circumstances the creditor may exercise his right of entering into possession and incur the expense of carrying out the necessary works of repair and maintenance, but there is a risk that the net price ultimately obtainable under deduction of that expense is less than the amount of the original unqualified offer. It would appear that the creditor is not bound to accept such a risk, particularly if the difference in price as between the two offers is relatively small: he is entitled to accept the best price obtainable for

---

[68]*Ibid.*, s. 25. See *Bank of Credit* v. *Thomson*, 1987 G.W.D. 10–341.
[69]*Ibid.*, s. 25.
[70]See para. 33–27.

the property in its existing condition without any suspensive or resolutive condition.

39–43 **Exposure to sale**. If the sale is made by public roup, the conditions in the articles of roup must not be such as will prejudice the price. On the general question of fair conditions and doing justice to the property, the decisions pronounced in relation to sales under the older forms of heritable security may be relevant.[71]

39–44 **Disposition on sale**. The contract of sale is carried into effect by a disposition by the selling creditor to the purchaser, which will bear to be granted in implement of the sale, and will be duly recorded or the interest of the purchaser registered. It will import an assignation to the purchaser of the warrandice contained or implied in the standard security and an obligation by the grantor of the standard security to ratify, approve and confirm the sale and disposition.[72] The creditor will have power to create common or mutual obligations on a sale in lots and for that purpose to execute and record a deed of declaration of conditions.[73]

Style 1

Disposition by creditor under a standard security

39–45   I, AB, (*designation*), whereas in virtue of a power of sale contained in a standard security for £   [or a maximum sum of £   ] (*or describe as in Note 2 to Schedule 4 to the 1970 Act*) by CD in my favour (*or in favour of GH to which I have now right*)[74] recorded in the Division of the General Register of Sasines for the County of   on   I advertised the subjects hereinafter disponed for sale [and sold the said subjects by private contract to JK, (*designation*), at the price of £   being the best price that could be reasonably obtained] *or* [and exposed the said subjects to public roup at   on   at the upset price of £   and that JK, (*designation*), being the only (*or* highest) offerer for the subjects was by the judge of the roup preferred to the purchase at the price of £   all as the (articles of roup dated   and relative minute of enactment and preference thereon dated   ) more fully bear]; and whereas the said JK has paid to me the said price of £   of which I acknowledge receipt, therefore I have sold and hereby dispone to the said JK heritably and irredeemably

---

[71] *Beveridge* v. *Wilson* (1829) 7 S. 279; *Wilson* v. *Stirling* (1843) 8 D. 1261; *Kerr* v. *McArthur's Trs.* (1848) 11 D. 301; *Park* v. *Alliance Heritable Security Co.* (1880) 7 R. 546; *Stewart* v. *Brown* (1882) 10 R. 192, *per* Lord Shand at 208; *Baillie* v. *Drew* (1884) 12 R. 199; *Shrubb* v. *Clark* (1897) 5 S.L.T. 125; *Davidson* v. *Scott*, 1915 S.C. 1120; *Aberdeen Trades Council* v. *Shipconstructors and Shipwrights Association*, 1949 S.C. (H.L.) 45, *per* Lord Reid at 65; 1949 S.L.T. 202 at 209; *Rimmer* v. *Thomas Usher & Son Ltd.*, 1967 S.L.T. 7.
[72] Conveyancing (Scotland) Act 1924, s. 41(1).
[73] 1970 Act, s. 37 applied to standard security by s. 32. As to procedure see para. 33–32.
[74] If the grantor does not have a recorded title to the standard security, insert here particulars of the last recorded title and specify the links in title whereby the grantor acquired right.

ALL and WHOLE   together with the whole
right, title and interest of the said CD and myself in and to the
said subjects; (*Reference to burdens, if any*); With entry at
          : And I assign the writs and have delivered those
specified in the inventory annexed and subscribed as relative
hereto (*special provisions re standard security being made
available to disponer, if required*): And I assign the rents: And I
bind myself to free and relieve the said JK of all feuduties and
public burdens: And I grant warrandice from my own facts and
deeds only and bind the said CD in absolute warrandice: [*stamp
duty clause*].

          (*To be attested*) (*Stamp as conveyance on sale*).

Protection of purchasers

39–46   When a creditor has sold the security subjects under a power
contained in a standard security and has granted a disposition bearing
to be in exercise of the power, which has been duly recorded, the
purchaser has certain statutory protections.

39–47   **(1) Pupillarity, minority or legal disability**. The proceedings for sale
under the powers contained in a standard security will be effectual
notwithstanding that any person on whom a calling-up notice or notice
of default was served was in pupillarity or minority or was subject to
any legal incapacity.[75]

39–48   **(2) Irregularities in procedure or debt having ceased to exist**. Where the
exercise of the power has been *ex facie* regular the title of a *bona fide*
purchaser for value will not be challengeable on the ground that the
debt secured has ceased to exist unless that fact appeared on the
record or was known to the purchaser prior to payment of the price.
Nor will the title be challengeable on the ground of any irregularity
relating to the sale or in any procedure preliminary thereto.[76] The
protection may extend to a failure by the creditor in his duty to
advertise the subjects adequately, but not if there has been no
advertisement at all since that would be *ex facie* irregular. If there is
any irregularity in procedure or breach of duty by the creditor, the
debtor may have a remedy in interdict or damages.[77]

Disburdenment of subjects sold

39–49   The effect of a sale by the creditor of the security subjects, followed
by a disposition to the purchaser or his nominee bearing to be granted
in implement of the sale and duly recorded or entered in the Land
Register, is that the subjects of sale are disburdened of all other
heritable securities and diligences ranking *pari passu* with, or

---

[75]Conveyancing (Scotland) Act 1924, s. 41(1) applied by s. 32 of the 1970 Act.
[76]Conveyancing (Scotland) Act 1924, s. 41(2) as amended by the 1970 Act, s. 38.
[77]*Park* v. *Alliance Heritable Security Co.* (1880) 7 R. 546; *Shrubb* v. *Clark* (1897) 5 S.L.T. 125.

postponed to, the security of the selling creditor.[78] There is no need in the case of a sale under a standard security to record certificates of surplus or no surplus as under the procedure in relation to existing bonds and dispositions in security.

Application of proceeds of sale

39–50   Section 27(1) of the 1970 Act sets out the order of priorities of ranking upon the proceeds of a sale of the security subjects by the creditor in a standard security. Payment should be made from the moneys available in the following order:

(1) all expenses properly incurred by the creditor in connection with the sale or any attempted sale;

(2) the whole amount due under any prior security to which the sale is not made subject;

(3) the whole amount due under the standard security held by the selling creditor and, in due proportion, the whole amount due under any recorded security ranking *pari passu* with it;

(4) any amounts due under any securities with a ranking postponed to that of the security of the selling creditor, according to their order of ranking;

(5) any balance will be paid to the person entitled to the security subjects at the time of the sale of the subjects, or any person authorised to give receipts for the proceeds of sale thereof.

Commentary on sections 26 and 27 of the 1970 Act

39–51   It is a reasonable deduction from section 27(2) that a *pari passu* creditor may sell under the powers in his standard security without the need to apply to the sheriff for a warrant to sell under section 11 of the Heritable Securities (Scotland) Act 1894 where another *pari passu* creditor is unwilling to co-operate. The recording of the disposition on sale disburdens the property of other *pari passu* securities, but the selling creditor must in terms of section 27(1)(c) give effect to the rights of other *pari passu* creditors in the application of the proceeds of sale.

Section 27 imposes upon the selling creditor the duty of adjudicating upon the order of ranking of other securities. That will usually be reasonably clear: if there is any doubt the matter can be resolved by an action of multiplepoinding. As to ranking of heritable securities generally, reference may be made to Chapter 42 *infra*.

The security subjects are not disburdened of a security which ranks prior to that of the selling creditor,[79] but the selling creditor has the same right as the debtor to redeem it. It is possible that the prior security was for a fixed term which has not expired so that the debtor is not entitled to redeem it, but in most circumstances the prior creditor

---

[78] 1970 Act, s. 26(1).
[79] *Ibid.*, s. 26.

will usually be prepared to accept early repayment so that the purchaser will obtain an unburdened title.

Consignation

39–52   It may not be possible to obtain a receipt or discharge for a payment which the selling creditor is required to make in terms of section 27(1) of the Act. For example, another creditor may be dead or absent, or the person who is entitled to the security subjects may be untraceable. In such circumstances the creditor may consign the amount due, so far as ascertainable, in the sheriff court[80] for the person appearing to have the best right thereto and lodge in court a statement of the amount consigned.[81] The Act offers no guidance as to the contents of the statement, but it is suggested that it should be reasonably informative. The relevant information will be available to the creditor at the time of consignation and it may save subsequent research if details of it are recorded when the money is consigned. Where the full amount due to another secured creditor is being consigned, the statement need only specify the amount consigned and the particulars of the recorded security in respect of which it is due. Where only partial payment is being made to a *pari passu* or postponed creditor, or where a balance is being consigned for the person entitled to the security subjects, the statement should record the price received and any interest received thereon and should show as deductions the amount of the expenses of the sale and any previous attempted sale and the amount paid to any prior creditor, and continue with the amounts paid in order of priority to the selling creditor, any *pari passu* creditor and any postponed creditor so far as necessary to bring out the amount of the payment or balance consigned.

Consignation thus made will operate as a discharge of the payment of the amount due and a certificate under the hand of the sheriff clerk will be sufficient evidence thereof.[82]

2. Entering into Possession

Legal basis of creditor's right

39–53   Under a bond and disposition in security, the legal basis of the creditor's right to take possession of the security subjects is the clause of assignation of rents which grounds an action of maills and duties. The standard security contains no clause of assignation of rents, but the creditor has a statutory right under standard condition 10(3) of the 1970 Act to enter into possession and uplift rents. The statutory right arises only on default within the meaning of standard condition 9, and

---

[80]The court of the sheriff having jurisdiction in terms of s. 29(1).
[81]s. 27(2).
[82]s. 27(3).

so it will only be on the occurrence of a default within the meaning of that condition that the right of entering into possession will be available to the creditor. The circumstances in which a creditor may be entitled to enter into possession and the powers available to him when he does so may have been varied or extended by contract when the standard security was granted. For example, it may have been stipulated that failure to make payment of interest or instalments of principal for a stated period after the due date would constitute default and entitle the creditor to take possession and the debtor may have undertaken to remove whenever default, either conventionally or in terms of the Act, occurred and may have agreed that a warrant of summary ejection might be taken against him in that event. It is thought that contractual arrangements of that kind are competent: although the standard conditions relating to the exercise of the powers of sale and foreclosure cannot be varied, there is no prohibition against altering the powers relating to the taking of possession. Further, apart from the creditor's statutory powers and any variations of them which may have been the subject of such antecedent contractual arrangements, the debtor may concede possession by agreement with the creditor at the time when the creditor wishes to take possession.

When right exercisable

39–54   The right of the creditor in a standard security to enter into possession under standard condition 10(1) and (3) of Schedule 3 to the 1970 Act will emerge:

(1) where there has been failure to comply with a calling-up notice,[83]

(2) where there has been failure to comply with any other requirement arising out of the security and the court has granted a warrant to the creditor to exercise the right,[84]

(3) where the proprietor of the security subjects has become insolvent and the court has granted a warrant to exercise the right.[84]

39–55   **(1) Non-compliance with calling-up notice.** When a calling-up notice has not been complied with the creditor may exercise the right of entering into possession without the need of any action in court.[85] As a matter of practice, however, an action declaratory of the right may be found necessary. Under the older procedure the creditor in a heritable security might interpel tenants from paying rents to the proprietor by a notice intimating the raising of an action of maills and duties, and the decree in the action, when also intimated, was authority to the tenants to make payment to the creditor.[86] It would appear that tenants would still be entitled to require a decision of court to authorise payment of rents to a person other than the proprietor.

[83]s. 20(1).
[84]s. 24(1).
[85]s. 20(1).
[86]Heritable Securities (Scotland) Act 1894, s. 3.

39–56   **(2) Non-compliance with requirement of security**. Standard condition 9(1)(*b*) refers to non-compliance with a "requirement arising out of the security." It is thought that this phrase is intended to refer primarily to a requirement made in a notice of default which has not been complied with.[87] When there has been such non-compliance, the creditor may apply to the court for a warrant to enter into possession and would normally seek also authority to exercise his rights under standard condition 10(4) and (5).[88] The court would presumably have discretion as to issuing the warrant and might perhaps allow the debtor time to purge the default. As regards onus of proof, the 1970 Act provides[89] that a certificate in accordance with the requirements in Schedule 7 to the Act may be lodged in court by the creditor and will be *prima facie* evidence of the facts contained in it. The certificate specifies the name and address of the creditor, the relevant standard security and the nature of the default alleged with full details of it, and is signed by the creditor or his solicitor.[90] The opinion is expressed that it would be competent for the creditor when making such an application to give notice by registered letter to tenants interpelling them from paying rents to the proprietor of the security subjects.[91] The decree of the court granting the application or counter-application will, when intimated to tenants, be authority for payment of rents to the creditor.[92]

39–57   **(3) Insolvency of proprietor**. The rights of the creditor as regards entering into possession in the circumstance that the proprietor of the security subjects has become insolvent are similar to the rights arising on non-compliance with a requirement arising out of the security. An application to the court for a warrant to enter into possession is required.

Specialities as to creditor and security subjects

39–58   **(1) Pari passu creditors**. A creditor in a standard security which ranks *pari passu* with another standard security may exercise the remedy of entering into possession notwithstanding that the creditor in the other security takes no action.[93]

39–59   **(2) Postponed creditors**. A postponed creditor may also exercise the right under his standard security, but a prior creditor may exercise his preferential right to take possession at any time.

---

[87] See para. 39–35.
[88] s. 24(1).
[89] s. 24(2).
[90] Sched. 7.
[91] A creditor taking an action of maills and duties under s. 3 of the Heritable Securities (Scotland) Act 1894 has such a right, and that section is not excluded in Sched. 8 to the 1970 Act.
[92] See para. 39–64.
[93] See para. 39–51.

39–60	**(3) Superiorities, ground annuals and registered leasehold property**. The right to enter into possession is available *mutatis mutandis* to a creditor in a standard security over a superiority, a ground annual or a registered lease.[94]

Style 2

Summary application for warrant to exercise remedies under section 24(1) of the 1970 Act[95]

39–61	Sheriffdom of			at
AB, (*designation*), Pursuer
against
CD, (*designation*), Defender

The pursuer craves the court
To find and declare (1) that the pursuer has right to enter into possession of the subjects known as (*identifying postal address*) being the subjects described in a standard security for £
[a maximum sum of £			] [*or otherwise describe as in note 2 to Schedule 4 of the 1970 Act*] by the said CD [*or EF, (designation)*,] in favour of the said AB [*or in favour of GH, (designation)*], to which the said AB has now right] recorded in the Register for the County of			on
[*or* the interest of the said AB as creditor by virtue of the said standard security being registered in the Land Register of Scotland in terms of Charge Certificate No.			] and to receive and recover the rents [feuduties] [ground annuals] of and from the said subjects, [(2) to ordain the said CD and any other persons occupying the said subjects to vacate the said subjects and to grant warrant for his and their summary ejection therefrom] and (3) that the pursuer has right to exercise in relation to the said subjects all other powers competent to a creditor in lawful possession of the said subjects by virtue of the Conveyancing and Feudal Reform (Scotland) Act 1970; and to find the defender liable in expenses.

CONDESCENDENCE

1. The pursuer is the creditor in a standard security for £			(*or as the case may be*) granted by the defender [*or EF*] in favour of the pursuer [*or in favour of GH, (designation)*, to which the pursuer has now right]. The pursuer's title to the said standard security is recorded in the Register of Sasines for the County of			on			[*or is registered in the Land Register of Scotland conform to Charge Certificate No.			*][96]
2. The defender is the proprietor of the property known as			being the subjects over which the said standard security was granted.
3. The pursuer served upon the defender on			a calling-up notice requiring payment of the sum of £

---

[94]1970 Act, ss. 9(8)(*b*) and 30(1) and (2).

[95]As to the remedies which may be sought by a summary application see para. 39–37.

[96]If the pursuer does not have a recorded or registered title, specify the last recorded or registered title and the links constituting the pursuer's right.

being the amount then due under the said standard security with interest thereon at the rate of   per cent per annum from the   day of   . A copy of the said notice with [an acknowledgment of receipt endorsed thereon] [or a certificate of posting attached thereto] is produced (or will be produced in the process to follow hereon). The said calling-up notice was not complied with timeously and has not since been complied with.

or

[3. The pursuer served on the defender on   a notice of default requiring fulfilment of certain obligations specified in a schedule thereto. A copy of the said notice with [an acknowledgment of receipt endorsed thereon] [or a certificate of posting attached thereto] is produced (or) [will be produced in the process to follow hereon.] The requirements of the said notice were not complied with timeously and have not been complied with.]

or

[3. The estates of the defender have been sequestrated conform to award by the [Court of Session] [Sheriff of   at   ] dated   or [The defender executed a trust deed in favour of JK, (designation), for behoof of his creditors dated   ].

PLEA IN LAW

The pursuer being entitled by virtue of section 20 (or 24) of the Conveyancing and Feudal Reform (Scotland) Act 1970 to apply for decree [and warrant] as craved and in the circumstances condescended on it is proper that the same should be granted, decree [and warrant] should be pronounced as craved.

In respect whereof

Proprietor in occupation

39–62   The creditor in a bond and disposition in security may bring an action of ejection against the proprietor of the security subjects who is in personal occupation of them but only if (a) there has been default by him in the punctual payment of interest or (b) there has been failure by him to pay the principal sum after requisition.[97] Where the security takes the form of an *ex facie* absolute disposition the right to eject the proprietor in occupation depends upon the contract, but usually a right to eject the proprietor on default is included in the qualifying agreement. Under a standard security the right to enter into possession is conferred, when the debtor is in default, by standard condition 10(3) of Schedule 3 to the 1970 Act. So, where there has been non-compliance with a calling-up notice, an action of ejection will be competent since the remedy in section 5 of the Heritable Securities (Scotland) Act 1894 is available.[98] Where there has been default within

---

[97] Heritable Securities (Scotland) Act 1894, s. 5.
[98] 1970 Act, s. 32.

the meaning of standard condition $9(1)(b)$, or the proprietor of the security subjects is insolvent, and in either case there has been default in punctual payment of interest, or where the contract relating to the security has included a condition that the creditor if entitled to enter into possession[99] may eject the proprietor who is in personal occupation, a separate action of ejection may be competent. In view of the decisions already cited[1] the action of ejection should be a separate action since a crave for ejection cannot competently be included in a summary application under section 24.[2]

Powers of creditor in possession

39–63   The powers of a creditor in possession of the security subjects will depend upon the process by which the right to take possession was obtained. (1) If possession has been taken by agreement with the debtor or proprietor, the powers of the creditor will be regulated by the terms of the agreement. (2) If possession follows on non-compliance with a calling-up notice, the creditor will have right to exercise all the powers conferred by standard condition 10, but only in accordance with the 1970 Act and any other enactment applying to heritable securities.[3] (3) If possession follows on a warrant issued by the court on default within the meaning of standard condition $9(1)(b)$ or on insolvency of the proprietor, the creditor will have the powers which the warrant authorises him to exercise.[4] In the following sub-paragraphs it is assumed that, where possession has been by arrangement or after warrant of the court, the full statutory powers have been given.

39–64   **(1) To recover feuduties, ground annuals or rents**. The creditor may receive or recover feuduties, ground annuals or rents of the security subjects or any part thereof.[5] His authority to do so will be the mandate of the proprietor (where possession is by agreement), the decree of declarator of his right (where there has been non-compliance with a calling-up notice and a mandate from the proprietor has not been given voluntarily) or the warrant of the court issued on an application made under section 24(1) of the Act. Intimation of the right should be made, where necessary, to the feuars, debtors in the ground annual or tenants. The right of the creditor, when duly intimated, will give him a preference over arresters or assignees whose diligence or title is used or acquired later than the recording date of

---

[99]See para. 39–37(B).
[1]In para. 39–37.
[2]See *Mountstar Metal Corporation* v. *Cameron*, 1987 S.L.T. (Sh.Ct.) 106.
[3]s. 20(1) and s.c. 10(1).
[4]s. 24(1).
[5]s.c. 10(3).

the standard security.[6] The creditor may pursue for payment by any appropriate form of action. In a question with the creditor recovering rents a tenant may set off any proper claims against the proprietor arising out of the tenancy,[7] but not claims arising from transactions unconnected with the tenancy.[8]

39–65   (2) **To let or grant leases.** A creditor who is in lawful possession of the security subjects (*i.e.* by agreement or due legal process), may let the security subjects or any part of them for a period not exceeding seven years.[9] If he wishes to let for any longer period, he may apply to the sheriff for a warrant to do so. The application will state the proposed tenant and the duration and conditions of the proposed lease, and will be served on the proprietor of the subjects and on any other heritable creditor having interest as such a creditor in the subjects.[9] The court has discretion to grant, vary or refuse the application.[10] The creditor in lawful possession will be deemed to hold an assignation of all rights and obligations of the proprietor relating to leases, or any permission or right of occupancy, granted in respect of the subjects or any part thereof[11] and, subject to the limitation above-mentioned as to leases for more than seven years, he has all the rights of the debtor in relation to the granting of leases or rights of occupancy over the security subjects and to the management and maintenance of those subjects.[12]

3. Repair, Reconstruction and Improvement

Basis of the right

39–66   In terms of standard condition 10(6) of Schedule 3 to the 1970 Act a creditor in a standard security may, where the debtor is in default within the meaning of standard condition 9, (1) effect such repairs and make good such defects as are necessary to maintain the security subjects in good and sufficient repair, (2) effect such reconstruction, alteration and improvement on the subjects as would be expected of a prudent proprietor to maintain their market value, and (3) enter on the subjects at all reasonable times for those purposes.

Practice

39–67   In practice this right will normally be exercised as incidental to or in preparation for exercise of the power of sale or leasing. A creditor who

---

[6] *Lang* v. *Hislop* (1854) 16 D. 908.
[7] *Marshall's Trs.* v. *Banks*, 1934 S.C. 405; 1934 S.L.T. 309.
[8] *Chambers' J.F.* v. *Vertue* (1893) 20 R. 257.
[9] 1970 Act, s. 20(3).
[10] *Ibid.*, s. 20(4).
[11] *Ibid.*, s. 20(5)(*a*).
[12] *Ibid.*, Sched. 3, s.c. 10(5). Standard condition 10(5) transfers the rights of the *debtor*, but, where the debtor is not the proprietor, the creditor may rely on the wider wording of s. 20(3) and (5) as regards letting and upon that of standard condition 10(6) as regards maintenance.

is in lawful possession of the security subjects has a similar right in terms of section 20(5)(*b*) of the 1970 Act. Usually the right will be exercised, except perhaps when the operations are carried out as preliminary to a sale of the subjects, after the authority of the court to enter into possession has been obtained. When the condition of a property has been allowed to deteriorate it is often difficult to differentiate between work required to repair or maintain it and operations which amount to reconstruction, alteration or improvement. The breadth of the powers given to the creditor obviate the need for such distinctions so long as the property remains substantially the same and the work can be justified as reasonable for the maintenance or restoration of its market value.

4. Poinding of the Ground

39–68   The right of a heritable creditor to poind the ground, *i.e.* to attach moveables on the security subjects, depends upon the existence of a *debitum fundi*.[13] The 1970 Act is silent on the matter but plainly a standard security will create a *debitum fundi*, and the rights available to the creditor under the Act are expressly in addition to any right conferred by any rule of law or otherwise.[14] The circumstances in which the right to poind the ground may be exercised and the extent of the preference obtained are unchanged by the Act.[15]

5. Adjudication

39–69   Adjudication also will be available to the creditor in a standard security as an additional remedy already existing. The Act makes no reference to it and the existing procedure (now very little used by a heritable creditor) remains unchanged.[16]

6. Foreclosure

The statutory provisions

39–70   Section 28 of the 1970 Act restates the procedure upon foreclosure in the exercise of rights arising from a standard security, and the provisions of the Act in that matter cannot be varied conventionally.[17]

When right exercisable

39–71   Foreclosure requires a decree of the sheriff court in an application for it made by the creditor. Such an application may be made where

---

[13]Ersk., *Inst.*, IV, i, 11.
[14]ss. 20(1) and 21(1).
[15]For an account of these, see Burns, 512 *et seq.*; *Encyclopaedia of the Laws of Scotland*, Vol. 11, 361 *et seq.*
[16]See Burns, 533, 534.
[17]s. 11(3).

the creditor has exposed the security subjects to sale: it is not competent if there has only been an attempt to sell by private bargain. The price at which the subjects were exposed must not have exceeded the amount due under the security and under any security ranking prior to or *pari passu* with it. The creditor must have failed to find a purchaser at that price or, having so failed, have succeeded in selling only a part of the subjects at a price which is less than the amount due under his security and under any prior or *pari passu* security. Further, a period of two months must have elapsed from the date of the first exposure before application to the court for a decree of foreclosure can be made.[18]

Exposure

39–72   It appears from the 1970 Act that there must in the first instance be an exposure of the *whole* security subjects in one lot. The exposure must be at a price not exceeding the actual amount due under the security and any prior or *pari passu* security. There is no objection to an exposure being tried in the first instance at a greater price, but, before an application for a decree of foreclosure will be competent, it must have been preceded by an unsuccessful exposure at a price which is equal to or less than the amount due under the security and any prior or *pari passu* security. In such a case it is suggested that the period of two months would run from the date of the first exposure at a price not exceeding the amount due, not the first exposure actually made at a higher price. On failure to find a purchaser for the whole subjects at a price not exceeding the amount due, exposure in lots may follow. If the price received for a part sold is insufficient to repay the amount due, an application for decree of foreclosure may be made.

Collateral securities

39–73   Where there is collateral security, such as a life policy, and the order of realisation of the securities held is not affected by contractual agreement or by the rules relating to catholic and secondary securities, the creditor may elect to realise the collateral security first, in which case the balance of the debt will then be the amount due for the purposes of foreclosure proceedings. Alternatively he may proceed by way of exposure of the heritable security in the first place, since he has the option of enforcing either of the securities, in which case it is thought that the full amount due is the relevant amount for the purposes of foreclosure. Normally the first method will be more convenient, but there could be circumstances in which it would be disadvantageous to realise the collateral security at the time when the creditor seeks repayment of the debt, *e.g.* if surrender of a life policy before maturity would involve significant loss.

---

[18] 1970 Act, s. 28(1).

Application to court

39–74   The creditor must lodge in court a statement setting out the whole amount due under the standard security. The debtor or proprietor may challenge the statement, but it will be sufficient for the purposes of the application if the creditor establishes to the satisfaction of the court that the amount stated is not less than the price at which exposure has been made or the price received on a sale of part.[19] These provisions introduce an element of flexibility. If there is room for argument as to the precise amount brought out in the statement, the decree of foreclosure will not be delayed so long as the disallowance of the charges in dispute will not result in the amount due being reduced to less than the price at which exposure has been made or a part sold, as the case may be. The only relevance of the argument as to adjustment of the amount in the statement will be in respect of the balance due under the personal obligation after imputing the value of the subjects.

Style 3

Application for decree of foreclosure

39–75   Sheriffdom of   at
AB, [*designation*], Pursuer
against
CD, [*designation*], Defender
The pursuer craves the court:
To grant a decree finding and declaring that, on the extract of such decree being duly recorded in the Register of Sasines [*or* the interest of the Pursuer under an extract of such decree being registered in the Land Register of Scotland] the Defender's right of redemption under a standard security for £   [*or* a maximum sum of £   ] [*or otherwise describe as in Note 2 to Schedule 4 to the Act*] by the said CD [*or* EF] in favour of the said AB [*or* in favour of GH to which the said AB has now right] recorded in the Register for the County of   on   has been extinguished, and that the said AB has right to the security subjects described in the said standard security, namely, ALL and WHOLE [*describe as in standard security*[20]] [*or where part has been sold* under exception of the part of the said subjects which has been sold in the exercise of the power of sale contained in the said standard security, namely, ALL and WHOLE (*describe part sold*)], but always with and under so far as valid and subsisting [*reference to conditions or clauses affecting security subjects (or unsold part thereof)*[21] *notwithstanding that the conditions or clauses are not referred to in the standard security*] and that at the price of £   [*last price at which exposed (or that price less price received for part sold)*]; and to direct that the expenses incurred and to be incurred by the

---

[19]*Ibid.*, s. 28(2).
[20]The description in the standard security should meet with the requirements as to description in s. 28(5) since they are the same as those required in a standard security (Note 1 to Sched. 2).
[21]See Land Registration (Scotland) Act 1979, Sched. 2, para. 4(*b*).

REMEDIES AGAINST SECURITY SUBJECTS

Pursuer in connection with this application and the proceedings to follow hereon be treated as expenses of sale; and to decern; and to grant warrant to record an extract of the decree to follow hereon in the Register of Sasines[21a]; and to find the Defender in the event of his appearing and offering opposition hereto liable in expenses.

CONDESCENDENCE

1. The Pursuer is the creditor in a standard security for £   [or as the case may be] granted by the defender [or by EF, (designation),] in favour of the Pursuer [or in favour of GH, (designation), to which the Pursuer has now right]. The Pursuer's title to the said standard security is recorded in the Register of Sasines for the County of   on   [or the interest of the pursuer as creditor by virtue of the said standard security is registered in the Land Register of Scotland in terms of Charge Certificate No.   ] [if the Pursuer does not have a recorded title, specify the last recorded title and deduce the pursuer's right].

2. The security subjects contained in the said standard security are as described in the crave.

3. So far as known to the Pursuer there is no heritable security secured over the said subjects other than the said standard security [if there are any prior or pari passu securities adjust accordingly].

4. The Pursuer served upon the Defender a calling-up notice [or notice of default] on   . A copy of the said notice with an acknowledgment of receipt endorsed thereon [or certificate of postage attached thereto] is produced. The said calling-up notice has [or the requirements of said notice of default have] not been complied with.

5. The said subjects were advertised for sale conform to certificate(s) of advertisement produced herewith.

6. The said subjects were exposed for sale within on   at a price of £   . The said price did not exceed the amount due under the said standard security [if any prior or pari passu securities add and the said prior and pari passu securities] as the said amount due is set out in the statement produced herewith. No offer was made for the subjects and the sale was adjourned. The articles of roup, with minute of adjournment annexed, are produced herewith. [If any part sale made, narrate appropriately specifying part sold and price.]

7. The Pursuer wishes to acquire an irredeemable vested right to the said subjects and he makes this application in terms of section 28 of the Conveyancing and Feudal Reform (Scotland) Act 1970.

PLEA IN LAW

The Pursuer having exposed the subjects described in the said standard security for sale at a price not exceeding the amount due under the said standard security [and under the said (prior or pari passu securities)] and having failed to find a purchaser [if part

---

[21a]If the security subjects are situated in an area which has become operational for the purposes of registration of title the interest of the pursuer as proprietor will induce first registration in the Land Register or the title of the defender may already have been registered therein: in such circumstances the crave should be amended to authorise registration in the Land Register.

sold add narrative of part sold and price] decree ought to be granted as craved.

In respect whereof

Service of application

39–76   The application should be served on the debtor, the proprietor of the security subjects (if a different person) and the creditor in any other heritable security affecting the security subjects as disclosed by a search of the Register of Sasines for 20 years preceding the last date to which the minute book of the Register has been completed at the time of the application or by an examination of the title sheet of the security subjects in the Land Register of Scotland.[22]

Remit

39–77   The court may order such intimation and inquiry as it thinks fit.[23] It is thought that this will, in accordance with the practice adopted in foreclosure proceedings under the Heritable Securities (Scotland) Act 1894, involve a remit to a reporter to inquire into the facts, examine the titles and satisfy himself as to the regularity of the procedure.

Allowance of time to debtor

39–78   The court has discretion to allow the debtor a period of not more than three months in which to pay the whole amount due.[24] This is a new provision: there is no corresponding discretion conferred in the Heritable Securities (Scotland) Act 1894.

Re-exposure

39–79   The court may appoint the security subjects or the unsold part thereof to be re-exposed to sale at a price to be fixed by the court. On re-exposure the creditor, if he wishes to acquire the subjects, must bid and purchase and obtain a title by granting a disposition in his own favour in implement of the sale: he is not entitled to adjourn the sale and seek a decree of foreclosure at the upset price on the re-exposure.[25]

Decree of foreclosure

39–80   The court may, instead of appointing re-exposure, grant a decree of

---

[22]1970 Act, s. 28(3) as amended by the Land Registration (Scotland) Act 1979, Sched. 2, para. 4(*a*).
[23]1970 Act, s. 28(4).
[24]*Ibid.*, s. 28(4).
[25]*Ibid.*, s. 28(4). It would appear that paras. (*a*) and (*b*) of the subsection are alternatives, so that a decree of foreclosure is inappropriate when the court has ordered the subjects to be re-exposed. But this may be too strict a construction.

foreclosure.[26] The decree will contain a declaration that, on due recording of the extract decree or registration of the pursuer's interest thereunder in the Land Register, any right to redeem the standard security has been extinguished and that the creditor has right to the security subjects or the unsold part thereof. In view of the express terms of subsection 28(5) it would seem incompetent for the creditor to use the extract decree unrecorded as a link in title, since it is only upon the extract decree being recorded or registration in the Land Register having followed upon it that the creditor has right to the security subjects. The subjects will be described by a particular description or by reference to a description as in Schedule D to the Conveyancing (Scotland) Act 1924 or in Schedule G to the Titles to Land Consolidation (Scotland) Act 1868 or in Schedule B to the Land Registration (Scotland) Rules 1980. A reference to burdens and conditions (if any) should be inserted. The price at which the creditor will have right to the subjects will be the price at which they were last exposed, under deduction of the price received for any part sold. The decree will contain a warrant authorising recording of the extract of the decree in the Register of Sasines,[26] or registration of the pursuer's title in the Land Register.

39–81 **Effect of decree.** When the extract of the decree is recorded in the Register of Sasines or its effect registered in the Land Register:

(1) any right to redeem the security will be extinguished and the creditor will have right to, and be vested in, the subjects as if he had received an irredeemable disposition of them, duly recorded, from the proprietor of the subjects at the date of recording of the extract decree,[27]

(2) the subjects will be disburdened of the standard security and all securities and diligences postponed to it, and

(3) the creditor will have the same right as the debtor to redeem any security prior to, or *pari passu* with, his own security.

Although stamp duty on standard securities and assignations and discharges thereof has been abolished,[28] it should be noted that an extract decree of foreclosure still requires to be stamped as a conveyance on sale, *ad valorem* duty being based on a sum equal to the value of the property.[29]

Personal obligation

39–82 A decree of foreclosure does not extinguish the personal obligation as regards any balance that may remain due after imputing towards the amount due the price at which the subjects have been acquired, *i.e.* by

---

[26]*Ibid.*, s. 28(5) as amended by Redemption of Standard Securities (Scotland) Act 1971, s. 1(f).
[27]*Ibid.*, s. 28(6) as amended by Redemption of Standard Securities (Scotland) Act 1971, s. 1(f).
[28]Finance Act 1971, s. 64.
[29]Stamp Act 1891, s. 54 as amended by Finance Act 1898, s. 6.

vesting in the creditor by virtue of the decree, and the price received for any part sold.[30] The creditor may pursue under the personal obligation for any such balance.

Title of creditor

39–83 The title acquired by the creditor under a decree of foreclosure will not be challengeable on the ground of any irregularity in the proceedings for foreclosure or on calling-up or default which preceded it.[31] The right to the debtor or proprietor to claim damages against the creditor in respect of any such irregularity, however, remains unaffected.[31]

39–84 **Infeftment**. As regards the procedure of foreclosure under the Heritable Securities (Scotland) Act 1894, the opinion has been expressed[32] that the decree will not give a feudalised title to the property unless the creditor is already infeft under his bond and disposition in security. It is suggested that the same effect will not result under the new procedure if the pursuer is a creditor who has right to a standard security but has not a recorded title. The reason for the distinction is that the effect of a recorded extract decree under section 8 of the 1894 Act was as if the disposition in security had been an irredeemable disposition as from the date of the decree: whereas the effect of the recorded extract decree under the 1970 Act is as if the creditor had received an irredeemable disposition from the proprietor of the subjects, duly recorded.[33] The effect of such a disposition is independent of the state of the creditor's security title.

39–85 **Effective date of creditor's absolute title**. The 1970 Act avoids the doubt which arose under the 1894 Act as to the effective date of the creditor's acquisition of an absolute title.[34] It is clear that the effective date of the creditor's absolute title is the date of recording of the extract decree, or entering the creditor's interest thereunder in the Land Register.[35]

---

[30]1970 Act, s. 28(7).
[31]*Ibid.*, s. 28(8).
[32]Burns, 539.
[33]1970 Act, s. 28(6)(*a*).
[34]See Burns, 539, 540.
[35]1970 Act, s. 28(6).

CHAPTER 40

SUBSEQUENT VARIATION, ASSIGNATION, TRANSMISSION, RESTRICTION, REDEMPTION AND DISCHARGE OF STANDARD SECURITIES

TRANSMISSIONS

(A) Creditor

(B) Debtor

RESTRICTION

REDEMPTION

DISCHARGES

REGISTERED INTERESTS IN RELATION TO
STANDARD SECURITIES

SUBSEQUENT VARIATIONS

The statutory facility

40–01   The Conveyancing and Feudal Reform (Scotland) Act 1970 provides for variation of the terms of a standard security in accordance with section 16 of the Act. The facility of effecting such variations is *not* available (1) if the alteration is one which may appropriately be effected by an assignation, discharge or deed of restriction or (2) if it involves an addition to, or extension of, the security subjects. In the latter case a new standard security will be required. Subject to these qualifications, any change in the terms of a standard security, whether in the personal obligation or the standard conditions, may be effected by a variation.

Recorded and unrecorded variations

40–02   The scheme of the legislation is that, if the alteration is being made in a recorded provision of a standard security, then the variation should also be recorded.[1] The recorded variation may be either separate from or endorsed on the standard security.[1] It has already been pointed out[2] that if the standard security has been originally framed in terms which permit of variation of any of its elements, an alteration of any of these will not require a recorded variation. That would not be an alteration *in* the provisions of the standard security but an alteration *made within* the existing provisions of it.

40–03   Where the personal obligation or any other provision of a standard security has been created in a separate unrecorded instrument, any variation *in the personal obligation or that provision* may be made in any appropriate form of deed, which need not be recorded.[3] If it is desired to alter a provision which is contained in the standard security itself, however, then a recorded variation will be the proper method. So, if the standard conditions have been varied in the recorded standard security, then, even if the personal obligation was contained in an unrecorded document, any change in the standard conditions should be recorded. It will avoid confusion if, in any standard security where the personal obligation is constituted by a separate instrument, any variations originally made in the standard conditions are not recorded.

40–04   Section 16 is not mandatory and alterations in the separate contract between creditor and debtor may be made in any other way. For example, an additional personal obligation may be granted in the form of a bond of corroboration. Singular successors in the creditor's

---

[1] 1970 Act, s. 16(1).
[2] In para. 37–10.
[3] 1970 Act, s. 16(2).

interest in the standard security are not affected, since an assignation carries to the assignee the benefit of all corroborative or substitutional obligations, however effected.[4] One major advantage of the section, however, is that it enables provisions created by unrecorded documents to be altered by unrecorded documents and the altered contract or conditions will be covered by the heritable security. In this connection it should be observed that subsection (2) of section 16 only applies where "the personal obligation or any other provision (including any standard condition) relating to the security has been created or specified in a deed which has not been recorded," and permits variation by unrecorded document only in respect of "an alteration in that personal obligation or provision." If an unrecorded deed of variations has been prepared at the time when the standard security was granted and alters some, but not all, of the standard conditions, it may be contended that the unaltered standard conditions cannot subsequently be varied so as to be covered by the security unless by way of a recorded variation. The unaltered conditions have been imported expressly in the recorded standard security, but have neither been created nor specified in the unrecorded deed of variations. To avoid any such question it is suggested that the whole of the standard conditions should be "specified" by a general reference in the unrecorded deed of variations.[5]

Deduction of title in variations

40–05   In recorded variations deduction of title is required where either the creditor is not the original creditor and does not have a recorded title to the security[6] or the grantor of the variation does not have a recorded title to the security subjects.[7] In the case of an unrecorded variation in such circumstances there is no need to narrate or deduce the title of the creditor to the security nor the title of the debtor to the security subjects.[8] So long as the parties to an unrecorded variation have right to grant and consent to it respectively, the variation will be effective. As a matter of sound conveyancing practice, however, it is recommended that the devolution of the title of either party who is not the original debtor or creditor should be narrated in order to provide within the variation *prima facie* evidence of title to enter into it.

---

[4]*Ibid.*, s. 14(2).
[5]See for example styles in paras. 37–27 and 38–29.
[6]1970 Act, Sched. 4, Note 1.
[7]*Ibid.*, Sched. 4, Note 6.
[8]Notes 1 and 6 to Sched. 4 apply only to recorded variations.

Styles of Variations[8a]

Style 1

Recorded variation (endorsed)—additional advance by creditor—both parties infeft[9]

40–06   I, AB, (*designation*), agree that the foregoing standard security granted by me in favour of CD recorded in the Register for the County of   on   (*if any previous variation*, as varied) shall with effect from   be varied so that the sum undertaken to be paid by me and thereby secured shall be increased by £   to a total sum of £   : And I, CD, (*designation*), consent to the variation hereby effected.

(To be attested)

Style 2

Recorded variation (endorsed)—increase in rate of interest—grantor infeft—creditor uninfeft

40–07   I, AB, (*designation*), agree that the foregoing standard security granted by CD in favour of EF recorded in the Register for the County of   on   (*if any previous variation*, as varied) shall with effect from   be varied so that the rate of interest payable thereunder shall be increased from   per centum per annum to   per centum per annum: And I, GH, (*designation*), the sole trustee now acting under deed of trust by JK, (*designation*), in favour of me the said GH and LM, (*designation*), dated   and registered in the Books of Council and Session on   and as such trustee the creditor now in right of the said standard security consent to the variation hereby effected: Which standard security was last vested in the said JK whose title thereto was recorded in the said Register of Sasines on   and from whom I as trustee foresaid acquired right by (one) the said deed of trust and (two) minute of resignation by the said LM dated   and registered in the Books of Council and Session on   .[10]

(To be attested)

Style 3

Recorded variation (endorsed)—original debtor having died and loan continued to his widow (uninfeft)

[8a]Styles 1 to 3 and 5 and 6 are applicable where the standard security is recorded in the Register of Sasines. For appropriate variations where the interest of the creditor is registered in the Land Register see para. 40–75.

[9]This form is appropriate where the standard security was for a fixed amount and the personal obligation did not extend to further advances. Where the personal obligation in the original standard security was wide enough to cover further advances a receipt or other unrecorded document evidencing the further advance is sufficient—see para. 40–09.

[10]1970 Act, Sched. 4, Note 1.

40-08

I, Mrs. BB, (*designation*), widow of AB, (*designation*), agree that the foregoing standard security granted by the said AB in favour of the X Building Society recorded in the Register for the County of   on   shall with effect from   be varied so that I the said BB undertake the whole obligations undertaken by the said AB in the said standard security so far as they remain outstanding, the balance due thereunder as at   (*date from which variation effective*) being £   , and shall be entitled to the whole rights competent to the said AB thereunder and that on the whole terms and conditions contained in the said standard security, the security subjects to which the said standard security relates being last vested in the said AB whose title thereto was recorded in the said Register of Sasines on   and from whom I acquired right by (one) confirmation by the sheriff of   in favour of me the said BB as executor-nominate of the said AB dated at   on   and (two) docket on certificate of said confirmation by me as executor foresaid in favour of myself as an individual dated   [11]: And I the said BB consent to registration for execution.[12] And we the said X Building Society, (*designation*), consent to the variation hereby effected, [and we discharge the said AB and his executors and representatives of all liability under the said standard security].[13]

(*To be attested*)

Unrecorded variations—form

40-09

The 1970 Act imposes no requirements of form upon a deed giving effect to a variation which is not recorded, save that it will be in any appropriate form.[14] Since the document making the variation will alter the terms of a probative deed and will relate to the heritable security, the normal rule of conveyancing practice is that it should be executed with the same solemnities as the deed which it alters.[15] It is recommended that that practice be adopted and that the variation should be executed in duplicate, one copy to be retained by the creditor with the titles of the security and the other by the debtor. Where the personal obligation in the standard security has been expressed in terms wide enough to cover further advances, these may

---

[11]*Ibid.*, Sched. 4, Note 6.

[12]In law, without any deed effecting the variation, liability for the amount of the advance outstanding at the date of death of AB will have transmitted against Mrs BB, at least to the extent of the value of the whole estate bequeathed to her, as a person who has taken the security subjects by bequest, but unless she signs an agreement to transmission of the obligation summary diligence against her may not be competent (Conveyancing (Scotland) Act 1924, s. 15(2)). Moreover, the obligation undertaken by her in the variation will extend to her whole assets, not only the estate bequeathed to her by AB.

[13]The above style may be used where the security subjects have been bequeathed absolutely to the widow and she desires the loan to continue. A notice of title can be expede on behalf of the widow subject to the security, although the style is prepared on the basis that title has not yet been so completed. The discharge of the personal obligation of the deceased will enable the administration of his estate to be completed. Since the variation is endorsed on the standard security it may be preferred to have the discharge of the deceased's personal obligation in the form of a separate document.

[14]1970 Act, s. 16(2).

[15]A.G. Walker and N.M.L. Walker, *Law of Evidence in Scotland*, 303.

be evidenced by a simple receipt or other unrecorded document which is not technically a variation at all. The principle is that the debtor has, in the standard security, undertaken personal liability for any further advances and the grant of security covers these also. So all that is required on the occasion of a further advance being made is to record in writing evidence of the further advance having been made, when the original obligation and grant of security will automatically extend to the further advance.[16] Two qualifications should be made of that general statement, *viz.*— (1) A search in the property and personal registers should be instructed on the occasion of the further advance being made to ensure that there have been no deeds or diligences registered which may affect the security subjects or the debtor. (2) If intimation of the creation of a further security has been made to the creditor, section 13 of the 1970 Act will have restricted his preference under the existing standard security and the further advance should in practice be secured by a new standard security which will rank after the intimated security and should in turn be intimated to the creditor in the second security. Similarly, where the creditor has a reserved power to alter any obligation of the debtor, *e.g.* where a building society has a reserved power to increase the rate of interest or monthly payments, no agreement by the debtor is required: an official letter to the debtor notifying the increase will suffice.

Style 4

Unrecorded variation (endorsed)—alteration of repayment period

40–10   C Holdings Limited, (*designation*), ("C"), B and Company Limited (*designation*), ("B"), and A and Company Limited, (*designation*), ("A") the parties to the foregoing Agreement dated   WHEREAS four of the eight six-monthly instalments specified in Clause   of the said Agreement have been duly paid and C has agreed to extend the period of repayment of the balance of the Loans THEREFORE the parties AGREE—

1. B and A jointly and severally undertake to repay the balance of the Loans amounting to £   by six equal six-monthly instalments, each instalment being one sixth of the said balance, on or before (*one year later than original final payment date*), the first such instalment to be repaid on and the last such instalment to be repaid on [unless the loans are repaid earlier in accordance with the said Agreement]. The said Clause   shall no longer apply.

2. For   (*original final payment date*) where it occurs in each of Clauses   there shall be substituted (*one year later*).

3. The whole other provisions of the said Agreement shall apply to the said Agreement as hereby varied.

(*To be attested*)

---

[16] For a style of receipt see Style 6, para. 40–12.

Style 5

Unrecorded variation—to accumulate interest[17]

40–11   I, AB, (*designation*), WHEREAS I granted a standard security
in favour of CD, (*designation*), recorded in the Register for the
County of   on   for all sums due
and that might become due by me to the said CD in terms of an
agreement between me and the said CD dated
with interest thereon as provided in the said agreement AND
WHEREAS the said interest is now in arrears to the extent of
£   and I have agreed to grant these presents THEREFORE
I agree that (1) the said sum of £   shall be added to the
principal sum now due by me to the said CD amounting to
£   making a total sum of £   and that with effect from
             interest shall be payable at the rate provided in
the said agreement upon the said last mentioned sum of £
until repayment thereof and (2) these presents shall in no way
prejudice my liability for all other sums that may become due by
me to the said CD and the security created by the said standard
security shall extend to the said sum of £   and all such other
sums: [And I consent to registration hereof for execution]: And I
the said CD agree to the variation hereby effected.[18]

(To be attested)

Style 6

Receipt for further advance—building society[19]

40–12   I, AB, (*designation*), hereby acknowledge to have received
from   Building Society, (*designation*), a further
advance of £   on the terms of and secured by the standard
security granted by me in favour of the said Society over
(*description of property by postal address or other identifying
description*) and recorded in the Register for the County of
             on   : And I agree that the
monthly payment due by me to the said Society under the said
standard security shall as from   be £   .

(To be attested)

ASSIGNATIONS

The statutory provisions

40–13   In terms of section 14 of the 1970 Act a standard security may be
transferred, in whole or in part, by an assignation either in Form A
(separate) or Form B (endorsed) of Schedule 4 to the Act. When the
assignation is recorded the security, or the part assigned, will be vested

---

[17]Applicable where the standard security is for all sums due and to become due but no provision
for compound interest.
[18]In a case where the creditor has changed, insert narrative of devolution of title from original
creditor.
[19]Appropriate where the standard security has embraced further advances. This is not strictly a
variation—see para. 40–09.

in the assignee as effectually as if the security, or the part of it, had been granted in his favour. The assignation conveys to the grantee, without special mention, (1) the grantor's right to the writs, (2) the benefit of all corroborative or substitutional obligations for the debt, whether contained in any deed or arising by operation of law or otherwise, (3) the right to recover from the debtor expenses properly incurred by the creditor in connection with the security, and (4) the benefit of all notices served and all procedure instituted by the creditor in respect of the security.

Personal obligation

40–14   Where the personal obligation has been created in the standard security, an assignation of the standard security transfers both the debt and the security and all corroborative or substitutional obligations. Where the personal obligation has been constituted in a separate instrument, the effect of an assignation of the security in the statutory form is less clear. Section 14(1) makes it clear that the security is assigned and section 14(2) includes corroborative or substitutional obligations within the scope of what is transferred, but the original principal obligation does not fall appropriately within any of these terms. It will probably be seldom that a standard security in Form B is assigned, but it is suggested that, to avoid doubts, an assignation of a standard security of that kind should contain also (either in the recorded assignation or in a separate document) an assignation of the debt and any variations of it.[20]

Securities for maximum or uncertain amounts

40–15   Where the standard security has been granted for a maximum or uncertain amount, it can only be assigned to the extent of the sum outstanding at the time of assignation.[21] That is in accordance with former law and practice.[22] The amount outstanding should be stated in the assignation.

Deduction of title

40–16   Where the grantor of the assignation, although not the original creditor, has a recorded title to the standard security assigned, no specification of his title is necessary.[23] Where the grantor of the assignation is not the original creditor and does not have a recorded title, a deduction of title should be inserted.[24]

---

[20]See Style 10, para. 40–24.
[21]1970 Act, Sched. 4, Forms A and B and Note 2.
[22]See Burns, 576.
[23]1970 Act, Sched. 4, Note 1, last para.
[24]Ibid., Sched. 4, Note 1.

Advantages and disadvantages of assignation

40–17   One of the demerits of the *ex facie* absolute conveyance as a security
was the difficulty of assigning it. The introduction of the standard
security largely removes that difficulty, but conveyancers will now have
to consider the advantages and disadvantages of taking a simple
assignation as an alternative to a discharge and a new standard
security. The principal considerations for and against taking an
assignation are:

Benefits. (1) Retention of existing ranking. (2) Reduced expense.

Disadvantages. (1) The liability upon the assignor of warranting the
validity of the security.[25] (2) The risk to the assignee of the debt having
been repaid, in whole or in part, by payments not appearing on
record.[26] In the case of debts for a fluctuating amount the assignee
should require a formal certificate determining the amount outstanding
as provided for in the standard security and it may be prudent to
confirm that the debtor agrees with the amount. (3) If the owner of the
security subjects was not the grantor of the standard security and the
personal obligation has not transmitted against him, the assignee will
not have the owner's personal obligation, unless a bond of corroboration is taken.[27]

Right to assignation

40–18   The legal principles relating to the right of the debtor upon
repayment to require an assignation instead of a discharge as already
settled in connection with bonds and dispositions in security,[28]
probably apply also to a standard security. Where the debt is a
fluctuating amount the assigning creditor will be accepting the
responsibility of certifying and warranting the balance due, and it may
be advisable to provide in the original standard security that the
creditor will not be obliged to grant an assignation. If it is granted the
account should be frozen during the period between the certification of
the amount due and the recording of the assignation.

Assignation of standard security for fluctuating amount

40–19   In general an assignation of a standard security for a fluctuating
amount is undesirable. The personal obligation of the debtor will have
been created in favour of the original creditor and will have covered
sums becoming due to him by the debtor: after assignation of the
standard security there will normally be no further course of dealing
between these parties. So if any further advances are to be made by

---

[25]*Reid* v. *Barclay* (1879) 6 R. 1007.
[26]*Jackson* v. *Nicoll* (1870) 8 M. 408.
[27]See para. 33–45 for discussion of policy in relation to assignation of bond and disposition in
security.
[28]See para. 33–45(2).

the assignee and are to be covered by the security, then (a) if the personal obligation was contained in the original standard security either a recorded variation or a new standard security will be necessary to secure the further advances or (b) if the personal obligation was contained in a separate instrument an unrecorded instrument will be necessary to constitute the new personal obligation for the further advances or a new standard security may be granted in respect of them. In practice it will probably be simpler and clearer to discharge the existing standard security and have a new comprehensive standard security.

Confusion

40–20   Since a standard security is on the face of it a security deed, it will be extinguished *confusione*. This may be of importance in a reconstruction of associated companies where there is an inter-company loan secured by a standard security which is to remain after the reconstruction. It will be necessary to ensure that at no stage in the procedure do the assets and liabilities of the creditor and debtor companies merge, even for a brief period; if that happens it will be necessary to create the standard security afresh.

<h2 style="text-align:center">Styles of Assignations[29]</h2>

Style 7

Assignation (separate)—fixed amount—grantor infeft

40–21   I, AB, *(designation)*, in consideration of £   hereby
            assign to CD, *(designation)*, a standard security for £   by
            EF in my favour (*or if grantor is not original creditor* in favour of
            GH)[30] recorded in the Register for the County of
            on   (*if only part assigned*, but only to the extent
            of £   of principal): With interest from   .
                                                            (*To be attested*)

Style 8

Assignation (endorsed)—fixed amount—grantor infeft

40–22   I, AB, *(designation)*, in consideration of £   hereby
            assign to CD, *(designation)*, the foregoing standard security by
            EF in my favour (*or if grantor is not original creditor*, in favour of
            GH) recorded in the Register for the County of

---

[29]Styles 7 to 16, based on the 1970 Act, Sched. 4, Forms A and B, are applicable where the standard security is recorded in the Register of Sasines. For appropriate variations where the interest of the creditor has been registered in the Land Register see para. 40–76.

[30]No specification of title required since grantor infeft—1970 Act, Sched. 4, Note 1, last para.

on   [31] (*if only part assigned*, but only to the extent
of £   of principal)[32]: With interest from   .

(*To be attested*)

Style 9

Assignation (separate)—uncertain amount—grantor original creditor[33]

40–23   We, C Finance Company Limited (*designation*), in consideration of £   hereby assign to D Limited, (*designation*), a
standard security by A Limited in our favour for all sums due and
to become due by the said A Limited to us in respect of moneys
lent in connection with a building development on subjects at
recorded in the Register for the County of
on   to the extent of £
being the amount now due thereunder[34]: With interest from

(*To be attested*)

Style 10

*Assignation (endorsed)—uncertain amount—original personal obliga-
tion in separate instrument—grantor infeft*[35]

40–24   We, C Holdings Limited, (*designation*), in consideration of
£   hereby assign to D Finance Company Limited,
(*designation*), the foregoing standard security by A and Company
Limited, (*designation*), in our favour for securing the obligation
to us of B and Company Limited, (*designation*), and the said A
and Company Limited in terms of Agreement between us and the
said B and Company Limited and A and Company Limited dated
, the said standard security being recorded in the
Register for the County of   on   ,
to the extent of £   being the amount now due under the
said Agreement: With interest from   : [And we
assign to the said D Finance Company Limited our whole rights
and interests under the said Agreement and also the said
Agreement itself, to the effect of substituting the said D Finance
Company Limited in our full right and place in the premises with
effect from   ].[36]
(*To be attested*)

---

[31]Even in the endorsed form the standard security should be described by reference to parties and
recording date. That facilitates identification for recording purposes.
[32]The endorsed form will not usually be advisable if the assignation is partial unless the balance has
been discharged.
[33]Assignation of standard security in Style 12, para. 37–26.
[34]1970 Act, Sched. 4, Form A: see para. 40–15.
[35]Assignation of standard security in Form B with separate Agreement.
[36]It may be necessary to assign also the loan agreement so that D Finance Co. Ltd. will have right
to the personal obligation. That may be combined with the assignation of the standard security but it
will probably be desired to keep the personal obligation unrecorded. It should be intimated to B &
Co. Ltd. and A & Co. Ltd. If further advances are to be made by the assignee and covered by the
security the assignation of the loan agreement should also include the creation of the personal
obligation of B & Co. Ltd. and A & Co. Ltd. for further advances. See para. 40–19.

Style 11

Assignation (separate)—fixed amount—uninfeft executor of original creditor

40–25   I, AB, (*designation*), executor nominate of GH, (*designation*), conform to confirmation[37] by the sheriff of   dated at   on   in consideration of £   hereby assign to CD, (*designation*), a standard security for £   by EF in favour of the said GH recorded in the Register for the County of   on   (*if only part assigned*, but only to the extent of £   of principal): With interest from   : Which standard security was last vested in the said GH as aforesaid and from whom I as executor foresaid acquired right [to the extent foresaid] by the said confirmation.

(*To be attested*)

Ranking clauses

40–26   It may be desired to create different rights of ranking when a standard security is partially assigned, the ranking being determined either as between the grantor for the retained part and the assignee, or between different assignees of parts.

Style 12

Clause of ranking

40–27   [*Insert in partial assignation before the testing clause*] Declaring that these presents shall have the effect of granting to the said (*assignee*) a security and preference over the subjects described in the said standard security and the rents thereof and the price thereof in the event of a sale prior and preferable [*or* after and postponed] to the security and preference held by me [*or* held by XY, (*designation*)], as in right of the remainder of the sum secured by the said standard security.

Alterations in personal obligation, security subjects or ranking

40–28   Since warrandice *debitum subesse* is implied in an assignation, the release of any previous personal obligants for the amount secured should be referred to in an assignation. Similarly reference should be made to any part of the original security that has been released. Also, if any deferment of the original ranking has been made, that should also be mentioned.

Style 13

Clause where personal obligation has been discharged

40–29   [*Insert before testing clause*] But declaring that the personal

---

[37]The confirmation must include the whole debt assigned.

obligation of the said (*original grantor*)[38] has been discharged conform to discharge by me [*or* XY] dated , the obligation of LM, (*designation*), having previously[38a] been substituted therefor conform to agreement by him *in gremio* of disposition by PQ, (*designation*), in his favour recorded in the said Register of Sasines on [*or* bond of corroboration by him dated , *or agreement or other document, as the case may be*].

Style 14

Clause where part of security subjects released

40–30   [*Insert before testing clause*] but excepting from the security hereby assigned that part thereof disburdened by deed of restriction granted by me [*or* XY] recorded in the said Register of Sasines on namely, ALL and WHOLE (*describe part disburdened*).

Style 15

Clause where part of sum due has already been assigned with prior ranking

40–31   [*Insert before testing clause*] But these presents shall have the effect only of conferring on the said (*assignee*) a security and preference over the subjects described in the said standard security and the rents thereof and the price thereof in the event of a sale after and postponed to the security and preference held by XY, (*designation*), as in right of the remainder of the sum secured by the said standard security.[39]

Style 16

Combined partial assignation and partial discharge

40–32   I, AB, (*designation*), (first) in consideration of £ hereby assign to CD, (*designation*), a standard security for £ by EF, (*designation*), in my favour [*or if grantor is not original creditor* in favour of GH] recorded in the Register for the County of on but only to the extent of £ of principal: With interest from ; and (second) in consideration of £ paid by the said EF [*or if debtor not original debtor* JK, (*designation*)], hereby discharge the said standard security, but only to the

---

[38]If any other person has become bound under the personal obligation, *e.g.* a purchaser of the security subjects—see para. 40–42—and his obligation has been discharged, that should also be mentioned in the assignation by an appropriate adjustment of the style.

[38a]Necessary to avoid extinction of standard security.

[39]A fuller narrative of the assignation whereby the prior ranking was constituted may be inserted if desired.

extent of the balance of £   of principal: (*Clause of deduction of title, if required*).[40]

(*To be attested*)

Arrears of interest

40–33 The right to arrears of interest will not be carried to the assignee by an assignation in the statutory form. If the assignee is to have right to arrears of interest, they must be specifically assigned, *e.g.* "with interest from   and also all arrears and accumulations of interest due and unpaid at the date of this assignation."

Variations

40–34 Where the personal obligation has been constituted in the standard security itself, any subsequent variation will usually be in the nature of a corroborative or substitutional obligation and will be carried by an assignation of the standard security without requiring to be specially mentioned. Where the personal obligation has been created in a separate instrument and has subsequently been varied then (1) if the debt is assigned in a deed separate from the assignation of the standard security, the variations should be specified or referred to, and (2) if the debt is assigned in the assignation of the security it is suggested that the safest practice is to specify the variations although that may not be strictly necessary.

TRANSMISSIONS[41]

(A) Creditor

Succession—heritable or moveable—legal rights

40–35 The provisions of enactments relating to a bond and disposition or assignation in security apply to a standard security so far as not inconsistent with the 1970 Act or excluded in Schedule 8 to that Act. So the provisions of section 117 of the Titles to Land Consolidation (Scotland) Act 1868 as amended by section 34 of and Schedule 3 to the Succession (Scotland) Act 1964 are applicable to a standard security. Accordingly a standard security is moveable in the creditor's succession but remains heritable as regards the fisc and for the purposes of legal rights. Since there are no legal rights in heritable property, it follows that standard securities are not subject to legal rights and should be excluded from the computation for the purpose of calculating *jus relictae*, *jus relicti* or legitim.[42]

---

[40]To be recorded with two warrants of registration, one on behalf of CD and one on behalf of EF (or JK).

[41]This chapter relates to successions opening on or after September 10, 1964: for successions opening before that date see Vol. IV.

[42]See Meston, *The Succession (Scotland) Act 1964*, 46.

Procedure

40–36   A standard security forming part of the estate of a deceased creditor should be entered in the inventory of the estate and included in the confirmation. The executor, if he desires to complete title to the standard security, may expede a notice of title in appropriate form using the confirmation as a link and record the notice of title in the Register of Sasines. If the standard security has been transferred by the executor to a beneficiary by a docket in accordance with section 15(2) of the Succession (Scotland) Act 1964 the beneficiary may complete title by expeding a notice of title using the confirmation and the docket as links and record the notice of title in the Register of Sasines. In the above cases the notice of title will be in Form No. 3 of Schedule B to the Conveyancing (Scotland) Act 1924 (where the deceased had a recorded title to the standard security) or Form No. 5 of that Schedule (where the deceased did not have a recorded title to the standard security). If the interest of the deceased as creditor in the standard security had been registered in the Land Register the number of the charge certificate should be specified in the inventory and confirmation and the executor or beneficiary, as the case may be, can register his interest by making application on Form 2 with production of the appropriate links evidencing his right, no notice of title being required.[43]

It will seldom be necessary to complete title to standard securities for fluctuating or uncertain amounts, since these are normally granted in favour of banks or commercial lenders or companies, but if the creditor was an individual who has died the above procedure may be followed but the amount outstanding at the date of death should be specified in the confirmation and in any notice of title which follows.

Style 17

Notice of title—standard security for fixed amount—Form A—trustees or executors nominate of creditor

40–37   Be it known that AB, (*designation*), CD, (*designation*), and EF, (*designation*), as testamentary trustees [*or* executors nominate] of GH, (*designation*), have right to a standard security for the sum of £   by JK, (*designation*), in favour of the said GH dated   and recorded in the division of the General Register of Sasines for the County of on   ; which standard security was last vested in the said GH as aforesaid and from whom the said AB, CD and EF as trustees [*or* executors] foresaid acquired right by his trust disposition and settlement dated   and registered in the Books of Council and Session on   [*or* confirmation by the sheriff of   dated at on   ]: Which last recorded title

---

[43]Land Registration (Scotland) Act 1979, s. 3(6).

and an extract of which subsequent writ [*or* and subsequent writ] have been presented to me XY, (*designation*), Notary Public [*or* solicitor].

(*To be attested*)

Style 18

Notice of title—standard security for uncertain amount—Form A— executor dative

40–38   Be it known that AB, (*designation*), as executor dative of EF, (*designation*), has right to a standard security for all sums due and that might become due by CD, (*designation*), in respect of moneys advanced by the said EF to the said CD in connection with his business of   , the amount due thereunder at the date of death of the said EF being £   of principal, granted said standard security by the said CD in favour of the said EF dated   and recorded in the division of the General Register of Sasines for the County of   on   ; which standard security was last vested in the said EF as aforesaid and from whom the said AB as executor foresaid acquired right by confirmation by the sheriff of   dated at   on   ; Which standard security and subsequent writ have been presented [*as in Style 17*].

(*To be attested*)

Style 19

Notice of title—standard security for uncertain amount—Form B— executor

40–39   Be it known that AB, (*designation*), as executor [nominate] [dative] of EF, (*designation*), has right to a standard security by CD, (designation), in favour of the said EF dated   and recorded in the division of the General Register of Sasines for the County of   on   for all sums payable and that might become payable by the said CD to the said EF in terms of an Agreement between the said CD and the said EF dated   , the amount due thereunder at the date of death of the said EF being £   of principal; which standard security was last vested in the said EF as aforesaid and from whom the said AB as executor foresaid acquired right by confirmation by the sheriff of   at   on   ; Which standard security and subsequent writ have been presented to me XY, (*designation*), Notary Public [*or* solicitor].

(*To be attested*)

Style 20

Notice of title to standard security—Form A—beneficiary

40–40   Be it known that AB, (*designation*), has right to a standard

security for the sum of £   by CD, (*designation*), in favour of the now deceased EF, (*designation*), dated
and recorded in the division of the General Register of Sasines for the County of   on   ; which standard security was last vested in the said EF as aforesaid and from whom the said AB acquired right by (1) confirmation by the sheriff of   at   dated
in favour of GH, (*designation*), as executor [nominate] [dative] of the said EF and (2) docket on certificate of said confirmation by the said GH as executor foresaid in favour of the said AB dated
     ; which standard security and subsequent writs have been presented to me XY, (*designation*), Notary Public [*or* solicitor].

(To be attested)

(B) Debtor

Transmission on death of the debtor

40–41   The liability of the debtor under a standard security is heritable in succession on the death of the debtor, but is a debt of the deceased which must be satisfied from his general estate even if the security is insufficient. It will be inserted in the inventory of the debtor's estate as a burden on the security subjects. If summary diligence is to be competent against the successor who becomes liable for the debt, an agreement executed by him will be required as in the case of a bond and disposition in security.[44] The agreement may be in the same form as in paragraph 33–56 *supra*, with the substitution of references to the standard security for references to the bond and disposition in security.

Transmission on sale of security subjects

40–42   When the security subjects are sold under burden of the standard security the position is similar to that under the former law when the heritable security was in the form of a bond and disposition in security.[45] The sale of the security subjects will not discharge the personal obligation of the seller as the grantor of the standard security. The provisions for transmission of the obligation against the purchaser by agreement in the disposition contained in section 47 of the Conveyancing (Scotland) Act 1874 as amended by section 15 of the Conveyancing (Scotland) Act 1924 apply to a standard security. Alternatively, the new personal obligation can be created in a bond of corroboration which will not require to be recorded even if the original personal obligation has been expressed in the recorded standard security.[46] Where the debt is of uncertain amount neither of these methods is recommended: the standard security should be discharged and a new one granted.

---

[44]See paras. 33–53 and 33–54.
[45]See paras. 33–53 and 33–55.
[46]s. 16(1) of the 1970 Act is enabling, not mandatory.

Style 21

Clause in disposition transmitting personal obligation in standard security—fixed amount

40–43   (*To be inserted after statement of cash consideration*) and in consideration also of the said [EF (*disponee*) undertaking as by his signature hereto he undertakes] *or* [EF and GH (*joint disponees*) undertaking as by their signatures hereto they jointly and severally undertake] the personal obligation [contained in a standard security for the sum of £   ] [*if in separate instrument* contained in (*describe shortly the instrument containing the personal obligation* for the sum of £   and secured by a standard security] granted by AB, (*designation*), in favour of CD, (*designation*), dated   and recorded in the division of the General Register of Sasines for the County of   on   ,[47] do hereby dispone, etc.

If the interest of the creditor in the standard security has been registered in the Land Register the standard security should be described by reference to the title number of the registered interest of the subjects conveyed, which should also appear in the description of them in the dispositive clause of the disposition.

RESTRICTION

The statutory provisions

40–44   Section 15 of the Conveyancing and Feudal Reform (Scotland) Act 1970 prescribes a form of deed of restriction[48] and a form of a combined partial discharge and deed of restriction.[49] The effect of such deeds when recorded is to restrict the security to the remainder of the security subjects other than the part disburdened. A restriction may be effected by a separate recorded deed or by a provision in the style of restriction prescribed in the Act[50] which is incorporated in a disposition of the disburdened part of the security subjects and is executed by the creditor.[51]

Deduction of title

40–45   The rules for deduction of title in a deed of restriction are the same as in the case of an assignation.[52]

---

[47]The fuller description of the standard security is to comply with the terms of Form No. 2 of Sched. A to the Conveyancing (Scotland) Act 1924: that form is not altered by the 1970 Act.

[48]Sched. 4, Form C.

[49]Sched. 4, Form D.

[50]By Sched. 4, Form C.

[51]See Style 24, para. 40–49.

[52]See para. 40–16.

<h1 align="center">Styles of Deeds of Restriction[52a]</h1>

<h2 align="center">Style 22</h2>

Deed of restriction—no consideration—creditor infeft

40–46   I, AB, (*designation*), at the request of CD, (*designation*), but without any payment to me, hereby disburden of a standard security for £   (*or* a maximum sum of £   ; *in other cases describe as in Note 2 to Schedule 4 to 1970 Act*) by the said CD [*or* by EF[53]] in my favour [*or* in favour of GH to which I have now right[54]] recorded in the Register for the County of   on   (*adding if necessary but only to the extent of £   of principal*) ALL and WHOLE (*describe the subjects disburdened as directed in Note 1 to Schedule 2 to 1970 Act in the case of a description of security subjects*).

(*To be attested*)

<h2 align="center">Style 23</h2>

Partial deed of restriction—price—creditor uninfeft

40–47   I, AB, (*designation*), executor (nominate) (dative) of CD, (*designation*), conform to confirmation by the sheriff of   at   dated   in consideration of £   hereby disburden of a standard security for £   by EF, (*designation*),[55] in favour of the said CD in the Register for the County of   on   ALL and WHOLE (*describe the part of the security subjects disburdened so as to identify them*) being part of the subjects described in the said standard security: Which standard security was last vested in the said CD as aforesaid and from whom I as executor foresaid acquired right by the said confirmation.

(*To be attested*)

<h2 align="center">Style 24</h2>

Combined partial discharge and deed of restriction—creditor infeft

40–48   I, AB, (*designation*), in consideration of £   paid by CD, (*designation*), hereby discharge a standard security for £   by the said CD [*or* by EF] in my favour [*or* in favour of GH] recorded in the Register for the County of   on   , but only to the extent of £   of

---

[52a]Styles 22 to 25 are applicable where the title to neither the security subjects nor the standard security has been registered in the Land Register. For appropriate variations of the styles where either title has been registered in the Land Register, see para. 40–77.

[53]Where CD not original debtor.

[54]Where AB not the original creditor, but no specification of title required since AB has a recorded title to the standard security.

[55]Designation not required by 1970 Act, but convenient since deed will be recorded in favour of EF.

principal; And I disburden of the said standard security ALL and WHOLE (*describe as in Style 22*).

(*To be attested*)

Style 25

Deed of restriction in gremio of disposition with deduction of title

40–49 [*Insert before "do hereby dispone"*] with consent of AB, (*designation*), and CD, (*designation*), the trustees acting under trust deed by EF, (*designation*), dated   and registered in the Books of Council and Session on to the effect of disburdening as by their signatures hereto they hereby disburden of a standard security for £   by me the said GH (*grantor of disposition*) [*or* JK[56]] in favour of the said EF recorded in the Register for the County of on   the subjects hereinafter disponed, which standard security was last vested in the said EF as aforesaid and from whom the said AB and CD as trustees foresaid acquired right by the said trust deed, do hereby dispone, etc.

REDEMPTION

Right of redemption

40–50 Subject to any agreement to the contrary, the debtor is entitled to redeem a standard security in accordance with the provisions of section 18 of the Conveyancing and Feudal Reform (Scotland) Act 1970 and standard condition 11 of Schedule 3 to the Act. The right can be varied conventionally,[57] but the procedure on redemption specified in standard condition 11, as amended,[58] remains applicable in all cases.

Persons entitled to redeem

40–51 Subject to any special agreement on the matter, the debtor in the standard security or, where the debtor is not the proprietor of the security subjects, then such proprietor is entitled to redeem the security.[59] Moreover, "debtor" includes any successor in title, assignee or representative of the debtor.[60] It has been decided in the case of a bond and disposition in security that a postponed bondholder was entitled to redeem a prior bond and disposition in security[61] and the same principle will apply in the case of a standard security.[62]

---

[56]If standard security granted by former proprietor of security subjects.
[57]1970 Act, s. 18(1A) substituted by the Redemption of Standard Securities (Scotland) Act 1971.
[58]Redemption of Standard Securities (Scotland) Act 1971, s. 1(*g*).
[59]1970 Act, s. 18(1) as amended by 1971 Act, s. 1(*b*) and (*c*).
[60]1970 Act, s. 30(1).
[61]*Adair's Tr.* v. *Rankin* (1895) 22 R. 975; *Reis* v. *Mackay* (1899) 6 S.L.T. 331.
[62]1970 Act, s. 26(2).

Notice of redemption—amount

40-52 The parties may now by agreement regulate the arrangement between them as to redemption of the security and notice of redemption but, subject to any such special arrangement, the debtor or the proprietor may redeem the security on giving two months' notice in writing to the creditor of intention to do so.[63] It would appear that, apart from any special agreement, the whole sum due must be repaid[64] and that there is no right to make partial repayment unless that has been contracted for originally. Notice may be given to redeem at any time: redemption is not restricted, as under a bond and disposition in security, to a term of Whitsunday or Martinmas.[65] If the notice of redemption states that a specified amount is to be repaid and it is subsequently ascertained that the whole amount due is different, the notice is effective as a notice of repayment of the correct amount due.[66]

Several creditors

40-53 It is clear that, where there are several creditors each having a separate standard security then, subject to any special agreement, the debtor is entitled to redeem any one or more of them he may select. The position is more doubtful where a standard security has been divided by partial assignations to different assignees. In the case of a bond and disposition in security, the opinion has been expressed[67] that the debtor may compel a partial creditor to accept repayment of his part although the other parts, due to other creditors, remain unpaid. It is doubtful whether this will apply in the case of a standard security. *Prima facie* the right of redemption is expressed in relation to a standard security[68] and "creditor" is defined as including any successor in title, assignee or representative of a creditor.[69] In practice the point will seldom become an issue; a partial creditor will normally be willing to accept payment.

Form of notice

40-54 The form of notice of redemption prescribed in Form A of Schedule 5 to the 1970 Act is:

> To AB (address)
> TAKE NOTICE that on (*date of repayment*) CD, (*designation*), will repay the sum of £   [*or*, the whole amount due] secured by a standard security by the said CD (*or* by EF) in your favour (*or* in favour of GH) recorded in the Register for the

---

[63] *Ibid.*, s. 18(1) as amended by 1971 Act, s. 1(*b*).
[64] See 1970 Act, s. 18 and s.c. 11(5).
[65] Conveyancing (Scotland) Act 1924, s. 32.
[66] 1970 Act, s.c. 11(4).
[67] Burns, 593, 594.
[68] 1970 Act, s. 18.
[69] *Ibid.*, s. 30(1).

County of   on   .
   Dated this   day of   .

The notice should be signed by the debtor or proprietor, or by his agent. If it is signed by an agent he should add his designation and the words: "Agent of the said (*name of debtor or proprietor*)."

Where the standard security has been granted for an obligation which does not consist in the payment of money, the form of notice should be adapted appropriately, *e.g.*

> TAKE NOTICE that on   CD, (*designation*), will implement the obligation to construct and deliver six prefabricated building units in terms of contract between the said CD and you dated   , which obligation is secured by a standard security etc.

It is difficult to envisage that in practice a notice will be served in relation to a non-monetary obligation.

Service of notice

40–55   A notice of redemption may be delivered to the creditor or sent by registered post or recorded delivery to him at his last known address.[70] In practice a duplicate copy of the notice will be sent to facilitate acknowledgment and a further copy will be retained for attachment of a certificate of posting. If the address of the creditor is not known, or if the packet containing the notice is returned to the sender with an intimation that it could not be delivered, a notice of redemption may be sent to the Extractor of the Court of Session.[71] Notice will be held to have been given on the day immediately following the date of posting.[72]

Evidence of service

40–56   Service may be evidenced by:

(1) An acknowledgment signed by the creditor or his agent.[73] A form of acknowledgment is provided in the Act[74] for endorsement on a copy of the notice, which runs:

> I, AB above named, hereby acknowledge receipt of the Notice of Redemption of which the foregoing is a copy.
> Dated this   day of   .

It should be signed by the creditor or his agent. If an agent signs he should add his designation and the words: "Agent of the said (*name of creditor*)." It is not, however, necessary that an acknowledgment

---

[70] 1970 Act, s.c. 11(3)(*a*).
[71] *Ibid.*, s.c. 11(3)(*b*).
[72] *Ibid.*, s.c. 11(3)(*c*).
[73] *Ibid.*, s.c. 11(3)(*a*).
[74] *Ibid.*, Sched. 5, Form B.

should be in that precise form: an acknowledgment signed by the creditor or his agent is sufficient evidence.[75]

(2) A certificate of postage by the person giving the notice accompanied by the postal receipt.[76] A form of certificate is also provided in the Act which runs:

> Notice of Redemption, of which the foregoing is a copy, was posted to AB above named on the   day of

It should be signed by the debtor or proprietor or by his agent, the latter adding his designation and the words: "Agent of the said (*name of debtor or proprietor*)," and the postal receipt should be attached.

(3) An acknowledgment of receipt by the Extractor of the Court of Session in cases where service has been made on the Extractor.[77]

Waiver of notice or shortening of period

40–57 The creditor may waive the necessity of notice of redemption or may agree to a period of notice of less than that to which he is entitled.[78]

Discharge

40–58 On payment of the whole amount due, which means the debt to which the security relates and any other sums due under the standard security including interest, expenses, etc.,[79] the creditor is bound to grant a discharge in the statutory form.[80]

Consignation

40–59 Where the debtor or proprietor is entitled to redeem the security but a discharge cannot be obtained by reason of the death or absence of the creditor or for any other cause, the whole amount due (other than unascertained expenses of the creditor) may be consigned by the debtor or proprietor in any bank in Scotland incorporated by or under Act of Parliament or by Royal Charter for the person appearing to have the best right thereto.[81] That person will normally be the creditor, but the statutory phraseology permits consignation to be effected where doubt or dispute may exist as to the person or persons having right to the amount due.

40–60 **Certificate of consignation.**[82] On consignation being made a certificate of consignation may be expede by a solicitor in the following form:

---

[75] *Ibid.*, s.c. 11(3)(*a*).
[76] *Ibid.*, Sched. 5, Form C.
[77] *Ibid.*, s.c. 11(3)(*b*).
[78] *Ibid.*, s.c. 11(2) as amended by 1971 Act, s. 1(*g*).
[79] *Ibid.*, s. 18(4).
[80] *Ibid.*, s.c. 11(5) as amended by 1971 Act, s. 1(*g*).
[81] *Ibid.*, s. 18(2)(*a*) as amended by 1971 Act, s. 1(*d*).
[82] *Ibid.*, s. 18(3) and Sched. 5, Form D, No. 1.

I, AB, (*designation*), solicitor, certify that consignation of the whole amount due under the standard security aftermentioned was made as after stated and was necessitated by reason of a discharge being unobtainable after due notice of redemption had been given.

STANDARD SECURITY for £   [*or a maximum of* £   ] [*or all sums due or to become due in respect of advances made in connection with a building development at*] by CD in favour of EF recorded in the Register of Sasines for the County of   on   .

AMOUNT CONSIGNED £   , being £   of principal, £   of interest and £   in respect of ascertained expenses.

BANK IN WHICH CONSIGNED (*specify bank or branch, with address, in which consignation made*) conform to deposit receipt dated   in name of the person appearing to have the best right thereto (*specifying name and designation if known*) (*or if he is only a partial creditor* to the extent of £   ).

(To be attested)

The certificate of consignation should then be recorded in the Register of Sasines with a warrant on behalf of the proprietor of the security subjects. Upon the certificate being so recorded the security subjects will be disburdened of the standard security.[83]

Declarator of performance

40–61   Where the obligation secured by the standard security does not consist, or does not wholly consist, in the payment of money, and a discharge cannot be obtained owing to the death or absence of the creditor or for any other cause, the debtor or proprietor may apply to the sheriff having jurisdiction over any part of the security subjects for a declarator that the whole obligations under the contract to which the security relates have been performed.[84] On a declarator to that effect being pronounced, a certificate of declarator may be expede by a solicitor in the form No. 2 of Form D of Schedule 5 to the 1970 Act, and the recording of the certificate in the Register of Sasines will disburden the security subjects of the standard security.[85]

Right of redemption under section 11 of Land Tenure Reform (Scotland) Act 1974

40–62   A special right to redeem a standard security in particular circumstances is conferred upon the debtor in terms of section 11 of the Land Tenure Reform (Scotland) Act 1974 in order to counter a possible device to evade the prohibition of leases of dwelling-house

---

[83]*Ibid.*, s. 18(3).
[84]*Ibid.*, ss. 18(2)(*b*) and 29(1).
[85]*Ibid.*, s. 18(3).

property for more than 20 years. It would be possible for the owner of a dwelling-house to create something akin to a long lease by sale under burden of a standard security granted by the purchaser in favour of the seller for the full price or a substantial part of it. If the security was not redeemable for a lengthy fixed period, or redeemable only on penal conditions, the interest was payable at a flexible rate subject to review based on current values and a clause of redemption in favour of the seller at the end of the period of the security was inserted in the disposition, the general effect of the transaction would be similar to a long lease. Accordingly the 1974 Act provided (in section 11) that the debtor would have a statutory right to redeem a standard security after 20 years and (in section 12) that the period within which a right to redeem the property was exercisable was restricted to 20 years.

Section 11 applies to a standard security executed after September 1, 1974 where (i) the security subjects are used as or as part of a dwelling-house, and (ii) that use was not in contravention of a conventional condition of the security or, if it was, the creditor has approved of the contravention expressly or by his actings. If these conditions are satisfied the debtor will be entitled to redeem the security at any time not less than 20 years after the date of its execution. The amount payable on redemption will not exceed the amount remaining unredeemed of (i) any excess of the value of the security subjects at the date of execution of the security over the amount paid for the subjects, (ii) any sums actually advanced under the security, (iii) any expense or charge reasonably incurred by the creditor in the exercise of a right to perform any obligation which the debtor has failed to perform and which was reasonably necessary for the protection of the security, and (iv) interest outstanding at redemption at the rate applicable in terms of the security immediately before notice of redemption was given. In practice the legislation has achieved its objective and transactions of the kind which it was intended to discourage have been virtually unknown.

DISCHARGES

Form of discharge

40–63   Section 17 of the Conveyancing and Feudal Reform (Scotland) Act 1970 authorises discharge of a standard security and disburdenment of the security subjects by a discharge in conformity with Form F of Schedule 4 to the Act, duly recorded. It may be separate or endorsed on the standard security.[86]

Cautionary obligations and collateral securities

40–64   In law ancillary or cautionary obligations for payment of the amount

---

[86] 1970 Act, Sched. 4, Form F.

due under a standard security and collateral security given for the obligations of the debtor will fall when the principal obligation is extinguished by payment or discharge. For the reasons already explained,[87] creditors may take advantage of the flexibility of the standard security to frame the personal obligation as covering additional sums that may become due, even when a loan of fixed amount is all that is contemplated at the time of the original advance.[88] It would appear that, in the interest of debtors and co-obligants, it is desirable to obtain formal discharges as soon as the original loan has been repaid. Suggested rules for practice are: (1) to obtain a recorded discharge of the standard security whenever the amount secured has been repaid, (2) to procure at the same time a discharge of any co-obligations or guarantees, either incorporated in the discharge of the standard security or in a separate document,[89] and (3) to obtain a retrocession or discharge of any collateral security, moveable or heritable, in order to disburden the title to the collateral asset.

Styles of Discharges[89a]

Style 26

Discharge (separate)—fixed amount—grantor infeft

40–65   I, AB, (*designation*), in consideration of £   paid by CD, (*designation*), hereby discharge a standard security for £   by the said CD in my favour (*or* in favour of EF) recorded in the Register for the County of   on

(*To be attested*)

Style 27

Discharge (endorsed)—fixed amount—grantor infeft

40–66   I, AB, (*designation*), in consideration of £   paid by CD, (*designation*), hereby discharge the foregoing standard security by the said CD in my favour [*or* in favour of EF] recorded in the Register for the County of   on   .[90]

(*To be attested*)

---

[87] See para. 37–10.

[88] *e.g.* Style 9, para. 37–21.

[89] s. 17 of the 1970 Act does not provide (as s. 14(2) does in relation to assignations) that corroborative and substitutional obligations are covered by a discharge, but it is unnecessary to do so on account of the rule of law that a discharge of the relevant debt will extinguish them.

[89a] The Styles 26 to 33 are applicable where the titles to the security subjects and the standard security have been recorded in the Register of Sasines. For variations where either of these titles has been registered in the Land Register, see para. 40–76.

[90] It should be noted that, even in an endorsed discharge, specification of the names of the parties and the recording date of the standard security is *required* by the Act.

Style 28

Discharge (separate)—maximum or uncertain amount—grantor infeft

40–67   We, X Limited, (*designation*), in consideration of £
being the whole amount secured by the standard security
aftermentioned[91] [now and formerly] paid by AB, (*designation*),
hereby discharge a standard security for [a maximum sum of
£   ] [all sums due and to become due in respect of
advances made in connection with the purchase of plant and
equipment for the business of engineering contractor carried on
by the said AB] granted by the said AB in our favour recorded in
the Register for the County of   on   .

(*To be attested*)

Style 29

Partial discharge—fixed amount—by uninfeft executors of assignee

40–68   We, AB, (*designation*), and CD, (*designation*), executors
nominate of EF, (*designation*), conform to confirmation by the
sheriff of   at   dated
in consideration of £   paid by GH, (*designation*), hereby
discharge a standard security for £   by the said GH in
favour of JK recorded in the Register for the County of
          on   , but only to the extent of
£   of principal; Which standard security was last vested in
the said EF whose title thereto was recorded in the said Register
of Sasines on   and from whom we as executors
foresaid acquired right [to the extent aforesaid] by the said
confirmation.

(*To be attested*)

Style 30

*Discharge of one standard security by three partial creditors—two
infeft—one uninfeft*

40–69   We (first) AB, (*designation*), (second) CD, (*designation*), and
(third) EF, (*designation*), executor dative of GH, (*designation*),
conform to confirmation by the sheriff of   at
          dated   in consideration of (one)
£   paid to me the said AB, (two) £   paid to me
the said CD and (three) £   paid to me the said EF as
executor foresaid, in all cases by JK, (*designation*), hereby, but
each for our respective rights and interests only, discharge a
standard security for £   by the said JK in favour of the
trustees of LM recorded in the Register for the County of
          on   ; which standard security to
the extent of £   was last vested in the said GH whose title

---

[91]The statement as to the whole amount secured is required where the sum is expressed as a
maximum or uncertain amount. It should be inserted even where the original advance was a single
sum if the standard security was expressed in terms wide enough to cover additional advances, *e.g.* as
in Style 9, para. 37–21. It need not be included, however, where only the interest rate is variable.

thereto was recorded in the said Register of Sasines on and from whom I the said EF as executor foresaid acquired right to the extent of £ aforesaid by the said confirmation.

(To be attested)

Style 31

Discharge where there has been subsequent recorded variation substituting new obligant[92]

40–70   We, X Building Society, (*designation*), in consideration of £   , being the whole amount secured by the standard security aftermentioned, now and formerly paid partly by AB, (*designation*), and partly by Mrs BB, (*designation*), hereby discharge a standard security for £   and all other sums due and that might become due granted by the said AB in our favour recorded in the Register for the County of on   ; and we discharge the liability for the debt secured by the said standard security undertaken by the said BB conform' to Variation by her with our consent recorded in the said Register of Sasines on   .[93]

(To be attested)

Style 32

Discharge where there have been subsequent unrecorded variations[94]

40–71   We, A Limited, (*designation*), in consideration of £   , being the whole amount secured by the standard security aftermentioned, paid by CD, (*designation*), hereby discharge a standard security by the said CD in our favour recorded in the Register for the County of   on for all sums due and that might become due by the said CD to us in respect of balances on trading accounts in connection with goods supplied by us in terms of an agreement between us and the said CD dated   as varied by two subsequent agreements between us and the said CD dated respectively and   .

(To be attested)

Style 33

Discharge incorporating retrocession of life policy—grantor infeft[95]

40–72   I, AB, (*designation*), in consideration of £   paid by

---

[92]As in Style 3, para. 40–08.

[93]The discharge of the obligation of BB may not strictly be necessary but it clears the record specifically of the recorded variation.

[94]Where the effect of an unrecorded variation has been to incorporate additional obligants, a specific discharge on the lines of Style 31, para. 40–70 is recommended. For other alterations made in unrecorded variations this form of discharge will generally be adequate.

[95]Where life policy has been assigned by separate assignation, a separate retrocession will be more convenient. The above style is for use where the assignation of the life policy has been incorporated in the standard security.

CD, (*designation*), hereby discharge a standard security for
£   by the said CD in my favour recorded in the Register
for the County of   on   ; and I
reassign to the said CD a policy of assurance of the
Assurance Company Limited effected by the said CD on his own
life for the sum of £   number   dated
      , which policy was assigned to me in security in
the said standard security, together with all bonus additions
accrued or that may accrue thereon and the whole benefit
thereof, present and future[96]: And I warrant the foregoing re-
assignation from fact and deed only.

(*To be attested*)

REGISTERED INTERESTS IN RELATION TO HERITABLE SECURITIES

The statutory provisions

40–74   In terms of section 4(2)(*d*) of the Land Registration (Scotland) Act
1979, an application for registration in the Land Register of a deed
which relates to a registered interest and is executed after that interest
has been registered will be rejected by the Keeper if it does not bear a
reference to the title sheet of that interest. Accordingly if any such
deed relating to a heritable security is being submitted with an
application for registration in the Land Register it must contain a
reference to the title number of the burdened subjects. In practice such
an application will be made where (1) a new standard security is being
granted over a registered interest, or (2) any deed or writ is being
granted which relates to a heritable security and the interest of the
creditor has already been registered in the Land Register. If by
inadvertence the reference to the title number has been omitted in the
deed it will be sufficient if it is clearly marked at the top of the first
page of the deed (*not* on the backing).[97] In cases where the title to the
security subjects has been registered in the Land Register but the title
to an existing security remains recorded in the Register of Sasines, a
related deed or writ may continue to be recorded in that Register, but
in practice will normally be entered or its effect registered in the Land
Register.[98] Since many such deeds, *e.g.* assignations or discharges,
contain no description of the security subjects a note of the title
number of the registered interest of the proprietor of the security
subjects should be placed at the top of the first page of the deed.

In cases where the interest of the creditor in a heritable security has
been registered in the Land Register so that the effect of the
subsequent deed or writ relating to the security will also be so
registered, variations in the styles contained in this chapter are
suggested in the following paragraphs.

---

[96]To be intimated to assurance company.
[97]R.T.P.B., para. D.1.15.
[98]See para. 42–05.

Registrable variations

40–75   In Styles 1, 2, and 3 the reference to the standard security should run:

> standard security for £   (*or otherwise as the case may be*) by (*name of grantor*) in favour of (*name of grantee*) registered on (*date*) over the subjects in Title Number(s)   .

In Styles 2 and 3 no clause of deduction of title is required but the links in title should be produced with the application for registration on Form 2.

Registrable assignations and discharges

40–76   In Styles 7 to 11 and 16 (assignations) and Styles 26 to 33 (discharges) the reference to the standard security should run:

> standard security for £   (*or otherwise as the case may be*) by (*name of grantor*) in favour of (*name of grantee*) registered on (*date*) over the subjects in Title Number(s)   .

Where the grantor of the assignation or discharge is not the person having a registered title to the interest of the creditor no deduction of title is required, but the links in title should be produced with the application for registration on Form 2.

Registrable deeds of restriction

40–77   In the case of deeds of restriction the subjects disburdened (if the whole security subjects) should be described by reference to the number of the title sheet: if part only of the security subjects is disburdened it should be described, preferably by reference to a plan, so that its precise boundaries can be identified on the Ordnance Map, and stated to be part of the security subjects identified by reference to the number of their title sheet as in the examples below.

Whole subjects disburdened

> hereby disburden of a standard security for £   (*or otherwise as the case may be*) by AB in favour of CD registered on (*date*) the whole subjects in Title Number(s)   .

Partial disburdenment

> hereby disburden of a standard security for £   (*or otherwise as the case may be*) by AB in favour of CD registered on (*date*) ALL and WHOLE (*describe disburdened part so as to enable it to be identified on Ordnance Map, preferably by reference to plan annexed to the deed of restriction*) being part of the subjects in Title Number   .

In circumstances where the interest of the proprietor of the security subjects, but not that of the heritable creditor, has been registered in the Land Register, and the deed of restriction is to be recorded in the Register of Sasines the description of the disburdened property or the part of it which is disburdened may be in the form contained in Styles 22 to 25 but, since the registered interest of the proprietor is being wholly or partially disburdened, it is particularly desirable that a note be placed at the top of the first page of the deed of restriction containing a reference to the title number of the registered interest of the proprietor.[99]

Heritable securities over long leases

40–78   Where the interest of a heritable creditor over a long lease has been registered in the Land Register, the same principles already explained in paragraphs 40–74 to 40–77 *supra* are applicable to subsequent deeds or writs relating to the security. The suggested variations in the description of the subjects of the standard security in paragraphs 40–75 to 40–77 *supra* remain appropriate, since the description of the subjects registered under the title number specified will refer to the registered interest of the tenant under the lease.

---

[99]See para. 40–74.

CHAPTER 41

FLOATING CHARGES

ATTACHMENT OF FLOATING CHARGES

APPOINTMENT OF RECEIVER

Introduction

41–01   Before 1961 it was impossible to create a security over corporeal moveable property under Scots law without delivery of the property to the creditor[1] or to create a security over incorporeal moveable rights except by assignation of the rights and intimation of the assignation to the obligants.[2] The concept of a floating charge was alien to the principles of Scots law and did not create a security.[3]

The Companies (Floating Charges) (Scotland) Act 1961 made it competent for an incorporated company to create a floating charge over all or any of its property, heritable or moveable, for the purpose of securing any existing or future debts, but did not provide for the appointment of receivers.

The Companies (Floating Charges and Receivers) (Scotland) Act 1972 superseded the 1961 Act and provided for the appointment of receivers.

The legislation regarding companies and insolvency of 1985/1986 repealed the 1972 Act, and the principal provisions with regard to floating charges are now contained in the Companies Act 1985 and, with regard to receivers, in the Insolvency Act 1986 and relative regulations. Briefly these are:

Floating Charges

Creation, effect, ranking and alteration of floating charges	Companies Act 1985, ss. 462–466
Registration of floating charges	ss. 410–424

Receivers

Appointment, powers and duties of receivers	Insolvency Act 1986, ss. 50–71
Cross-border operation of receivership provisions	Insolvency Act 1986, s. 72
Statutory regulations	The Receivers (Scotland) Regulations 1986 (S.I. 1986 No. 1917) (S.141); The Insolvency (Scotland) Rules 1986 (S.I. 1986 No. 1915) (S.139)

Nature and effect of floating charge

41–02 There is no precise definition of a floating charge save that which can be deduced from the terms of section 462 of the Companies Act 1985, *viz.*— "It is competent under the law of Scotland for an incorporated company (whether a company within the meaning of this Act or not), for the purpose of securing any debt or other obligation (including a cautionary obligation) incurred or to be incurred by, or

---

[1]There were a limited number of exceptions to that rule, *e.g.* hypothecs and statutory mortgages of ships or aircraft under the Merchant Shipping Act 1894 or the Mortgaging of Aircraft Order 1972—see Vol. I, paras. 8–55 and 8–57.

[2]Also subject to certain statutory exceptions where special systems of registration operated, such as patents. See Vol. I, paras. 7–48 to 7–52.

[3]*Carse* v. *Coppen*, 1951 S.C. 233.

binding upon, the company or any other person, to create in favour of the creditor in the debt or obligation a charge, in this Part referred to as a floating charge, over all or any part of the property (including uncalled capital) which may from time to time be comprised in its property and undertaking." In effect a floating charge gives the creditor a form of security over the property, moveable or heritable, of the granting company which is subject to the charge without the need for delivery or intimation in the case of moveable property or recording or registration in the Register of Sasines or the Land Register in the case of heritable property.[4]

Until a receiver is appointed or the company is wound up the charge is dormant and the company may, subject to any specific contractual restrictions imposed by the charge, deal with its property by burdening it or disposing of it, and any new property which it acquires will become subject to the charge. Upon the appointment of a receiver, or on commencement of the winding-up of the company, the charge attaches to the property of the company then comprised in the subjects over which the charge has been expressed to extend (frequently all assets) as if it were a fixed security over that property, subject only to the rights of any person who has effectually executed diligence on the property or any part of it or who holds a fixed security or another floating charge over the property or any part of it which has a prior ranking.[5]

CONSTITUTION OF FLOATING CHARGES

Form and execution of floating charges

41–03   Under the Companies (Floating Charges) (Scotland) Act 1961[6] a floating charge by a company which the Court of Session had jurisdiction to wind up required to be as nearly as practicable in the form of the First Schedule to the Act, but that requirement was not renewed in the Companies (Floating Charges and Receivers) (Scotland) Act 1972 which repealed the 1961 Act, so that the charge may now be in any appropriate form. It is necessary, however, that the instrument creating the charge granted by a company which the Court of Session has jurisdiction to wind up[7] is executed under seal of the company or by an attorney authorised for that purpose by writing under its common seal.[8]

---

[4]Companies Act 1985, s. 462(5).
[5]*Ibid.*, s. 463: Insolvency Act 1986, ss. 53(7) and 54(6).
[6]s. 2.
[7]These include companies registered in Scotland on incorporation and also under Pt. XXII (bodies corporate subject or becoming subject to the Companies Act 1985 otherwise than by original formation) or Pt. XXIII thereof (overseas companies) and unregistered companies in the circumstances (mainly relating to their principal place of business) under s. 666 of the 1985 Act.
[8]Companies Act 1985, s. 462(2) and (3).

Styles of floating charges

41–04   The style of floating charge varies according to circumstances and the bargain between the parties. In general floating charges are most commonly used to provide security to banks or finance houses for advances on current account or by instalments: sometimes the personal obligation of the debtor company is constituted in a separate bond of cash credit[9] when the floating charge deals primarily with the security, but in some cases both the personal obligation and the floating charge are incorporated in one instrument. The style and specimen clauses given in the example in paragraph 41–05 incorporate both elements. The style contains

1. The undertaking of the personal obligation.

2. Conditions relative to the personal obligation (Clause FIRST).

3. The grant of the security and the ranking and scope thereof (Clause SECOND).

4. The obligations of the granter in relation to the security during its subsistence (Clause THIRD).

5. Appointment and powers of a receiver (Clause FOURTH).

6. Right of the creditor to redeem or acquire other prior or *pari passu* securities (Clause FIFTH).

7. Discharge of the security on repayment (Clause SIXTH).

8. Definition and notices (Clause SEVENTH).

9. Expenses, warrandice and consent to registration (Clause EIGHTH).

The style is intended to be comprehensive: some of its provisions may be varied or omitted by arrangement of parties.

Specimen style of bond and floating charge

41–05   We, AB Limited, incorporated under the Companies Acts and having our registered office at   Hereby BIND and OBLIGE ourselves to pay on demand to the X Bank, (*designation*), (hereinafter called "the Bank") all sums which are now and which may at any time hereafter become due to the Bank in any manner of way whatever by us and for which we may at any time become liable to the Bank, whether solely or jointly with any person or persons and whether as principal debtors or guarantors or sureties including, without prejudice to the foregoing generality, all sums for which we are or may become liable to the Bank upon any current or other accounts, wherever operated, and upon bills, promissory notes, orders, drafts, letters of credit, guarantees and other

---

[9] See Vol. I, para. 5–44 (but granted by a company).

documents of any kind and all discounts, commissions and banking charges, costs and expenses, with interest on all such sums from the respective times of advance or becoming due until payment at the rate or rates charged or computed in accordance with the ordinary practice of the Bank from time to time or as may be provided in any separate agreement, such interest to include interest as well before as after any decree obtained by the Bank for said sums.

FIRST

IT IS PARTICULARLY AGREED THAT

(1) A certificate signed by (*specify signing officials of Bank*) or any other signing official authorised by the Bank at any of their offices shall ascertain and constitute conclusively the whole amount, principal, interest and others, that may at any time be due by us to the Bank hereunder and no suspension of a charge or of a threatened charge for payment of the amount so constituted shall pass nor any sist of execution thereon be granted except upon consignation;

(2) Nothing herein contained shall prejudice or affect any securities or guarantees which the Bank may at any time hold for any of the said sums or interest and the Bank shall have full power in their discretion to discharge or release any such securities or guarantees in whole or in part, or to sell, dispose of or otherwise deal with any such securities or any property to which they relate without applying the same or the proceeds thereof towards payment of any sum hereby secured, and the whole obligations hereby undertaken by us shall remain in full force and effect as if no such securities or guarantees had existed;

(3) The Bank may at all times in their sole discretion without prejudice to our liability and their rights hereunder or affecting any securities, guarantees or other rights available to them (i) grant to us or to any other person or persons liable with or for us any time or other indulgence, (ii) compound with us or them, (iii) accede to any trust deed and draw dividends and (iv) exercise any right competent to us to redeem any security over our heritable or moveable property ranking prior to or *pari passu* with any security held by the Bank over that property or any part thereof and to charge

the cost thereof against us which shall form part of the sums due by us hereunder, with interest thereon as aforesaid, and to do all or any such things without notice to us or to any other person concerned;

(4) The whole sums and obligations which may be due by us or for which we may have become liable to the Bank at any time with all interest, charges and expenses shall be repaid or satisfied by us to the Bank upon the occurrence of any of the following events:

(a) on an order being made or a resolution being passed for our winding up or liquidation, compulsory or voluntary,

(b) on our stopping payment or ceasing to carry on business,

(c) on a receiver of our assets or any part thereof being appointed, or

(d) the Bank requiring us in writing at any time to so repay or satisfy such sums or obligations; and

(5) As at the date or dates upon which any of the said sums or obligations shall fall to be repaid or satisfied in terms of sub-clause (4) of this clause, or at any time thereafter, the Bank may in their option (a) capitalise the interest, discounts, commissions and banking charges then accrued or outstanding, and all sums of principal (including such interest and others so capitalised) shall bear interest computed as aforesaid as well after as before any decree obtained by the Bank for the said sums and (b) if the Bank shall have more than one account for us in their books, transfer all or any part of a credit balance on any account to any other of such accounts then in debit without prior notice to us but subject to notifying us of any such transfer having been made.

SECOND

IN SECURITY of our whole obligations hereunder we hereby GRANT in favour of the Bank a FLOATING CHARGE over the whole of the property (including uncalled capital) which is, or may be from time to time while this Instrument is in force, comprised in our property and undertaking   PROVIDING   AND DECLARING THAT

(1) Except as otherwise agreed in writing by the Bank the Floating Charge hereby created shall rank in priority to any fixed security as defined in section 70 of the Insolvency Act 1986 or any statutory amendment or re-enactment thereof for the

time being in force (which Act as so amended or re-enacted is hereinafter referred to as "the Act") and any other floating charge, being a fixed security or floating charge which shall have been created by us after our execution hereof, but with the exception that any fixed security in favour of the Bank shall rank in priority to the floating charge hereby created, and

(2) The security hereby created shall be a continuing security and shall extend to cover all sums and obligations which may be due by us from time to time or for which we may become liable to the Bank and shall not be affected by any fluctuations in such sums or by the existence at any time of a credit balance on any current or other account.

THIRD

WE UNDERTAKE to procure that while this security is in force:

(1) Without prejudice to the foregoing provisions we shall not, except with the previous consent in writing of the Bank, (i) create or permit to be created any security, mortgage or charge upon or affecting our property or assets or any part thereof, heritable or moveable, real or leasehold and wherever situated, (ii) call up or receive in advance of calls any uncalled capital, (iii) create or issue any debentures, debenture stock or other form of loan capital or (iv) raise or permit to be raised either by us or any of our subsidiaries any sums of money secured in any way over the assets of us or any of such subsidiaries;

(2) We shall, on being so requested in writing by the Bank, forthwith grant, or procure the granting in favour of the Bank of, a fixed security or securities in the usual form adopted by the Bank over any heritable, real or leasehold property or over any book or other debts, securities for money or any other moveable property which may from time to time belong to us or any of our subsidiaries;

(3) We shall, if so requested by the Bank, deposit with the Bank the title deeds and documents of title to all our heritable, real and leasehold property and all incorporeal moveable property to which there is a document of title;

(4) We shall not, except with the consent in writing of the Bank, sell or otherwise dispose of any part of the heritable, real or

leasehold property which may from time to time belong to us or any of our subsidiaries nor create or permit to be created any servitudes, wayleaves or other rights over any such property nor shall any part of the assets of us or our subsidiaries be sold or otherwise disposed of unless in the ordinary course of business;

(5) We shall keep all buildings, machinery, fixtures, fittings and trade utensils which may from time to time form part of our assets in good repair and in proper working order and condition and in the event of any of the same being destroyed, injured or in a state of deterioration we shall forthwith repair or replace and make them good; and

(6) (i) We shall insure and keep insured the whole property and corporeal assets which may from time to time belong to us or our subsidiaries for their full replacement value against loss by fire and such other risks as the Bank may reasonably require with such insurers as shall be approved by the Bank and the relative policy or policies shall be endorsed, if the Bank so require, to show the interest of the Bank, and we shall produce to the Bank, if so required, within fifteen days after becoming due and payable in each year receipts for the current premiums, failing which the Bank shall be entitled at our expense to effect or renew any such insurances as the Bank may decide.

(ii) All moneys which may be received or receivable at any time by virtue of any such policy or policies shall be applied in replacing, restoring or making good the loss or damage in respect of which such moneys may have been received or in the option of the Bank in discharge or reduction of the sums and obligations hereby secured.

FOURTH (1) At any time after the sums and obligations hereby secured shall fall to be paid or satisfied as aforesaid or after the Bank shall have been requested by us in writing to do so,[9a] the Bank shall have power by instrument in writing to appoint any person or persons to be a receiver or receivers of our property and assets and

---

[9a] If the floating charge specifies the official of the company who may make such a request, a demand signed by any other official is invalid—*Elwick Bay Shipping Co. Ltd.* v. *Royal Bank of Scotland Ltd.*, 1982 S.L.T. 62 (a decision relating to an official of the creditor bank).

may in like manner appoint any person or persons to be a receiver or receivers in place of any receiver removed by the court or otherwise ceasing to act.

(2) Every receiver appointed by the Bank shall have the powers conferred on a receiver by the Act.

(3) Every receiver appointed by the Bank hereunder shall be our agent and we shall be solely responsible for his acts or defaults and for his remuneration, costs, charges and expenses.

(4) The Bank and every receiver appointed by the Bank hereunder shall be entitled to be indemnified out of the property and assets covered by this security in respect of all liabilities incurred by them or him in the execution [or purported execution] of any of the powers vested in them or him by the Act or these presents and against all actions, proceedings, expenses and claims arising from anything done or omitted to be done in any way in relation to the said property and assets and the Bank and any such receiver may retain and pay all sums in respect of the same out of any moneys received in the exercise [or purported exercise] of the powers so vested in him.

FIFTH

Without prejudice to their whole other rights and powers hereunder the Bank shall be entitled in their sole discretion, at any time after the said sums and obligations fall to be paid or satisfied as aforesaid or after any power conferred by any fixed security or floating charge ranking in priority to, or *pari passu* with, the floating charge hereby created shall become exercisable, to redeem or procure the transfer to the Bank of that fixed security or floating charge so ranking and all sums and expenses paid by the Bank in consideration of such redemption or transfer shall be charged to and repayable by us as provided for in respect of the whole sums and obligations due to the Bank hereunder with interest thereon from the date or dates of payment by the Bank computed as aforesaid.

SIXTH

On repayment and satisfaction to the Bank of the whole sums and obligations and all interest, charges and expenses due and that may become due hereunder the Bank shall on our request and at our expense discharge the security hereby created and discharge or release any other security granted by us to the Bank or held by the Bank in virtue of Clause THIRD hereof.

SEVENTH (1) In this deed "subsidiary" shall have the meaning ascribed to it by section 736 of the Companies Act 1985.

(2) Any demand or notice to be given by the Bank to us in connection with or arising from these presents may be left at or sent by post to us at our registered office or place of business last known to the Bank.

EIGHTH We bind and oblige ourselves for the whole proper and reasonable expenses of creating and enforcing this security and also for the proper expenses of any assignation thereof. And we warrant these presents at all hands and against all mortals. And we consent to registration hereof and of any certificate under Clause FIRST hereof for preservation and execution.

(To be sealed with the Common Seal and subscribed by two Directors or one Director and the Secretary)

Debentures and debenture stock

41–06 Floating charges may also be incorporated in debentures or debenture stock. For styles of these reference may be made to *Butterworth's Company Precedents*, Volume 2.

REGISTRATION OF FLOATING CHARGES

Registrable charges

41–07 In terms of section 410 of the Companies Act 1985 the following charges created by an incorporated company are registrable:

(a) a charge on land wherever situated, or any interest in land (not including a charge for any rent, ground annual or other periodical sum payable in respect of the land, but including a charge created by a heritable security within the meaning of section 9(8) of the Conveyancing and Feudal Reform (Scotland) Act 1970),

(b) a security over the uncalled share capital of the company,

(c) a security over incorporeal moveable property of any of the following categories—

  (i) the book debts of the company,

 (ii) calls made but not paid,

(iii) goodwill,

(iv) a patent or a licence under a patent,

 (v) a trademark,

(vi) a copyright or a licence under a copyright,

(d) a security over a ship or aircraft or any share in a ship, and
(e) a floating charge.

The deposit of a negotiable instrument to secure the payment of any book debts of a company is not to be treated as a charge on those book debts for the purposes of registration under section 410 of the 1985 Act.[10]

The requirement of registration

41–08 **(a) Scottish companies**. Charges, including floating charges, which are created by an incorporated company registered in Scotland, require to be registered with the Registrar of Companies in Scotland within the time or times aftermentioned.[11]

(b) English and foreign companies. A floating charge created by a company which is registered in England and Wales over property situated in Scotland is sufficiently registered if registration is effected within the prescribed period with the Registrar of Companies in England and Wales.[12]

If a charge on property in Scotland is created, or an existing charge on property in Scotland is acquired, by a company incorporated outside Great Britain which has a place of business in Scotland, then registration of the charge with the Registrar of Companies in Scotland is required within the 21-day period from creation of the charge or acquisition of the property.[13]

Procedure on registration

41–09 Prescribed particulars of a floating charge together with a copy (certified in the prescribed manner to be a correct copy) of the instrument by which the charge is created or evidenced must be delivered to or received by the Registrar of Companies within 21 days after the date of creation of the charge, *i.e.* the date on which the instrument creating the floating charge was executed by the company creating it.[14] The prescribed particulars of a floating charge comprise (i) the name of the company creating the charge and its company number, (ii) the date of creation of the charge, (iii) a description of the instrument creating or evidencing the charge, (iv) the amount secured by the charge, (v) the name and address of the person entitled to the charge, (vi) short particulars of the property charged, (vii) a statement of any restrictions on power to grant further securities and any ranking provision, and (viii) particulars of any commission, allowance or discount paid (usually nil in the case of a floating charge).[15]

---

[10] 1985 Act, s. 412.
[11] *Ibid.*, s. 410. As to time limit see para. 41–09.
[12] *Ibid.*, s. 395.
[13] *Ibid.*, s. 424.
[14] *Ibid.*, s. 410(2) and (5).
[15] See Companies Form No. 410 (Scot.).

Where the charge is created out of the United Kingdom and comprises property situated outside the United Kingdom the period of 21 days is extended to 21 days after the date on which the copy of the instrument creating it could (in due course of post and if despatched with due diligence) have been received in the United Kingdom.[16] Where a charge is created in the United Kingdom but comprises property outside the United Kingdom no extension of the period for registration is allowed, but the copy of the instrument creating or purporting to create the charge may be sent for registration notwithstanding that further proceedings may be necessary to make the charge valid or effectual according to the law of the country in which the property is situated.[17]

Failure to register timeously

41–10   If the registration requirements are not complied with timeously the floating charge is void against the liquidator and any creditor of the company and the money secured by it immediately becomes payable.[18] It is the duty of the company which grants the floating charge to effect registration and penalties are imposed on the company and every officer who defaults in doing so,[19] but the interest of the creditor to obtain a valid security is paramount and in practice he should be vigilant to ensure that registration of the floating charge is effected within the period prescribed by the 1985 Act. As to the power of the court to extend the time for registration of a charge in appropriate circumstances, see paragraph 41–15 *infra*.

Charges associated with debentures

41–11   Where a charge is incorporated in a debenture or series of debentures the requirement of registration with the Registrar of Companies applies similarly and details of the particulars which should be included are set out in section 413 of the 1985 Act.

Charges by way of heritable securities qualified by agreements

41–12   Where a charge has been created in the form of an *ex facie* absolute disposition qualified by a back letter or other agreement or in the form of a standard security qualified by an agreement, registration of the charge in the Register of Charges does not of itself render the charge unavailable as security for indebtedness incurred after the date of registration. If, however, the amount secured by the charge is purported to be increased by a further back letter or agreement, a further charge is held to have been created by the original *ex facie*

---

[16] 1985 Act, s. 411(1).
[17] *Ibid.*, s. 411(2).
[18] *Ibid.*, s. 410(2) and (3).
[19] *Ibid.*, s. 415.

absolute disposition or standard security as qualified by the further back letter or agreement and particulars of the further charge must be registered within 21 days after execution of the further back letter or agreement.[19a]

Registration of existing charges on property acquired

41–13   Where a company acquires any property which is subject to a charge of any kind which would, if it had been created by the company after the acquisition of the property, have been required to be registered by the company under Chapter II of the 1985 Act, the company must cause prescribed particulars of the charge, together with a copy (certified in the prescribed manner to be a correct copy) of the instrument by which the charge was created or evidenced to be delivered to the Registrar of Companies for registration within 21 days after the transaction was settled. If, however, the property is situated and the charge was created outside Great Britain, the said period of 21 days is extended to 21 days after the date on which the copy of the instrument could (in due course of post and if despatched with due diligence) have been received in the United Kingdom. Failure to comply timeously does not render the charge void, but the company and every officer who is in default are liable to fines.[20]

Certificates of registration

41–14   The duties of the Registrar of Companies to keep for each registered company a register in prescribed form and the particulars of charges to be entered therein are set out in section 417 of the 1985 Act. A copy of the charge itself is not contained in the Register, but a copy of the instrument creating the charge can be examined in the company's own register.[21]

Upon registration of a charge the Registrar issues a certificate of registration which is conclusive evidence that the statutory requirements as to registration of the charge have been complied with.[22]

Extension of time for registration

41–15   The court may in certain circumstances, on the application of the company concerned or any person interested, order that the time for registration of a floating charge be extended or that any accidental omission or misstatement in the particulars registered with respect to the charge or in a memorandum of satisfaction shall be rectified, on such terms and conditions as seem to it just and expedient. The circumstances in which the court may exercise this power are that the

---

[19a]*Ibid.*, s. 414.
[20]1985 Act, s. 416.
[21]See para. 41–16.
[22]1985 Act, s. 418.

failure to register timeously was due to inadvertence or some other sufficient cause, or is not of a nature prejudicial to the position of creditors or shareholders of the company, or that it is on other grounds just and equitable to grant relief.[23,24] In England it has been decided that an extension of time will not be granted after the commencement of winding up save in exceptional circumstances[25] or when winding up is imminent.[26] In practice where there has been omission to register a floating charge timeously it may be simpler, if nothing has intervened to affect the priority of the charge, to cancel the existing charge and create it anew by a fresh instrument which can be registered within the time limit.

Registration in the company's own register

41–16   Every company must keep at its registered office a register of charges and enter in it all floating charges on any property of the company and all charges specifically affecting property of the company. In each case there should be inserted in the register a short description of the property charged, the amount of the charge and, except in the case of securities to bearer, the names of the persons entitled to it. Omission to enter a charge does not invalidate it, but an officer of the company who knowingly and wilfully authorises or permits such omission is liable to a fine.[27] Copies of the instruments creating charges may be inspected by any person during business hours on payment of a fee not exceeding 5p per inspection.[28]

AVOIDANCE, RANKING, ALTERATION, ASSIGNATION AND SATISFACTION OF OR RELEASE FROM FLOATING CHARGES

Avoidance of floating charges

41–17   Section 245 of the Insolvency Act 1986 (repealing and replacing provisions in earlier statutes) provides that a floating charge created on the undertaking or property of a company is invalid except to the extent aftermentioned if created within certain periods before the company becomes insolvent.

41–18   The date at which a company becomes insolvent (the onset of insolvency) is (i) where an administration order is made, the date of presentation of the petition on which the order is made or (ii) where the company goes into liquidation, the date of commencement of the winding up.

---

[23]*Ibid.*, s. 420.

[24]For an illustration of circumstances in which late registration was permitted under the corresponding provision of the 1961 Act, see *Amalgamated Securities Ltd., Petrs.*, 1967 S.L.T. 273.

[25]*Re Resinoid and Mica Products Ltd.* [1982] 3 All E.R. 677, C.A.

[26]*Victoria Housing Estates Ltd.* v. *Ashpurton Estates Ltd.* [1982] 3 All E.R. 665, C.A.

[27]1985 Act, s. 422.

[28]*Ibid.*, s. 423.

41–19   The periods prior to the onset of insolvency within which a floating charge, to be vulnerable under the section, has been created are (i) in the case of a charge created in favour of a person connected with the company,[28a] two years, or (ii) in the case of a charge created in favour of any other person, 12 months, or (iii) in either case between the presentation of a petition for making an administrative order and the making of an order on that petition. Where the floating charge is created in favour of a person who is not a connected person the charge is not invalidated although created within 12 months of the onset of insolvency unless the company was at the time when the charge was created unable to pay its debts within the meaning of section 123 of the Insolvency Act 1986 or becomes so by the transaction under which the charge was created.

41–20   The floating charge is so invalidated except to the extent of the aggregate of (i) the value of so much of the consideration for the creation of the charge as consists of money paid or goods or services supplied at the same time as, or after, the creation of the charge, (ii) the value of so much of that consideration as consists of the discharge or reduction, at the same time as, or after, the creation of the charge, of any debt of the company, and (iii) the amount of such interest (if any) as is payable on the amount falling within (i) or (ii) above in pursuance of any agreement under which the money was so paid, the goods or services were so supplied, or the debt was so discharged or reduced. For the purpose of (i) above the value of any goods or services supplied by way of consideration for a floating charge is the amount in money which at the time they were supplied could reasonably have been expected to be obtained for supplying the goods or services in the ordinary course of business and on the same terms (apart from the consideration) as those on which they were supplied to the company.

Commentary on section 245 of the Insolvency Act 1986

41–21   The policy of the legislature with regard to the avoidance of floating charges has undergone several changes in detail since 1972. The following points in the latest version incorporated in section 245 of the 1986 Act should be noted:

(1) The exceptions from the extent of invalidity now extend not only to cash paid as consideration for the creation of the charge but also to the value of any consideration given in the form of goods and services supplied and the discharge or reduction of any debt of the company.

(2) The period within which the validity of a floating charge may now be challengeable dates back, not only from the commencement of winding up of the company, but alternatively from the presentation of a petition for the making of an administration order.

[28a] As defined in the Insolvency Act 1986. ss. 249, 435.

(3) The period for challenge is extended to two years where the charge was created in favour of a connected person and in that case the "inability to pay its debts" test does not apply.

(4) In the case of a charge in favour of any other person the old period of 12 months is applicable and the challenge can be made only if the company at the time was unable to pay its debts within the statutory meaning of that phrase or was made so by the transaction under which the charge was created.

(5) The right to challenge a floating charge as a gratuitous alienation or unfair preference, originally excluded as a ground of challenge by the Companies (Floating Charges and Receivers) (Scotland) Act 1972[29] and also by the Companies Act 1985,[29a] was not so excluded in the Insolvency Act 1985[30] nor is excluded in section 245 of the Insolvency Act 1986. Accordingly a floating charge is now open to challenge, not only under section 245 of the 1986 Act, but also as a gratuitous alienation or unfair preference under section 242 or 243 of that Act or at common law.

(6) The effect of avoidance of a floating charge is only to reduce the charge or security as such: the debt remains exigible unless its continued enforceability can be challenged on other grounds, *e.g.* as a fraudulent preference.[31]

(7) The provisions of the 1986 Act are not retrospective in their application and so the vulnerability of a floating charge to avoidance is tested by reference to the relevant statutory provisions in force at the time of its creation.[32]

Ranking of floating charges and extent of security—the statutory rules

41–22   The main statutory rules with regard to the ranking of floating charges over all or any part of the company's property are contained in section 464 of the Companies Act 1985. That section provides that:

(1) Subject to subsection (2), a floating charge may contain (a) provisions prohibiting or restricting the creation of any fixed security or any other floating charge having priority over, or ranking *pari passu* with, the floating charge[33] or (b) provisions regulating the order in which the floating charge shall rank with any other subsisting or future floating charges or fixed securities over that property or any part of it.[34]

(2) Where all or any part of the property of a company is subject both to a floating charge and to a fixed security arising by operation of

---

[29]s. 8.
[29a]s. 617(3).
[30]s. 104.
[31]*Parkes Garage (Swadlingcote) Ltd.* [1929] 1 Ch. 139; *Mace Builders (Glasgow) Ltd.* v. *Lunn* [1985] 3 W.L.R. 465.
[32]Insolvency Act 1986, Sched. 11, para. 9.
[33]For an example see style in para. 41–05, Cl. Third (1).
[34]For an example see style in para. 41–05, Cl. Second (1).

law, the fixed security has priority over the floating charge.

(3) Where the order of ranking of the floating charge with any other subsisting or future floating charges or fixed securities over all or any part of the company's property is not regulated by provisions contained in the instrument creating the floating charge, the order of ranking is determined in accordance with the following provisions of the section.

(4) Subject to the provisions of the section—

(a) a fixed security, the right to which has been constituted as a real right before a floating charge has attached to all or any part of the property of a company, has priority over the floating charge;

(b) floating charges rank with one another according to the time of registration in accordance with Chapter II of Part XII of the Companies Act 1985;

(c) floating charges which have been received by the registrar for registration by the same postal delivery rank with one another equally.

(5) Where the holder of a floating charge over all or any part of the company's property which has been registered in accordance with Chapter II of Part XII above has received intimation in writing of the subsequent registration in accordance with that Chapter of another floating charge over the same property or any part thereof, the preference in ranking of the first-mentioned floating charge is restricted to security for—

(a) the holder's present advances;

(b) future advances which he may be required to make under the instrument creating the floating charge or under any ancillary document;

(c) interest due or to become due on all such advances; and

(d) any expenses or outlays which may reasonably be incurred by the holder.

(6) The section is subject to section 614(2) of the 1985 Act (preferential debts in winding up).

Conventional provisions as to ranking in floating charges

41–23   The prohibition in a floating charge against the creation of any fixed security or other floating charge ranking in priority to or *pari passu* with it will, it is thought, be effective to enable the grantee of the charge to challenge any fixed security or floating charge subsequently created in breach of that negative pledge. Since the prohibition will be disclosed in the Register of Charges any person who seeks to obtain a fixed security or floating charge in contravention of it may not be in good faith and any such purported security or floating charge will be challengeable so far as restricting the preference of the holder of the first charge.

The declaration regulating the ranking of the floating charge cannot affect the ranking of an existing security or another floating charge save one created in favour of the grantee of the floating charge: it is effective, however, *quoad* future fixed securities or floating charges in favour of third parties.

Priority of fixed securities arising by operation of law

41–24 The preservation of the priority of fixed securities arising by operation of law applies to such securities, whether existing or future. So a lien or a landlord's hypothec[35] is preferable to the floating charge.

Priorities of fixed and floating charges in the absence of conventional ranking provisions

41–25 Where priority in ranking is not regulated by conventional provisions in floating charges (1) a fixed security which has been constituted as a real right before a floating charge has crystallised or attached to all or any of the property of the company is preferable to the floating charge, and (2) floating charges rank with one another in accordance with the respective times of their registration, those which have been received by the same post ranking *pari passu*. It would appear that a floating charge received for registration by an earlier postal delivery ranks in priority to one so received by a later postal delivery on the same day.[36]

Intimation of creation of subsequent floating charge

41–26 The restriction in the preference of the holder of a floating charge who has received written intimation of the subsequent registration of another floating charge in terms of subsection (5) of section 464 of the 1985 Act is usually elided by a "fluctuating advances" clause in a formal ranking agreement among the creditors.[37] Where there is no such clause the preference of the holder of the first floating charge is restricted as provided in the subsection.[37a] It is not the *security* of the holder of the first floating charge that is restricted, but only his *preference* in a question with the holder of the second floating charge.[37b]

Additional interest

41–27 Special problems may arise where the holder of a floating charge has

---

[35] The contrary was decided in *Cumbernauld Development Corporation v. Mustone Ltd.*, 1983 S.L.T. (Sh.Ct.) 55, but the corresponding s. 5(2) of the Companies (Floating Charges and Receivers) (Scotland) Act 1972 was not cited to the court.

[36] Contrast with the position as to recording or registration of heritable securities where those received at any time on the same day rank equally—Land Registration (Scotland) Act 1979, s. 7; Titles to Land Consolidation (Scotland) Act 1868, s. 142 as amended.

[37] For a style, see Greene and Fletcher, App. 15.

[37a] See para. 41–22.

[37b] The effect is similar to that where fixed securities are involved—see para. 36–20(3).

stipulated for additional interest becoming payable in certain circumstances. The test as to the legal effectiveness of such a stipulation is whether it amounts to a penalty and so is unenforceable.[38] Broadly, if the additional interest is not payable on an event which involves breach of contract, or even if made conditional on such an event bears some reasonable relation to the loss suffered by the holder of the charge, payment of the additional interest will be enforceable and covered by the security, but otherwise if it is not so related and amounts to a penalty.[39]

Effectually executed diligence

41-28   The effect in ranking of effectually executed diligence in relation to a floating charge is treated in paragraphs 41-34 to 41-38 *infra*.

Alteration of floating charges

41-29   An instrument creating a floating charge or any ancillary document may be altered by an instrument of alteration executed by (i) the company, (ii) the holder of the charge and (iii) the holder of any other charge (including a fixed security) which would be adversely affected by the alteration.[40] Execution of the instrument of alteration should be formal unless execution in some other manner is provided for in the floating charge.[41] An instrument of alteration which (a) prohibits or restricts the creation of any fixed security or any other floating charge having priority over, or ranking *pari passu* with, the floating charge, or (b) varies, or otherwise regulates the order of, the ranking of the floating charge in relation to fixed securities or to other floating charges, or (c) releases property from the floating charge, or (d) increases the amount secured by the floating charge, requires registration with the Registrar of Companies within 21 days of execution of the instrument of alteration.[42] The effectiveness of the alteration as being valid against a liquidator or creditor of the company is conditional upon timeous registration of the instrument which makes the alteration.

The style of an instrument of alteration varies with the nature of the changes effected but (1) it requires execution by all three parties above mentioned and (2) provisions in it which effect several of the alterations (a), (b), (c) and (d) above should, as a matter of clear drafting, be contained in separate clauses with appropriate headings.

---

[38]*Clydebank Engineering and Shipbuilding Co. Ltd.* v. *Castaneda* (1904) 7 F. (H.L.) 77.
[39]*Bell Brothers (H.P.) Ltd.* v. *Aitken*, 1939 S.C. 577; *Granor Finance Ltd.* v. *Liqdr. of Eastore Ltd.*, 1974 S.L.T. 296; *Export Credits Guarantee Dept.* v. *Universal Oil Products Co.* [1983] 1 W.L.R. 399.
[40]Companies Act 1985, s. 466(1).
[41]*Ibid.*, s. 466(2).
[42]*Ibid.*, s. 466(4) and (5).

Assignation of floating charges

41–30   A floating charge is assignable.[43] The assignation should be
sufficiently executed in accordance with the relevant law applicable to
assignation of an incorporeal moveable right. In the *Libertas-Kommerz*
case informal intimation to the liquidator of the debtor company was
held sufficient, but in practice it is recommended that intimation of the
assignation should be made formally to the debtor company, which
should note on its own register of charges particulars of the assignee
who is now entitled to the benefit of the charge. Registration of the
assignation with the Registrar of Companies is not appropriate unless
the assignation incorporates any such alteration in the terms of the
instrument creating the charge as would require registration under
section 466 of the Companies Act 1985.

Style of assignation of floating charge

41–30A   We, AB Limited, (*designation*), the holders of a Bond and
          Floating Charge granted by GH Limited, (*designation*), in our
          favour dated   In consideration of £   paid
          to us by CD Limited, (*designation*), [*if not cash consideration
          narrate other cause of granting*] hereby ASSIGN to the said CD
          Limited and its assignees whomsoever the said Bond and Floating
          Charge but that only to the extent of £   being the sum
          due thereunder at the date of delivery of these presents conform
          to certificate in terms of the said Bond and Floating Charge, with
          interest to accrue on the said sum of £   thereafter,
          together with our whole right, title and interest present and
          future therein: And we warrant the foregoing assignation from
          fact and deed only: And we have herewith delivered the said
          Bond and Floating Charge and the said certificate.
                              (*To be sealed with the common seal
                              of AB Limited and signed by one
                              director and the secretary or by
                              two directors*)

NOTE. The priority of the floating charge assigned will be retained in
respect of the balance due as shown in the certificate plus interest
thereon. If CD Limited propose to make further advances an
additional bond and floating charge will be required, but the priority of
the security for such further advances made under it will be regulated
by its date of creation.

Satisfaction and relief

41–31   Where the debt for which a floating charge was granted has been
paid or satisfied in whole or in part, or a part of the property has been
released from the charge or has ceased to form part of the company's
property, the Registrar of Companies, on receipt of a statutory
declaration in prescribed form verifying the fact, will enter a

[43] *Libertas-Kommerz GmbH* v. *Johnson*, 1977 S.C. 191.

memorandum of satisfaction (in whole or in part) on the Register of Charges. The Registrar will do so only if the creditor entitled to the benefit of the charge, or a person authorised to do so on his behalf, certifies as correct the particulars submitted to the Registrar with respect to such entry or, if such certification cannot readily be obtained, the court directs him to make the entry. It is unnecessary for the company to submit particulars with regard to such an entry where it has simply disposed of part of the property subject to the charge.[44]

ATTACHMENT OF FLOATING CHARGES

Circumstances in which floating charge attaches to security property

41–32   Initially, as already explained,[45] a floating charge simply "floats" over the property of the company over which it extends leaving the company free, subject to any contractual restrictions imposed by the charge, to deal with its property, but when in certain circumstances the charge attaches to the property which is subject to it, the charge has effect as if it were a fixed security over that property.[46] These circumstances are:

(1) The appointment of a receiver by the holder of the floating charge which may be made on the occurrence of any event which, in terms of the instrument creating the charge, entitles the holder to do so, or so far as not otherwise provided in that instrument, on (a) the expiry of a period of 21 days after the making of a demand for payment of the whole or any part of the principal sum secured by the charge, without payment having been made, or (b) the expiry of a period of two months during the whole of which interest due and payable under the charge has been in arrears, or (c) the making of an order or the passing of a resolution to wind up the company, or (d) the appointment of a receiver by virtue of any other floating charge created by the company.[47]

(2) The appointment of a receiver by the court may be made on the occurrence of any of the events specified in subparagraph (1) of this paragraph other than (d) above or where the court, on the application of the holder of the charge, pronounces itself satisfied that the position of the holder of the charge is likely to be prejudiced if the appointment is not made.[48]

(3) The commencement of winding up of the company.[49]

---

[44]Companies Act 1985, s. 419.
[45]In para. 41–02.
[46]See para. 41–33.
[47]Insolvency Act 1986, s. 52(1).
[48]*Ibid.*, s. 52(2).
[49]Companies Act 1985, s. 463(1).

Effect of attachment

41–33   When a floating charge attaches to the property subject to the charge the effect is "as if the charge was a fixed security over the property to which it has attached."[50] A "fixed security" is defined as meaning any security, other than a floating charge or a charge having the nature of a floating charge, which on the winding up of the company in Scotland would be treated as an effective security over that property and (without prejudice to that generality) includes a security over that property being a heritable security within the meaning of the Conveyancing and Feudal Reform (Scotland) Act 1970.[51] Moreover, the Companies Act 1985[52] provides that a floating charge has effect in relation to heritable property in Scotland notwithstanding that the instrument creating it is not recorded in the Register of Sasines or registered in accordance with the Land Registration (Scotland) Act 1979. These provisions to some extent clarify the problems hitherto presented by the less specific terms of section 13(7) of the Companies (Floating Charges and Receivers) (Scotland) Act 1972 which were the subject of consideration in previous cases.[53] In general it appears that the holder of a floating charge upon its attachment has a completed security in the case of property consisting of corporeal moveables as if he had a security completed by delivery, in the case of incorporeal moveable property as if he had a security constituted by assignation and intimation or in the case of heritable property a security constituted by a standard security duly recorded in the Register of Sasines or registered in accordance with the Land Registration (Scotland) Act 1979. It may be observed, however, that as a matter of practice there are still certain advantages to the holder of a floating charge in taking also a recorded or registered standard security, *viz.*— (1) it automatically restricts the power of the debtor company to sell or let its heritable property without the consent of the creditor, (2) the creditor can enforce his rights without having to appoint a receiver, and (3) his claim is not postponed to the rights of preferential creditors.[54]

Attachment and diligence

41–34   The powers of a receiver in dealing with the property of a company to which the floating charge has attached are subject to the rights of any person who has effectually executed diligence.[55] The extent of the limitation on the powers of a receiver imposed by the corresponding provision of the Companies (Floating Charges and Receivers)

---

[50]Insolvency Act 1986, ss. 53(7), 54(6).
[51]*Ibid.*, s. 70(1).
[52]s. 462(5).
[53]*Lord Advocate* v. *Royal Bank of Scotland Ltd.*, 1977 S.C. 155 at 178, 179; *Forth & Clyde Construction Co. Ltd.* v. *Trinity Timber & Plywood Co. Ltd.*, 1984 S.L.T. 94 at 96, 97.
[54]See para. 41–59.
[55]Companies Act 1985, s. 471(2).

(Scotland) Act 1972 has been the subject of considerable litigation, and the effect of the leading judicial decisions is summarised in the following paragraphs.[56]

41-35 **(1) Arrestments**. The rights of a receiver prevail over those of a creditor who has arrested moneys due to the company after the attachment of the floating charge.[57] Even if the arrestment has been made before attachment by the appointment of a receiver, the right of the receiver is preferable unless the arrestment has been followed by a decree of forthcoming.[58]

41-36 **(2) Inhibitions**. The effect of an inhibition upon heritable property which is the subject of a floating charge which has attached, where the inhibition has antedated or postdated the creation of a charge, has already been considered.[59] In *Armour and Mycroft, Petitioners*,[60] where the floating charge was created before the inhibition but the inhibitor refused to discharge it and the joint receivers petitioned the court under section 21 of the 1972 Act (now replaced by an amended version in section 61 of the Insolvency Act 1986) seeking power to sell heritable property free of the encumbrance, the court rejected the inhibiting creditor's claim that its debt prevailed over the right of the receivers but held that it should be satisfied from the proceeds of sale of·the property in priority to the claims of the ordinary creditors. It may be observed, however, that the decision was pronounced in a situation where there was no other receiver or secured creditor and that the only other person in right of the free proceeds was the company itself which had been inhibited.

41-37 **(3) Sequestration for rent**. It is thought that sequestration by a landlord for rent made after the attachment of a floating charge is preferable to the right of the receiver, not as being effectually executed diligence, but as a fixed security arising by operation of law under section 464(2) of the Companies Act 1985.

41-38 **(4) Sale by receiver of property which is subject to effectually executed diligence**. Where a receiver wishes to sell or dispose of property falling under the charge by virtue of which he was appointed but is restricted from doing so by reason of effectually executed diligence upon it or the existence of a prior or *pari passu* security over it and the consent of the diligence creditor or secured creditor cannot be obtained, he may apply to the court for authority to sell or dispose of the property.[61] The

---

[56]For a fuller analysis of these decisions see Greene and Fletcher, paras. 2.13 to 2.17.
[57]*Forth & Clyde Construction Ltd.* v. *Trinity Timber & Plywood Co. Ltd.*, 1984 S.L.T. 94.
[58]*Lord Advocate* v. *Royal Bank of Scotland Ltd.*, 1977 S.C. 155. The decision has been strongly criticised; W.A. Wilson, *The Law of Scotland relating to Debt*, 233; James R. Campbell, "Receivers' Powers" (1978) 23 J.L.S. 275; A.J. Sim, "The Receiver and Effectually Executed Diligence," 1984 S.L.T. (News) 25; *contra* J.A.D. Hope, 1983 S.L.T. (News) 177.
[59]See Vol. II, para. 21–80.
[60]1983 S.L.T. 453.
[61]Insolvency Act 1986, s. 61: *Armour and Mycroft, Petitioners, supra*.

conditions on which such authorisation may be given, the requirement of registration of a copy of the authorisation with the Registrar of Companies and the effect of a disposition or document of transfer granted by the receiver in disencumbering the property and freeing it from the diligence are set out in the 1986 Act.[62]

Acquirenda

41–39   Whether or not property acquired by a company after appointment of a receiver is attached depends primarily upon the wording of the floating charge. If that wording bears to create the charge over "the whole of the property (including uncalled capital) which is or may be from time to time while this instrument is in force comprised in our property and undertaking" property which accrues after the attachment of the charge is included in the property attached.[63] The *ratio* of the decision was that the charge covered all property of the company existing and from time to time emerging while the instrument creating it was in force and the instrument did not cease to be in force on attachment of the charge. On that view money or goods recovered by a receiver on reduction of an unfair preference would fall within the scope of the security. It must be emphasised that the decision in *Ross* v. *Taylor* was based on the particular terms of the relevant floating charge,[64] but the terminology of the instrument in that case is now generally adopted[65] so that the decision will be applicable in many cases. The decision in *Ross* v. *Taylor* was pronounced principally in relation to the provisions of section 13(7) of the 1972 Act: the corresponding provision is now section 53(7) of the Insolvency Act 1986 but its terms are not materially different.

Set-off

41–40   In *Taylor, Petitioner*[66] it was held that on attachment of a floating charge the receiver acquired a *jus crediti* to recover on behalf of the company debts due to it, and the debtor was entitled to set off against it any valid counterclaim. It is thought that, notwithstanding an earlier decision to a different effect,[67] the principle applied in *Taylor* is correct.

Powers of directors

41–41   The effect of the appointment of a receiver upon the powers of the directors of the company has been considered in several Scottish and

---

[62] s. 61.
[63] *Ross* v. *Taylor*, 1985 S.L.T. 387.
[64] For an English decision based on the terms of a debenture, see *Yagerphone Ltd.* [1935] Ch. 392.
[65] See style in para. 41–05, Cl. Second.
[66] 1982 S.L.T. 172.
[67] *McPhail* v. *Lothian Regional Council*, 1981 S.L.T. 173.

English cases.[68] For a review of these decisions reference may be made to the undernoted text[69] but, at the risk of over-simplification, their effect may be summarised thus: (1) the appointment of a receiver effectively relieves the directors of their powers of management of the company and its business and assets falling under the charge, but (2) the directors may still do any acts which do not interfere with the exercise by the receiver of his functions and which would not prejudicially affect the assets subject to the charge, and (3) the directors are not relieved of their statutory obligations such as maintaining accounting records.

Effect on fixed securities, other floating charges and liquidation

41–42 The attachment of a floating charge on the appointment of a receiver does not affect the rights of the holder of a valid fixed security, e.g. a standard security, having priority over or ranking *pari passu* with the charge, and the creditor under that security may exercise the powers available to him over the subjects of his security.[70] Likewise it does not affect the rights of the holder of another floating charge having priority over, or ranking *pari passu* with, the floating charge which has attached.[70] The attachment of a floating charge does not automatically effect crystallisation of other floating charges, but it entitles the holder of another floating charge to appoint a receiver so far as not otherwise provided by the instrument creating it.[71]

Normally the attachment of any floating charge is the signal for appointment of a receiver also by holders of other floating charges granted by the company. Precedence among receivers is regulated statutorily.[72] Normally all the holders of floating charges for obvious reasons of convenience of administration appoint the same receiver or joint receivers, although sometimes where charges cover only part of the company's property different receivers may be appointed. If a liquidator is appointed on winding up of the company, whether before or after the appointment of a receiver, the liquidator must deliver or make available to the receiver the property subject to the charge.[73]

APPOINTMENT OF RECEIVER

Persons qualified for appointment as receiver

41–43 Sections 388 to 398 of the Insolvency Act 1986 provide for the

---

[68]*Imperial Hotel (Aberdeen) Ltd.* v. *Vaux Breweries Ltd.*, 1978 S.C. 86; *Newhart Developments Ltd.* v. *Co-operative Commercial Bank Ltd.* [1978] Q.B. 814; *Macleod* v. *Alexander Sutherland Ltd.*, 1977 S.L.T. (Notes) 44; *Hastings Black Construction Ltd.* v. *AIR (Air Conditioning and Refrigeration) Ltd.* (1984) Oct. 4, Glasgow Sheriff Court (unreported).
[69]Greene and Fletcher, paras. 2.18 to 2.25.
[70]Insolvency Act 1986, s. 55(3)(b).
[71]*Ibid.*, s. 52(1)(d).
[72]*Ibid.*, s. 56. See para. 41–50.
[73]*Manley, Petitioner*, 1985 S.L.T. 42.

persons who may become qualified insolvency practitioners (including receivers). Briefly a qualified person must be an individual who has been authorised by a recognised professional body to act as an insolvency practitioner and the relevant professional body may have its own rules or code which regulate the persons who will be so authorised, *e.g.* The Institute of Chartered Accountants of Scotland adopts a policy that it is improper for a practice, or a partner in or an employee of the practice, having, or during the previous two years having had, a continuing professional relationship with a company to accept appointment as receiver of that company, so that the auditors of the company are ineligible to accept appointment as a receiver of its property. In terms of section 51(3) of the Insolvency Act 1986 a body corporate, an undischarged bankrupt or a Scottish firm is disqualified from appointment as a receiver.

Administrative receivers and receivers

41–44   In terms of section 29 of the Insolvency Act 1986 a person who is appointed a receiver and manager of the whole (or substantially the whole) of a company's property is known as an administrative receiver: in any other circumstances he will be known as a receiver. The distinction is mainly of importance in relation to administration orders.

Method of appointment of receiver by holder of floating charge

41–45   In almost all cases a receiver is appointed by the holder of a floating charge or a person authorised by the holder to do so in pursuance of powers conferred in the floating charge.

41–46   Instrument of appointment by holder of floating charge

>   We, (*name and address*), the holder of a [Floating Charge] [Bond and Floating Charge] granted by (*name and registered office*), ("the Company") in our favour dated
>   WHEREAS an event has occurred whereby we are entitled to appoint a receiver of the property which is subject to the floating charge created by the said [Floating Charge] [Bond and Floating Charge] THEREFORE in exercise of the powers conferred on us by the said [Floating Charge] [Bond and Floating Charge] and relevant statutory powers we hereby APPOINT (*name, professional qualification and address*) to be receiver of the whole property which is, or may be from time to time, while the said [Floating Charge] [Bond and Floating Charge] is in force, comprised in the property and undertaking of the Company [including its uncalled capital for the time being].
>
> > (*To be sealed and subscribed by one director and the secretary or by two directors of the appointing company*)[74]

---

[74]Insolvency Act 1986, s. 53(3)(*a*).

The instrument of appointment may be executed on behalf of the holder of the floating charge, if a company, in accordance with section 36 of the Companies Act 1985.[74] Alternatively it may be executed on behalf of such holder by any person duly authorised in writing by the holder, or, in the case of a series of secured debentures, by any person authorised by resolution of the debenture holders to do so.[75] Where execution is by an authorised person his signature to the instrument of appointment should be attested by two witnesses in accordance with the requirements of law for execution of a probative deed,[76] and the document of authorisation or the resolution should be specified in the instrument of appointment.

41–47 **Registration of appointment.** Within seven days of the execution of the instrument of appointment a copy (certified by or on behalf of the person executing it to be a correct copy)[77] must be delivered by or on behalf of the person making the appointment to the Registrar of Companies, and must be accompanied by a notice (Form 1, Scot.) of the making of the appointment.[78] The Registrar will then enter particulars of the appointment in the Register of Charges.[79] Failure to comply with the requirements for registration timeously does not invalidate the appointment of the receiver but renders the person responsible for the failure liable to fines.[80]

41–48 **Acceptance of appointment.** The appointment to be effective must be accepted by the receiver before the end of the business day following that on which the instrument appointing him is received[81] and the acceptance (which need not be in writing) must be intimated by him to the holder of the floating charge or his agent within that period. As soon as possible thereafter the receiver must endorse on the instrument of appointment a docquet that the instrument was received on a day and time specified and also a docquet of acceptance of the appointment and deliver a copy of the instrument so endorsed to the holder of the charge or his agent.[82] That procedure with minor adjustments applies also to joint receivers.[83] The appointment is deemed to have been made on the day and at the time on which the instrument of appointment was so received.[84]

Appointment of receiver by the court

41–49 A receiver may also be appointed by the court on application by the

---

[75]*Ibid.*, s. 53(4).
[76]*Ibid.*, s. 53(3)(*b*).
[77]Receivers (Scotland) Regulations 1986 (S.I. 1986 No. 1917) (S.141). r. 4.
[78]Insolvency Act 1986, s. 53(1).
[79]*Ibid.*, s. 53(5).
[80]*Ibid.*, s. 53(2).
[81]*Ibid.*, s. 53(6).
[82]Insolvency (Scotland) Rules 1986 (S.I. 1986 No. 1915) (S.139) r. 3.1. (1) to (3).
[83]*Ibid.*, r. 3.1.(4).
[84]Insolvency Act 1986, s. 53(6)(*b*).

holder of a floating charge.[85] Details of the procedure, registration of the interlocutor making the appointment and the effective date of the appointment are contained in section 54 of the Insolvency Act 1986 and the relevant Rules of Court.[86]

Precedence among receivers

41–50   Where there are two or more floating charges over all or part of the property of a company the holder of each charge is entitled to appoint a receiver, but the receiver appointed by the holder of a floating charge having priority over any other floating charge has the powers of a receiver under the Insolvency Act 1986 to the exclusion of any other receiver. Where two or more floating charges rank *pari passu* with each other the receivers appointed by the respective holders of the charges are deemed to have been appointed as joint receivers.[87] Joint receivers act jointly unless the instruments of appointment otherwise provide,[88] but as a matter of convenience of administration it is desirable that the instruments of appointment authorise each receiver to act individually.

Notification of appointment of receiver

41–51   The registration of particulars of the appointment of a receiver by the holder of the floating charge[89] gives public notice of it, but in addition the Insolvency Act 1986 requires the receiver himself to publish his appointment in various ways. Every invoice, order for goods or business letter issued by or on behalf of the company or the receiver must contain a statement that a receiver has been appointed.[90] Further, the receiver forthwith after his appointment must send to the company and publish notice of his appointment.[91] Usually the receiver shortly after his appointment publishes in the *Edinburgh Gazette* and in a newspaper circulating in the district where the company carries on business the statutory notice for preferential claims.[92] The receiver must also within 28 days after his appointment send notice thereof to all the creditors of the company (so far as he is aware of their addresses), unless the court otherwise directs.[93]

Powers of receiver

41–52   The powers of a receiver are listed in Schedule 2 to the Insolvency

---

[85]The procedure is by petition to the Outer House of the Court of Session.
[86]Act of Sederunt (Rules of Court Amendment No. 11) (Companies) 1986 (S.I. 1986 No. 2298) (S.170); Act of Sederunt (Sheriff Court Company Insolvency Rules (1986) (S.I. 1986 No. 2297) (S.169).
[87]Insolvency Act 1986, s. 56(1) and (2).
[88]*Ibid.*, s. 56(3).
[89]See para. 41–47.
[90]Insolvency Act 1986, s. 64(1).
[91]*Ibid.*, s. 65(1)(*a*); Form 4 (Scot).
[92]*Ibid.*, s. 59(2).
[93]*Ibid.*, s. 65(1)(*b*).

Act 1986. Any additional special powers that may be required should be specified in the floating charge, but the statutory powers will be adequate in most cases. These include powers in relation to the subjects falling under the charge to take possession of and collect and get in property and to take any necessary proceedings, to sell, feu, hire or otherwise dispose of property, to borrow money on the security of property, to appoint a solicitor or accountant or other professional adviser, to bring or defend actions or other legal proceedings in the name and on behalf of the company, to refer questions affecting the company to arbitration, to effect and maintain insurances in respect of the business and property of the company, to use the company's seal, to do all acts and to execute documents in name and on behalf of the company, to draw, accept, make and endorse any bill of exchange or promissory note in the name and on behalf of the company, to appoint agents and employ and dismiss employees, to do all such things (including the carrying out of works) as may be necessary for realising property, to make any payment necessary or incidental to the performance of his functions, to carry on the business of the company or any part of it, to grant or accept the surrender of a lease or tenancy of property, to make any arrangement or compromise on behalf of the company, to call up uncalled capital of the company, to establish subsidiaries of the company, to transfer to subsidiaries of the company the business of the company or any part of it and any of the property, to rank and claim in the bankruptcy, insolvency, sequestration or liquidation of any person indebted to the company and accede to trust deeds by creditors of any such person, to present a petition for winding up the company, to change the situation of the company's registered office and to do all other things incidental to the exercise of the powers in section 55(1) of the 1986 Act or above. Some of these powers which involve more particularly conveyancing matters are considered in paragraphs 41–56 to 41–58 *infra*.

Liability of receiver on contracts

41–53   As a preliminary to consideration of the exercise by a receiver of his powers it is essential to have a clear view of the liabilities which he may incur under contracts into which he may enter.

41–54   **Pre-receivership contracts**. Contracts entered into by the company before appointment of a receiver do not terminate on such an appointment being made unless the contract so provides. If a contract continues, the receiver is not automatically liable personally under it unless by his actings he adopts the contract, which is a question of fact. Often the appointment of a receiver disables the company from continuing a contract: the courts will not normally grant to the other contracting party a decree of specific implement in such circumstances[94] save in exceptional cases where there is no question of the receiver incurring personal liability.[95] If a receiver adopts a contract, he will incur personal liability but is entitled to be indemnified from the property covered by the charge in respect of which he was appointed.[96] In practice a receiver must exercise his judgment as to whether adoption of a pre-receivership contract will clearly benefit the company: if in such circumstances he decides to adopt it but some element of risk of loss may be involved, he should either (i) be satisfied that the net assets under his charge are ample to recoup any possible loss or (ii) obtain an indemnity from the creditor who appointed him against any loss from adoption of the contract.

41-55 **Post-receivership contracts.** In terms of section 57(1) of the Insolvency Act 1986 a receiver is deemed to be the agent of the company in relation to the property of the company attached by the charge by virtue of which he was appointed. Accordingly the receiver in entering into a contract relating to such property, if he does so expressly in his capacity as receiver, is acting as the agent of a disclosed principal and does not incur personal liability. On the other hand if he enters into a contract in the performance of his functions otherwise than as agent for the company then he is personally liable thereunder unless the contract otherwise provides[97] and he cannot contractually exclude that liability if the contract is one of employment, *e.g.* liability for wages. He has the same right to be indemnified against personal liability out of the property covered by the charge in respect of which he was appointed. In the circumstances that the company is in receivership another party will seldom be willing to enter into a contract involving the performance of works or the supply of goods on the basis that the personal liability of the receiver is excluded, and so the receiver will frequently face a conflict between the desirability of entering into a contract which should be profitable and the risk of incurring personal liability for loss if it turns out not to be so. Again the problem is similar to that already considered in the preceding paragraph, and may be resolved in the way there suggested.

Sale or feu of heritable property

41-56 In a sale or feu of heritable property of the company the receiver has a wide discretion as to method, which may be by private bargain or public exposure. As a party disposing of subjects held under a fixed security he has a duty to obtain the best price that can reasonably be obtained,[98] and there should be adequate advertisement in such form

---

[94] *Macleod* v. *Alexander Sutherland Ltd.*, 1977 S.L.T. (Notes) 44; *Airlines Airspares Ltd.* v. *Handley Page Ltd.* [1970] Ch. 193.
[95] *Freevale Ltd.* v. *Metrostore (Holdings) Ltd.* [1984] 1 All E.R. 495.
[96] Insolvency Act 1986, s. 57(3).
[97] *Ibid.*, s. 57(2).
[98] *Forth & Clyde Construction Co. Ltd.* v. *Trinity Timber & Plywood Co. Ltd.*, 1984 S.L.T. 94 at 97.

as will do justice to the property. Where the sale is by private bargain the missives should be entered into by the receiver expressly in that capacity, and should contain all the conditions appropriate to a contract for the sale of a property of the kind involved.

Letter of obligation by solicitor for receiver

41–57   In the circumstances of a sale by a receiver who excludes his personal liability, the granting of a letter of obligation by his solicitor which imposes obligations on the solicitor personally requires care. The problems with regard to obligations of solicitors in sales of heritable property by a company have already been considered and suggestions made as to possible solutions in practice.[99] When the sale is by a receiver, however, there is a special element, namely, that on attachment of the floating charge the creditor by whom the receiver was appointed has a fixed security over the property and the receiver has power to sell it.

(a) Property register. Where the relevant register is the Register of Sasines an obligation by the solicitor acting for the receiver may cover a considerable period between the last date to which the search is available and the date of the transaction of sale: the period is much less when the title to the property has been registered in the Land Register. The receiver's solicitor will normally have received the title deeds of the property from the company's solicitors, however, who will usually be aware of any transactions affecting the property which have been effected within either period and be prepared to communicate information on the matter to the solicitor for the receiver so that the risk of any adverse deed having been recorded in the Register of Sasines or entered in the Land Register is little greater than in the situation where the title deeds of the property have been held throughout the relevant period by a seller's solicitor. Subject to obtaining such information from the solicitor who acted for the company (which he will usually co-operate in supplying) the solicitor for the receiver may with reasonable safety give an obligation with regard to entries in the relevant property register in respect of the period between the last date to which reports are available and the date when the disposition to the purchaser is recorded provided that is done without delay after settlement of the transaction.

(b) Personal register. (i) If the report on the personal register discloses an inhibition against the company which is prior in date to the creation of the floating charge by virtue of which the receiver was appointed, it must be cleared, and that should be done before a binding contract of sale is concluded. Normally the receiver should negotiate with the inhibitor to obtain either a discharge of the inhibition or release of the

[99]See Vol. II, para. 21–87.

property from it, but the practicability of procuring a discharge or release will depend upon the amount of the debt due to the inhibitor and the value of other properties under the control of the receiver which are also affected by the inhibition. If it is impracticable to obtain a discharge or release on reasonable terms it may be possible for the receiver, particularly where the value of such other subjects is ample to secure repayment of the debt due to the inhibitor, to obtain the authority of the court to the proposed sale by application under section 61 of the Insolvency Act 1986 on conditions which may be more acceptable.

(ii) If the date of the inhibition was after the creation of the floating charge it does not prevail over the receiver's right[1]; nevertheless the purchaser may decline to proceed until the record is cleared of the inhibition[2] and an application by the receiver under section 61 of the 1986 Act may still be required.[3] Preferably the application should be made before the missives of sale are concluded but, if there is urgency to have the bargain completed, the receiver may do so since, because his right is prior to that of the inhibitor, he can be reasonably assured of obtaining the authority of the court on conditions as to the inhibitor which will not preclude the granting of a valid disposition. In those circumstances, however, the responsibility of obtaining authority is that of the receiver; any letter of obligation granted by his solicitor should be expressed as subject to any rights of the inhibitor.

(iii) If the date of the inhibition is after the receiver's appointment, it is thought that the receiver, as the creditor in a pre-existing fixed security, may grant a disposition to the purchaser which, when recorded in the Register of Sasines or when the purchaser's interest is registered in the Land Register, will disburden the property of the diligence of the inhibition.[4] In those circumstances the receiver's solicitor, if he is granting a letter of obligation, need not qualify it by reference to the inhibition.

If the inhibition is of so recent a date that it may be rendered wholly ineffectual by liquidation of the company within 60 days after the inhibition was effected, it may be cut down if the receiver quickly exercises his power to present a petition for the winding up of the company.[4a] The appointment of a liquidator may be administratively inconvenient to the receiver in his conduct of the receivership and may have tax disadvantages,[5] but on the other hand, if the amount of the inhibitor's debt is substantial, it may be preferable to have any right

---

[1] See Vol. II, para. 21–80.

[2] *Dryburgh* v. *Gordon* (1896) 24 R. 1.

[3] As in *Armour and Mycroft, Petitioners*, 1983 S.L.T. 453.

[4] Conveyancing and Feudal Reform (Scotland) Act 1970, s. 26(1). It may be argued that, since the 1986 Act, s. 61 prescribes a particular remedy, that is the appropriate procedure to adopt, but that seems unnecessary since the attachment of the floating charge has been equiparated to a recorded security—see para. 41–33.

[4a] Insolvency Act 1986, s. 185; Bankruptcy (Scotland) Act 1985, s. 37(2).

[5] See Greene and Fletcher, para. 7.73.

obtained by the reducible inhibition wholly removed rather than take the risk of the court according to the inhibitor some kind of preference over ordinary creditors upon a decision made under section 61 of the Insolvency Act 1986. So, if the inhibition is of recent date and in respect of a debt of substantial amount and affects several properties of the company which the receiver will require to sell, it may be sensible, subject to consideration of the administrative and taxation disadvantages, for the receiver to take immediate steps to have a liquidator appointed.

(c) **Companies Charges Register**. A purchaser sometimes stipulates for a clear search in the Companies Register of Charges. Such a stipulation cannot normally be accepted for the following reasons:

(i) *The floating charge by virtue of which the selling receiver was appointed*. The secured debt may not be fully satisfied by the sale of the property and indeed may never be fully satisfied. A request for a memorandum of full or partial satisfaction of the charge in order to disburden the property of the fixed security created by its attachment is unnecessary since a disposition by the creditor under powers contained in a heritable security, when recorded or when it enters the Land Register, automatically disburdens the property conveyed of *inter alia* that heritable security[6] and if it is contended that the analogy of a receiver selling in the exercise of the powers conferred by the fixed security of the attached charge to that of a heritable creditor selling under his security is not complete, it is thought that, on ordinary principles of personal bar, the holder of the floating charge could not subsequently maintain successfully that his charge still constituted a security over a property which the receiver appointed by him had conveyed for value by a disposition which did not except the charge from warrandice.

(ii) *Prior floating charges*. A prior floating charge does not automatically crystallise on the appointment of a receiver by the holder of a postponed floating charge, but the holder of the prior charge may appoint a receiver who will have powers which will exclude those of a receiver appointed by virtue of the postponed charge.[7] So a letter should be obtained from the holder of any prior charge that it has not crystallised and that there are no circumstances in which it is contemplated that a receiver will be appointed under it within the period in which the disposition to the purchaser will be recorded in the Register of Sasines or submitted for registration in the Land Register, as the case may be.

On the whole the solicitor for the receiver should not be required to give a letter of obligation with regard to the Companies Charges Register.

---

[6]Conveyancing and Feudal Reform (Scotland) Act 1970, s. 26(1).
[7]Insolvency Act 1986, s. 56(1).

Disposition by receiver

41–58   As to the form of a disposition by a receiver on sale see Volume II, paragraph 22–50.

Distribution of proceeds of sale by receiver

41–59   In terms of section 60(1) of the Insolvency Act 1986 the order of priority of claims to the proceeds of sale of property realised by a receiver (subject to any directions given by the court on an application under section 61 of that Act) is:

(1) the holder of any fixed security over property subject to the floating charge and which ranks prior to, or *pari passu* with, the floating charge;

(2) all persons who have effectually executed diligence on any part of the property of the company which is subject to the charge by virtue of which the receiver was appointed[8];

(3) creditors in respect of all liabilities, charges and expenses incurred by or on behalf of the receiver;

(4) the receiver in respect of his liabilities, expenses and remuneration, and any indemnity to which he is entitled out of the property of the company; and

(5) the preferential creditors entitled to payment under section 59 of the 1986 Act.[9]

Subject to satisfaction of those claims the receiver pays moneys received by him to the holder of the floating charge by virtue of which he was appointed in or towards satisfaction of the debt secured by the floating charge. Any balance remaining is to be paid in accordance with their respective rights and interests to (a) any other receiver, (b) the holder of a fixed security which is over property subject to the charge, and (c) the company or its liquidator, as the case may be.[10] Where any question arises as to the person entitled to a payment, or where a receipt or discharge cannot be obtained in respect of any such payment, the receiver must consign the amount of it in any joint stock bank of issue in Scotland in the name of the Accountant of Court for behoof of the person or persons entitled thereto.[11]

Cross-border operation of receivership provisions

41–60   Section 72 of the Insolvency Act 1986 (broadly re-enacting the provisions of earlier statutes[12]) provides that a receiver appointed under the law of either part of Great Britain in respect of the whole or

---

[8]See paras. 41–34 to 41–38.

[9]These are creditors within the categories specified in Sched. 6 to the Act which after six months from advertisement for claims in the *Edinburgh Gazette* and a newspaper circulating in the district have been intimated or become known to the receiver.

[10]Insolvency Act 1986. s. 60(2).

[11]*Ibid.*, s. 60(3).

[12]Companies (Floating Charges and Receivers) (Scotland) Act 1972. s. 15(4); Administration of Justice Act 1977. s. 7; Companies Act 1985, s. 724.

any part of any property or undertaking of a company and in consequence of the company having created a charge which, as created, was a floating charge may exercise his powers in any other part of Great Britain so far as their exercise is not inconsistent with the law applicable there. Section 7 of the Administration of Justice Act 1977 (which has not been repealed) is wider in its application and makes identical provision in relation to the United Kingdom, not merely Great Britain. In *Gordon Anderson (Plant) Ltd.* v. *Campsie Construction Ltd. and Anglo Scottish Plant Ltd.*,[13] the Court of Session held that the appointment of a receiver in England effected attachment of the charge to the property of the company in Scotland so that a fixed security over that property was created.

Further reference works

41–61   It has been practicable within the scope of this work to deal only with those aspects of the law relating to floating charges and receivers which have important conveyancing implications. For more detailed study, reference may be made to Palmer, *Company Law* (23rd ed.), *Halsbury's Laws of England* (4th ed.), Volume 7, and Greene and Fletcher, *The Law and Practice of Receivership in Scotland*.

---

[13]1977 S.L.T. 7.

CHAPTER 42

RECORDING AND REGISTRATION AND RANKING OF HERITABLE SECURITIES

PART I: RECORDING AND REGISTRATION
OF HERITABLE SECURITIES

Introduction

42–01   Part I of this chapter treats of the recording in the Register of
Sasines of deeds or writs relating to heritable securities or the
registration in the Land Register of Scotland of interests in heritable
securities. Initially the practice is affected by the situation where (1)
the area in which the security subjects are situated has not yet been
designated as operational for the purposes of registration of title (a
non-operational area) or (2) the area has been so designated (an
operational area). Within the second category there are distinctions in
practice between recording or registration arising from transactions in
respect of heritable securities which existed before first registration of
the title to the security subjects in the Land Register has occurred and
those which continue to subsist or are created after such registration.
In this chapter the term "old securities" refers to those which cannot

now be created in that form for debts as defined in the Conveyancing and Feudal Reform (Scotland) Act 1970,[1] *e.g.* bonds and dispositions in security, cash credit bonds and dispositions in security, *ex facie* absolute dispositions and ground annuals.

Non-operational Areas

Recording in Register of Sasines

42–02   Where the security subjects are situated in an area which has not yet been designated as operational for the purposes of registration of title all new standard securities and all deeds or writs relating to existing heritable securities, whether old securities or standard securities, will, with warrants of registration in appropriate terms, continue to be recorded in the Register of Sasines.[2]

Contemporaneous discharge of heritable security and sale

42–03   Normally the discharge with a warrant of registration signed by or on behalf of the seller and a covering letter to the Keeper instructing registration of the discharge are delivered at settlement to the purchaser's solicitor who then forwards them to the Keeper with the disposition having a warrant of registration signed by or on behalf of the purchaser and the discharge and disposition are recorded contemporaneously.[3] Where for any reason the discharge is not available at settlement, the seller's solicitor will normally grant a letter of obligation to deliver it and when it is available will deliver the executed discharge with a warrant of registration signed by or on behalf of the seller to the purchaser's solicitor and a covering letter to the Keeper, and the purchaser's solicitor will forward it to the Keeper to be recorded.[3a]

Contemporaneous purchase and new loan

42–04   Usually the disposition in favour of the purchaser with a warrant of registration signed by or on behalf of the purchaser and a covering letter instructing registration are delivered to the solicitor for the lender (if other than the solicitor acting for the purchaser), who then forwards it with the standard security in favour of the lender with an appropriate warrant of registration signed by or on behalf of the lender to the Keeper to be recorded contemporaneously.[4] If the disposition and standard security are recorded together the recording dues payable in respect of the standard security are at a reduced rate. Late or

---

[1] s. 9.
[2] See Vol. II, Chap. 24.
[3] As to steps in procedure, see Vol. II, para. 23–02.
[3a] It should be emphasised that in proper practice the discharge should be delivered at settlement.
[4] As to steps in procedure, see Vol. II, para. 23–02.

separate recording of the standard security will therefore be more costly to the client.

Operational Areas

General rules

42–05   Where the security subjects are situated in an area which has been designated as operational for the purposes of registration of title, the following general rules in relation to recording or registration of transactions relating to heritable securities may be stated:

(i) Before the interest of the proprietor of the security subjects has been registered in the Land Register, new standard securities granted and deeds or writs relating to existing heritable securities will be recorded in the Register of Sasines, save in the case of the exceptional transactions in rule (iii).

(ii) Once the interest of the proprietor of the security subjects has been registered in the Land Register, then

(a) as regards all new standard securities and subsequent dealings with them, the interest of the creditor must be registered in the Land Register;

(b) deeds or writs which created or related to existing heritable securities and were recorded in the Register of Sasines before the interest of the proprietor of the security subjects became registered in the Land Register may remain recorded in the Register of Sasines: as to the legal effect of that course and the alternative of applying for voluntary registration of the creditor's interest in the Land Register see paragraphs 42–15 and 42–16 *infra*. Subsequent dealings with such heritable securities (*i.e.* existing heritable securities which remain recorded in the Register of Sasines) should as a matter of policy be entered or their effect reflected in the Land Register. Section 2(4)(*c*) of the Land Registration (Scotland) Act 1979 makes registrable any transaction which is capable of affecting the title to a registered interest. Clearly a discharge or deed of restriction of the heritable security affects the interest of the proprietor of the security subjects, a deed of variation of the security may do so and even a simple assignation of the security has some effect upon the security subjects as identifying the creditor in a burden affecting them. Even if a transfer or transmission of the creditor's interest is not such as is technically registrable under section 2(4)(*c*), the Keeper has the power to disclose it on the title sheet of the security subjects under section 6(1)(*g*) of the 1979 Act and it is understood that he would welcome applications to do so. Two related matters require consideration, *viz.*— (1) Where the heritable security covers also subjects other than those comprised in a registered interest, the subsequent deed should be recorded also in the Register of Sasines. (2) Technically there could be a question whether an assignation or deed of variation requires to be recorded in the

Register of Sasines in order to complete the title of the creditor to the security as transferred or varied. It would appear that, where an unregistered creditor's interest remains, recording in the Register of Sasines would be competent under section 8(2)(c) of the 1979 Act, but to avoid duplication of registration the best course might be to seek voluntary registration of the creditor's interest when that interest remains after the subsequent transaction affecting the security.

(iii) Transactions relating to heritable securities which existed before first registration of the interest of a proprietor of the security subjects and which have the effect of altering the interest of the proprietor or *ex facie* proprietor of the security subjects as transfers of that interest for valuable consideration will be given effect by registration in the Land Register whether such transactions occur before or after first registration of the interest of the proprietor.

1. Interest of Proprietor of Security Subjects not yet Registered in Land Register

Security transactions where relevant deed recorded in Register of Sasines

42–06   If the security transaction consists of the granting of a new standard security or a dealing with any existing heritable security which does not itself induce first registration of the interest of a proprietor of the security subjects the relevant deed will, in accordance with the general rule (i) in paragraph 42–05 *supra*, be recorded in the Register of Sasines. So a new standard security or an assignation, deed of restriction or discharge of a bond and disposition in security or of a standard security will be so recorded.

Security transactions which may induce first registration of the interest of the proprietor of the security subjects

42–07   **(a) Enforcement of security and extinction of security**. Certain transactions relating to heritable securities have themselves the effect of inducing first registration of the title to the security subjects in the Land Register. Examples are: (1) a disposition of the security subjects on sale by a heritable creditor in the exercise of his power of sale, (2) an extract decree of foreclosure, or (3) a disposition by a heritable creditor in his own favour after re-exposure under section 8 of the Heritable Securities (Scotland) Act 1894 or section 28(4) of the Conveyancing and Feudal Reform (Scotland) Act 1970. All these transactions are in effect transfers of the interest in the security subjects for valuable consideration which induce first registration of the title to the security subjects in the Land Register and in all cases the heritable security is extinguished. Application for registration should be made by the new proprietor or his solicitor on Form 1 accompanied by (i) the relevant disposition or extract decree which induces first registration (no warrant of registration is required), (ii) an inventory (Form 4) in duplicate, (iii) a prescriptive progress of the property and security titles together with any deeds whereby rights, burdens or conditions affecting the security subjects have been or are created, varied or discharged (other than deeds common to several titles), all of which should be included in the inventory, (iv) any additional documentary evidence, *e.g.* a feuduty redemption receipt or any necessary separate consent or affidavit obtained in pursuance of the Matrimonial Homes (Family Protection) (Scotland) Act 1981 when the security was created and (v) any plan which may be required to enable identification of the security subjects on the Ordnance Map. Where in relation to any of those transactions ancillary documents require to be recorded or registered, *e.g.* certificates of surplus or no surplus on a sale under power contained in an old security, the advice of the Keeper should be sought as to the appropriate register, but *prima facie* they should be entered in the Land Register.[5]

42–08 **(b) Transactions relating to ex facie absolute dispositions or assignations.** Where the creditor's interest under an *ex facie* absolute disposition (feudal property) or *ex facie* absolute assignation (leasehold property) is transferred by a disposition or assignation difficult theoretical problems as to recording or registration of the relevant deed can arise, and in all cases the Keeper should be consulted as to the appropriate procedure. Subject to the Keeper's advice in the circumstances of the particular transaction the following views are expressed: (1) If the transfer is not for valuable consideration (and frequently it is not) it is not registrable under section 2(1)(*a*)(ii) of the 1979 Act and the disposition or assignation should be recorded in the Register of Sasines. (2) If the back letter or agreement qualifying the original disposition or assignation has been recorded, the fact that the original transaction was truly one of security will have been published on record and so the subsequent transfer of the creditor's interest (whether for value or not) will be a dealing with a security and so section 2(2) of the 1979 Act applies and again the disposition or assignation will be recorded in the Register of Sasines. (3) If the fact that the original transaction was truly one of security has not been disclosed on record but the transferee of the creditor's interest is aware that he is acquiring a security (as he almost always will be) and discloses that fact to the Keeper, then probably the procedure for recording will be as in case (2) above. (4) In the very unusual situation where the facts are as in case (3) above but the transferee does not disclose the true nature of the original transaction and the transfer is for value, then the disposition or assignation is *prima facie* a transfer of the subjects which induces first registration under section 2(1)(*a*)(ii) of the 1979 Act, application should be made on Form 1 and the

---

[5]Land Registration (Scotland) Act 1979, s. 29(2).

procedure on registration will be as outlined in paragraph D.4.01 of the *Registration of Title Practice Book*. (5) In the very rare case where the *ex facie* absolute disponee or assignee grants a security over his interest the subsequent standard security, if the title of the *ex facie* absolute disponee or assignee is still recorded in the Register of Sasines, will also be recorded in that Register, but if the interest of the original creditor under the *ex facie* absolute disposition or assignation has been assigned to a new creditor whose title has been registered as in case (4) above, then the grant of the standard security over it, being a security over a registered interest, will fall to be registered under section 2(3) of the 1979 Act and application for its registration should be made on Form 2.[6]

Contemporaneous discharge of heritable security and sale

42–09 Where a transaction involves the discharge of an existing heritable security, in whatever form, and sale of the security subjects, first registration of the security subjects is induced by the sale. In these circumstances where the discharge relates to the whole interest acquired by the purchaser and accompanies the application for registration of the purchaser's interest (or follows immediately upon it) and is listed on the inventory (Form 4), the Keeper will give effect to the discharge although it contains no warrant of registration nor is accompanied by an application for registration and the discharge will not be recorded in the Register of Sasines at all.[6a] The same procedure applies to a deed of restriction, or a discharge or reconveyance by an *ex facie* absolute disponee, provided that the deed relates solely to the interest acquired by the purchaser.[7,8]

42–10 Where the discharge is not available at settlement the application for registration of the purchaser's title induced by the sale transaction (Form 1) should include the discharge in the accompanying inventory (Form 4) marked "to follow." In due course when the executed discharge is available it should be delivered to the purchaser's solicitor in pursuance of the obligation granted by the seller's solicitor at settlement along with an application (Form 2) for registration completed and signed by the seller or his solicitor, an inventory (Form 4) in duplicate and (where the granter of the discharge does not have a recorded title to the security) any links in title connecting the granter's right to the last recorded title to the security.

The purchaser's solicitor will then mark on the top of the front page of the discharge the title number of the registered interest of the purchaser (which will already have been allocated and of which he will have been notified) and forward the application for registration, the

---

[6] See R.T.P.B., para. D.4.01.
[6a] Technically, unless the discharge is received before the application for registration of the purchaser's interest, it cannot be recorded in the Register of Sasines.
[7] See R.T.P.B., para. G.2.40.
[8] As to steps in procedure, see Vol. II, para. 23–17.

executed discharge, the inventory and any necessary links in title to the Keeper.[9] In this event a separate registration fee will be payable in respect of the discharge.

42–11 If the discharge affects other subjects the title to which is still recorded in the Register of Sasines, *e.g.* a partial discharge and deed of restriction, effect will require to be given to it both in the Register of Sasines and the Land Register and so a warrant of registration will require to be endorsed on it and, if the granter of the discharge does not have a recorded title to the security, a clause of deduction of title should be incorporated in it. If the discharge accompanies the application for registration of the purchaser's interest (Form 1) an application on Form 2 is not required but the Keeper should be requested in an accompanying letter to record the deed in the Register of Sasines.[10]

Where the deed is not available at settlement it should be listed in the inventory (Form 4) accompanying the application (Form 1) for registration of the purchaser's interest. Then, when the executed deed is available, it should be delivered by the seller's solicitor, with the warrant of registration signed by him, to the purchaser's solicitor in implement of the letter of obligation granted at settlement along with an application for registration on Form 2 completed and signed by the seller's solicitor, a relative inventory (Form 4) in duplicate and any supporting documents. The purchaser's solicitor should then mark on the front page of the deed the title number of the registered interest of the purchaser (which will by then have been notified to him) and submit the application with the duplicate inventory and the executed deed and any other documents in order that the deed be recorded in the Register of Sasines.[11] An additional fee for registration of the deed will be payable.

Contemporaneous purchase and new secured loan

42–12 First registration is induced by the purchase, and the standard security in respect of the new loan, being a dealing with a registered interest, must also be registered in the Land Register. The application (Form 1) for registration of the purchaser's interest and the application (Form 2) for registration of the lender's interest will be adjusted by the solicitors for the seller, the purchaser and the lender, and any additional information or evidence that may be required by the Keeper

---

[9] R.T.P.B., para. G.2.41. In strict logic Form 2 should be completed and signed by or on behalf of the purchaser who is now the proprietor of the subjects disburdened by the discharge, but in practice the Keeper will accept the application completed by or on behalf of the seller.

[10] R.T.P.B., para. G.2.42.

[11] See n. 9 to para. 42–10. It is thought that the warrant of registration should be signed by or on behalf of the seller in accordance with previous practice in sasine transactions, but the Keeper would probably accept Form 2 completed by or on behalf of the purchaser.

obtained.[12,13] After settlement there should be forwarded to the Keeper by the solicitor acting for the purchaser and the lender (if the same) or by the solicitor for the lender (if different solicitors act for the purchaser and the lender) the following: (i) Form 1 duly completed by or on behalf of the purchaser, (ii) the executed disposition (no warrant of registration is required), (iii) the relative inventory (Form 4) in duplicate, (iv) all deeds and documents detailed in the inventory (which should include a prescriptive progress of titles and deeds whereby rights, burdens or conditions are created, varied or discharged other than deeds common to several titles), (v) any Form P.16 report and any supplementary plan required to enable the Keeper to identify the subjects on the Ordnance Map (which plan should be listed in the inventory), (vi) any additional documentary evidence, e.g. a feuduty redemption receipt and separate consent or affidavit required by the Matrimonial Homes (Family Protection) (Scotland) Act 1981 (these also should be included in the inventory), (vii) Form 2 being the application for registration of the creditor's interest under the standard security, and (viii) the executed standard security (no warrant of registration required).[14] Where the standard security is granted by a company, the certificate of registration of the charge in the Register of Charges should also be sent when it becomes available later.[15]

When the registration has been completed the Keeper will issue to the purchaser's solicitor a land certificate in name of the purchaser and to the lender's solicitor a charge certificate in the name of the lender. The standard security itself will be attached to the charge certificate. All deeds and other evidence exhibited to the Keeper will be returned to the purchaser's solicitor. As to subsequent procedure in relation to the checking of the land certificate and the charge certificate and delivery and disposal of the title deeds, reference may be made to paragraphs G.2.45 to G.2.47 of the *Registration of Title Practice Book*.[16]

2. Proprietor's Interest already Registered in Land Register

New standard securities

42–13   After the interest of the proprietor of the security subjects has been registered in the Land Register any standard security granted by him is registrable in that Register. Application should be made by the creditor on Form 2 with an inventory (Form 4) in duplicate

---

[12]R.T.P.B., para. G.2.27.
[13]As to the forms of the disposition and the standard security, see R.T.P.B., paras. G.2.29 to G.2.31.
[14]See R.T.P.B., para. G.2.34.
[15]See para. 42–21.
[16]See also Vol. II, para. 23–17.

accompanied by the relevant land certificate, the new standard security (which should describe the security subjects by reference to the title number of the proprietor's interest) duly executed, any links in title establishing the granter's right to the security subjects if he is not the registered proprietor and any other documents or evidence that may be required by the Keeper, *e.g.* a consent or affidavit required under the Matrimonial Homes (Family Protection) (Scotland) Act 1981 in respect of any proprietor formerly infeft and any person intervening between him and the grantor of the standard security (matrimonial homes evidence is not required at this stage in respect of the grantor of the standard security himself). Upon registration of the creditor's interest, the Keeper will issue to him a charge certificate to which the standard security will be annexed.

If the standard security is created over a part only of the registered interest the description of the security subjects in the standard security should be sufficient to enable the Keeper to identify the part on the Ordnance Map or a separate plan should be supplied which provides the necessary description. Application for registration should be made by the creditor, again on Form 2, with the accompanying documents as in the preceding subparagraph.

Dealings with registered standard securities

42–14   Once the interest of the creditor under a standard security has been registered in the Land Register any subsequent dealing with the security should also be registered in that Register. Applications in respect of a dealing with the whole or a part should be made on Form 2; if the dealing affects a part only of the security subjects the part should be described so as to enable it to be identified on the Ordnance Map. In either case the application should be accompanied by the relevant deed, the charge certificate and any links in title establishing the right of the granter of the deed (if other than the creditor named in the charge certificate).

Transactions relating to existing heritable securities which remain recorded in Register of Sasines

42–15   Upon first registration of the interest of the proprietor of security subjects which are burdened by a proper security previously recorded in the Register of Sasines, the Keeper will enter the security in the charges section of the title sheet and the entry in the charges section will reflect the effect of any subsequent deeds relating to the security, *e.g.* assignations, deeds of restriction or discharges. The entry in the charges section, however, merely discloses that the subjects are burdened by a security which on the face of the record is valid and preserves the rights of the creditor to that extent, but is not equivalent to the registration of the interest of the creditor in the Land Register and no charge certificate will be issued. The position is simply that the security, subject to any existing defects, remains, but without the protection of an indemnity. If the creditor wishes to have his interest registered in the Land Register with that protection, or if the person of the creditor changes or his rights are altered by some subsequent transaction,[17] he may apply for registration of his title to the security on Form 2 when, if the Keeper is satisfied as to the existence and validity of the security, the creditor's interest will be registered in the Land Register and a charge certificate issued supported by the Keeper's indemnity.

Paragraph D.4.08 of the *Registration of Title Practice Book* contains a warning that a creditor who decides to seek registration of his title to the security should consider carefully the effect of section 7 of the Land Registration (Scotland) Act 1979 on the ranking of his existing security with any other subsequent securities already registered in the Land Register, since it is not clear from that section that the creditor will retain the priority accorded by his original recording date. It is thought, however, that the existing ranking of the respective securities will not usually be affected, since subsection (2) of section 7 (which provides for ranking in accordance with the respective dates of registration of the interests in the Land Register) is in terms of subsection (1) to be without prejudice to any express provision as to ranking in any deed or having effect by virtue of any enactment and, where the respective securities had originally been recorded in the Register of Sasines, the express provision of section 120 of the Titles to Land Consolidation (Scotland) Act 1868 will already have determined that in competition the securities were preferred according to their original dates of recording in the Register of Sasines.

42–16   In the case of transactions relating to existing heritable securities which remain recorded in the Register of Sasines which have the effect of altering the ownership of the registered interest of the proprietor of the security subjects, *e.g.* any of the three types of transaction exemplified in paragraph 42–07 *supra*, the relevant deed must contain a description of the security subjects by reference to their title number but no deduction of title or warrant of registration is required. Application for registration will be made on Form 2 with production of the land certificate and any links in the title of the creditor to the security if he is not infeft therein.

Transactions relating to creditor's interest under ex facie absolute disposition or assignation

42–17   Where first registration of the interest of the reversionary proprietor has already been induced, *e.g.* by a disposition of that interest for valuable consideration under burden of the security created by an *ex*

---

[17]See para. 42–05, r. (ii)(b).

facie absolute disposition or assignation, the Keeper will usually have accepted an application for registration of the purchaser's interest in the reversion despite the fact that doubt may exist whether such an interest is an interest in land within the meaning of section 2(1)(*a*) of the Land Registration (Scotland) Act 1979.[18] If the transfer of the reversionary proprietor's interest was not made for valuable consideration the Keeper will normally have accepted it for voluntary registration. Where the transfer was of a part only of the interest it is recommended, whether the transfer was for value or not, that application should have been made for voluntary registration of the interest remaining in the reversionary proprietor under section 2(1)(*b*) of the 1979 Act so that the whole interest would appear on the Land Register.[19] Upon registration of the interest of the reversionary proprietor he will have been entered in the proprietorship section of the title sheet as proprietor in reversion and there will also have been noted in that section the existence of the sasine title in favour of the *ex facie* absolute proprietor, and to that extent indemnity will have been excluded. Where the title to the creditor's security has remained in the Register of Sasines but is now entering the Land Register, *e.g.* by a transaction of the kind mentioned in subclause (4) of paragraph 42–08 *supra*, application should be made on Form 2 but the Keeper should be consulted as to the procedure and documents to be produced.

Contemporaneous discharge of heritable security and sale

42–18 Where a heritable security recorded in the Register of Sasines is being discharged in connection with a sale of the registered interest of the proprietor of the security subjects the Keeper will not require a separate application to be submitted in respect of the discharge of the security if it relates solely to the registered interest, provided that the discharge is presented along with the application for registration of the purchase of that interest and is listed on the inventory (Form 4) which accompanies the application. The Keeper will give effect to the discharge which does not additionally require to be presented for recording in the Register of Sasines.

42–19 Where for any reason the discharge of the heritable security is not available when settlement of the sale transaction is effected the discharge should be listed in the inventory (Form 4) which accompanies the application for registration of the purchaser's interest and marked "to follow."[20] In due course when the discharge is available it should be sent with an application for registration (Form 2) by the seller along with an inventory (Form 4) in duplicate and (if the granter of the discharge does not have a recorded title to the security) any

---

[18]See R.T.P.B., para. D.4.02.
[19]*Ibid.*
[20]The Keeper will not wait indefinitely for submission of the discharge and may exercise his powers under Rule 12—see R.T.P.B., para. D.2.21. In proper practice the discharge should be delivered at settlement—see n. 3a *supra*.

links in title which establish his right to the security. The application for registration should be completed and signed by the seller or his solicitor[21] and delivered to the purchaser's solicitor along with the executed discharge and other supporting documents and the purchaser will then forward the application and those other documents to the Keeper. The discharge should have marked on the front page the title number of the registered interest of the proprietor. A separate registration fee will be payable in respect of the discharge.

42–20   If the deed of discharge affects also other subjects the title to which is still recorded in the Register of Sasines, *e.g.* a partial discharge and deed of restriction, effect will require to be given to it both in the Register of Sasines and the Land Register and so a warrant of registration requires to be endorsed upon it and, if the granter does not have a recorded title to the security, a clause of deduction of title should be incorporated in it. The deed should also specify, either *in gremio* or marked at the top of the front page, the title number of the registered interest of the proprietor. The Keeper should be requested in the accompanying letter to record the deed in the Register of Sasines.

Where the partial discharge and deed of restriction is not available at settlement the procedure to be followed is similar to that already outlined in the second subparagraph of paragraph 42–11 *supra*, save that the title number of the registered interest of the proprietor will already appear in the body of, or marked upon, the deed.

Particular Transactions

Standard securities granted by companies

42–21   In order to comply with the provisions of section 410(2) of the Companies Act 1985 it is necessary that a standard security granted by a company is delivered to or received by the Registrar of Companies for registration within 21 days of the creation of the charge, *i.e.* within 21 days of the date when the standard security is recorded in the Register of Sasines or the creditor's interest is registered in the Land Register. The prescribed particulars of the charge (Companies Form No. 410) together with a certified copy of the standard security must be furnished to the Registrar of Companies within that period.

Where the standard security is recorded in the Register of Sasines the date of the Keeper's acknowledgment of the deed normally constitutes the *terminus a quo* the period of 21 days commences to run.

Where the interest of the creditor is registered in the Land Register the procedure for obtaining confirmation of the date of registration is described in detail in paragraphs D.4.40 to D.4.45 of the *Registration of Title Practice Book* and should be carefully followed. The position

---

[21]See n. 11 to para. 42–11.

as to exclusion of indemnity and the procedure for having the exclusion deleted are described in paragraph D.4.46 of the *Practice Book*.

Standard securities over long leases

42–22   As has already been explained,[22] once an area has become operational for the purposes of registration of title the tenant under a long lease or an assignee or partial assignee of the tenant's interest under a long lease can obtain a real right only by registration of his interest in the Land Register. Where, however, a lessee whose title has already been made real by recording in the Register of Sasines grants a standard security over his interest then, even although in the meantime the area in which the leasehold subjects are situated has become operational, the standard security will still be recorded in the Register of Sasines.[23] On the other hand, if the interest of the tenant has already been registered in the Land Register, a standard security granted over that interest, being a dealing with a registered interest, will be the subject of registration in the Land Register.

Registration of standard securities in the Books of Council and Session

42–23   Normally registration of a standard security in the Books of Council and Session is not desired at the time when it is being recorded in the Register of Sasines or the interest of the creditor is being registered in the Land Register. If, however, registration in the Books of Council and Session is desired at that time, then (1) where the standard security is being recorded in the Register of Sasines it should bear a warrant of registration directing such registration in appropriate terms,[24] or (2) where the interest of the creditor is being registered in the Land Register the applicant should instruct the Keeper in a covering letter stating the purpose for which registration in the Books of Council and Session is required (preservation or preservation and execution) and the number of extracts required.[25]

If registration in the Books of Council and Session for execution is desired at some time after recording or registration, then (1) if the standard security has been recorded in the Register of Sasines it, or if it has already been registered for preservation an extract of it, should be sent to the Keeper with a warrant of registration for execution endorsed thereon, or (2) if the interest of the creditor under the standard security has been registered in the Land Register the charge certificate with the standard security attached should be returned to the Keeper with a request to have the deed registered for execution

---

[22]See para. 26–11.
[23]Land Registration (Scotland) Act 1979, s. 8(2)(c): R.T.P.B., para. D.4.19.
[24]For form of warrant, see Vol. I, para. 4–75.
[25]R.T.P.B., para. D.1.24.

(an office copy is not enough), when the Keeper will remove the standard security, register it in the Books of Council and Session and reissue the charge certificate with the Books of Council and Session extract of the standard security attached.[26]

Absorption in relation to security subjects

42–24   **(a) Feudal property**. When consolidation of the superiority and the property occurs, a heritable security over either estate remains valid.

If the titles to both estates are recorded in the Register of Sasines, no action by a heritable creditor holding a security over either of them is required.

If, however, the title to either or both estates has been registered in the Land Register, some procedure in respect of a heritable security over either or both estates may be required. Reference may be made to the *Registration of Title Practice Book*, paragraphs C.15 and D.4.25 to D.4.31 as to the procedures in the Register of Sasines and the Land Register with regard to the proprietorship titles when consolidation occurs. Further variants are involved where heritable securities exist over either estate and the titles to them are registered in either register. The total number of possible permutations is considerable. Suffice to say that, when the title to either or both estates is registered in the Land Register and is burdened with a heritable security and consolidation of the two estates takes place, the advice of the Keeper should be sought as to any procedures which may be necessary in relation to the heritable security.

42–25   **(b) Long leases**. Similar problems can arise where the interest of the landlord and/or the tenant under a long lease is registered in the Land Register, either interest is burdened with a heritable security and absorption of the interest occurs. In this case the problem as to registration of the security will occur less often since, when the landlord acquires the tenant's interest or *vice versa*, the heritable creditor may have participated in the transaction and his security will either have been discharged or reconstituted over the united estate. If, however, the heritable security subsists in its original form, the Keeper should be consulted as to any appropriate procedure in relation to its continued registration.

Adjudication in execution

42–26   Where a heritable creditor adjudges the security subjects in execution (now a somewhat rare procedure since a sale under the powers in the security or foreclosure is more effective and gives an immediate title to the purchaser or the foreclosing creditor) the legal

---

[26]R.T.P.B., para. D.1.25.

result is that (a) if he proceeds under the personal obligation the creditor does not obtain the same ranking as the heritable security, other adjudications within a year and a day rank *pari passu* and the absolute title subsequently acquired by declarator of expiry of the legal does not clear the record of other securities effected between the adjudging creditor's security and the adjudication, but (b) if the heritable creditor proceeds on the *debitum fundi* he takes a decree of poinding of the ground followed by letters of poinding of the ground and formal execution by a messenger-at-arms bearing that he could not find moveables sufficient to repay the debt before proceeding to obtain a decree of adjudication which then has the same ranking as the heritable security and a decree of declarator of expiry of the legal cuts out any subsequent heritable securities.

As regards recording or registration:

(1) If the subjects are situated in a non-operational area, the extract decree of adjudication and the extract decree of declarator of expiry of the legal, when later obtained, should be recorded in the Register of Sasines.

(2) If the subjects are situated in an operational area but the title of the proprietor has not yet been registered in the Land Register, it would appear that the grant of a decree of adjudication, the legal effect of which is to create a *pignus praetorium* or a type of judicial security, would not induce first registration in the Land Register and the extract decree should be recorded in the Register of Sasines. When a decree of expiry of the legal is later obtained, the transaction effectively becomes a transfer of a proprietorship interest for valuable consideration and will induce first registration in the Land Register. Application should be made on Form 1 with production of the two extract decrees and any other relevant documents which the Keeper may require.

(3) If the title of the proprietor or debtor has already been registered in the Land Register, application should be made on Form 2 for registration of the extract decree of adjudication. The entry in the proprietorship section showing the debtor as proprietor will remain, and another entry will be made showing the adjudger as proprietor but with exclusion of indemnity in respect that the legal has not yet expired. In addition another entry will be made in the charges section to show the position of the adjudger in relation to other heritable securities. On subsequent registration of the extract decree of expiry of the legal the entry showing the debtor as proprietor will be deleted from the proprietorship section, the exclusion of indemnity as affecting the adjudger's title will be removed and the entry in the charges section relating to the extract decree of adjudication will be deleted.[26a]

[26a]R.T.P.B., paras. D.4.13. and D.4.14.

PART II: RANKING OF HERITABLE SECURITIES

The general rule

42–27   In the absence of any express ranking agreement,[27] the general rule is that the priority in ranking of heritable securities is regulated by the order in which or the dates on which they are respectively recorded in the Register of Sasines or the interest of the creditor is registered in the Land Register. In the case of heritable securities which were recorded in the Register of Sasines before April 4, 1981, the criterion of preference was the order in which the deeds appeared in the presentment book, so that a deed was preferred in ranking to one which was received later on the same day, with the qualification that deeds received by the same post ranked *pari passu*.[28] Since April 4, 1981, however, priority of ranking, both as regards heritable securities recorded in the Register of Sasines and heritable securities where the interest of the creditor is registered in the Land Register, is determined only by the day of recording or registration,[29] *i.e.* deeds recorded or registered at any time on the same day rank *pari passu*.

Section 7 of the Land Registration (Scotland) Act 1979

42–28   Section 7 of the 1979 Act provides that (a) titles to registered interests in land shall rank according to the date of registration of those interests, (b) a title to a registered interest and a title governed by a deed recorded in the Register of Sasines shall rank according to the respective dates of registration and recording, and (c) where the date of registration or recording of the titles to two or more interests in land is the same, the titles to those interests shall rank equally.[30] These provisions, however, are without prejudice to any express provision as to ranking in any deed or any other provision as to ranking in, or having effect by virtue of, any enactment or rule of law.[31] The terms of the section are broadly consonant with the general rule stated in the immediately preceding paragraph.

The saving provision of subsection (1) of section 7 may be of importance in certain circumstances. For example, (1) if the preferences of two heritable creditors have been regulated by a ranking agreement, the recording or registration of their respective titles on different dates does not affect their preferences under the ranking agreement or (2) if two heritable securities have been recorded on different dates in the Register of Sasines, the subsequent voluntary registration in the Land

---

[27]See para. 42–35.
[28]Register of Sasines Act 1693; Land Registers (Scotland) Act 1868, s. 6; Titles to Land Consolidation (Scotland) Act 1868, s. 142.
[29]Land Registration (Scotland) Act 1979, ss. 7, 29(1) and (4) and 30(2) and Land Registration (Scotland) Act 1979 (Commencement No. 1) Order 1980 (S.I. 1980 No. 1412) (S.113).
[30]1979 Act, s. 7(2), (3) and (4).
[31]*Ibid.*, s. 7(1).

Register of their respective titles in a different chronological order does not alter the preferences already established.[31a]

Partial assignations

42-29   The former rule of law was that partial assignations of one heritable security, although recorded on different dates, ranked *pari passu* in the absence of any ranking or other provision to the contrary.[32] The underlying reasoning was that, when the first partial assignation was granted, the effect was to transfer the part assigned with its original ranking *pari passu* with the retained part: when subsequently the retained part or any portion of it was assigned, its original *pari passu* ranking was also retained. It is thought that this rule is not displaced in relation to registered interests in heritable securities by section 7 of the Land Registration (Scotland) Act 1979 since subsection (2) is qualified by subsection (1), but to avoid doubt it is recommended that in partial assignations a clause of ranking should be inserted or, if partial assignations which are intended to rank equally are granted at the same time, care should be taken to ensure that the dealings are registered on the same day.

Standard security subject to burden of existing heritable security— warrandice

42-30   Under the former law relating to bonds and dispositions in security, where two bonds were granted to A and B respectively and the bond in favour of B excepted from warrandice the bond in favour of A, the exception from warrandice did not confer upon A a preference over the security subjects but only regulated the rights and liabilities of the parties under the personal obligation of warrandice.[33] The respective preferences of the parties over the security subjects were regulated by any ranking clause or, in its absence, priority of registration. The point was observed by the framers of the Conveyancing and Feudal Reform (Scotland) Act 1970 which provides[34] that where the security subjects are burdened by any other heritable security the grant in any subsequent standard security should be expressed as subject to the former heritable security with appropriate qualification of warrandice, and that, where the standard security is to rank prior or postponed to, or *pari passu* with, any other existing heritable security or any other standard security, a ranking clause may be inserted in appropriate terms immediately prior to the warrandice clause and the warrandice clause shall, if necessary, be amended appropriately. It is arguable that the "subject to" clause does not *per se* determine the ranking of the two securities and that the proper application of the clause is in

---

[31a]See para. 42–15.
[32]Burns, 444.
[33]Burns, 446; *Leslie* v. *McIndoe's Trs.* (1824) 3 S. 48.
[34]Sched. 2, Note 5.

circumstances where the priority in ranking of the existing heritable security has already been established, *e.g.* by prior recording or registration of the creditor's interest. It is understood that this view is provisionally adopted by the Keeper so that, if the position as to preference in ranking is doubtful, the charge certificate issued in respect of the standard security will not necessarily include as a prior burden the heritable security which is stated to burden it. Until the matter is clarified by judicial decision the safe practice, unless the respective preferences of the two securities have already been clearly established, is to insert a ranking clause or clauses in appropriate terms or to execute a separate ranking agreement or deed of postponement which is duly registered.

Notification of creation of subsequent heritable securities or floating charges

42–31   The effect upon the preference for future advances of the creditor under an existing heritable security of the subsequent creation of another heritable security notified to the existing creditor has already been considered.[35]

The effect upon the preference for future advances of the creditor in a floating charge of the subsequent creation of another floating charge has also been considered.[36]

Where the creditor under an existing heritable security which extends to future advances receives notification of the subsequent creation of a floating charge over assets which include the security subjects then, if there has been no agreement as to the ranking of the securities, the preference of the creditor under the existing heritable security remains unaffected, even when the charge subsequently crystallises.[37]

In the converse case where the holder of an existing floating charge which has not yet crystallised receives notification of the subsequent creation of a standard security over property which is included in the assets falling under the charge it would appear that, in the absence of any special provisions in the relevant deeds or an agreement which regulates the ranking of the securities, the creditor under the standard security has preference.[38] It is improbable that this problem will occur in practice, since lenders on current account secured by a floating charge almost always include provisions in the charge which prohibit the creation of subsequent fixed securities and contract for the priority of ranking of the charge over any securities subsequently created, or the various creditors execute a ranking agreement incorporating a

---

[35] para. 36–19.
[36] para. 41–26.
[37] Companies Act 1985, s. 464(4)(*a*).
[38] Ibid., s. 464(4)(*a*).

"fluctuating advances" clause which overrides the effect of notification.[39]

Ranking clauses and agreements

42–32 An effective ranking clause or ranking agreement must be entered into by parties who have power to grant it. In practice:

(1) A standard security over subjects as yet unburdened by any other heritable security does not require a ranking clause unless another standard security is being granted contemporaneously: the rule of priority of recording or registration sufficiently creates a preference.

(2) A standard security over subjects already burdened by another heritable security may contain a clause which postpones it to the existing security, but that is not necessary since the ranking of the two securities will be established by the order of their recording or registration. If, however, the second standard security is to rank in priority to, or *pari passu* with, the existing heritable security it is necessary to have the consent of the creditor under the existing security either incorporated in the second standard security executed also by him or in a separate deed of postponement granted by him or in a ranking agreement amongst the debtor and both creditors.

(3) Where two standard securities are being granted contemporaneously ranking clauses in consistent terms may be inserted in each or a separate ranking agreement may be entered into by the debtor and both creditors.

(4) In all the above cases the deed or deeds incorporating ranking clauses or the separate deed of postponement or ranking agreement should be recorded in the Register of Sasines or enter the Land Register.

(5) An unrecorded or unregistered ranking agreement may create a contractual arrangement between the creditors *inter se*, but does not affect the ranking of their respective securities as such.

(6) Where a floating charge or charges and a heritable security or securities are involved, it is recommended that a ranking agreement be executed by the debtor and all creditors, but it is not the practice to have it recorded or registered in the Register of Sasines or the Land Register unless more than one fixed heritable security is involved.[40] It should be registered in the Companies Register of Charges since it effects an alteration.[40a]

Styles

Ranking clauses

42–33 As to styles of ranking clauses in standard securities see paragraphs

---

[39]For an example of such an agreement see Greene and Fletcher, App. 15.
[40]For an example of a ranking agreement relating to standard securities and floating charges, see Greene and Fletcher, App. 15.
[40a]See para. 41–29.

37–54 and 37–55 *supra*, and as to a style of ranking clause in a partial assignation see paragraph 40–27 *supra*.

Deed of postponement

42–34   I, AB, (*designation*), Whereas I hold a standard security for the sum of £   granted by CD, (*designation*), in my favour over the property known as (*brief identifying description*) [recorded in the Register for the County of   on   ] [registered on   over the said property being the subjects registered under Title Number   ], And whereas EF, (*designation*), holds a standard security for the sum of £   granted by the said CD in favour of the said EF [over the said property recorded in the said Register on   ] [registered on   over the said property being the subjects registered under Title Number   ], and I have agreed to postpone my security to the said security in favour of the said EF, Therefore I hereby postpone the security and preference held by me over the said property in virtue of the said standard security in my favour to the security and preference held by the said EF in virtue of the said standard security in his favour: And I agree and declare that the said standard security in favour of the said EF and the whole sums, principal, interest and expenses due and to become due thereunder shall have the same preference and priority over the said standard security in my favour and the whole sums, principal, interest and expenses due and to become due thereunder as if the said standard security in favour of the said EF had been duly [recorded] [registered] prior to the recording [registration] of the said standard security in my favour: But I reserve the full force and effect of the said standard security in my favour in all other respects: And I warrant this postponement absolutely to the said CD and EF.

(*To be attested*)

Ranking agreement

42–35   AGREEMENT
                              amongst
                    A Bank plc, (*designation*), (hereinafter
                    called "the Bank")
                    B Limited, (*designation*), (hereinafter
                    called "B") and
                    C Limited, (*designation*), (hereinafter
                    called "the Company").
WHEREAS

(A) The Company in security of all sums due and to become due by it to the Bank has granted in favour of the Bank a standard security ("the Bank's Security") over the Company's heritable property at 4 King Street, Glasgow ("the Property") [recorded in the Register for the County of   on   ] [registered on   over the Property being the subjects registered under Title Number   ];

(B) the Company has granted in favour of B a standard security ("B's Security") for the sum of £20,000 over the Property which is about to be [recorded in the said Register of Sasines] [registered in the Land Register]; and

(C) the parties have agreed that the Bank's Security and B's Security should rank as follows:—

1. Notwithstanding the terms of the documents constituting the Bank's Security and B's Security or the respective dates of their granting or [recording] [registration] the parties hereto agree that the sums, principal, interest and expenses, secured or to be secured by the Bank's Security and B's Security respectively shall rank and be preferred in the event of a sale of the Property or any part thereof in the following order of priority:

(i) The Bank's Security shall rank in priority to the extent of £30,000 of principal with interest thereon and expenses;

(ii) B's Security shall rank next in priority to the extent of £10,000 of principal with interest thereon and expenses; and

(iii) The Bank's Security and B's Security shall in respect of the remaining sums due to the Bank and B respectively rank *pari passu* to the effect that the proceeds of sale of the Property, after payment of the expenses of sale, and payment of the amounts due to the Bank and B respectively in accordance with the order of priority in sub-paragraphs (i) and (ii) above, shall be payable to the Bank and B *pro rata* according to the proportion which the amount remaining due to each of them bears to the aggregate of these amounts.

2. The Bank's Security shall rank as hereinbefore provided as a continuing security for repayment of the amounts owing to the Bank from time to time and shall not be affected by any fluctuation in such amounts or by the existence at any time of a credit balance on any current or other account.

3. The Bank shall be entitled at any time in its discretion and without consulting the Company or B to transact and deal with any other securities or guarantees of any kind held or that may be held by it for any obligations of the Company and may sell, dispose of or realise such other securities in any order which it may determine and this agreement shall remain in full force and effect notwithstanding such transactions or dealings to the same extent and effect as if no such other securities or guarantees had ever existed.[41]

(*To be attested*)

Catholic and secondary securities

42–36 There are equitable rules applicable to a situation where one creditor (the catholic creditor) has prior securities over two subjects belonging to his debtor and another creditor (the secondary creditor) has a postponed security over one of these subjects. The rules apply

---

[41]This clause is designed to negative any obligations which might be implied by law in respect of catholic securities.

whether the securities are heritable or moveable, but are applicable most frequently in relation to heritable securities. The *ratio* of the rules is that the catholic creditor's only interest is to secure payment of his debt, the debtor's liability is to have both of the debts paid as fully as possible and so the catholic creditor must use his securities so as to leave the maximum balance available for the secondary creditor. Accordingly, if the catholic creditor A elects to obtain payment of his debt by realising the subjects over which the secondary creditor B has a postponed security, A must assign to B his security over the other subject.[42] Such an assignation will be assumed in any process for the distribution of the balance remaining after the catholic debt is paid, and so if the debtor becomes bankrupt and both subjects are realised B has a secured right in a question with the trustee in bankruptcy to the balance of the proceeds of sale of both subjects which remains after A's debt is satisfied.[43] The principle applies also to more complex situations. For example, if A has a catholic security over two properties and B has a postponed security over one property and C has a postponed security over the other, the burden of A's security, in a question between B and C, is apportioned rateably according to the value of each property without regard to the respective dates of creation of the securities of B and C.[44]

The rules, however, do not extend to giving a secondary creditor control over the actions of the catholic creditor in relation to his own security and in particular do not require the catholic creditor to deal with his security in a way which would adversely affect his own interests. So the secondary creditor cannot object to a discharge by the catholic creditor of the security over the subjects which are not burdened by his own security.[45] And if A holds a catholic security for a particular debt over two properties X and Y, and also a security for another debt over Y only, he is entitled to lay the whole burden of the catholic debt upon X even although X is burdened by a postponed security in favour of B.[46,47]

Heritable securities and inhibitions

42–37 **(a) Inhibitions against debtor.** Where there are several heritable securities and the debtor is inhibited (1) securities created before the inhibition are unaffected by it,[48] but (2) securities created after the inhibition are struck at by the inhibition with the result that the inhibitor is entitled to draw back from these posterior heritable

---

[42] Bell, *Comm.*, II, 417.
[43] *Littlejohn* v. *Black* (1855) 18 D. 207; *Nicol's Tr.* v. *Hill* (1889) 16 R. 416.
[44] *Ferrier* v. *Cowan* (1896) 23 R. 703.
[45] *Morton (Liddell's Curator)* (1871) 10 M. 292.
[46] *Preston* v. *Erskine* (1715) Mor. 3376.
[47] For a fuller treatment of the rules governing catholic and secondary securities, see Gloag and Irvine, *Rights in Security*, 58–65.
[48] *Campbells' Tr.* v. *De Lisle's Exrs.* (1870) 9 M. 252.

creditors the amount which he would have obtained had their debts not existed; if there are several posterior heritable creditors having different rights of priority the amount required to satisfy the inhibitor's right is drawn back from the heritable creditors in inverse order of their respective priorities. This process of double ranking is described in detail in Bell, *Commentaries*, II, 413 and has been judicially approved.[49]

42–38 **(b) Inhibitions against heritable creditor**. As to the effect of inhibitions used against a heritable creditor see Volume II, paragraph 21–80 *supra*.

Heritable securities on sequestration of debtor

42–39 The respective rights of heritable creditors and the trustee in the sequestration of the debtor to sell the security subjects are discussed in Volume II, paragraph 22–24 *supra*.

Heritable securities on liquidation of debtor

42–40 The respective rights of heritable creditors and the liquidator of the debtor company to sell the security subjects are discussed in Volume I, paragraphs 2–92 to 2–94 and 2–108 and paragraph 22–26 of Volume II. The relevant current statutory provision is now section 185 of the Insolvency Act 1986 but there is no significant difference: the respective rights of heritable creditors and the liquidator are as provided in subsections (3), (4), (7) and (8) of section 39 of the Bankruptcy (Scotland) Act 1985 with appropriate substitution of references to make these subsections applicable to liquidation and a liquidator.

Heritable creditors and receivers

42–41 The rights of heritable creditors whose securities were constituted prior to the debtor company being placed in receivership are not affected by the appointment of the receiver. Where the receiver wishes to sell heritable property which is subject to a prior heritable security and is unable to obtain the consent of the heritable creditor, he may apply to the court for authority to do so.[50]

---

[49]*Baird & Brown* v. *Stirrat's Tr.* (1872) 10 M. 414.
[50]Insolvency Act 1986, s. 61. See Vol. I, paras. 2–112 and 2–113 relating to the corresponding s. 477 of the Companies Act 1985 and *Armour and Mycroft Petrs.*, 1983 S.L.T. 453.

INDEX